BEYOND HEROES AND HOLIDAYS:

A Practical Guide to K-12 Anti-Racist, Multicultural Education and Staff Development

Edited by
Enid Lee, Deborah Menkart
and Margo Okazawa-Rey

NETWORK OF EDUCATORS ON THE AMERICAS
WASHINGTON, DC

ACKNOWLEDGMENTS

On the inside cover we list the many people who donated their time and services to this publication. In addition to their in-kind support, we received the financial support needed to get this book to the printer from the people and organizations listed below. Our deepest appreciation for their support and patience.

COLLABORATORS

The Center for Language Minority Education and Research (CLMER) at California State University, Long Beach (CSULB) provided financial, technical and content support for this publication. This support was made possible by (1) the ARCO Foundation to assist in improving teacher preparation and instructional practices for meeting the needs of California's linguistically and racially diverse students; and (2) the Pacific Southwest Regional Technology in Education Consortium (PSRTEC), funded by a grant from the U.S. Department of Education's Office of Educational Research and Improvement.

MAJOR DONORS

Boston Foundation   Janice Dressel   Humanities Council   Jennifer Ladd
Heleny Cook   of Washington DC

DONORS

Antonio Abad
John Allocca
Applied Research Center
Celia Wiehe Arnade
Aurora (CO) Public
    Schools Multicultural
    Education
Mary Ball
Dr. Katie Barak
Pat Barbanell
Bill Bliss
Paddy Bowman
Barbara Foulks Boyd
Dr. Susan C. Brown
William Brown
Keith Buchanan
Molly Bunnell (Santa
    Catalina School)
Mary Burke-Hengen
Ilene Carver
Patricia Chalco
Margarita Chamorro
David Christiano
Constance Chubb
Donald and Patricia
    Clausen
Bonny M. Cochran
Abby Cohen
Kenneth Danford
Lorri Davis
Maria T. DeFelice
Eleanor Duckworth

Debi Duke
Carole Edelsky
Jackie Ellenz
Peter Elliston
James F. Ford
Steven Friedman
Christian Gerhard
Jan M. Goodman
Helen Gym and Bret
    Flaherty
Rachell Brett Harley
Joseph Hawkins
Aida Heredia
Susan Hersh
Bartlett G. Hewey
Judi Hirsch
Marlene Hoffman
Sarah Hudelson
Jean Ann Hunt
Gregory Jay
Sara D. Jonsberg
Stan Karp
Gwyneth Kirk
Rob Koegel
Connie Kriehn
Carlene B. Larsson
Bob and Kris Libon
Mark and Joanne Libon
Catherine Long
Lutheran Human
    Relations Association
Lutheran Immigration
    and Refugee Service

Elizabeth Mahan
Sharon Martinas
Martha Matlaw
Dody S. Matthias
Sylvia McGauley
Arona McNeill-Vann
Andrew Menkart
Margaret K. Menkart
Mennonite Central
    Committee
Edgardo Menvielle
Diana Mitchell
Gina Murphy
Andrea Nash
Honey W. Nashman
Sonia and Angel Nieto
Ray Nosbaum
Joy Kreeft Peyton
Diana Porter
Marijane Poulton
Mary Louise Pratt
Susan E. Randall
Marcia A. Rautenstrauch
Andrew Reich
Rachelle Resnick
Grace Rissetto
Dr. Faith Rogow
Pam Root
Laurie Rubin
Dell Salza
Deborah Santana
Betsy Sason
Mary C. Savage

Stephanie Schmid
Nancy Schniedewind
Carol Schulkey
Sarah Sehnert
Donna Sharer
Renee H. Shea
Ira Shor
Betty Sitka (AU SIS)
Christine E. Sleeter
Betty Ansin Smallwood
Lisa Sparaco
Sylvia Stalker
Charles W. Stansfield
Richard Sterling (NWP)
Lally Stowell
Ruth Tamaroff
Grace Taylor
Mary Frances Taymans
Patricia Thompson
Lynda Tredway
Jenice View
Donna Villareal
Athena Viscusi
Marilyn Watkins
Debbie Wei
Jim Weiler
Jean Weisman
Karel Weissberg
Patricia L. Williams
Marshall J. Wong
Michael Wong
Claudia Zaslavsky

Beyond Heroes and Holidays:

A Practical Guide to K-12 Anti-Racist, Multicultural Education and Staff Development

TABLE of CONTENTS

© RICK REINHARD

INTRODUCTION

If you are trying to make sure that multicultural education in your school is more than just a celebration of heroes and holidays, this book is for you. We believe that multicultural education should help students, parents, teachers and administrators understand and relate to the histories, cultures and languages of people different from themselves. But multicultural education must be much more than that. It must be transformative; that is, encourage academic excellence that embraces critical skills for progressive social change. Therefore, multicultural education must:

▶ instill the importance of academic excellence;

▶ examine the history and underlying causes of racism and its institutional features;

▶ teach the connections between racism and other forms of inequality;

▶ analyze the ways in which schools and education, as an institution of our society, have helped to support and perpetuate racism;

▶ teach how racism hurts both peoples of color and White people, and prevents us from being effective allies;

▶ show how White people and peoples of color throughout history have indeed worked together,

and celebrate those efforts;

▶ provide opportunities to collectively envision just and fair schools, communities and the larger society; and

▶ inspire and empower us to do the necessary work to make those visions come true.

OUR VISION OF A MULTICULTURAL SOCIETY

Our ideas about multicultural education rest on our vision of a multicultural society. In a genuinely multicultural society, everyone would recognize and honor differences in race, ethnicity, gender, culture, class, language, sexual orientation, religion, abilities and so on, while also acknowledging the similarities of experiences and interests across these social categories. We also believe that a truly multicultural society would be a just society. People controlling societal institutions would do everything within their power to provide to *all people* the sources for meaningful livelihoods, ensure true physical and emotional safety and security, and create an ecologically sustainable environment for the survival of future generations.

We designed *Beyond Heroes and Holidays* to serve as a practical guide. We share strategies that educators are using in K-12 classrooms in many disciplines and in staff development. These strategies can be used directly, but more important, they serve as examples of transformative education. These examples make the goals of anti-racist, multicultural education tangible, and offer ideas and frameworks for the reader's own school reform efforts.

OUR EDUCATIONAL PHILOSOPHY

Our work is guided by the philosophy of critical pedagogy, pioneered by Brazilian educator, Paulo Freire. This philosophy is grounded in the beliefs that (1) the purpose of education in an unjust society is to bring about equality and justice, (2) students must play an active part in the learning process, and (3) teachers and students are both simultaneously learners and producers of knowledge.

Therefore we believe that schools should work to ensure that the barriers to student achievement are removed and that schools should promote cross-cultural dialogue and respect. But just as importantly, schools should be the place where students can analyze the forces which maintain injustice and develop the knowledge, hope and strategies needed to create a more just society for us all.

There is no formula for multicultural education from a critical perspective, only several general guiding principles. We kept these in mind as we searched for lessons and articles to include in this book. We asked ourselves, does the lesson:

▸ Draw on the knowledge and experience of the students?

▸ Help reveal the diversity and complexity of the issues and fields it addresses?

▸ Use a variety of instructional methods to stimulate students' multiple ways of learning and understanding?

▸ Reinforce the idea that students have individual and collective agency and help to develop that agency?

▸ Convey a politics of possibility and hope?

Additionally, because we focus specifically on race and racism, we also asked, does the lesson:

▸ Challenge stereotypes and correct mis-information about peoples of color?

▸ Expose the deep historical and institutional roots of racism and its devastating effects on both peoples of color and White people?

▸ Require a recognition of racism and its connections to other forms of inequalities?

FOCUS ON RACE

We agree with many who argue that race is "both an empty category and one of the most destructive and powerful forms of social categorization" (Toni Morrison, *Race-ing Justice, En-Gendering Power*, 1992). Race is not a biological construct, with clearly definable features and characteristics, as most of us were taught to think. Yet, as it has been constructed in our society, race plays a critical role in many social interactions in general. Racism is pervasive and has an impact on all aspects of society.

Moreover, many of us know that race is always present as an issue in the organization, life and curriculum of schools, even all-White schools. But because the presence of race and racism is often neither acknowledged nor critically examined, students of color and White students are often left to assume that whiteness is the norm; students of color experience racism and often have no language acceptable to school teachers and administrators to discuss it, or spaces to address it; and many staff and parents find themselves without support or allies when tackling racism and general concerns about race.

In *Beyond Heroes and Holidays* we attempt to expose race and racism as they operate in schools by including lessons that help students, parents and school staff pay attention to race. For example, "The Cherokee/Seminole Removal Role Play" introduces students to one of the strong alliances formed between Africans and Native Americans in the early-1800s. The lesson "Exclusion — Chinese in 19th Century America" looks at the period of the Gold Rush through the eyes of the often-ignored Chinese immigrants who, contrary to the westward movement of European immigrants, began their journey from the west coast of the United States and moved eastward. "A Native Perspective on Thanksgiving" turns on its head the notion, still prevalent in many schools, that Pilgrims prepared a wonderful dinner for Native Americans who showed up with only corn. Through "The Institutionalization of Racism" students see the concerted and systematic effort required to institutionalize racism in the United States, which included teaching European immigrants to be White. Students explore how this served to oppress not only people of color but also working-class White people with the time-old strategy of divide and conquer. This lesson also makes clear that racism is not "natural" because it requires the force of multiple institutions to establish and maintain it. This analysis of racism conveys hope; if something was con-

Young author in the Books Project shares a book he wrote.

structed, as opposed to being natural, it can be changed.

We also encourage the application of this lens of race to school-wide events. During Women's History month, for example, event-organizers can look for racial diversity in the women featured in posters or assemblies. Or, in deciding which play to produce for the annual theatre production, producers should remember the works by African American, Asian American, Latino/a, and Native American playwrights.

In addition to analyzing school curriculum and activities, staff and parents can work separately and together to uncover and understand the racial and cultural biases embedded in how the school is organized. For instance, they can analyze the ways the school is governed. Questions such as the following are useful in this task:

▶ Who has what kinds of power, influence and authority?

▶ How does race affect who has power, influence and authority?

▶ How is decision-making shaped by race?

The section on working with school staff, family, and community includes readings that can open up a dialogue among school staff and parents about the impact of race on the school as a whole as well as on individual children. An example is "Do You Know Where the Parents of Your Children Are?" which documents the successful efforts of one school to create a meaningful relationship with parents.

In our experiences with multicultural education, we have noticed that most of it focuses on racial and ethnic groups except Whites. By ignoring White people, and the underlying concept of Whiteness, it is implied that they have no race or that their experiences require no examination because they are the standard. We challenge that notion by including a number of lessons for staff development and the classroom that examine the formation and maintenance of White racial identity and the particular role White people have played and can play in challenging racism. The readings by Sandra Lawrence and Beverly Tatum, Cynthia Cohen, Christine Sleeter, Peggy McIntosh, Ruth Anne Olson and others suggest ways that pre-service and in-service teacher education courses can help white teachers look honestly at racism and white racial identity. In focusing on whiteness, we do not assume that teachers and staff of color do not need to examine their identities, attitudes, prejudices and internalized racism. The "Personal Cultural History Exercise" helps both White staff and staff of color explore the impact of race and culture on their own lives.

Although we chose to focus on race, we argue that many dynamics of racial oppression can easily be applied to other forms of inequality such as sexism and heterosexism, and so forth. We, therefore, included several works that address those issues. "Girl Power" was developed by social workers and counselors to allow girls to explore their experiences of being female in a middle school. The discrimination faced by gay and lesbian students is discussed in "Growing Up Gay." It is important to give more in-depth attention to these and all other forms of oppression and inequality as well as to develop curricula that examine and challenge their intersections.

INEQUALITY IN EDUCATION: THE CONVERGENCE OF RACE AND CLASS

Issues of race, combined with class, undergird questions of educational inequality. The structures of inequality in the larger society — patterns of employment, the differential social, political, and economic status of neighborhoods, to name two — result in uneven distribution of resources to schools. In low-income communities of color, teachers may have very good intentions and progressive ideas, but inadequate resources or skills to address the needs of their students. Racial and class differences and inequalities influence even who becomes a teacher. Therefore, teachers and students seldom share the same neighborhood, similar cultural backgrounds, or life experiences. It is no wonder that teachers often do not see their students' strengths, competencies, and areas of expertise. If we all recognize these areas, we have to ask, for example, Why are the students who are consistently late to class on time for other things? Or, why is it that some students seem lackadaisical about coming to school but take very seriously their family responsibilities in minding their younger brothers and sisters? Some of the lessons and readings in this book, such as "Students' Stories in Action Comics" and "Portrait Poems," are designed to help us see and appreciate the complexity of each other's lives. There are also lessons which demonstrate how one can create the kind of schools and classrooms that actively engage students. These include the "The Business of Drugs" and "Cultural Clubs in Public Schools."

How we analyze academic and social problems in schools is influenced by two fundamental questions: What is the purpose of schooling? How is this purpose conceived differently according to the racial and socioeconomic characteristics of the students, school and school district? For example, in higher-income, predominantly-White schools, students are socialized, encouraged, and trained to become professionals and leaders. From early years of schooling, children are prepped to fare well on standardized tests, with the aim of gaining entrance to "better" colleges. By contrast, in lower-income, primarily African American and Latino schools, students are often taught to accept lower status occupations or positions outside the mainstream, including prisons. Teachers and counselors explicitly advise college-bound high school students of color to settle for community college rather than university. Students with discipline problems, even in elementary schools, are described as "repeat offenders," a term usually used to describe criminals.

WAYS OF SEEING

As we stated above, multicultural education is much more than learning facts and information about people's experiences, cultures and histories. It includes a serious examination of the Euro-centric cultural values, norms, and expectations that form the dominant perspectives through which many of us theorize about education and develop curriculum. Eurocentrist perspectives and methods and multicultural education are inherently in contradiction. It is impossible to develop genuinely multicultural curricula from only the dominant perspective because it illuminates only one set of experiences. As we worked on this book, we identified several key features of the dominant culture that severely limit the possibilities for a genuinely multicultural curriculum.

FOCUS ON THE INDIVIDUAL

Dominant North American culture is centered primarily on the individual as opposed to many other cultures that place much higher value on family and community. This focus on the individual leads people to see themselves without a context of a tradition-bearing community. As Robert Bellah explains in *Habits of the Heart* (UCP, 1985), for example, most North Americans imagine that we autonomously select our religious beliefs, even though the great majority of us are the same denomination as our parents.

This focus on individuals is embedded in dozens of curricula that view racism as simply a matter of individual biases, ignorance and prejudice, and deal with racism as "prejudice reduction," similar to a weight-loss program. It is up to the student, the individual, to shed their biases and ignorance. Students are told that it is up to them individually and personally to get along with people who are different from themselves. Primarily working at the individual/personal level does not lead to long-term change. While we learn to respect each other's differences, the economic, political and social forces in the larger community and society further fuel the inequalities between us. For this book we looked for lessons and articles that address three levels of analysis: individual/personal (micro), community (meso), and societal (macro). These levels are explained in more detail in "Educating for Critical Practice."

© RICK REINHARD

An example of focusing on the individual, rather than also looking at the community and societal context is how we, as educators, cover history and contemporary events. Poster series of famous scientists, artists and historical figures now feature African Americans, women, Asian Americans and Latinos/as. But the focus is still on the individual. Applying all the levels of analysis, we would begin to look at the groups, both formal and informal, that have made great inventions, historical events and even works of art possible. Herbert Kohl (*Rethinking Schools*, Vol. 5, No. 2) has noted how little of the actual life and work of Rosa Parks is illuminated when viewed through the dominant lens. She was an old woman, too tired to go to the back of the bus. Looking through a wider perspective, we see that she was actually tired everyday after work, that her decision not to go to the back of the bus on that particular day was one part of a whole strategy designed and supported by activists in Birmingham to challenge the entire system of segregation, and that she studied and worked at the Highlander Center in Tennessee with other activists from different parts of the country to become a more effective political organizer.

THE SYSTEM WORKS

The dominant culture promotes the myth that the basic structures and institutions of the society — economic, social, educational — are fair and democratic. So whenever problems are identified, one's strategic imagination only embraces "solutions" that address the symptoms. To address language differences we only need to put a sign on the door in many languages to tell parents they are welcome. We don't need to look at how the school curriculum and policies treat language. In reality the basic structure may have to undergo substantive changes as recommended in the articles by James A. Banks, Sonia Nieto and Enid Lee.

QUICK 'N EASY

"Buy this item now, it will make your life simpler." Five minutes of commercials provide ample proof that the dominant culture places a value on things that are quick, easy or simple. Unless we consciously rethink this cultural value, it will continue to shape many of our school practices. For example, if a child's family name is difficult for teachers or classmates to pronounce, it is often suggested that the name be changed to something that the rest of the class is more familiar with. "It will make the child's life easier," is stated as the rationale. Who could argue with that — unless we decide that maybe making life easier should not be the goal. What if instead we choose to make it richer, deeper, more complex? What if instead of setting a goal of learning a name quickly, we set the goal taking the time to learn it correctly? "Para Teresa," "Redefining the Norm" and "Looking Through an Anti-Racist Lens" provide examples of how one can take a more complex look at the world around us.

MYTH OF THE WHITE SETTLER

Growing up in the United States or Canada, most of us have learned, consciously or subconsciously, that White men made our country's history and that other people (forcibly or by choice) helped out. Whites are at the center. It is this myth that compels educators, even multiculturalists, to see the need for multicultural education as a response to "the growing diversity" in North America. The truth is that this continent has always been culturally diverse. There were many Native American nations with diverse languages, systems of government and ways of life even before the Europeans arrived, and some of their ways of life continue today, even under great threat from the outside. The first European settlers included people from England, France, Germany, Holland, Ireland, Italy, Scotland and Spain. Early inhabitants also included free Africans, and Africans may have come as explorers even earlier. The children of Spaniards, Native Americans and Africans constituted the large Latino population in the southwestern United States that predates the Declaration of Independence. Asian Americans have a history of over 150 years in this country. The lessons "Lies My Textbook Told Me," "Exclusion — Chinese in 19th Century America" and "Violence, the KKK and the Struggle for Equality" provide a more accurate picture of U.S. history.

ONE-DIMENSIONAL LIVES

Argentinean author Luisa Valenzuela once commented that she could never write a book in the United States because everything here is flat, one-dimensional and linear. Time always moves forward in a straight line. Dichotomized thinking prevails so things are either one thing or another, good or bad, right or wrong, and so forth. It is this perspective that makes it easy to divorce ourselves from history, to move only in one direction at a time, to use only a singular perspective to see and understand the world around us.

Our capacity to deal with and understand complex realities is shaped by the perspectives we employ to do so. For example, effective multicultural education requires a critical reflection on the meaning and effect of our own racial and cultural identity and categories. This means coming to terms with the contradictory relationship of privilege and disadvantage most of us experience based on our race, gender and class. We may reside in the dominant group with one aspect of our lives, and yet be oppressed for another. For instance, a White, middle-class woman has access to many privileges because she is White and middle-class. Yet she also is subject to many forms of discrimination and disadvantage because she is female. For example, if her middle-class status is dependent upon her partnership with a middle-class man, it may very well change as a result of separation, divorce, or death. A third-generation, working-class, Chinese American man may be disadvantaged by race and class, but advantaged by gender. And so on.

FORMAT OF THE BOOK

The book is divided into ten sections: School Staff, Family and Community Development; Reading Between the Lines: Critical Literacy; Language; Lessons for the Classroom; Technology; School-wide Activities; Holidays and Heritage; Talking Back; Glossary; and Resource Guide. The Staff, Family and Community Development section provides lessons and readings for staff development, and articles by practitioners sharing insights from their work. Many of the teaching ideas in this section could easily be adapted for use at the secondary level. The Lessons for the Classroom section includes teaching suggestions for early-childhood through secondary school. These range from lessons about the genocide of Native Americans to understanding the electoral process. In Talking Back there are lessons for school staff and students on how to respond to injustices. There are also stories of how students, teachers, parents and administrators in Canada and the United States have spoken out against racism. The Resource Guide includes a list of relevant print and audio visual materials, and a guide to Internet sources.

INVITATION TO CONTINUE THE DIALOGUE

This book does not pretend to be all inclusive; we are keenly aware of its gaps. We would like to have included more on the intersection of racism and other forms of oppression such as sexism, heterosexism and classism. We included many lessons for social studies, but very few for math, science, technology, language arts and the visual arts. We are limited by our own perspectives, particular connections to the field, and lack of time. Thus, if you have articles and lessons to address these or other gaps you see, please submit them to NECA for consideration for our next edition.

We hope this guide will assist you in your work as educators committed to both the specific goals of multicultural education and the overarching purpose of transformative education: to be part of collective efforts aimed at helping all students become creative, caring, and responsible human beings and creating a secure and sustainable world for us all.

SCHOOL STAFF, FAMILY & COMMUNITY DEVELOPMENT

EDUCATING FOR EQUALITY: FORGING A SHARED VISION

BY LOUISE DERMAN-SPARKS

All multicultural curriculum guides and classroom practices rest on key beliefs and assumptions about the causes of and solutions to racial problems and conflicts. They may be clearly stated and conscious; they may remain unnamed and unexamined. Whether explicit or implicit, these beliefs profoundly influence the why, what, and how of multicultural education at all grade levels. Teachers, therefore, must look closely at these underlying beliefs and assumptions to ensure what they are teaching is congruent with their own values and visions of a just society. And, if teachers are to do this, they must first uncover and examine their own beliefs and assumptions. They can begin by asking such questions as, What do I believe are the causes of racism and other "isms"? What do I really think should be done to address these "isms"? What do I believe are the appropriate goals, content, and methods of multicultural education, and whom do I think needs it?

Today, there are numerous multicultural curriculum guides and materials available for us. However different they may look on the surface, when you explore the underlying value base and assumptions on which they are constructed, most can be categorized into two fundamentally different schools of thought: the "Tolerance" paradigm, and the "Transformation" paradigm. In a 3-page chart accompanying this article I describe some of the major themes and practices that characterize each paradigm. Of course one must recognize that within each paradigm there is considerable variation in the specifics of curriculum content and methods, and that there is some overlap between them. The article also suggests challenges to forging a shared vision faced by educators who are working or wish to work, within the transformation paradigm. My discussion of these issues comes out of my experiences and reflections as an anti-bias educator and author whose work falls within the transformation paradigm.

FORGING A SHARED VISION

Furthering the development of effective transformational multicultural education requires solutions to several current problems.

1. Fragmentation and competition

Curricula within the transformation paradigm frequently focus on only one of the several arenas of diversity, such as race or ethnicity or gender or disabilities. This may lead to a competition among diversity issues, "My problem is more important than yours," rather than endeavoring to address all forms of discrimination and prejudice. Another serious consequence of fragmentation is attempting to implement a transformational curriculum without ensuring that the methods are culturally relevant to the children and families being served. Conversely, a program may be culturally relevant, and yet not directly address issues of bias and injustice.

2. Lack of clarity and depth in our understanding of how the various arenas of diversity and the "isms" interconnect.

To overcome and solve the problems generated by a fragmented approach to equity issues, we need to do much more work together towards conceptualizing and articulating the interconnections, as well as the differences between the key "isms" in our society. Moreover, we need a more coherent and unified plan of action for implementing a transformation model of multicultural education. No one can do this work alone. Honest and respectful conversations, collaborative practice, and critical analyses of our practice are essential. This, however, requires letting go of competitiveness among advocates for the various arenas of diversity.

3. Lack of clarity and depth in our understanding of how Euro-Americans fit in at the "multicultural table."

Considerable confusion reigns on the issue of the nature of Euro-American culture. Many "Whites" see themselves as without an identifiable culture because they come from families that fused into the mythological "melting pot" of U.S. society. This makes it difficult to unravel the complex knot of the culture of power created by racism and the other aspects of Euro-American culture. Americans of European descent need a clear understanding and self-acceptance of their own racial and cultural identities, as well as awareness of how they participate in maintaining racism if they are to participate effectively in forging a vision for and carrying out transformation education.

4. Lack of a coherent, developmental view and plan for education from preschool onwards.

Multicultural curricula, like other aspects of educational planning, tend to focus on specific age or grade levels. To date, a coherent overall view of what it would mean to implement the goals of a transformational-based multicultural curriculum does not exist. This creates discontinuity and fragmentation. Children need continuous and age-appropriate opportunities throughout their school years to learn about themselves and others, to do critical thinking, and to practice acting in the face of bias.

The absence of a coherent, developmental plan also produces an "I must do it all by myself" anxiety for teachers. If I am a kindergarten teacher who embraces education for equality but the other teachers in my school do not, then, I want to give my children as much as I possibly can in the one year I have them. This anxiety may result in curriculum that is developmentally inappropriate.

5. Relationship between educational work in the classroom and organizing for social justice outside of the classroom.

The transformation paradigm of multicultural education calls on teachers to place their work in the larger context of societal change. We must understand the sometimes contradictory functions of schools in our society: to train children to fit into prescribed societal relationships on the one hand, and to teach children, as citizens of a democracy, how to challenge and change unjust aspects of the society on the other. Educators must work both within and outside their classrooms as advocates and activists for the conditions in which all children can grow to their fullest, wonderful potential.

Those of us working to forge a shared vision of educating for equality must be good at presenting what we are for, not just what we are against, explaining the many ways that a true multicultural education ultimately benefits all children, and devising effective strategies for organizing not just to stem the rising tide of right wing groups but, more important, to promote our own agendas. We must help people recognize that so long as some groups are excluded and alienated from educational and occupational opportunities, our world is precarious. We must also articulate a vision of how *everyone* will be enriched by a more inclusive, and just society. We have to seek ways to broaden the dialogue about educational, as well as other social reforms, to include people who are afraid they may be left

out, because for them, change means turning current power relationships upside down, whereby, for example, people of color will be in charge and oppress White people. We must continue to articulate the vision that a real multicultural society will have, at its center, a fundamentally equitable structure of power relations.

As we prepare ourselves and the children we teach for the 21st century, can we, with our sisters and brothers in this, and every country around the world, build societies where diversity and equity thrive? Can we each learn how to live our own deeply felt beliefs and values while also respecting and supporting others to do the same? Can we figure out how to build social and economic institutions that do not rest on privilege for some at the expense and degradation of the many?

One of the great wonders of creation is its diversity: no one culture has a monopoly on goodness, value, and worth, nor on understanding all the complexities of our world. A second great wonder is the common thread that binds all life together in mutual interdependency. Survival for all of us depends on each new generation getting increasingly better at creating societies in which "liberty and justice for all" really is for *all*. As Alice Walker aptly writes in *The Temple of My Familiar*, "Keep in mind always the present you are constructing. It should be the future you want" (Walker, 1989).

Louise Derman-Sparks is a faculty member of Pacific Oaks College in Pasadena, California. She teaches courses on anti-bias education for K-12 and adult educators, and on the sociopolitical context of human development. She is the director of the Anti-Bias Education Leadership Project and offers lectures and workshops on anti-bias education at conferences nationally and internationally. She is the author of the most widely read book on anti-bias education for early childhood, Anti-Bias Curriculum: Tools for Empowering Young People *(w/ the ABC Task Force, NAEYC, 1989) and the co-author of* Teaching/Learning Anti-Racism: A Developmental Approach *(w/Carol Brunson Phillips, Teachers College Press, 1997).*

REFERENCES

Derman-Sparks, L. & the ABC Task Force. 1989. *Anti-Bias curriculum: Tools for empowering young children.* Washington, DC: NAEYC

Lee, E. 1995. *Rethinking our classrooms.* Milwaukee: Rethinking Schools.

Walker, A. 1989. *The temple of my familiar.* New York: Harcourt Brace Jovanovich

TOLERANCE VS. TRANSFORMATION

A. ASSUMPTIONS ABOUT THE SOURCES OF RACIAL PROBLEMS AND CONFLICTS

THE TOLERANCE PARADIGM

▸ Racial problems and conflicts exist because of prejudice.

▸ Prejudice is an individual problem. Some individuals are more inclined to be strongly prejudiced because of their personality type or their particular growing up and life experiences.

▸ Prejudice appears when there is contact and interaction among people who are racially and culturally different from each other.

▸ Prejudice, which results from lack of knowledge about each other and from stereotypes that occur "naturally," is a way to make sense out of unfamiliar and complex situations when there is little knowledge.

TRANSFORMATION PARADIGM

▸ Racial problems and conflicts are rooted in racism, a systemic problem that functions at both institutional and interpersonal levels.

▸ Racism is created as a method for one society or group of people in a society to rule and control another society or groups of people within a society on the basis of racial differences or characteristics. As Asa Hilliard (1992) points out, its source is greed, and its consequences are economic, political and cultural benefits to the group that holds the power and exploitation and physical, emotional, and spiritual degradation of those who are the targets of the racism.

▸ All individuals born into a society that practices institutional racism get lessons, in how to participate in its many forms. Families, schools, and the media, play major roles in this socialization process, and teach all of us to participate — actively by being direct perpetrators and passively by quiet acceptance of benefits and acquiescence to racism directed against one's own group, or even another racial group.

B. ASSUMPTIONS ABOUT WHAT NEEDS TO CHANGE

TOLERANCE PARADIGM

▸ Changing individual attitudes and behaviors leads to the elimination of prejudice and discrimination.

▸ People learn to be non-prejudiced through gaining more facts and information about different cultures and through increased interaction with people different from themselves.

TRANSFORMATION PARADIGM

▸ Individual changes in attitudes and behavior are necessary, but not sufficient to eliminate racism. Knowledge, respect, and appreciation of different cultures are necessary, but also not sufficient.

▸ Eliminating racism requires restructuring power relationships in the economic, political, and cultural institutions of the society, and creating new conditions for interpersonal interactions. Examining the dynamics of oppression and power and how individuals participate in these dynamics are essential.

▸ Individuals can learn to be anti-racist activists, developing the skills to work with others to create systemic, institutional changes. Conversely, institutional change will result in greater opportunities to foster the development of more people who strongly support diversity and social, economic, and political justice.

C. Assumptions about who needs multicultural education

Tolerance paradigm

▸ Children from groups that are the targets of racial prejudice need multicultural education to build-up their "low self-esteem."

▸ Children in mixed/integrated settings need multicultural education to learn about each other.

▸ Children in all-White settings do not usually need multicultural education because problems of prejudice do not arise when children of color are not present.

Transformation paradigm

▸ *Everyone* needs multicultural, anti-bias education in all educational settings.

▸ The issues and tasks will vary for children depending on their racial and cultural background as well as their family and life experiences.

▸ Teachers and parents, as well as children, need to engage in multicultural, anti-oppression education.

D. Working with parents

Tolerance paradigm

▸ Teachers occasionally ask parents to share special cultural activities, such as cook a holiday food, dress in traditional clothing, show pictures of their country of origin.

▸ Teachers may read about or ask for information about the most visible aspects of each family's cultures, such as foods, music, and favorite objects, but usually do not learn about the underlying aspects, like beliefs and rules about teacher-child interaction and preferred learning styles. Nor, even if known, are these incorporated into daily classroom life.

Transformation paradigm

▸ Parents/family caregivers collaborate in curriculum development, implementation and evaluation.

▸ Teachers use a variety of strategies that actively and regularly involve parents, including provisions for languages other than English.

▸ Parents'/family caregivers' knowledge about their home culture is essential information for adapting curriculum to each child's needs.

▸ Parents regularly share their daily life experiences at home and work, as well as special holiday events. Parents who are activists in any aspect of social justice work also share these experiences.

E. Goals

Tolerance paradigm

▸ Teaching about "different" cultures, that is, cultures of racial and ethnic groups dissimilar to the dominant European American culture.

▸ Advocating for appreciation, enjoyment, and tolerance of other cultures.

Transformation paradigm

▸ Fostering the development of people of all ages to be activists in the face of injustice directed at them or others.

▸ Constructing a knowledgeable and confident self-identity

▸ Developing empathetic, comfortable, and knowledgeable ways of interacting with people from a range of cultures and backgrounds

▸ Learning to be critical thinkers about various forms of discrimination.

▸ Working with others to create concrete changes at the institutional and interpersonal levels.

▸ Instilling the idea that multicultural education is a process, rather than an end in itself, and is a life-time journey.

F. METHODS AND CONTENT

TOLERANCE PARADIGM

- Curriculum usually consists of activities for use with any and all children — a "one size fits all" approach — which is also "teacher proof."

- Content focuses on learning discrete pieces about the cultures of various racial and ethnic groups. The particular cultures selected for study are usually either those that are presented in a curriculum guide or ones a teacher knows about and likes.

- Multicultural activities tend to be add-ons to the curriculum — a special holiday activity, a multicultural bulletin board, a week-long unit, a multicultural education course in a teacher training program. In essence, students "visit" other cultures from time to time, then return to their existing Euro-American-based curriculum.

- Critics sometimes refer to this approach as "tourist" curriculum. Tourists do not get to see the daily life of the cultures they visit, nor do they delve into the societal practices that may be harmful and unjust. Moreover, tourists may not even like the people they are visiting, but only appreciate their crafts, or music, or food.

TRANSFORMATION PARADIGM

- All aspects of the curriculum integrate multicultural, critical thinking and justice concepts and practice. As Enid Lee points out, "It's a point of view that cuts across all subject areas and addresses the histories and experiences of people who have been left out of the curriculum. It's also a perspective that allows us to get at explanations for why things are the way they are in terms of power relationships, in terms of equality issues" (Lee, 1995).

- Teachers actively incorporate their children's life experiences and interests and tailor curriculum to meet the cultural, developmental and individual needs of their children.

- Content includes diversity and justice issues related to gender, class, family forms and disabilities, as well as ethnicity and culture.

- Teachers view children as active learners who learn from each other as well as from adults. They also consider cooperative learning and participation in the governance of their classroom as crucial components of educating for equality.

G. TEACHER PREPARATION

TOLERANCE PARADIGM

- Training content typically consists of information about various cultures and a compilation of multicultural activities to use with children. Training occurs in a separate module or course, rather than being integrated into the "regular" curriculum class.

- Methods tend to emphasize providing information through readings and "spokespeople" from various ethnic groups.

- Training does not require teachers to uncover or change their own biases and discomforts, or to learn about the dynamics and manifestations of institutional racism.

TRANSFORMATION PARADIGM

- Teacher training challenges students to uncover, face, and change their own biases, discomforts, and misinformation and identify and alter educational practices that collude with racism and other institutionalized discrimination and prejudice.

- Training also enables students to understand their own cultural identity and behaviors, and develop culturally sensitive and relevant ways to interact with people.

- Diversity and equity issues are integrated into all aspects of the teacher-training curriculum.

- Training methods rely on experiential and cooperative peer learning, as well as on information giving and gathering.

REFERENCES

Hilliard, A. January, 1992. "Racism: Its origins and how it works." Paper presented at the meeting of the Mid-West Association for the Education of Young Children, Madison WI.

Lee, E. 1995. "Taking multicultural, anti-racist education seriously." In *Rethinking Schools: An agenda for change*. New York: New Press.

Affirmation, Solidarity and Critique: Moving Beyond Tolerance in Education

BY SONIA NIETO

"We want our students to develop **tolerance** of others," says a teacher when asked what multicultural education means to her. "The greatest gift we can give our students is a **tolerance** for differences," is how a principal explains it. A school's mission statement might be more explicit: "Students at the Jefferson School will develop critical habits of the mind, a capacity for creativity and risk-taking and tolerance for those different from themselves." In fact, if we were to listen to pronouncements at school board meetings, or conversations in teachers' rooms, or if we perused school handbooks, we would probably discover that when mentioned at all, multicultural education is associated more often with the term tolerance than with any other.

My purpose in this article is to challenge readers and indeed the very way that multicultural education is practiced in schools in general, to move beyond tolerance in both conceptualization and implementation. It is my belief that a movement beyond tolerance is absolutely necessary if multicultural education is to become more than a superficial "bandaid" or a "feel-good" additive to our school curricula. I will argue that tolerance is actually a low level of multicultural support, reflecting as it does an acceptance of the *status quo* with but slight accommodations to difference. I will review and expand upon a model of multicultural education that I have developed elsewhere in order to explore what multicultural education might actually look like in a school's policies and practices. (See Sonia Nieto, *Affirming Diversity: The Sociopolitical Context of Multicultural Education*, Longman, 2000.)

Levels of Multicultural Education Support

Multicultural education is not a unitary concept. On the contrary, it can be thought of as a range of options across a wide spectrum that includes such

> **TOLERANCE: THE CAPACITY FOR OR THE PRACTICE OF RECOGNIZING AND RESPECTING THE BELIEFS OR PRACTICES OF OTHERS.** — *THE AMERICAN HERITAGE DICTIONARY*, AS QUOTED IN *TEACHING TOLERANCE*, SPRING, 1993.

diverse strategies as bilingual/bicultural programs, ethnic studies courses, Afrocentric curricula, or simply the addition of a few "Holidays and Heroes" to the standard curriculum (see James A. Banks, *Teaching Strategies for Ethnic Studies,* Allyn & Bacon, 6th ed., 1997), just to name a few. Although all of these may be important parts of multicultural education, they represent incomplete conceptualizations and operationalizations of this complex educational reform movement. Unfortunately, however, multicultural education is often approached as if there were a prescribed script.

The most common understanding of multicultural education is that it consists largely of additive content rather than of structural changes in content and process. It is not unusual, then, to hear teachers say that they are "doing" multicultural education this year, or, as in one case that I heard, that they could not "do it" in the Spring because they had too many other things to "do." In spite of the fact that scholars and writers in multicultural education have been remarkably consistent over the years about the complexity of approaches in the field (see, especially, the analysis by Christine E. Sleeter & Carl A. Grant, "An Analysis of Multicultural Education in the United States," *Harvard Educational Review,* November, 1987), it has often been interpreted in either a simplistic or a monolithic way. It is because of this situation that I have attempted to develop a model that clarifies how various levels of multicultural education support may actually be apparent in schools.

Developing categories or models is always an inherently problematic venture and I therefore present the following model with some hesitancy. Whenever we classify and categorize reality, we run the risk that it will be viewed as static and arbitrary, rather than as messy, complex and contradictory, which we know it to be. Notwithstanding the value that theoretical models may have, they tend to represent information as if it were fixed and absolute. Yet we know too well that nothing happens exactly as portrayed in models and charts, much less social interactions among real people in settings such as schools. In spite of this, models or categories can be useful because they help make concrete situations more understandable and manageable. I therefore present the following model with both reluctance and hope: reluctance because it may improperly be viewed as set in stone, but hope because it may challenge teachers, administrators and educators in general to rethink what it means to develop a multicultural perspective in their schools.

The levels in this model should be viewed as necessarily dynamic, with penetrable borders. They should be understood as "interactive," in the words of Peggy McIntosh (see her *Interactive Phases of Curricular Revision: A Feminist Perspective,* Wellesley College Center for Research on Women, 1983). Thus, although these levels represent "ideal" categories that are internally consistent and therefore set, the model is not meant to suggest that schools are really like this. Probably no school would be a purely "monocultural" or "tolerant" school, given the stated characteristics under each of these categories. However, these categories are used in an effort to illustrate how support for diversity is manifested in schools in a variety of ways. Because multicultural education is primarily a set of beliefs and a philosophy, rather than a set program or fixed content, this model can assist us in determining how particular school policies and practices need to change in order to embrace the diversity of our students and their communities.

The four levels to be considered are: **tolerance; acceptance; respect**; and, finally, **affirmation, solidarity and critique.** Before going on to consider how multicultural education is manifested in schools that profess these philosophical orientations, it is first helpful to explore the antithesis of multicultural education, namely, **monocultural education,** because without this analysis we have nothing with which to compare it.

In the scenarios that follow, we go into five schools that epitomize different levels of multicultural education. All are schools with growing cultural diversity in their student populations; differences include staff backgrounds, attitudes and preparation, as well as curriculum and pedagogy. In our visits, we see how the curriculum, interactions among students, teachers and parents and other examples of attention to diversity are either apparent or lacking. We see how students of different backgrounds might respond to the policies and practices around them. (In another paper entitled "Creating Possibilities: Educating Latino Students in Massachusetts, in *The Education of Latino Students in Massachusetts: Policy and Research Implications,* published by the Gaston Institute for Latino Policy and Development in Boston, which I coedited with R. Rivera, I developed scenarios of schools that would provide different levels of support specifically for Latino students.)

MONOCULTURAL EDUCATION

Monocultural education describes a situation in which school structures, policies, curricula, instructional materials and even pedagogical strategies are primarily representative of only the dominant culture. In most United States schools, it can be defined as "the way things are."

We will begin our tour in a "monocultural school" that we'll call the George Washington Middle School. When we walk in, we see a sign that says "NO UNAUTHORIZED PERSONS ARE ALLOWED IN THE SCHOOL. ALL VISITORS MUST REPORT DIRECTLY TO THE PRINCIPAL'S OFFICE." The principal, assistant principal and counselor are all European American males, although the school's population is quite diverse, with large numbers of African American, Puerto Rican, Arab American, Central American, Korean and Vietnamese students. As we walk down the hall, we see a number of bulletin boards. On one, the coming Christmas holiday is commemorated; on another, the P.T.O.'s bake sale is announced; and on a third, the four basic food groups are listed, with examples given of only those foods generally considered to be "American."

The school is organized into 45 minute periods

of such courses as U.S. history, English, math, science, music appreciation, art and physical education. In the U. S. history class, students learn of the proud exploits, usually through wars and conquest, of primarily European American males. They learn virtually nothing about the contributions, perspectives, or talents of women or those outside the cultural mainstream. U.S. slavery is mentioned briefly in relation to the Civil War, but African Americans are missing thereafter. In English class, the students have begun their immersion in the "canon," reading works almost entirely written by European and European-American males, although a smattering of women and African-American (but no Asian, Latino, or American Indian) authors are included in the newest anthology. In music appreciation class, students are exposed to what is called "classical music," that is, European classical music, but the "classical" music of societies in Asia, Africa and Latin America is nowhere to be found. In art classes, students may learn about the art work of famous European and European American artists and occasionally about the "crafts" and "artifacts" of other cultures and societies mostly from the Third World.

Teachers at the George Washington Middle School are primarily European American women who have had little formal training in multicultural approaches or perspectives. They are proud of the fact that they are "color-blind," that is, that they see no differences among their students, treating them all the same. Of course, this does not extend to tracking, which they generally perceive to be in the interest of teaching all students to the best of their abilities. Ability grouping is a standard practice at the George Washington Middle School. There are four distinct levels of ability, from "talented and gifted" to "remedial." I.Q. tests are used to determine student placement and intellectually superior students are placed in "Talented and Gifted" programs and in advanced levels of math, science, English and social studies. Only these top students have the option of taking a foreign language. The top levels consist of overwhelmingly European-American

© EARL DOTTER/ALEC

Many schools provide little space for teachers to call parents.

and Asian-American students, but the school rationalizes that this is due to either the native intelligence of these students, or to the fact that they have a great deal more intellectual stimulation and encouragement in their homes. Thus, teachers have learned to expect excellent work from their top students, but little of students in their low-level classes, who they often see as lazy and disruptive.

Students who speak a language other than English as their native language are either placed in regular classrooms where they will learn to "sink or swim" or in "NE" (non-English) classes, where they are drilled in English all day and where they will remain until they learn English sufficiently well to perform in the regular classroom. In addition, parents are urged to speak to their children only in English at home. Their native language, whether Spanish, Vietnamese, or Korean, is perceived as a handicap to their learning and as soon as they forget it, they can get on with the real job of learning.

Although incidents of racism have occurred in the George Washington Middle School, they have been taken care of quietly and privately. For example, when racial slurs have been used, students have been admonished not to say them. When fights between children of different ethnic groups take place, the assistant principal has insisted that race or ethnicity has nothing to do with them; "kids will be kids" is the way he describes these incidents.

What exists in the George Washington Middle School is a monocultural environment with scant reference to the experiences of others from largely subordinated cultural groups. Little attention is paid to student diversity and the school curriculum is generally presented as separate from the community in which it is located. In addition, "dangerous" topics such as racism, sexism and homophobia are seldom discussed and reality is represented as finished and static. In summary, the George Washington School is a depressingly familiar scenario because it reflects what goes on in most schools in American society.

TOLERANCE

How might a school characterized by "tolerance" be different from a monocultural school? It is important here to mention the difference between the **denotation** and the **connotation** of words. According to the dictionary definition given at the beginning of this article, tolerance is hardly a value that one could argue with. After all, what is wrong with "recognizing and respecting the beliefs or practices of others"? On the contrary, this is a quintessential part of developing a multicultural perspective. (*Teaching Tolerance*, a journal developed by the Southern Poverty Law Center, has no doubt been developed with this perspective in mind and my critique here of tolerance is in no way meant to criticize this wonderful classroom and teacher resource.) Nevertheless, the connotation of words is something else entirely. When we think of what tolerance means in practice, we have images of a grudging but somewhat distasteful acceptance. To **tolerate** differences means that they are endured, not necessarily embraced. In fact, this level of support for multicultural education stands on shaky ground because what is tolerated today can too easily be rejected tomorrow. A few examples will help illustrate this point.

Our "tolerant" school is the Brotherhood Middle School. Here, differences are understood to be the inevitable burden of a culturally pluralistic society. A level up from a "color-blind" monocultural school, the "tolerant" school accepts differences but only if they can be modified. Thus, they are accepted, but because the ultimate goal is assimilation, differences

Student collaboration.

in language and culture are replaced as quickly as possible. This ideology is reflected in the physical environment, the attitudes of staff and the curriculum to which students are exposed.

When we enter the Brotherhood School, there are large signs in English welcoming visitors, although there are no staff on hand who can communicate with the families of the growing Cambodian student population. One prominently placed bulletin board proudly portrays the winning essays of this year's writing contest with the theme of "Why I am proud to be an American." The winners, a European-American sixth grader and a Vietnamese seventh grader, write in their essays about the many opportunities given to all people in our country, no matter what their race, ethnicity, or gender. Another bulletin board boasts the story of Rosa Parks, portrayed as a woman who was too tired to give up her seat on the bus, thus serving as a catalyst for the modern civil rights movement. (*Rethinking Our Classrooms* includes a powerful example of how people such as Rosa Parks have been decontextualized to better fit in with the U.S. mainstream conception of individual rather than collective struggle, thus adding little to children's understanding of institutionalized discrimination on our society; see "The Myth of 'Rosa Parks the Tired;'" by Herbert Kohl, in which Kohl reports that based on his research most stories used in American schools present Rosa Parks simply as "Rosa Parks the Tired.")

Nevertheless, a number of important structural changes are taking place at the Brotherhood School. An experiment has recently begun in which the sixth and seventh graders are in "family" groupings and these are labeled by family names such as the Jones family, the Smith family and the Porter family. Students remain together as a family in their major subjects (English, social studies, math and science) and there is no ability tracking in these classes. Because their teachers have a chance to meet and plan together daily, they are more readily able to develop integrated curricula. In fact, once in a while, they even combine classes so that they can team-teach and their students remain at a task for an hour and a half rather than the usual three quarters of an hour. The students seem to like this arrangement and have done some interesting work in their study of Washington, D.C. For instance, they used geometry to learn how the city was designed and have written to their congressional representatives to ask how bills become laws. Parents are involved in fundraising for an upcoming trip to the capital, where students plan to interview a number of their local legislators.

The curriculum at the Brotherhood School has begun to reflect some of the changes that a multicultural society demands. Students are encouraged to study a foreign language (except, of course, for those who already speak one; they are expected to learn English and in the process, they usually forget their native language). In addition, a number of classes have added activities on women, African-Americans and American Indians. Last year, for instance, Martin Luther King Day was celebrated by having all students watch a video of the "I Have a Dream" speech.

The majority of changes in the curriculum have occurred in the social studies and English departments, but the music teacher has also begun to add a more international flavor to her repertoire and the art classes recently went to an exhibit of the work of Romare Bearden. This year, a "multicultural teacher" has been added to the staff. She meets with all students in the school, seeing each group once a week for one period. Thus far, she has taught students about Chinese New Year, *Kwanzaa, Ramadan* and *Dia de los Reyes*. She is getting ready for the big multicultural event of the year, Black History Month. She hopes to work with other teachers to bring in guest speakers, show films about the civil rights movement and have an art contest in which students draw what the world would be like if Dr. King's dream of equality became a reality.

Students who speak a language other than English at the Brotherhood School are placed in special English as a Second Language (E.S.L.) classes where they are taught English as quickly, but sensitively, as possible. For instance, while they are encouraged to speak to one another in English, they are allowed to use their native language, but only

as a last resort. The feeling is that if they use it more often, it will become a "crutch." In any event, the E.S.L. teachers are not required to speak a language other than English; in fact, being bilingual is even considered a handicap because students might expect them to use their other language.

The principal of the Brotherhood School has made it clear that racism will not be tolerated here. Name-calling and the use of overtly racist and sexist textbooks and other materials are discouraged. Recently, some teachers attended a workshop on strategies for dealing with discrimination in the classroom. Some of those who attended expect to make some changes in how they treat students from different backgrounds.

Most teachers at the Brotherhood School have had little professional preparation to deal with the growing diversity of the student body. They like and genuinely want to help their students, but have made few changes in their curricular or instructional practices. For them, "being sensitive" to their students is what multicultural education should be about, not overhauling the curriculum. Thus, they acknowledge student differences in language, race, gender and social class, but still cannot quite figure out why some students are more successful than others. Although they would like to think not, they wonder if genetics or poor parental attitudes about education have something to do with it. If not, what can explain these great discrepancies?

ACCEPTANCE

Acceptance is the next level of supporting diversity. It implies that differences are acknowledged and their importance is neither denied nor belittled. It is at this level that we see substantial movement toward multicultural education. A look at how some of the school's policies and practices might change is indicative of this movement.

The name of our school is the Rainbow Middle School. As we enter, we see signs in English, Spanish and Haitian Creole, the major languages besides English spoken by students and their families. The principal of the Rainbow School is Dr. Belinda Clayton, the first African American principal ever appointed. She has designated her school as a "multicultural building," and has promoted a number of professional development opportunities for teachers that focus on diversity. These include seminars on diverse learning styles, bias-free assessment and bilingual education. In addition, she has hired not only Spanish and Haitian Creole speaking teachers for the bilingual classrooms, but has also diversified the staff in the "regular" program.

Bulletin boards outside the principal's office display the pictures of the "Students of the Month." This month's winners are Rodney Thomas, a sixth grader who has excelled in art, Neleida Cortes, a seventh grade student in the bilingual program and Melissa Newton, an eighth grader in the special education program. All three were given a special luncheon by the principal and their homeroom teachers. Another bulletin board focuses on "Festivals of Light" and features information about *Chanukah, Kwanzaa* and Christmas, with examples of *Las Posadas* in Mexico and Saint Lucia's Day in Sweden.

The curriculum at the Rainbow Middle School has undergone some changes to reflect the growing diversity of the student body. English classes include more choices of African American, Irish, Jewish and Latino literature written in English. Some science and math teachers have begun to make reference to famous scientists and mathematicians from a variety of backgrounds. In one career studies class, a number of parents have been invited to speak about their job and the training they had to receive in order to get those positions. All students are encouraged to study a foreign language and choices have been expanded to include Spanish, French, German and Mandarin Chinese.

Tracking has been eliminated in all but the very top levels at the Rainbow School. All students have the opportunity to learn algebra, although some are still counseled out of this option because their teachers believe it will be too difficult for them. The untracked classes seem to be a hit with the students and preliminary results have shown a slight improvement among all students. Some attempts have been made to provide flexible scheduling, with one day a week devoted to entire "learning blocks" where students work on a special project. One group recently engaged in an in-depth study of the elderly in their community. They learned about services available to them and they touched on poverty and lack of health care for many older Americans. As a result of this study, the group has added a community service component to the class; this involves going to the local Senior Center during their weekly learning block to read with the elderly residents.

Haitian and Spanish-speaking students are tested and, if found to be more proficient in their native language, are placed in transitional bilingual education programs. Because of lack of space in the school, the bilingual programs are located in the basement, near the boiler room. Here, students are taught the basic curriculum in their native language while learning English as a second language during one period of the day with an ESL specialist. Most ESL teachers are also fluent in a language other than English, helping them understand the process of acquiring a second language. The bilingual program calls for students to be "mainstreamed" (placed in what is called a "regular classroom") as quickly as possible, with a limit of three years on the outside. In the meantime, they are segregated from their peers for most of the day but have some classes with English-speaking students, including physical education, art and music. As they proceed through the program and become more fluent in English, they are "exited" out for some classes, beginning with math and social studies. While in the bilingual program, students' native cultures are sometimes used as the basis of the curriculum and they learn about the history of their people. There is, for instance, a history course on the Caribbean that is offered to both groups in their native languages. Nevertheless, neither Haitian and Latino students not in the bilingual program nor students of other backgrounds have access to these courses.

Incidents of racism and other forms of discrimination are beginning to be faced at the Rainbow Middle School. Principal Clayton deals with these carefully, calling in the offending students as well as their parents and she makes certain that students understand the severe consequences for name-calling or scapegoating others. Last year, one entire day was devoted to "diversity" and regular classes were canceled while students attended workshops focusing on discrimination, the importance of being sensitive to others and the influence on U.S. history of many different immigrants. They have also hosted a "Multicultural Fair" and published a cookbook with recipes donated by many different parents.

The Rainbow Middle School is making steady progress in accepting the great diversity of its students. They have decided that perhaps assimilation should not be the goal and have eschewed the old idea of the "melting pot." In its place, they have the "salad bowl" metaphor, in which all students bring something special that need not be reconstituted or done away with.

RESPECT

Respect is the next level of multicultural education support. It implies admiration and high esteem for diversity. When differences are respected, they are used as the basis for much of what goes on in schools. Our next scenario describes what this might look like.

The Sojourner Truth Middle School is located in a midsize town with a changing population. There is a fairly large African-American population with a growing number of students of Cape Verdean and Vietnamese background and the school staff reflects these changes, including teachers, counselors and special educators of diverse backgrounds. There is, for example, a Vietnamese speech pathologist and his presence has helped to alleviate the concerns of some teachers that the special needs of the Vietnamese children were not being addressed. He has found that while some students do indeed have speech problems, others do not, but teachers' unfamiliarity with the Vietnamese language made it difficult to know this.

When we enter the Sojourner Truth Middle School, we are greeted by a parent volunteer. She gives us printed material in all the languages represented in the school and invites us to the parents' lounge for coffee, tea and danish. We are then encouraged to walk around and explore the school. Bulletin boards boast of students' accomplishments in the Spanish Spelling Bee, the local *Jeopardy* Championship and the W.E.B. DuBois Club of African American history. It is clear from the children's pictures that there is wide participation of many students in all of these activities. The halls are abuzz with activity as students go from one class to another and most seem eager and excited by school.

Professional development is an important principle at the Sojourner Truth Middle School. Teachers, counselors and other staff are encouraged to take courses at the local university and to keep up with the literature in their field. To make this more feasible, the staff gets release time weekly to get together. As a consequence, the curriculum has been through tremendous changes. Teachers have formed committees to develop their curriculum. The English department decided to use its time to have reading and discussion groups with some of the newly available multicultural literature with which they were unfamiliar. As a result, they have revamped the curriculum into such overarching themes as **coming of age, immigration, change and continuity and individual and collective responsibility.** They have found that it is easier to select literature to reflect themes such as these and the literature is by its very nature multicultural. For instance, for the theme **individual and collective responsibility** they have chosen stories of varying difficulty, including *The Diary of Anne Frank, Bridge to Terabithia* (by Katherine Paterson), *Morning Girl* (by Michael Dorris) and *Let the Circle be Unbroken* (by Mildred D. Taylor), among others. The English teachers have in turn invited the history, art and science departments to join them in developing some integrated units with these themes. Teachers from the art and music departments have agreed to work with them and have included lessons on Vietnamese dance, Guatemalan weaving, Jewish Klezmer music and American Indian story telling as examples of individual and collective responsibility in different communities.

Other changes are apparent in the curriculum as well, for it has become more antiracist and honest. When studying World War II, students learn about the heroic role played by the United States and also about the Holocaust, in which six million Jews and millions of others including Gypsies (Romani people), gays and lesbians, people with disabilities and many dissenters of diverse backgrounds, were exterminated. They also learn, for the first time, about the internment of over a hundred thousand Japanese and Japanese Americans on our own soil.

It has become "safe" to talk about such issues as the crucial role of labor in U.S. history and the part played by African-Americans in freeing themselves from bondage, both subjects thought too "sensitive" to be included previously. This is one reason why the school was renamed for a woman known for her integrity and courage.

The Sojourner Truth Middle School has done away with all ability grouping. When one goes into a classroom, it is hard to believe that students of all abilities are learning together because the instruction level seems to be so high. Upon closer inspection, it becomes apparent that there are high expectations for all students. Different abilities are accommodated by having some students take more time than others, providing cooperative groups in which students change roles and responsibilities and through ongoing dialogue among all students.

Students who speak a language other than English are given the option of being in a "maintenance bilingual program," that is, a program based on using their native language throughout their schooling, not just for three years. Changing the policy that only students who could not function in English were eligible for bilingual programs, this school has made the program available to those who speak English in addition to their native language. Parents and other community members who speak these languages are invited in to classes routinely to talk about their lives, jobs, or families, or to tell stories or share experiences. Students in the bilingual program are not, however, segregated from their peers all day, but join them for a number of academic classes.

A participant in a writing project for youth in Washington, DC called The Books Project proudly displays a story he wrote in Spanish, "El Gusano Perdido" ("The Lost Worm").

Teachers and other staff members at this middle school have noticed that incidents of name-calling and interethnic hostility have diminished greatly since the revised curriculum was put into place. Perhaps more students see themselves in the curriculum and feel less angry about their invisibility; perhaps more teachers have developed an awareness and appreciation for their students' diversity while learning about it; perhaps the more diverse staff is the answer; or maybe it's because the community feels more welcome into the school. Whatever it is, the Sojourner Truth Middle School has developed an environment in which staff and students are both expanding their ways of looking at the world.

AFFIRMATION, SOLIDARITY AND CRITIQUE

Affirmation, solidarity and critique is based on the premise that the most powerful learning results when students work and struggle with one another, even if it is sometimes difficult and challenging. It begins with the assumption that the many differences that students and their families represent are embraced and accepted as legitimate vehicles

for learning and that these are then extended. What makes this level different from the others is that conflict is not avoided, but rather accepted as an inevitable part of learning. Because multicultural education at this level is concerned with equity and social justice and because the basic values of different groups are often diametrically opposed, conflict is bound to occur.

Affirmation, solidarity and critique is also based on understanding that culture is not a fixed or unchangeable artifact and is therefore subject to critique. Passively accepting the status quo of any culture is thus inconsistent with this level of multicultural education; simply substituting one myth for another contradicts its basic assumptions because no group is inherently superior or more heroic than any other. As eloquently expressed by Mary Kalantzis and Bill Cope in their 1990 work *The Experience of Multicultural Education in Australia: Six Case Studies,* "Multicultural education, to be effective, needs to be more active. It needs to consider not just the pleasure of diversity but more fundamental issues that arise as different groups negotiate community and the basic issues of material life in the same space — a process that equally might generate conflict and pain."

Multicultural education without critique may result in cultures remaining at the romantic or exotic stage. If students are to transcend their own cultural experience in order to understand the differences of others, they need to go through a process of reflection and critique of their cultures and those of others. This process of critique, however, begins with a solid core of solidarity with others who are different from themselves. When based on true respect, critique is not only necessary but in fact healthy.

The Arturo Schomburg Middle School is located in a midsize city with a very mixed population of Puerto Ricans, Salvadorans, American Indians, Polish Americans, Irish Americans, Chinese Americas, Filipinos and African Americans. The school was named for a Black Puerto Rican scholar who devoted his life to exploring the role of Africans in the Americas, in the process challenging the myth he had been told as a child in Puerto Rico that Africans had "no culture."

The school's logo, visible above the front door, is a huge tapestry made by the students and it symbolizes a different model of multicultural education from that of either the "melting pot" or the "salad bowl." According to a publication of the National Association of State Boards of Education *(The American Tapestry: Educating a Nation),* "A tapestry is a handwoven textile. When examined from the back, it may simply appear to be a motley group of threads. But when reversed, the threads work together to depict a picture of structure and beauty" (p. 1). According to Adelaide Sanford, one of the study group members who wrote this publication, a tapestry also symbolizes, through its knots, broken threads and seeming jumble of colors and patterns on the back, the tensions, conflicts and dilemmas that a society needs to work out. This spirit of both collaboration and struggle is evident in the school.

When we enter the Schomburg Middle School, the first thing we notice is a banner proclaiming the school's motto: LEARN, REFLECT, QUESTION, AND WORK TO MAKE THE WORLD A BETTER PLACE. This is the message that reverberates throughout the school. Participation is another theme that is evident and the main hall contains numerous pictures of students in classrooms, community service settings and extracurricular activities. Housed in a traditional school building, the school has been transformed into a place where all children feel safe and are encouraged to learn to

the highest levels of learning. While there are typical classrooms of the kind that are immediately recognizable to us, the school also houses centers that focus on specific areas of learning. There is, for instance, a studio where students can be found practicing traditional Filipino dance and music, as well as European ballet and modern American dance, among others. Outside, there is a large garden that is planted, cared for and harvested by the students and faculty. The vegetables are used by the cafeteria staff in preparing meals and they have noticed a marked improvement in the eating habits of the children since the menu was changed to reflect a healthier and more ethnically diverse menu.

We are welcomed into the school by staff people who invite us to explore the many different classrooms and other learning centers. Those parents who are available during the day can be found assisting in classrooms, in the Parents' Room working on art projects or computer classes, or attending workshops by other parents or teachers on topics ranging from cross-cultural child-rearing to ESL. The bulletin boards are ablaze with color and include a variety of languages, displaying student work from critical essays on what it means to be an American to art projects that celebrate the talents of many of the students. Learning is going on everywhere, whether in classrooms or in small group collaborative projects in halls.

What might the classrooms look like in this school? For one, they are characterized by tremendous diversity. Tracking and special education, as we know them, have been eliminated at the Schomburg Middle School. Students with special needs are taught along with all others, although they are sometimes separated for small group instruction with students not classified as having special needs. All children are considered "talented" and special classes are occasionally organized for those who excel in dance, mathematics or science. No interested students are excluded from any of these offerings. Furthermore, all students take algebra and geometry and special coaching sessions are available before, after and during school hours for these and other subjects.

Classes are flexible, with an interdisciplinary curriculum and team-teaching resulting in sessions that sometimes last as long as three hours. The physical environment in classrooms is varied: some are organized with round worktables, others have traditional desks and still others have scant furniture to allow for movement. Class size also varies from small groups to large, depending on the topic at hand. Needless to say, scheduling at this school is a tremendous and continuing challenge, but faculty and students are committed to this more flexible arrangement and willing to allow for the problems that it may cause.

There are no "foreign languages" at the Schomburg Middle school, nor is there, strictly speaking, a bilingual program. Rather, the entire school is multilingual and all students learn at least a second language in addition to their native language. This means that students are not segregated by language, but instead work in bilingual settings where two languages are used for instruction. At present, the major languages used are English, Spanish and Tagalog, representing the common languages spoken by this school community. It is not unusual to see students speaking these languages in classrooms, the hallways or the playground, even among those for whom English is a native language.

Students at the Schomburg Middle School seem engaged, engrossed and excited about learning. They have been involved in a number of innovative long-range projects that have resulted from the interdisciplinary curriculum. For instance, working with a Chinese-American artist in residence, they wrote, directed and produced a play focusing on the "Know-Nothing" Movement in U.S. history that resulted in, among other things, the Chinese Exclusion Act of 1882. In preparation for the play, they read a great deal and did extensive research. For example, they contacted the Library of Congress for information on primary sources and reviewed newspapers and magazines from the period to get a sense of the climate that led to Nativism. They also designed and sewed all the costumes and sets. In addition, they interviewed recent immigrants of many backgrounds and found that they had a range of experiences from positive to negative in their new country. On the day of the play, hundreds of parents and other community members attended. Students also held a debate on the pros and cons of continued immigration and received up-to-date information concerning immigration laws from their congressional representative.

The curriculum at the Schomburg Middle School is dramatically different from the George Washington School, the first school we visited. Teachers take very seriously their responsibility of **teaching complexity**. Thus, students have learned that there are many sides to every story and that in order to make informed decisions, they need as much information as they can get. Whether in English, science, art, or any other class, students have been encouraged to be critical of every book, newspaper, curriculum, or piece of information by asking questions such as: **Who wrote the book? Who's missing in this story? Why?** Using questions such as these as a basis, they are learning that every story has a point of view and that every point of view is at best partial and at worst distorted. They are also learning that their own backgrounds, rich and important as they may be, have limitations that can lead to parochial perceptions. Most of all, even at this age, students are learning that every topic is fraught with difficulties and they are wrestling with issues as diverse as homelessness, solar warming and how the gender expectations of different cultures might limit opportunities for girls. Here, nothing is taboo as a topic of discussion as long as it is approached with respect and in a climate of caring.

What this means for teachers is that they have had to become learners along with their students. They approach each subject with curiosity and an open mind and during the school day they have time to study, meet with colleagues and plan their curriculum accordingly. Professional development here means not only attending courses at a nearby university, but collaborating with colleagues in study groups that last anywhere from half a day to several months. These provide a forum in which teachers can carefully study relevant topics or vexing problems. Some of these study groups have focused on topics such as Reconstruction and the history of the Philippines, to educational issues such as cooperative learning and diverse cognitive styles.

Especially noteworthy at this school is that **multicultural education** is not separated from **education;** that is, all education is by its very nature multicultural. English classes use literature written by a wide variety of people from countries where English is spoken. This has resulted in these classes becoming not only multicultural, but international as well. Science classes do not focus on contributions made by members of specific ethnic groups, but have in fact been transformed to consider how science itself is conceptualized, valued and practiced by those who have traditionally been outside the scientific mainstream. Issues such as AIDS education, healing in different cultures and scientific racism have all been the subject of study.

One of the major differences between this school and the others we visited has to do with its governance structure. There is a Schomburg School Congress consisting of students, faculty, parents and other community members and it has wide decision making powers, from selecting the principal to determining reasonable and equitable disciplinary policies and practices. Students are elected by their classmates and, although at the beginning these were little more than popularity contests, in recent months it has been clear that students are beginning to take this responsibility seriously. This is probably because they are being taken seriously by the adults in the group. For instance, when students in one class decided that they wanted to plan a class trip to a neighboring city to coincide with their study of toxic wastes and the environment, they were advised to do some preliminary planning: what would be the educational objectives of such a trip? How long would it take? How much would it cost? After some research and planning, they presented their ideas to the Congress and a fundraising plan that included students, parents and community agencies was started.

The Schomburg School is a learning center that is undergoing important changes every day. As teachers discover the rich talents that all students bring to school, they develop high expectation for them all. The climate that exists in this school is one of possibility, because students' experiences are used to build on their learning and expand their horizons. Students in turn are realizing that while their experiences are important and unique, they are only one experience of many. A new definition of "American" is being forged at this school, one that includes everybody. Above all, learning here is exciting, engrossing, inclusive and evolving.

Conclusion

One might well ask how realistic these scenarios are, particularly the last one. Could a school such as this really exist? Isn't this just wishful thinking? What about the reality of bond issues rejected by voters?; of teachers woefully unprepared to deal with the diversity in their classrooms?; of universities that do little more than offer stale "Mickey Mouse" courses?; of schools with no pencils, paper and chalk, much less computers and video cameras?; of rampant violence in streets, homes and schools?; of drugs and crime?; of parents who are barely struggling to keep their families together and can spare precious little time to devote to volunteering at school?

These are all legitimate concerns that our society needs to face and they remind us that schools need to be understood within their sociopolitical contexts. That is, our schools exist in a society in which social and economic stratification are facts of life,

Elementary school students at PS205 in Brooklyn, New York learn conflict resolution skills.

where competition is taught over caring and where the early sorting that takes place in educational settings often lasts a lifetime. Developing schools with a multicultural perspective is not easy; if it were, they would be everywhere. But schools with a true commitment to diversity, equity and high levels of learning are difficult to achieve precisely because the problems they face are pervasive and seemingly impossible to solve. Although the many problems raised above are certainly daunting, the schools as currently organized are simply not up to the challenge. In the final analysis, if we believe that all students deserve to learn at the very highest levels, then we need a vision of education that will help achieve this end.

The scenarios above, however, are not simply figments of my imagination. As you read through the scenarios, you probably noticed bits and pieces of your own school here and there. However, because the "monocultural school" is the one with which we are most familiar and unfortunately comfortable, the other scenarios might seem farfetched or unrealistic. Although they are **ideal** in the sense that they are not true pictures of specific schools, these scenarios nevertheless describe **possibilities** because they all exist to some degree in our schools today. These are not pie-in-the-sky visions, but composites of what goes on in schools every day. As such, they provide building blocks for how we might go about transforming schools. In fact, were we to design schools based on the ideals that our society has always espoused, they would no doubt come close to the last scenario.

It is not, however, a monolithic model or one that can develop overnight. The participants in each school need to develop their own vision so that step by step, with incremental changes, schools become more multicultural and thus more inclusive and more exciting places for learning. If we believe that young people deserve to be prepared with skills for living ethical and productive lives in an increasingly diverse and complex world, then we need to transform schools so that they not only teach what have been called "the basics," but also provide an apprenticeship in democracy and social justice. It is unfair to expect our young people to develop an awareness and respect for democracy if they have not experienced it and it is equally unrealistic; to expect them to be able to function in a pluralistic society if all we give them are skills for a monocultural future. This is our challenge in the years ahead: to conquer the fear of change and imagine how we might create exciting possibilities for all students in all schools.

Sonia Nieto is Professor of Education in Language, Literacy and Culture in the School of Education, University of Massachusetts at Amherst. Dr. Nieto has published numerous books and articles on curriculum issues in multicultural and bilingual education, the education of Latinos in the United States and Puerto Ricans in children's literature. Two of her widely used books are Affirming Diversity: The Sociopolitical Context of Multicultural Education *(Addison-Wesley, 2000) and* The Light in Their Eyes: Creating Multicultural Learning Communities *(Teachers College Press, 1999). E-mail: snieto@educ.umass.edu*

Reprinted with permission from Multicultural Education Magazine, *Spring 1994.*

EDUCATING FOR CRITICAL PRACTICE

BY MARGO OKAZAWA-REY

At the San Francisco State University, School of Social Work, our mission is to educate students to become social work practitioners committed to working with peoples of color, women, children, gays and lesbians, people with disabilities, poor people and others in oppressed communities, with the aim of empowering individuals, families and communities and being active participants in progressive social change. Our hope is that social workers we graduate would not only know the history of how social workers have helped perpetuate oppression in communities of color but would work with their clients to empower them, or would examine the overall climate in schools for youth of color and work with them to improve un-supportive conditions. To this end, we have a required two-semester course on racism, oppression and social work practice with peoples of color, in our Foundation Curriculum for Master of Social Work students, called "Ethnic and Cultural Concepts I and II."[1] The overall goals of the course are to:

▸ define and present a critical[2] analysis of racism, and examine its connections to other forms of oppression, in the United States;

▸ understand the relationship of racism to capitalism;

▸ assist students in becoming aware of and examining their own attitudes, beliefs, biases and in knowing their position in this society, based on race, class, gender and other social ascriptions;

▸ encourage students to connect what happens to individuals and families (the micro level of interaction) with what happens in their community settings (the meso level) and at the larger institutional level and global level (the macro level). That is, we encourage students to think about personal problems as public issues;

▸ examine both the gate-keeping and helping functions of social work by gaining a critical understanding of theories and practice models, and how the biases and perspectives embedded in them, by definition, may be discriminatory or oppressive;

▸ create alternative theories and practice models that help empower and liberate oppressed individuals, families and communities;

▸ be inspired to become critical social work practitioners and activists who, by working collectively with others in the communities, will help transform our society into a just society.

COURSE CONTENT

The first semester of the course is focused on macro analysis; that is, we look at the "big picture" of oppression and racism, and the connections between racism and other forms of oppression such as sexism, classism and heterosexism. The key questions that frame the course are:

▸ What is oppression? What is racism and how does it work in the United States?

▸ How is racism connected to other forms of oppression, such as sexism and classism?

▸ How do racism and other forms of oppression manifest in social policies?

▸ What does it mean to be of a particular race, class, gender, sexual orientation, etc.? How are we individually privileged and disadvantaged according to a particular set of social characteristics we embody?

The semester is divided into three sections: a) definition of terms, such as oppression and racism, and analysis of institutions; b) analysis of the impact of racism on peoples of color and White people; and c) analysis of social policies. In the first section, the students learn about the nature, role and function of societal institutions, such as education, religion, government, the media and family, and examine them for bias and discrimination. It is here many students begin to see, for the first time, the institutionalized nature of discrimination, and equally significant, the interlocking/re-enforcing features of institutions.

I also include a good amount of the history of racism and its relationship to European and U.S. imperialism and colonialism[3], and to the development of capitalism. Students learn, for example, the socially constructed nature of the concept of race and racial categories, including the creation of whiteness. Many are surprised when they read that the pseudo-scientific racial categories ("Negroid, Caucasoid, Mongoloid") we all were taught in school

Families write stories together at the Mt. Pleasant Library, Washington, DC.

© RICK REINHARD, 1993

were originally invented to create a social hierarchy that placed White people on top and Black people on the bottom and to justify the exploitation of peoples of color around the globe for the purpose of gathering raw materials needed for the industrial era in Europe and the United States. In this discussion students are also exposed to the fact that the overarching capitalist principles of turning everything, including human beings and intangibles such as love, into commodities ("commodification") for sale, and of maximizing profits have been practiced at the expense of human life and human spirit, the environment and whatever else necessary. From this section, students then begin to make the connections between early the history of Western expansionism with contemporary globalization of the economy and multinational corporations.

In the second segment of the course I move the focus to the effects of racism on both peoples of color and White people. I begin by asking the question, what does it mean to be a person of color, mixed-race person, or White person in the United States? Not surprisingly, students of color have thought about this question time and again, but not neces-

sarily beyond the experience of individual and group victimization. Also not surprising, many White students have never thought about what it means to be White. Instead they most typically approach the analysis of their personal experiences from the lens of gender, ethnicity, class, or sexual orientation. These White students soon come to realize that not thinking about being White is an example of having privilege based on race.

This section on the effects of racism is a particularly significant marker for most people in the class. Above all else, it is the first time that many have had the opportunity to discuss their experiences, both racial and nonracial, in a mixed-race setting. They are forced to confront ideas, experiences and feelings they may have been able to avoid, due to the segregation of many social settings. In particular, the most eye-opening experiences are those that compel students to see and understand the contradictory nature of many people's lives, which breaks down the monolithic ways they typically perceive and understand the experiences of other persons or groups. For example, students of color are shocked when they hear of an experience of White students who were tracked into lower achievement levels due to their class background; most everyone looks in amazement when an African American woman shares her connections to Buddhism. Out of these kinds of encounters, the students and I are impelled to identify both differences and commonalties among us; recognize contradictions, such as how one often is both privileged[4] and disadvantaged structurally, e.g., upper-middle-class, heterosexual, Latina and working-class, gay, White man; and search for possibilities for alliance-building given all they have discovered.

The third section is learning about and examining various social policies and institutional practices, such as Affirmative Action, immigration policies and standardized testing in schools. This is also the opportunity for the class to think about alternative policies and practices that could better address the issue the established policy is attempting to address.

In the second semester, we focus on social work practice. The key questions that frame this semester are:

▸ How is it possible for well intentioned practitioners to do not-so-helpful things in oppressed communities?

▸ What constitutes "good practice" in oppressed communities?

▸ What is our vision of empowerment practice?

The semester is divided into four sections. We begin by spending several class meetings analyzing the historical and contemporary construction of professionalism, the ideology of "blaming the victim," and the effect of unequal distribution of institutional and personal power in the context of social workers' relationships with clients. We also critically analyze how individual and social problems are defined by mainstream practitioners, social service agencies and institutions, including asking questions such as, who benefits from a particular definition? Next we examine the development of existing social work theories and practice models designed to address certain problems, and critique them for racial, gender, class and other biases. In the third section, I have students examine three major contexts in which people live their lives: family, community and school. Finally, I choose several current problem areas, such as work and employment, crime and violence, immigration, health and interethnic conflicts (conflicts between communities of color, such as Asian/African American), that we explore in great detail. Finally, after the critique and analysis, students are asked to redefine a particular problem of their choosing and design an alternative practice model that takes into account much of what they discovered and learned during the year.

During the second semester, it becomes plain to everyone how difficult it is to imagine possibilities for change that are outside the individualist/capitalist framework. For example, a group working on improving the welfare-to-employment transitions programs could only think about micro-enterprise — a woman owning her business in her community — as a viable option for her to become economically independent. Out of this awareness, we are then able to discuss in great detail what it would take for us to first imagine, then build, a truly egalitarian, economically and socially just society. Although this discussion may seem utopian and pie-in-the-sky to some, maybe to us all at some moments, it raises the important point that currently progressive people, as a whole, have no clearly articulated vision of what kind of society we all want to be a part of. It soon becomes clear to us that, in fact, many of our actions are reactive, whether at the local or national level; that is reacting to or countering a "Contract with America," instead of articulating and publicizing our own visions and agendas.

TEACHING PRINCIPLES

The course is an immersion experience. Students are required to engage at the intellectual, emotional and spiritual levels of their being, as the class discussion and activities, as well as homework assignments, demand total involvement and participation. They must engage with subject matter, with their own intellectual and emotional reactions to information that is new, unfamiliar and challenges their taken-for-granted views of the world, and with other students and their reactions. As the teacher, I inundate students with difficult analytical questions at every turn. Most of all, I challenge them to think about and understand our society, and people's situations within it, from the macro perspective: institutional, political, sociological and "Big Picture." This is to counter the dominant ideological perspectives that are most often taught in schools, which often cover up racism and all other forms of oppression, and with which students are most familiar and comfortable: the individual and the psychological. To these ends, I attempt to apply the following teaching principles I have formulated and modified, based on experiences during the past eight years of teaching, and drawn heavily from the work of Paulo Freire and other critical educational theorists.

1. **Use a variety of materials as "text."** I use practically everything as material we can learn from. This includes the usual analytical and theoretical books and articles; fiction and poetry; and newspaper and magazine articles from the popular press. The most interesting material for text, however, comes many times from students' rich experiences and their observations of everyday life and from the conversations and dynamics of the classroom. For example, in a typical class of 35 students, about one-third to one-half are peoples of color, both immigrant and U.S.-born; one-fourth are gay, lesbian or bisexual; they span the range of economic classes; and most are in their late-20s to late-30s. Even just from a demographic standpoint, one can imagine the wealth of experiences and perspectives they bring to the classroom! When people begin sharing their experiences, exploring new, and often very controversial, ideas and information and listening to other students' divergent views, the classroom is transformed into a very exciting forum for learning.

2. **Employ a variety of activities.** Many college and graduate school classrooms are filled to the windows with one-way talk: from the teacher to the students, where teacher pumps the students with lots of information, with little room for discussion or critical reflection of what is being presented. I do very little lecturing. Instead, I use a combination of conversational and experiential methods, audio-visual aids, student presentations and practical activities outside the classroom. Role plays, simulations, group problem-solving exercises and community research projects all require students to engage with the subject matter, and with one another, on a variety of levels (see activity below). Students are also required to keep a weekly journal, which I collect three times during each semester, responding to the assigned readings, analyzing their observations of events and incidents related to racism and reflecting on what and how they are learning in the course. This also becomes a vehicle by which each student and I can have a kind of private discussion about whatever she or he is experiencing.

3. **As much as possible, relate the course work to everyday life, and theory with practice.** For each content area I ask students to apply the analyses and theories to "real life" by asking them to provide examples from their own experiences and observa-

DEFINITION OF RACISM ACTIVITY

The purpose of this activity is to generate a common definition of racism. This role play works on the principle of using participants' experience, knowledge and observation as "text."

IDEAL NUMBER OF PARTICIPANTS
Any number larger than five.

MATERIALS NEEDED
Chalkboard or newsprint.

TIME
Approximately two hours for a group of up to 20 or so people; longer if the group is significantly larger.

METHOD

1. Divide the whole group into smaller groups of at least five but not more than eight members.

2. Ask each group to come up with a collective definition of racism. Ask them to generate as pre-cise a definition as they possibly can.

3. Instruct them to make up a five-minute skit that illustrates their definition. Give the group approximately 30 minutes to complete these two parts.

4. When all are finished, ask for groups to volunteer for the presentation. After each group completes its skit, ask the observers to identify what they saw as examples of racism.

5. After all the presentations, have the whole group synthesize their definitions and observations.

ROLE OF FACILITATOR
The primary role of the facilitator is to make sure the group arrives at a definition that includes the micro, meso and macro levels of racism. The tendency, at least in the beginning, is for participants to identify primarily individual actions as racism.

© Sam Deaner

tions as well as to take into their own situations what they have learned in class. In the section on the media, for example, I ask them to analyze one medium of their choice — TV sitcoms, evening news, weekly news magazines, academic journals, children's books, etc. — for racist content. Here they are compelled to reexamine everyday sources of information (they soon come to discover much misinformation, distortion and lies) using the analytical framework they learned in class, then theorize from their findings.

4. **Ask critical questions.** I inundate the classroom with difficult questions, not just about the whats (descriptions), but also whys (analyses) and hows (processes). Moreover, I frame the questions in ways that will require them to engage intellectually and emotionally, challenge their usual ways of understanding a phenomenon or situation, compel them to think about how they themselves, both personally and professionally, stand on issues and to recognize the contradictions in what they believe and how they actually behave and push them to envision possibilities for change. In our discussion about the Republican Party's "Contract with America," I asked them to analyze the content, point by point, asking questions such as:

▸ What are the underlying assumptions?

▸ What is fact, opinion, belief, etc.?

▸ Who is the audience that is being courted?

▸ How do you think the points outlined in the Contract were formulated?

▸ Why these particular points, at this time in U.S. history?

I then instructed them to switch the focus of their analysis to themselves and the people around them, such as their families, friends, significant others, colleagues and people in their neighborhoods. I generated questions such as:

▸ Which points are attractive to you and why?

▸ If you were sitting at the dining table with your family of origin talking about the Contract, what would the various members of your family be saying? Why?

▸ Was there ever a time in your life when you believed or thought exactly, or similarly, to what is being promoted? Did you change? How?

5. **Require students to work in groups.** Many students have never worked in groups, even in their professional roles. The best they might have done is attend staff meetings or worked with one other person. Some who do have group experience often describe it as having been an unpleasant one. Both inexperienced and experienced students carry around with them two interesting assumptions about group work: individual effort yields better

results; the group will hold individual members back. These two assumptions, of course, are embedded in the dominant ideology of individualism in the larger society. Thus, working on a group project becomes a major learning experience for most of them. I devise one group project assignment each semester wherein the members have to do both analytical and creative work. I also frequently assign group papers, in-class problem-solving exercises, presentations and so forth. As an integral part of the group work, students are asked to analyze and reflect on their group's process during the semester, which is presented to me in writing in the form of a report, or in person, as a group, during a conference. The content of this includes description and analysis of process, issues related to class, race, gender, etc., that influenced the dynamics, the main things they learned and what they would do differently next time.

6. **Apply democratic principles in the classroom.** Although the structural inequality between teacher and students heavily influences the dynamics in the class, I attempt to make it as democratic as possible. I use participatory decision making methods, encourage input in course content (often switch topics mid-semester if deemed necessary or appropriate), structure time students spend only with themselves and generally support open dialogue with both content and classroom dynamics. I have also experimented with allowing students to grade themselves at the end of the semester, based on the nonnegotiable criterion that a student may do so only if she or he has missed no more than one class.

Outcomes

"770/771," as the course is often referred to, is an informative, intense, overwhelming, and ultimately, for some students, a transformative experience. Throughout the five years of having taught this course, I have identified several consistent outcomes: a) understanding the importance of macro level and global level analysis; b) new understanding of racism as institutionalized discrimination, bound up in interlocking institutions that re-enforce each other; c) the global reach of racism; d) sustained ongoing working relationships among students after leaving the School; and e) renewed commitment to progressive social change.

The most frequently repeated comment at the end of the course is, "I never used to think macro until this class!" This, I think, attests to the thorough indoctrination we receive about the individual being the final and ultimate location of whatever oc-

curs in this society. We are all taught to see everything from the perspective of the individual, with the assumption that each of us ultimately controls our own lives, good or bad. Accordingly, we have been socialized to understand racism as an individual psychological phenomenon, where someone (anyone) hates or mistreats another due to her or his skin color, or as the work of extremist groups such as the neo-Nazis or the Ku Klux Klan. We often explain the former as the result of some psychological problem, as in "low self-esteem," and the latter as a horrible deviation. There is little acknowledgment and awareness that racism is the ideology of White supremacy embedded in every institution in this country, which does its discriminatory work, irrespective of, and despite, individuals' good intentions. Students come to realize that unless one truly comprehends the institutionalized character of racism, it will be impossible to transform it.

Related to understanding racism at the macro level is becoming cognizant that the ideology of White supremacy embedded in racism has been spread globally as an outgrowth of the globalization of the economy, which began with European, and continued with the later U.S. colonization around the world. The fact that Europe and the United States used racial and cultural differences to justify the massive exploitation, sometimes the genocide, of peoples of color, and appropriation of rich natural and human resources, around the world horrifies students but also provides them a starting point from which to make connections between the exploitation of one group with that of another. They reach the conclusion that the profit motive of capitalism is contrary to the life-enhancing and life-affirming principles, such as interdependence, wholeness of body, mind and spirit, necessary for sustainable life on this planet. They also begin to see the importance of alliance-building, and the necessity of avoiding identity politics, where a group is interested only in its own welfare or issues, and of creating a hierarchy of oppression by asserting certain groups are categorically worse off than others.

Another important outcome of the course, supported by the experience of being in school together, is the long-lasting relationships that develop as a result of intensive group work during the year. Many students have continued working with members of their original groups to complete their culminating experience project for fulfilling their degree requirements. Others work closely after graduation in their professional settings to continue the work begun in the course. In one notable case, three students working in three different school sites, one in Alameda County, another in San Francisco and the third in Marin County, annually organize a combined multicultural in-service for their staff and interns that is a condensed version of 770/771. This gathering is unique because the organizing of it cuts across school district and social service agency bureaucratic lines and because the composition of the group is multiracial, mixed-class and gender and intergenerational. It would take tremendous more effort to organize this kind of event if we were to follow strict bureaucratic procedures and protocol, rather than use the informal connection between the former SFSU students!

Last, many students leave the course inspired to become active participants in community organizing activities. This interest often starts by becoming involved in school related activism, such as stronger participation in school governance issues like inclusion of gay and lesbian content into the MSW curriculum. Many times also students initiate a schoolwide involvement in activism in the community, such as organizing against anti-immigration legislation. This kind of involvement gives me the hope that the work we began in class will continue long after class is over.

The following comments, taken from students' self-evaluations from the Fall, 1995 SW 770 class, illustrate some of the points I have made in this paper. These comments are answers to the question, What were the most important things you learned about the course content?

The way the course broke down racism from a macro to a micro level gave me a perspective on racism that was revolutionary. I was able to see a world view of economics and racism and how it affects people of color. Opening up this makes the connections clear on how racism is a vital part of how this government and many governments operate around the world.

One thing I learned that has been significant and powerful for me is how our capitalistic economic system feeds and feeds on exploitation of poor and working-class people, including those in developing countries. I had not previously understood that capitalism requires keeping a large group of people

in extreme poverty, and is deliberately and purposefully racist, promoting divisions among people in order for the dominant group to maintain political, economic and social power and control....I also learned that all the institutions in this country...are inherently racist and exist for the purpose of maintaining the power and wealth of the dominant group, and the much larger group...as a result live in poverty. The [White] people in the so-called "middle-class" have no real power, but buy into the system in exchange for wages and an illusion of power largely through identification with the dominant group on the basis of race.

The most important thing I really got was that I have not considered this [racism] my issue/my struggle and I have been wrong.

Throughout the semester I have thought a lot about what it means to speak out against racism to get acknowledgment or separate myself from other Whites. This keeps the focus on me and is one way I have distanced myself from racism. Instead, I am trying to work on being an ally by using my privilege to confront situations without putting myself in the center.

I learned that we have reason for "critical optimism." There have been allies who have resisted the dominant system, and with organizing and joining together with all oppressed groups, it's possible to change the system.

Notes

1. Students in the Undergraduate Program are required to take a one-semester course on sexism and another one-semester course on racism, heterosexism and able-bodyism.

2. The term *critical* is used throughout the paper to describe theories, analytical frameworks and ways of understanding and being in the world that challenge social hierarchies, institutionalized discrimination, capitalism and ethnocentric thoughts and perspectives.

3. It has been quite an eye-opener to discover how little students know of the real history of the United States, or in the words of historian Howard Zinn, "the people's history." For further information, see *A People's History of the United States*, (New York: Harper & Row, 1995).

4. Privilege refers to unearned benefits people accrue based on race, class, gender, sexual orientation and other ascriptions. We are most often unaware of the various ways in which we may be privileged; instead, we assume certain benefits are simply givens, or "just normal." For a detailed description of the concept, see "White Privilege: Unpacking the Invisible Knapsack," by Peggy McIntosh.

ANTI-RACIST EDUCATION: PULLING TOGETHER TO CLOSE THE GAPS

BY ENID LEE

This essay is based on a keynote address to the annual METCO conference in Boston, Massachusetts in March 1996.

I attended school in a time and a place in which being academically successful and being Black were not seen as contradictory states. That experience has no doubt influenced the stance I take as an anti-racist consultant working with teachers, schools and school districts across Canada and the United States to improve the academic performance of students of color and of African American students in particular. In many districts, this activity is referred to as "closing the racial gap" in academic achievement. In this essay I will describe the anti-racist framework and process which I use in helping parents, students, teachers and administrators close a variety of gaps created by systems of inequality in schools and society.

THREE GAPS

Whenever I go to a school district, a major concern is the racial gap in academic performance. Generally African American, Latino/Hispanic and Native American students as groups are seen to be performing less well than White students and some Asian students as groups. This is one gap. However there are at least two other equally important and related gaps which are seldom mentioned.

The second is the individual gap. Within the social groups of African American, Native American and Latino students, there are individual students who are experiencing a gap at the personal level. Some students of color, and a growing number of immigrant students, come to school as confident learners, with strong self-esteem, knowing more than one language in some cases, having several skills from home and community life ranging from mathematical to musical. When some students leave our schools they are less capable and less confident. Their self-esteem has been eroded by the experiences of subtle racism — the low expectations of teachers and the culturally-invalidating classrooms they inhabit day after day. They have been "de-skilled" because some of their skills are devalued or unrecognized. Too often they lose their "curiosity to know" which is an essential characteristic of the engaged learner. They lose their belief in their ability to learn. Sometimes they lose the languages they knew when they came to school because their use has been discouraged in the school setting. In short, there is a major gap between the student's state upon entering school and his or her state at the time of departure. It is the accumulation of these gaps at the individual level which results in the social group gap that concerns many school district officials and classroom teachers. To close the gap at the *group* level, we need to monitor and address the needs of *individual* students within the racial groupings we have in our school.

The third and most important gap is at the community level. There is a shortfall between the way we are now as nations and the way we could be if all cultural and racial communities were to achieve their full human potential. One of the outcomes in a society structured by racism is that certain communities are robbed of the basic conditions that other communities take for granted: a good education; long and healthy lives; and equal protection under the law. For example, when we look at the statistics offered by the Children's Defense Fund in the Children's Yearbook for 1996, we are reminded that *every day* in America:

▶2,833 high school students drop out

▶6 children under the age of 20 commit suicide

▶15 children under 20 are killed by firearms

▶518 babies are born to mothers with little or no prenatal care

▶6,042 children under 18 are arrested

These are disproportionately the experiences of people in communities of color. For example, in 1995, of the total number of school dropouts, 1.3 million were Hispanic/Latino students. This number represented 33% of all Latino students between the ages of 16 and 24 (U.S. Department of Commerce, Bureau of Census, Current Population Survey, October 1995, unpublished data). In some parts of the country, for example San Diego and St. Paul, the dropout rate is as high as 60% among Southeast Asians (*New York Times*, November 9, 1997). Although African Americans represent 12% of the population, they constitute at least 44.9% of the prison population (*Two Nations: Black and White, Separate, Hostile, Unequal*, Andrew Hacker, Ballantine, 1995).

This gap at the community level is intimately related to the school-based academic gap at the group and individual levels. Whatever processes we engage in to close the gaps at schools must ultimately include the gaps we find at the community level. We simply cannot ignore the color-coded statistics that point to the ravages of institutional racism in our communities.

DEFINITIONS

I'm described as an anti-racist educator. Let me say something about the term "anti-racist." Sometimes people will not attend a workshop if it's called "anti-racist." In one city I asked people what went through their minds when they saw the title of a workshop I was presenting, "Building an Anti-Racist, Multicultural Curriculum." Several people said they just ignored the word "anti-racist" because it was too severe. They came anyway because the workshop title had "multicultural" in it. I learned that part of the process of closing the gaps with an anti-racist approach is to use language that will give teachers and others a place to begin, while keeping them firmly focused on the task at hand — dismantling racist structures.

A White Canadian student linked racism and multiculturalism very well when he said, "Multiculturalism can work as soon as racism is abolished." *Multiculturalism* is the ideal state in which people's culture, language, heritage and humanity are fully valued and not mired in the kind of statistics reflected on the previous page. *Racism* is the use of institutional power to deny or grant people and groups of people rights, respect, representation and resources based on their skin color. Racism in action makes Whiteness a preferred way of being human. By Whiteness I am referring to the civilization, language, culture and the skin color associated most often with European-ness. *Racism* is reflected in a hierarchy in which beauty, intelligence, worth and things associated with Whiteness are at the top.

The school is one site in which this hierarchical arrangement of skin power is confirmed daily. It is also a site where it can be undone. We can contribute to the building of communities and societies in which all the ways of being human are equally valued. That humanity includes our identities of gender, language, class, ableness and sexual orientation. These other aspects of our identity are embedded in our racial identity. As we pay attention to dismantling the barriers that limit us on the basis of race, we must ask how are sexism, classism and linguicism are part of this oppression called *racism*.

For example, how is racism a part of the linguicism that bilingual students face? If the Latino/Hispanic students we work with had their origins in Spain rather than Mexico or El Salvador, would they still be negatively stereotyped? Would school staff still be assuming that the parents of these children do not care about their education and that the students are not capable of succeeding? I think not. These students by and large are associated with countries deemed to be "third world" which is a fondly used euphemism for countries and communities peopled largely by those with black or brown skin.

This relationship between race and language was brought home to me when a teacher told me the other day about a parent who was praising the school for a bilingual program. The parent was reported to have said, "It's great you have a bilingual program, but it's such a pity that the language you are teaching is Spanish." When the teacher inquired as to why he thought that Spanish was an unfortunate choice, he replied, "It should be something like Russian. Look at who speaks Spanish around here, a bunch of drug pushers." Race is entwined with every aspect of identity, and as we close gaps we must be mindful of the way in which racism itself seeps into every subject in schools. Anti-racism is a proactive strategy for dismantling racist structures and for building racial justice and equality. It must become a perspective that cuts across all subjects areas and institutional practices.

PROCESS, FRAMEWORK AND PRINCIPLES

I do this gap-closing work in a variety of settings. They include on-site classroom consultations with individual teachers; school-wide meetings of faculty, staff, parents and students; district-wide workshops; and in sessions with policymakers and consultants who support and inspire teachers' work in schools. The approach that has the most immediate impact on the academic gap is the classroom consultation. There I observe the actual teaching, the content of the formal curriculum and the climate of the classroom or the informal curriculum as it is sometimes understood. I discuss my observations with the teacher, always focusing on the curriculum and how it is experienced by individual students and groups, and the ways it is interconnected with the communities from which they come.

After our conversations, teachers attempt new

© Marie Moll, 1996

and the systemic inequalities.

2. The work must emphasize good teaching.

3. The work must emphasize the belief and realization that all teachers, and indeed everyone involved in educating our children, can learn to do what we do even better.

4. The work must identify inequalities based on race, as well as equity measures, as the path to racial equality.

Closing the Gaps

1. Situational and Systemic

Gaps are produced by systemic inequities and the related practice of individual teachers at very specific times and situations. Racism is systemic and not episodic and must be addressed as such. But every episode of racism must and can be confronted and interrupted at every turn as a means of reaching back to its systemic roots. I stress both of these aspects of change since an exclusive reliance on either the systemic or the situational will result in frustration and widening gaps. If we focus only on the situations in front of us, for example, on a group of students doing poorly on a test, we might overlook where key decisions are made, such as the use of time blocks in the school that affect the very situations we are trying to change. If we look only at the massive and oppressive systems in which we work, we become paralyzed, unable to make the changes which are right within our reach. With the urgency of the gaps before us, we cannot afford the luxury of choosing between the system and the situation. We must grapple with both at every moment of our lives.

Let me share a gap-closing story in which I had the privilege of participating. As part of its reform goal, a high school wanted to increase the number of African American and Latino/Hispanic students in Advanced Placement classes. The school, like so many others across the nation, although multiracial in its student population, was predominantly White in Advanced Placement classes. We wanted to close this gap in the school.

When this goal was discussed, concerns were expressed that this might mean lowering academic standards. It was quickly established that to the con-

strategies and sometimes report immediate changes. A teacher shared with me that after one of our conversations about using language of high expectations, she spoke with her class about what she expected from them with respect to conduct and class work. She also invited them to talk about their expectations of her and exactly how she could help them meet these expectations. In addition, she publicly praised her class to anyone who dropped by. At first the students were quite unused to this praise. When she said, "They are good hard-working kids," the students would contradict her, exclaiming, "We are not really like that!" But the teacher persisted on both fronts in conversations with the students themselves and with the school community. She was pleased to report that over a six week period, she saw a marked improvement in several of the students, their willingness to live up to her expectations, to work together and to produce work that could be proudly displayed for visitors.

This approach to work with teachers is based on a social, political and historical understanding of the issues of racism. In practice it is directed to the policies and structures in institutions; the professional and personal growth of teachers; and their practice in classrooms, in hallways, in parent meetings and all areas of school life. Power and theories about the conflict that arises over the unequal distribution of that power are at the heart of the efforts to close the gaps. On an everyday basis, this anti-racist framework is undergirded by four principles:

1. The work must emphasize both the situational

trary, this effort was aimed at raising the standards. More students would be working at a higher level and more importantly, a more diversified group of students would be working at the higher level.

Because of my own anti-tracking stance, I hoped that this initiative would be one step towards eliminating the lower tracks in the school — a method of detracking the school by removing its lowest level classes. At that point, however, I was content to begin with the situations that seemed to require immediate remedy.

Some members of the guidance department felt that the absence of a certain kind of parental involvement was a major cause for the small number of students of color in the Advanced Placement classes. There was a sense that the parents of the African American and Hispanic/Latino students were not aware of the way the system worked. They did not attend the meetings at which the students made decisions about the subjects they were going to take. Working on the assumption that all parents, regardless of ethnic background, are interested in the education of their children, I encouraged the guidance department to come up with a communication strategy which they believed would be effective for the parent population they were targeting. They did. The school sent a special invitation to parents for a meeting to discuss the participation of their child in Advanced Placement classes. Each parent was given a specific time slot in which they were asked to attend a meeting.

The perception surrounding entry criteria to Advanced Placement classes also needed to be addressed. According to the counselors, expression of interest in the classes and a willingness to try were at least as important as grades. A focus group with students revealed a variety of perceptions and realities about entry into this program. While there were some variety of experiences within groups, by and large the students' perceptions and experiences followed racial lines. White students appeared to have the same sense of the entry criteria as the guidance counselors. In contrast, some Hispanic/Latino students did not know that Advanced Placement classes were an option for them. They could not remember being actively encouraged to consider them. Some African American students indicated that they had to do a lot more than express interest; some felt that they had been actively discouraged from entering the program.

Clearly there were several realities operating, as is often the case in any school. The guidance department decided to use the parent meeting to ensure that a consistent and strong invitation was communicated to the parents and their children.

At the systemic level, there was a redistribution of three key organizational resources: human beings, money and time. The principal freed up the necessary financial resources to allow the guidance counselors to remain until eight o'clock at night to accommodate more working parents. In this way more time was devoted to this important encounter between parents and the school. At about the same time, the faculty voted to adopt block scheduling which can allow teachers to work individually with students and can allow students to have longer blocks of time to consolidate their learning.

But the parent meeting, which was a direct response to the situation, proved to be pivotal in changing the landscape at the school. The African American parents came in significant numbers. Some had to take several busses to get to the meeting. In the process of this change, once and for all (or perhaps at least for that moment) the stereotype of the disinterested parent was struck down. The African American parents encouraged, and in some cases, insisted their children sign up for the Advanced Placement classes. The number of students in the Advanced Placement classes increased by thirty percent that year. Over the past three years, the data reflect that this increase has been maintained.

There are many other pieces to this account, but what is clear is that as each situation arose, we attempted to address it and to look at ways of institutionalizing our efforts. For example, today there is systematic checking on the perceptions of students about

© Marie Moll, 1996

entry requirements to the program and yearly monitoring of the percentages of student participation across racial lines. This gap has begun to close. The work must continue to make detracking and academic excellence a reality for all schools and all children.

2. Emphasis on Good Teaching

Visiting hundreds of classrooms each year has confirmed for me the importance of good teaching in closing the gaps. In much the same way that a musician or a sports person is delighted to hear a fine piece of music or a watch a beautiful hook shot, so it is with me when I see a lesson well taught. I am happy, I want to celebrate. I want to dance. In order to move beyond my subjective pleasure in this area, I will offer a composite picture drawn from several situations that include some of the elements of good teaching and their role in closing gaps at the social, individual and community levels.

The focus here is on one small aspect of teaching, questioning and eliciting answers. Simply by concentrating on the type of questions asked and the process used for inviting answers we are able to increase participation and change the environment of the classroom. In many classrooms the questions asked are at the level of recall. Students are required to give back in their answers exactly what we have told them or what is recorded in the textbooks. It is not surprising to find that the result is sometimes frustration born of being silenced. I cannot tell you the number of times that I have sat in classrooms where kids keep putting their hands up and, because the questioning stops as soon as the first person demonstrates the ability to recall, do not have the opportunity to participate. One time a student who was sitting next to me, after putting her hand up for every question, stamped in frustration and said, "They never ask me!" Unfortunately the teacher heard only the stamping but not the statement that accompanied it. The student was reprimanded. Had the questioning and the method of questioning allowed for more participation, this instance of what was described as "bad behavior" might not have occurred. For example, students can make up the questions, present the questions, be allowed to comment on and extend other students' answers, jot down their answers and share them with their neighbors or with the whole class. More voices. Deeper thinking.

The language we use to address our students and to help them extend their thinking is an important part of teaching. An Algebra teacher said to me, "I never thought these kids could learn Algebra, but I see them differently now, now that I have found a way to teach them." I have seen this teacher work with students. One of the ways in which he encourages success is that he treats every student in the class like a mathematician. He says to them, "We mathematicians have many ways of solving problems. How would you as a mathematician yourself solve this?" This language in the classroom helps students build positive identities as learners. In keeping with this approach, he is able to use language well, to clarify what they have understood so far and to provide a question or an example that offers the scaffolding to move them to the next level of thought. In contrast, I have heard teachers use unhelpful words such as, "Look at it, look at it," when students are stumped by a difficult Algebra problem. An alternative would be to use language that would help the student know how to look at it and some clue as to what they might be looking for. Affirming and clarifying language is part of good teaching and can help close gaps with individual learners.

Good teaching is made better when we create opportunities for our students to show us what they have accomplished outside of the school and when we incorporate their teaching into our teaching. A group of Hispanic/Latino students offered to show their art teacher the best art work in town which they thought had great potential for a school mural. This teacher took a walk with his students under a city bridge where he was shown some very elaborate artwork (which some would call graffiti) that they had helped to create. The teacher was able to use some of the under-the-bridge art in the above-ground work they did on the school walls. Not only did the teacher learn about the students' work outside of school, he made use of it in teaching.

We know that linking students' lives to the school and the formal curriculum in a serious way enhances our opportunities of reaching and teaching them. My mind goes back to the grade six teachers in a school in Manitoba Canada. It has a significant population of Native Canadians, also known as First Nations. The team of grade six teachers used the video *For Angela* with all of their classes. This video portrays the experiences of racism and recovery on the part of a Native Canadian woman and her daughter living in an urban setting. There is an episode in which the young girl cuts her hair in order to avoid racist taunts. One teacher reported that after the post-viewing discussion, two of the First Nations students returned to school with their hair neatly braided and their heads held high. Their transformation was so significant that the rest of their classmates applauded when these students entered the room. The students shared the positive feelings they had derived from the discussion about the film. They shared experiences similar to those of the girl in the video and explained the importance of their braids. The video showing was just one part of a broader school-wide anti-racist program, during which the staff had been discussing their expectations of academic achievement for students of the First Nations.

In addition to making links with students' lives, good teaching, like that described here, must also validate and elevate the marginalized cultures and experiences that many inner-city, working class students of color bring into the classroom. Such an approach is essential to reducing the individual and group gaps with respect to academic achievement, and the community gap with respect to empowerment and self-determination.

In one classroom, children were reading about a tourist visiting a museum in Spain. The teacher wanted to help the students in her class make connections between this lesson and their own lives. Her questions went well beyond recall and introduced the element of application. She asked them where they would take someone who came to visit them in their communities. One student said, "I would take them to a shopping mall." Another said, "to a restaurant." A third student indicated that she would take her guest to a local festival connected to the cultural and racial group of which she was a member. To these answers the teacher politely replied, "Yes," "Mmm," "OK". At that point a bright youngster realized that this was not the kind of answer that the teacher was looking for. He answered, "the museum." To that he got an affirming "Right." The subsequent answers continued to reflect what one might call "high culture," in comparison to the inner-city working class lived culture that was reflected by the earlier answers.

What difference, you might ask, does it make to academic achievement which examples are used and what culture is acknowledged, as long as the skill is acquired? The difference is: That which is validated by school becomes that which is worth knowing and writing about. Over a period of time, the teacher in this class began to validate more of what students brought into the classroom. She learned about their lives and made use of it in her teaching. The children's communities began to be seen by the teacher and by some of the students as places of power and possibility; as places where OK things happened. The deficit language so often used to describe inner-city communities became less common and the students began to rely on the knowledge they had acquired in their communities. They wrote more about their communities. They began to write more and to become more confident writers. In some instances, the test scores in writing even improved.

Very frequently I am asked about Black History Month and where that fits in helping to close the academic gap and in fostering racial harmony and equality in schools. I am in full agreement with the often-made critique that the add-on approach of to Black History, Chinese New Year, and Cinco de Mayo is unsatisfactory. I generally offer this strategy for integrating the curriculum, using Black History as an example: Do not wait until January or February to begin to work on Black History Month. Integrate the themes of Africa and African people throughout the year throughout the curriculum in subjects from English to economics. Let us return to Carter G. Woodson's plan which was to celebrate in February what has been done for the entire year. Black history would be integrated into the full curriculum. The community and its history would be raised to a level of respect. The gap between word and deed would be narrowed.

Finally, good teaching can remedy many of the discipline issues that contribute to poor academic performance. When students are engaged in challenging learning experiences they have less time to become discipline problems. Some philosophies of change focus on changing the student and leaving the learning environment as toxic as ever. The theory of change guiding my work emphasizes changing the context in order to change what the child does. The difference in these philosophies was made clear in conversations I had with two teachers. I asked, "What it is that you want to accom-

plish when you discipline a student in a particular way?" One teacher said, "I want to change the student. I want to deal with that student's behavior." The other teacher said, "I want to find a way of working with the environment in the classroom to bring out the best behavior out of this child." The second approach would significantly lower the suspension rate in many of our urban schools and among students of color. It would also help to change the penitentiary-like atmosphere which pervades some urban classrooms. Schools could be converted into places where young people can learn from their mistakes. As one student said to me, "We want teachers to pull us up when we slip up, not kick us out." "To go where?" he asked me.

3. All Teachers Can Learn

"All students can learn," is a common slogan in urban schools to raise expectations and by extension academic performance. I believe it to be equally true that: "All teachers can learn." All teachers can become better teachers. I am convinced of this. Modeling a constructivist approach, co-creating staff development curriculum with the teacher participants, I always begin with teachers' questions and comments. When I begin here, we can move forward together with gap-closing strategies for the students.

The most frequently asked question is: Well Enid, do you believe that White teachers *can* teach Black kids? I suggest that the question which we want to consider is *what* it is that they can teach them. Clearly, in many circumstances, teachers of all backgrounds are teaching kids of all colors many things. It is really not whether they can teach these students, but rather what it is that they can and cannot teach them. One must recognize both strengths and limitations based on personal and collective racial history. What a good teacher does is acknowledge one's location and point students to other sources of support.

Also related to this knowledge of self in a social sense is the responsibility to educate ourselves about our students and the communities from which they come. One should also work actively for a more racially diversified faculty. Such a faculty can be a source of learning for students and teachers of all backgrounds.

In these discussions, I always ask teachers to look at the history of race and racism in education and the history of relationships between and among racial groups. This leads them to ask questions about power and also about the record of White controlled school districts with regard to the education of Black and other students of color. Teachers have shown themselves willing and able to examine these questions, especially when linked to their immediate concerns. This examination helps them to have a better understanding of how we have come to be in these situations, and it is the beginning of an analysis of their practice as teachers within an institutional framework. This exploration then leads us to look at advantages and disadvantages that various groups have in society along racial and other lines. They also learn from stories about the growth and struggle of other White teachers who have taught Black and other students of color and have allowed themselves to be taught by those students and their parents. They not only learn, but they change their practice when they begin to chronicle their observations and experiences with their own students. Teachers are then able to see where their individual fears come from and are also able to recognize the resources they have at their disposal to make a difference in students' lives.

A very common statement that I hear is: I never noticed you were Black. It is generally meant in a complimentary way. As soon as I hear this, I know that we have a great deal of work to do moving from the color-blind state to the color-conscious state. I understand that it is part of the socialization of many participants. It is an attempt to treat people of color fairly, but it is a misguided notion. We will never address racism in education if we do not look at how skin color plays a part in what people do or do not receive or experience in the educational process.

Sometimes not noticing race if you are White means that you do not have to acknowledge the privileges and opportunities you have by virtue of your skin color. Sometimes not acknowledging race if you are a person of color means that you are denying the existence and perhaps pain of racism or that you want to have others focus on your strengths, your individual effort or your ability to be resilient. By addressing fears about skill and identity on the part of teachers, we are able to begin the process of freeing them up to learn from their students, from others around them, from their own history and the histories of other groups as they work to educate a multiracial student body for academic excellence and social justice.

4. Equity and Equality

The final principle is concerned with equity and equality, and their relationship to each other. Eq-

of people of color in learning material.

2. The under-representation of people of color on school faculties and in Advanced Placement classes.

3. The undervaluing and ignoring of home and community knowledge, language and experience of students of color in the teaching process.

4. The use of assessment procedures which never get at what some students of color know.

5. The absence of intellectual challenge in the learning activities given to some students of color.

6. The inadequate numbers of computers and even textbooks in some of their schools.

7. The poor maintenance of some of their school buildings.

8. The mechanisms for school governance which do not include their parents' voices.

9. The concern about, if not the outright prohibition against, African American, Latino/Hispanic, Asian American and other students of color assembling to socialize at lunch and in other informal places.

10. The practice of punishing and frequently suspending students of color, particularly African American and Latino males for minor infractions.

11. The miseducation of White students through inaccurate information in school materials and the structured inequalities that they witness in relationships and the institutional practices around them.

12. The unexamined myth that some cultural and racial groups do not value education and that the children from those groups do not have the intellectual ability to succeed in schools.

uity measures — or extra measures — must be taken in order to bring about the desired goals of fairness, same status and at least the same academic outcomes among students of color as are found among White students as a group. These outcomes are an important part of educational equality.

Equity is a rather misunderstood concept even though it has been around in English law since at least the twelfth century. According to the *Hutchinson Encyclopedia*, "Equity is a system of law supplementing the ordinary rules where application of these (ordinary rules) would operate harshly in a particular case; sometimes it is regarded as an attempt to achieve natural justice." The spirit of equity is at the heart of all gap-closing measures since inequity is being acknowledged if equity is being discussed. A participant in a workshop, once put it in these words, "Equity does not mean treating everyone in the same way. It means doing whatever it takes to get everyone to the same place." This is difficult to convey since many people feel that being equitable means: "I treat everyone in the same way — red, yellow, blue, green, black." This is a very popular statement in some educational circles. But in order to address, indeed to change the outcomes of a racist system, one simply cannot do the same with and for every group of students.

Many of the gaps we have talked about are the outcomes of a racist system and to change them requires equity measures. Let me list some other outcomes of a racist system in the four areas mentioned in my definition of racism — representation, respect, rights and resources. My top twelve examples are:

1. The under-representation and misrepresentation

To overturn and alter these conditions and ideas, with their deep historic roots in the nation's history, one simply cannot apply "the ordinary rules" of treating everyone in the same way and doing what we have always done. At best, the ordinary rules will perpetuate the situation. At worst, they will cause things to deteriorate. Equity measures then, are required from every teacher, administrator, every secretary, every custodian, every business partner, every trustee, every person engaged in educating our children.

I provided several examples of teachers and administrators engaged in equity measures. Like the grade two teacher who told me that she checks her equity systems everyday, we must make sure that ours are ready and operating fully to roll back the years of racial injustice in our schools. We have numerous opportunities everyday to do equity work. When we select learning materials, we can think of the current imbalance and of the damaging impact this has on students of every race. We can provide additional and corrective information. I think of a teacher who was preparing her students for one of the many tests that are given in public schools these days. They had to cover a rather Eurocentric account of Columbus' activities in preparation for this test. After the teacher had reviewed the material with the students, she said, "I did not write this text book and although I do not agree with what is here we have to cover it for the test. Now that we are ready for the test, let us look at Columbus from another view." These are some of the contradictory and difficult situations faced by teachers every day, but let them not prevent us from undertaking equity measures and working for real equality in all aspects of education.

Like the math teacher who used statistics on race and employment when teaching statistics one year, we too can find moments for equity in every subject area and all areas of school life. In addition to helping the students understand how statistics worked, he also helped them understand how the gaps of inequality are created. He helped them measure the resistance of communities in the face of these injustices and their struggle for dignity and self-determination. He also helped them to see their education as a tool to change things in their communities and not to be educated away from community interests as often happens with some of the brightest and most successful students of color. Some of the students of color have achieved a kind of academic excellence but have also become miseducated misfits, wanting to have nothing to do with the communities from which they came. This math teacher with his equity work was ensuring that his students learned that academic excellence included applications of one's learning for community empowerment.

But "for how long must this equity work continue?" you might ask, as did a participant in one of the workshops I was conducting. He pointed out that I had said that equity had been on the books since the twelfth century and he was wondering why we had not brought every one to the same place yet. I assured him that as soon as we had closed all of the gaps and that we had a mechanism in place to keep them from widening again, then we could stop, but not before that. Until then, we have to press on!

PRESSING ON TO VICTORY

As I think of how long and hard the struggle is to close these gaps created by systems of inequality, I am reminded of a story by African American writer, scholar and historian John Henrik Clarke. The story reminds me of how costly it can be to try to close these gaps, but also how much dignity one can experience with each victory. In this story, a student in one of the southern United States brought to school a picture he had made of Christ painted Black. The principal of the school displayed it in the hall. He thought that it was important that children incorporate their culture and their history and their race into their work. When the school district supervisor visited for an inspection, he was not amused by this display of what he called "nonsense, sacrilegious nonsense." The story goes that when the supervisor questioned his judgement, the principal sternly replied that the time was long overdue for the world and certainly for the children in the school to know that African people had erected and enjoyed the benefits of a splendid civilization long before the people of Europe had a written language. The principal was eventually relieved of his responsibilities because he was told that he was not paid to teach such things in schools. That story was set in the 1940s. We are almost at the end of the twentieth century, and the same Eurocentrism that the principal and the student were trying to address then is still very much with us.

I hope that our own stories will be filled with many gaps closed at the individual, group and community levels. Every gap we close is a victory won and a small piece of our humanity regained.

LESSONS LEARNED

TEACHING WHITES ABOUT RACISM

BY CHRISTINE SLEETER

As student populations become increasingly diverse in racial and cultural composition and as the teaching force becomes increasingly White, interest in training teachers in multicultural education is growing. Many educators conceptualize this task as helping White teachers and preservice students replace negative attitudes about race with positive attitudes, and as helping them acquire a knowledge base about race and various racial groups. I see the task as more complex than that: as White women, many of whom have worked themselves up from working-class origins, these teachers already have considerable knowledge about social stratification in America, but it tends to be fairly conservative. Part of the task for teacher educators is to help them examine and reconstruct what they know. Otherwise, they simply integrate information about race into the knowledge they already have and in the process distort it. This article describes a process I have used with White preservice students to help them recognize the limits of what they know about social stratification so that they can begin to reconstruct what they know.

HOW WHITE TEACHERS THINK ABOUT SOCIAL STRATIFICATION AND RACE

Anthony Giddens (1979) advanced his analysis of social theory on the premise that "every social actor knows a great deal about the conditions of reproduction of the society of which he or she is a member." Regardless of how little experience with racial or cultural diversity White teachers have had, they enter the classroom with a considerably rich body of knowledge about social stratification, social mobility, and human differences based on their life experiences. The analogies they draw between racism and what they know about sexism, class mobility, and the White ethnic experience tend to minimize the importance of race as they see it.

Race is one axis of oppression in America; social class and gender are equally important axes. About 90% of the teaching population is White, and most teachers, as Whites, are members of the dominant racial group. As such, most never have been victims of racism in America nor have experienced racial minority communities in the same way Americans of color do. Whites draw on their own experience to understand inequality, and their interpretation of that experience usually upholds their belief that the rules of society apply roughly the same to everyone. Haves and have-nots rise or fall by their own merit or effort, for the most part.

White Americans and Americans of color grow up in different locations in the racial structure, although Whites usually deny that there is a significant racial structure. Based on his study of White perceptions of race, David Wellman (1977) argued that a contradiction Whites face is how to interpret racial inequality in a way that defends White interests in publicly acceptable terms. Generally, sociobiological explanations for inequality are not acceptable today, so Whites construct alternative explanations, resolving "the contradiction by minimizing racism. They neutralize it," viewing racism as individual prejudice and inequality as due mainly to cultural so called deficiencies.

While denying structural racism, Whites usually spend their lives in White-dominated spheres, constructing an understanding of race and social equality from that vantage point. According to Wellman (1977), "Given the racial and class organization of American society, there is only so much people can 'see.' The positions they occupy in these structures limit the range of their thinking. The situation places borders on their imaginations and restricts the possibilities of their vision." Consequently, they assume the opportunity structure works the same for all Americans.

A large proportion of teachers are women, and a large proportion have also worked their way up from lower or working-class origins. In that regard, they are members of oppressed groups, and their experiences with social class and gender provide teachers with a perspective about how they believe social stratification works.

Historically, teaching has provided members of the lower- and working-class entree into middle-class status; many teachers have experienced working their way up by attaining education (Lortie, 1975). For example, Patricia Ashton and Rodman Webb (1986) noted that, "The life experiences of most teachers demonstrate their allegiance to the ethic of vertical mobility, self-improvement, hard work, deferred gratification, self-discipline and personal achievement. These individualistic values rest on the assumption that the social system...works well, is essentially fair, and moves society slowly but inevitably toward progress." For example, I interviewed twenty-three teachers about their parents' occupations (Sleeter 1992). Four of their fathers had held jobs that normally require college education, two had owned small businesses, and the fathers of the other seventeen had worked as laborers of various sorts. Some of the teachers had experienced the stigma of being poor. But they had raised their own social class standing by earning college degrees and becoming teachers. Education had served them as an effective vehicle of upward mobility and personal betterment. Several teachers also talked about their European ethnic backgrounds (or those of their spouses). Their parents or grandparents had come to America very poor and had worked hard; gradually the family had moved up the social ladder. These life experiences taught teachers that the social system is open to those who are willing to work regardless of ethnicity (a view that equates White ethnicity with race). Many Americans regard their own social standing as higher than that of their parents. While most social mobility has been due to an expansion of middle-class jobs and widespread improvement of the living standard of Americans in general, people tend to attribute their own improved status to their own individual efforts (Kluegel and Smith, 1986).

Teachers' experience with sexism also provides them with an experiential basis for thinking about social stratification. As women, many teachers have experienced prejudice and stereotyping. Therefore, they perceive themselves as knowledgeable about how discrimination works. They locate sexism (and classism) mainly in biased attitudes of individuals who limit the opportunities of others by treating them stereotypically. The main solution to discrimination from this perspective is to try to eliminate stereotyping so that all may strive as individuals.

Most teachers' understanding of sexism and social class is cast within a conservative framework that emphasizes individual choice and mobility within a relatively open system. One's progress may be hindered by prejudices and stereotypes, as well as by meager economic and cultural resources from home. However, these blocks can be compensated for by hard work. Structural bases for gender and social class oppression are rarely studied in school

in any depth, so most teachers' understanding of their personal experience stays rooted within a naive individualistic framework. But it is important to recognize the power of personal experience in reinforcing this framework.

When concerned White teachers define classism, sexism, and by extension racism as a matter of individual prejudice, they then strive to keep racial prejudices and stereotypes from coloring their interactions with individuals. I interviewed twenty-six teachers over a period of time as they participated in a two-year staff development project in multicultural education. How to think about race, color, and culture was a major issue they grappled with and often discussed in interviews and in the staff development sessions. Many of them upheld the "color-blind" perspective, believing that one is not participating in racism if one learns to ignore color and feel comfortable around children of color. Yet most White teachers had an unresolved dilemma: how to accept all children regardless of race while explaining their difficulties in school without seeming racist. Some blamed the "culture of poverty," asserting that race was not the issue. Several tried to ignore explanations that "blamed the victim." But they unconsciously used such explanations anyway for lack of means to explain children's classroom behavior and achievement. First, they mentioned the racial and socioeconomic composition of their students; then they immediately described those students (for a complete report on the study, see Sleeter, 1992).

Those who attempt to teach White teachers about racism commonly encounter defenses that are difficult to penetrate. Convinced that individual attitudes and stereotypes form the basis of racism, Whites try very hard not to see color and therefore not to hear race-related information; Whites also experience guilt when confronted with information about racism. Reducing social organization to individual relationships, many Whites define "getting along" in face to-face interactions as the solution to racism, then maintain that they already do this well. Many Whites equate race with what they know about White ethnicity, drawing on what they know about their own ancestors' experiences pulling themselves up "by the bootstraps." The European ethnicity analogy assumes that every group faced difficulties but that

> WHILE DENYING STRUCTURAL RACISM, WHITES USUALLY SPEND THEIR LIVES IN WHITE-DOMINATED SPHERES, CONSTRUCTING AN UNDERSTANDING OF RACE AND SOCIAL EQUALITY FROM THAT VANTAGE POINT.

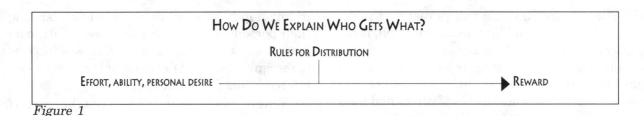

Figure 1

most overcame those difficulties through hard work; it ignores the importance of skin color in perpetuating racial discrimination. However, drawing parallels between racism, sexism, and classism, many Whites resentfully interpret civil rights laws and social interventions as people of color wanting "special attention and privileges."

The European ethnic immigrant experience provides a template for thinking about diversity that White teachers commonly use to try to construct race in what they construe as a positive rather than negative manner. According to the ethnicity paradigm, members of diverse groups voluntarily came to America to partake in its freedom and opportunity; while systems were not always fair in the past, opportunity has gradually been extended to everyone. In his study of how Euro Americans think about ethnicity, Alba (1990) found them to view it as voluntary participation in a group, in which the meaning of ethnicity is tied mainly to family history and expressions of so-called old world culture, especially cuisine, holidays and ethnic festivals. Among Euro Americans, ethnic differences no longer define opportunities or social participation: marriage, housing, employment, education and so forth are almost unrelated to European ethnic background. So, it makes sense for Euro Americans to view their own ethnicity as voluntary and to define it as they do. However, colonized groups as well as immigrant groups who are visibly identifiable have not had the same history; the European ethnic experience does not provide an appropriate framework for understanding non-European groups (Omi and Winant,1986; Ringer and Lawless, 1989). Trying to apply it to everyone, in fact, is another defense Whites use.

One approach to penetrating these defenses is to affirm to Whites that their beliefs are valid — for Whites, but not necessarily for people of color. Since Whites tend to deny that a racial structure locates them differently from people of color, one can begin by helping them recognize structural racism and the importance of visible differences among people when defining access. This shifts attention away from feelings of guilt, reliance on the White ethnic experience, or the possibility of being color-blind.

In what follows, I describe a process I have used to help White preservice students articulate some of what they know about the social system, recognize that what they know may be true for White people but does not necessarily generalize to Americans of color, and develop some sensitivity to how the rules of American society work differently for people of color than they do for Whites. It is significant to my teaching that I am White. I deliberately use my race and my background to try to relate to the White students, for example, by telling them that I used to think X until I experienced Y, that "we as Whites" experience advantages we are often aware of, or that I have made some big mistakes that Whites commonly make.

Professors of color can draw on different advantages than White professors to teach about race. A lifetime of personal experience with a group and with racial discrimination arms a professor of color with a rich repertoire of experiences and examples (as an African American friend put it to me once, "I've been Black all my life and taking notes"). Students may attempt to dismiss professors of color as advocating a cause (as well as women professors who teach about gender); this avoidance technique should be pointed out directly, and students should be redirected to the information the professor is attempting to teach.

ANALYTIC FRAMEWORK

Before describing some specific teaching strategies, I will present a framework that structures how I teach about race and other axes of oppression. I share this framework with students, referring back to it repeatedly. The framework directs them to analyze social institutions rather than characteristics of individuals and groups, and to examine how institutions work differently for different groups; it is based on conflict theory.

In a fair social system individuals generally get what they strive for according to predictable rules that apply equally to everyone. This is a tenet of U.S. society that most citizens, regardless of race or any other ascribed characteristic, believe ought to be the case. Figure 1 represents this visually, in which "Reward" refers to whatever an individual is

DIFFERENT PERSPECTIVES

	Dominant Groups	Oppressed Groups
Nature of society	Fair, Open	Unfair, Rigged
Nature of *have not* groups	Lack ambition, effort, culture, language, skills, education	Strong, resourceful, work to advance

Figure 2

striving for (such as a job, or a decent place to live or food), and the arrow indicates the social rules governing distribution of that resource.

However, in reality the rules do not work the same way for everyone. Conflict theorists postulate that dominant groups make the rules in order to retain control over the resources of society. Different groups actually experience society's rules differently, and as a consequence, view society and *have not* groups differently. Figure 2 illustrates this. Since it repeats what has been said thus far in this article, I will not elaborate on it here. But the figure helps orient students visually to a major idea of the course: that society operates differently for different groups, and consequently different groups construct opposing explanations for inequality.

Most Americans analyze who gets what only in terms of individual effort and ability. Figure 3 illustrates two additional levels of analysis that explain group differences in status: the institutional level and the cultural level. At the institutional level, one examines both written and unwritten rules and procedures that are used to regulate human behavior; one can also examine the degree to which any given reward (such as housing or higher education) is actually available to everyone who works for it. At the cultural level, one examines beliefs people have about society and diverse groups, how and by whom those beliefs are encoded and how and to

whom they are transmitted. The relationship between cultural beliefs and individuals, and between cultural beliefs and institutions is reciprocal; both levels influence one another.

When teaching Whites about racism, my main goal is to help them ask and begin to answer questions about racism at the institutional and cultural levels, those levels that people of color generally direct their attention toward to explain racial disparities. Such analyses are foreign to the way most White people think about racial disparities, and it takes a good deal of practice to be able to think in institutional and cultural terms. As Whites gain practice in doing so, however, they begin to understand (sometimes for the first time) what people of color are saying about racism. Below, I will describe some specific strategies I use to help students learn to ask and answer questions at the institutional and cultural levels.

HELPING WHITE PRESERVICE TEACHERS RETHINK RACE

I begin the semester by having students describe and discuss some of their beliefs about teaching and about how society works. They do this first in writing, then in small group discussions, addressing questions such as the following. What is proper student behavior in the classroom? What does it mean to be late and how do you interpret someone who is late?

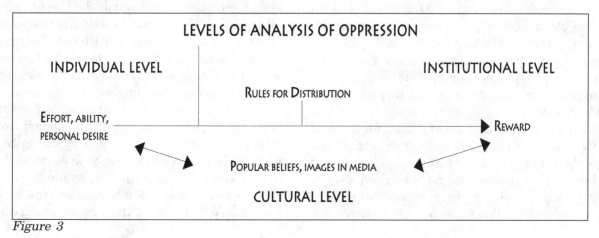

LEVELS OF ANALYSIS OF OPPRESSION

INDIVIDUAL LEVEL   INSTITUTIONAL LEVEL

Rules for Distribution

Effort, ability, personal desire ——————————————▶ Reward

Popular beliefs, images in media

CULTURAL LEVEL

Figure 3

Why do most people live in racially homogeneous neighborhoods? What do you consider to be the greatest works of literature? I also have students fill out a questionnaire examining how much contact they have had with members of other racial groups and social class backgrounds in various areas of their lives, including school, college, work, neighborhood, and religious practice.

Students generally approach this task puzzled by the obviousness of it. On the one hand, their beliefs have a transparently "obvious" character. For example, they believe proper classroom behavior consists of students showing respect and interest by attending to the teacher, asking questions politely, obeying, sitting quietly, and so forth. Most believe people live in relatively homogeneous neighborhoods because they prefer to do so. In small group discussions about their beliefs, there is usually so much agreement (especially when groups are all White) that they are unclear why they are doing this. On the other hand, the questionnaire about their backgrounds shows the extent to which the great majority have had fairly little contact with people of a different background; this, too, has a certain obviousness about it. Some students at this point maintain that they are not prejudiced; others admit that their beliefs are limited by their backgrounds, though they do not know to what extent.

I then tell the class that all their answers are correct, but also that multiple correct answers exist for every question they have been discussing, ones that vary by race, culture and other factors. At this point, I introduce two related but somewhat different ideas that subsequent class sessions will develop.

First, all social behavior is culturally constituted, often differently across cultural groups. One example of how something that seems obvious can be viewed differently across cultures is interpretation of time. I ask students what time they would arrive someplace if told to come at 9:00. Even within an all-White class, students suggest different appropriate arrival times. Someone always asks whether the event is an appointment or a social gathering, which leads to consideration of time as culturally interpreted. I provide examples of correct arrival times in contexts that do not surface in the discussion, such as on an Indian reservation, for a Black as opposed to White party, or in Switzerland. I then discuss the concept of code switching, emphasizing that they (and everyone else) have learned a set of correct cultural codes in their own environment, that the codes they know are not the only correct

ones, and that anyone can learn another set of codes if taught.

Second, I suggest that a color line exists, in addition to gender and social class lines, that differentiates those who make the rules of society and for whom the rules operate fairly consistently from those who do not make the rules and for whom they do not operate consistently. I point out that we all see color and that visible differences become important social marks of who belongs on which side of the line. The line is socially constructed, although we may associate it with biological features. Over time (and in different cultures) the line may be positioned differently. For example, southeastern Wisconsin (where I taught) was a popular destination for eastern and southern European immigrants historically, and some of their descendants usually are in the class; I ask students whether Italians are White or not. Those who are familiar with the history of discrimination against Italians locally can point out that they were not considered White for a long time but generally (although not universally) are now. When Latinos are class members, we discuss whether class members view Latinos as White; students usually emphasize the importance of visible characteristics, especially to White people, in making this determination. I then comment that education is supposed to pay off equally for everyone and show statistical information illustrating that it actually pays off (in terms of income and employment) differently based on race and sex. Students' main reaction at this point is that this is not fair, and they begin asking why.

I then assign students to read the book *The Education of a WASP* (Stalvey, 1988) which traces the experience of a White, middle-class, Protestant woman as she relearns how race in America works for African Americans. The book is autobiographical. It opens with Stalvey's description of her growing up in Milwaukee during the 1940s and 1950s and of her naive beliefs about the essential fairness and justice of American society. At this point, most of my students can identify with her. The book then chronicles her life and the change in her perspective over a four-year period as she became increasingly involved with struggles within the Black community. She describes how she learned about institutional racism in a variety of areas: housing, schooling, media coverage, job opportunities, and so forth. Over the four years, Stalvey crossed a color line that most White Americans never cross, and she learned firsthand how African Americans experience America, from the other side of a color line that Stalvey earlier had believed did not exist.

When I first assigned the book, I was afraid my White students would find it too offensive, too angry, or even too dated to take seriously. Generally, this is not their reaction, and many of them cannot put it down once they start reading it. Overwhelmingly, they tell me that it is very interesting and eye-opening. Some say it made them cry; some say it was the first textbook they had read cover-to-cover; a few confess they are not reading assignments for other classes because they want to finish it. Some loan it to friends and neighbors. One class commented that there will probably be few used copies in the bookstore because this is one book no one would want to sell. One student who had studied about racism in high school, wrote later:

I must admit now that I have received this education with my eyes and heart closed. For example, I know how Blacks were historically forced into slavery and about the Black inventors who made many contributions for American society.... I am sure that I can go on with more historical knowledge but the point is that even though I have been taught these accounts, I have never experienced any of them. This is because I am White and have never really had any contact with people outside of my race until after I entered college.

The Education of a WASP provokes a strong reaction from most White readers. Many students find themselves emotionally engaged in a struggle against racism for the first time in their lives. The engagement is vicarious but strongly felt. Students of color also find the book worth reading, commenting that it made them think about issues they had not thought deeply about for a while and that it gave them a better idea of how White people think. As one African American student put it, "I knew White people were naive, but I didn't know they were *that* naive."

The book focuses on institutional racism as well as media production of imagery that rationalizes racist actions. It provides a very different template for thinking about race than the European ethnic immigrant experience does. But it also describes one woman's experience, almost three decades ago. Subsequent activities engage students in examining the same factors the book describes, here and now, focusing on institutional processes and on cultural beliefs and images.

I have found two simulations very helpful. The one I use first, because it is the less threatening of the two is BaFa BaFa (Shirts, 1977). In this simulation, the class is divided into two groups in two different rooms where each learns and practices a different culture. After each group has mastered its culture, observers and visitors are exchanged for a few minutes at a time and are encouraged to share with members of their own culture what they saw. The simulation is followed by a discussion. During the simulation itself, which lasts about one hour, contact experiences with the other culture invariably produce a set of stereotypes, antagonisms, and feelings of confusion. Members of each culture rather quickly learn to view theirs as best and most sensible, and they use it as a benchmark to judge others negatively. After discussing their reactions to each other, we draw parallels between the simulation and real-life denigration of members of other groups. The example I provided earlier about cultural differences in time orientation is helpful again here. Often, White students comment that this was the first time they experienced feeling left out and confused by encountering a different set of cultural rules and that now they have a sense of what code-switching means.

The other simulation I use, usually two or three weeks later, is Star Power (Shirts, 1969). In this simulation, participants are divided into three groups (Squares, Circles, and Triangles) to play a trading game, the purpose of which (they are told) is to compete in the accumulation of points. The trading game in the simulation is rigged so that one group continues to accumulate more than the rest, but they are led to believe their success is due to their skill. Part way through the simulation the top group (Squares) is given power to make rules for the rest of the simulation. The Squares invariably use this power to further their own advantages (e.g., they restrict membership, impose taxes, make rules for themselves that differ from rules for everyone else, and sometimes establish a welfare system to keep everyone else playing). The other two groups react in a variety of ways to their powerless position; sometimes they stop playing, usually they find ways to subvert the rules, sometimes they revolt. The discussion that follows the simulation helps participants move from their own particular experiences with the simulation to broader issues of power and social structure. In the discussion, I try to draw from the group as many real-life examples that parallel the simulation as possible. I have also found the simulation helpful in providing the class with a common vocabulary and set of experiences I can use throughout the semester to make points (such as, Why might this set of parents be behaving like Triangles?). Typically students need help connecting both simulations to racial issues around them; some draw parallels easily, but others need to have me walk them through specific examples (such as race relations in the university) before they start to make connections.

Some students dismiss the book as outdated

do contribute to neighborhood crime. Therefore, although he personally does not agree with this view, he honors it. Another student telephoned several local industries and banks to find out how many people of color they had hired in management positions. Most of the individuals he tried to talk to refused to answer his questions or gave him a run-

and the simulations as unreal. Therefore, I also ask students to investigate some aspect of racism for themselves, locally. We use the framework in Figure 3 to generate questions, brainstorming questions one could ask at each of the three levels of analysis. I instruct students to focus on the institutional or cultural levels. For example, they can interview a realtor to find out if color is taken into account when selling a house, investigate whether there is a relationship between racial composition of neighborhoods and accessibility of voting places, ask university students of color why students at the university are disproportionately White, and so forth.

For example, in one class a White student interviewed a family friend who is a realtor. This individual explained to her that he does not care who he sells a house to, but the neighbors often do, believing that Blacks do not keep up their houses and

around; he interpreted their refusal to discuss this with him as indication that few if any people of color occupy management positions. Still another student asked a Black university student about obstacles he encountered to getting into college and was told that a major one was money. The part-time jobs that paid most were located in the suburbs (near where this White student lived), too far away from him and most other Blacks to be accessible. The White student realized that he held a part-time job that the Black student did not have access to. Yet another student counted the racial representation of people on cereal boxes, then shared his findings with an African American friend. She found his figures interesting, but suggested things that were more important, from her perspective, such as the preponderance of White women used to portray beauty.

I encourage students to share what they find out. I also supplement their sharing with a barrage of statistical information on distribution of income across racial lines, unemployment, housing discrimination, life expectancy, access to health insurance, and so forth. By then, they are usually willing to listen to me, especially if their own personal investigations have validated the idea that society's rules operate differently for people of color than they do for Whites, just as Stalvey found out.

I also show a videotape of Dr. Charles King talking about racism on the Phil Donahue show several years ago. In the videotape, Dr. King (who is Black) deliberately shows his anger and impatience toward White racism and White denials of racism, and he attempts to direct viewers away from blaming Blacks for their condition toward examining the racist structures that are responsible for the condition in which Blacks find themselves. Since Dr. King does not mince words with the audience and shows his emotion, most Whites find the videotape offensive unless they have been prepared for it. Having prepared students with the above activities, most are able to listen to him fairly non-defensively. In a follow-up discussion, one of the main points I stress is the difficulty we as Whites experience listening to people of color talking honestly about racism but our need to listen nonetheless in order to learn, just as Stalvey did.

In May of 1992, I showed Dr. King's videotape to a class shortly after the riots in Los Angeles following the acquittal of White police officers accused of police brutality and after we had completed the rest of the activities above. Many class members told me that the idea of racism finally made sense: they were for the first time able to see what people of color were angry about. The combination of the book, the class activities, and the videotape — so very directly connected to a current issue — finally came together.

I teach a two course sequence in Multicultural Education; this describes only the beginning. In subsequent sessions I have students examine how schools institutionalize racism, as well as classism and sexism and then explore things they can do differently. I also direct White students to find out more about students of color from people of the students' own racial background, including community members, teachers, and scholars. (White preservice students are often very resistant to seeking information from anyone other than teachers they encounter, the great majority of whom are White.)

I also try to help students move beyond their understanding of sexism and classism as matters of individual stereotyping. Discussion of these areas is beyond the scope of this paper, but I will note that most students are quite resistant to examining institutional sexism or the social class structure outside the school itself. To many of them, questioning the class structure sounds like what they call "socialism" or "communism," which they have been trained to regard as anti-American. Questioning sexism leads to an analysis of family roles and structures; young women who are preoccupied with establishing their own families resist this tenaciously. Further, many young women have learned to associate a gender analysis with "feminism," a term they perceive as militantly anti-male.

TEACHING WHITES ABOUT RACISM

I have found the process described above to be fairly effective, although it does antagonize a few students to a point where some drop out. I judge its effectiveness based on connections students make in papers and class discussions and on receptivity to ideas that build upon this foundation over the two-course sequence. I believe the approach is effective with many students for several reasons.

First, I begin by having students articulate some beliefs, and then I attempt to validate that what they know is correct for themselves but at the same time not correct for all Americans. Students often become angry and defensive when told their experience is wrong; they are much more receptive when shown that it is right but limited. While it is difficult for many people to accept that there are multiple perspectives and multiple experiences, it is even more difficult for an individual to accept that she or he is completely wrong. Multicultural education is about multiple realities, not about one "correct" reality.

Second, I direct students' attention toward barriers to access, rather than characteristics of people of color, which is where Whites normally direct their attention; and I encourage them to investigate some barriers for themselves. I try to show them how stereotypes arise from the consequences of barriers, then are used to justify the barriers. The books, the simulations, and their own investigations help to reinforce this point and help keep their attention directed toward access barriers. A student's paper about *The Education of a WASP* illustrates the focus: "We learned that the Black people learn at a very early age just where their place in society is, and the consequences for stepping over that line. Their reactions are a form of self preservation." Later I explore strengths and resources among oppressed groups (such as community self-help groups, or linguistic resources in one's first language or dialect, upon which a second language or dialect can be built), and I contrast this view with the *cultural deficiency view*.

Third, I try to involve students actively in constructing a sense of how discrimination works, drawing ideas out of their experience with the simulations and their investigations rather than imposing ideas on them. Again, this approach validates their ability to construct for themselves an understanding of how society works, but it introduces a different set of questions and materials on which to draw than most have used previously.

The approach I have described is not a panacea. I strongly suspect that many White students continue to regard it as an academic exercise, giving me what I want but not taking it very seriously. Some who are actively interested and engaged at the time shift their attention to other things later on in their preservice program; Whites have the luxury of being able to forget about racism, and my students are no exception. A variation of the forgetfulness is that many students learn the vocabulary I have used to examine racism without connecting it with much in their own lives; instead they revert to blaming "cultural deficiencies" of students of color when they get into schools and are confronted with behavior they do not really understand.

However, I also believe that the emotional impact of the book and the experiential basis of the simulations and their own investigations, interpreted through a vocabulary and set of concepts I try to provide, equip many White preservice students with a foundation on which they can continue to rethink how racism works and their own participation in racist institutions. (Contact I have had with some former students who are now teaching supports this belief.) As a student concluded in a paper, "After having some exposure to the harsher realities of life, I now hope that I will not be as blind to them as I was before, and that my education never stops, for my sake and the sake of others."

Christine Sleeter is a professor at the Center for Collaborative Education and Professional Studies, California State University — Monterey Bay. She is the author and editor of dozens of books and articles on multicultural education including Multicultural Education and Critical Pedagogy: The Politics of Difference *(w/P. McLaren, SUNY, 1995),* Empowerment Through Multicultural Education *(SUNY, 1991),* Turning on Learning, 2nd ed. *(w/C. Grant, Macmillan, 1997),* Making Choices for Multicultural Education: Five Approaches to Race, Class, and Gender, 2nd ed. *(w/ C. Grant, Prentice-Hall, 1994), and* Multicultural Education as Social Activism *(SUNY, 1996). Her research addresses the theoretical foundations of multicultural education, White racism, critical pedagogy, and special education as a social construct. E-mail: Christine_Sleeter@Monterey.edu*

Reprinted with permission from Practicing What We Teach: Confronting Diversity in Teacher Education, *ed. Renee J. Martin. Albany, NY: SUNY Press, 1996.*

REFERENCES

Alba, R.D. 1990. *Ethnic identity.* New Haven: Yale University Press.

Ashton, P.T. and R.B. Webb. 1986. *Making a difference: Teachers' sense of efficacy and student achievement.* New York: Longman.

Giddens, A. 1979. *Central problems in social history.* Berkeley: University of California Press.

Kluegel, J.R. and E.R. Smith. 1986. *Beliefs about inequality: Americans' views of what is and what ought to be.* New York: Aldine de Gruyter.

Lortie, D.C. 1975. *Schoolteacher.* Chicago: University of Chicago Press.

Orni, M. and H. Winant. 1986. *Racial formation in the United States.* New York: Routledge and Kegan Paul.

Ringer, B. B. and E. R. Lawless. 1989. *Race-ethnicity and society.* New York: Routledge.

Shirts, G. 1969. *Star power.* La Jolla, CA: Western Behavioral Sciences Institute.

—— 1977. *BaFa BaFa.* La Jolla, CA: Western Behavioral Sciences Institute. *Note that there is a version that can be used at the elementary school level called RaFa RaFa.*

Sleeter, C. E. 1992. *Keepers of the American dream.* London: Falmer Press.

Stalvey, L. M. 1988. *The education of a WASP.* Madison: University of Wisconsin Press.

Wellman, D. T. 1977. *Portraits of White racism.* Cambridge, MA: Cambridge University Press.

White Racial Identity and Anti-Racist Education: A Catalyst for Change

BY SANDRA M. LAWRENCE
AND BEVERLY DANIEL TATUM

Although race and race-related issues permeate and influence every social institution, many White teachers currently teaching in schools have had little exposure to a type of education in which the impact of race on classroom practice and student development was systematically examined (Sleeter, 1992; Zeichner, 1993). Some teacher education programs have responded to this disparity by providing teacher education students with courses dealing with multicultural issues as well as with experiences in diverse classroom settings. Similarly, some school districts have provided school faculty with multicultural professional development workshops and programs. Despite these pre- and in-service attempts to address this "deficiency" in White teachers' education, few studies of these programs have been conducted. And because both undergraduate and professional development efforts to prepare teachers to teach in a diverse world vary greatly in substance and duration, the limited research that has been conducted on these endeavors shows mixed results. While some findings reveal that White teachers have more positive feelings about people of color after participating in multicultural courses and programs (Bennet, Niggle & Stage, 1990; Larke, Wiseman & Bradley, 1990), it seems that few of these programs have had the ability to influence either prospective or current teachers' views about themselves as racial beings or to alter existing teaching practices (McDiarmid & Price, 1993; Sleeter, 1992).

Even though the number of studies that point to successful multicultural and anti-racist courses continues to be low, we believed that what we were doing in our courses with our students was more successful than what we had read about in formal studies. Sandra's teaching in multicultural educa-

> FOR WHITES, THE PROCESS INVOLVES BECOMING AWARE OF ONE'S "WHITENESS," ACCEPTING THIS ASPECT OF ONE'S IDENTITY AS SOCIALLY MEANINGFUL AND PERSONALLY SALIENT, AND ULTIMATELY INTERNALIZING A REALISTICALLY POSITIVE VIEW OF WHITENESS WHICH IS NOT BASED ON ASSUMED SUPERIORITY.

tion with undergraduate students and Beverly's teaching with practitioners in an anti-racist professional development course were guided by a belief that anti-racist pedagogy based on the principles of racial identity development could bring about changes in teachers' fundamental beliefs about race and racism. This article stems from that belief. What follows is a brief description of the essential elements of our teaching, as well as the results of our efforts to assess the impact of multicultural and anti-racist courses on White participants specifically.

Understanding White Racial Identity Development

Since much of our work with White teachers is guided by our understanding of Janet Helms' White racial identity development model (1990, 1995), it may be useful to briefly describe it here. In general, racial identity development theory refers to the belief systems that evolve in response to the racial group categorizations given meaning by the larger society. In societies like the U.S., where racial-group membership is an important determinant of social status, it is assumed that the development of a racial identity will occur, to some degree, in everyone. For Whites, the process involves becoming aware of one's "Whiteness," accepting this aspect of one's identity as socially meaningful and personally salient, and ultimately internalizing a realistically positive view of whiteness which is not based on assumed superiority.

Helms (1995) has identified six identity statuses (formerly called stages) which characterize a White individual's pattern of responding to racial situations in his or her environment. Though a person may use more than one strategy or pattern in responding to racial situations, one pattern often predominates.

The first status, **Contact**, is best described as obliviousness. Being White is viewed as a "normal" state of being which is rarely reflected upon, and the privileges associated with being White are simply taken for granted. A shift from this pattern to the second status, **Disintegration**, is often precipitated by increased interactions with people of color and/or exposure to new information about the reality of racism, heightening awareness of White racial privilege and the systematic disadvantages experienced by people of color.

This greater awareness is often accompanied by feelings of guilt, anger and sadness. These emotions can lead to denial and resistance to this new learning, but they can also be a catalyst for action. People operating from this standpoint often try to "convert" others to their new way of thinking. Such actions are not always well-received and individuals may feel considerable social pressure to "not notice" racism, and to maintain the status quo.

The discomfort of the learning process and fear of social isolation can result in a psychological shift to the third status, **Reintegration**. Feelings of guilt and denial may be transformed into fear and anger toward people of color. Resentful "blaming the victim" may be used as a strategy to avoid dealing with the uncomfortable issue of racism, as well as avoiding the struggle to abandon racist assumptions and define a new, anti-racist identity.

However, further development often takes place if one remains engaged in the personal examination of these issues. The fourth status, **Pseudoindependence**, is marked by an intellectual understanding of the unfairness of racism as a system of advantage and a recognition of the need to assume personal responsibility for dismantling it. The individual may seek to distance him/herself from other Whites, and actively seek relationships with people of color as a way of reducing the social isolation experienced earlier. These cross-racial interactions may heighten the individual's awareness of the need to actively examine and redefine the meaning of his/her own whiteness.

This process of redefinition is central to the fifth status, **Immersion/Emersion**. Actively seeking answers to the questions, "Who am I racially? What does it really mean to be White in society?," the individual needs information about White allies, those Whites who have worked against racism, as role models and guides for a new way to thinking about White identity (Tatum, 1994).

The last status, **Autonomy**, represents the internalization of a positive White racial identity and is evidenced by a lived commitment to anti-racist activity, ongoing self-examination and increased interpersonal effectiveness in multiracial settings.

Though described as the last status, it is important to note that an individual may operate from more than one status at a time, and which status predominates may vary with particular situations. However, as one's cross-racial experiences increase and understanding about racism deepens, the latter statuses are more likely to be the ones shaping an individual's behavior. Because the ideology of White racial superiority is so deeply embedded in our culture, the process of "unlearning racism" is a journey we need to continue throughout our lives.

DESIGN OF THE COURSES

Both the undergraduate and graduate courses were racially mixed, though predominantly White. Of the twenty-four female students in the undergraduate course, there were two African American students and three Latinas. There was also one White man. Most students were from middle-class backgrounds with a few from low-income families. Of the forty educators enrolled in the in-service course, there were twenty-eight White participants, eleven African Americans and one Latina.

A major focus of both courses was to help these current and future educators, both White and of color, become more aware of the effects of institutional as well as individual forms of racism and to prepare them to become agents of change by challenging racist practices and policies both in their teaching and in their daily lives. Topics central to the courses included: an examination of White privilege, the cultural and institutional manifestations of racism, theories of racial identity development for Whites and people of color (Helms, 1990) and the connections between racism and other systems of oppression.

Required readings included selections from books such as *Affirming Diversity: The Sociopolitical Context of Education* (1992) and *Freedom's Plow: Teaching in the Multicultural Classroom* (1993). Other readings central to both courses included "White Racism" by Christine Sleeter (1994); "White Privilege: Unpacking the Invisible Knapsack" by Peggy McIntosh (1989); "Talking about Race, Learning about Racism: The Application of Racial Identity Development Theory in the Classroom" (1992) and "Teaching White Students about Racism: The Search for Allies and the Restoration of Hope" (1994) by Beverly Daniel Tatum; "Being, Not Doing" by Andrea Ayvazian (1990); and "Ten Quick Ways to Analyze Children's Books for Racism and Sexism" (1980). Since we continue to revise and update our course syllabi, more recent additions to the required reading list include, among others, *The Dream Keepers* (1995) by Gloria Ladson-Billings and *Rethinking Our Classrooms: Teaching for Equity and Justice* (1994).

Class sessions were designed to be highly interactive and involved both discussion and written reflection. For example, films depicting the roots and manifestations of racism were usually followed by small or large group discussions. Films such as *Ethnic Notions*, *A Class Divided* and *A Tale of O* helped participants understand more fully the destructive ways in which subtle (and not so subtle) racist behaviors and attitudes influence the daily lives of children in and out of schools.

Specific group and individual exercises were also used both in and out of the classroom. For example, one classroom exercise that seemed to function as a turning point for many undergraduate White students in their understanding of racism and their own White privilege involved a read-aloud and writing activity (Lawrence, 1996) focused on Peggy McIntosh's "White Privilege: Unpacking the Invisible Knapsack" (1989). During the class, students seated in a circle were asked to select an index card on which was written one of McIntosh's "privileges." Students were then asked to read aloud, one at a time, the statement on the card with one qualification. White students are asked to read the card as written while students of color are asked to read the card with a "not" before the verb. Any student could "pass" if she/he wished. After all privileges had been read, students were asked to reflect in writing about their experience reading or listening to the read-aloud of "privileges." Oral sharing of experiences was then used to initiate class discussion, a discussion which, though emotional, enabled students to reevaluate their relationship to racism.

One particular exercise in the professional development course that was pivotal for many White educators involved a taped self-interview (Tatum, 1992). For this assignment, participants were asked to interview themselves near the beginning of the course according to a specific interview guide which assessed, among other things, their prior experience and contact with people of color, their attitudes about race and racial issues, their images of people of color and their personal identity in terms of race. Near the conclusion of the course, participants were asked to listen to their tape and then to compose a written analysis of their views as expressed at the time of the interview as well as any new perspectives on their responses.

Through this assignment, White participants were able to see the racism embedded in their attitudes, racism which previously was "invisible" to them. They realized that by avoiding thinking about their "whiteness" they had been able to perceive racism as something external to their lives. They experienced a new recognition of themselves as race-privileged, capable of racist thoughts and behaviors. Some educators were able to move beyond feelings of complicity with racism, to recognize their need to take action to interrupt the oppression now so obvious to them.

Other curricula common to both courses involved weekly written reflection papers, analyses of classroom materials for racial bias and small group sharing of instructional practices and ideas. Through these and related activities, participants received feedback on their views either privately from the instructor in writing or orally from class members in small and large group formats.

DESIGN OF STUDIES

Not only did we design and teach these courses, but we also conducted separate research studies involving the participants of the courses. Specifically, the goal of both studies was to determine the impact of the multicultural and anti-racist courses on the racial identity development and related behavioral changes of the White enrollees. Because we believed that new learning about race is a process that develops over time, we wanted to see whether and how thinking changed and shifted and whether new thinking led to new behaviors.

In order to assess such changes, we used qualitative approaches to data collection and analysis. For one course, Sandra, with the assistance of one of her honors' students, Takiema Bunche, gathered and analyzed interview data and collected samples of student writing. They wanted to determine how and in what ways her undergraduate course in multicultural education influenced her White students' racial identity development (Lawrence & Bunche, 1997). Using a similar design, the authors collected interview and writing sample data from educators enrolled in the professional development course taught by Beverly in order to determine not only how teachers' racial identity changed throughout the course, but to what extent they acted on those changes in their classrooms with their students (Lawrence & Tatum, 1997).

Two sets of interviews were used for the studies. For the first interview, questions focused on prior educational experiences, family and community characteristics, previous experiences with people of color and attitudes about race and racial issues in society and education. Interviews at the conclusion of the course involved the learning the students had experienced, the feelings they had during the course and their opinions of the course content. Other forms of data included samples of students' writing which focused on class discussions and required readings. These data were coded, categorized and thematically analyzed according to comments, attitudes and behaviors detailed in Helms's six statuses of White racial identity development (1995).

INITIAL CHARACTERISTICS OF RACIAL IDENTITY

Data from both courses reveal that pre-service and in-service teachers entered these courses at different stages of racial identity development. At the beginning of the undergraduate course, for example, White students tended to exhibit thinking consistent with the "contact status" of development: they generally thought of themselves as "prejudice-free" and believed they treated all people fairly, regardless of their skin color. Other White people were racist, but not them. In addition, undergraduates seem to lack awareness of the existence or effects of institutional racism; instead, they thought of racism in purely individual terms.

Many of the White veteran teachers entering the in-service course, on the other hand, presented attitudes characteristic of the "pseudo-independent status." They realized that people of color were treated differently than Whites; they were not "color-blind" and were genuinely concerned about the racial oppression that people of color experience in this country. But like the undergraduates, they had given little thought to their racial privilege or how their own complacency in regards to racism could reinforce and perpetuate racist policies and practices. In fact, both groups of participants seemed to have a limited awareness of the pervasiveness of cultural racism, the extent to which they were influenced by stereotypes, or the degree to which people of color were invisible in the school curriculum. For example, few had thought about the racial implications of tracking, the educational system's overreliance on standardized testing for placement decisions or the ways in which cultural stereotypes could influence teacher expectations.

MOVING TOWARDS AN ANTI-RACIST WHITE IDENTITY

Regardless of their initial racial identity "status," all participants moved along Helms' continuum through the course as they gained new insight into the differential treatment accorded to them because of their race and the ways in which experiences of people of color have been either distorted or omitted from the history of this country. For example, one of the most profound learning experiences for both teachers and teacher education students was acknowledgment of their own White privilege. Susan, one of the undergraduate students, reflected on this pivotal new learning in a response paper:

After the powerful realization that people of color do not have the same advantages as I, I am upset and angry. I realized that I, like so many White women, decided that it was easier to be kept in the dark. As long as I did not think about the fact that grave oppression exists, I had no responsibility to take any course of action. This self-imposed decision was not a conscious one, but a decision nonetheless.

Pam, an elementary school teacher, remarked that she had never given her racial privilege any consideration:

I do admit that I have rarely thought of the position I hold because of my race. I have taken for granted the power and in most cases the security that my whiteness has given me.

Neither the graduates nor the undergraduates had previously examined the social power conferred on them because of their whiteness.

Many undergraduates and graduates alike were surprised to discover how "sanitized" their prior education had been and to what extent the experiences of Native Americans, African Americans, Chinese Americans and other people of color were left out of the social studies curriculum. One undergraduate was so "outraged that we spent so much time reviewing the ships that Columbus sailed on" in her private school education that she decided to write letters to her former teachers and administrators to inform them that her social studies education was "inadequate due to all the errors of omission in the social studies curriculum," so that other students would not be as "miseducated in the future" as she believed she was. Teachers in the in-service course also acknowledged their "miseducation" and realized that they had a lot of catching up to do if they wanted their students to be more informed. As one middle school teacher remarked,

I am also trying to learn the history I was never taught in school. I am more questioning of the history I learned and more reflective on how issues and concepts are presented. I no longer believe everything I read!

Their new understanding of racial privilege and institutional manifestations of racism did not come easily, however. Many undergraduates, especially,

struggled with feelings of guilt and shame which accompanied their new perspective. This discomfort, typical of persons in the "disintegration status," caused some students to retreat from the new information and become defensive. Tracey, for example, tried to minimize the burden she felt at recognizing her White privilege by returning to her view of racism as individual acts of discrimination, which she too had experienced:

When we were learning about racism and discrimination and things, it seemed like the focus was on Black people or Puerto Ricans or other minorities that are discriminated against, but I've been discriminated against too and I'm a White person.

Tracey's inability to acknowledge the reality of institutional racism, combined with her selective perception of discrimination, is typical of thinking that characterizes Helms's "reintegration" status. Unfortunately, Tracey seemed firmly implanted in this thinking and by the end of the course did not seem to have experienced any further development of her racial identity.

Veteran teachers also experienced painful moments as they recognized their White privilege. Teachers, like Evelyn, repeatedly wrote about the "guilt associated with unearned advantages." But unlike some of the undergraduates, most teachers did not retreat from the burden of their feelings.

Instead, they acknowledged their roles in maintaining institutional racism and recognized the need to do something differently. Rita captures this view of moving beyond awareness in a reflection paper:

I do indeed have a long way to go on this journey. Awareness is only the beginning, now I have to make real changes.

PUTTING WORDS INTO ACTIONS

Many of the participants in the courses, both students and veteran teachers, were able to stick with the course content through the help and support of instructors and classmates. They were able to deal with their uncomfortable feelings and channel their need to "make changes" by taking action to challenge racism. Reading and talking explicitly about White "allies" and empowered people of color working as change agents helped pre- and in-service teachers see ways they could take responsibility to address the racism they witnessed in their lives. To further facilitate participants' thinking in this direction, we required the class members to design an "action plan" to address racism within their own sphere of influence. Cynthia, one of the undergraduates, wrote about how she felt she had been living "in blinders" referring to her obliviousness to racism. She resolved to continue learning about White racism and about how to be a better White anti-racist ally, and to come out of silence when she heard racist jokes and comments. In fact, by the end of the course she had already put her words into action:

I actually have people that I don't invite over [to my house] anymore. I like Jane, but her husband is a bigot, and I won't put up with it.

Like the teacher education students, veteran teachers also wrote action plans that involved further educating themselves and educating others. Since they were already working in classrooms, they also wrote about changing their teaching practices. Throughout the course, many White teachers acknowledged that they seldom brought the issue of race into their teaching even though they taught in racially-mixed schools. As their awareness grew, they sensed that students were eager to talk about race, but some still felt uncomfortable facilitating discussions that could be "emotionally-charged." With time and experience engaging in similar conversations themselves in the course, they came to realize that they too could conduct such discussions with their students.

Some of their action plans reflected their new race-conscious thinking about the importance of addressing issues of race both in classroom interactions and in the curriculum. Two middle-school teachers, for example, decided to address racial stereotypes with their students while they taught them the fundamentals of essay writing. They had students read and analyze a newspaper essay (one which they had read as part of the course) entitled, "Calling the Plays in Black and White," by Derrick Jackson, a Black journalist, which dealt with the stereotypical language used by sports announcers during professional sports events. Through the use of this essay, the teachers intended both to "raise students' awareness of racial stereotyping" and make their curriculum more inclusive by using models of good writing that included writers of color.

Greg, a third-grade teacher, also attempted to make his curriculum more inclusive after realizing that his current Euro-centric curriculum might be "sending messages that Black cultures are not important." One way that might add a different perspective to his teaching is to use African countries to illustrate points and concepts in his geography curriculum instead of references to Europe or the United States. By teaching students that "Accra is on the coast as opposed to Boston on the coast," Greg felt that he would be validating cultures different than his own.

REFLECTING ON OUR FINDING

Not all the teacher education students nor all the teachers who enrolled in these anti-racist education courses experienced the same degree of movement along Helms's continuum as presented in this brief glimpse of our research and our teaching. While we believe that everyone's thinking shifted to some degree, individual factors such as initial level of resistance, previous exposure to the content and prior multicultural life experiences influence the amount of learning and change that can occur. Although one course can serve as a catalyst that helps White educators to progress through the statuses of White racial identity, we also realize that one course cannot do it all. In fact, both undergraduates and veteran teachers often spoke and wrote about their need for more information, more support and more time to help them to stay on the path of change.

We believe that teacher education students need not just one course in anti-racist education but a series of courses where anti-racist and multicultural concepts build upon one another. Likewise, educators currently teaching need more than a one-semester shot of anti-racist professional development. Follow-up workshops and institutes would help those teachers committed to change to maintain their momentum and confront opposition from a society that denies the existence of institutional racism. Leadership at the school level is also an important factor in maintaining momentum. White educators working to alter the status quo need the support of others like them to discuss and evaluate their continued growth as anti-racist White allies (Ayvazian, 1995).

Our small-scale studies of our courses have confirmed for us our belief that anti-racist teaching built upon a sound blend of psychological and pedagogical theories can be instrumental in assisting White educators, both in development of their racial identities and in a re-visioning of their current curriculum. While we are certain that more is needed, we continue to be encouraged by the changes that we see in our pre-service and in-service teachers, and in ourselves as we work to prepare teachers who will challenge racist and ethnocentric school practices that may seem to benefit some but are, in reality, a detriment to us all.

Sandra M. Lawrence, Associate Professor of Pychology and Education at Mount Holyoke College. Dr. Lawrence teaches courses in anti-racist education to preservice and inservice teachers and directs the middle and secondary education programs at Mount Holyoke. Among her most recent publications are: "Beyond Race Awareness: White Racial Identity and Multicultural Teaching" (1997) in the Journal of Teacher Education and "Bringing White Privilege Into Consciousness" (1996) in Multicultural Education. E-mail: SLAWRENC@MTHOLYOKE.EDU

Beverly Daniel Tatum, Professor of Psychology and Education, Mount Holyoke College. Dr. Tatum speaks nationally on the psychology of racism and has published numerous articles in journals including the Harvard Educational Review and Women's Studies Quarterly. She is the author of "Why Are All the Black Kids Sitting Together in the Cafeteria?" And Other Conversations About Race (1997).

REFERENCES

Ayvazian, A. 1995. "Interrupting the cycle of oppression: The role of allies as agents of change." *Fellowship*. January/February: 6-9.

Bennet, C. T., T. Niggle, and F. Stage. 1990. "Preservice multicultural teacher education: Predictors of student readiness." *Teaching and Teacher Education*. 8.1: 243-254.

Council on Interracial Books for Children. 1980. "Ten quick ways to analyze children's books." Bigelow, B., et al. 1994. *Rethinking our classrooms: Teaching for equity and justice*. Rethinking Schools.

Helms, J. E. 1995. "An update of Helms's White and people of color racial identity models". In J.G. Ponterotto, J.M. Casas, L.A.Suzuki, C.M. Alexander, eds. *Handbook of multicultural counseling*. Thousand Oaks, CA: Sage.

Helms, J. E., ed. 1990. *Black and White racial identity: Theory, research and practice*. Westport, CT: Greenwood Press.

Jackson, D. 1989. "Calling the plays in black and white: Will today's Super Bowl be Black brawn vs. White brains?" *Boston Sunday Globe*. January 22, p. A25.

Ladson-Billings, G. 1995. *The Dreamkeepers: Successful teachers of African American children*. San Francisco: Jossey Bass.

Larke, P., J., D. Wiseman; and C. Bradley. 1990. "The Minority mentorship project: Changing attitudes of preservice teachers for diverse classrooms". *Action in Teacher Education*, 12.3: 5-11.

Lawrence, S. M. Spring, 1996. "Bringing White privilege into consciousness." *Multicultural Education: The Magazine of the National Association for Multicultural Education*, pp. 46-48.

Lawrence, S. M. and T. Bunche. 1997. "Feeling and dealing: Teaching White students about racial privilege." *Teaching and Teacher Education*, 12.5: 531-542.

Lawrence, S. M. and B.D. Tatum. 1997. "White educators as allies: Moving from awareness to action". In M. Fine, L. Weiss, L. Powell & M. Wong. eds. *Off-white: Readings on society, race and culture*. NY: Routledge.

McDiarmid, G.W., and J. Price.1993. "Preparing teachers for diversity: A study of student teachers in a multicultural program". In M. J. O'Hair and S. J. Odell, eds. *Diversity and teaching: Teacher education yearbook I*. Forth Worth, TX: Harcourt Brace Jovanovich.

McIntosh, P. 1989. "White privilege: Unpacking the invisible knapsack."*Peace and Freedom*. July/August: 10-12.

Nieto, S. 1992. *Affirming diversity: The sociopolitical context of multicultural education*. NY: Longman.

Perry, T. and J. Fraser, eds. 1993. *Freedom's plow: Teaching in the multicultural classroom*. NY: Routledge.

Sleeter, C. A. 1992. *Keepers of the American dream: A study of staff development and multicultural education*. London: Farmer.

Sleeter, C. A. Spring, 1994. "White racism." *Multicultural Education*, pp 5-8.

Tatum, B. D. 1992. "Talking about race, learning about racism: The application of racial identity development theory in the classroom." *Harvard Educational Review*. 62 .1: 1-24.

Tatum, B. D. 1994. "Teaching White students about racism: The search for White allies and the restoration of hope." *Teachers College Record*. 95 .4: 462-476.

Zeichner, K. 1993. *Educating teachers for cultural diversity*. Paper presented at the annual meeting of the American Educational Research Association, Atlanta.

ADDITIONAL READINGS

Cross, Jr., W.E. 1991. *Shades of black: Diversity in African American identity*. Temple, PA: Temple University Press.

Tatum, B. 1997. *"Why are all the Black kids sitting together in the cafeteria?" and other essays*. NY: Basic Books/Harper Collins.

The True Colors of the New Jim Toomey: Transformation, Integrity, Trust in Educating Teachers About Oppression

BY CINDY COHEN

Jim Toomey[1] was a student in Contemporary Educational Perspectives, a foundations course for pre-service teachers I taught in the fall of 1993. In the portfolio in which he reflected on his learning, Jim included a composition essay he had written two years previously along with a current response:

The Old Jim Toomey

...The problem is "there aren't enough Maya Angelo's [sic] in these happy-go-lucky people. Who grow up to be drug users and amount to nothing as far as I'm concerned. They meander the streets of my old neighborhood shooting one another, which my father thinks is just smashing. He feels that this is the answer to the Massachusetts budget problem. Wall off Roxberry [sic], Mattapan and certain parts of Dorchester and dump 10,000 machine guns and let them do their thing. In a week the state will be back on its feet."

—*Jim Toomey, 3/91[2]*

Response to the Old Jim Toomey

This paper [I wrote two years ago] is living proof that I have come a long way in regards to my view on issues of difference. I believe this paper...is barbaric. I'm embarrassed to say that I wrote it, and believed in it. ...Cindy, there are many people like the old Jim Toomey not only "out there" but right here in Durham. It's horrifying to me. I notice it especially back home. ... I almost can't wait to go home and show the true colors of the new Jim Toomey.

—*Jim Toomey, 12/93*

Like Jim, I, too, was horrified to read the violent, racist assumptions that permeated his earlier writing. I was deeply moved, however, that he trusted me enough to reveal them, and heartened by his enthusiasm about his changing awareness. Jim's writing documented exactly the kind of reexamination of learned prejudices I had hoped the course would engender.

As I read their portfolios at the end of the semester, I realized that, like Jim, most of his 27 classmates had earnestly implicated themselves within our exploration of differences and oppressions. Their writing was passionate. It documented moments of transformation, but also revealed awareness of resistances, questions and confusions. Although the semester had had its share of tensions and problems, somehow we had created enough trust to allow for this work.

The importance of "trust" becomes apparent upon reading accounts of classes that seek, whether successfully or not, to engage students in addressing issues of oppression. Few practical or theoretical accounts[3], however, offer either a conceptual framework to help us understand the nature and significance of trust, nor any practical guidance for nourishing relationships that actually warrant it.[4]

In general, I believe we deserve students' trust when we relate in ways that promote their capacity for integrity. We do this when we elicit and honor their voices[5]; when we challenge them to seek consistency among their actions, beliefs, knowledge and values; and when we support critical thinking. But when we ask students to implicate themselves in dynamics of oppression — to analyze critically the narratives out of which their world views have been woven — we invite them into extreme disjunctures between values and actions. They find themselves torn, for instance, between commitments to family and openness to new understandings. How do we nourish their integrity, while simultaneously provoking confusion and conflict? How do we engage them in transformative and radicalizing curricula without falling into the trap of indoctrination?

In this article, I propose some initial answers to these questions by reflecting on Contemporary Educational Perspectives, a course that challenged prospective teachers, in an environment of political conservatism and racial homogeneity, to review their own lives through the lens of oppression. The syllabus drew heavily on pedagogical models I developed

© RICK REINHARD

with colleagues at The Oral History Center, a community-based cultural organization in the Boston area.[6] I describe specific activities and assignments in some detail, in case readers wish to adapt elements of the course to their own circumstances. Also, with help from my students' writing and several contemporary feminist philosophers, I consider the concepts of "integrity" and "trust" in ways that have helped me negotiate the risky ethical terrain that almost always accompanies meaningful education about oppression.

CREATING A COMMUNITY OF INQUIRY

Parker Palmer, a Quaker educator and writer, asserts that academic institutions must play a stronger role in developing within our citizenry a "capacity for relatedness" (1987). He claims that the epistemological assumptions that dominate academia — objectivist, analytic and experimental modes of knowing — foster intellectual and ethical habits of detachment and control. As an alternative, he suggests we invite "our students to intersect their autobiographies with the life story of the world," so that they come to know intimately and passionately as well as objectively. To support critical thinking and constructive conflict, we must create classrooms characterized by strong relationships.

During the first three weeks of Contemporary Educational Perspectives I introduced students, through both activities and readings, to the concepts of "community of inquiry" and "language of story," and to the importance of listening. The primary activity of the first three weeks was the creation of a paper quilt, in which each student created a patch depicting a scene from his or her own life.[7] The activity is based on several key ideas about story: every person has a story to tell; respectful listening elicits the stories that need to be told; we shape the meaning of our experiences through the telling of stories; we honor each other's stories by responding to them; and a community grows stronger when all its stories are celebrated. I hoped that we were stitching a "compassionate fabric of human caring," (Palmer, 1987) strong enough to sustain the creative conflict that inevitably accompanies meaningful encounters with issues of oppression.

In order to generate stories and images for their quilt patches, as well as to help them begin to reflect on their own experiences as teachers and learners, I asked students to write briefly about nine different memories of learning and teaching such as a time when you felt proud of learning something new; a time when you felt connected to people through learning something; a time when you felt excited about teaching someone something; and so forth. In class, students wrote about a time when they felt a part of a community. Then, offering brightly colored, square-shaped origami paper as background, and lots of pipe cleaners, tissue paper, glitter, chalk, markers and crayons, I asked each student to create a visual image based on one of their ten stories.

To introduce students to attentive listening, I asked them to observe me interviewing one student about the story behind his patch. We discussed techniques of listening, and how oral history helps people discover and give voice to the stories they wish (and need) to tell. I emphasized their role as interviewer: to be present as a listener and to seek to understand the other's map of the world. Students interviewed each other, and then each one wrote again, in poetry or prose, about his or her own story and the story of the other.

The next week, we listened as the twenty-seven students presented their quilt patches, read or told their stories and then listened as the interviewers offered responses. The activity had engaged students in a conscious exercise of their listening skills and allowed them to experience how a community grows closer when all of its members' stories are acknowledged and celebrated. These brief narratives — about childhood fights on the playground, favorite teachers, family outings, first successes during the previous semester's teaching internships, for instance — provided windows into students' lives. We glimpsed the diversity among our ranks. Susan, the one Jewish student in the class, for instance, depicted her isolation at the time of the yearly Christmas play. In her presentation, she indicated that she hesitated to use the word "discrimination" to describe her experience, because it had become such a buzzword. Dale, her interviewer, responded with the following poem: "Discrimination is not just a buzz word./It is like a buzz saw./It separates and it hurts."

At the end of the first three-week unit, students wrote a letter to me, synthesizing their thoughts about the theme of "community of inquiry," looking for connections among their own stories, class activities and the assigned readings. I responded to each student, answering questions about the course, acknowledging reservations and surfacing the pedagogical and political implications I saw in their stories. I responded to Jim Toomey, the student whose end-of-the-semester writing I quoted above, in part by finding points of connection between his resistances to learning and my own:

It's interesting to me that there is a voice in you that "already knows" about these questions [of pedagogy and curriculum.] I have that voice inside of me, too...I don't want to have to absorb the ways of thinking of these other people, I want to pursue models that I've already developed. But learning does require being willing to change, to reexamine. ...[I've found that] there is no way to get through resistances until we can name them, acknowledge them and consciously let them go.

At the end of Jim's letter, he made a passing reference to his ethnicity, attributing his stubbornness to "the Irish in me." Knowing that we were soon to engage in deeper explorations of identity, I wrote:

I'm interested in your understanding of what is the "Irish" in you. As we move into the third unit of this course and begin to explore our own cultures and our interactions with people of different cultures, I hope to hear more about this. In your paper you attach your stubbornness to your Irishness. (I've often attached my proclivity for suffering to my Jewishness.) What else do you attach to your Irishness? What do you like and not like about what you've absorbed from Irish culture?

I also used this letter to ask political questions that were raised for me by his quilt patch, which depicts him beating up a playground bully, a time he felt proud of learning something new:

Your story about striking Jacob Schwartz in the third grade stuck in my mind after class. Having spent many years working on nonviolent conflict resolution...I found myself wondering: Is it INEVITABLE that young boys use violence to resolve conflicts, to prove themselves? How has it come to be so acceptable, so much a standard part of young boys' lives?...Do we require boys to develop emotionally in such a way that they have the capacity to be soldiers later in life? What's gained and what is lost?

Throughout the semester, students monitored their learning by creating portfolios of samples of their work accompanied by a reflection on its significance. Many students developed the themes they first named during the paper quilt project. Trevor, for instance, depicted himself in the second grade, squirming and wiggling during the required hour-long religion class. His poem about the quilt patch ended with these lines: "I believe in the Lord, don't get me wrong/but an hour of religion is just too long." His portfolio essay used this image merely as a point of entry to explore several aspects of his identity. He was the only Protestant student in a Catholic private school, a circumstance which led him to feel very much an outsider. His early years at school were difficult, in part because he witnessed the physical abuse of his mother by his alcoholic father; in part because of his outsider status at school; in part because he experienced a sense of shame about his economic class (exacerbated when one of his teachers missed a home visit claiming she couldn't find the trailer park where he lived.) These memories informed Trevor's subsequent reading of theory about class and gender. They helped him interpret Theodore Sizer's statement: "Good schools are thoughtful places. The people in them are known....No one is ridiculed" (Sizer, p. 128).

AMPLIFYING FEELINGS OF PRIDE

On a preliminary worksheet on issues of difference, Jane wrote: "I've lived my entire life in Union, New Hampshire. Sad, isn't it?" Like Trevor's story about feeling ashamed of living in a trailer, Jane's response reminded me why it is important to help students name and explore positive aspects of their backgrounds.[8] In order for students to truly appreciate the story of the other they must first have a sense of themselves as people with stories, with voice, with awareness of rootedness. They need a sense of belonging or pride associated with family, place, a particular relationship, heritage, experience, competency, or struggle.

I offered another oral history activity through which students could connect with or generate a sense of pride in their own identities. Students brought from home objects connected to special people, rituals, traditions, or places. They shared stories about their objects first in small groups, then in writing, and, the next week, according to their request, each student told a brief version of the story to the entire class. Many pictures of these objects and students writings about them appeared at the end of the semester in their portfolios.

I discovered several students had little sense of having stories to tell; amplifying their voices became an important first step in engaging them in this inquiry. This group included mostly women. For instance, Amelia, a senior art major and a single-mother from a nearby working-class community, at first seemed to have difficulty simply completing assignments and juggling family responsibilities in order to attend class. Her quilt patch was, to my eyes, visually the most striking in the class, but, when interviewed by a classmate, she wasn't able to verbalize much about its meaning. In response to the assignment to bring in an object that would help her tell a story, she brought in pictures of her daughter. Once her role as a mother was visible and validated within the classroom community, she became much more engaged in our work. Later, in her portfolio, she wrote:

One picture, at the harbor, shows a continuation of my childhood. I have gone to New Harbor every summer of my life and Emily has also. It's significant now because my grandfather, who was a big part of that tradition, just died two weeks ago....Emily and I are a team...When I was pregnant with her, I felt as if she was destined to do great, important things for the world. I still think

that way!

These past eight months have been hard for me....I just about stopped fighting....Taking this class helped me regain the fire and energy in my soul that I had lost....Something Cindy said to the class helped tremendously: that everybody's story of their life is okay. We shouldn't feel bad about it. We should be proud of our lives and our family histories. It made me realize, even more, how important it is to be a teacher and what you say, as a teacher/adult, effects children....I think [this idea] has given me more respect for other people and their way of life. It makes me look at people in a different way, a more positive way.

Several of the men in my class had a different need. They didn't quite know how to engage with an inquiry into issues of difference and oppression without seeing themselves as bad people. Mike actually articulated his doubts about his own goodness in a story he wrote about becoming friends with the only African American man on his lacrosse team. When his friend revealed to him the poverty of his family, the fact that he couldn't even "ask his father for $10, I mean shit man $10," Mike didn't know how to respond:

What could I say to my friend? Don't worry, everything will work out? Easy for me to say, a White guy who has school, an apartment, books and a nice car paid for. I had mixed emotions. Should I help? Should I feel guilty for what I have? Am I the bad guy? Why should I care? Well I did care and I did feel bad that I was more privileged than he.

By engaging students with a sense of pride, and by supporting them to articulate their fears and their resistances, I hoped to help them reach through their defensiveness, to strengthen their capacity to acknowledge both their oppression and their privilege. In order to have the strength and flexibility to acknowledge their complicity in racist and sexist dynamics, they first needed to reaffirm the valuable aspects of their backgrounds and the goodness of their persons.

ENCOUNTERING THE OTHER

After these activities of self-affirmation, we read autobiographical essays written by people of diverse backgrounds. My intention was for students to imagine the lives of people different from them (by virtue of sexual orientation, religion, ethnicity, race, or class) to enable them to understand not only the insidious effects of oppressive dynamics but also to realize the sources of strength that exist within every group

Counter demonstraters in New Hope, Pennsylvania protest Neo-Nazi and KKK "Gay Bash '93" rally.

whose story has been suppressed. For some members of the class, reading autobiographical essays[9] proved to be effective in opening windows onto the worlds of people they'd never before encountered. This was especially true for several students who read essays by lesbian women:

...It was weird (strange, different) to read how in between her two relationships with women, she was planning on marrying a man to have a family. I guess it's weird because it's one thing to be homosexual — which is something that I don't understand, but it's another to say you're homosexual, but still want to be with someone of the opposite sex. I guess I've always thought that if you're gay — you're gay and if you're straight — you're straight. But obviously I was wrong.

....When the author revealed that she was a lesbian my first reaction was to go back and reread the essay to pick up hints of it. I stopped myself from doing this, however, because I realized that it didn't matter. I am ashamed to say that I was actually afraid to admit that I could see the point of view of this author. I had always thought of myself as fairly open-minded, but my reaction to learning that she is a lesbian proves that I have a long way to go before I am accepting of others' differences When I realized I was distancing myself from her views, I began to think about how isolated lesbians and gay men must feel.

These essays, along with our class discussions, led several students to write about ways in which their own lives had already brought them into relationship with people who are different. Several of these stories appeared in students' portfolios. Jane, the student who felt sad about having lived her whole life in a small New Hampshire town, responded to the essays by lesbian authors Minnie Bruce Pratt and Leslie Lawrence with this story:

In my family, my brother's wife left him to be with a woman. My brother had been married for eight years and they had two children. The wife (I will call her Sara, not her real name) decided to leave my brother and he got custody of the children. Sara went to Vermont where she married her lover. They had a child, not Sara, but the other woman. The baby is now two years old and she is a beautiful child.

My brother was devastated, their two children had to deal with so many issues and I am sure Sara had many, many issues to deal with, too.

The students' stories revealed the extent to which, even within this apparently homogeneous class, in this racially homogeneous university, many students had already encountered issues of oppression in personally meaningful ways. Dwight wrote about his struggle to understand an incident in which an African American woman had falsely accused him of keeping her son under surveillance in the sports store where he worked as a cashier. "I was so hurt," he wrote. "This lady must have had one hell of a life to be so bitter and accusing." Vicki wrote this telling story about a more intimate encounter with racism in rural New Hampshire:

Life in the town of Greenfields isn't exactly what you would call worldly. I had little or no contact with other cultures during the first 18 years of my life...I don't recall ever meeting or talking with a Black person until my brother, Rob, started seeing Jessica.

Nobody at my school thought twice about making racial jokes or saying "What am I, Black?" when asked to do something, or was excluded from some activity. My stepfather, Roger was one of the biggest culprits of this type of behavior. When Rob sent us a picture of Jessica, we weren't sure how we were going to break the news to Roger. We weren't sure how he'd react to the fact that Jessica was Black. I can't remember how he did react when we told him, but I do remember her first visit.

I was unsure what to say or how to act when she came. I had never been around a Black person and I didn't want to say or do anything that would offend or embarrass her or myself. I also wanted to make her feel like she was comfortable and part of the family. I'm not sure that she could be completely comfortable meeting the whole family and on top of it all we were all White.

Everything seemed to work out that first weekend. Roger was on his best behavior and discovered that even he could like a Black person. The only real embarrassing moment came on another visit where my father gave the patented response to a request by my mother, "What am I, Black?" He tried to cover up by listing out colors as fast as he could while his face turned from its normal pale skin color to a bright shade of red. Although we were embarrassed, Jessica seemed to ignore the comment and once Roger's original color returned it was as if nothing had happened.

By now we've gotten to the point where we're all comfortable with each other. The questions come easily and without too much embarrassment to get rid of some of those curiosities that we have. An example of this was at my camp when my mom asked Jessica if she tanned when out in the sun. There was a little embarrassment that was eased quickly by Jessica's answer "Black as the ace of spades."

. . . I would never give up the chance to see my little three year old niece, Rob and Jessica's daughter, smile and call me "Auntie Ricky." I'm glad that I got the chance to get to know and love Jessica before prejudice from my environment caused me to dislike or fear all Blacks.

PLACING OURSELVES WITHIN A POLITICS OF LOCATION

Once students had begun to affirm aspects of their own identities and to encounter the world-views of others, I asked them to reflect on how the dynamics of oppression operate in their own lives, to implicate themselves within a "politics of location."[10] They completed personal timelines, in which they responded to questions about the presence and absence of different kinds of people in their lives, and about their formal and informal education concerning the history and cultures of different groups. The assignment helped them identify ways they'd been both hurt and privileged by oppressive dynamics, as well as goals they had for themselves as persons and as educators. These timelines became a shorthand way for students to record and analyze memories that arose throughout this unit of the course; students also used them to generate stories and essays for their portfolios. As a model of self-reflection, I assigned Vivian Paley's *White Teacher*.

Many students experienced great resistance to the idea that "oppression" could have any relevance to their lives. For instance, on his preliminary worksheet on issues of difference, Gregg wrote: "This word [oppression] evokes very negative connotations to me....If we view society solely in terms of a struggle between the oppressors and oppressed we oversimplify and fail to recognize the heterogeneity of society, the complexity of some of these issues and the values of individuals. Such a bipolar view helps to construct walls, and makes it difficult to move forward...." Dale echoed his emphasis on the importance of individuals:

Sometimes I feel like the issues of multiculturalism get analyzed and discussed to death and get made into something much more complicated than they really are. I don't see the problem as complex. I see it simply as people not accepting other people who are different from them.

Dale, Gregg and many other students in the class were exhibiting forms of resistance analyzed by Beverly Tatum (1992) in her article "Talking About Race, Learning About Racism: The Application of Racial Identity Development Theory in the Classroom." They were uncomfortable challenging the myth that America is essentially a just society; they saw racism and other forms of oppression, to the extent they actually exist, primarily as problems of individuals, especially individuals other than themselves.

Marilyn Frye's (1993) essay "On Oppression" evoked more controversy than any other reading. In the essay, Frye uses the image of a birdcage to explain how oppression works. To paraphrase Frye, she asserts that it isn't possible to understand the nature of oppressive systems by studying any one aspect of discrimination; that would be like trying to understand how a birdcage constrains by examining only one wire in its structure. In order to understand a cage, it is necessary to step back and see all the wires and the webbed pattern they form. Similarly, in order to understand sexism, for instance, one must look at patterns of discrimination in employment, education, family roles, athletics, corporate styles of communication and decision-making, etc. Amelia drew a model of the cage that circumscribes her life as a young, single-mother. She labeled its wire bars as follows: "job," "child care," "welfare," "education," "child's needs for mother's attention," "generalizations" and "criticalizations [sic] of [single mothers]," "money/expenses," "father of child (whether involved or not)," "guilt for having child out of wedlock/guilt for having abortion." While her analysis reveals her awareness of how her options have been constrained by issues of both gender and class, she also acknowledges her relative privilege as a White person:

Oppression (or My Life As a Single Mother)

As I was reading "Oppression" by Marilyn Frye I found my life being described. It startled me because even though being a single mother is hard, being oppressed never entered my mind. I guess not knowing more about the word kept me from realization. Even though I've found that single mothers, let alone being female, are oppressed, I'm not going to dwell on it and feel sorry for myself. It puts fire in my soul and makes me want to push even further past the odds. I can just imagine how hard it must be to be a single, Black mother.

I was inspired by the sincerity with which most students engaged in this inquiry. Students wrote about their own experiences as targets of oppressive dynamics and as outsiders — for instance when visiting other countries, as they grappled with having been adopted, and when they had been labeled as "learning disabled." Rosanne, for instance, wrote:

I was sitting in this small room with one opaque window, it felt like a jail. I had just been told I had a learning disability, and I would be working with a UNH student on my reading comprehension.... I tried to tell these brilliant minds, whom [sic] decided on my education, that my only disability was my lack of interest in school. Their response was "that is caused by your learning disability."

I felt stuck, and more frustrated in academics then I had ever been before. I was in this caving room with a person who made me feel stupid and more disinterested....Forced, I sat everyday and told her exactly what she wanted to hear, so when the bell rang I could leave immediately and be with my friends. I have never felt so disinterested and resistant to the learning process and my education, as I did that day.

The timelines and the portfolios allowed many students to explore the ways in which they were both victims of and privileged by oppressive dynamics. They also worked to help students name and begin to address their confusions and their questions. For instance, Mike (the same student whose friendship with an African American athlete had raised feelings of guilt) wrote about the day when, as a teenager, he realized that two of his neighbors were lesbian women.

"This is the bathroom and through the kitchen is the back porch..." said Morgan, a 7 year old, only child. The little tow-headed blond, blue-eyed boy tugged at my shirt to follow him to the back part of the house. "And this is where mom and Jan sleep and this...is my...bed...r...o...o...m" As his voice drifted away into the next room I looked down at the large queen sized bed. Morgan's words....rang through my hollow head like someone shouting across the Grand Canyon....It had never clicked that Morgan's mother (Sara) and her friend? roommate? work associate? (Jan) were lesbians. I didn't know how to feel at 14 years old. I liked them very much, yet weren't lesbians bad in some way? Taboo? They weren't supposed to be nice, cool, and well, fun-loving.

...Jan, a short blond haired rolly polly woman with a great sense of humor always made me feel as if I was a knight in shining armor. Jan would say things like, "Gosh how did you ever lift that box? I could never had done that in a million years." She would then squeeze my bicep and say, "a true hunk, yah, right here." I was confused. Why would they act this way? Weren't homosexual women supposed to hate men and their masculinity?

Mike found himself filled with questions about lesbianism and homosexuality. The idea of physical and sexual expressions of love between two people of the same gender was not in his "schema," not in his "vocabulary." "It is a complete voice which I'm positive will not change," he wrote. But then, he wondered if his attitude was discriminatory.

Is it wrong to feel awkward around homosexuals because I don't understand? Am I paranoid or homophobic because I don't understand? If so, is being homophobic bad? Does it parallel bigotry, racism? I think that it is the mere fact that I need more education on the subject.

The night before the portfolios were due, Mike called me and asked for suggestions of articles to read about lesbianism. He began to educate himself on issues of homosexuality and homophobia by reading "The Death of Fred Astaire," an essay by Leslie Lawrence (1993) in the anthology we'd been using in class, *daily fare: essays from the multicultural experience.*

A question which was always at the forefront of my brain when I was near Sara was; did you just fall out of heterosexual love? Do you still find your ex-husband attractive? How are the emotional feelings with a woman different? Or are there different feelings?

By reading this essay, Mike found some initial and partial answers to his questions. Perhaps more important, he experienced the power of literature to help him find answers to his questions about people who are different from him. Having embarked on the process of educating himself, he could acknowledge that the barrier between himself and homosexual men and women was his own ignorance; the problem resided in him, not in gays and lesbians:

....Leslie Lawrence shows her lifestyle, feelings and the conflict which surrounds it as honest and openly as a writer can. This story creates and transfers knowledge to people like me who have trouble comprehending homosexuality. Literature, as well as open, honest talk are significant starting points in gaining knowledge, and breaking down often ignorant barriers. Barriers which contain multitudes of misunderstanding.

It was near the end of the semester, and Jim, the student whose writing appears in the introduction to this article, didn't have much to enter into his portfolio. He took me up on an offer to meet, and our discussion turned to the questions I'd raised in my letter weeks earlier. What was his experience of being Irish? What did he think about the inevitability of violence among boys? I could feel the tension between the loyalty and love he felt for his parents, on the one hand, and his growing awareness of the injustices of their racist beliefs on the other. I encouraged him to use the portfolio to write about his family and his experiences

of culture and class. His first entry was about his father:

Power

The man who is loved by many and hated by few. He travels with a smile on his face, his heart on his shirt but his emotions in his pocket. I have never been able to complain about my lack of upbringing. Hell, anything I had was twice what he had, especially when you're talking about a man who never had hot running water until he was eighteen. So here I sit at twenty-three seeing in the glass of the computer his reflection staring back at me.

....He'll be the first to admit that as a child growing up he was not the nicest kid in the parish....I get the feeling from his friends from the old days that he was the man, nobody messed with him, if they did, they lost. He was known as the "quickest hands in Dorchester." As I grew up and began to understand my father and his acceptance for aggression and fighting, I too began to talk more with my fists than my mouth. To this day I still have a hard time keeping my hands in my pockets when confronted by someone.

....Like my father I moved. I entered Academy Ave. School knowing few people at the time I was confronted by the school bully, and I did not know what to do. Upon returning home I explained what had happened. My father was just full of advice, I had come to the right man. I remember his telling me how to slightly bend the wrist so that when I hit him my fist would not give. He also told me that day in the dining room by the buffet that if I lost it was okay. He told me that I should go back and fight Jacob Schwartz each day until I won or until he eventually got sick of fighting me. As Jacob Schwartz approached me at the tender age of eight, I stood there looking up at this monster when out of my pocket my slightly bent fist blasted toward his face. It was as if my fist had eyes, I had won the war. To see Jacob Schwartz belly up crying, holding his blood filled face in his hands left me at the moment satisfied. I learned a valuable lesson which helped shape the person I am today. Don't let anyone push you around, bend but don't break. However horrible as it may sound, I learned a simple way to resolve problems ...violence....I realize that this is not the proper way of handling situations of conflict. It's much easier now at twenty-three to see it as such.

My father had always tried to provide for the family. One night back in '78 while he was cruising along in his police car, his obligation as bread-winner ended. *While riding in the passenger seat he filled out paperwork, the front right wheel fell into an uncapped manhole. It's almost as if this hole that the car fell in still surrounds him today.*

Jim explained how his father's forced retirement limited his capacity to earn money, and wondered how this has affected his sense of his own worth:

Right now nobody will hire him, as he is approaching sixty and retired on disability....He is a strong man, full of pride: how does he feel sprawled out on the recliner, each day seeing his wife of fifty-one come home from work, pass by him and plop into bed.

...I had a roommate at college whose father only made it to probably four of our lacrosse games in four years. If my dad missed four games in a season it was a shocker...Kev's father made at least six figures; my dad made no figures. But the biggest and difference between the two father-son relationships is this....I knew my dad. I could talk the way I wanted to talk. I could go out and be a human being around him. He is my friend. I kiss him, I hug him, I tell him that I love him, He is my Dad.

The second entry in Jim's portfolio is about his Mom:

Strength

She is the strongest woman I know, bar none. She is like the stitching that bind the seams of a complex mitt. Without her we would fall apart, unable to work as a unit.

....My mother was born the daughter of two Galway immigrants, both of whom were dead by the time she was barely eighteen. Her mother died of Cancer brought on, my mother says, by the cleaning solutions she used in the banks on weekends. Her father died two years later in his sleep, (God rest their souls) my mother claims from loneliness.

....She is a woman of high standards and who always wanted the best for her boys. It has always been my mother's dream to put the three boys through college. None of her brothers and sisters ever went to college the same goes for my father's side. This dream became etched in stone one day when I came home to find out that she had lost her job. My father was unemployed and had exhausted his unemployment benefits. Our net income for that period of time was nil. She was out having a few drinks when I found out. That night she came home

late. *She was about forty-three at the time. I sat there and listened as she explained that they replaced her with an attractive young woman, who only had two years of college experience. My mother had been working there for roughly five years, she knew her job, there was no one more qualified that she. The promise she made that night was that this would never happen to her kids, nobody would treat her boys in the way that she was mistreated. There I was at seventeen looking at my mother, the backbone of our household, through flushed eyes wishing there was something I could do. I was helpless. The memory is so vividly carved in my brain, the strongest woman I know, the woman who brought me into this world and provided for me in a way that no other mother could, hunched there in front of me weeping like a child. She promised me that if she had to work five jobs to put us through school she would. I believe her.*

Jim's essays about his parents honor his Irish, working-class history and culture, and affirm his love and respect for them. He gives voice to the humiliations and the constraints that have circumscribed their lives. At the same time, he celebrates their strengths, the bonds of family loyalty, their willingness to work in support of each other, their capacity for intensity and intimacy.

As he worked on his portfolio, Jim read "Listening," an essay in which Sey Chassler (1992) documents his growing awareness of sexist dynamics in his own household. Reading this essay helped Jim name, for the first time, similar patterns operating in his family:

I have seen my parents argue at home.... They're both pretty good at pointing the finger at someone else, who usually isn't around. Other times they may argue over something like who fed the cat last. And believe me these fights were worth the price of admission. They never fought over whose turn it was to do the dishes, or who would do the laundry that day, or who would take Danny to South Shore Hospital. These were things the mother did. Upon finishing dinner, my father would strike-up a butt, get up without saying a word and slip into the living-room. On the way to his throne (recliner) he would pass by the sink, he wouldn't even lift the plate and drop it off along the way. As Sey Chassler would say, there was a "click" in my head.

I think it is no coincidence that Jim honored his parents' suffering and celebrated their culture before he was able to think and write critically about the racism and sexism he had learned from them. In fact, Jim recapitulated in his own portfolio the pedagogy that had informed the entire semester: first, students celebrated aspects of their own heritage and then acknowledged the ways they themselves (and their families) have been targeted by discrimination. These reflections were intended to create a foundation of self-respect upon which they could acknowledge the inadequacy of their education about differences, and the ways they had internalized and participated in oppressive dynamics. I believe these were the steps that allowed Jim to reveal and critique his earlier, racist writing.

In subsequent semesters, students have worked in small groups to produce anthologies, rather than individual portfolios. The anthologies create a structure which requires students to make comparisons among their different stories and experiences. In some cases, students' writing in individual portfolios reflects deeper introspection than their anthology entries.

INTEGRITY, RADICAL CHANGE AND WARRANTING STUDENTS' TRUST

In her essay "Transforming Pedagogy and Multiculturalism," bell hooks acknowledges the discomfort and pain that accompany shifts in the paradigms that have defined students' worlds. White students often come to recognize their parents' nonprogressive thinking; "it hurts them that new ways of knowing may create estrangement where there was none" (1993).

As I worked with Jim on his portfolio, I appreciated the emotional labor required for his sincere engagement with the course. He came face to face with his parents' pain, their sacrifice, and how, as a teenager, he'd disappointed them. Furthermore, as his awareness enlarged, he began critically to observe the dynamics within his family and the ideology that informed his parents' world views. Jim realized that, although he respected much about his parents' values, he was no longer fully at ease in their house or in his old neighborhood. He would henceforth always see his family's community in part through the lens of an outsider.

The conflict Jim felt between his Irish working-class self and his developing reflective, anti-racist, anti-sexist self reminded me of the tension described by the feminist philosopher Maria Lugones as she "travels" between the "worlds" of her Latin-American and lesbian communities. Lugones felt herself shifting "from being one person to being a different person" in contexts characterized by different vocabularies and different norms, in which she experienced different degrees of human bondedness and the presence or absence of a shared history (1987). Lugones's "world-traveling" challenged a second feminist philosopher, Victoria Davion, to seek an understanding of integrity that allows for such multiplicitous persons and for radical change.

Enlarging traditional definitions of integrity that refer to "unchanging, unconditional commitments," Davion seeks integrity within the process of change itself (1991). She proposes a conception of "integrity" that involves monitoring the processes of our transformations, so that no part of ourselves is left out. Multiplicitous beings can have integrity, she asserts, so long as the two selves (each in community) are connected. Each self can understand and critique the other, and must work to avoid betraying the other. Davion writes that "the two selves are part of a larger self that constitutes the multiplicitous being. This being keeps the two beings working together for its survival. . . . They have at least one fundamental goal in common — the preservation of the identity of the being as multiplicitous. . . . It is the commitment to monitoring oneself . . . . that forms the basis for integrity."

When students from politically conservative, racially homogeneous communities implicate themselves in the study of oppression, their new awareness often creates considerable tension between the world of their homes and the world of progressive discourse and activism. Several students in Contemporary Educational Perspectives indicated that their new perspectives were so different from their previous world views, they didn't quite know how to behave or what to think, especially when they returned to their parents' homes and their conservative communities. I don't think it would be an exaggeration to say that they found themselves with two distinct selves, unsure whether they would quite fit in to either the worlds they were glimpsing or the worlds they had previously known.

As educators involved in challenging racism, we have likely experienced the losses involved in becoming aware of our own participation in oppressive dynamics; many of us have experienced exactly the kind of painful alienation described by bell hooks. As she suggests, we can use insights from our experiences to bring a quality of compassion to our work with our students. Reminding them of aspects of their own cultures that they cherish is more than a strategy to anticipate and minimize the effects of resistance. It is a way of helping them bring "all of themselves" into the process of change, and to ensure that the new selves they are becoming won't betray those aspects of their old selves that they value and choose to sustain.

Following Davion's conception of integrity, it is also important for students to monitor their transformations. In Contemporary Educational Perspectives, the end-of-the-semester portfolios offered a structure to support these reflections. The portfolios consisted of more than samples of stories, essays, responses to readings, poems and drawings. Students also wrote reflections on each of these entries, noting points of resistance, moments of transformation, as well as unresolved questions and reservations. These reflective pieces became tools for metacognitive awareness through which they observed and named their own processes of and resistances to change.

When we ask students to engage meaningfully in the study of oppression, we are asking them to make vulnerable something about which they care very deeply: the stories they have constructed that give a sense, coherence and meaning to their lives. We ask them to reveal their uncertainties and their prejudices, and to reflect critically on the ways they've made sense of their worlds. In short, we ask them to relate to us with a high degree of trust.[12] I feel more certain that I've warranted students' trust when I encourage them to both bring all of themselves into the process of change and to monitor their own transformations.

In this article, I've described an approach to educating pre-service teachers about oppression that balances the imperatives to challenge and transform with concerns about integrity and trust. The approach is built on a foundation of strong relationships, nurtured by attentive listening, sharing stories and sincere response. I hope other educators engaged in this difficult work find these reflections useful.

Cindy Cohen is an educator and co-existence facilitator affiliated with the International Center for Ethics, Justice and Public Life, Brandeis University and the Seeds of Peace International Camp for Conflict Resolution. As a community oral historian and folklorist, she founded the Boston-based Oral History Center in 1980. Cindy is completing doctoral work in Education at the University of New Hampshire, where she is writing about the distinctive contributions of the aesthetic domain to the educational work of reconciliation. E-mail: cynthiacohen@ LOGOS.CC.BRANDEIS.EDU

References

Aguero, K., ed. 1993. *daily fare: essays from the multicultural experience*. Athens and London: University of Georgia Press.

Baier, A. 1986. "Trust and antitrust." *Ethics*. 96: 231-260.

Berlak, A. 1994. "Antiracist pedagogy in a college classroom: mutual recognition and a logic of paradox." In R. Martusewicz and W. Reynolds, eds. *Inside out: Contemporary critical perspectives in education*. New York: St. Martin's Press.

Boyd, D. 1989. "The Moral Part of Pluralism as the Plural Part of Moral Education." In F. C. Power and D.K. Lapsley, eds. *Moral education in a pluralist society*. Notre Dame, IN: Notre Dame Press.

Burbules, N. and Rice, S. 1991. "Dialogue across differences: continuing the conversation." *Harvard Educational Review* 61:393-416.

Chassler, S. 1992. "Listening." In P. Rothenberg, ed. *Race, Class and Gender in the United States: An Integrated Study*. New York: St. Martin's Press.

Clair, M. 1993. Word up: Oral tradition in the pedagogy of creative writing. *Women's Studies Quarterly* 3-4:69-74.

Cohen, C. 1983. "Using oral history to build multicultural and intergenerational networks." *Frontiers: A Journal of Women's Studies* VII.1:98-102.

—— 1987. *Designing an oral history project: A workbook for teachers and community workers*. Cambridge: The Oral History Ctr.

—— 1987. "Using the arts in political education: The model of the Oral History Center." *Radical Teacher* 33:2-7.

—— 1994. "Removing the dust from our hearts: The search for reconciliation in the narratives of Palestinian and Jewish women." *National Women's Studies Association Journal* 6.2:97-233.

—— 1995. "A patchwork of our lives: Oral history quilts in inter cultural education." In M. Salazar and A. Jennison, eds. *Reweaving the myths of the past: A resource guide to using multicultural storytelling throughout the curriculum*. Lee, NH: Anne Jennison and Melinda Salazar.

Cohen, C. & Watrous, B. G. 1990. "The lifelines project." In B.G. Watrous, ed. *Drawing from the well: Oral history and folk arts in the classroom and community*. Greenfield, MA: The Pioneer Valley Folklore Society.

Davion, V. M. 1991. "Integrity and radical change." In C. Card (Ed.) *Feminist ethics: Problems, projects, prospects*. Kansas: University Press of Kansas.

Ellsworth, E. 1989. "Why doesn't this feel empowering? Working through the repressive myths of critical pedagogy." *Harvard Educational Review* 59.3:297-324.

Fisher, B. 1993. "The heart has its reasons: feeling, thinking, and community-building in feminist education." *Women's Studies Quarterly* 3&4:75-87.

Govier, T. 1991. "Trust, distrust, and feminist theory." *Hypatia: A Journal of Feminist Philosophy* 7.1:16-33.

Frye, M. 1993 "Oppression." In *The politics of reality: Essays in feminist theory*. Trumansberg, New York: The Crossing Press.

hooks, b. 1990 "Choosing the margin as a space of radical openness." *Yearning: race, gender and cultural politics*. Boston: South End Press. 145-154.

hooks, b. 1993. Transformative pedagogy and multiculturalism. In T. Perry and J. Fraser, eds. *Freedom's plow: Teaching in the multicultural classroom*. NY: Routledge.

Jackson, F. R. 1993-1994. "Seven strategies to support a culturally responsive pedagogy." *Journal of Reading* 37.4:298-303

Lawrence, L. 1993. "The death of Fred Astaire." In K. Aguero, ed., *daily fare: essays from the multicultural experience*. Athens and London: University of Georgia Press.

Lugones, M. 1990. "Playfulness, 'world-travelling,' and loving perception." In G. Anzaldua, ed *Making face, making soul/Haciendo caras: Creative and critical perspectives by women of color*. San Francisco: Aunt Lute Books.

Maher, F. A. and Tetreault, M. 1993. "Frames of positionality: constructing meaningful dialogues about gender and race." *Anthropological Quarterly* 66:118-126.

Paley, V.G. 1989. *White teacher.* Cambridge, Mass: Harvard University Press.

Palmer, P. J. 1987. "Community, conflict, and ways of knowing: Ways to deepen our educational agenda." *Change* 19.5:20-25.

Pratt, M. B. 1993. "Books in the closet." In K. Aguero, ed. *Daily fare: Essays from the multicultural experience.* Athens and London: University of Georgia Press.

Rich, A. 1986. "Notes toward a politics of location." *Blood, bread, and poetry: Selected prose 1979 - 1985.* New York: W.W. Norton and Company.

Shabatay, V. 1991. The stranger's story: Who calls and who answers? In C. Witherell and N Noddings, eds. *Stories lives tell: Narrative and dialogue in education.* New York: Teachers College Press.

Sizer, T.R. 1992. *Horace's school: Redesigning the American high school.* Boston: Houghton Mifflin Company.

Swilky, J. 1993. "Resisting difference: student response to multicultural texts." *The Writing Instructor* 13.1:21-33.

Tatum, B.D. 1992. "Talking about race, learning about racism: The application of racial identity development theory in the classroom." *Harvard Educational Review* 61:1-24.

NOTES

1. All references to students and to the people they name in their writing are pseudonyms.

2. The racist attitudes revealed in this journal excerpt are cited to document the intensity of the bigotry that characterized many students' beliefs when they entered the course. I trust that these references will serve to minimize and not perpetuate the harm caused by such language.

3. For a sample of practical and theoretical accounts of teaching about issues of oppression, see Berlak (1994), Boyd (1989), Burbules and Rice (1991), Clair (1993), Ellsworth (1989), Fisher (1993), hooks (1993; 1990), Jackson (1993), Maher and Tetreault (1993), Paley (1989), Shabatay (1991), Swilky (1993) and Tatum (1992).

4. For discussion on the notion of warranted and unwarranted trust, see Govier (1991).

5. By honoring students' voices I refer to the need to respond to their stories — emotionally, intellectually, morally — with thoughtfulness and care.

6. The Oral History Center model, and its application in several community-based settings, are described in several articles and a workbook by Cohen, all listed in the references. Oral History Center, 403 Richards Hall, Northeastern University, Boston, MA, 02115; 617-373-4814.

7. For a detailed description of this paper quilt activity geared towards younger students, see Cohen (1990 and 1995). The 1990 article is available from The Pioneer Valey Folklore Society, PO Box 710, Greenfield, MA 01302. The 1995 article is available from A. Jennison, 34 High Road, Lee, NH 03824.

8. There are particular reasons why this is true for White students. First, they begin to explore the complexity of being "White," and to understand that the term White often masks religious, ethnic, or regional affiliations, communities with folk knowledge and traditions that can add texture to their lives. Students can acknowledge aspects of their identities which have been silenced; in this process they find common ground with people of color and members of other oppressed groups whose stories have also been suppressed. It is important for all students — even those who make meaning in reference to the symbols of the dominant culture, to recognize that they have a culture. Otherwise, they begin to see their own way of being as "normal" or "natural," the standard against which all others are compared. Alternatively, students who feel that they have no culture often appropriate aspects of other cultures (frequently Native American cultures) in ways that are disrespectful. Finally, I find anecdotal evidence in my students' writing that students can more easily acknowledge participating in oppressive dynamics once they've celebrated aspects of their own cultures and identities.

9. The text we used was *daily fare: essays from the multicultural experience.* Students were assigned to read any three essays of their choice, and keep "reading logs" of their responses to the stories.

10. "Politics of location" is a phrase used by Adrienne Rich (1986), bell hooks (1990) and others to refer to critical awareness of the dynamics of power inherent in one's positions within social structures, and the perspectives and knowledge related to those positions.

11. For a philosophical inquiry into "trust," see Baier (1986).

Activities for Workshops,
Courses and Institutes

PERSONAL CULTURAL HISTORY EXERCISE

BY MARGO OKAZAWA-REY

Many exercises and activities used in multicultural staff development workshops focus on teachers, mostly White, learning about cultures different from their own. They are presented histories and generalized characteristics of racial and cultural groups, such as "Asian Americans value family ties," which often serve only to reinforce old stereotypes or form new ones and to maintain a distance as the Other. Teachers, particularly Whites, are rarely asked to think about the histories of their own racial/ethnic groups or about their own racial and cultural identities and the experiences that shaped those identities. This exercise is an opportunity to explore their histories and identities. For teachers of color, who are frequently confronted with questions and challenges about their identities, this is a chance to examine their experiences from a critical perspective. The purposes of the Personal Cultural History exercise are to have the participants:

▸ recall and reflect on their earliest and most significant experiences of race, culture and difference;

▸ think about themselves as cultural beings whose lives have been influenced by various historical, social, political, economic and geographical circumstances;

▸ make connections between their own experiences and those of people different from themselves.

Although it is important to maintain the goal of having teachers reflect on their own racial and cultural identities, the specific wording of questions in the procedure may be altered to suit your participants the best way possible.

IDEAL NUMBER OF PARTICIPANTS
10-15

MATERIALS NEEDED
Large size newsprint; bright markers and crayons; masking tape.

TIME
Two and a half to three hours, depending on number of participants; 15-20 minutes for drawing; the rest for presentation and discussion.

PROCEDURE

1. Give each participant a sheet of newsprint. Ask all of them to answer the following questions using drawings, symbols and colors, rather than words.

▸ What is your racial and ethnic identity?

▸ What is your earliest recollection of observing someone being excluded from your group based on race or culture?

▸ What is your earliest recollection of being different or excluded, based on race or culture, from those around you?

2. After the drawings are completed, discuss with the whole group the process of doing this exercise. How did it feel to think about and answer the questions? How did it feel to use a medium most are not accustomed to using? Next, ask each person to stand up with the drawing and tell his or her story in about ten minutes. Other listeners may ask only factual questions, such as the name of the town where the person lived and demographics of the community. When the person's turn is over, ask her or him to tape the drawing on the wall or some other appropriate place in the room where it can be seen by all.

3. After all have shared their histories, ask participants to analyze their collective experiences, drawing on such factors as geography, historical time period, race, class, religion and gender. Ask questions such as:

▸ What similarities and differences do you notice in everyone's experiences?

▸ What are some of the major forces — in families, communities, society, historical time period — that shaped each person's experiences?

▸ How did oppression, discrimination and prejudice affect the participants' lives?

▸ If they were not noticeably affected, why weren't they?

▸ In what ways were people privileged and disadvantaged? Why?

▸ What does it mean to be a person of color in the United States?

▸ What does it mean to be a White person in the United States?

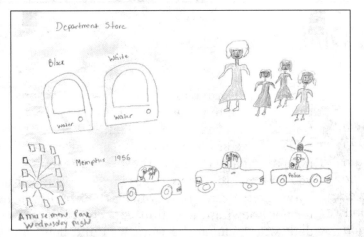

In my own neighborhood I always felt comfortable and supported by my family and friends. It was in elementary school that I had my first experience of feeling I was different. I had always been taught the history of Mexico from my mother as she had learned it, but when I went to school and was being taught U.S. history, I was totally confused. I never contradicted my teachers because I thought I might get into trouble....Everything I had learned at home didn't seem to matter. If historical events I was taught at home did come up, they seemed twisted to make Europeans settlers out to be the heroes and the Mexicans made to seem so insignificant....

4. From this discussion ask participants to think about the three levels at which social phenomena occur: the individual/family (micro), community (meso) and institutional (macro) levels. Here use three concentric circles with micro at the center, then meso and finally macro, with arrows going from one to another, that illustrate the relationship of one level to another. After explaining this concept, have them draw some conclusions about the dynamics of oppression at all three levels across racial and cultural groups. For example, many people identify school (an example of micro, the individual, coming together with meso, the community) as the place where they first noticed differences. At school they were made to feel inferior or insecure (or secure and superior), or watched another child treated that way, with the teacher being one of the main perpetrators of discrimination, prejudice and indifference. If this were the case, you would want to ask the group what role schools play in the dynamics of oppression. Similar analysis can be done on any other institution, such as the media,

criminal justice, government, religion and so forth. Also have participants think about how communities, families and individuals resisted, countered and transformed oppressive actions and institutions. Ask questions such as:

▶ How did schools (and other institutions such as the media, religion, etc.) support and promote oppressive practices?

▶ How was what happened in one institution supported by others?

▶ What strategies did communities, families and individuals use to resist discrimination or organize on their own behalf?

5. Finally, ask the participants to think about how their personal experiences have shaped their conceptions of themselves as teachers. Ask questions such as:

▶ How, if at all, did your experiences influence your decision to become a teacher?

▶ How have your cultural and racial experiences influenced your view of yourself as a teacher?

▶ How have they shaped your views of your students who are from racial and cultural groups different from your own?

▶ How have they shaped your views of your students who are from racial and cultural groups different from your own?

My earliest images of race and color are from television, particularly shows like Sesame Street. These shows provided me with very little information about how to deal with racial issues...I suppose my being White gave me the privilege of being oblivious to what was going on around me, if I wanted to be. I am a White, Jewish, gay male. I know that if any one of these four characteristics were not the case, I would be a very different person....

De-Tracking the Tracking Dialogue

BY DEBORAH MENKART

Opinions about tracking are influenced by our own schooling. As educators, many of us went through school on the upper or college-bound track. So did our children. Therefore, although we may have some intellectual sympathy for children in the lower tracks, it is difficult to truly empathize with their situation. There is often the nagging assumption that maybe they deserve to be there, that if they applied themselves more they could move to the more advanced classes. Prior to a discussion of tracking in schools, I find it is very helpful to stage a simulation of a tracked class. In less than fifteen minutes, illusions are shattered about the mobility within tracks and the impact of tracking on students of all levels. Following is how I stage the simulation.

MATERIALS

Copies of "My Name" by Sandra Cisneros from *The House on Mango Street* (Vintage, 1989)

PROCEDURE

1. In advance:
- Select 5 words from the short story and write them on the board or a flip chart to use as a vocabulary list.
- Ask one participant to be the 'advanced' teacher. Explain that, when you divide the class, she or he should gather the advanced students in a circle. S/he should invite them to read "My Name" and then share stories about their own name. The teacher should ensure that the students have a positive learning experience.

2. Divide the participants into two, unequal groups. Place about 25% into the advanced group and the rest into the basic group. If possible, try to place participants so that their own experiences with schooling are reversed. That is, if there are students who may have experienced the lower track at some point in their schooling, select them for the advanced group and vice-versa.

3. The advanced group is asked to go with the advanced teacher. The rest of the group stays with you. While seated in rows, point to the vocabulary words on the board. Ask them to write the words in alphabetical order and then write definitions for them. (It's up to you whether they can refer to dictionaries.) As they do this, walk around the room and criticize students for how they are seated, for not having a heading on their paper (even though you have not told them to put on a heading), for not leaving a two-finger margin, for their handwriting, for not knowing the definitions, etc. Find one student who is doing the work well and point out to everyone that she or he should be their role model.

When 'students' begin to snicker, complain, or generally misbehave — which they inevitably do — tell them that they will never be promoted to the upper level with that behavior.

As students complete their vocabulary assignment, ask them to wait until everyone else is finished. About a minute later (whether or not they are all finished) ask a few to read out the list of words in alphabetical order and their definitions. Then distribute the story, "My Name." Tell them to find the vocabulary words and underline them. As they are busy working, alert the advanced teacher that you are about to regroup.

4. End the simulation and bring the participants back together. Don't be surprised if there is a little animosity from the 'basic' towards the 'advanced' group. Solicit participants' comments on how they felt about themselves as learners and how they felt about the school and the teacher. Record these comments on a flip chart for all to see. Begin with the advanced group. Their comments are generally: "enjoyed the lesson," "felt respected," "wanted the lesson to continue," etc. Members of the basic group on the other hand generally say they felt: "frustrated," "stupid," "bored," "so caught up with the rules that they weren't sure what they were learning," "angry at the teacher," "no desire to be like the student presented as the role model," and had "no desire to go to the advanced class."

5. If a participant does not bring up the following, you can add that:
- The lower track's comments are very similar to comments made by students when asked why they dropped out of school.
- They felt all these things after only 15 minutes. Imagine how more deeply entrenched these feel-

ings would be after many years!

▸ As people are placed in the lower group a few may say they really belong in the upper track. Seldom does anyone question whether we should track the group at all. This indicates that the culture of schools has taught us to look out for ourselves as individuals but not to question systemic inequities.

WHAT IS TRACKING?

Tracking is a way of sorting students. Sorting determines the kinds of skills, knowledge and resources available to students. Although tracking is often known as ability grouping, it has very little to do with ability. Rather, tracking is usually based on achievement as measured by standardized tests or estimates of a child's ability. Even when tracking is based on the judgment of teachers, students and/or parents, it rarely accounts for differences in family education or circumstances, past school experiences and other factors. It fails to fully consider each student's strengths, weaknesses and potential.

The result is an education system that duplicates inequalities among races, classes and sexes that continue to tear our society apart. The most vicious forms of tracking close off opportunities for certain students, most often the poor and children of color. These students end up spending years repeating mindless drills in English, math and other so-called basic classes.

Teachers and parents sometimes believe tracking is beneficial because it seems to respect differences among students. However, in the long run tracking is harmful — once a child is in a low track it is almost impossible to get out. Every day children spend in the low track they lose ground to students in more advanced groups. Following is a list of questions to help you decide if negative forms of tracking are being used.

WHAT DOES TRACKING LOOK LIKE?

You may not immediately recognize tracking practices if your school system claims it does not track. However, if you answer "no" to any of the questions below, you may want to talk to others about your concerns and investigate further.

1. Do most classes have a racial and ethnic mix similar to the school as a whole? For instance, if the school is 2/3 Black and 1/3 White, are most of the classes the same or are some 90% Black and others 90% White?

2. Do most classes have roughly equal numbers of boys and girls?

3. Do students in most classes have backgrounds similar to those found in the school as a whole? For example, are there classes where students' parents are professionals and others where most students come from poor or working class families?

4. Are students with varied language backgrounds and students with disabilities in mainstream classes?

5. Can you see that your children are progressing? Grades may not be the best indicator; notice whether children are reading and writing more, moving beyond basic math skills, expressing more complicated ideas, taking on more responsibility, developing skills or talents and so on.

6. Do your children's teachers seem to know your children's weaknesses and strengths and have a plan for addressing them?

7. When you attend school programs or extracurricular activities, do the participating students seem to reflect the racial, ethnic and class mix found in the school as a whole?

8. If your school or school system has special programs or schools, do the students who are part of them seem to reflect the mix found in the school or system as a whole?

9. What kinds of homework do your children have? Ask questions if they:

▸ Have no homework

▸ Get many worksheet drills

▸ Are reading and answering questions on paragraphs instead of whole stories and books

▸ Have lots of multiple choice questions rather than thoughtful writing assignments

Reprinted from Maintaining Inequality, *with permission from the National Coalition of Education Activists (NCEA). Contact NCEA (see "Resource Guide") to order the complete packet and for ideas on how your school can challenge tracking.*

TRACKING TEACHER EXPECTATIONS & STUDENT OUTCOMES

BY NONI MENDOZA REIS AND IRENE McGINTY

This activity helps participants evaluate the impact of tracking on teacher expectations and student outcomes. It can help to initiate a dialogue about tracking in the participants' school district.

MATERIALS

Make copies of the Quadrant Worksheet and the Teachers and Students on Tracking handouts for all the participants.

PROCEDURE

If this is not part of a broader unit or session on tracking, an introduction will be needed as to what tracking is and why you are discussing it.

1. Explain that temporary and flexible grouping is different from the practice of tracking which is the *long-term* placement of students in classes of matched ability or the formation of homogeneous groups within a classroom. Examples of long-term tracking include: reading tracking; leveled subject area classes in middle school and high school; and specific programs such as college prep or vocational classes.

2. Tell participants that they will be referring to some of the data collected in Jeannie Oakes' study entitled "Keeping Track: How Schools Structure Inequality," which contributed significantly to an understanding of how tracking affects students and teachers in junior and senior high schools. The schools Oakes studied followed a pattern of racial composition with disproportionately large percentages of White students in high-track classes and disproportionately large percentages of students of color in low-track classes. In the study, Oakes addressed what students are actually receiving in the different tracks. She studied over 13,000 students. The study investigated:

    (a) *Who Learns What?* Students were asked: What is the most important thing you have learned so far in this class?; and

    (b) *Learning Beyond Content* Teachers were asked: What are the five most critical things you want the students in your class to learn this year? By learn, we mean everything that the student should have upon leaving the class that (s)he did not have upon entering.

3. Distribute the Teachers and Student on Tracking handouts, explaining that these responses were collected during Oakes' research.

4. Hand out the Quadrant Sheet. Ask half of the participants to work together in pairs to fill out the top (high track) portion of the worksheet, and the other half to fill out the bottom (low track) portion of the sheet.

5. Have pairs share their insights with an opposite pair. Did anything surprise them? What trends did they see? How would they analyze the information? Ask these small groups to identify one issue/ concern/question they have about tracking. Ask them to consider how to overcome or resolve that issue, concern or question. Say that in five minutes each group will be asked to share a group insight that resulted from the discussion. After five minutes, ask each group to share their insight. Chart responses.

6. Ask participants to discuss the questions below with their partner, in terms of their own classroom or school.

    ‣ What are the ways in which students are inappropriately tracked or grouped?

    ‣ How might you change your practice, influence your school's practice or explore more information about untracking?

7. Ask participants to write a reflection about their thoughts and plans. Save these for later reference if participants are to develop an overall Action Plan at the end of your workshop or course.

Noni Mendoza Reis *and* ***Irene McGinty*** *have taught in the public schools for over 20 years and co-edited the guide listed below. E-mail: NoniR@aol.com*

Reprinted from Reis, N. M. & McGinty, I. A Guide to Becoming Culturally Responsive and Responsible Educators. Sacramento: California State Department of Education.

TRACKING QUADRANT SHEET

What characterizes the expectations of teachers of high track students?	**What characterizes the educational/academic outcomes for students in the high track groups?**
What characterizes the expectations of teachers of low track students?	**What characterizes the educational/academic outcomes for students in the low track groups?**

Teachers on Tracking

QUESTION: WHAT ARE THE FIVE MOST CRITICAL THINGS YOU WANT THE STUDENTS IN YOUR CLASS TO LEARN THIS YEAR?

HIGH TRACK STUDENTS

Interpreting and identifying. Evaluation, investigating power. Science; Junior High

Ability to reason logically in all subject areas. Math; Senior High

Investigating technology, investigating values. Social Science; Junior High

To think critically — to analyze, ask questions. Social Science; Junior High

Logical thought processes. Analysis of given information. Ability to understand exactly what is asked in a question. Ability to perceive the relationship between information that is given in a problem, in a statement and what is asked. Science; Senior High

Determine best approaches to problem solving. Recognize different approaches. High track English; Senior High

Problem solving situations — made to think for themselves. Realizing the importance of their education and use of time. Easy way is not always the best way. Science; Senior High

EXPECTATIONS OF LOW TRACK STUDENTS

Develop more self-discipline — better use of time. English; Junior High

I want them to respect my position — if they get this, I'll be happy. Math; Junior High

I teach personal hygiene — to try to get the students to at least be aware of how to keep themselves clean. Vocational Education; Junior High

Ability to use reading as a tool — e.g. how to fill out forms, write a check, get a job. Low track English; Junior High

Understanding the basic words to survive in a job. Being able to take care of their own finances — e.g. banking, income tax, etc. Being able to prepare for, seek and maintain a job. To associate words with a particular job. English; Senior High

To be able to work with other students. To be able to work alone. To be able to follow directions. English; Junior High

More mature behavior (less outspoken). Low track Science; Junior High

Good work habits. Math; Junior High

STUDENTS ON TRACKING

QUESTION: WHAT IS THE MOST IMPORTANT THING YOU HAVE LEARNED SO FAR IN THIS CLASS?

FROM HIGH TRACK CLASSES

Learning political and cultural trends in relation to international and domestic events. Social Studies; Senior High

Learned to analyze famous writings by famous people, and we have learned to understand people's different viewpoints on general ideas. English; Junior High

About businesses — corporations, monopolies, oligopolies, etc. and how to start, how they work, how much control they have on the economy — prices, demand, supply, advertising. We've talked about stocks and bonds — and business in the USA. Vocational Education; Junior High

The most important thing is the way other countries and placers govern themselves economically, socially and politically. Also different philosophers and their theories on government and man and how their theories relate to us and now. Social Studies; Junior High

I learned things that will get me ready for college entrance examinations. English; Junior High

I have learned quite a deal about peoples of other nations, plus the ideas of creation and evolution, ideas that philosophers have puzzled over the years. Social Science; SH

Learning to change my thought processes in dealing higher mathematics and computers. Math; Senior High

Probably the most important thing I've learned is the understanding of the balance between man and his environment. High track Science; Senior High

FROM LOW TRACK CLASSES

The most important thing I have learned in this class I think is how to write checks and figure the salary of a worker. Another thing is the tax rate. Math; Senior High

I learned that English is boring. English; Senior High

I have learned just a small amount in this class. I feel that if I was in another class, that I would have a challenge to look forward to each and every time I entered the class. I feel that if I had another teacher I would work better. Math; Junior High

I can distinguish one type of rock from another. Low track Science; Senior High

To spell words you don't know, to fill out things where you can get a job. English; Junior High

Learned how to get a job. English; Junior High

Spelling worksheets. Science; Junior High

How to sew with a machine and how to fix a machine. Vocational Education; Junior High

APPROACHES TO MULTICULTURAL CURRICULUM REFORM

Dr. James Banks is one of the leading scholars in the field of multicultural education and is the Director of the Center for Multicultural Education at the University of Seattle-Washington. In this article he outlines four levels of curriculum reform. The first level, the Contributions or 'Heroes and Holidays' Approach, provided the inspiration for this book's title. As Dr. Banks explains, we should develop a curriculum which goes beyond heroes and holidays, one that is transformative and teaches decision-making and social action skills.

These levels can be a useful tool as we examine our own curriculum. Present the four levels in a workshop or staff meeting. Have participants discuss at which level they would categorize their overall school curriculum. It helps to point out that most school districts are at level one — the Contributions Approach. Then ask participants to describe a particular lesson or unit that they teach and brainstorm strategies for moving it up a level.

BY JAMES A. BANKS

THE CONTRIBUTIONS APPROACH

Several identifiable approaches to the integration of ethnic content into the curriculum have evolved since the 1960s. The Contributions Approach to integration is one of the most frequently used and is often used extensively during the first phase of an ethnic revival movement. This approach is characterized by the addition of ethnic heroes into the curriculum that are selected using criteria similar to those used to select mainstream heroes for inclusion into the curriculum. The mainstream curriculum remains unchanged in terms of its basic structure, goals, and salient characteristics.

The Heroes and Holidays Approach is a variant of the Contributions Approach. In this approach, ethnic content is limited primarily to special days, weeks and months related to ethnic events and celebrations. *Cinco de Mayo*, Martin Luther King's birthday, and Black History Week are examples of ethnic days and weeks that are celebrated in the schools. During these celebrations, teachers involve students in lessons, experiences, and pageants related to the ethnic groups being commemorated. When this approach is used, the class studies little or nothing about the ethnic groups before

or after the special event or occasion.

The Contributions Approach is the easiest approach for teachers to use to integrate the curriculum with ethnic content. However, it has several serious limitations. Students do not attain a global view of the role of ethnic and cultural groups in U.S. society. Rather, they see ethnic issues and events primarily as an addition to the curriculum, and consequently as an appendage to the main story of the development of the nation and to the core curriculum in the language arts, the social studies, the arts, and to other subject areas. The teaching of ethnic issues with the use of heroes, holidays, and contributions also tends to gloss over important concepts and issues related to the victimization and oppression of ethnic groups and their struggles against racism and for power. Issues such as racism, poverty, and oppression tend to be evaded in the Contributions Approach to curriculum integration. The focus, rather, tends to be on success and the validation of the Horatio Alger myth that every American who is willing to work can go from rags to riches and pull himself or herself up by the bootstrap.

The Contributions Approach often results in the trivialization of ethnic cultures, the study of their strange and exotic characteristics, and the reinforcement of stereotypes and misconceptions. When the focus is on the contributions and unique aspects of ethnic cultures, students are not helped to understand them as complete and dynamic wholes.

THE ETHNIC ADDITIVE APPROACH

Another important aspect to the integration of ethnic content to the curriculum is the addition of content, concepts, themes, and perspectives to the curriculum without changing its basic structure, purposes, and characteristics. The Additive Approach allows the teacher to put ethnic content into the curriculum without restructuring it, which takes substantial time, effort, training and rethinking of the curriculum and its purposes, nature, and goals. The Additive Approach can be the first phase in a more radical curriculum reform effort designed to restructure the total curriculum and to integrate it with ethnic content, perspectives, and frames of reference. However, this approach shares several disadvantages with the Contributions Approach. Its most important shortcoming is that it usually results in the viewing of ethnic content from the perspective of mainstream historians, writers, artists, and scientists because it does not involve a restructuring of the curriculum. The events, concepts, issues, and problems selected for study are selected using Mainstream-Centric and Euro-Centric criteria and perspectives. When teaching a unit such as "The Westward Movement" in a fifth-grade U.S. History class, the teacher may integrate her unit by adding content about the Lakota (Sioux) Indians. However, the unit remains Mainstream-Centric and focused because of its perspective and point of view. A unit called "The Westward Movement" is Mainstream and Euro-Centric because it focuses on the movement of European Americans from the eastern to the western part of the United States. The Lakota Indians were already in the West and consequently were not moving west. The unit might be called, "The Invasion from the East," from the point of view of the Lakota. An objective title for the unit might be, "Two Cultures Meet in the Americas."

The Additive Approach also fails to help students to view society from diverse cultural and ethnic perspectives and to understand the ways in which the histories and cultures of the nation's diverse ethnic, cultural, and religious groups are inextricably bound.

THE TRANSFORMATIVE APPROACH

The Transformative Approach differs fundamentally from the Contributions and Additive Approaches. This approach changes the basic assumptions of the curriculum and enables students to view concepts, issues, themes, and problems from several ethnic perspectives and points of view. The key curriculum issue involved in the Transformation Approach is not the addition of a long list of ethnic groups, heroes, and contributions, but the infusion of various perspectives, frames of reference, and content from various groups that will extend students' understandings of the nature, development, and complexity of U.S. society. When students are studying the Revolution in the British colonies, the perspectives of the Anglo Revolutionaries, the Anglo Loyalists, Afro-Americans, Indians, and the British are essential for them to attain a thorough understanding of this significant event in U.S. history. Students must study the various and sometimes divergent meanings of the Revolution to these diverse groups to fully understand it.

When studying U.S. history, language, music, arts, science, and mathematics, the emphasis should not be on the ways in which various ethnic and cultural groups have "contributed" to mainstream U.S. society and culture. The emphasis, rather, should be on how the common U.S. culture and society emerged from a complex synthesis and interaction of the diverse cultural elements that originated within the various cultural, racial, ethnic, and religious groups that make up American society. One of the ironies of conquest is that those who are conquered often deeply influence the culture of the conquerors.

THE DECISION-MAKING AND SOCIAL ACTION APPROACH

This approach includes all of the elements of the Transformation Approach but adds components that require students to make decisions and to take actions related to the concept, issue, or problem they have studied in the unit. In this approach, students study a social problem such as, "What actions should we take to reduce prejudice and discrimination in our school?" They gather pertinent data, analyze their values and beliefs, synthesize their knowledge and values, and identify alternative courses of action, and finally decide what, if any, actions they will take to reduce prejudice and discrimination in their school. Major goals of the Decision-Making and Social Action Approach are to teach students thinking and decision-making skills, to empower them, and to help them acquire a sense of political efficacy.

MIXING AND BLENDING THE APPROACHES

The four approaches to the integration of ethnic content into the curriculum that I have described are often mixed and blended in actual teaching situations. One approach, such as the Contributions Approach, can also be used as a vehicle to move to other and more intellectually challenging approaches, such as the Transformation and the Decision-Making and Social Action Approaches. It is not realistic to expect a teacher to move directly from a highly Mainstream-Centric curriculum to one that focuses on decision making and social action. Rather, the move from the first to the higher levels of ethnic content integration into the curriculum is likely to be gradual and cumulative.

Reprinted with permission of James A. Banks from the Multicultural Leader *Volume 1, Number 2. Published by the Educational Materials & Services Center Spring, 1988.*

WHAT IS THE BIAS HERE?: STAFF DEVELOPMENT FOR CRITICAL LITERACY

An important skill for parents, school staff and students is to be able to recognize bias in textbooks, children's literature and the media. A number of articles speak to this aspect of multicultural education in another section of this book titled "Critical Literacy: Reading Between the Lines."

One way to introduce the topic of critical literacy is to give teachers the opportunity to analyze children's books and textbooks in a course session or workshop. The sequence below is based on workshops developed by educators Linda Christensen and Bill Bigelow.

PROCEDURE

1.   Create and distribute a worksheet to participants with headings such as: women, men, working people, people of color and Whites. (Add other headings depending on material to be critiqued.)

WOMEN	MEN	WORKERS	PEOPLE OF COLOR	WHITES

2.   Read a children's book or show an excerpt from a cartoon to the group. A children's book that everyone is familiar with, such as *Cinderella*, is ideal. While the book is read or video shown, ask participants to use their chart to document the portrayal of the groups listed for each column. (Or use the *Rethinking Columbus Slide Show* listed in Additional Resources below.)

3.   Share and discuss participants' insights regarding the portrayal of people of color, Whites, women, men and working people. This is important to do even if, or especially if, any one of these groups is missing. We need to notice who is consistently left out of stories.

4.   Brainstorm a list of values that children learn from the material presented. For example, participants will usually come to the conclusion that *Cinderella* teaches children that:

▸ Good girls are meek, obedient and grateful;

▸ Pretty is defined as blond and petite;

▸ Happiness for a girl is finding a rich man;

▸ If you are unhappy with your conditions, wish for a fairy godmother or some form of magic to solve your problem. In other words, do not complain or organize.

5.   Ask participants to create a critical reading check-list. Based on the item they critiqued as a group, what questions would they ask as they critique other materials. (For example, whose perspective is the story told from? What are the credentials of the author? How are people of color, women, men and working people portrayed? How does change happen?)

6.   Divide the participants into groups of four or five. Give each group a different item to critique. It could be textbook used in your district, a collection of news articles on a particular topic, a course description (see hand-out following this lesson), a children's book, or a collection of advertisements. Circulate as the particpants work in small groups and ask critical questions. If the text is short, ask them to critique and then rewrite it. For example, one of the resources shared in workshops in Washington, DC is an excerpt from a 5th grade history textbook. It says:

Only the very wealthy lived on plantations. Most people in Virginia were small farmers. They had a few slaves, if any. They raised most of their own food and traded very little (The United States and Its Neighbors, Silver Burdett, 1982).

Often participants' first rewrite is very close to the original. If this is the case, encourage them to try again. For example, with the text above, their first rewrite may be something like the following:

Wealthy people lived on plantations along with their slaves.

If this is the case, ask participants to reword it again. Ask them to make it clear that everyone being talked about is a human being. Using the word *slaves* all by itself makes it sound as if a class of people truly are slaves instead of a people who are enslaved. Also, shouldn't the plantation owners be identified as White? Subsequent rewrites may read:

The majority of people living and working on the plantations were enslaved Africans. In the minority were the White landowners who lived well from the profits made from the work of the enslaved Africans. Most Whites in Virginia were not large landowners. They were small farmers. A few had enslaved Africans working for them, but most worked their own land. They raised most of their own food and traded very little. Blacks and Native Americans were not allowed to own land.

For groups with longer texts, ask them to rewrite just one section of it or analyze the impact that this text would have on the values and beliefs of children.

7. After about 20-30 minutes, have the groups share some of their insights.

8. Discuss ways that critical literacy can be introduced in the participants' classrooms.

ADDITIONAL RESOURCES

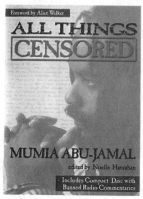

Abu-Jamal, M. 2000. *All Things Censored*. New York: Seven Stories Press. Mumia Abu-Jamal's major new release with 79 writings on a host of topics, including the U.S. prison system, NAFTA, South Africa, and his own case. Accompanied by the CD "Banned" with 19 recorded essays by Mumia and recorded comments by writers and activists including Alice Walker, Cornel West and Howard Zinn. An especially fine resource for exploring with students issues of capital punishment. Available from NECA.

Adbusters. Website and magazine with innovative critiques of mass consumerism. Great resource for interdisciplinary media literacy, art and social studies classes. (See examples on page 332.) www.adbusters.org

Bigelow, B. 1992. *Rethinking Columbus Slide Show*. Washington, DC: NECA. Fifty-four slides of text and visual exerpts from textbooks and children's literature along with a 10-page script for the facilitator. This provides the basis for an extremely successful workshop which has been presented to educators all over the country. The slide show can be used instead of the children's book or cartoon excerpt in step two of this lesson. Available from NECA.

Boihem, H. and and Emmanouilides, C. 1996. *The Ad and the Ego*. San Francisco: California Newsreel. This video offers a comprehensive examination of advertising and the U.S. culture of consumption. The film intercuts clips from hundreds of familiar television ads with insights from media critics. Available from NECA.

Center for Media Literacy. Web site and publication with resources such as: Media Literacy Workshop Kits. Titles include: News for the 90s, Images of Conflict, Selling Addiction, Break the Lies That Bind: Sexism in the Media, and Global Questions. www.medialit.org

Christensen, L. 1994. "Unlearning the Myths That Bind Us" in *Rethinking Our Classrooms*. Milwaukee: Rethinking Schools. An article on how to help students critique racism, sexism and classism in literature.

The Cola Conquest. 1999. DLI Productions. This video shows how a soft drink, more than 99% sweetened water, comes to wield enormous power and assume such significance in so many people's lives. *The Cola Conquest* begins with Coke's invention by a morphine-addicted Civil War vet and continues through a century of image-making with master artists — including the creation of our modern version of Santa — as Coke sheds its patent medicine image to become the most recognized brand name on earth. Available from NECA.

Extra! Website and bimonthly journal with well-documented criticism of media bias produced by Fairness and Accuracy in Reporting. www.fair.org

Ferreira, E. & J. 1997. *Making Sense of the Media: A Handbook of Popular Education Techniques*. NY: Monthly Review. Lessons for high school and adult education on how to critique the media and how students can make their own media.

Hazen, D. and Winokur, J. (Eds.) 1997. *We the Media: A Citizen's Guide to Fighting for Media Democracy*. New York: New Press. Tired of ten-second soundbites and news from sources you can't trust? Concerned that the American media are turning into a national entertainment state controlled global corporations? We the Media offers help and hope. Filled with facts, figures and commentary, the book features over 100 of the leading journalists, media critics and experts in the country on: who owns and controls the media; how the rapidly expanding empires of Disney, TimeWarner, etc. affect what you see and hear; the influence of the right; and how advertising pervades virtually every second of your life. *We the Media* also highlights alternatives. The 80 illustrations, charts and graphs make this book extremely useful for lessons on the media, advertising and American culture. Available from NECA.

Phillips, P. 2000. *Censored 2000: The Year's Top 25 Censored Stories*. New York: Seven Stories Press. Every year an increasing number of important news stories are not reported in the mainstream media. This book presents important, under-covered news stories on topics such as NATO, pharmaceutical companies, nuclear testing, toxic racism, and more. Students love to read stories that have been censored by the press.

Teaching for Change. The NECA web site, www.teachingforchange.org, has a section titled "Behind the Headlines." Here you can find the stories behind the news, and links to other sites with up-to-date, accurate information on domestic and international news.

— Note that all items "Available from NECA" can be purchased on the NECA web site shopping cart: www.teachingforchange.org

READING FOR BIAS IN A COURSE DESCRIPTION

Following is a sample of one of the many resources which can be analyzed in a critical literacy workshop. It can be copied and shared with teachers along with the instructions below.

Course Description
Eurasian Geography – Europe and Asia
(GEO 231)

Areas of Study: Social and Environmental Studies
                       Canadian Studies

Prerequisite: None

For a Canadian student, the study of geography of Eurasia offers an opportunity to investigate the fascinating variety of different people and places that make up the world's largest continent. The struggling and crowded masses of South Asia, the successful Japanese and the highly advanced Western Europeans all provide highly interesting examples of people with a different approach to life from we Canadians.

A wide variety of resources such as films, maps, games and case studies will be utilized to help make the study of the various environments and cultures realistic.

PROCEDURE

1.   Read the description above of a course offered in Canada.

2.   Answer the following questions:
  a. What would it mean to describe Canadians as fascinating?
  b. What constitutes success?
  c. What is the purpose of a course description?

3.   Rewrite the description so that it sounds interesting to the student without reinforcing stereotypes.

4.   What biases might you find if you examine the course descriptions from your school?

Reprinted from Lee, E. 1985. Letters to Marcia: A Teacher's Guide to Anti-Racist Education. *Toronto: Cross Cultural Communication Centre.*

White Privilege: Unpacking the Invisible Knapsack

This article is now considered a 'classic' by anti-racist educators. It has been used in workshops and classes throughout the United States and Canada for many years. While people of color have described for years how Whites benefit from unearned privileges, this is one of the first articles written by a White person on the topic.

It is suggested that participants read the article and discuss it. Participants can then write a list of additional ways in which Whites are privileged in their own school and community setting. Or participants can be asked to keep a diary for the following week of White privilege that they notice (and in some cases challenge) in their daily lives. These can be shared and discussed the following week.

BY PEGGY MCINTOSH

Through work to bring materials from Women's Studies into the rest of the curriculum, I have often noticed men's unwillingness to grant that they are overprivileged, even though they may grant that women are disadvantaged. They may say they will work to improve women's status, in the society, the university, or the curriculum, but they can't or won't support the idea of lessening men's. Denials which amount to taboos surround the subject of advantages which men gain from women's disadvantages. These denials protect male privilege from being fully acknowledged, lessened or ended.

Thinking through unacknowledged male privilege as a phenomenon, I realized that since hierarchies in our society are interlocking, there was most likely a phenomenon of White privilege which was similarly denied and protected. As a White person, I realized had been taught about racism as something which puts others at a disadvantage, but had been taught not to see one of its corollary aspects, White privilege, which puts me at an advantage.

I think Whites are carefully taught not to recognize White privilege, as males are taught not to recognize male privilege. So I have begun in an untutored way to ask what it is like to have White privilege. I have come to see White privilege as an invisible package of unearned assets which I can count on cashing in each day, but about which I was 'meant' to remain oblivious. White privilege is like an invisible weightless knapsack of special provisions, maps, passports, codebooks, visas, clothes, tools and blank checks.

Describing White privilege makes one newly accountable. As we in Women's Studies work to reveal male privilege and ask men to give up some of their power, so one who writes about having White privilege must ask, "Having described it, what will I do to lessen or end it?"

After I realized the extent to which men work from a base of unacknowledged privilege, I understood that much of their oppressiveness was unconscious. Then I remembered the frequent charges from women of color that White women whom they encounter are oppressive. I began to understand why we are justly seen as oppressive, even when we don't see ourselves that way. I began to count the ways in which I enjoy unearned skin privilege and have been conditioned into oblivion about its existence.

My schooling gave me no training in seeing myself as an oppressor, as an unfairly advantaged person, or as a participant in a damaged culture. I was taught to see myself as an individual whose moral state depended on her individual moral will. My schooling followed the pattern my colleague Elizabeth Minnich has pointed out: Whites are taught to think of their lives as morally neutral, normative, and average, and also ideal, so that when we work to benefit others, this is seen as work which will allow "them" to be more like "us."

I decided to try to work on myself at least by identifying some of the daily effects of White privilege on my life. I have chosen those conditions which I think in my case *attach somewhat more to skin-color privilege* than to class, religion, ethnic status, or geographical location, though of course all these other factors are intricately intertwined. As far as I can see, my African American co-workers, friends and acquaintances with whom I come into daily or frequent contact in this particular time, place, and line of work cannot count on most of these conditions.

1. I can if I wish arrange to be in the company of people of my race most of the time.

2. If I should need to move, I can be pretty sure of renting or purchasing housing in an area which I

can afford and in which I would want to live.

3.   I can be pretty sure that my neighbors in such a location will be neutral or pleasant to me.

4.   I can go shopping alone most of the time, pretty well assured that I will not be followed or harassed.

5.   I can turn on the television or open to the front page of the paper and see people of my race widely represented.

6.   When I am told about our national heritage or about "civilization," I am shown that people of my color made it what it is.

7.   I can be sure that my children will be given curricular materials in their schools that testify to the existence of their race.

8.   If I want to, I can be pretty sure of finding a publisher for this piece on White privilege.

9.   I can go into a music shop and count on finding the music of my race represented, into a supermarket and find the staple foods which fit with my cultural traditions, into a hairdresser's shop and find someone who can cut my hair.

10.   Whether I use checks, credit cards or cash, I can count on my skin color not to work against the appearance of my financial reliability.

11.   I can arrange to protect my children most of the time from people who might not like them.

12.   I can swear, or dress in second hand clothes, or not answer letters, without having people attribute these choices to the bad morals, the poverty or the illiteracy of my race.

13.   I can speak in public to a powerful male group without putting my race on trial.

14.   I can do well in a challenging situation without being called a credit to my race.

15.   I am never asked to speak for all the people of my racial group.

16.   I can remain oblivious of the language and customs of persons of color who constitute the world's majority without feeling in my culture any penalty for such oblivion.

17.   I can criticize our government and talk about how much I fear its policies and behavior without being seen as a cultural outsider.

18.   I can be pretty sure that if I ask to talk to "the person in charge," I will be facing a person of my race.

19.   If a traffic cop pulls me over or if the IRS audits my tax return, I can be sure I haven't been singled out because of my race.

20.   I can easily buy posters, postcards, picture books, greeting cards, dolls, toys and children's magazines featuring people of my race.

21.   I can go home from most meetings of organizations I belong to feeling somewhat tied in, rather than isolated, out-of-place, outnumbered, unheard, held at a distance, or feared.

22.   I can take a job with an affirmative action employer without having coworkers on the job suspect that I got it because of race.

23.   I can choose public accommodation without fearing that people of my race cannot get in or will be mistreated in the places I have chosen.

24.   I can be sure that if I need legal or medical help, my race will not work against me.

25.   If my day, week, or year is going badly, I need not ask of each negative episode or situation whether it has racial overtones.

26.   I can choose blemish cover or bandages in "flesh" color and have them more or less match my skin.

I repeatedly forgot each of the realizations on this list until I wrote it down. For me White privilege has turned out to be an elusive and fugitive subject. The pressure to avoid it is great, for in facing it I must give up the myth of meritocracy. If these things are true, this is not such a free country; one's life is not what one makes it; many doors open for certain people through no virtues of their own.

In unpacking this invisible backpack of White privilege, I have listed conditions of daily experience which I once took for granted. Nor did I think of any of these perquisites as bad for the holder. I now think that we need a more finely differentiated taxonomy of privilege, for some of these varieties are only what one would want for everyone in a just society, and others give license to be ignorant, oblivious, arrogant and destructive.

I see a pattern running through the matrix of White privilege, a pattern of assumptions which were passed on to me as a White person. There was one main piece of cultural turf; it was my own turf, and I was among those who could control the turf.

My skin color was an asset for any move I was educated to want to make. I could think of myself as belonging in major ways, and of making social systems work for me. I could freely disparage, fear, neglect, or be oblivious to anything outside of the dominant cultural forms. Being of the main culture, I could also criticize it fairly freely.

In proportion as my racial group was being made confident, comfortable, and oblivious, other groups were likely being made unconfident, uncomfortable, and alienated. Whiteness protected me from many kinds of hostility, distress, and violence, which I was being subtly trained to visit in turn upon people of color.

For this reason, the word "privilege" now seems to be misleading. We usually think of privilege as being a favored state, whether earned or conferred by birth or luck. Yet some of the conditions I have described here work to systematically overempower certain groups. Such privilege simply *confers dominance* because of one's race or sex.

I want, then, to distinguish between earned strength and unearned power conferred systematically. Power from unearned privilege can look like strength when it is in fact permission to escape or to dominate. But not all of the privileges on my list are inevitably damaging. Some, like the expectation that neighbors will be decent to you, or that your race will not count against you in court, should be the norm in a just society. Others, like the privilege to ignore less powerful people, distort the humanity of the holders as well as the ignored groups.

We might at least start by distinguishing between positive advantages which we can work to spread, and negative types of advantages which unless rejected will always reinforce our present hierarchies. For example, the feeling that one belongs within the human circle, as Native Americans say, should not be seen as a privilege for a few. Ideally it is an *unearned entitlement.* At present, since only a few have it, it is an *unearned advantage* for them. This paper results from a process of coming to see that some of the power which I originally saw as attendant on being a human being in the U.S. consisted in *unearned advantage* and *conferred dominance.*

I have met very few men who are truly distressed about systemic, unearned male advantage and conferred dominance. And so one question for me and others like me is whether we will be like them, or whether we will get truly distressed, even outraged, about unearned race advantage and conferred dominance and if so, what will we do to lessen them. In

any case, we need to do more work in identifying how they actually affect our daily lives. Many, perhaps most, of our White students in the U.S. think that racism doesn't affect them because they are not people of color; they do not see "whiteness" as a racial identity. In addition, since race and sex are not the only advantaging systems at work, we need similarly to examine the daily experience of having age advantage, or ethnic advantage, or physical ability, or advantage related to nationality, religion, or sexual orientation.

Difficulties and dangers surrounding the task of finding parallels are many. Since racism, sexism, and heterosexism are not the same, the advantaging associated with them should not be seen as the same. In addition, it is hard to disentangle aspects of unearned advantage which rest more on social class, economic class, race, religion, sex and ethnic identity than on other factors. Still, all of the oppressions are interlocking, as the Combahee River Collective Statement of 1977 continues to remind us eloquently.

One factor seems clear about all of the interlocking oppressions. They take both active forms which we can see and embedded forms which as a member of the dominant group one is not taught to see. In my class and place, I did not see myself as a racist because I was taught to recognize racism only in individual acts of meanness by members of my group, never in the invisible systems conferring unsought racial dominance on my group from birth.

Disapproving of the systems won't be enough to change them. I was taught to think that racism could end if White individuals changed their attitudes. [But] a "white" skin in the United States opens many doors for Whites whether or not we approve of the way dominance has been conferred on us. Individual acts can palliate, but cannot end, these problems.

To redesign social systems we need first to acknowledge their colossal unseen dimensions. The silences and denials surrounding privilege are the key political tool here. They keep the thinking about equality or equity incomplete, protecting unearned advantage and conferred dominance by making these taboo subjects. Most talk by Whites about equal opportunity seems to me now to be about equal opportunity to try to get into a position of dominance while denying that *systems* of dominance exist.

It seems to me that obliviousness about White advantage, like obliviousness about male advantage, is kept strongly inculturated in the United States so as to maintain the myth of meritocracy, the myth that democratic choice is equally available to all. Keeping most people unaware that freedom of confident action is there for just a small number of people props up those in power, and serves to keep power in the hands of the same groups that have most of it already.

Though systemic change takes many decades, there are pressing questions for me and I imagine for some others like me if we raise our daily consciousness on the perquisites of being light-skinned. What will we do with such knowledge? As we know from watching men, it is an open question whether we will choose to use unearned advantage to weaken hidden systems of advantage, and whether we will use any of our arbitrarily-awarded power to reconstruct power systems on a broader base.

Peggy McIntosh is Associate Director of the Wellesley College Center for Research on Women.

Reprinted by permission of the author. This essay is excerpted from her working paper, "White Privilege and Male Privilege: A Personal Account of Coming to See Correspondences Through Work in Women's Studies," copyright © 1988 by Peggy McIntosh. Available for $6 from the address below. The paper includes a longer list of privileges. Permission to excerpt or reprint must be obtained from Peggy McIntosh, Wellesley College Center for Research on Women, Wellesley, MA 02181; 781-283-2520, fax: 781-283-2504.

THE S.E.E.D. PROJECT ON INCLUSIVE CURRICULUM (SEEKING EDUCATIONAL EQUITY & DIVERSITY) A STAFF DEVELOPMENT PROGRAM FOR K-12 EDUCATORS

The National SEED Project is entering its twelfth year of establishing teacher-led faculty development seminars in public and private schools throughout the United States and in English-speaking International Schools. A week-long SEED Summer Leaders' Workshop prepares school teachers to hold year-long reading groups with other teachers to discuss making school curricula more gender-fair and multicultural.

SEED reading and discussion groups meet monthly during a school year for three hours at a time. They enroll ten to twenty teachers from all subject areas and from one or more schools, public and private. Each group is coordinated by one or more educators who have attended the Learners' Workshop during the previous summer. The SEED project provides each leader with a small library of books, access to video resources, and numerous packets of materials from new multicultural scholarship on women and men.

Project directors are Peggy McIntosh, Associate Director of the Wellesley College Center for Research on Women, who has taught in schools and colleges, and Emily Style, an English teacher who has taught in private school, urban and suburban public schools in New Jersey and is currently adjunct teaching for Cornell and NYU. They are joined each year at the Leaders' Workshop by experienced SEED seminar leaders in various disciplines who have diverse ethnic backgrounds. The Project provides various types of technical assistance throughout the year for SEED seminars, which have now been led by coordinators in many U.S. states, Hong Kong, Jakarta, Kuala Lumpur, Manila, Singapore, Taipei, Tokyo, and Vancouver. Once SEEDed, many seminars continue meeting for years.

Key questions for all participants in SEED seminars are: What would curriculum and pedagogy look like if the diverse lives of women and girls were seen as co-central with the diverse lives of men and boys? And how can curriculum and teaching methods provide, in the metaphor of Emily Style, both windows into others' experiences, and mirrors of each student's own reality and validity?

SEED seminar, leadership and participation carry optional graduate credit. For application forms, contact project co-directors Peggy McIntosh, Wellesley College Center for Research on Women, Wellesley, MA 02181, (781) 283-2520 or fax (781) 283-2504; or Emily Style, 286 Meeker Street, South Orange, NJ 07079, (973) 763-6378 or fax (973) 763-5670.

WHITE PRIVILEGE IN SCHOOLS

BY RUTH ANNE OLSON

It is important to distinguish between prejudice and privilege. Where as racial prejudice is negative action *directed against* an individual, privilege is passive advantage that *accrues to* an individual or group. Good teachers recognize and actively address prejudice. But as Peggy McIntosh (1988) points out, most White people are blind to the privileges accorded to White children and parents in schools.

I tried to identify my own family's experience of White privilege in schools and without much effort, it became clear that we have, indeed, benefited from privileges to which we have given little thought. Using McIntosh's format I could elaborate on her work and add observations from my own experience.

▸ Whatever topics my children choose to study, they are confident that they will find materials that link people of their race to the accomplishments in those areas.

▸ My children know that they will always see faces like their own liberally represented in the textbooks, posters, films and other materials in the hallways, classrooms and media centers of their schools.

▸ When my children talk about celebrations, holidays or family observances in show-and-tell or in other informal exchanges at school, they know that their teachers will have experienced similar events and will be able to reinforce their stories.

▸ My children are confident that the musical instruments, rhythms, harmonies, visual design forms and dramatic traditions of their culture will be generously recognized in the formal and informal uses of music, theater and visual arts in their schools.

▸ The color of my children's skin causes most adults in school offices, classrooms and hallways to have neutral or positive assumptions about them.

▸ My children know that the vast majority of adults in their schools will be of their same racial background, even in classrooms where many or most of their fellow students are of races different from theirs.

▸ My children are confident that they will never be embarrassed by being called on to tell the class about their race, culture or special ways of celebrating events.

▸ When I visit their schools, my children know that school staff members will reserve judgement about my economic class, my level of education and my reason for being in the school until I make them known.

▸ My children take for granted that the color of any crayons, bandages, or other supplies in their classrooms labeled "flesh" will be similar to their own.

▸ I take for granted that the tests used to judge my children's achievement and to determine placement in special classes have been developed with groups that included significant numbers of students who share our racial history and culture.

▸ My children are confident that they will never be embarrassed by hearing others suggest that the problems of the school (low levels of achievement, the need for special support services, etc.) are caused by the high numbers of children of their race.

▸ I am confident that policy decisions that affect my children's school experience will be made by state and local bodies dominated by people who understand our racial history and culture.

This list can go on. My family never asked for these privileges; principals and teachers didn't purposely create them for us; and, frankly neither they nor we have been consciously aware these privileges exist.

But stating that no one is to blame does not erase the fact that privilege has allowed my family to take for granted things that others must spend time, energy and resources trying to earn. And while I have been blind to the existence of our privileges, people who don't share them cannot help but see them and feel resentment, puzzlement, disappointment and rage at the fact that their children are excluded from the privileged class.

Ruth Anne Olson is a Co-Director of Supporting Diversity in Schools (SDS) at the Saint Paul Foundation in Saint Paul, Minnesota.

SEE DISCUSSIONS QUESTIONS ON THE NEXT PAGE.

Reprinted with permission from: Olson, R.A.1992. Eliminating White privilege in schools: an awesome challenge for White parents and educators. *Available from: SDS (Supporting Diversity in Schools Through Family and Community Involvement) 1120 Northwest Center, St. Paul, MN 55101.*

REFERENCES

McIntosh, P. 1988. "White privilege and male privilege: A personal account of coming to see correspondences through work in women's studies." Wellesley, MA: Working Paper Series, Wellesley College.

▸ Can you think of other privileges that could be added to this list?

▸ What are the implications for children of color if Whites have these privileges?

▸ How can the system be changed so that these 'privileges' become rights for everyone?

▸ What actions can you take to help the system change?

■ ■ ■ A CLOSER LOOK AT WHITE PRIVILEGE ■ ■ ■ ■

Helping parents, students and educators examine White privilege is a crucial step towards supporting equity in education. In addition to reviewing the lists of school privileges by Ruth Anne Olson, one can also examine statistical data about current economic realities of race, gender, wealth and ownership, labor and government spending, education, welfare, health and the environment. *The New Field Guide to the U.S. Economy* by Nancy Folbre and the Center for Popular Economics is full of graphs, charts and statistics such as the sample below. These charts can be duplicated and distributed for review in small groups. Ask each group to share some of the facts they learned from their chart, what surprised them and what they can conclude about the ways in which Whites still have privilege in this country. (*The New Field Guide* is available from the Teaching for Change catalog. Ordering information is provided in the Resource section.)

LAST HIRED

High unemployment rates afflict African Americans and Latinos more than Whites. In 1994, 11.8% of Black workers and 10.2% of Latinos could not find jobs, while only 5.4% of Whites were in the same predicament. Teenagers had an even harder time. The unemployment rate among Black youths was 36%; for Whites, it was 16%.

Persistently high unemployment rates discourage people from looking for work. Black male labor force participation rates have dropped considerably in recent years.

When people of color bear a large share of the burden of unemployment, they buffer Whites against the ups and downs of the business cycle.

Unemployment rate, by race and Latino origin
(civilian workers age 16 and above)

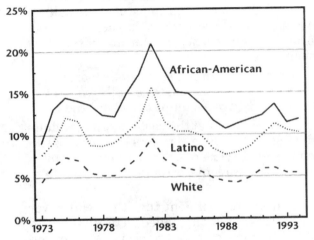

DEVELOPING POSITIVE RACIAL ATTITUDES

This handout was developed by the Council on Interracial Books for Children (CIBC). It can be used in joint parent/teacher workshops. Divide the participants into small groups and give each group one or two numbered points for discussion. Ask groups to do the following.

1. *Discuss what the point means and your own experiences with that issue as a child.*
2. *Share experiences with the point in your life as a parent and/or school staff person.*
3. *Share strategies, questions and concerns.*
4. *Select one insight or question to share with the other groups.*

BY CIBC

A healthy racial/cultural identity, plus skills to aid in recognizing and combatting racism, are essential to all children's self-esteem and ability to function productively in our society. Fostering growth in this direction is therefore, a major parental and teacher responsibility. Adults need to be able to not only respond to children's concerns but also to initiate activities and discussions.

Race is a social concept, not a scientific term. But racism is a social reality, and the concept is used to categorize and oppress large groups of people. It is with this understanding in mind that we offer the following suggestions.

1. Initiate activities and discussions to build a positive racial/cultural self-identity.

▶ Do not wait for the child to ask questions; initiate discussions.

▶ Talk about the child's skin color, features and hair texture in positive ways.

▶ Admire physical characteristics of other children and adults in the same racial group.

▶ Discuss leaders or members of the child's racial group of whom you are especially proud; make books about them available and display photographs or paintings of them in the home and classroom.

▶ Talk about White leaders who are anti-racist activists, not just the traditional leaders popularized at most schools.

▶ Offer a selection of books that depict the child's heritage and racial group in a positive way.

▶ Visit museums, parades, rallies and concerts that emphasize racial/cultural heritage and pride.

▶ Talk about the difference between feelings of superiority and feelings of racial pride.

2. Initiate activities and discussions to develop positive attitudes toward racial/cultural groups different from the child's.

▶ Expose children to a large variety of experiences, information, and images about each cultural group in order to develop an understanding of rich cultural patterns and diversity.

▶ Make clear that ALL shades of skin, types of hair and other racial features are beautiful, and are of equal value.

▶ Place multicultural pictures and posters around the house and in the classroom.

▶ Attend multicultural art exhibits.

▶ Involve children in your own anti-racist activities.

▶ Provide opportunities for children to interact with a mixed racial/cultural group of people.

▶ Seek out the services of adults of color (i.e., doctors, dentists, instructors.)

▶ Remember, "Action speaks louder that words." Children are quick to recognize contradictions in adult behaviors. White adults, for example, who talk about appreciation of other groups but live in a totally White environment teach double message regardless of their intent.

3. Always answer a child's questions about race when the questions are asked.

▶ Don't sidestep the issue by saying, "We'll talk about it later," or "It's not polite to ask about that."

▶ Don't over-respond. Do offer information and feedback appropriate to what the child is asking at the moment.

▶ Acknowledge and appreciate differences. Don't deny them.

▶ Practice possible answers with family, colleagues and friends.

▸ Don't worry if you don't say everything there is to say on the subject at once. It will come up again.

4. Listen carefully (in a relaxed manner) to questions and comments. Be sure you understand what a child means and wants to know.

▸ Distinguish between children's curious, age-relevant questions and comments about race and color from questions that indicate children are learning negative attitudes about themselves or others. A curious question meant to gather information should be treated as such. e.g. Young White children may associate dark skin with dirt, and commonly ask, "Will the black wash off in the tub?" An appropriate answer might be, "Skin comes in a range of beautiful colors, just like the color of our hair, and thankfully it does not wash off. We all take baths to wash off dirt."

▸ Be aware that children learn the practice of name-calling at age. Make very clear that this is unacceptable.

▸ If a child says, "I don't want to play with Tommy because he's ____," a good first response is to say, "That is not a good reason." Further investigation may reveal that there is another reason, unrelated to race, having to do with the interaction which can then be addressed.

5. Pay attention to feelings.

▸ It is important for children to get effective, informational feedback which includes expressions of support and positive reinforcement for who they are.

▸ Openly express disapproval of children's racist (sexist, heterosexist, etc.) remarks and behavior, but the child should not be made to feel rejected. Express your approval of anti-racist behavior.

6. Provide truthful explanations appropriate to the child's level of understanding.

▸ Be aware that children will be exposed to materials that are insulting to children of color and/or misinforming to all children. Help children identify inaccuracies. e.g. "Columbus discovered America." Columbus was a European explorer, but this continent had already been discovered and occupied by Native Americans. -or- "People

thought of slaves as possessions. like dogs, cattle or furniture." Adults can help children see that the ethnocentric phrasing of that sentence implies that all "people" are White. The adult might say, "Some ignorant or greedy White people treated enslaved Blacks as less than human, which was unfair, but the enslaved people, free Blacks, and some Whites always fought for justice and equality."

▸ It is natural to want to shield children of color from the truth about racism, but avoidance does not give children tools they can use to effectively deal with the realities they will face.

7. Help children recognize racial stereotypes.

▸ With your help, children quickly grow adept at spotting racial (and sex-role) stereotypes in books, TV programs, greeting cards, etc.

▸ As children get older, they can be helped to see how stereotypes are used to justify oppression.

▸ Encourage children to write letters protesting stereotypes to authors, publishers and TV stations.

8. Encourage children to challenge racism by your own example.

▸ It is important that adults provide children with anti-racist behavioral models, by responding to racist jokes, for example.

▸ When a child has been hurt by a racial slur, the adult must always support the child and show disapproval of the perpetrator. Don't deny the racism.

▸ Racial incidents involving a child should be thoroughly discussed within the family or classroom. A range of appropriate responses can be suggested to the child for future use.

9. Cultivate the understanding that racism does not have to be a permanent condition — that people are working together for a change.

▸ Adult role models are critical here. The benefits are great. In one study, children of activist families showed greater self-identification and pride and were better able to withstand societal stereotyping.

10. Keep in mind that learning about racial identity and racism is a lifelong process.

Adapted from "Suggestions for Developing Positive Racial Attitudes" Bulletin. 11:3-4.

READINGS

DO YOU KNOW WHERE THE PARENTS OF YOUR CHILDREN ARE?

BY HUGH MCKEOWN

As a school principal, it has always intrigued me to see which parents are involved in the life of the school and *which are not.* Our schools, particularly in larger urban centers, represent a multi-cultural, multi-racial, multi-linguistic and multi-faith community where children of various racial, ethnic, linguistic and faith backgrounds learn together. Yet invariably, parental involvement is limited for the most part to White, English speaking mothers of Judeo-Christian background. It's not because the school plans it that way, but "They're the only ones who come," and we speak about other parents as if it's their fault. Parents often refer to the school as the school in the community rather than their school. *Language is not neutral.*

Several years ago, I was asked by the principal of a neighboring school to facilitate a meeting of Greek-speaking parents. He was asked to do this by his superintendent. Although fifty percent of the families spoke Greek, he advised me that only a handful of parents would come and the meeting would be in a staff room that would hold approximately twenty people. "Those parents just don't show," he said.

I knew two or three families of Greek ancestry in that district and asked them to mount a telephone campaign to encourage Greek-speaking parents to attend. A week before the meeting, the principal asked if parents from a second school could be invited. That principal had been asked to do the same thing and felt that by combining the two meetings, a reasonable turnout could be expected. "We may get two dozen," he said. Again parents were helpful in issuing invitations by telephone.

The principals of the schools arranged to have the school board coordinators of English as a Second Language and Special Education as well as a respected leader of the local Greek community attend to say a few words and respond to questions. "They're the ones the parents would be most interested in hearing," they said. I was to be the facilitator for the evening and sit at the front of the room with one principal on either side. A half hour before the meeting was to begin, there was standing room only in the staff room. The meeting was switched to the gymnasium where, within a very short time, all seats were filled and people stood at the back. *To the surprise of the principals,* the parents were interested in the teaching of reading and mathematics, homework and discipline. Greek translation was provided throughout. As the meeting progressed, one principal handed a note through me to the other principal which read "Do you know any of these people?" The reply came back, "No ! Do you?" At the end of the evening, one father stood up and thanked the principals for organizing the meeting and said he felt he was speaking for the majority when he said that it was the first time they felt really welcome in the school.

Why was that? It was the first time they were truly valued as a group and the school was taking the time to ask their views as to how the system was impacting on their children. Most of the time, we send invitations to all parents to come to the school. That's the fairest thing to do. Everyone has the same opportunity. We don't even think of group dynamics. The dynamics of first meeting in a group with which we can identify racially, ethnically, linguistically or by faith are quite different than meeting with a cross-cultural group with people of diverse backgrounds. *It's an issue of power.* In our society, White, English-speaking parents have the power, dominate and are allowed to dominate a group. Their issues will be considered. They become de facto spokespersons for the others. Other parents keep quiet. They either do not attend or stop attending. Why should they? They are effectively marginalized.

I have tried this theory on numerous occasions. In one school, forty percent of the parents were followers of Islam. It was during the Gulf War. I asked a friend who was a local Imam to come to the school one evening to help me talk with Muslim parents. I wanted them to tell the staff, and me, the impact of the school and its programs on their children. I had done this before, in other schools, but this staff needed to hear what parents would say and more importantly create a climate in which parents could talk with us. Our meeting began with the Imam talking about how Muslims and Arabs in particular were stereotyped in Canadian society. After about twenty minutes, he stopped and said, "I want you to talk to the staff

© Rick Reinhard, 1993

and tell them your story. It's all right. This is a staff you can trust. They will make a difference."

The parents asked if we knew why many of the children didn't participate in "hot dog" days. Did we know why some children in kindergarten didn't eat their cookies during snack time? They told us they were unsure of what the hot dogs were made of and whether lard was used in making the cookies. They were unwilling to take the risk their children would eat pork or pork products. Their children were not participating in special lunches and other activities involving food during fundraising activities in March. We had to be told that Ramadan occurred during that period and people were fasting. We learned so much more during that meeting: from ways in which the curriculum could be made more inclusive to how the dress code for physical education could be altered — from the policies and practices of the school to how language used inadvertently could create stereotypes that other children could latch on to and tease their classmates. Parents were empowered to talk with us. *It wasn't so much that we had said they couldn't talk with us, it was just that we hadn't created the climate in which they could.* We didn't need the Imam again.

We made a breakthrough because we focused on parents with something in common — their faith. They told us they were used to Christian influences in the curriculum and in the practices of the school. In our society, other faiths are not given the same prominence. Why would they expect us to be interested? *We had to say we were.* We had to do it in an *explicit* way by holding a faith-specific meeting rather than implicitly getting our message out in a cross-cultural meeting. It was the first time they had had a school wanting to ask about its impact on children with respect to their culture and their faith.

About the same time, one of the school custodians approached me and asked if it would be all right if she painted the windows at the front of the school at Christmas with a Christmas motif. I said she could as long as she would do the same thing in celebration of other faiths when their significant celebrations took place. She replied that she would do that if someone showed her what to do. We created parent committees. As each celebration occurred, she would meet with parents representing that particular faith and with their help, the windows were decorated. Thus, we began involving non-teaching staff with our approach with parents. Now that parents were coming to the school, we began meeting around both Christmas concerts and other faith celebrations. Groups of parents were enthusiastic about meeting and working with us to organize the celebrations. During the first year, only Christian parents and their children participated in Christmas and Easter celebrations. Muslim parents and their children participated in Eid celebrations and Hindu parents and their children in Diwali celebrations. Each time, we had an evening concert preceded by a potluck dinner. The staff came back in the evening to participate. During the second year, children of other faith backgrounds asked if they could attend the celebrations of their friends. They, along with their parents, began to join their neighbors. That year, Easter and Eid fell two weeks apart. As the committee of Muslim parents met in one room and Christian parents in another, I was asked to join the Muslim parents. They asked if there was any reason why the Eid celebration couldn't be delayed a week and the Easter celebration moved up a week so they could all celebrate together. The other committee agreed. It was a wonderful time. The only request made was to label the food each family brought. This way, Muslim parents could avoid any pork.

What was important here was that each community needed to meet separately and to feel valued for themselves before they could meet and participate together. A climate was created here, where they could meet each other on a more even footing. That climate was helped by the staff saying it was important enough to attend as well. They were helping to validate through their attendance. Society believes that what is really important, happens at school. Schools wouldn't promote things that were not important. When you can see yourself reflected in the life of the school, you are validated. When you are not there or there as a token, you are marginalized. It was also important to continue to highlight Christmas and Easter. Christian parents who were used to being in *the privileged group were eager to accept other faith celebrations when they realized their own was not going to be abandoned or threatened.*

I have tried to learn how to greet parents in the language of their home. When new parents arrive, I ask how to pronounce the appropriate greeting. We had one child in the first grade who was accompanied to school by his grandfather. The grandfather would walk the boy to the classroom door, never looking up and never acknowledging the presence of others. I knew he spoke Punjabi. One day, as he was entering the school, I stopped, placed my hands together in the traditional form for greeting in many South Asian cultures and greeted him with the only Punjabi phrase I knew. He looked up, smiled and replied in English, "And how do you do, sir." The next day, he greeted me in both languages as he entered the school. On the third day, he asked if he could meet with me after taking his grandson to his class. He explained that he had been a professional bookbinder in India. He was now retired. He asked if he could offer his services. He would pick up damaged books from our library, once a week, on Friday, repair them and return them on Monday. He became a regular fixture in our library, so much so, that he appeared to be a member of staff.

Many parents don't identify with the school as their own, but as the "Canadian" school and do not see that they can or are welcome to participate. They see it as an institution that educates their children and hope that it will make their children "Canadian" but still see themselves as outsiders. They believe their background is different. Their feelings about their command of language can make them feel less confident. Their faith is not that of the majority. They aren't the same skin color as those making the decisions. They have had enough experiences to suggest to them, they had better not rock the boat if their children are going to succeed. Society here has not been set up to include them in a meaningful way. *The school must find ways to empower them, if they are going to be equal, active, participating parents in the school community.*

At a meeting of African Canadian parents we were asked why all of the library books their children were bringing home featured characters that were White. Shortly thereafter, the librarian proudly produced two books, both biographies, and declared them to be two of the most popular books in the school. They were the biographies of Wilt Chamberlain and Bill Cosby. She was perplexed when the parents told her that those books in isolation compounded the problem rather than helped. They continued the stereotype of Blacks only being suited for athletics, music or the theater. A third book about Black Canadians was suggested by a committee of school librarians for use in our schools. The committee was well meaning — and all White. When viewed by our parents, we were able to see again how a book can be written in such a way as to continue to stereotype, not so much by what is included but what is excluded or by the particular focus such a book can take through what is or is not there. When a parents' committee of parents of African heritage was formed specifically to recommend purchases for our library, the collection began to change. Not only did the collection change, but so did the amount of time children read at home, were read to by family members and in the increase in the number of volunteers reading to children in our library. Parents were empowered to speak out at a race-specific meeting, listened to, were part of the solution to inequities they saw in the library collection and developed ownership of the solution.

We need to understand we are not all starting from the same point. We don't have a level playing field. It is not a fair race. A race is just to decide a winner and many losers. Furthermore, the race is designed for a select group. Is that our goal in education? Educators believe the goal is to make *all students winners*. To do that, we need to look at where each is starting and what factors are impacting on their chances for success. That means treating people differently at times in order to level the playing field. As we do, we still have to consider the part of the community who has held the power. We have to continue to provide validation for the White, Christian, English-speaking part of the community. Some schools throw the baby out with the bath water. We need to continue to celebrate Christmas while celebrating other faiths. We need to continue to select materials which feature White characters or feature the contributions of Europeans to our country. We need to guard against excluding in order to bring another part of the community into the equation. *However, it's a matter of proportion.* It's a matter of finding ways to share that power. It means consciously focusing on marginalized groups in order to level the playing field. It also means making a conscious effort to help the whole community understand the course the school is

© Rick Reinhard, 1993

following and why. Make clear the benefits to all students and to the community of including everyone and not continuing to marginalize those who have been traditionally outside the curriculum. We have to be explicit. We have to talk out loud and often and then we have to walk the talk. We must find ways to talk to all our parents. We can and must take the mystique out of inclusion. Parents who are included and reflected in the life of the school see the school as their school, not just the school in the community. *Then you will know where the parents of your students are.*

Hugh McKeown *is a former elementary principal in North York, Ontario and is currently an anti-racist consultant to school boards developing and implementing anti-racism and enthnocultural equity.*

WHY DO YOU FORCE YOUR WAYS?

BY FRANK FINGARSEN

Matthew was a maddening student. He never did what I asked of him and his school work was dismal. Parents' Night was coming up and I planned to bring this situation to a head. A special letter had even been sent out to his parents because I felt there was a need to confront them about the boy's attitude, and in fact, his complete lack of learning.

It was going to be touchy but it was something I had to do. Matthew was a big worry. He and I got along well enough outside of school but the classroom seemed to transform him into something else altogether. This young adolescent's learning skills were very low indeed. His work was of poor quality, his study habits were atrocious, and his attitude towards school was even worse. He was never successful because he never seemed to care. If he wasn't dozing, he was joking around; if he wasn't joking around, he was bothering other students. He was a problem I was determined to solve. Parents' Night was going to be a showdown.

Thomas, Matthew's father, would be the epitome of attentiveness, I thought. It was about 8:30 in the evening when things began to take shape. Parents' Night had been slow and the staff was ready to close up shop. I was sorting report cards back into a pile and compiling a list of the visitors for the office. I was feeling quite sorry that Thomas hadn't been there.

Matthew had been acting up lately and his work was at a standstill. I wanted so much to change this situation and hoped that his father could help.

I guess I must have been dozing (meditating) at my desk when I was jarred awake.

"Tansi [commonly used greeting in Cree meaning "Hello" or "Hi"], boy, hello. You got some time for me?"

His disarming smile poked its way through the doorway. He seemed concerned and wanted to talk. But I was ready for him.

We joked around for a while as I waited for the right time to put my master plan into action. I was really prepared: I had Matthew's books (such as they were) in a little pile; my planbook was ready to disgorge the lack of accomplishments by date, subject, and mark. My audiovisual aids were there to impress this man with proof of my work ethic; the machines were lined up in a corner to show that I've tried every conceivable piece of equipment available to humans. All for that son of his who couldn't learn and didn't want to, anyway.

MINOSINS

He was impressed when I discussed flashcards and listening centers; the videotape machine seemed to interest him and he especially liked the prerecorded stories that I had on cassette tapes. He muttered his "minosins" [Cree for fine, wonderful, that's good] and I thought, "Isn't this great!"

I mentally patted myself on the back and felt that I had finally found an ally who I could use against the boy! An ally who would convince his lazy son that I, the teacher, was right, after all. I was ecstatic.

Then out of nowhere, this question:

"Can you set a snare?"

My expression must have shown a need for repetition.

"I said, can you set a rabbit snare?"

Hesitantly, not knowing the reason for his sudden change of topic, I answered, "Uhh... no, I can't."

"Can you set a beaver trap?....How 'bout a net under the ice?... Can you cook bannock on a rock?"

"No, I can't...but what's that got to do with your son?"

"Well Matthew can and so can I. His little brother is learning fast and pretty soon he'll know it good. And I'll teach you, too, if you want but I'd never force you to do it. Why do you force your ways?"

He smiled, then, as only he could, knowing that he had reached into my soul. I didn't seem to fully understand, so he continued.

"My Matthew is special. He's the very best young trapper around — even sometimes better than me! How come you say that he can't learn? He's learned lots. Maybe not your stuff — but lots!"

He talked as he slowly rose from the too small desk that I had dutifully provided for the parents and he backed his way toward the door, his hands gesturing as he spoke.

"You know, we don't want to be exactly like you

and I know you don't want to be like us.

"Show my kid how to learn. Show him how to use his mind. He has a good one. I know! I've known him much longer than you have. Don't just try to drag him into your world. He doesn't want to be there. He has his own."

Weesagaychuk

"Matthew doesn't like to read about your fancy world but he loves stories about the bush and about hunting and about Weesagaychuk. [A common character in Cree legends — mischief maker, can change form in some stories.] He also loves to draw about his life but he says he is not allowed. How come? How come his pictures make my trapline come alive and he can tell so many things with his art and you tell me he can't learn? Maybe he doesn't read so good here but he can say more than anyone I know, in his own way.

"Maybe if you gave him stuff that he knows about, he would try harder for you. He reads at home and he's pretty good. Don't make him into something he's not. Help him to become a better Matthew...Please."

Our eyes captured each other's intensity and we both knew, at that moment, that there was a bond: an understanding between two people who wanted the best for this Matthew.

He touched the brim of his cap with his index finger as his way of bidding farewell. Smiling, he left me with "Matt will never be a Mistigoosoh [Cree word for non-native, usually used for Caucasian] — he doesn't want to be one. Please don't try and make him into something he's not. Help him become a better him and I will be grateful always."

Great Lesson

He disappeared out the door taking his smile with him. There I sat, transfixed and deep in thought. This weather-beaten trapper had just shown me what educating is supposed to be all about. I'll never forget him nor his great lesson.

I had tried all kinds of methods to reach into Matt's psyche. I used basal readers, SRA Language Labs High-Interest/Low-Vocabulary reading series. I made him listen to prerecorded tapes while having the book in front of him. I threatened, I pleaded, I bribed — all to no avail.

What I didn't really attempt was that which would come from the boy himself. His father provided the key that unlocked it all.

With this new-found knowledge, I began to work with Matthew and — wonder of wonders — he began to learn. I took advantage of his artistic abilities and his own experiences. He began to work and he began to learn. He didn't become the class "Einstein" but he did begin to read and find out about things and he did progress. I was his guide and he was my tutor, at times. I learned much about northern life-styles and the people. I owe it to that late evening lesson that Thomas gave me that night at the school.

From that day on, I taught the "Matthews" in all my classes from a different point of view. My lessons evolved from their perspective as well as from mine. Their experiences, their lives, their needs, their abilities all became part of the learning experience for them. I began, finally and realistically, to teach by taking them from the known to the unknown. Teaching has never been the same.

Frank Fingarsen has taught in northern Manitoba for more than 20 years. He is presently a special education consultant, based in Brandon, for the Department of Indian Affairs.

Reprinted from Education Manitoba, *February, 1988.*

GROWING UP GAY

BY KATHERINE WHITLOCK

"A child's personality cannot grow without self-esteem, without feelings of emotional security, without faith in the world's willingness to make room for him [or her] to live as a human being." These are the words of Lillian Smith, a civil rights activist in the 1940s. Smith urged her audiences to become aware of the ways in which behaviors and attitudes directed against particular groups (in this instance African Americans) placed so many children in jeopardy.

Basic elements necessary to our children's emotional well-being and development are denied, Smith said, when dominant groups single out others for separate and less-than-equal treatment. Healthy development, for both individuals and societies, is not possible in settings where certain children learn that they are fair game for mistreatment while others learn that it is permissible to mistreat them.

Today, homophobia — defined as the fear or hatred of lesbians and gay men — is so interwo-

ven in our society that lesbian and gay youth face especially difficult struggles for self-esteem, emotional security and a sense of caring community. Most gay and lesbian young people are not open: they are in the closet, which is to say that they hide an important part of themselves from others (perhaps even from themselves) because they are afraid of what will happen to them if they tell the truth.

Even today it is not unusual for lesbian or gay young people never to have heard of homosexuality, to be unable to put a name to their feelings. They know only that they are "different," and that their difference is unacceptable.

A small number of young people do acknowledge their sexual orientation, at least to some important people in their lives, or are labeled by others as lesbian or gay. These identifiable youth face many of the same fears as their sisters and brothers in the closet, and they also become more obvious targets for homophobic mistreatment.

Whether in hiding or not, gay and lesbian youth know they live in a society which, in large mea-

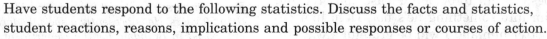

EYE-OPENING STATISTICS

Have students respond to the following statistics. Discuss the facts and statistics, student reactions, reasons, implications and possible responses or courses of action.

a) As many as 7.2 million Americans under age 20 are lesbian or gay.

b) Half of all lesbian and gay youths interviewed in a 1987 study reported that their parents rejected them for being gay.

c) 97% of all students surveyed reported hearing anti-gay comments in school.

d) Nearly half of all gay men and 1 in 5 lesbians are harassed or assaulted in secondary schools.

e) Gay and lesbian youth account for 30% of completed youth suicides and are 2-3 times more likely than other students to commit suicide.

f) Research at University of South Carolina showed that 8 out of 10 teachers in training harbored anti-gay attitudes.

g) 28% of students who drop out of schools are gay or lesbian.

h) 25% of all youth living on the streets are gay.

i) In 1993, Massachusetts became the first and only state in the U.S. to outlaw discrimination against lesbian and gay students in public schools.

j) Nationally, there were more than 100 gay/straight alliances in public and private high schools as of 1995.

From "Making Schools Safe for Gay and Lesbian Youth," published by the Massachusetts Governor's Commission on Gay and Lesbian Youth (February 1993), and from Gay & Lesbian Stats: A Pocket Guide of Facts and Figures *by Bennett Singer and David Deschamps (The New Press, 1994).*

BLACK AND GAY

I can still vividly remember my first few days at school. On that very first day no one spoke to me; I felt like a goldfish in a bowl. I decided I was never coming back. On the second day at the end of school I was suddenly surrounded by a group of about ten kids. They began to chant and call me names that I had never heard before, things like "blackie," "wog" and "nig-nog." Knocking them out of my path, I ran home crying to my mother. I couldn't understand why they were being so horrible to me. I explained to my mother that they had called me "blackie," and the fact that I wasn't black at all, I was brown! My mother tried to explain to me that I wasn't any different from the rest of the kids at school, apart from the fact that my skin was a different color. How do you explain to a child of five about racial prejudices? It would be nice to think that this was an isolated case, but it was not; at primary school there were taunts such as "nigger go home." My father told me to tell them that I had been born in this country and had as much right to be there as they.

It must have been in my early teens that I realized that I was gay. This was the time when boys discovered girls and that kissing wasn't sissy. I felt no desire whatsoever to kiss a girl. I remember sitting in science class listening to one of my friends describing giving his girlfriend a "frenchie"; I felt more of a desire to practice my "frenchie" on the science teacher. I then went through a period of self-denial. I went out with girls, got involved in so-called manly sports like rugby and baseball. Even whilst kissing these girls, I'd imagine it was a man; usually my science teacher...

Being Black can be hard enough on its own, but being Black and gay is a double hurdle. Choosing cookery as an option brought this point home to me. Whilst the rest of the lads at school did what was deemed, in their opinion, boys' options such as woodwork, metalwork, technical drawing etc., myself and two other lads decided to take homecraft as we had decided on careers in the catering industry. For the first few months we became outcasts; abuse was hurled at us; "here come the three benders" or "backs to the walls, here come the girls."

I can recall one day being cornered in the cloakroom by three friends — or boys who I thought were friends. They said I really shouldn't be doing cookery as there were no Black puffs.

They thought that because I was doing homecraft and being called "queer" I was bringing down the Black community at school, and that Blacks had enough problems without me adding to them. They hadn't guessed that I was gay, it was just the fact that I was doing a subject that was considered to be for girls. I think that the possibility of jibes from your friends about your sexuality puts many people off from choosing to do "non-standard" option subjects. I didn't let this deter me. I remember saying that some of the best chefs in the world were men, this seemed to eventually stop the name calling.

Living at home during these troubled times was very difficult for me. My mother would give me the third degree on school. On one occasion she said that I hadn't brought any girls home in a long time and was I turning queer? Although this was said in a joking way, I found it very hurtful to be referred to as queer. If she had said gay it would not have made me feel as though there was something wrong with me...

The only time that sex could be discussed seriously was at school. We had an hour per week to discuss social issues. These classes were very good as we could ask any related questions we liked. Looking back now, I am angry that the only sort of relationships that were discussed were those of heterosexuals. There were never any references to gay and lesbian relationships, not that I would have dared ask any questions for fear of showing a far too zealous interest. It has taken me seven years to begin to feel positive about being gay. I'd always thought that gay relationships had to be carried out in private for fear of going to prison. The idea that you might go to prison came from a friend of my mother who, after reading a case in a daily paper about a young child being sexually assaulted decided, quite rightly, that these people should be locked away, but went on to include that gays should be locked up as well. The fact that this man was a heterosexual didn't seem to change her mind in the slightest.

The feelings of isolation are now gone. Through meeting other gay people, one can share one's experiences and it soon becomes apparent that experiences you have been through are common to many gay people. Although I now have positive images about being gay I am not quite ready to let the door of that proverbial closet swing wide open, but as each week passes it gets a little wider.

From Outlaws in the Classroom: Lesbians and Gays in the School System, *1987. City of Leicester Teachers Association (NUT).*

sure, condemns them solely on the basis of their sexual orientation. Once homosexual orientation is disclosed or even suspected, it is treated as the most important thing about that young person, even though it is only one aspect of self. It is as if the young person has ceased to exist as a complete human being with the same questions, doubts and needs as heterosexual peers.

Lesbian and gay youth learn that they are seen as somehow less than human; that the quickest way to safety is to lie about themselves; that if they are found out, they will have to survive in a world that often fears and despises them.

These messages are so much a part of daily life that they go unnoticed. In schools across the country, even very young children learn the codes, passed on in joking whispers: don't wear certain colors to school on a particular day, or you're "queer." Lessons are learned each time a child discovers that one of the surest ways to deliver an insult is to accuse another of being a *lezzy,* a *faggot,* a *sissy.* Children may not always know what these words mean, but they know the pejorative power of this language; they know it is meant to belittle others.

Lessons are learned each time a homophobic joke is told and tolerated; each time adults speak and act as if everyone in the world is heterosexual, or should be.

Such manifestations of homophobia may seem inconsequential. Yet each time they go unchallenged, hostility and fear grow in their power to dominate our lives and those of our children. Possibilities for human understanding are diminished. Worse, adult acquiescence in homophobia places lesbian and gay youth at great emotional and sometimes physical risk....

Perhaps one of the most bitter examples of recent years occurred in 1984, when a group of teenagers in Bangor, Maine taunted and harassed a young gay man named Charlie Howard, finally pitching him over a bridge to his death. A group of high school students in central Maine, together with one of their teachers, responded by planning a Tolerance Day program intended to spotlight the special concerns of groups who had been persecuted as minorities and to increase awareness of the human costs of intolerance. The program, including a lesbian speaker along with representatives of the Jewish, Black, Native American and other minority communities, was cancelled by the school board on the grounds that presence of a lesbian might provoke violence. The board's move was later upheld by the state Supreme Court.

School environments are not unique. Damien Martin, executive director of the Hetrick-Martin Institute, observes: "[We] have to deal every day with teenagers who have been kicked out of their homes because they are gay. We have to find a bed for the 'sissy kid' who has been raped or beaten up in the last few shelters he has gone to and who would rather risk being killed by a kinky john than going back. We have to deal with the sixteen-year-old with a temperature of 104 who would rather take his chances on disease than risk the humiliation he is used to getting from social service agencies." Martin knows of one case where a sixteen-year-old gay youth was gang-raped in a youth shelter and then thrown out of the shelter because the staff said "it wouldn't have happened if he wasn't gay."

Not every gay or lesbian young person experiences homophobia so violently, but all live with the risks. Moreover, such outright expressions of hostility are only the most obvious indicators of an entire atmosphere permeated with fear. Violence comes in many forms, some less tangible than physical brutality. It can be inflicted with words and actions or through silence, indifference and neglect, wounding a young person's heart and spirit...

Today, there is an increase in reports of harassment of gay/lesbian students on college campuses. The incidence of verbal or physical abuse in high schools has been and remains high. Notes the Hetrick-Martin Institute: "Much of the violence is carried out by groups of fourteen to nineteen-year-olds and such violence is escalating sharply. Attacks by young people represent a clear failure of our schools and other social institutions to educate against violence and against homophobia."

Each time adults in positions of responsibility remain silent or look the other way when homophobic harassment occurs, children are learning that it is acceptable to tolerate violence, even to participate in it. The damage is all the worse when adults in authority actively participate in homophobic behavior.

Indifference to the destructiveness of homophobia can have another deadly, but preventable, consequence. Suicide, or attempted suicide, is one all-too-frequent choice for many lesbian/gay-identified young people who experience pain and isolation as unending; whose despair of being accepted for who they really are is almost absolute; who anticipate nothing but harm or loss — loss of family, friends — if they are honest about themselves... Many young gays and lesbians who have attempted suicide say they were afraid to tell anyone about the attempt, or about subsequent suicidal thoughts, fearing that disclosure would be met only with more rejection.

As parents, youth service providers, educators and community leaders, it is our job to ensure a safe and humane environment for all young people and to say, through our work, that each of them matters. There are obstacles ahead, and so we must be prepared to confront the fears and stereotypes that stand in the way of constructive change.

RESPECTING DIVERSITY AND DIFFERENCES

In learning about lesbian and gay youth, it is vital to recognize that they are by no means a monolithic population, distinguished only by sexual orientation. Though they are stigmatized on that basis, there are other important facets to their lives and experiences. We are far better able to address their needs when we acknowledge and pay attention to their diversity.

For example, though there are many Black, Latino, Asian/Pacific and Native American gay and lesbian youth, the myth persists that homosexuals are predominantly White. Lesbian and gay youth of color must contend with the ways in which homophobia and racism reinforce one another. They face discriminatory treatment not only because of sexual stereotyping but also on the basis of race and culture. Few environments provide safe spaces that support healing from the pains of both forms of oppression.

Young lesbians and gays of color know that racism is as prevalent within White-dominated les-bian/gay circles as it is in the larger society. Forms of expression may be subtle or overt; one common experience is that gays and lesbians of color are admonished not to be "divisive" in predominantly White gay/lesbian settings by bringing up racial concerns. This push for "color-blindness" obscures the experiences and histories of people of color, establishing a context in which the meaning of those experiences is diminished or simply ignored.

Similarly, it is not uncommon for gay and lesbian youth of color to feel pressured to conceal or downplay their sexual orientation in families and groups that offer support for resisting the harms of racism. In our society, no racial or ethnic group is immune to homophobia.

In either case, lesbian/gay youth are pressured to choose which community they will identify with. This dichotomy is absolutely untenable for young people who need support for claiming both sexual and racial/cultural identities.

Reprinted with permission from chapters one and three of Whitlock, K. 1989. Bridges of Respect: Creating Support for Lesbian and Gay Youth. *Philadelphia: American Friends Service Committee. © American Friends Service Committee, Philadelphia, PA.*

The "Eye Opening Statistics" were included in a teaching guide for Bennett, S.L. 1994. Growing Up Gay/Growing Up Lesbian. *New York: New Press. The book contains more than fifty coming-of-age stories by established writers and teenagers. An excellent classroom resource.*

For more information about resources and advocacy for gay and lesbian youth and teachers, contact the Gay, Lesbian and Straight Education Network (GLSEN), 121 West 27th Street, Suite 804, New York, NY 10001, 212-727-0135, http://www.glsen.org

Understanding the Needs of Youth:
"Who 'You Calling Violent?"

BY LUIS RODRIGUEZ

Pedro* is a thoughtful, articulate and charismatic young man; he listens, absorbs and responds. His movements are quick, well-developed during his years surviving in the streets of Chicago. Pedro is a 20-year-old gang leader. For most of his life, he has lived off and on between his welfare mother and an uncle. He has been kicked out of schools and has served time in youth detention facilities. He is also a great human being.

For four months in 1993, the courts designated me as his guardian under a house arrest sentence. He was respectful and polite. He meticulously answered all my messages. He was loved by my 6-year-old son. His best friend happens to be my 19-year-old son Ramiro.

During his stay, I gave Pedro books, including political books to help him become more cognizant of the world. One of these was *Palante,* a photo-text about the Young Lords Party of the 1970s. Pedro, whose family is from Puerto Rico, began to open up to an important slice of history that, until then, he'd never known about. Pedro read *Palante* from cover to cover — as he did other books, for the first time ever.

When Pedro was released from house arrest, he moved out of the neighborhood with his girlfriend and her small boy. He found a job. He remained leader of the gang, but was now talking about struggle, about social change, about going somewhere.

Last November, Pedro was shot three times with a .44. He was hit in his back, leg and hand. Ramiro and I visited him at the Cook County Hospital. He lived, but he was not the same after that. One day during Pedro's hospital stay, the same gang that had shot him ambushed and killed Angel, a friend of Ramiro and Pedro. Angel, an honor student at one of the best schools in the city, was on his way to school; a news account the next day failed to mention this, reporting only that he was a suspected gang member, as if this fact justified his death.

I tried to persuade Pedro to get his boys to chill.

I knew that Ramiro and the others were all sitting ducks. Pedro went through some internal turmoil, but he decided to forbid retaliation. This was hard for him, but he did it.

Unfortunately, the story doesn't end there. Earlier this year, Pedro allegedly shot and killed one of the guys believed to be behind Angel's murder and his own shooting. Pedro is now a fugitive.

I tell you this to convey the complexity of working with youths like Pedro, youths most people would rather write off, but who are also intelligent, creative and even quite decent. The tragedy is that it is mostly young people like these who are being killed and who are doing the killing. I've seen them in youth prisons, hospitals and courts throughout the land: young people who in other circumstances might have been college graduates, officeholders or social activists. Unfortunately, many find themselves in situations they feel unable to pull out of until it's too late.

I've long recognized that most youths like Pedro aren't in gangs to be criminals, killers or prison inmates. For many, a gang embraces who they are, gives them the initiatory community they seek and the incipient authority they need to eventually control their own lives. These are things other institutions, including schools and families, often fail to provide. Yet without the proper guidance, support and means to contribute positively to society, gang involvement can be disastrous.

This August, a media storm was created when 11-year-old Robert Sandifer of Chicago, known as "Yummy" because he liked to eat cookies, allegedly shot into a crowd and killed a 14-year-old girl. A suspected member of a Southside gang, Yummy disappeared; days later he was found shot in the head. Two teenage members of Yummy's gang are being held in his death. Hours before his murder, a neighbor saw Yummy, who told her, "Say a prayer for me."

This is a tragedy, but without a clear understanding of the social, economic and psychological dynamics that would drive an 11-year-old to kill, we can only throw up our hands. Yet it isn't hard to figure out the motive forces behind much of this violence.

Luis Rodriguez (with glasses) and some YSS members in South Dakota's Badlands en route to meet with youth at the Pine Ridge Lakota Indian Reservation.

Sandifer, for example, was a child of the Reagan years, of substantial cuts in community programs, of the worst job loss since the Great Depression, of more police and prisons and of fewer options for recreation, education or work. Here was a boy who had been physically abused, shuttled from one foster home to another, one juvenile justice facility after another. At every stage of Robert's young life since birth, he was blocked from becoming all he could be. But there was nothing to stop him from getting a gun. From using it. And from dying from one.

No "three strikes, you're out," no trying children as adults, no increased prison spending will address what has created the Pedros and Yummys of this world. Such proposals deal only with the end results of a process that will continue to produce its own fuel, like a giant breeder reactor. This is not a solution.

Gangs are not new in America. The first gangs in the early 1800s were made up of Irish immigrant youths. They lived as second-class citizens. Their parents worked in the lowest-paid, most menial jobs. These youths organized to protect themselves within a society that had no place for them. Other immigrants followed identical patterns. Today the majority of gang members are African-American and Latino and they face the same gen-

eral predicaments those early immigrants did. But today something deeper is also happening. Within the present class relations of modern technology-driven capitalism, many youths, urban and rural, are being denied the chance to earn a "legitimate" living. An increasing number are White, mostly sons and daughters of coal miners, factory workers or farmers.

Los Angeles, which has more gang violence than any other city, experienced the greatest incidence of gang-related acts during the 1980s and early 1990s, when 300,000 manufacturing jobs were lost in California. According to the Gang Violence Bridging Project of the Edmund G. "Pat" Brown Institute of Public Affairs at California State University, Los Angeles, the areas with the greatest impoverishment and gang growth were those directly linked to industrial flight.

At the same time, the state of California suffered deep cuts in social programs — most of them coming as a result of the passage in 1978 of Proposition 13, which decreased state funding for schools after a slash in property taxes. Since 1980, while California's population has jumped by 35 percent, spending for education has steadily declined. Yet there has been a 14 percent annual increase in state prison spending during the past decade; the state legislature has allocated $21 billion over the next ten years to build twenty new prisons.

Almost all areas in the United States where manufacturing has died or moved away are now reporting ganglike activity. There are seventy-two large cities and thirty-eight smaller ones that claim to have a "gang problem," according to a 1992 survey of police departments by the National Institute of Justice. Chicago, also hard hit by industrial flight, has many large multigenerational gangs like those in L.A.

What has been the official response? In Chicago "mob action" arrests have been stepped up (when three or more young people gather in certain proscribed areas, it is considered "mob action"), as have police sweeps of housing projects and "gang infested" communities. Recently there have been calls to deploy the National Guard against gangs, which is like bringing in a larger gang with more firepower against the local ones. This, too, is not a solution.

I agree that the situation is intolerable. I believe most people — from the Chicago-based Mothers Against Gangs to teachers who are forced to be police officers in their classrooms to people in the community caught in the crossfire — are scared. They are bone-tired of the violence. They are seeking ways out. First we must recognize that our battle is with a society that fails to do all it can for young people — then lays the blame on them.

It's time the voices for viable and lasting solutions be heard. The public debate is now limited to those who demonize youth, want to put them away, and use repression to curb their natural instincts to recreate the world.

I have other proposals. First, that we realign societal resources in accordance with the following premises: that every child has value and every child can succeed. That schools teach by engaging the intelligence and creativity of all students. That institutions of public maintenance — whether police or social services — respect the basic humanity of all people. That we rapidly and thoroughly integrate young people into the future, into the new technology. And finally, that we root out the basis for the injustice and inequities that engender most of the violence we see today.

Sound farfetched? Too idealistic? Fine. But anything short on imagination will result in "pragmatic," fear-driven, expediency-oriented measures that won't solve anything but will only play with people's lives.

Actually, the structural/economic foundation for such proposals as I've roughly outlined is al-

CHICAGO YOUTH PEACE PLAN: YOUTH STRUGGLING FOR SURVIVAL

Members of YSS met in 1996 to develop recommendations regarding education, the economy, discrimination and the legal system. Following is an excerpt from the section on education.

EDUCATION

Problems

Our schools look like prisons.

The conditions of our schools are terrible. There are few resources, such as books. The buildings are also run down and falling apart.

Programs are being cut, such as sports, arts and shop classes.

There is a lack of education that is engaging, meaningful and well-taught.

There is overcrowding of students. Sometimes there are not enough chairs; many students have to sit on the floor.

The youth are not included in solving the problems.

Instead, the police are given millions of dollars to patrol the schools.

There is no proper day care for children. They are often not monitored. No educational programs are offered. The ones that are good are too expensive.

Solutions

More money should be given to improve the conditions of the schools, instead of policing the schools. No more metal detectors in schools. All this discourages people from being comfortable in schools.

No more dress codes that impose a "standard" of appearance.

Students need counselors that listen, that care, and have the time to answer any problem. Teachers should be more interested in students. Both should get adequate pay so they can devote more time to their work.

Schools should not make money off students.

Youth should be used to help prevent problems such as mediator programs. The students obviously know how to relate to the problems of their peers. They can offer better solutions.

Schools should be opened up to the community so that their resources are utilized by everyone.

Good day care should be available for everyone.

© Marie Moll

ready laid. The computer chip has brought about revolutionary shifts in the social order. The only thing that isn't in place is the non-exploitative, non-oppressive relations between people required to complete this transition.

I know what some people are thinking. What about being tough on crime? Let me be clear: I hate crime. I hate drugs. I hate children murdering children. But I know from experience that it doesn't take guts to put money into inhumane, punishment-driven institutions. In fact, such policies make our communities even less safe. It's tougher to walk these streets, to listen to young people, to respect them and help fight for their well-being. It's tougher to care.

For the past two years, I've talked to young people, parents, teachers and concerned officials in cities as far flung as Hartford, Brooklyn, Phoenix, Seattle, Lansing, Denver, Boston, El Paso, Washington, Oakland, San Antonio and Compton. I've seen them grope with similar crises, similar pains, similar confusions.

Sometimes I feel the immensity of what we're facing talking to Teens on Target in Los Angeles, a group made up of youths who have been shot, some in wheelchairs; or to teenage mothers in Tucson, one child caring for another; or to incarcer-

ated young men at the maximum security Illinois Youth Center at Joliet. I felt it when a couple of young women cried in Holyoke, Massachusetts, after I read a poem about a friend who had been murdered by the police, and when I addressed a gym full of students at Jefferson High School in Fort Worth and several young people lined up to hug me, as if they had never been hugged before.

Because I have to deal with people like Yummy and Pedro every day, I decided this summer to do something more than just talk. With the help of Patricia Zamora from the Casa Aztlan Community Center in Chicago's Mexican community of Pilsen, I worked with a core of young people, gang and nongang, toward finding their own solutions, their own organizations, their own empowerment.

In the backyard of my Chicago home, some thirty people, mostly from the predominantly Puerto Rican area of Humboldt Park (my son's friends, and Pedro's homeys) and Pilsen, were present. They agreed to reach out to other youths and hold retreats, weekly meetings and a major conference. All summer they worked, without money, without resources, but with a lot of enthusiasm and energy. They hooked up with the National Organizing Committee, founded in 1993 by revolutionary fighters including gang members, welfare recipients, trade unionists, teachers and parents from throughout the United States. The N.O.C. offered them technical and educational assistance.

The young people's efforts culminated in the Youth '94 Struggling for Survival Conference, held in August at the University of Illinois, Chicago. More than a hundred young people from the city and surrounding communities attended. They held workshops on police brutality, jobs and education, and peace in the neighborhoods. A few gang members set aside deadly rivalries to attend this gathering.

Although there were a number of mishaps, including a power failure, the youths voted to keep meeting. They held their workshops in the dark, raising issues, voicing concerns, coming up with ideas. I was the only adult they let address their meeting. The others, including parents, teachers, counselors, resource people and a video crew from the Center for New Television, were there to help with what the young people had organized.

Then the building personnel told us we had to leave because it was unsafe to be in a building without power. We got Casa Aztlan to agree to let us move to several of their rooms to continue the workshops; I felt we would probably lose about half the young people in the fifteen-minute ride between sites. Not only did we hang on to most of the youths, we picked up a few more along the way. In a flooded basement with crumbling walls in Casa Aztlan we held the final plenary session. The youths set up a roundtable, at which it was agreed that only proposed solutions would be entertained. A few read poetry. It was a success, but then the young people wouldn't let it be anything else.

Youth Struggling for Survival is but one example of young people tackling the issues head-on. There are hundreds more across America. In the weeks before the November 8 elections in California, thousands of junior high and high school students, mostly Latino, walked out of schools in the Los Angeles area. Their target: Proposition 187, intended to deny undocumented immigrants access to education, social services and non-emergency health care.

These young people need guidance and support; they don't need adults to tell them what to do and how to do it; to corral, crush or dissuade their efforts. We must reverse their sense of helplessness. The first step is to invest them with more authority to run their own lives, their communities, even

their schools. The aim is to help them stop being instruments of their own death and to choose a revolutionary service to life.

We don't need a country in which the National Guard walks our children to school, or pizza-delivery people carry sidearms, or prisons outnumber colleges. We can be more enlightened. More inclusive. More imaginative.

And, I'm convinced, this is how we can be more safe.

*Some of the names in this article were changed.

Luis J. Rodriguez, *formerly of Los Angeles, now writes from Chicago, where he directs Tia Chucha Press. His most recent book is* Always Running: La Vida Loca, Gang Days in L.A. *(Touchstone, 1993).*

Rodriguez, L. "Turning Youth Gangs Around," The Nation magazine. © 1994 The Nation Company, LP. Reprinted with permission.

YOUTH STRUGGLING FOR SURVIVAL

Youth Struggling for Survival, founded in August of 1994, is a youth empowerment not-for-profit organization. We have incorporated authentic and respectful relationships, spirituality, political education, arts and ritual, as well as leadership training to assist gang and nongang youth from ten impoverished communities in Chicago. Our aim is to get highly-marginalized and often forgotten young people to relate to each other across gang, racial and sexual barriers and along their own immediate interests. We have also worked to incorporate indigenous teachings from the United States and Mexico as well as Africa and other traditional cultures. In addition, we hope to re-establish some long-severed relationships with parents, mentors, elders and other adults. Some related activities in YSS have included job placement, sanctuary, court advocacy, poetry and arts mentoring, and participating in speaking engagements, retreats, conferences and forums around the country, and, in some cases, Europe and Latin America.

YSS

PO Box 477446
Chicago, IL 60647
312-409-6696

A B.S. in Education

by Toni Blackman

small brown circular
looking pieces
eye my presence
blushing at the thought of their
admiration
while enjoying
the height of my pedestal
status

i stand with captive audience
prisoners in a cell they call
school
this classroom shields them
from bullets for now
miss teacher wipes
perspiration from her brow
tears from her eyes
frustration rests on her shoulders
she is without rest

her radio blares
unfortunate headlines
sleep thoughts to
keep her company at night
the kids on capitol hill
play mortal kombat
the kids downtown
play gin rummy
drunkenly sipping
on the lives of teachers
and little people

powerless little people
asking unanswered
why questions
not knowing
not understanding
why paper is rationed
why losing a crayon causes chaos
why teacher brings her own tools to make repairs
why the heat is without temperature control
 why schools doors are being shut

Toni Blackman is a rapper, vocalist and poet. She has a Masters in Organizational Communication from Howard University and is the director and founder of the Freestyle Union. The Freestyle Union brings together youth from various backgrounds and with various levels of experience to assist in their development as hip-hop artists.

Reprinted by permission of the author, Toni Blackman © March 12, 1996.

WHEN THE FRAME BECOMES THE PICTURE

BY CLEM MARSHALL

Most of us walk taller when we catch our reflection in a mirror. For those of us who work as teachers, the mirrors that matter most are the eyes of our students. This is especially true when dealing with students who are working through their personal experiences of discrimination and racism. Racism contracts the space — economic, material, physical, emotional, intellectual, psychological, moral and aesthetic — in which members of some groups can express their humanity. It has the power to distort and deform every human image, and none of us escape it entirely as we teach and learn. In this article, I would like to offer some of the experiences and reflections that have been important in my own development of an anti-racist teaching approach over a period of more than 15 years.

Peeling back the layers of class, ethnicity, gender and race in the school demands that we constantly check back with the learners, our students. As adults and as educators, we have no reliable maps for exploring this terrain. Sudden mountains of misunderstanding and precipices of self-doubt are bound to loom up. When they do, our differential years of lived experience mean that we are usually looking over the heads of our students.

For many years I taught French at a downtown Canadian public school. The diversity-rich student body included newly-arrived Vietnamese refugees, descendants of the First Nations and sixth-generation English, French and Afrikan Canadians from working-class backgrounds. My colleagues and I were faced with the challenge of meeting their many distinct academic needs. Less tangible but equally pressing, however, was the need to prepare the students, especially the students of colour, to deal with the pervasive racism that exists in North American society. One of my colleagues was convinced that our students needed to be reading at least two years above grade level by grade three in order for them to have a real chance for success in school. It also seemed to us that they could benefit

> RACISM CONTRACTS THE SPACE IN WHICH MEMBERS OF SOME GROUPS CAN EXPRESS THEIR HUMANITY

from a strong base of race-proofing. Students of colour needed some hands-on practice dealing with racist slurs, over-the-counter abuse in local malls and frequent harassment from those appointed to "serve and protect." White students needed to develop an understanding of the advantages conferred upon them by the simple fact of their skin colour; they needed a framework that would help them avoid or subvert the power of racism. As one student of colour remarked during an interview: "The White kids know the teacher will believe them. They think they can get you in trouble..." And as many of us had observed, some students' skin colour legitimized their movements throughout the school as effectively as a written pass. Our challenge as educators then, as it is now, was to create a climate in which all students learn how to protect their dignity inside the school and out.

When we move beyond the words, however, we know in our gut that our ability to create safe spaces for our students is tied to our feeling safe ourselves. Teachers who feel that their dignity is under attack make poor protectors of their students' self-respect. Understanding this, a small group of us began to meet regularly to hone our skills and to share our experiences and our teaching strategies. The group included individuals who had experienced exclusion after arriving as refugees from Eastern Europe in the fifties, West Asian (Middle Eastern) immigrants who had come to Canada via the United States, and others with roots in diverse Canadian and Caribbean communities.

Of course there were tensions. However, as we worked we built trust. In the end, we felt able to talk safely through many of our painful experiences around social identity. Over time our language changed and became more direct and respectful. Rather than ignore our differences in public until they turned into a bitter stew in private, we offered alternative information. By planning our curriculum together, we learned to work together. I also remember the intense discussions on social policy and learning theory which kept us excited as we worked to define and refine our goals. I must confess that talking about it today feels a bit pompous, but it's probably not a mis-representation to admit that we thought of our-selves as poised somewhere on the cutting edge of anti-racist pedagogy, beaming in a kind of ultra-modern, deep-dish multiculturalism. Not all the staff joined our working group, but we were able to provide a cooperative space which others could enter. As it turned out, this proved to be a crucial space for inviting our students to work with us as well.

In order to create a safe learning space for our students and for ourselves, we had to change the curriculum. We also helped elect and select pro-gressive school trustees and administrators. We held evening meetings with the parents and care-givers of our students, and we were political thorns in the sides of power and the status quo. When a newspaper headline stooped to slander with "DOWNTOWN KIDS DUMB!" we took to the streets, banners unfurled.

WORDS ARE NOT ENOUGH

It took a student's passing remark in the hall one day, however, to help me grasp the truth about what and how the young people in our school were really learning about race, diversity and respect — both in and outside the classroom.

Trinh, Vietnamese and just two years in Canada, had in his short life been a victim of war and witnessed some pretty frightening betrayals of our common humanity. "They're just pretending," he said in passing. He was referring to yet another public pronouncement on inter-group affection. Then, as though reading the unspoken question in my eyes, he continued: "But you guys are really dif-ferent; you're like brothers."

He was, I presumed, making comparisons be-tween the way his home-room teacher and I treated each other and other relationships he had observed between staff members. What must have been sig-nificant for him was that I was Black and his home-room teacher was White. From our behaviour he inferred that we liked each other. More importantly, he could see that we treated each other with the respect of equals. Day after day he could see us shar-ing information, books and equipment and doing so without tension and with collegial affection. He had no way of knowing how hard we had worked to get there, but clearly, this informal and unrehearsed behaviour meant more to him than the official words which spoke, over the P.A., of being tolerant and respecting each other. He saw our mutual respect as a model of a world where his own self-respect would also be safe.

In a way, he was also putting me on notice that he was making an investment of trust in us and we were not to let him down. Sometimes young people are the most subtle of strategists in getting their wants and needs fulfilled. Trinh had learned to read the anxious eyes behind smiling faces and to hear the music of fear under pleasant words and ritu-alized protestations of common humanity.

UNDERSTANDING HISTORY

Twelve-year old Merlisa heard the accusation behind a careless remark and looked for reassur-ance in the eyes of her teacher. She sought me out one day to tell me how uncomfortable she felt when a White female student complained of being tired of hearing about the bad things White people had done to Black and Aboriginal people. Merlisa's White teacher had gravely nodded his head in as-sent. When she came to see me, she was still feel-ing discomfort and a pain she could not safely name. "I didn't say *she* did those things. I read them in that book you showed me," she said, "and he made me feel I was picking on her."

In fact I wasn't sure which particular book or story she was referring to. I had taken most of my collection of Black books to school so both staff and students could use them. The books ranged from standards like the story of the African-American genius George Washington Carver, to a biography of Mary Ann Shadd. [In the 1850s, this Black free-dom fighter moved to Canada from Delaware, hav-ing grown up in a home which was a station on the Underground Railroad. She soon became the edi-tor of the *Provincial Freeman* in Ontario and is be-lieved to have been among the first women to pub-lish a newspaper in North America.] But for Merlisa, her teacher's discouraging nod of the head was far more meaningful to her learning curve than all the words and pictures in all the books I had provided.

The problem was discussed, without naming names, with the school librarian. That move made sense, given the fact that she saw all the students and was also a strong force for change. Scottish by birth, she was a seasoned navigator in steering her own history through troubled English waters. Her approach, on this occasion, was to revisit the same topics Merlisa and her White classmate had faced, integrating them into her ongoing discus-sions and research.

The whole subject was broadened and thus less easily personalized. It became safer, therefore, for students to bring their anxieties and ambivalences to the table. I won't pretend that it was a microwave event getting to that point of feeling relatively safe. Using the teacher-librarian as a model, they often borrowed the words and phrases until they had created a respectful language of their own.

WITH MY OWN EYES

Pictures, quite literally, shaped another encounter which drove home for me the power of the unwritten curriculum. This time skin power reared its head in my French class.

It isn't easy to be a Francophone in a dominant English world, and after a long and bitter struggle, Francophones in Ontario had won the right to a French-language education. Most Francophone students attended the French-language school in the neighbourhood. However, one student, René, had come back to us after a short spell there. His accounts of his experiences at that school caused us to suspect that he may in fact have felt pushed out by the class bias of both the students and the staff. Although in the public system, the school catered largely to the children of professionals, diplomats and international business executives.

But class is only one petal in the flower of social power. At an unconscious level, this White student of deep working class roots understood that White people, even students, and even those from a minority culture, own power in our society. He also understood at some level that that power was available to him for use against people of colour.

One day, René looked at the pictures on the wall and said: "How come you only have Jamaicans* on your wall?" *Moi?* Was he really challenging my commitment to diversity? I swallowed hard and asked him why he had said that. "Well! just look," he said, pointing to the wall.

René in fact gave us a great lesson. We set out to check on his observations and assumptions as a class. Using *"Combien de..."* ("How many?"), we counted the number of images on the wall and the number of representations of different racial and ethnic groups. In fact, because he was unaccustomed to seeing pictures of Blacks on the school walls, they became all he saw.

We checked out shades of skin colour and re-

viewed our vocabulary on colours. Our close observation showed that the pictures represented Black, White, Asian and Aboriginal people from diverse ethnic groups. We noted the absence of people with disabilities in active roles. Some of the students revealed for the first time that their parents were from different racial groups. Others said they saw themselves as biracial. One student talked about the conflict in her family because her Chinese mother had married her Vietnamese father.

That discussion changed the way we all looked at the curriculum and at each other. It led us to examine how easy it is to make the wrong assumptions about people's origins. And I learned that I not only needed to provide examples of diversity but to point them out, again and again, so that stu-

Here are questions which some teachers have found useful in dealing with situations that challenge their own practice. You will no doubt have developed many of your own.

1. Am I aware of how others see me and what patterns frame my behaviour?

2. How does it affect my practice when students or colleagues not of my descent challenge me in private or in public?

3. Do students not of my descent feel free to discuss with a colleague issues of identity which they choose not to share with me?

4. What is the method by which student experiences in the school yard, on the street, in the community or at home enter and inform my work with them in school?

5. In my work with colleagues or students, are there some people whose contribution is named and appreciated more than others?

6. Do I accept White colleagues playing the parent role in the group because of their greater access to social power or resources?

7. Do I explain clearly why I choose individuals to perform tasks of status or service (reading the announcements or cleaning the chalk board) so that everyone understands and accepts the process as fair?

---

* A commonly held stereotype in Toronto is that all Blacks are Jamaican.

dents would get the reinforcement they needed to see beyond the images already planted in their heads. And in a school system with a very diverse population, the task of explaining becomes harder.

MAKING THE LINKS

I have felt on occasion that we are squandering the legacy of such words as "I have a dream..." from Martin Luther King, Jr.'s most famous civil rights speech. Like so many teachers, I have watched students squirm through endless assemblies where those powerful words are spoken stripped of the images of pain, sacrifice and resistance which could give them faces of flesh and blood. Were our students really being informed by such events? Were these formal presentations a good approach in helping young people to embrace the goals of a truly just society? Or did all that formality feel like hypocrisy to them? I worried sometimes that some of our efforts might turn students into cynics at an early age. Did the frame in which the events were presented distort the picture itself?

This time our learning as educators was facilitated by the experience of some female students. What we discovered, or learned again, was how easy it was to destroy positive images even when we felt certain that we were building them up.

A group of senior students attended a special event in celebration of Black History Month in the gym. One of the visiting speakers, an engineer who had been a student in the school years earlier, cited an encounter she had had with anti-Black racism in the biggest encyclopedia in the school library. She told of anxiously searching out the word "Negro," only to find that the ugly stereotypes, written down with ultimate authority, confirmed her worst doubts and fears. Her distress lived on in her voice as she recalled the pain those words had caused her long ago.

The whole audience was moved by the story. It was all the female students could talk about when they went back to their home room. Trying to perhaps provide some perspective on the issues discussed, their teacher commented: "That's all very well, but we can't go on living in the past!" The irony of her remark did not escape the young women. For the past week, the class had been studying the fight for women's equality and the life of Canada's first female Member of Parliament. Agnes Macphail, who had been elected in 1921,

was of European heritage.

Later, one of the students revealed her confusion and conflict over the mixed messages she and her classmates had received. They liked their teacher and looked up to her. She herself was a feminist who was helping them learn how to deal with sexism in their lives. Yet she had misjudged the depth of their feelings about the differential treatment accorded to Black and White histories.

Would I be betraying my colleague if I discussed the issue with the student before hearing what she had to say? And could I, as a Black male adult, afford the risk of betraying a Black girl's trust by discussing what she had told me with her teacher? What lesson would all the students learn if I remained silent and pretended that nothing had happened?

In the end I told the student I would bring up the subject without mentioning any names. I knew that I had to share the information I had with my colleague. "That's not what I meant them to understand," she said. "I was just trying to get them back on track. I didn't know that they would take it that way. But I can see how they could. I'll explain to them the next time we meet."

> RACISM IS LIKE GRAVITY: IT WORKS FOR US OR AGAINST US EVEN WHEN WE'RE STANDING STILL

For my White colleague, it was a rare moment; she was close to those students and thought she knew them well. But clearly their reading of her actions was framed by what they had already learned about the racist society in which we all live. I always feel I've received a gift when colleagues not of my descent let me look through their eyes.

Often, when incidents occur across racial or cultural lines, students pre-test the impact of their views and feelings on teachers from their own background. As colleagues, when we have ways of sharing this information easily, we can often provide the bridge of communication the students are hoping to find.

FRAMING THE PICTURE

These experiences convinced me that skin and social power do not always respond readily to our good intentions or our determination to treat each other as equals. Racism is like gravity: it works for us or against us even when we're standing still. Some of us in our anti-racist group at school had learned and internalized the idea that we should be wary of setting up hierarchies of oppression. "I don't rank oppression" can still be a powerful silencer when there are competing needs within a diverse group. Did it really mean that we could never point out the differences in the collective weight of vulnerability that groups experience within society? Were women creating a hierarchy of oppression by pointing out the differential attention given to the fight against AIDS as against breast cancer? And if these questions are so hard for us to even ask as adults, where do we find the skill to help our students grow through facing and understanding them? How do we help them see, for instance, that Black History Month is not a reflection of privilege for Black students but an expansion of equity for all students?

The hierarchy of skin makes it easier for White teachers to assume the role of expert, for both staff and students, when working alongside their Aboriginal, Afrikan, Asian or Hispanic colleagues. Colour is a powerful persuader in convincing students who is competent to teach them what. Similarly, stereotypes in the popular culture make it easier for Asian educators to be more credible as experts in science or math than Afrikan or Aboriginal educators of equal experience. Even within groups, whatever colour they happen to be, White is often the standard. Our students don't learn measurement by slide rules alone. From observing the adult world, they learn to measure and judge identity as well.

Along the way, my colleagues and I discovered that discussions around stressful issues were not easy to deal with on an episodic basis. The very intensity of the passions and the pain they aroused would make the group reluctant to handle them. Unless there is a process in place, when pressure comes we grow apart and all communication systems come crashing down. One of the tools we developed as we worked was a set of questions which we could use, on our own, to prepare for problems and repair damage when it occurred.

The questions were not easy; they challenged us to push the limits of our self-knowledge. But over the years, we found that the questions we developed became a ritualized part of the way we dealt with the difficult issues of conflicting perceptions and unequal power.

It is now widely documented that an important part of the contemporary picture in education is built-in inequity. It has also been demonstrated again and again that, for teachers, the most difficult aspect of inequity to uproot is the ubiquitous weed of racism. In admitting that part of the picture is racism, we cannot afford to forget, for even an instant, that in our role as teachers, in every interaction, we provide that picture with its living, breathing frame. Our students don't create the world or the classrooms in which they must function. But when they step into them we can support them so they can reshape those living sites through their living presence. As adults, it is our duty to our students to provide a frame which at least affirms their worth, supports their community identity, challenges them to full growth and protects their human dignity.

Clem Marshall is an African-Canadian educator, with teaching experience in French and English. He wrote and directed the film All Eyes on Africa, *which explores aspects of the global cultural impact of African art. He also designed and taught the course* Anti-Racist Research and Practice in Canadian Schools *at York University in Toronto. At present he is part of the equity team of Enidlee Consultants Inc., working with schools in Canada and the United States.*

Dear High School Teacher

BY KAI JAMES

December 1995.

I am a new high school student and I am looking forward to these next years of my schooling. I feel the need to write this letter because I seek a different experience in high school from that of elementary school. One of the things I would like to see changed is the relationship between students and teachers. I feel that a relationship that places students on the same level as teachers should be established. By this I mean that students' opinions should be taken seriously and be valued as much as those of teachers, and that together with the teachers we can shape the way we learn and what we learn.

Currently, discussion about issues that affect us directly is so rare that school becomes for us boring and irrelevant. Teachers should ensure that students have access to a wide range of resources and encourage independence in study so that creativity may blossom. Teachers should listen to students with an open mind and speak on our behalf when we are not given the opportunity to express ourselves to the school authorities.

Our curriculum is one which breeds stereotypes and does not address the issues that affect our lives every day. What we need is a curriculum that all students can relate to and that will motivate us to be the best we can be by introducing people like us in all kinds of occupations. We need curriculum that will not shield us from reality but will prepare us for life.

Like all other students, Black students come to school with expectations that they will do well. But so much emphasis is placed on athletics for us that we are looked upon as athletes alone and teachers believe that we are more likely to succeed in sports than in academics. Let me relate an example of this. This happened when I was in elementary school. We were celebrating Black History Month for the first time. A student brought in a documentary about Malcolm X. We were told that the head office doesn't allow certain films to be shown in school, so we would have to settle for a video about the Harlem Globetrotters basketball team instead.

Apart from sports, whenever we discuss math, geography, science and even music, reference is constantly made to White Europeans such as Pascal, Newton and Mozart instead of Matthew Henson, George Washington Carver and Louis Armstrong. It is only when we discuss basketball or track and field that we hear about a Black person. By the end of that day many students left the class not knowing who Malcolm X was or what he did.

Occurrences similar to this one went on throughout my years at elementary school. This probably didn't affect me as much as it did other students whose entire school years revolved around basketball and track, which was all right with the teachers.

I am interested in athletics but do not want teachers to assume that it will be my major interest in school or that I will be participating in every sport that comes along, because while I may participate in a sport, I am aware of the importance of a balance between sports and academics and will keep that in perspective.

After years of being ignored, what the students need, and what Black students in particular need, is curriculum that we can relate to and that will interest us. We need appropriate curriculum that will motivate us to be the best we can be. We need to be taught to have a voice, and have teachers who will listen to us with an open mind and not dismiss our ideas simply because they differ from what they have been told in the past. We need to be made aware of all of our options in life. We need to have time to discuss issues of concern to the students as well as the teachers. We must be able to talk about racism without running away from it, or disguising the issue. We must also be taught to recognize racism instead of denying it and then referring to those who have recognized it as "paranoid." We also need to be given the opportunity to influence our education and in turn our destinies.

We should also be given the right to assemble and discuss issues without having a teacher present to discourage us from saying what we need to say. Teachers must gain the trust of their students and students must be given a chance to do the same. We need teachers who will not punish us just because they feel hostile or angry. We need teachers who will allow us to practice our culture without being ridiculed.

The school office has been turned into a place that students dread. It is where we are sent for doing anything from fighting to expressing disagreement. It is a place where we are lectured to and made to feel like we are criminals. A place where we may speak only when we are apologizing to whomever we have hurt, which is in most cases a teacher. Instead, the office should be a place where we can be heard, a place where we have the opportunity to point out how a teacher could have dealt with the situation differently and a place where we are advised on how to handle future incidents.

My expectations of high school are that more issues will be open for discussion and that students will be given a more active role in the school community. I also trust that the changes I have proposed will be taken into consideration and that we will get the respect and recognition we deserve. I'm hoping that high school will be a change for the better from what I have experienced in elementary school. Hopefully, high school will be an opportunity to voice my opinion as someone who is as valuable to the school community as all other members, including the teachers.

This is a change I look forward to.

Sincerely,

Kai James

Kai James *is currently in 11th grade and lives in Toronto, Canada. He is a member of his school basketball team, chess club and math club.*

Reprinted by permission of the author from Brathwaite, K. S. & James, C.E. Eds. 1996. Educating African Canadians. *Toronto: Our Schools/Our Selves, James Lorimer and Company Ltd.*

DEAR PRINCIPAL

BY MURIEL CLARKE

I would like to introduce myself to you as the mother of a Grade Six student who recently enrolled in your school. I believe in good communication between the home and the school, and hope that you and my child's teacher will communicate with me as I will try to work with you in the interest of my child.

As a parent, I take my role seriously and consider myself as an important partner in the education of my child. I have learned through experience that Black parents have to be very vigilant when we enroll our children in school due to low expectations and negative attitudes some teachers have of Black students. I have already experienced some of this in my child's previous schooling, for even though she performed well, she sometimes felt excluded and passed over in the classroom. Like other parents, I wish that my child will feel part of the school, that she will see herself reflected in the curriculum and in the composition of the teaching body. I do not want school to be an alienating experience for her, as it has been for so many of our students over the years.

I would also like to share with you some of my observations about the education of Black students. My involvement in the Black community in Toronto and in the Organization of Parents of Black Children (OPBC) has exposed to me the depth of the problems Black students generally face in schools due to racism, exclusion, stereotyping and low expectations of many teachers. I have listened to parents discuss their children's difficulties in school, and have tried to counsel and support some who felt intimidated by the system. Because of my knowledge of the research on Black students as well as the discussions in the conferences and workshops in which I have participated, I am very fearful about my child's education and future. I do not want her to become a high school dropout statistic nor do I want her to be streamed [tracked] and be limited in any way. I have expectations of her completing her education and allowing herself options in terms of future studies and careers. So please, allow me to be involved in her education so that I can work with the school to help her accomplish her goals.

In my child's previous schools, even though I tried to be part of the school activities and attended all the meetings, I still felt a sense of unease. I felt that the schools are not sufficiently welcoming of us as parents in general, and especially of Black parents. Many of us feel that the atmosphere in the school does not include us. This exclusion of our African heritage must impact negatively on our children's self-esteem, and must affect their academic performance, I believe. Let us be fair to the students. It is important that the school reflects all of them, including my child and other Black students. Her connection to her studies is very important to my daughter, as well as to me.

Just as I encourage my child to do her best in school, so I am asking the school to provide the best support for her in every area: the curriculum, the activities, the attitudes and expectations of the teacher, and involvement of parents. The kind of support she needs can be provided only in an anti-racist, inclusive environment in which she can grow and blossom.

I hope that my daughter will enjoy attending your school and will achieve good academic success as I know she is capable of. I hope that she will be taught by caring teachers who will appreciate her heritage and support her aspirations.

Let us work together for the good of my child.

Sincerely,

Muriel Clarke, Parent

Muriel Clarke is the former Chair and founding member of the Organization of Parents of Black Children (OPBC) and supports parents who are experiencing difficulties with the school system.

Reprinted by permission of the author from Brathwaite, K. S. & James, C.E. (Eds.) 1996. Educating African Canadians. *Toronto: Our Schools/Our Selves, James Lorimer and Company Ltd.*

WHAT I'VE LEARNED ABOUT UNDOING RACISM

BY ANDREA AYVAZIAN

I remember the first Unlearning Racism Workshop I attended, over a decade ago. I can picture myself in the predominantly White group, everyone gathered in a circle. I remember feeling self-conscious, guilty, fearful and cautious lest I say the wrong thing and thus appear racist. The mental image I retain of my presence that day is of me sitting with my arms and legs crossed, my brow knitted together in a tight and pensive look, my whole body fortressed, my mind sharp and ready to monitor my speech and defend my actions.

It was a difficult day for me; I resisted and rebelled. The armor I used to keep the issues at arm's length was my hypercritical self. I managed to find fault with almost everything the trainers presented, thereby making myself somewhat superior and impervious to their points. I struggled with them. But more sunk in and took hold than I realized. Bits of their presentation would rattle around inside for me some time to come.

I did not realize then how much that day was a beginning for me, a baptism of sorts. I was starting on a journey. Since then, events and decisions have propelled me forward — quietly and nervously at first, but forward nonetheless — to work on issues of oppression, and especially on racism.

Sometimes we have a sensation that we have been called to do something — not with thunder and lightning, but with a whisper from within. For me, the whisper was barely audible ten years ago — but it grew in volume and clarity, and I have been able to "follow a leading," as Quakers say, to speak, teach and wrestle with others on issues of racism and White privilege.

For the past five years, I have been leading workshops on Unlearning Racism. I have been the trainer perched in front of the group coaxing other White people to confront the issue of racism. I have had to deal with participants' resistance, I have been the target of their rebellion, and I have had to look at crossed arms, thinking to myself that I alienated more people than I touched — that folks *say* they want to work on this issue but they don't — and that I hate this work anyway. But some days I have packed up my materials and headed home feeling renewed hope — that we did get somewhere, and that folks like us can and will change the world.

Over the years of attending and leading Unlearning Racism workshops, I have observed certain patterns emerging among White participants and with predominantly White groups.

▸ I have noticed in numerous settings that White people often spend considerable time and energy doing battle with the basic definition of racism now used in most anti-racism workshops, that is: Racism equals Social Power plus Prejudice. This concept serves as a cornerstone for the work that follows. It is interesting to discover how much argument this simple definition often causes in groups. White people work hard explaining how little social power they have, defending their status as ordinary individuals with no special advantages or benefits in society. These discussions can become quite passionate. However, it ignores institutional racism and White privilege. These two concepts are tough ones for some Whites to hear and accept.

Another issue that arises around the "Power plus Prejudice" definition, which causes considerable distress, is that it precludes people of color from being racist because they have limited social power in a White-dominated society. (People of color may be prejudiced, some may have ugly feelings about folks in other ethnic groups, but they are not racist.) White people can spend the entire first hour of a workshop explaining why people of color can be and are racist. This argument must bring some relief to guilt that surfaces when White people look directly at racism, confront it as a *White* problem and start to wrestle with it.

▸ Beneath the struggle that erupts over the definition of racism is the difficulty many Whites seem to have in accepting the degree of privilege that White skin brings. Asking White people to become aware of their privilege as Whites seems to be like asking fish to become aware of water; it is all around us and yet very difficult to see. Racism, a system of advantage based on race, bestows advantages on White people *daily* — privileges and advantages given without our asking and often received without our being aware of it. We live in a very racist society — most Whites agree with that point. But grasping the subtle yet profound level of privilege that each White individual has received throughout her/his life is difficult for many folks to absorb.

▶ Another pattern I have seen emerge is the number of well-intentioned groups, deeply committed to working on issues of racism, that deal with the topic by designing programs focused on the targeted group — people of color — rather than on the dominant group — White people — as the source of the problem. Striving to be inclusive and overvaluing "dialogue," Whites attempt to put people of color under the microscope as a way of solving their own White racism. White people need to work with other White people on our racism. People of color have a role to play in dismantling racism, but it is not in showing us White people the way, forever being our teachers on this issue.

Racism is a White issue and White people need to work together to confront it directly and move to a place where we can be active agents of change. A parallel can be made to sexism. Sexism is an issue that men must address — women are the victims of sexism, not the cause. Women cannot serve as the teachers and experts on sexism for men to work out their issues. Women's work is our own liberation and empowerment — and the same is true of people of color. (In fact, people of color often do gather together to work on issues of internalized oppression.)

▶ Another issue that hampers our forward movement toward dismantling racism is the belief that onetime experiences — even when they are emotionally powerful and full of insights — can transform individuals or organizations. Unlearning personal racism and working towards the dismantling of institutional racism require long-term plans, sustained vigilance and "daily practice" (as one participant explained it). Too often groups look for or hope for a quick fix — a single workshop or a dramatic event that will solve the problem in one fell swoop.

Racism is *learned,* and it can be *unlearned,* but it takes a commitment to stay aware, to keep working and to accept the unlearning as a lifelong journey. White people absorbed racist images and messages early on in life — in schools, houses of worship, children's books, through television and through our families and neighborhoods. Clearing out the distorted images and stereotypes we absorbed as children and replacing the misinformation with accurate information requires time and attention — it does not just happen, and it does not happen quickly. Examining the racism inherent in the institutions we are a part of, and analyzing how those institutions maintain their Whiteness, also takes time and focused attention. There are no quick fixes.

Once on the road to liberation, we see that the journey stretches out far ahead. Because we live in a racist society, we are seduced into looking the other way, losing our attention and slipping back into business as usual. But there is no such thing as a passive anti-racist. Business as usual, or quietly complying with the status quo, means colluding with a racist society.

A trainer of color, with whom I worked to prepare myself to lead these workshops, once told me that of all the things that I could teach White people, the single most important concept to convey in my work was to help Whites understand that the key to dismantling racism is to "keep paying attention." Keep paying attention to the racism that pervades our society. It is so tempting for White people to pay attention for a while, to attend a workshop and to think: "Work on dismantling racism? I *did* that." We must remember our charge: to keep paying attention, and then say instead: "Work on dismantling racism? I *do* that."

Andrea Ayvazian, PhD is an anti-racism educator and social justice activist. She is currently the Protestant Chaplain at Mount Holyoke College in South Hadley, Mass. Email: aayvazia@mhc.mtholyoke.edu

Reprinted with permission of the author.

DISCUSSION QUESTIONS

1. What were your reactions to the essay? Have you had any of the experiences that the author describes?

2. In what ways over the last few weeks have you "paid attention"?

3. How do you plan to "pay attention" in the weeks to come?

Distancing Behaviors Often Used by White People

By James Edler and Bruce Irons

As Whites work on the issue of racism, certain avoidance or distancing behaviors invariably arise. These behaviors may be unconscious and arise from a universal need for safety, security and a positive self-image. However they minimize the impact of the workshop, since racism cannot be confronted at a distance. To really understand and deal with racism entails experiencing various levels of personal questioning, discomfort and bewilderment about personal responsibility. Becoming aware of one's armor of distancing behaviors can allow one to move past such struggles and begin a constructive effort to confront personal and societal racism.

1. Definitions Game

This behavior prevents people from addressing the problem of racism by requesting a "clear," absolute definition of racism and related terms, which often leads to involved, abstract discussions. This is not to be confused with an actual need to clarify differences among concepts like racism, discrimination, prejudice and the like.

2. Where are the People of Color?

Many White people believe that until they can discuss racism with people of color directly, the issue can't be addressed. This belief also suggests that if there are only a limited number of minorities representing a particular organization or community, racism isn't a problem. Racism, however, may be the very reason they are not present.

3. Racism Isn't the Only Problem

Frequently, White people insist that racism is part of a larger societal problem, and must therefore be discussed within the context of other problems such as sexism, crime, and poverty. While it is true that many forms of oppression are deeply intertwined, this behavior is one way to avoid confronting racism directly.

4. Being an Expert

While White people spend numerous hours theorizing about what it is like to be oppressed, they seem to take little action in their communities to combat the problem. This manifests as "some of my best friends are..." or "I'm the okay White person in this group," and leads to denying the need to change racist views they may embrace.

5. Instant Solutions

Advocates sometimes simplify the problem of racism by promoting single solutions such as "Change the Schools" which have their value, but can be self-limiting. In order to effectively combat problems such as racism, advocates must look at how things are rather than "how they should be."

6. Find the Racist

One of the most destructive behaviors transpire when members of a White group working on the issue of racism attack one another for their "racist comments." This generates a climate of uncertainty among the group and may prevent further discussions about how to constructively address racism in White communities.

7. After I...

Those people who do nothing or only minimally invest in the area of combatting racism justify their actions by focusing on all the things that prevent them from taking action. For example, one might say, "I will challenge racism when I get my degree" or "It's too big a problem. I don't know what to do!" Excuses like these are common and become a routine way to avoid fighting racism.

8. Geography

Racism is a sickness that prevails in most areas regardless of the size of the minority population. For this reason, White people must ask themselves what it is that keeps minorities from living and working in their White communities, and avoid focusing strictly on those areas that have developed reputations for overt "race problems."

9. You've Come a Long Way

Developing rationales that emphasize what changes have or may have occurred among people of color, slow down and even prevent White people from confronting racism. This strategy implies that these groups should be satisfied with certain improvements that have indeed occurred in their communities. Though victories hard won must be acknowledged, it is important not to discount what is left to be done and the retrogression that has occurred during the past decade.

Adapted from an article by James Edler and Bruce Irons.

"EVERY ONE OF OUR TEACHERS BELIEVED IN US."

This essay describes what can happen when teachers, and the community as a whole, place a priority on education. After reading the essay, discuss how schooling would change if that same sense of urgency and commitment were present in your school district.

BY DEBBIE WEI

My experience has taught me another interesting lesson. Some of the most motivated and highest achieving ESOL students I ever taught were from Eritrea and Ethiopia. Time and again, Eritrean and Ethiopian students entered my classroom, with incredible skills for academic performance well implanted in their first languages — Tigrinia and Amharic. But I knew these were the children of war, children of guerilla fighters who had spent years in the underground, running from bombs and massacres. They had lived in makeshift shelters, walked through deserts, survived in refugee camps. Many of the kids had missed four, five or even six years of formal schooling. I asked them how they had managed to learn so much, to remember so much.

The Eritrean students told me, "Oh, Miss Wei, we were taught. Whenever there was a pause in the bombing, people in the Eritrean Peoples Liberation Front took turns teaching us. We didn't have a school, of course. We sat under trees usually. We did our lessons in the dirt with sticks. We learned when we could."

I asked them why they thought they and their friends learned with so few resources, and why many of their classmates in the U.S., with many more resources, were not learning.

"Miss Wei, here there are more things, it is true," the students answered, "But two things are very different. One, in Eritrea every one of our teachers believed in us. They believed not only that we could learn, but that we had to learn for the future of the country. Two, even though we had so little, we had all that our community could give us. We had the best of what was available. No one had time for anything when you live on the run, but they made time for our schooling. We knew we were important.

"Here, this country is so rich, but the schools are so poor in comparison to what the country has. Here, students see they are not important. They don't matter. No one really cares. They only open schools because they have to, because it's the law. No one will learn if people don't believe in them."

Reprinted from the Philadelphia Public School Notebook, *Volume 3, Number 1, Fall 1995.*

BUTTERFLIES

This story highlights the importance of understanding the social and cultural contexts that frame students' experiences and actions. It suggests that we consider their life and work through the lens of their culture. In order to do this, we can ask questions to learn more about the context of the situation before jumping to pass judgement.

Any study of the environment also requires an examination of the larger context. Sometimes the environment is described as only including plants and animals. On the other hand, some ideologies place ultimate value on people, at the expense of the environment. The more complex yet beneficial approach is to see the environment as a dynamic and delicate relationship among people, animals, plants, water, the land and the air we breathe.

What questions could the teacher in this story have asked that would have turned the days' lesson into a lesson for both the student and teacher?

BY PATRICIA GRACE

The grandmother plaited her granddaughter's hair and then she said, "Get your lunch. Put it in your bag. Get your apple. You come straight back after school, straight home here. Listen to the teacher," she said. "Do what she say."

Her grandfather was out on the step. He walked down the path with her and out onto the footpath. He said to a neighbor, "Our granddaughter goes to school. She lives with us now."

"She's fine," the neighbor said. "She's terrific with her two plaits in her hair."

"And clever," the grandfather said. "Writes every day in her book."

"She's fine," the neighbor said.

The grandfather waited with his granddaughter by the crossing and then he said, "Go to school. Listen to the teacher. Do what she say."

When the granddaughter came home from school her grandfather was hoeing around the cabbages. Her grandmother was picking beans. They stopped their work.

"You bring your book home?" the grandmother asked.

"Yes."

"You write your story?"

"Yes."

"What's your story?"

"About the butterflies."

"Get your book then. Read your story."

The granddaughter took her book from her schoolbag and opened it.

"I killed all the butterflies," she read. "This is me and this is all the butterflies."

"And you teacher like the story, did she?"

"I don't know."

"What your teacher say?"

"She said butterflies are beautiful creatures. They hatch out and fly in the sun. The butterflies visit all the pretty flowers, she said. They lay their eggs and then they die. You don't kill butterflies, that's what she said."

The grandmother and the grandfather were quiet for a long time, and their granddaughter, holding the book, stood quite still in the warm garden.

"Because you see," the grandfather said, "your teacher, she buy all her cabbages from the supermarket and that's why."

Patricia Grace, a Maori New Zealander, is author of eight books. Her prizewinning novel, Potiki, *was published in 1986. This story is from* Electric City and Other Stories. *(Penguin N.Z.)*

READING BETWEEN THE LINES

Lies My Textbook Told Me: Racism and Anti-Racism in U.S. History

James Loewen spent two years at the Smithsonian surveying twelve leading high school textbooks of American history. What he found was an embarrassing amalgam of bland optimism, blind patriotism, and plain misinformation. In response, he has written Lies My Teacher Told Me: Everything Your American History Textbook Got Wrong, *a telling critique of existing textbooks and a wonderful retelling of American history as it should be told. Including events and characters as diverse as the Alamo, John Brown, Reconstruction, Helen Hunt Jackson, the U.S. secret war with the U.S.S.R., the Civil Rights Movement, and the My Lai Massacre,* Lies *supplies the conflict, suspense and connections with current-day issues so appallingly missing from textbook accounts. The editors of this publication highly recommend* Lies My Teacher Told Me *as essential reading for all teachers, and for anyone else who wants to know the real story of America's history.*

The following excerpt from Lies My Teacher Told Me *examines textbook coverage (or omission) of racism and anti-racism in United States' history.*

BY JAMES LOEWEN

THE AMERICAN OBSESSION

Perhaps the most pervasive theme in our history is the domination of Black America by White America. Race is the sharpest and deepest division in American life. Issues of Black-White relations propelled the Whig Party to collapse, prompted the formation of the Republican Party, and caused the Democratic Party to label itself the "white man's party" for almost a century. The first time Congress ever overrode a presidential veto was for the 1866 Civil Rights Act, passed by the Republicans over the wishes of Andrew Johnson. Senators mounted the longest filibuster in United States history, more than 534 hours, to oppose the 1964 Civil Rights bill. Thomas Byrne Edsall shows how race prompted the seeping political realignment of 1964-72, in which the White South went from a Democratic bastion to a Republican stronghold. Race still affects politics, from the notorious Willie Horton commercial used by

George Bush in the 1988 presidential campaign to the more recent candidacies of the Ku Klux Klan leader David Duke. Race riots continue to shake urban centers from Miami to Los Angeles.

Almost no genre of our popular culture goes untouched by race. From the 1850s through the 1930s, except during the Civil War and Reconstruction, minstrel shows, which derived in a perverse way from plantation slavery, were the dominant form of popular entertainment in America. During most of that period, *Uncle Tom's Cabin* was our longest-running play, mounted in thousands of productions. America's first epic motion picture, *Birth of a Nation*; first talkie, *The Jazz Singer*; and biggest blockbuster novel ever, *Gone with the Wind*, were substantially about race relations. The most popular radio show of all time was "Amos 'n' Andy," two White men posing as humorously incompetent African Americans. The most popular television mini-series ever was "Roots," which changed our culture by setting off an explosion of interest in genealogy and ethnic background. In music, race relations provides the underlying thematic material for many of our spirituals, blues numbers, reggae songs, and rap pieces.

The struggle over racial slavery may be the predominant theme in American history. Until the end of the nineteenth century, cotton — planted, cultivated, harvested, and ginned by enslaved Africans — was by far our most important export. Our graceful antebellum homes, in the North as well as in the South, were built largely by enslaved Africans or from profits derived from the slave and cotton trades. Black-White relations became the central issue in the Civil War, which killed almost as many Americans as died in all our other wars combined. Black-White relations was the principal focus of Reconstruction after the Civil War; America's failure to allow African Americans equal rights led eventually to the struggle for civil rights a century later.

Studs Terkel is right: race is our "American obsession." Our society has repeatedly been torn apart and sometimes bound together by this issue of Black-White relations.

SLAVERY WITHOUT RACISM

While textbooks now show the horror of slavery and its impact on Black America, they remain largely silent regarding the impact of slavery on White America, North or South. Textbooks have trouble acknowledging that anything might be wrong with White Americans, or with the United States as a whole. Perhaps telling realistically what slavery was like for slaves is the easy part. After all, slavery as an institution is dead. We have progressed beyond it, so we can acknowledge its evils. Without explaining its relevance to the present, however, extensive coverage of slavery is like extensive coverage of the Hawley-Smoot Tariff — just more facts for hapless eleventh graders to memorize.

Slavery's twin legacies to the present are the social and economic inferiority it conferred upon Blacks and the cultural racism it instilled in Whites. Both continue to haunt our society. Therefore, treating slavery's enduring legacy is necessarily controversial. Unlike slavery, racism is not over yet.

To function adequately in civic life in our troubled times, students must learn what causes racism. Although it is a complicated historical issue, racism in the Western world stems primarily from two related historical processes: taking land from and destroying indigenous peoples, and enslaving Africans to work that land. To teach this relationship, textbooks would have to show students the dynamic interplay between slavery as a socioeconomic system and racism as an idea system. Sociologists call these the social structure and the superstructure. Slavery existed in many societies and periods before and after the African slave trade. Made possible by Europe's advantages in military and social technology (described in Chapter Two of *Lies*), the slavery started by Europeans in the fifteenth century was different, because it became the enslavement of one race by another. Increasingly Whites viewed the enslavement of Whites as illegitimate, while the enslavement of Africans was acceptable. Unlike earlier slaveries, children of African American slaves would be slaves forever and could never achieve freedom through intermarriage with the owning class. The rationale for this differential treatment was racism. As Montesquieu, the French social philosopher who had such a profound influence on American democracy, ironically observed in 1748: "It is impossible for us to suppose these creatures to be men, because, allowing them to be men, a suspicion would follow that we ourselves are not Christian."

Historians have chronicled the rise of racism in the West. Before the 1450s Europeans considered Africans exotic but not necessarily inferior. As more and more nations joined the slave trade, Europeans came to characterize Africans as stupid, backward, and uncivilized. Amnesia set in: Europe gradually found it convenient to forget that Moors from African had brought to Spain and Italy much of the learning that led to the Renaissance. Europeans had known that Timbuctu, with its renowned university and library, was a center of learning. Now, forgetting Timbuctu, Europe and European Americans perceived Africa as the "dark continent." By the 1850s many White Americans, including some Northerners, claimed that Black people were so hopelessly inferior that slavery was a proper form of education for them; it also removed them physically from the alleged barbarism of the "dark continent."

The superstructure of racism has long outlived the social structure of slavery that generated it. The very essence of what we have inherited from slavery is the idea that it is appropriate, even "natural," for Whites to be on top, Blacks on the bottom. In its core our culture tells us — tells all of us, including African Americans — that Europe's domination of the world came about because Europeans were smarter. In their core, many Whites and some people of color believe this. White supremacy is not only a residue of slavery, to be sure. Developments in American history since slavery ended have maintained it. Textbooks that do not discuss White involvement in slavery in the period before 1863, however, are not likely to analyze White racism as a factor in more recent years. Only five of twelve books list racism, racial prejudice, or any term beginning with race in their indexes.

Only two textbooks discuss what might have caused racism. The closest any of the textbooks comes to explaining the connection between slavery and racism is this single sentence from *The American Tradition*: "In defense of their 'peculiar institution,' Southerners become more and more determined to maintain their own way of life." Such a statement hardly suffices to show today's students the origin of racism in our society — it doesn't even use the word! *The American Adventure* offers a longer treatment: "[African Americans] looked different from members of White ethnic groups. The color of their skin made assimilation difficult. For this reason they remained outsiders." Here Adventure has retreated from history to lay psychology. Unfortunately for its argument, skin color in itself does not explain racism. Jane Elliot's famous experiments in Iowa classrooms have shown that children can quickly develop discriminatory behavior and prejudiced beliefs based on eye color. Conversely, the leadership position that African Americans frequently reached among American Indian nations from Ecuador to the Arctic show that people do not automatically discriminate against others on the basis of skin color.

Events and processes in America history, from the time of slavery to the present, are what explain racism. Not one textbook connects history and racism, however. Half-formed and uniformed notions rush in to fill the analytic vacuum textbooks thus leave. *Adventure's* three sentences imply that it is natural to exclude people whose skin color is different. White student may conclude that all societies are racist, perhaps by nature, so racism is all right. Black students may conclude that all Whites are racist, perhaps by nature, so to be anti-White is all right. The elementary thinking in *Adventure's* three sentences is all too apparent. Yet this is the most substantial treatment of the causes of racism among all twelve textbooks.

In omitting or treating it so poorly, history textbooks shirk a critical responsibility. Not all Whites are or have been racist. Levels of racism have changed over time. If textbooks were to explain this, they would give students some perspective on what caused racism in the past, what perpetuates it today, and how it might be reduced in the future.

Although textbook authors no longer sugarcoat how slavery affected African Americans, they minimize White complicity in it. They present slavery virtually as uncaused, a tragedy, rather than a wrong perpetuated by some people on others. Textbooks maintain the fiction that planters did the work on the plantations. "There was always much work to be done," according to *Triumph of the American Nation*, "for a cotton grower also raised most of the food eaten by his family and slaves." Although managing a business worth hundreds of thousand of dollars was surely time-consuming, the truth as to who did most of the work on the plantation is surely captured more accurately by this quotation from a Mississippi planter lamenting his situation after the war: "I never did a day's work in my life, and don't know how to begin. You see me in these coarse old clothes; well, I never wore coarse clothes in my life before the war."

The emotion generated by textbook descriptions of slavery is sadness, not anger. For there's no one to be angry at. Somehow we ended up with four million slaves in America but no owners! This is part of a pattern in our textbooks: anything bad in American history happened anonymously. Everyone named in our history made a positive contribution (except John Brown, as is explained later). Or as Frances Fitzgerald put it when she analyzed textbooks in 1979, "In all history, there is no known case of anyone's creating a problem for anyone else."

The climate of race relations has improved, owing especially to the civil rights movement. But massive racial disparities remain, inequalities that can only briefly be summarized here. In 1990

John Brown

HISTORICAL PICTURE SERVICES, CHICAGO

African American median family income averaged only 57 percent of White family income; Native Americans and Hispanics averaged about 65 percent as much as Whites. Money can be used to buy many things in our society, from higher SAT scores to the ability to swim, and African American, Hispanic and Native American families lag in their access to all these things. Ultimately, money buys life itself, in the form of better nutrition and heath care and freedom from danger and stress. It should therefore come as no surprise that in 1990 African Americans and Native Americans had median life expectancies at birth that were six years shorter than Whites'.

On average, African Americans have worse housing, lower scores on IQ tests, and higher percentages of young men in jail. The sneaking suspicion that African Americans may be inferior goes unchallenged in the hearts of many Blacks and Whites. It is all too easy to blame the victim and conclude that people of color are themselves responsible for being on the bottom. Without casual historical analysis, these racial disparities are impossible to explain.

When textbooks make racism invisible in American history, they obstruct our already poor ability to see it in the present. The closest they come to analysis is to present a vague feeling of optimism: in race relations, as in everything, our society is constantly getting better. We used to have slavery; now we don't. We used to have lynchings; now we don't. Baseball used to be all White; now it isn't. The notion of progress suffuses textbook treatments of Black-White relations, implying that race relations have somehow steadily improved on their own. This cheery optimism only compounds the problem, because Whites can infer that racism is over. "The U.S. has done more than any other nation in history to provide equal rights for all," *The American Tradition* assures us. Of course, its authors have not seriously considered the levels of human rights in the Netherlands, Lesotho, or Canada today, or in Choctaw society in 1800, because they don't mean their declaration as a serious statement of comparative history — it is just ethnocentric cheerleading.

Educators justify teaching history because it gives us perspective on the present. If there is one issue in the present to which authors should relate the history they tell, the issue is racism. But as long as history textbooks make White racism invisible in the nineteenth century, neither they nor the students who use them will be able to analyze racism intelligently in the present.

ANTI-RACISM: WHERE ARE THE HEROES?

The opposite of racism is anti-racism, of course, or what we might call racial idealism or equalitarianism, and it is still not clear whether it will prevail. In this struggle, our history textbooks offer little help. Just as they underplay White racism, they also neglect racial idealism. In so doing, they deprive students of potential role models to call upon as they try to bridge the new fault lines that will spread out in the future from the great rift in our past.

Consider their treatment of the most radical White anti-racist of them all, John Brown. The treatment of Brown, like the treatment of slavery, has changed in American history textbooks. From 1890 to about 1970, John Brown was insane. Before 1890 he was perfectly sane, and after 1970 he has regained his sanity. Since Brown himself did not change after his death, his sanity provides an inadvertent index of the level of White racism in our society.

Discovering American History describes Brown's 1859 Harpers Ferry raid:

John Brown, son of an abolitionist, envisioned a plan to invade the South and free the slaves. In 1859, with financial support from abolitionists,

Brown made plans to start a slave rebellion in Virginia, to establish a free state in the Appalachian Mountains, and to spread the rebellion through the South. On October 16, 1859, Brown and eighteen of his men captured the federal arsenal at Harpers Ferry, in the present state of West Virginia... He and his men were captured by a force of marines. Brown was brought to trial and convicted of treason against Virginia, murder, and criminal conspiracy. He was hanged on December 2, 1859.

In all, seven of the twelve textbooks take this neutral approach to John Brown. Their bland paragraphs don't imply that Brown was crazy, but neither do they tell enough about him to explain why he became a hero to so many Blacks and nonslaveholding Whites.

Three textbooks still linger in a former era. "John Brown was almost certainly insane," opines *American History. The American Way* tells a whopper: "Later Brown was proved to be mentally ill." The American Pageant has him "deranged," "gaunt," "grim," "terrible," and "crack-brained," "probably of unsound mind," and says that "thirteen of his near relatives were regarded as insane, including his mother and grandmother." Two other books finesse the sanity issue by calling Brown merely "fanatical." No textbook has any sympathy for the man or takes any pleasure in his ideals and actions.

For the benefit of readers who, like me, grew up reading that Brown was at least fanatic if not crazed, let's consider the evidence. To be sure, some of his lawyers and relatives, hoping to save his neck, suggested an insanity defense. But no one who knew Brown thought him crazy. He favorably impressed people who spoke with him after his capture, including his jailer and even reporters writing for Democratic newspapers, which supported slavery. Governor Wise of Virginia called him "a man of clear head" after Brown got the better of him in an informal interview. "They are themselves mistaken who take him to be a madman," Governor Wise said. In his message to the Virginia legislature he said Brown showed "quick and clear perception," "rational premises and consecutive reasoning," "composure and self-possession."

After 1890 textbook authors inferred Brown's madness from his plan, which admittedly was far-fetched. Never mind that John Brown himself presciently told Frederick Douglass that the venture would make a stunning impact even if it failed. Nor that his twenty-odd followers can hardly all be considered crazed too. Rather, we must recognize that the insanity with which historians have charged John Brown was never psychological. It was ideological. Brown's actions made no sense to textbook writers between 1890 and about 1970. To make no sense is to be crazy.

Clearly, Brown's contemporaries did not consider him insane. Brown's ideological influence in the month before his hanging, and continuing after his death, was immense. He moved the boundary of acceptable thoughts and deeds regarding slavery. Before Harpers Ferry, to be an abolitionist was not quite acceptable, even in the North. Just talking about freeing slaves — advocating immediate emancipation — was behavior at the outer limit of the ideological continuum. By engaging in armed action, including murder, John Brown made mere verbal abolitionism seem much less radical.

After an initial shock wave of revulsion against Brown, in the North as well as in the South, Americans were fascinated to hear what he had to say. In his 1859 trial John Brown captured the attention of the nation like no other abolitionist or slave owner before or since. He knew it: "My whole life before had not afforded me one half the opportunity to plead for the right." In his speech to the court on November 2, just before the judge sentenced him to die, Brown argued, "Had I so interfered in behalf of the rich, the powerful, it would have been all right." He referred to the Bible, which he saw in the courtroom, "which teaches me that all things whatsoever I would that men should do to me, I should do even so to them. It teaches me further, to remember them that are in bonds as bound with them. I endeavored to act up to that instruction." Brown went on the claim the high moral ground: "I believe that to have interfered as I have done, as I have always freely admitted I have done, in behalf of His despised poor, I did no wrong but right." Although he objected that his impending death penalty was unjust, he accepted it and pointed to graver injustices: "Now, if it is deemed necessary that I should forfeit my life for the furtherance of the ends of justice, and mingle my blood further with the blood of my children and with the blood of millions in this slave country whose rights are disregarded by wicked, cruel, and unjust enactments, I say, let it be done."

Brown's willingness to go to the gallows for what he thought was right had a moral force of its own. "It seems as if no man had ever died in America before, for in order to die you must first

School children assembled to march in a parade with the scrap metal they have collected for war. San Juan Bautista, California. May, 1942. The photograph exemplifies our multicultural society and also our nationalist education in action.

have lived," Henry David Thoreau observed in a eulogy in Boston. "These men, in teaching us how to die, have at the same time taught us how to live."

Quite possibly textbooks should not portray this murderer as hero, although other murderers, from Christopher Columbus to Nat Turner, get the heroic treatment. However, the flat prose that textbooks use for Brown is not really neutral. Textbook authors' withdrawal of sympathy from Brown is perceptible; their tone in presenting him is different from the tone they employ for almost everyone else. We see this, for instance, in the treatment of his religious beliefs. John Brown was a serious Christian, well read in the Bible, who took its moral commands to heart. Yet our textbooks do not credit Brown with religiosity — subtly they blame him for it. "Believing himself commanded by God to free the slaves, Brown came up with a scheme...," in the words of *Land of Promise*. The *American Pageant* calls Brown "narrowly ignorant," perhaps a euphemism for overly religious, and "God's angry man." "He believed that God had commanded him to free the slaves by force," states

American History. God never commanded Brown in the sense of giving him instructions; rather, Brown thought deeply about the moral meaning of Christianity and decided that slavery was incompatible with it. He was also not "narrowly ignorant," having traveled widely in the United States, England and Europe and talked with many American intellectuals of the day, Black and White.

The textbook's withdrawal of sympathy from Brown in also apparent in what they include and exclude about his life before Harpers Ferry. "In the 1840s he somehow got interested in helping black slaves," according to American Adventures. Brown's interest is no mystery: he learned it from his father, who was a trustee at Oberlin College, a center of abolitionist sentiment. If *Adventures* wanted, it could have related the well-known story about how young John made friends with a Black boy during the War of 1812, a friendship that convinced him that Blacks were not inferior. Instead, its sentence reads like a slur.

Our textbooks also handicap Brown by not letting him speak for himself. Even his jailer let Brown put his pen to paper! *American History* includes three important sentences; American Adventures gives us almost two. *The American Pageant* reprints three sentences from a letter Brown wrote his brother. The other nine books cannot bring themselves to provide even a phrase. Brown's words, which moved a nation, therefore do not move students today.

While John Brown was on trial, the abolitionist Wendell Phillips spoke of Brown's place in history. Phillips foresaw that slavery was a cause whose time was passing, and he asked "the American people" of the future, when slavery was long dead in the "civilization of the twentieth century," this question: "When that day comes, what will be thought of these first martyrs, who teach us how to live and how to die?" Phillips meant the question rhetorically. He never dreamed that Americans would take no pleasure in those who had helped lead the nation to abolish slavery, or that textbooks would label Brown's small band misguided if not fanatic and Brown himself possibly mad.

Anti-racism is one of America's great gifts to the world. Its relevance extends far beyond race relations. Anti-racism led to a "new birth of freedom" after the Civil War, and not only for African Americans. Twice it reinvigorated our democratic spirit, which had been atrophying. Throughout the world, from South Africa to Northern Ireland, movements of oppressed people continue to use tactics and words borrowed from our abolitionist and civil rights movements. Iranians used nonviolent methods borrowed from Thoreau and Martin Luther King, Jr., to overthrow their hated shah. On Ho Chi Minh's desk in Hanoi on the day he died lay a biography of John Brown. Yet we in America seem to have lost these men and women as heroes. Our textbooks need to

present them in such a way that we might again value our own idealism.

Reprinted with permission of the author. Excerpted from Loewen, J. 1995. Lies My Teacher Told Me. *New York: New Press.*

James W. Loewen *is an independent researcher and writer with affiliations at the Catholic University of America and the Smithsonian Institution. He co-wrote the first integrated state history textbook,* Mississippi: Conflict and Change, *and created* The Truth About Columbus, *a subversively true posterbook, which also stemmed from his Smithsonian research on American history textbooks. He is the author of* Lies My Teacher Told Me *originally published by New Press and issued in paperback by Simon and Schuster. E-mail: jloewen@zoo. uvm.edu. Web-site: www.uvm.edu/~jloewen/*

© EARL DOTTER/AMERICAN LABOR, 1989

Singing "We Shall Overcome" with Korean lyrics, hospital workers in South Korea strike for recognition of their union. Management turned firehoses on the sitdown strikers, but later agreed to negotiate when the union said it planned to create an alliance with the University students.

THE MEN

BY E. ETHELBERT MILLER

What then shall we say to this?
If God is for us, who is against us?
                    — Romans 8:31

I

Today I saw black men
carrying babies,
pushing carriages,
holding their own.

II

Our streets filled
with good news,
we must write
the headlines ourselves.

III

When the world
makes a fist
we duck and counterpunch,
we jab and swing.

IV

Black men
at construction sites
lifting black earth,
black hearts, black
hands.

V

The young men
dress in black,
their clothes
just big enough
for love.

E. Ethelbert Miller is *Director of the African American Resource Center at Howard University since 1974. Mr. Miller is the founder of the Ascension Poetry Reading Series, one of the oldest literary series in the Washington, DC area. Mr. Miller has published several books including* Migrant Worker, Season of Hunger/Cry of Rain, Women Surviving Massacres and Men, Where are the Love Poems for Dictators?, First Light *and* Whispers, Secrets and Promises.

Reprinted by permission of the author. "The Men" appears in I Am The Darker Brother *edited by Arnold Adoff (Simon & Schuster, 1997).*

Bias in Children's Movies: Pocahontas

by Tom Roderick, Laura McClure and Chief
Roy Crazy Horse

Pocahontas *Does* Educate — Falsely

by Tom Roderick

In 1995, children across the country packed into movie theaters to see a film in which the hero and heroine, representing peoples of different cultures who are in conflict, urge the leaders of the warring parties to "talk it out." This fall those children will come into our classrooms humming "Colors of the Wind."

Shouldn't we be happy that they were exposed to a message of nonviolence and racial harmony? Aren't we glad that for once there was a Disney cartoon in which the heroine didn't give up everything to run off with the prince? I wish I could answer yes to those questions, but I found the movie "Pocahontas" offensive. My reasons are connected to my understanding of conflict resolution, racial harmony and critical thinking.

On the surface, the film is innocuous enough. While Ratcliffe, the greedy leader of the English settlers, sets his men to ravaging the land in search of gold, Pocahontas is courageous, peace-loving and beautiful. Her father, Powhatan, is wise and flexible. After falling in love, she and John Smith prevent war between the settlers and Powhatan's confederacy. In the final scene, the settlers sail off to England with Ratcliffe in chains, while Pocahontas decides to stay with her people.

If this film were about fictional characters in an imaginary land, then we might indeed be able to take the story at face value and give two cheers to Disney. Pocahontas, however, was a real historical figure, and the Powhatans were and are real people. And so it matters that the film is as historically inaccurate as it seems to be "politically correct."

Pocahontas was a peacemaker, but not quite in the way depicted in the film. Whether she saved Smith or not is a matter of conjecture, but we do know that she was captured by the English at eighteen and held in Jamestown as security for English prisoners. There, colonist John Rolfe received consent to marry her from the governor and from Powhatan. Peace prevailed between the English and Powhatans for eight years thereafter. Pocahontas died in England of smallpox at about age twenty-two.

What is more disturbing than the license the filmmakers took with Pocahontas' life story are the distortions of the larger story of the European invasion. As we know, the English did not sail back to England with their leader in detention, but stayed on to establish tobacco as a cash crop (later bringing in enslaved Africans). Although the settlers' need for corn gave them an interest in peace during the early years, it wasn't long before they began pressing into Native American territory in search of farmland for tobacco. Led by Powhatan's successor, the Powhatans resisted these incursions, and the result was a long, bloody war. By 1644, twenty-seven years after Pocahontas' death, the power of the Powhatan confederacy had been broken.

In view of what really happened to Pocahontas and her people, the film's "pro-social" messages about racial tolerance and talking out disagreements ring hollow. The English invaded the territory they named Virginia, seized the lands that were home to the Powhatans and used force to define their relationship with the Powhatans strictly on their own terms.

To imply, as "Pocahontas" does, that the root of the conflict was a misunderstanding resulting from cultural differences and that each side had equal responsibility for making an enemy of the other is to forget that justice and fair play must form the basis for true racial harmony. Without a willingness to take the other party's needs into account, what is there to talk out, except the terms of surrender? The situation is analogous to wife battering, where negotiation or mediation between husband and wife are simply not appropriate until the physical abuse stops. For the Europeans, profits took precedence over racial harmony. They had the power to enforce their will; and they told the stories from which we and our children derive our cultural myths.

How we understand history affects decisions we make in the here and now. Since millions of young people and adults will see this film, concerns about its distortions of history are completely justified. "Pocahontas" preserves our self-image as a country that never engaged in empire-building and the ravaging of other cultures. The fact that selling this image makes millions for Disney is not a side issue. This perspective keeps us in denial about the plight of Native Americans today and serves the interests of those who want to maintain current economic and political arrangements, keeping the world safe for profit-making by American business.

Disney is not the only company using "entertainment" to promote ideology, but since "Pocahontas" is coming to our classrooms, we might as well take advantage of it. Let's use the film to point out that through "entertaining," the entertainment industry is educating, whether they like it or not. Let's use "Pocahontas" to illustrate the kinds of messages communicated by entertainment products. And let's give our students accurate information about Pocahontas and her people, and engage them in dialogue about the issues the true story raises.

The cliche is that those who do not know history are condemned to repeat it. Our history is more complex than any cartoon rendering, even well-intentioned ones. It is our responsibility as educators to help our students understand those complexities as part of our struggle to create a just, peaceful and truly democratic society.

© 1995 THE WALT DISNEY COMPANY

The Disney image of Pocahontas.

"POCAHONTAS" AS TEACHING TOOL

BY LAURA MCCLURE

The Pocahontas lunchboxes and notebooks and necklaces are everywhere, and some of us have heard boys taunting girls by yelling, "Hey, Pocahontas!" We've seen displays of packaged "Pocahontas" toys appearing in the local supermarkets — including little plastic "Indians" wearing the feather headdresses of traditional Plains Indians (Pocahontas was from an Eastern coastal tribe, the Powhatans). The Mattel toy company has already made over $40 million in Pocahontas sales, and hopes eventually to net as much on Pocahontas tie-in toys as they did on last year's "Lion King." The movie itself had grossed about $125 million by late

July, and for a while the "Pocahontas" soundtrack was number two on the album charts — selling more copies than Michael Jackson's latest.

Kids and adults may find themselves beguiled by the movie "Pocahontas," with its beautiful animation, its romance and its seeming message of peace. In its depiction of Native Americans, the Disney film is an improvement over old stereotypes of bad-guy "Indians" in feather headdresses. In making the film, Disney did consult with Native American activists, including Russell Means, who narrates the voice of Pocahontas' father in the film. But many Native American activists are very troubled by the film.

Teachers may want to use the opportunity presented by "Pocahontas" to help kids learn more about real Native American history, and to talk with young people about the difference between reality and what we see in the movies or on television.

Paula Rogovin, a first-grade teacher who has taught a Native American unit for two decades, sees "Pocahontas" as a chance to open up a good discussion. In talking about the film, Paula says, she wouldn't "just knock the movie down. I would say, 'This movie gave you a lot of information, and let's write down what we learned about Indians from it. After that, you get down to finding out how accurate that depiction really was.'"

After urging Educators for Social Responsibility (ESR) to address the issues raised by "Pocahontas," longtime ESR member Miriam Lyons and her daughter joined a group of ESR staff members to see the movie for ourselves one hot July afternoon. Afterwards we sat down in a coffee shop to talk about what we had seen.

All of us were immediately struck by the Barbie-doll image Disney gave to Pocahontas. She was in reality only 10 or 11 years old when John Smith came to her land; and Native American historians assure us she would not have been wearing a tight-fitting minidress.

Dr. Cornel Pewewardy of Cameron University argues that Pocahontas' Disnified image is "entirely a product of Western colonialism. The Indian princess stereotype is rooted in the legend of Pocahontas and is typically expressed through characters who are maidenly, demure and deeply committed to some White man." Pewewardy, a Comanche-Kiowa who has taught many Native American students, points out that this Hollywood image "forces young viewers to reevaluate their standards of beauty" to conform with "White middle class norms."

At points, the movie does portray some of the colonists as greedy, warrish and racist. This outlook was counterposed with the tolerance and peace urged by Pocahontas and John Smith in the film. But by making Smith himself out to be a peace-loving innocent, the film distorted history beyond recognition. At times, "Pocahontas" made warring Native Americans and English colonizers look like equal offenders, when in reality it was the English who were the aggressors.

The very selection of the mythologized Pocahontas story as a theme is problematic. Robert Eaglestaff, principal of the American Indian Heritage School in Seattle, told the *New York Times* he felt Disney's use of the Pocahontas story was "like trying to teach about the Holocaust and putting in a nice story about Anne Frank falling in love with a German officer. You can't pretend everything was okay between the Germans and the Jews."

Some might view as positive the portrayal of Pocahontas and her people as great respecters of nature, but this too has been turned into a bland stereotype. Pewewardy argues that the old John

Engraving by Simon van de Passe, 1616. As with Disney images, this picture may also be influenced by European perceptions of beauty.

Wayne Western stereotype of "Indians" as "savages" has now "shifted to that of the 'noble savage,' which portrays Indians as part of a once great but now dying culture that could talk to the trees like Grandmother Willow and to the animals like Meeko and Flit."

The film's finale, which seems to imply a joyful "blending" of cultures is a huge distortion of the history of genocide and forced isolation of Native Americans. Today, many Native Americans don't view assimilation as either possible or desirable.

Disney's ultimate goal for the movie was not to teach but to make a profit. Unfortunately, though, it does teach: It reinforces peoples stereotypes and misunderstandings. "Pocahontas" is about "selling the consumer goods based on imposed values," says Pewewardy. "When we challenge the motives, the response from corporations and their marketers is that it is nothing to do with racism, that it's simply good business principles. Disney says it's entertainment -- but at whose expense?"

Pewewardy, a former kindergarten teacher, thinks "Pocahontas" does present an opportunity for teachers to "talk about the issues. But I think that most elementary teachers, before they can even talk about it, need a knowledge base of historical information so that they can start a critical thinking discussion. I'd suggest a nonthreatening discussion of the film with kids about the imagery it uses and about the real people."

Students can research the real Pocahontas story (insofar as it is known) and then compare it to the film which is now at video stores. Seeing the movie on video allows the class to stop the action so they can discuss what's happening.

Paula Rogovin's experience learning about Native Americans with her young students might be helpful.

I usually start out by asking kids, 'What do you know about 'Indians'?' And they'll say, 'Oh, they wear feathers, they chant, they kill children...' They go through this whole horrendous list of what they have learned about Indians, and I write everything down, just so we know where we're starting from. Then I say 'How do you know so much?' And they say, 'Well, we learned from other people, from our parents, from TV, cartoons, shows.' So we make a list of our resources for learning.

Then I draw a TV and I say, 'You know, the cartoons and some of the movies about Indians have told many things that are really not true about Indians. And we are going to find out now what is true and what is not.'

Then Paula's class begins learning about Native American peoples.

Two years ago, Paula's class examined Disney's movie "Peter Pan."

We did an analysis of the section where Peter Pan has a confrontation with a group of Indians -- and it's the most bigoted, stereotypical garbage. The kids sat there with clipboards and with a partner and said, 'That's a stereotype! That's a stereotype!' when they saw the scenes of Indians dancing around a fire doing war whoops with the feathers, the face paint, and the tepees. These were all things we had researched. After that, we took action. We wrote to Disney and asked them to make a new version of the movie. They never answered our letter. But that's okay. We learned something.

POCAHONTAS: THE REALITY

BY CHIEF ROY CRAZY HORSE

This year, Disney decided to release an animated movie about a Powhatan woman known as "Pocahontas." In answer to a complaint by the Powhatan Nation, Disney claims the film is "responsible, accurate and respectful."

We of the Powhatan Nation disagree. The film distorts history beyond recognition. Our offers to assist Disney with historical and cultural accuracy were rejected. Our efforts urging Disney to reconsider its misguided mission were spurned.

"Pocahontas" was a nickname meaning "the naughty one" or "spoiled child." Her real name was Matoaka. The legend is that she saved a heroic John Smith from being clubbed to death by her father in 1607 — she would have been about 10 or 11 at the time. The truth is that Smith's fellow colonists described him as an abrasive, ambitious, self-promoting mercenary soldier.

Of all Powhatan's children, only "Pocahontas" is known, primarily because she became the hero of Euro-Americans as a "good Indian," one who saved the life of a White man. Not only is the "good Indian/bad Indian" theme inevitably given new life by Disney, but the history, as recorded by the English themselves, is badly falsified in the name of "entertainment."

The truth of the matter is that the first time John Smith told the story about his rescue was 17 years after it happened, and it was but one of three reported by the pretentious Smith that he was saved from death by a prominent woman. Yet in an account Smith wrote after his winter stay with Powhatan's people, he never mentioned such an incident. In fact, the starving adventurer reported he had been kept comfortable and treated in a friendly fashion as an honored guest of Powhatan and Powhatan's brother.

Most scholars think the "Pocahontas incident" would have been highly unlikely, especially since it was part of a longer account used as justification to wage war on Powhatan's Nation.

Euro-Americans must ask themselves why it has been so important to elevate Smith's fibbing to status as a national myth worthy of being recycled again by Disney. Disney even improves upon it by changing Pocahontas from a little girl into a young woman.

The true Pocahontas story has a sad ending. In 1612, at the age of 17, Pocahontas was treacherously taken prisoner by the English while she was on a social visit and was held hostage at Jamestown for over a year. During her captivity, a 28-year old widower named John Rolfe took a "special interest" in the attractive young prisoner. As a condition of her release, she agreed to marry Rolfe, who the world can thank for commercializing tobacco. Thus, in April 1614, Matoaka, also known as "Pocahontas" became "Rebecca Rolfe."

Rolfe, his young wife and their son set off for Virginia in March 1617, but "Rebecca" had to be taken off the ship at Gracesend. She died there on March 21, 1617 at the age of 21. It was only after her death and her fame in London society that Smith found it convenient to invent the yarn that she had rescued him.

Chief Powhatan died the following spring of 1618. The people of Smith and Rolfe turned upon the people who had shared their resources with them and had shown them friendship. During Pocahontas' generation, Powhatan's people were decimated and dispersed and their lands were taken over. A clear pattern had been set which would soon spread across the American continent.

DISNEY RESPONDS

"Pocahontas" producer James Pentecost, responded to his critics this way, in the *New York Times* (July 12, 1995):

"Nobody should go to an animated film hoping to get the accurate depiction of history. That's even worse than using Cliff's Notes to rely on giving you an in-depth understanding of a story. More people are talking about Pocahontas than ever talked about her in the last 400 years since she lived. Every time we talk about it, it's an opportunity to talk about what was, what was known about her, and what we created out of our imagination."

Chief Roy Crazy Horse is leader of the Powhatan Renape Nation.

Laura McClure is the Editor and Membership Coordinator for the New York Metropolitan Area chapter of Educators for Social Responsibility.

Tom Roderick is the Executive Director of the New York Metropolitan Area chapter of Educators for Social Responsibility.

Reprinted with permission. This article originally appeared in ESR Action News, *the newsletter of Educators for Social Responsibility (ESR), New York Metropolitan area. E-mail: esrmetro@igc.org*

EDUCATORS FOR SOCIAL RESPONSIBILITY

Educators for Social Responsibility's primary mission is to help young people develop the convictions and skills to shape a safe, sustainable and just world. ESR is nationally recognized for promoting children's ethical and social development through its leadership in conflict resolution, violence prevention, intergroup relations and character education. They support educators and parents with professional development, networks, and instructional materials.

For more information about ESR publications, staff development or local committees contact:

ESR
23 Garden Street
Cambridge, MA, 02138
800-370-2515
www.esrnational.org

So Mexicans Are Taking Jobs from Americans

BY JIMMY SANTIAGO BACA

O Yes? Do they come on horses
with rifles, and say,

        Ese gringo, gimmee your job?
And do you, gringo, take off your ring,
drop your wallet into a blanket
spread over the ground, and walk away?

I hear Mexicans are taking your jobs away.
Do they sneak into town at night,
and as you're walking home with a whore,
do they mug you, a knife at your throat,
saying, I want your job?

Even on TV, an asthmatic leader
crawls turtle heavy, leaning on an assistant,
and from a nest of wrinkles on his face,
a tongue paddles through flashing waves
of lightbulbs, of cameramen, rasping
"They're taking our jobs away."

Well, I've gone about trying to find them,
asking just where the hell are these fighters.

The rifles I hear sound in the night
are white farmers shooting blacks and browns
whose ribs I see jutting out
and starving children,

I see the poor marching for a little work,
I see small white farmers selling out
to clean-suited farmers living in New York,
who've never been on a farm,
don't know the look of a hoof or the smell
of a woman's body bending all day long in fields.

I see this, and I hear only a few people
got all the money in this world, the rest
count their pennies to buy bread and butter.

Below that cool green sea of money,
millions and millions of people fight to live,
search for pearls in the darkest depths
of their dreams, hold their breath for years
trying to cross poverty to just having something.

The children are dead already. We are killing them,
that is what America should be saying;
on TV, in the streets, in offices, should be saying,
    "We aren't giving the children a chance to live."

    Mexicans are taking our jobs, they say instead.
    What they really say is, let them die,
    and the children too.

***Jimmy Santiago Baca**, born in Santa Fe, New Mexico is the author of three books of poetry including* Immigrants in Our Own Lands *and* Martin & Meditations on the South Valley, *for which he won the 1988 American Book Award.*

Reprinted by permission of New Directions Publishing Corporation from Immigrants in Our Own Lands and Selected Early Poems *by Jimmy Santiago Baca* (New Directions Books, 1982).

Arab Stereotypes and American Educators

BY MARVIN WINGFIELD AND BUSHRA KARAMAN

When American children hear the word "Arab," what is the first thing that often comes to mind? It might well be the Arabian Nights fantasy imagery in the Disney film "Aladdin," a film which has been very popular in theaters and on video and is sometimes shown in school classrooms.

Yet Arab Americans have problems with this film. Although in many ways it is charming, artistically impressive and one of the few American films to feature an Arab hero or heroine, a closer look reveals some disturbing features.

The film's light-skinned lead characters, Aladdin and Jasmine, have Anglicized features and Anglo American accents. This is in contrast to the other characters who are dark-skinned, swarthy and villainous — cruel palace guards or greedy merchants with "Arabic" accents and grotesque facial features. The film's opening song sets the tone:

Oh, I come from a land,
From a faraway place
Where the caravan camels roam.
Where they cut off your ear
If they don't like your face.
It's barbaric, but hey, it's home.

Thus the film immediately characterizes the Arab world as alien, exotic and "other." Arab Americans see this film as perpetuating the tired stereotype of the Arab world as a place of deserts and camels, of arbitrary cruelty and barbarism.

Therefore, Arab Americans raised a cry of protest regarding "Aladdin." The American-Arab Anti-Discrimination Committee (ADC) challenged Disney and persuaded the studio to change a phrase in the lyrics for the video version of the film to say: "It's flat and immense, and the heat is intense. It's barbaric, but hey, it's home." While this is an improvement, problems remain.

Former ADC President Candace Lightner, founder of Mothers Against Drunk Driving, comments, "I was angry and embarrassed when I listened to the "Aladdin" lyrics while watching the movie. I could only hope that the audience was not paying close attention and would not take home with them a poor image of the Arab world." She adds, "I only wish Disney had consulted us first before they developed a movie reaching millions of people based on our culture. This is why there is an ADC."

Grassroots protest has also been successful in combatting the troubling elements of this film. In Illinois a 10-year old Arab American girl persuaded a music teacher leading the school chorus to discard the offensive "Aladdin" lyrics — although she had to explain three times why the lyrics were offensive before the teacher "got it."

Arabs In Popular Culture

Disney is by no means the only offender. Popular culture aimed at children is replete with negative images of Arab women as belly dancers and harem girls, and Arab men as violent terrorists, oil "sheiks" and marauding tribesmen who kidnap blond Western women.

Arabs are frequently cast as villains in Saturday morning TV cartoons — Fox Children Network's "Batman," for example. This cartoon portrayed fanatic, dark-complexioned Arabs armed with sabers and rifles as allies of an "alien" plotting to take over the Earth.

A few years ago, Spencer Gift stores sold "Arab" Halloween masks with grotesque physical features, along with their usual array of goblin, demon and vampire masks. The chain stocked no other ethnic masks.

Comic books frequently have Arab villains as a gratuitous element in their story line such as: Tarzan battles with an Arab chieftain who kidnaps Jane; Superman foils Arab terrorists hijacking a U.S. nuclear carrier or the Fantastic Four combat a hideous oil sheik supervillain. But, as Lebanese American media analyst Jack Shaheen comments, "There is never an Arab hero for kids to cheer." (Shaheen, 1980.)

Negative portraits of Arabs are found in numerous popular films, such as *True Lies*, *Back to the Future* and *Raiders of the Lost Ark*.

Numerous computer games on the market feature cartoon Arab villains. Children rack up high scores and win the games by "killing Arabs."

Ethnic stereotypes are especially harmful in

© BRUCE HARKNESS

the absence of positive ethnic images. Shaheen observes that in the media Arabs are "hardly ever seen as ordinary people, practicing law, driving taxis, singing lullabies or healing the sick." (Shaheen, 1988.)

ARAB STEREOTYPES AMONG EDUCATORS

Popular films and television imprint young children with numerous negative images of Arabs, and American educators do not do enough to correct this bias. Many do not even perceive anti-Arab racism as a problem. Educators who have not yet been alerted to this issue and are unaware of the potential harm being done are themselves part of the problem.

Despite the multicultural philosophy that currently prevails in American education, ADC has found many teachers and the public at large not yet sufficiently sensitized to the problem of anti-Arab and anti-Muslim stereotyping. While multicultural articles, books and curriculum teaching units may deal with the heritage of African American, Hispanic, Native American and Asian/Pacific American cultures, it is not unusual for them to ignore Arabs and the Middle East. One educator in Fairfax County, Virginia, commented that "The kids from the Middle East are the lost sheep in the school system. They fall through the cracks in our categories."

The Middle East Studies Association (MESA) and the Middle East Outreach Council (MEOC) have researched history and geography textbooks, and found "an over portrayal of deserts,

camels and nomads" in the chapters on the Middle East. Even some well-intentioned teachers use the Bedouin image as somehow typifying "Arab culture." In fact, only about 2% of Arabs are traditional Bedouin, and today there are probably more Arab engineers and computer operators than desert dwellers.

American textbooks are often Eurocentric, while Arab points of view regarding such issues as the nationalization of resources or the Arab-Israeli conflict are presented inadequately or not at all. The MESA/MEOC study concludes that "the presentation of Islam is so problematic that it is perhaps time for educators at the college and university level to send a red alert to their colleagues at the pre-collegiate level. Crude errors and distortions abound." (Barlow, 1994.) Some textbooks link Islam to violence and intolerance, ignoring its commonalities with Christianity and Judaism. While from a contemporary ecumenical or interfaith perspective, Yahweh, God the Father, and Allah (the generic word for God in Arabic) can be regarded as one God, textbooks sometimes discuss Allah as if the word referred to an alien god remote from Jewish and Christian tradition.

EFFECTS OF STEREOTYPING ON ARAB AMERICAN CHILDREN

What does it feel like for Arab American children to grow up surrounded by a culture that does not recognize their ethnic identity in a positive way? They may find that the messages about the Arab world in school conflict with the values and traditions passed on at home. The images of Arabs which are conveyed in the classroom may have nothing in common with their relatives and experiences at home, with their friends in the neighborhood, at their church/mosque or elsewhere. They also find their peers to be influenced by negative and inaccurate images and preconceptions about the Arab heritage. Obviously these circumstances will lead to hurtful experiences.

Dr. Shaheen remembers being taught in his Lebanese American home to be proud of his family's Arab heritage. But at school, he remembers teasing, taunts and epithets: "camel jockeys," "desert niggers," "greasy Lebs."

Shaheen reports that his children were deeply upset when eight students in the annual Halloween parade at their school dressed up as "Arabs," "with accessories such as big noses, oil cans or money bags to complete the costume." Later, at

© BRUCE HARKNESS

the school's ethnic festival, "our children were hesitant to wear ethnic costumes," he said. (Shaheen, 1980.)

Others report similar incidents. Carol Haddad, a second-generation American of Lebanese and Syrian ancestry, describes her experience at age ten: "Each time I left the security of my family house, I experienced the oppression of being darker and different." Her family was stared at on the street, and Irish and German American children in her neighborhood mocked her family for "eating leaves" when they served grape leaves stuffed with lamb, rices and spices. During an argument, a boy in her neighborhood called her a "nigger." (Haddad, 1994.)

An ADC staffer recalls that, when she was growing up, her class was taught about Jewish culture. "We danced the hora and I came home singing Jewish songs." But there was no equivalent teaching about Arab culture. "My father was so mad!"

Like other ethnics, Arab Americans frequently encounter negative stereotypes disguised in the form of "humor." When they object, they are told that the derogatory comments were "not meant to be taken seriously." Today there should be greater public awareness and acknowledgment that not

taking the identity of others seriously is just another form of racism.

More dangerous were the numerous incidents of anti-Arab hostility during the Gulf war with Iraq when schools and communities were swept by patriotic fervor. The flags, banners, yellow ribbons, patriotic songs and speakers from the military undermined teachers' efforts to encourage critical thinking about news reports and official statements. There was little chance of understanding Arab society or the humanity of the Iraqi people. Arab American students often felt intimidated and silenced, although the presence of students of Arab origin in classes served to heighten teachers' sensitivity to the human dimension of the conflict. (Knowles, 1993; Merryfield, 1993.)

In Dearborn, Michigan, a proposal was brought before the Wolverine A basketball conference to disband all sports competition for the year. Some schools did not want to play with the team from Fordson High School, where half of the students and most of the basketball team were Arab. Students from Fordson were told, "Go back to Saudi Arabia. You're not wanted here." A bomb threat was reported at the school. Students also reported fights with students from other schools during the previous year. (McCabe, 1991.)

Often as they mature, Arab American young people consciously reclaim their ethnic identity. Lisa Suhair Majaj, a Palestinian American doctoral student, at the University of Michigan, observes that "Once I claimed a past, spoke my history, and told my name, the walls of incomprehension and hostility rose, brick by brick: unfunny ethnic jokes, jibes about terrorists and kalashnikovs, about veiled women and camels; or worse, the awkward silences, the hasty shifts to other subjects. Searching for images of my Arab self in American culture I found only unrecognizable stereotypes. In the face of such incomprehension I could say nothing." (Majaj, 1994.)

EFFECTS ON SOME ARAB AMERICAN STUDENTS AND SOME CLASSROOM SOLUTIONS

What effect does this stereotyping have on the increasing numbers of Arab American students in U.S. schools. What can classroom teachers do about these problems? The following suggestions may help educators correct the bias.

It is recognized that the more positive a student's self-concept, the higher his or her achievement level will be. Teachers use various techniques to make students feel worthy and important. But when Arab students see negative and erroneous portrayals of Arabs in films and on television, they begin to feel inferior and ashamed, or perhaps belligerent and aggressive.

Students suffer as a result of this. And learning suffers. Caught in this spiral, Arab American students may begin to believe that they, as a people, are inferior. They may stop trying to do their best and become convinced that they can never amount to anything. For many it becomes a self-fulfilling prophecy. As educators we must break this cycle by finding ways to intervene effectively.

In Dearborn, Michigan the schools' bilingual programs use Arab language and literature to make students from homes in which Arabic is spoken feel more culturally comfortable. Special programs, however, are not enough. It is important for mainstream teachers to consciously rid themselves of negative and ill-informed media images of Arabs (and other ethnic groups). It is also important for them to learn about their students' histories and cultures and to be prepared to teach

© BRUCE HARKNESS

about them in their classes.

The historic achievements of Arab culture are rarely discussed in American schools or are perhaps limited to 6th and 10th grade world history courses. In the culturally sensitive classroom, there is no good reason why a historical and cultural dimension cannot be provided for classes in mathematics, for example. Math teachers can explain the cultural origins or development of "Arabic numerals," the decimal system, geometry and al-jabr (algebra) in ancient Greece, India and the medieval Arab world. Science teachers can present the history of astronomy in ancient Babylon, Hellenic culture, and medieval Arab civilization as the precursor of modern science. Music classes can teach about Arabic music. Home economics classes can teach about Arab cuisine and its cultural meanings.

The Arabic language, a major world language, is spoken by some 200 million people. The Middle East is a region of vital political, economic and strategic importance for the United States. Yet the Arabic language is taught in only a handful of U.S. schools. Even in Dearborn, where 30% of the students are Arab, Arabic is offered only in the high schools of East Dearborn attended by the Arab students. It is not offered in West Dearborn schools with a higher proportion of non-Arabs.

In schools with minority populations, teachers should make a particular effort to abandon political and cultural biases and build on students' personal histories and existing knowledge bases, rather than ignoring them or minimizing their importance. Dearborn schools have made an attempt to build on the existing strengths of the students, including their Arabic language skills.

Only when educators regard Arab students as having a rich and living culture, separate and distinct from the popular media images, can we have a proud new Arab American generation. And only then can we begin to liberate other American young people from the negative and distorted stereotypes of Arabs.

© National Council for the Social Studies. Reprinted by permission.

Marvin Wingfield is the Director of Educational Programs at the American-Arab Anti-Discrimination Committee (ADC). ADC is the largest grassroots Arab-American organization in the U.S. It is a nonsectarian, nonpartisan organization dedicated to the promotion of the civil and legal rights of people of Arab descent, including resistance to racism, discrimination and stereotyping of Arab Americans. ADC has an active outreach program to educators. For more information, contact: ADC, 4201 Connecticut Ave. NW, Suite 500, Washington, DC 20008, 202-244-2990.

Bushra Karaman, a Palestinian American teacher, is a resource consultant for the public schools in Dearborn, Michigan, the home of the largest population of Arab-Americans in the United States.

REFERENCES

Barlow, E., ed. 1994. *Evaluation of secondary-level textbooks for coverage of the Middle East and North Africa*. Ann Arbor, MI/ Tucson, AZ: Middle East Studies Association/Middle East Outreach Council. An analysis of 77 high school geography and world history textbooks.

Hayes, J. R., ed. 1983. *The genius of Arab civilization*. Cambridge, MA: MIT Press. These essays cover Arabic literature, philosophy, history, art, music, science, technology, and commerce.

Haddad, C. 1994. "In search of home." *Food for our grandmothers: Writings by Arab-American and Arab-Canadian feminists*, Kadi, J., ed. Boston, MA: South End Press. A personal account.

Kadi, J., ed. 1994. *Food for our grandmothers: Writings by Arab-American and Arab-Canadian feminists*. Boston, MA: South End Press. This book is an excellent collection of essays, poems and recipes, with sensitive autobiographical accounts that are at once "personal and political."

Knowles, T. 1993. "A missing piece of heart: Children's perceptions of the Persian Gulf War of 1991." *Social Education*. 57.1: 19-22.

Macron, M. 1992. "Arab contributions to civilization". Washington, DC: ADC Research Institute. A concise essay.

Majaj, L.S. 1994. "Boundaries: Arab/American." *Food for our grandmothers*, J. Kadi, ed. Boston, MA: South End Press, 65-86. A personal account.

McCabe, M. 1991. "Fordson confronts prejudice." *Detroit Free Press*. January 18:1E, 3E.

McCarus, E., ed. 1994. *The Development of Arab-American identity*. Ann Arbor, MI: University of Michigan Press.

Merryfield, M. M. 1993. "Responding to the Gulf War: A case study in instructional decision making." *Social Education*. 57(1): 33-41.

Shaheen, J. 1991. "The comic book Arab." *The Link*. 24(5): 1-11. A brief essay.

—— 1980. "The Influence of the Arab stereotype on American children." Washington, DC: American-Arab Anti-Discrimination Committee. A brief essay.

—— 1988. "The Media's image of Arabs." *Newsweek*. February 29:10 (Jack Shaheen, a Fulbright scholar, is one of the foremost analysts of the image of Arabs in the media. He was formerly Professor of Mass Communications at Southern Illinois University at Edwardsville. He is also the author of The TV Arab and is preparing a book on "the Hollywood Arab.")

Tobenkin, D. 1994. "Arab-American groups lobby for changes." Broadcasting and Cable. July 11.

MEDIA MYTHS CONTRIBUTE TO HUNGER IN AFRICA

BY DEBORAH MENKART

For many of us growing up in North America, our images of contemporary Africa have been shaped by front page photos of starving children, dying in their emaciated mother's arms. If there is any help in sight it is a White relief worker, bringing badly needed food or medical supplies. Other news photos feature wealthy African leaders. Consciously or subconsciously, we are left with an image of Africa as "backward", "corrupt" and in need of European and North American "assistance." No historical explanations are provided for the current economic and social crisis, so the reader is left to wonder, "What is wrong with *them*?" Even a class on the achievements of ancient African civilizations does not equip us to challenge the stereotypes about contemporary Africa.

This lesson is designed to help students analyze the hunger crisis in Africa from a global and historical perspective. It will counteract racist stereotypes about Africa and other regions of the world which suffer from the impact of neocolonialism. It can be used as an introductory lesson to a study of bias in the media or a study of any region of Africa.

OBJECTIVES

▸ Students will gain an understanding of the historical and contemporary causes of hunger in Africa

▸ Students will be able to identify Eurocentric biases in media reports on Africa

PROCEDURE

1. Introduce the lesson by asking students what words and images come to mind when they think about Africa. Invariably, hunger and starvation will be some of the terms students suggest. Tell them that you will focus on the image of hunger for this lesson.

2. Explain that it is true that hunger is a major problem in Africa (and has become increasingly so over the last 20 years), however it is very important to understand the root causes. Tell them that it is also important to know that in many areas of Africa food is as abundant as it is in the United States. Display photos to demonstrate this fact.

3. Place the three points listed below on the board. Ask students to vote for which one they consider to be the greatest cause of hunger in Africa today. Have students discuss the list in pairs first before they vote. Record the number of votes for each cause:

▸ Nature (droughts and other natural disasters)

▸ Overpopulation

▸ Corrupt local and national African governments

4. Announce that the students will have the opportunity to check their own answers. You will share with them a reading on the roots of hunger in Africa by Kevin Danaher and Abikok Riak. Before looking at the reading, point out that as we discuss this issue it is important to differentiate between famine and hunger. As Barbara Brown of the Boston University African Studies Center explains, "famine is an acute phase and hunger is a long-term problem. Even if famine relief is shipped in and adequately distributed, most people will continue to die of hunger, because hunger occurs in non-famine situations. Famines receive much attention from the media and relief agencies, but we need to address the crisis of hunger."

5. Divide the class into five groups. Have each group read one of the responses to the myths and develop a skit or poster to teach what they have learned to the rest of the class.

6. Then ask students to develop a post-list of what they now consider to be the major causes of hunger in Africa. Compare these to the list and votes and the beginning of this lesson. It is likely that they will identify a number of factors that they had not considered before. They will also see that there are many myths about hunger in Africa and that the issue is complicated. Ask students to write about how their understanding of the hunger crisis in Africa has changed as a result of this lesson.

7. The next step is to examine how our major sources of information present this issue. Have available social studies textbooks from different grade levels in your school which include Africa. Also bring in (or have students collect, depending on how much time you have available) an assort-

ment of articles on hunger in Africa from news journals such as *Time* and *Newsweek* and major newspapers. Divide the materials among small groups of students and ask them to evaluate the information and analysis presented in their book or article. Does it help the reader get a good understanding of the history, complexity and reality of the situation? Does it reinforce stereotypes? Which perspectives are included? Which are excluded?

8. Discuss why the media and textbooks present the perspective that they do. Who benefits and who loses from such a perspective? How have opinions in this country been shaped by the media? (If time permits, students could conduct a survey in their school and/or of their family members similar to the one conducted at the beginning of this lesson.)

9. If students determine that the resources they have examined present a stereotyped or inaccurate picture of the roots of hunger, ask them to: (a) plan how to teach other students at school about the realities of hunger in African and/or (b) share their critique in some way to the textbook or newspaper publishers.

ACKNOWLEDGMENT

Barbara Brown, Outreach Director of the Boston University African Studies Center, provided extensive feedback and resources for this lesson. She developed a similar lesson for use with teachers. For more information: African Studies Center, 270 Bay State Road, Boston, MA 02215, 617-353-3673. E-mail: buasc@acs.bu.edu

REFERENCES

The editors do not provide a list of books on Africa in this reference list because it could not compare with the detailed, annotated list provided by the Africa Access Review listed below. On the topic of hunger, we recommend the teaching guide by Kempf. Catalogs and journals with more information about Africa are listed in the Resource Guide.

Danaher, K. and Abikok Riak. 1995. *Backgrounder: Myths of African hunger.* SF: Food First/Institute for Food and Development Policy. This publication is the handout for this lesson. Food First produces many excellent documents for the lay-reader of the global economy and food. To get a free list of their resources, contact Food First, 398 60th Street, Oakland, CA 94618, 510-654-4400.

Kempf, S. 1997. *Finding solutions to hunger: A sourcebook for middle and upper high school teachers.* NY: World Hunger This curricula encourages students to discover causes and misconceptions about hunger, with anecdotes, role plays, simulations and statistics. Reproducible handouts, resource guide and glossary. Order from NECA.

Randolph, B. 1992. *Africa access review of K-12 materials.* Silver Spring, MD: Africa Access. Detailed, critical annotations of over 200 print and audiovisual materials for teaching about Africa from K-12. This is an essential resource for every school library and social studies department. Order from NECA.

Below is an additional, optional handout for students.

A RADICAL CHALLENGE TO SEVEN MYTHS ABOUT AFRICAN FAMINES

BY LIDWIEN KAPTEIJNS

1. African famines are **NOT** merely due to a deteriorating climatological and ecological environment. They are a function of an international division of labor which operates at Africa's expense.

2. Africans are **NOT** dying because they have not yet become "modern." Starvation is the price they pay for belonging to a modern economy imposed upon them during the colonial period.

3. Africans have **NOT** always starved in large numbers. While famines and epidemics are not unknown in the pre-colonial period, the frequency and scale of current famines have their roots in the complete reorientation of African economies by colonial powers.

4. Africans are **NOT** dying because they are not producing, but because they are producing for the needs of a world market that does not pay fair prices for their products.

5. Africa is **NOT** starving because it fails to curb a traditional, irrationally high birth rate. High birth rates were a relatively recent and rational response to the labor demands of a colonial economy that was not willing to pay for the reproduction and sustenance of its labor force.

6. African governments **CANNOT** be absolved from responsibility for exacerbating famine. However, corruption and tyranny are often encouraged by foreign alliances and politically motivated aid programs.

7. African famines will **NOT** just go away because private citizens in the North Atlantic world open their hearts and purses. While our generosity can save those who are threatened by starvation now, long-term solutions depend on narrowing the gap in wealth between the richer, more industrialized nations and the poorer, less industrialized nations.

MYTHS OF AFRICAN HUNGER

BY KEVIN DANAHER AND ABIKOK RIAK
INSTITUTE FOR FOOD AND DEVELOPMENT POLICY BACKGROUNDER

In 1990, approximately 4.2 million African children died as a result of malnutrition-related disease. An additional 30 million were underweight.[1] In the public discussion of African hunger, many myths and misconceptions have been created about why so many Africans go hungry. For those of us who want to put an end to needless suffering, it is important to understand the real causes of hunger in Africa.

MYTH ONE: NATURE IS THE MAIN CAUSE OF FAMINE IN AFRICA.

Drought and other natural disasters in many parts of Africa have intensified hunger, but poverty is the real cause of famine. Only the chronically impoverished die from the effects of drought, and Africa's impoverishment has been several hundred years in the making.

As European countries colonized Africa, they disrupted farming and herding systems that for centuries Africans had adapted to changing environmental conditions. Ecologically balanced food systems were undermined: the best agricultural lands were taken for growing coffee, sugar cane, cocoa, and other export crops that were viewed as the means to economic development according to the neoclassical theory of comparative advantage. Private and government funds were invested to develop these cash crops, while food production for the poor majority was neglected.

Colonial cash cropping ravaged the soil, reducing large areas to desert and semidesert. Millions of acres of brush and trees were cleared, robbing the soil of organic replenishment. Export crops such as cotton, peanuts, and tobacco absorbed large amounts of nutrients from the soil. After each year's harvest, the soil was left bare and unprotected leading to accelerated erosion.[2] As more land was put in cash crops, small farmers have been pushed further and further onto marginal land with scarce rainfall, decreasing their ability to produce food. It is this unfortunate, yet avoidable situation that has contributed to drought-induced famine.

Using the best land for export agriculture degraded the environment and impoverished the rural agricultural population, forcing many to work on plantations or crowd into cities seeking employment. Plantation owners and other commercial interests developed a large labor force that could be paid low wages, thus ensuring high profits.

Poor rainfall and other environmental hazards are indeed troublesome for farmers throughout the world. They push people into famine, however, where farmers and pastoralists have been made vulnerable by economic and political structures that impoverish the many while enriching the few.

[Editors' note: It is also important to consider what Jim Pritchett describes as the "myth of tropical exuberance." This is the myth that Africa was or is a tropical land of plenty where fruit just drops from the trees; and that therefore Africans have not developed good farming methods and need foreign consultants to teach them. In reality, much of the continent has always been a difficult place to farm. If available (maybe from a science or geography teacher), take a look at soil and weather maps of Africa to get an appreciation for the challenges farmers face. Africans have used great skill and energy to farm under these constraints. Therefore the impact of colonialism is all the more devastating. The methods developed by African farmers allowed for the long term use of the land. The practice of colonialism was to look only to the short term profit, undermining region specific methods developed by African farmers.]

MYTH TWO: AFRICAN HUNGER IS CAUSED BY OVERPOPULATION.

Contrary to popular opinion, hunger is not caused by extreme population density. If it were, we would expect to find widespread hunger in densely populated countries like Japan and the Netherlands and little or no hunger in sparsely populated countries like Senegal and Zaire where, in fact, malnutrition and hunger are widespread.[3]

Africa is not densely populated. Compare Africa's 23.7 persons per square kilometer to Europe's 108.6 and Asia's 122.9.[4] But of all continents, Africa ranks last in the use of irrigation, fertilizers, and tractors.[5] The problem is not a shortage of land but a shortage of money, training, and appropriate technology to develop the land.

Africans use a very small percentage of the globe's resources. For example, Africa's 600 million people (11.3 percent of the world's population) consume just 2.4 percent of the world's commercial energy, while the USA's 260 million people (4.9 percent of the world's population) consume 25.1 percent.[6]

It is true that Africa's population growth rate (3.0% per year) is higher than that of any other continent. It is important, however, for us to understand the real relationship between high population growth rates and hunger. High population growth rates do not cause hunger. Rather, they are both consequences of social inequities that deprive the poor majority — especially women — of the security and economic opportunity necessary for them to choose to have fewer children.

Having large families is a logical response to the conditions of poverty under which most Africans live. On the small family farms that produce most of Africa's food, the most important input is family labor. The high birth rate is partly a response by parents to this need for farm labor.

With the world's highest rate of death for children aged 0-4, Africa's high infant mortality rates lead to an even greater number of births as parents try to compensate.[7] For some mothers, however, the burden of raising another child under difficult circumstances is outweighed by the eventual benefits of another laborer in the family.

Data from around the world shows a close connection between rising living standards and falling birth rates.[8] If African parents were assured their children would survive, they would not need to have so many. If parents could earn enough from their labor, and were assured of support in old age, they would see it as being in their own interest to limit their number of children. And if women were empowered as equal members of society, they would be able to make better use of family planning technology.

The key problem is not too many people, it's too much inequality.

MYTH THREE: AFRICAN GOVERNMENTS BEAR THE MAIN RESPONSIBILITY FOR DECLINING FOOD PRODUCTION.

To lay all the blame on African governments is to imply that they alone control the destiny of their countries. The forces that have institutionalized hunger in Africa are made up of transnational corporations, Western governments, international agencies and African elites as well as the governments. Together they form a coalition whose life-styles and interests are very different from those of Africa's rural majority.

Over the decades, this coalition has implemented policies that have undermined food crops. Prices paid to farmers have been kept artificially low, thus providing cheap food to people in the cities, which reduced the likelihood of urban unrest and allowed urban employers to pay lower wages, but also stifled incentives for increased food production.[9] Policy makers direct most agricultural assistance to cash crops, mainly benefiting large commercial interests. For example, with the implementation of structural adjustment programs in the 1980s, credit availability for small farmers has decreased dramatically.

The fact that policy making is dominated by men, while most food (80%) is produced by women, also helps explain the low priority given to food crops. Most agricultural training and development assistance is directed towards men, neglecting women farmers. For example, agricultural extension services traditionally have been staffed by men, for men. A recent Food and Agriculture Organization (FAO) study found that under 11 percent of agricultural extension workers are women.[10]

But food production can be increased, as developments in Zimbabwe have shown. After years of guerrilla war against a White minority government, Zimbabwe achieved independence in 1980. During the first few years the government of Robert Mugabe raised the price paid for food crops and gave small farmers credit so that they could purchase seeds, fertilizers, and tools. Although they did not reach all the family farmers in need, these programs led to a massive increase in food production. In 1985, despite several years of drought, small farmers not only fed their families, but they marketed twice as much as before, exporting to neighboring countries.[11]

Africa is a diverse continent with over 50 governments ranging from some who are blatantly anti-farmer to those genuinely trying to help the poor majority. But in every nation it can be said that only when the majority gain control of their country's resources will we see an end to policies that systematically impoverish people and leave them vulnerable to natural disasters.

MYTH FOUR: THE "FREE MARKET" HOLDS THE SOLUTION TO AFRICA'S FOOD PROBLEMS.

Most people fail to realize that the world market is Africa's worst enemy. Almost all African countries are dependent on exporting minerals and cash crops. While real prices in the world market for these commodities have declined during the post-World War II period, the prices of manufactured imports from industrialized countries have steadily increased.[12]

Throughout sub-Saharan Africa, low commodity prices have affected markets and local communities that depend on a very narrow range of exports. Most Africans find themselves in what Oxfam calls a "trade trap" where they are forced to produce cash crops for income that is so low, they continue to live their lives in abject poverty.[13] In Côte d' Ivoire, exports of coffee rose by 26 percent in volume but fell by 21 percent in value between 1988 and 1990.[14] Similarly, in Rwanda, export earnings declined by 50 percent between 1987 and 1991.[15]

Recent studies have shown that under the Uruguay Round of the General Agreement on Tariffs and Trade (GATT), Africa will suffer more than any other geographical region. With the loss of special trading rights with the European Community (EC) and cuts in agricultural subsidies, it is estimated that Africa will lose an additional 3 billion dollars in trade income each year.[16]

The deterioration of Africa's terms of trade means that most African governments have been forced to spend more in the world market than they earn. They have filled this gap by borrowing. By 1992, external debt for sub-Saharan Africa was over $200 billion-a debilitating number that represents 109 percent of its GNP, an 80 percent increase since 1980.[17] The World Bank has concluded that "the bite that debt-service payments take out of a country's capacity to import each year is clearly unsustainable in an environment of low investment and stagnant GDP."[18]

The world financial system is a greater cause of hunger in Africa than is bad weather. Forced to produce foreign-exchange earning crops to pay off unpayable debts, African nations find themselves importing more and more food. Food imports, currently estimated at 10 percent of total imports, place considerable strain on Africa's balance of payments.[19]

Markets allocate food according to wealth, not nutritional need. The few large corporations that control 85 to 90 percent of world grain shipments are concerned with profits, not hunger. It is a cruel irony that 37 percent of world grain consumed goes to feed livestock, while widespread hunger affects millions of Africans.[20] We also find an increasing trend toward the substitution of grains in eastern and southern Africa. In Sudan, Tanzania and South Africa the production of wheat and rice for wealthy and upper classes has increased relative to the production of staple grains such as sorghum and millet, which are the staples of the poor majority. A similar trend exists in Kenya and Zimbabwe, where there has been a significant increase in the acreage used to grow export crops.[21]

Policy makers claim that economic progress will be achieved if markets are left alone. But the problem is not market intervention per se, it is the way in which institutions and governments intervene — against the interests of the poor majority, in favor of the rich and powerful. Markets can be tamed to serve the interests of the majority, but only when governments and institutions are genuinely committed to the poor.

MYTH FIVE: U.S. FOREIGN AID IS HELPING AFRICA'S HUNGRY.

The United States has donated large amounts of emergency food to Africa, food that has undoubtedly saved thousands of lives. But while it is essential to help people in need, we must remember that food aid, at best, only treats the symptoms of hunger and poverty, not its causes.

As discussed in Food First books *Aid as Obstacle* and *Betraying the National Interest*, most food aid from the U.S. government is not even intended for the hungry.[22] It is purchased by foreign governments using money loaned by the United States. Recipient governments then sell the food on the open market, which means the poor do not benefit.

Food aid can undermine local food production by flooding local markets and depressing food prices. Dumping large quantities of low-priced grain or other commodities can make it impossible for small farmers to compete in the marketplace. In Burkina Faso, heavily subsidized wheat from the EC is sold at about a third lower than the cost of producing and marketing locally grown staples such as sorghum and millet.[23] In addition, pastoralists in the Sahel region have seen their regional livestock trade fall by one-third due to the recent dumping of cheap EC beef on the local market.[24] Food aid can also create dependence on foreign aid or be used by recipient governments to manipulate the poor.

The concentration of U.S. aid on only a few countries shows that its objectives are strategic rather than humanitarian. Of all the U.S. aid to Africa, 60 percent goes to just one country: Egypt. Of U.S. aid to the 53 African countries other than Egypt, nearly one-half, (45 percent) goes to just six countries (South Africa, Mozambique, Ethiopia, Senegal, Liberia and Zambia).[25] These countries contain only

22 percent of Africa's population, and their governments historically did not follow policies favoring the majority, though they did have naval bases, CIA listening posts, and other strategic assets.

U.S. foreign aid has occasionally been eliminated to punish governments that refused to toe the U.S. line. Both Zimbabwe and Mozambique, for example, were cut off from U.S. food aid when their governments criticized U.S foreign policy. While punishing governments that have demonstrated a commitment to helping the poor, Washington has lavished aid on corrupt regimes such as those of Samuel Doe in Liberia, Mobutu Sese Seko in Zaire and Siad Barre in Somalia. In exchange for naval and military bases at the strategic Red Sea port of Berbera, the U.S. granted Somalia millions of dollars in economic and military aid, which in the early 1990s was used by the Barre government to wage war on its own people. This brutality by the U.S.-backed government ignited the civil war that destroyed Somalia as a nation.

Nearly all U.S. foreign aid is directed to repressive elites who have enriched the few while impoverishing the many. They use U.S. aid money to strengthen their hold on power. Given the undemocratic nature of these regimes, U.S. aid is more likely to perpetuate hunger and poverty than eliminate it.

SIGNS OF HOPE

Although economic and social conditions in Africa are worse now than twenty years ago, with real incomes at their lowest, and hunger and malnutrition at their highest, we must not lose sight of the positive developments that have taken place in Africa within the past few years. Armed conflict has come to an end in Angola, Ethiopia, Eritrea, and Mozambique, opening up new opportunities for growth and development. In South Africa, the demise of apartheid and the inauguration of Nelson Mandela as president also represent hope in a historically oppressive region. Grassroots organizations such as women's cooperatives, health initiatives and environmental movements have emerged as alternatives to elite coalitions and their failed top-down policies. In the face of formidable domestic obstacles such as limited resources, widespread poverty, government repression, and the international obstacles of trade and structural adjustment programs, these organizations represent hopeful attempts at development from the ground up. It is for this reason we as concerned citizens need to challenge those international institutions and policies that hinder the advancement of grassroots organizations.

Kevin Danaher is the Director of Public Education at Global Exchange in San Francisco. Abikok Riak is a research intern at Food First.

©Institute for Food and Development Policy (Food First)

NOTES

1. Oxfam UK. 1993. *Africa, make or break: Action for recovery,* Oxfam UK, 1.

2. See Chapters 3 and 4 of Richard W. Franke and Barbara H. Chasin, *Seeds of famine: Ecological destruction and the development dilemma in the West African Sahel.* Montclair, NJ: Allanheld Osmun, 1980.

3. For a more detailed analysis of the relationship between population growth and hunger, see Frances Moore Lappé and Joseph Collins, *World hunger: Twelve myths* (New York: Grove Press/Food First Books, 1986) See also Frances Moore Lappé and Rachel Schurman, *Taking population seriously* (San Francisco: Institute for Food and Development Policy, 1990).

4. World Resources Institute, *World Resources 1994-1995,* (New York: Oxford University Press, 1994), 284-285.

5. *World Resources 1994-1995,* 264-265.

6. *World Resources 1994-1995,* 334-335.

7. UNICEF, *State of the world's children,* 1994 (Oxford: Oxford University Press, 1994), 82.

8. *Hunger 1995: Causes of hunger* (Silver Springs: Bread for the World, 1994), 63.

9. For details see Robert H. Bates, *Markets and states in tropical Africa: The Political basis of agricultural policies* (Berkeley: University of California Press, 1981).

10. *World Resources 1994-1995,* 48-49.

11. Oxfam UK, 29.

12. Coote, Belinda. *The Trade trap: Poverty and the global commodity markets* (Oxford: Oxfam, 1992), 8.

13. Ibid., ix.

14. UNICEF 1994, 50-51.

15. Chossudovsky, M. *IMF-World Bank policies and the Rwandan Holocaust,* Third World Network Features, 1287/95.

16. Ritchie, M. *GATT Facts: Africa loses under GATT,* Institute for Agriculture and Trade Policy, (March, 1994).

17. Oxfam UK, 13.

18. Ibid.

19. UNDP, *Human development report 1994* (New York: Oxford University Press, 1994), 155.

20. *World Resources 1994-1995,* 296.

21. Barkin, D., Rosemary L. Batt and Billie De Walt. *Food crops vs. feed crops: Global substitution of grains in production,* (Boulder: Lynne Rienner Publishers, 1990), 73.

22. For a comprehensive overview of U.S. policy toward Africa from WWII to the present see Michael Clough, *Free at last? U.S. policy toward Africa and the end of the Cold War.* (New York: Council on Foreign Relations Press, 1992). For more global effects of U.S. foreign aid see Frances Moore Lappé, Joseph Collins and David Kinley, *Aid as obstacle: Twenty questions about our foreign aid and the hungry.* (San Francisco: Institute for Food and Development Policy, 1981) and Frances Moore Lappé, Rachel Schurman and Kevin Danaher, *Betraying the national interest,* (San Francisco: Institute for Food and Development Policy, 1987).

23. Oxfam, 28-29.

24. Gellen, K. "Africans blast European beef dumping," *African Farmer,* Oct. 1993, 44-45.

25. USAID Summary Tables FY 1992, 13.

Tips for Guiding Very Young Book Reviewers

BY PATRICIA B. CAMPBELL

The suggestions below may assist you in turning your students, the children who use your library or your own children into book reviewers.

Few children know or understand the *concept* of book reviewing; all need some discussion of the process. Reading a review of a book that is familiar to the children often helps to get the idea across. Asking children to discuss how *their* feelings about the book *differ* from those of the reviewer is a good way to validate their own ideas.

The reviewing process should make children more aware of the racism and sexism in what they read. In order to do this, discussions about racism and sexism should be held prior to doing the review. With very young children, the emphasis can be on how some people do not believe that other people can or should be able to do some things because of their sex or color — and how stupid that is. You can discuss how ideas like that hurt everybody, both the people who say, write or think them and the people about whom they are said. Examples frequently help. (For instance, ask a boy how he would feel if someone said that boys shouldn't play with trucks; if lots of people said that, would he stop playing with trucks? What would a student do if an adult decided that children with brown hair couldn't have snacks? Would that be fair?) Children usually find discussions of "fair" or "not fair" most relevant and soon generalize, with an adult's help, from the personal examples to the broader concepts of racism and sexism.

You might also discuss the people the students know. Talking about the racial composition of the class or community can sensitize them to the flaw in "all-White" books, for instance. Talking about the jobs and tasks done by their parents and other adults they know can lead to discussions of gender roles. (Picture books can also be used to spur such discussions.) Whether you use the words racism and sexism is up to you — and the age of the children. Frequently it is easier to get the concepts across without worrying about terms. Also, racism and sexism are very emotion-laden words that may bring negative responses from parents.

Talk with students about what constitutes a *good* book. Of course, it's helpful if children have been read to a lot and are familiar with depictions of positive role models. Help students develop some guidelines — perhaps five or six — for evaluating books. If the children don't include guidelines on racism and sexism, mention it yourself. Guidelines should be short and to the point, such as "is the book unfair to boys or girls?" (Don't just focus on sexism or racism; an anti-sexist, anti-racist book that is boring or poorly written has little value.)

Come out with a written product, even though you will have to write the review for younger children. It is important that the children see that their opinions have been written down and can be read. Base your review on the children's comments and be sure that they have the chance to react to it before it is "published" or disseminated.

Children need to know that reviewing is not just a make-work project and that their opinion is valuable and will be read by others. Although it is not always possible to have children's reviews published by the *Bulletin* or *The New York Times*, there are other possibilities, including class and school newspapers, library bulletins boards and PTA newsletters. Reviews can also be posted on a class bulletin board. Even if the reviews are only used to help classmates decide what books they want to read or have read to them, the sharing is important.

Good luck and have fun.

Patricia B. Campbell conducts educational research and evaluation.

Reprinted from the Council for Interracial Books for Children Bulletin.

LANGUAGE

"WHO IS TO SAY THAT ROBBING A PEOPLE OF ITS
LANGUAGE IS LESS VIOLENT THAN WAR?"
— RAY GWYN SMITH

THE BEST OF BOTH WORLDS

BY MARLENE CARTER

"Alvin, would you go next door and ask Ms. Bowton if she has any chalk?" Alvin nodded and left the room. He returned a minute later with Ms. Bowton's reply.

"She say she don't have none."

"She *doesn't* have *any*?" I asked, hoping he would hear my corrections.

"Yeah," he said, missing the point entirely.

I resisted the temptation to turn the favor into a grammar lesson and committed myself more firmly to finding answers to my questions about how to effectively teach speakers of Black English to speak and write standard English. Specifically, I wanted to know what effect the teaching of literature written in both Black dialect and standard English has on 1) the attitudes African American high school students have towards Black dialect and its speakers and 2) the ability of students who use Black dialect to distinguish Black dialect from standard English and to use standard English when appropriate. My questions did not stop here. I wondered if a literature based program was sufficient to effectively teach standard English. Would I need to resort to grammar lessons and drills? I also wondered if I would need to direct more attention to oral language in order to see any real improvement in written language.

My desire to research these questions grew from my observations as a resident of the community. As a resident, I was accustomed to hearing Black dialect in the grocery store and the mall, in the restaurants and at the post office in my neighborhood. The language communicated effectively. I felt students had a right to the culture transmitted through the use of their community language. I was also aware, however, of the necessity of speaking and writing standard English in college and outside of the community. I had graduated from Dorsey prepared to compete in college because my parents and teachers had required me to speak and write standard English. Being bi-dialectal would give my students an advantage; they could feel comfortable and accepted inside and outside of their community. I was committed to empowering my students to code switch when necessary and to value both languages.

For my teacher research I would be examining my own students in the Susan Miller Dorsey High School College Incentive Magnet. Although the program had been designed by the Los Angeles Unified School District to attract students of all races to the Dorsey campus, our "school within a school" was still 90% African American and 100% minority. Among my African American students there was diversity. Some students were from middle class families who owned homes in the expensive Baldwin Hills area; others relied on welfare for food and housing. Many students fell somewhere in the middle of these two groups, living with one or two working class parents. Family income was not necessarily an indication of a student's ability to use standard English, although the educational level of the parents was a key factor. Regardless of income, some students spoke and wrote only standard English, others moved easily between standard English and Black dialect and a third group spoke and wrote only Black dialect.

I had for years been teaching students the meaning of the word dialect as a part of the vocabulary of literary terms we regularly used. Dialect may be defined as a "regional variety of language distinguished by features of vocabulary, grammar, and pronunciation from other regional varieties" of language (*Webster's New Collegiate Dictionary*). As I read the literature dealing with Black dialect I found a variety of labels for the language. I determined that the terms Black dialect, Black English, Ebonics and Black language could be used interchangeably. The definition of Black language in the Los Angeles Unified School District publication *Proficiency in the English Program for the Black Learner* (PEP) provided me with the best definition of these terms. According to the PEP framework, Black language is a variety of English "spoken by many African Americans which differs from standard English in syntax, phonology, morphology, intonation, stress, and pronunciation and whose existence is explained by certain social, political, economic, and historical facts from Africa and the United States."

At the time of my study I determined that I would not use the term Ebonics because it suggested that Black dialect was a completely different language from mainstream or standard American English. I saw Black English as a dialect of English and did not want to confuse my students.

Researchers and educators are divided on the issue of Black dialect. Some voice the opinion that the child "has a right to his own language." We as educators are urged to accept the child and the dialect she speaks without asking the student to switch to standard English. Others see Black dialect as a hinderance, labeling it "poor English" and using every opportunity to attack it in their students' speech and writing. The result is a confusing message for students. They are praised by one teacher who values the content of the essay but ignores the inappropriate use of dialect. The next teacher is appalled by the grammar and ignores the content. I hoped that exposing students to literature written in both standard English and Black dialect would show them that each language has value and its appropriate uses.

DIALECT AND THE ADVANCED STUDENT

The subject of Black dialect entered into the curriculum of all my classes, even in the Advanced Placement English class comprised of seniors who regularly speak and write standard English. Each member of this college level class had to teach a poem to the rest of the class. Anne, who had taken my American Literature class the previous year, selected Paul Laurence Dunbar's *In the Morning*. She asked for volunteers to read the poem aloud. Students were understandably wary; a few lines from the poem may show why.

'lias! 'lias! Bless the Lawd!

Don' you know de day's erbroad?

Ef you don't git up you scamp

Dey'll be trouble in dis camp.

T'ink I gwine to let you sleep

W'ile I meks yo' boa'd an' keep?

Dat's a putty howdy — do —

Don' you hyeah me, 'lias — you? (p. 51)

I could see that students were having problems with the language. Few of them spoke Black English and although most were accustomed to hearing Black English spoken around campus and in their neighborhoods, Dunbar was not using the dialect of this community. His Black southern dialect was considerably harder for students to understand than the modern Black dialect prevalent in the lunch area.

Dialect is hard to read without practice, but following Anne's lead, students struggled through a first reading. In the ensuing discussion, Anne included the definition of dialect and pointed out its features using examples from the poem. She then asked why Dunbar had used dialect in this poem. The students were reluctant to respond to this question and were unusually silent during the entire presentation. I sensed that they felt this humorous monologue about a mother getting her children up in the morning was beneath them. They were unimpressed by Anne's choice of poems and Dunbar's use of dialect.

As I requested, Anne also taught *Sympathy*, a Dunbar poem written in standard English. Students were much more comfortable with the traditional language and subject matter.

I know what the caged bird feels, alas!

When the sun is bright on the upland slopes;

When the wind stirs soft through the springing grass

And the river flows like a stream of glass;

When the first bird sings and the first bud opens,

And the faint perfume from its chalice steals—

I know what the caged bird feels! (p. 356)

The discussion became lively as students noted the comparison Dunbar made between himself and the caged bird who sees freedom all around him and desperately tries to free himself. After the class had thoroughly analyzed the poem, I stepped in and asked students their thoughts about the use of Black dialect. Angela, who had attended a predominately White elementary school and who earned a full scholarship to Washington University in St. Louis said, "Why learn it? You'll never get a chance to use it." Devin, formerly of Louisiana and headed to the University of California at Santa Barbara, frowned as I suggested the value of dialect. I let the discussion drop, but I felt that the majority of the class was convinced that dialect had no place in literature or in American culture today.

Weeks later, as we read Ralph Ellison's *Invisible Man*, the subject of dialect arose again. This time Ellison taught the lesson, and he did so much more effectively than I had. Peter Wheatstraw asks Invisible Man, "Is you got the dog?" "Dog, what dog?" Invisible Man asks. "Now I know you from down home," Wheatstraw continues, "How come you trying to act like you never heard that before!... Why you trying to deny me?" (p. 170) Students were able to see that Ellison was using Black dialect as a symbol of Black heritage. In denying that he understood what Wheatstraw meant, Invisible Man was denying his heritage. On an intellectual level students were able to arrive at this conclusion. The real question was would they see their own negativity towards Black dialect as a denial of their heritage?

In other class discussions I sensed a softening of attitudes towards Black dialect, but it was not until graduation that my suspicions were confirmed. In her graduation speech Mesha, a member of the AP English class, recited the Langston Hughes poem *Mother to Son*. The poem opens with the line "Well, Son, life for me ain't been no crystal stair." Mesha developed a sizeable portion of her speech around that line, reminding her peers, "Well, seniors, life for us ain't been no crystal stair." The graduates and audience loved her adaptation. I knew it was not only the symbolism of the crystal stair, nor the advice the mother gave her son to encourage him that moved the listeners. It was also the dialect. Mesha had made a connection with the present community by using the language of the neighborhood. Her use of dialect in the midst of a formal speech demonstrated her ability to use both standard English and Black dialect appropriately. She had the best of both worlds.

BLACK DIALECT IN THE SOPHOMORE CLASS

In my tenth grade English class I saw a need to do more than foster an appreciation for Black dialect. More than half of my 20 students spoke Black dialect in class discussions and oral reports. Of the Black dialect speakers, only three were able to edit out the dialect from their written work. The others used dialect in formal written assignments even if they were asked to proofread to make sure they had used only standard English.

I began the semester by letting students feel comfortable with their language and with me. After three weeks, I launched into my project, hoping that awareness of the difference between Black English and standard English would be sufficient to cause many students to choose standard English when appropriate.

We were in the middle of our short story unit. The textbook *Question and Form in Literature* (Scott Foresman and Company, 1982) provided a variety of stories, three of which used Black dialect. As we read the first of these stories, I asked students to comment on the author's use of language. Some students said that the characters spoke "bad English" and that they probably didn't get a good education.

At this point I introduced the term dialect and had a student read a definition of the word from the dictionary. I explained that Black English dialect is a product of a blending of English and certain West African languages which occurred as Africans, mainly slaves, learned to speak English. Using a map, we discussed the differences in pronunciation, vocabulary and grammar found in various regions of the United States. Students shared examples of how their relatives from the south and east said certain words and phrases. We also discussed the dialect of our community. I explained the difference between slang and dialect. Slang changes quickly and varies from generation to generation. Students giggled as I shared phrases like "right on, brother" from my teen years. Then they enlightened me on the current slang. I told students that dialect, on the other hand, is constant and changes only slightly from generation to generation. A grandparent, parent and grandchild may all speak the same dialect of a language.

These younger students were more ready to accept the lesson on dialect than the seniors had been. The sophomores readily agreed that Black dialect deserved to be valued because it communicated effectively among the people who use it. They also agreed that it was necessary to speak and write standard English because this is the language many people expect to hear or read on the job or at school.

Then I asked students to find Black dialect in the stories we were reading. In William Melvin Kelley's *A Visit to Grandmother* they found the following:

"It Charles, Mama, That who it is." Aunt Rose, between them, led them closer.

"It Charles come all the way from New York to see you, and brung little Charles with him." (p. 115)

Students noticed the differences in verbs, "It Charles" rather than "It's Charles" and "brung" instead of "brought." They also noticed that the author used both standard English and dialect. Dialect was found in the dialogue; the narration was in standard English.

An awareness of the differences between Black dialect and standard English had some effect. I asked students to use standard English in class so that they could get more practice with the language. If a student used Black dialect I would say "How do you say that in standard English?" Soon students began policing each other. I overheard one student telling another, "Listen to what you just said, 'Yes he do.'" The friend smiled and said "does." In brief speeches students introduced themselves to the class. Ali said he could only give Kim a seven (out of ten) because even though the con-

©Elizabeth Crews

tent was okay, she had used Black dialect in her speech.

Still, I noticed five weeks later that some students had made no progress in using standard English in their speech or writing. These students were also having reading problems. I tried a few grammar exercises where students were asked to change Black dialect to standard English. I took care not to tell students to "correct" the sentences, for that implied that Black English was wrong. I told them that we were more or less translating into standard English.

With a busy schedule that included poetry, drama, mass media, novels and other English units, I did not spend very much time on formal grammar instruction. As it came time for the proficiency test in writing, I worried that my dialect speakers would do poorly on the test. I quickly reviewed a few verbs that had remained a problem for several students. I wrote on the board, "The horses was grazing in the field." Someone immediately said, "It should be the horses were."

"Why?" I asked.

"Because it's past tense," one student offered.

"Was is past tense," I said.

Another student said, "It's supposed to be *was*.

The horses was grazing. What's wrong with that?"

Finally, Freddie said the verb should be "were" because horses is plural. We practiced a few more was/were sentences, and I found myself wishing I had included more direct teaching of problem verbs in my lessons.

DIALECT IN THE LITERATURE CLASSROOM

I had originally thought that I would focus my study on my tenth grade students, but I eventually shifted my focus to my juniors. I found that the questions I wanted to answer could be best explored by looking at what I was already doing in my American Literature classes. I had launched my program enthusiastically in the fall teaching Black literature as it occurred chronologically in American Literature. Students responded well to contemporary author Lerone Bennett's account of slaves crossing the middle passage. Excerpts from *Before the Mayflower* graphically depicted the horrors faced by enslaved Africans. Bennett's style was accessible to students and worthy of imitation. He served as an excellent example of how standard English can be used effectively.

Encouraged by the interest and response, I looked forward to presenting poetry by Phillis

Wheatley. Students found *To S.M., a Young African Artist Upon Seeing His Work* too difficult. They complained constantly, but with the help of cooperative learning groups managed to write paraphrases of the poem and original poems addressed to their favorite artists.

I continued to introduce literature by Black and non-Black authors, pausing to have students write with each selection. I hoped that the reading of a lot of good literature written in standard English would cause speakers of Black dialect to acquire standard English grammatical structures. Also, I modeled standard English but seldom asked students to switch if they spoke Black dialect although I did call attention to dialect in their written work. I wanted students to feel comfortable with me before I set about making changes in their speech.

In the spring semester the title of the course changed and so did my approach. My American Literature students were now enrolled in my Contemporary Composition class. The focus this semester would be on writing. I decided to address the subject of Black dialect more directly and to ask students to switch if they used Black dialect inappropriately.

In February I had students read two stories in which the authors used Black dialect. In both "The Man Who Saw the Flood" by Richard Wright and "A Worn Path" by Eudora Welty, dialect is used in the dialogue, but the narration is in standard English. In addition to discussing the usual elements of fiction — plot, setting, character, theme, symbolism — we spent an entire class period discussing dialect. We defined the term, found examples and discussed its purpose in these stories.

The written assignment on the stories yielded proof that students understood the difference between "poor English" and Black dialect. I read a letter from Gladys Johnson (alias Marlene Carter), a parent who wanted the textbook banned because it contained stories that used bad language and atrocious spelling. Mrs. Johnson said that students should only read stories that modeled correct English. Students wrote business letters to Mrs. Johnson expressing their opinions on the topic.

Keisha explained:

The two stories which you critiqued are using southern dialect not bad English. The words in the story are spelled just as they are pronounced in southern states. I believe that students should be exposed to all types of literature using various dialects.

Rita wrote:

Black dialect is the style or way that some blacks talk. It is used among blacks everywhere. For example, 'I'm 'bout to go to the sto'' is black dialect. It is written the way it sounds to give more realistic qualities and effect.

I taped the discussion we had about Black dialect and Mrs. Johnson's letter. I found that because students knew we were being taped, those who spoke tended to make an effort to speak standard English. Students who spoke only Black dialect remained silent throughout the discussion. They let the more polished speakers control the conversation. Evidently, knowing that someone other than their classmates and their teacher would hear the tape inhibited them. This, unfortunately, is what often happens to Black dialect speakers in formal situations where standard English is expected. They fade into the background rather than call attention to their speech. They keep their ideas to themselves and are mistakenly thought to be disinterested or unintelligent. Listening to the tape, I decided that future lessons had to address both oral and written skills if I was to really empower students to be successful in this society.

I believed a research and debate unit would provide the opportunity for students to hone both their writing and speaking skills. Each student would work with a partner to research a current controversial issue, write note cards and an outline. Each student would then be responsible for drafting his own five page paper. The student and her partner would debate two other students who had researched the same topic. As I made my unit lesson plans, I envisioned writing groups that would help with revising and editing. These writing groups and practice sessions would provide, I hoped, plenty of opportunities for Black dialect speakers and writers to get assistance in using standard English.

The unit did not, however, go as planned. Students fell behind on their researching and instead of having three weeks from the start of the first draft to the due date for the final draft, many students were writing all drafts within a one week period. The result was research papers that were full of mechanical errors and inappropriate use of Black dialect. The content of most of the papers was good, however, and most students had enough information to carry on lively debates. We did not emphasize the importance of using standard English during the debates as I had planned, but most students instinctively made the effort to speak formal standard English. Still, I found that those students who spoke Black English most often did so during the debate although I could see that they were making an effort to speak formally. These students needed more direct instruction in order to speak and write standard English correctly.

Reluctantly, I decided to end the semester with a grammar and usage unit. Both my dialect and non-dialect speakers were making errors that would not disappear without some direct instruction. I questioned, though, whether the "correct the error" exercises I devised were really effective. I would have to wait until students wrote their final exam essays to find out.

My Contemporary Composition final included two writing samples. Students were given one week to write an essay comparing and contrasting themselves to one of the characters we had read about during the semester. I reminded students that I would be looking closely at content, style and mechanics and that they should use all resources to help them write the best possible paper. In class I encouraged students to read each other's papers and offer comments. The second writing sample was done in class on the day of the final exam. Students wrote letters advising a parent as to whether or not she should send her teenagers to Dorsey High School. Students were told that this paper would be evaluated on the basis of content, style and mechanics, but that I would take into account the time limitation.

The papers I received from Kareem are typical of those submitted by Black dialect speakers. He had a fairly good grasp of the material, but his errors and inappropriate use of dialect impede understanding. Kareem used Black dialect frequently at the beginning of the semester. His papers also contained many mechanical errors that were unrelated to dialect. I compared excerpts of Kareem's February and March essays with those he had written in June.

I feel that legal age for driving should remain at the age of sixteen. When a person reach sixteen the teen-ager has a strong body, good eyesight and fast reflexes, make young motorists potentially the best drivers on the road... If you raise the age to eighteen for a drivers licences you will crush the courage and determination of the teenagers who is striving for a drivers licences. (Kareem, February 8)

Kareems's use of "reach" instead of "reaches" and "teen-agers who is" rather that "teenagers who are" shows that he had not learned to edit out Black

dialect from his research paper. Other errors such as omitting "which" from the clause "make young motorists potentially the best drivers on the road" and using second person "you" in a formal paper cannot be attributed to dialect. Some errors are common among teenage writers without regard to the dialect they regularly speak.

A later writing sample shows some improvement, but it also contains both inappropriate dialect and grammatical errors.

The book to me is better than the movie because the book goes into more detail than the movie...After I finish viewing the movie I felt that the people who played in the movie didn't meet up to their expectation as they did in the book. For example Nick in the book was a kind of person that will listen to you, but in the movie he gave advice but the look on his face expresses he criticism. (Kareem, March 20)

Kareem's use of "finish" instead of "finished" is not just a verb tense problem. I see this as a dialect issue in that many Black dialect speakers do not put endings on verbs. The omission of the "s" on expectation is also a result of dialect as is the use of "he" rather than "his." The problems with clarity (What does Kareem mean when he says that characters didn't meet up to their expectation?) are not attributable to dialect.

Kareem's final exam papers contain errors, but fewer examples of inappropriate use of dialect.

The person that reflect the most of me is Nick. Nick is a type of person who does not judge people. I don't judge person by the way they act. I judge people by there personalities. For example, I met this girl for the first time. But the way she acted my have turned most people against her. I had the pleasure of talking with her on the phone. This girl was a very intelligent individual, whom I enjoyed talking with. She was an affable person as well. (Kareem's take home final, June 19)

I believe you son and daughter would have of the joyest times at Dorsey High School. We have one of the best academic programs in the nation. We push our kids to want to learn. We offer educational trips for our youngsters For example last month, (May 5) we had the pleasure of going to Alvera Street. It was very fun and educational We took a trip to Cal State LA, We went on a brief tour around the campus. (Kareem's in-class final, June 21)

Kareem was making an effort to eliminate Black dialect from his writing. He omitted the "s" from reflect but the errors in his final papers were not usually a result of Black dialect. The omission of punctuation in the in-class sample and the use of the wrong homonym (there instead of their) in the take home essay are mistakes common among teenage writers and not exclusive to Black dialect speakers. I could see that Kareem had made progress in editing out Black dialect from his formal writing.

I attributed most of the progress that he made to our individual conferences where I asked him to read his paper and circle any errors that he found. We had worked specifically on verb endings a few times. He was conscious of his problem in this area and had fewer subject-verb agreement problems as a result.

FINDINGS

My year of research led me to the following conclusions:

1. Presenting literature written in Black dialect is a valuable tool for helping both Black dialect speakers and non-dialect speakers value and respect Black dialect in literature and in America today.

2. Teaching literature in both Black dialect and standard English helps students to distinguish between the two. For some students this ability to distinguish is all they need to begin using standard English in their speaking and writing.

3. Just reading literature is not enough to help some Black dialect speakers become proficient in speaking and writing standard English. These students need specific lessons on verb tenses, subject-verb agreement, possessive forms and other structures that are not acquired simply from reading or hearing standard English. Mini-lessons of 10 to 15 minutes seem to be most effective for teaching specific grammatical structures in context so that students associate the lessons with the writing they have done or will be doing in the near future.

4. One-on-one conferencing appears to be very effective in helping a student focus on the structures that he/she has not yet acquired. Teaching students to locate and then switch Black dialect to standard English in their own writing empowers them to evaluate their own work and make adjustments as necessary.

IMPLICATIONS FOR THE CLASSROOM

What does this mean for the classroom teacher who instructs Black dialect speakers?

1. First, we have to show respect for the community language of our students. In doing so we build individual and collective self esteem and we encourage students to keep alive part of their cultural heritage. Students with a positive image of themselves and their culture will have fewer affective barriers to hinder learning.

2. We have to accept the fact that standard English is the language of power in this society. The people who have economic power dictate the language of power in this society. If we want to empower our students to be successful in college, to make positive impressions on job interviews, and to advance in their chosen careers we must help them become proficient in the language which colleges and employers expect to hear and read. We must respect the community language without neglecting to teach standard English.

3. We should integrate literature by Black (and other) minority authors into the curriculum throughout the year so that the language lessons learned from such literature are continuous. We do injustice to the literature and to our attempts to use Black literature to teach standard English when we present Black literature only during Black History Month or in a unit on Black or minority authors.

4. We must address the needs of those Black dialect speakers who need direct instruction in using standard English. After observing them during class discussions and evaluating their writing, we need to design specific mini-lessons to meet their needs. (For example, a teacher may decide to teach a lesson on the use of "do, did, and does.") The lesson needs to be taught in a context that helps students connect the information to their own writing or speaking.

5. In teaching about Black dialect, we should not assume that all African American students are Black dialect speakers. Some students speak only standard English or are already bi-dialectal. Lengthy lessons on standard English structures are unnecessary for a standard English speaker who has already acquired them. Also, we should not assume that all Black dialect speakers are African American. Many young people grow up in predominantly African American communities may learn the language from their peers.

I do not know exactly how teachers can best structure such lessons. It may be that the teacher will take advantage of a writing workshop day to work with a small group of Black dialect speakers

© Elizabeth Crews

while the rest of the class in involved in peer editing. During conferencing the teacher could spend
five or ten minutes helping an individual student
with the structures that are most problematic. We
have to be careful, though, that we don't segre-
gate Black dialect speakers and make them feel that
they are less intelligent or less able than other members of the class.

We need to take the subject of Black dialect out
of the political arena where we argue over its place
in our society and the linguistic realm where we
are satisfied with discussing its origins and features.
Teachers must continue to search for effective strategies that best help Black dialect speakers become
bi-dialectal, and we need to share our successes (and
failures) with our colleagues. We must continue to
work towards the goal of helping our students have
the best of both worlds.

Marlene Carter *is an English teacher at Dorsey High School
in the Los Angeles Unified School District. She is also the co-
Associate Director of the UCLA Writing Project. She lives in
Los Angeles with her husband and three sons. She can be
contacted at UCLA, Center X Office, GSE&IS, 1041 Moore
Hall, Los Angeles, CA 90095-1521.*

An earlier version of this article was printed in Power of
Context: Studies By Teacher-Researchers, *Volume II,
Peitzman, F. (Ed.) 1990. Copies can be ordered from the
Center X Office.*

REFERENCES

Dunbar, P.L. 1983. "In the Morning." *The black poets.* Randall,
    D. (Ed.) New York: Bantam Books.

Dunbar, P.L. 1982. "Sympathy." *United States in literature.* Miller,
    J. A., Jr., et al. (Eds.) Glenview, Illinois: Scott, Foresman and
    Company.

Ellison, R. 1972. *Invisible man.* New York: Vintage Books.

Kelley, W. M. 1982. "A Visit to Grandmother." *Question and
    form in literature,* Miller, J.A., Jr., et al. (Eds.) Glenview,
    Illinois: Scott, Foresman and Company.

LANGUAGE DIVERSITY AND LEARNING

BY LISA DELPIT

A brand-new Black teacher is delivering her first reading lesson to a group of first-grade students in inner city Philadelphia. She has almost memorized the entire basal-provided lesson dialogue while practicing in front of a mirror the night before.

"Good morning, boys and girls. Today we're going to read a story about where we live, in the city."

A small brown hand rises.

"Yes, Marti."

Marti and this teacher are special friends for she was a kindergartner in the classroom where her new teacher student-taught.

"Teacher, how come you talking like a White person? You talkin' just like my momma talk when she get on the phone!"

I was that first-year teacher many years ago, and Marti was among the first to teach me the role of language diversity in the classroom. Marti let me know that children, even young children, are often aware of the different codes we all use in our everyday lives. They may not yet have learned how to produce those codes or what social purposes they serve, but children often have a remarkable ability to discern and identify different codes in different settings. It is this sensitivity to language and its appropriate use upon which we must build to ensure the success of children from diverse backgrounds.

One aspect of language diversity in the classroom — *form* (the code of a language, its phonology, grammar, inflections, sentence structure and written symbols) — has usually received the most attention from educators, as manifested in their concern about the "nonstandardness" of the code their students speak. While form is important, particularly in the context of social success, it is considerably less important when concern is lodged instead in the area of cognitive development. This area is related to that aspect of language diversity reflected in Marti's statement — language *use* — the socially and cognitively based linguistic determinations speakers make about style, register, vocabulary, and so forth, when they attempt to interact with or achieve particular goals within their

environments. It is the purpose of this paper to address a broad conception of language diversity as it affects the learning environments of linguistically diverse students; it focuses on the development of the range of linguistic alternatives that students have at their disposal for use in varying settings.

ACQUIRING ONE LANGUAGE VARIETY AND LEARNING ANOTHER

The acquisition and development of one's native language is a wondrous process, drawing upon all of the cognitive and affective capacities that make us human. By contrast, the successful acquisition of a second form of a language is essentially a rote-learning process brought to automaticity. It is, however, a process in which success is heavily influenced by highly charged affective factors. Because of the frequency with which schools focus unsuccessfully on changing language form, a careful discussion of the topic and its attendant affective aspects is in order.

THE AFFECTIVE FILTER IN LANGUAGE LEARNING

Learning to orally produce an alternate form is not principally a function of cognitive analysis, thereby not ideally learned from protracted rule-based instruction and correction. Rather, it comes with exposure, comfort level, motivation, familiarity, and practice in real communicative contexts. Those who have enjoyed a pleasant interlude in an area where another dialect of English is spoken may have noticed a change in their own speech. Almost unconsciously, their speech has approached that of those native to the area. The evidence suggests that had these learners been corrected or drilled in the rules of the new dialect, they probably would not have acquired it as readily.

Stephen Krashen, in his work on second-language acquisition, distinguishes the processes of conscious *learning* (rule-based instruction leading to the monitoring of verbal output) from unconscious *acquisition* ("picking up" a language through internalizing the linguistic input-derived immersion in a new context — what happens, say, when the North American enjoys a visit to the Caribbean).[1] Krashen found unconscious acquisition to be much more effective. In further studies, however, he found that in some cases people did not easily "acquire" the new language. This finding led him to postulate the existence of what he called the "affective filter." The filter operates "when affective conditions are not optimal, when the student is not motivated, does not identify with the speakers of the second language, or is overanxious about his performance,... [causing] a mental block.... [which] will prevent the input from reaching those parts of the brain responsible for language acquisition."[2] Although the process of learning a new dialect cannot be completely equated with learning a new language, some processes seem to be similar. In this case, it seems that the less stress attached to the process, the more easily it is accomplished.

The so-called affective filter is likely to be raised when the learner is exposed to constant correction. Such correction increases cognitive monitoring of speech, thereby making talking difficult. To illustrate with an experiment anyone can try, I have frequently taught a relatively simple new "dialect" in my work with preservice teachers. In this dialect, the phonetic element "iz" is added after the first consonant or consonant cluster in each syllable of a word. (*Teacher* becomes tiz-ea-chiz-er and *apple,* iz-ap-piz-le.) After a bit of drill and practice, the students are asked to tell a partner why they decided to become teachers. Most only haltingly attempt a few words before lapsing into either silence or into "Standard English," usually to complain about my circling the room to insist that all words they utter be in the new dialect. During a follow-up discussion, all students invariably speak of the impossibility of attempting to apply rules while trying to formulate and express a thought. Forcing speakers to monitor their language for rules while speaking, typically produces silence.

Correction may also affect students' attitudes toward their teachers. In a recent research project, middle-school, inner-city students were interviewed about their attitudes toward their teachers and school. One young woman complained bitterly, "Mrs. _____ always be interrupting to make you 'talk correct' and stuff. She be butting into your conversations when you not even talking to her! She need to mind her own business."

In another example from a Mississippi preschool, a teacher had been drilling her three- and four-year-old charges on responding to the greeting, "Good morning, how are you?" with "I'm fine, thank you." Posting herself near the door one morning, she greeted a four-year-old Black boy in an interchange that went something like this:

Teacher: Good morning, Tony, how are you?
Tony: I be's fine.
Teacher: Tony, I said, How are you?
Tony: (with raised voice) I be's fine.
Teacher: No, Tony, I said how are you?
Tony: (angrily) I done told you I be's fine and I ain't telling you no more!

Tony must have questioned his teacher's intelligence, if not sanity. In any event, neither of the students discussed above would be predisposed, as Krashen says, to identify with their teachers and thereby increase the possibility of unconsciously acquiring the latter's language form.

ETHNIC IDENTITY AND LANGUAGE PERFORMANCE

Issues of group identity may also affect students' oral production of a different dialect. Nelson-Barber, in a study of phonologic aspects of Pima Indian language found that, in grades 1-3, the children's English most approximated the standard dialect of their teachers.[3] But surprisingly, by fourth grade, when one might assume growing competence in standard forms, their language moved significantly toward the local dialect. These fourth graders had the *competence* to express themselves in a more standard form, but chose, consciously or unconsciously, to use the language of those in their local environments. The researcher believes that, by ages 8-9, these children became aware of their group membership and its importance to their wellbeing, and this realization was reflected in their language. They may also have become increasingly aware of the school's negative attitude toward their community and found it necessary — through choice of linguistic form — to decide with which camp to identify.

A similar example of linguistic *performance* (what one does with language) belying linguistic *competence* (what one is capable of doing) comes from researcher Gerald Mohatt (personal communication), who was at the time teaching on a Sioux reservation. It was considered axiomatic among the reservation staff that the reason these students failed to become competent readers was that they spoke a nonstandard dialect. One day Mohatt happened to look, unnoticed, into a classroom where a group of boys had congregated. Much to his surprise and amusement, the youngsters were staging a perfect rendition of his own teaching, complete with stance, walk, gestures, *and* Standard English (including Midwestern accent). Clearly, the school's failure to teach these children to read was based on factors other than their inability to speak and understand

Standard English. They could do both; they did not often choose to do so in a classroom setting, however, possibly because they chose to identify with their community rather than with the school.

APPRECIATING LINGUISTIC DIVERSITY IN THE CLASSROOM

What should teachers do about helping students acquire an additional oral form? First, they should recognize that the linguistic form a student brings to school is intimately connected with loved ones, community, and personal identity. To suggest that this form is "wrong" or, even worse, ignorant, is to suggest that something is wrong with the student and his or her family. On the other hand, it is equally important to understand that students who do not have access to the politically popular dialect form in this country, that is, Standard English, are less likely to succeed economically than their peers who do. How can both realities be embraced?

Teachers need to support the language that students bring to school, provide them input from an additional code, and give them the opportunity to use the new code in a nonthreatening, real communicative context. Some teachers accomplish this goal by having groups of students create bidialectal dictionaries of their own language form and Standard

English. Others have had students become involved with standard forms through various kinds of role-play. For example, memorizing parts for drama productions will allow students to "get the feel" of speaking Standard English while not under the threat of correction. Young students can create puppet shows or role-play cartoon characters. (Many "superheroes" speak almost hypercorrect Standard English!) Playing a role eliminates the possibility of implying that the *child's* language is inadequate, and suggests, instead, that different language forms are appropriate in different contexts. Some other teachers in New York City have had their students produce a news show every day for the rest of the school. The students take on the persona of some famous newscaster, keeping in character as they develop and read their news reports. Discussions ensue about whether Walter Cronkite would have said it that way, again taking the focus off the child's speech.

ACTIVITIES FOR PROMOTING LINGUISTIC PLURALISM

It is possible and desirable to make the actual study of language diversity a part of the curriculum for all students. For younger children, discussions about the differences in the ways television characters from different cultural groups speak can provide a starting point. A collection of the many children's books written in the dialects of various cultural groups can also provide a wonderful basis for learning about linguistic diversity, as can audiotaped stories narrated by individuals from different cultures.[4] Mrs. Pat, a teacher chronicled by Shirley Brice Heath, had her students become language "detectives," interviewing a variety of individuals and listening to the radio and television to discover the differences and similarities in the ways people talked.[5] Children can learn that there are many ways of saying the same thing, and that certain contexts suggest particular kinds of linguistic performances.

Inevitably, each speaker will make his or her own decision about the appropriate form to use in any context. Neither teachers nor anyone else will be able to force a choice upon an individual. All we can do is provide students with the exposure to an alternate form, and allow them the opportunity to practice that form *in contexts that are nonthreatening, have a real purpose, and are intrinsically enjoyable.* If they have access to alternative forms, it will be their decision later in life to choose which to use. We can only provide them with the knowledge base and hope they will make appropriate choices.

ETHNIC IDENTITY AND STYLES OF DISCOURSE

Thus far, we have primarily discussed differences in grammar and syntax. There are other differences in oral language of which teachers should be aware in a multicultural context, particularly in discourse style and language use. Michaels and other researchers identified differences in children's narratives at "sharing time."[6] They found that there was a tendency among young White children to tell "topic-centered" narratives — stories focused on one event — and a tendency among Black youngsters, especially girls, to tell "episodic" narratives — stories that include shifting scenes and are typically longer. While these differences are interesting in themselves, what is of greater significance is adults' responses to the differences. Courtney Cazden reports on a subsequent project in which a White adult was taped reading the oral narratives of Black and White first graders, with all syntax dialectal markers removed.[7] Adults were asked to listen to the stories and comment about the children's likelihood of success in school. The researchers were surprised by the differential responses given by Black and White adults.

In responding to the retelling of a Black child's story, the White adults were uniformly negative, making such comments as "terrible story, incoherent" and "[n]ot a story at all in the sense of describing something that happened." Asked to judge this child's academic competence, all of the White adults rated her below the children who told "topic-centered" stories. Most of these adults also predicted difficulties for this child's future school career, such as, "This child might have trouble reading," that she exhibited "language problems that affect school achievement," and that "family problems" or "emotional problems" might hamper her academic progress.[8]

The Black adults had very different reactions. They found this child's story "well formed, easy to understand, and interesting, with lots of detail and description." Even though all five of these adults mentioned the "shifts" and "associations" or "nonlinear" quality of the story, they did not find these features distracting. Three of the Black adults selected the story as the best of the five they had heard, and all but one judged the child as exceptionally bright, highly verbal, and successful in school.[9]

When differences in narrative style produce differences in interpretation of competence, the pedagogical implications are evident. If children who produce stories based in differing discourse styles are expected to have trouble reading, and viewed as having language, family, or emotional problems, as was the case with the informants quoted by Cazden, they are unlikely to be viewed as ready for the same challenging instruction awarded students whose language patterns more closely parallel the teacher's. It is important to emphasize that those teachers in the Cazden study who were of the same cultural group as the students recognized the differences in style, but did not assign a negative valence to those differences. Thus, if teachers hope to avoid negatively stereotyping the language patterns of their students, it is important that they be encouraged to interact with, and willingly learn from, knowledgeable members of their students' cultural groups. This can perhaps best become a reality if teacher education programs include diverse parents, community members, and faculty among those who prepare future teachers, and take seriously the need to develop in those teachers the humility required for learning from the surrounding context when entering a culturally different setting.

QUESTIONING STYLES

Heath has identified another aspect of diversity in language use which affects classroom instruction and learning.[10] She found that questions were used differently in a southeastern town by young Black students and their teachers. The students were unaccustomed to responding to the "known-answer" test questions of the classroom. (The classic example of such questions is the contrast between the real-life questioning routine: "What time is it?" "Two o'clock." "Thanks." and the school questioning routine: "What time is it?" "Two o'clock." *"Right!"*[11]) These students would lapse into silence or contribute very little information when teachers asked direct factual questions which called for feedback of what had just been taught. She found that when the types of questions asked of the children were more in line with the kinds of questions posed to them in their home settings — questions probing the students' own analyses and evaluations — these children responded very differently. They "talked, actively and aggressively became involved in the lesson, and offered useful information about their past experiences."[12] The author concludes not only that these kinds of questions are appropriate for all children rather than just for the "high groups" with which they have typically been used, but that awareness and use of the kinds of language used in children's communities can foster the kind of language and performance and growth sought by the school and teachers.

ORAL STYLES IN COMMUNITY LIFE

I would be remiss to end this section without remarking upon the need to draw upon the considerable language strengths of linguistically diverse populations. Smitherman and many others have made note of the value placed upon oral expression in most African-American communities.[13] The "man (person) of words," be he or she preacher, poet, philosopher, huckster, or rap song creator, receives the highest form of respect in the Black community. The verbal adroitness, the cogent and quick wit, the brilliant use of metaphorical language, the facility in rhythm and rhyme, evident in the language of preacher Martin Luther King, Jr., boxer Muhammad Ali, co-

medienne Whoopi Goldberg, rapper L.L. Cool J., singer and songwriter Billie Holiday, and many inner-city Black students, may all be drawn upon to facilitate school learning.

Other children, as well, come to school with a wealth of specialized linguistic knowledge. Native American children, for example, come from communities with very sophisticated knowledge about storytelling, and a special way of saying a great deal with a few words. Classroom learning should be structured so that not only are these children able to acquire the verbal patterns they lack, but they are also able to strengthen their proficiencies, and to share these with classmates and teachers. We will then all be enriched.

THE DEMANDS OF SCHOOL LANGUAGE — ORALITY AND LITERACY

There is little evidence that speaking another dialectal form per se, negatively affects one's ability to learn to read.[14] For commonsensical proof, one need only reflect on nonstandard-dialect-speaking slaves who not only taught themselves to read, but did so under threat of severe punishment or death. But children who speak nonmainstream varieties of English do have a more difficult time becoming proficient readers. Why?

One explanation is that, where teachers' assessments of competence are influenced by the dialect children speak, teachers may develop low expectations for certain students and subsequently teach them less.[15] A second explanation which lends itself more readily to observation, rests in teachers' confusing the teaching of reading with the teaching of a new dialect form.

Cunningham found that teachers across the United States were more likely to correct reading miscues that were dialect related ("Here go a table" for "Here is a table") than those that were nondialect related ("Here is the dog" for "There is the dog").[16] Seventy-eight percent of the dialect miscues were corrected, compared with only 27 percent of the nondialect miscues. He concludes that the teachers were acting out of ignorance, not realizing that "here go" and "here is" represent the same meaning in some Black children's language.

> THERE IS LITTLE EVIDENCE THAT SPEAKING ANOTHER DIALECTAL FORM PER SE, NEGATIVELY AFFECTS ONE'S ABILITY TO LEARN TO READ. FOR COMMONSENSICAL PROOF, ONE NEED ONLY REFLECT ON NONSTANDARD-DIALECT-SPEAKING SLAVES WHO NOT ONLY TAUGHT THEMSELVES TO READ, BUT DID SO UNDER THREAT OF SEVERE PUNISHMENT OR DEATH.

In my observations of many classrooms, however, I have come to conclude that even when teachers recognize the similarity of meaning, they are likely to correct dialect-related miscues. Consider a typical example:

Text: Yesterday I washed my brother's clothes.

Student's Rendition: Yesterday I wash my bruvver close.

The subsequent exchange between student and teacher sounds something like this:

T: Wait, let's go back. What's that word again? [Points at walked.]

S: Wash.

T: No. Look at it again. What letters do you see at the end? You see "e-d." Do you remember vhat we say when we see those letters on the end of a word?

S: "ed"

T: OK, but in this case we say washed. *Can you say that?*

S: Washed.

T: Good. Now read it again.

S: Yesterday I washed my bruvver. . .

T: Wait a minute, what's that word again? [Points to brother.]

S: Bruvver.

T: No. Look at these letters in the middle. [Points to th.] *Remember to read what you see. Do you remember how we say that sound? Put your tongue between your teeth and say* /th/...

The lesson continues in such a fashion, the teacher proceeding to correct the student's dialect-influenced pronunciations and grammar while ignoring the fact that the student had to have comprehended the sentence in order to translate it into her own dialect. Such instruction occurs daily and blocks reading development in a number of ways. First, because children become better readers by having the opportunity to read, the overcorrection exhibited in this lesson means that this child will be less likely to become a fluent reader than other children who are not interrupted so consistently. Second, a complete focus on code and pronunciation blocks children's understanding that reading is essentially a meaning-making process. This child, who understands the text, is led to believe that she is doing something wrong. She is encouraged to think of reading not as something you do to get a message, but something you pronounce. Third, constant corrections by the teacher are likely to cause this student and others like her to resist reading and to resent the teacher.

Robert Berdan reports that, after observing the kind of teaching routine described above in a number of settings, he incorporated the teacher behaviors into a reading instruction exercise that he used with students in a college class.[17] He put together sundry rules from a number of American social and regional dialects to create what he called the "language of Atlantis." Students were then called upon to read aloud in this dialect they did not know. When they made errors he interrupted them, using some of the same statements/comments he had heard elementary school teachers routinely make to their students. He concludes:

The results were rather shocking. By the time these Ph.D. candidates in English or linguistics had read 10-20 words, I could make them sound totally illiterate. By using the routines that teachers use of dialectally different students, I could produce all of the behaviors we observe in children who do not learn to read successfully. The first thing that goes is sentence intonation: they sound like they are reading a list from the telephone book. Comment on their pronunciation a bit more, and they begin to subvocalize, rehearsing pronunciations for themselves before they dare to say them out loud. They begin to guess at pronunciations....They switch letters around for no reason. They stumble; they repeat. In short, when I attack them for their failure to conform to my demands for Atlantis English pronunciations, they sound very much like the worst of the second graders in any of the classrooms I have observed. They also begin to fidget. They wad up their papers, bite their fingernails, whisper, and some finally refuse to continue. They do all the things that children do while they are busily failing to learn to read. Emotional trauma can result as well. For instance, once while conducting this little experiment, in a matter of seconds I actually had one of my graduate students in tears.[18]

The moral of this story is not to confuse dialect intervention with reading instruction. To do so will only confuse the child, leading her away from those intuitive understandings about language that will promote reading development, and toward a school career of resistance and a lifetime of avoiding reading. For those who believe that the child has to "say it right in order to spell it right," let me add that English is not a phonetically regular language. There is no particular difference between telling a child, You may *say* /bruvver/, but it's spelled b-r-o-*t*-*h*-e-r," and "You say /com/, but it's spelled c-o-m-*b*."

For this and other reasons, writing may be an arena in which to address standard forms. Unlike unplanned oral language or public reading, writing lends itself to editing. While conversational talk is spontaneous and must be responsive to an immediate context, writing is a mediated process which may be written and rewritten any number of times before being introduced to public scrutiny. Consequently, writing is amenable to rule application — one may first write freely to get one's thoughts down, and then edit to hone the message and apply specific spelling, syntactical, or punctuation rules. My college students who had such difficulty talking in the "iz" dialect, found writing it, with the rules displayed before them, a relatively easy task.

STYLES OF LITERACY

There are other culturally based differences in language use in writing as well. In a seminal article arguing for the existence of "contrastive rhetoric," Robert Kaplan proposes that different languages have different rhetorical norms, representing different ways of organizing ideas.[19]

Such style differences have also been identified in public school classrooms. Gail Martin, a teacher-researcher in Wyoming, wrote about her work with Arapaho students:

One of our major concerns was that many of the stories children wrote didn't seem to "go anywhere." The stories just ambled along with no definite start or finish, no climaxes or conclusions. I decided to ask Pius Moss [the school elder] about these stories, since he is a master Arapaho storyteller himself. I learned about a distinctive difference between Arapaho stories and stories I was accustomed to hearing, reading, and telling. Pius Moss explained that Arapaho stories are not written down, they're told in what we might call serial form, continued night after night. A "good" story is one that lasts seven nights....

When I asked Pius Moss why Arapaho stories never seem to have an "ending," he answered that there is no ending to life, and stories are about Arapaho life, so there is no need for a conclusion. My colleagues and I talked about what Pius had said, and we decided that we would encourage our students to choose whichever type of story they wished to write: we would try to listen and read in appropriate ways.[20]

Similarly, Native Alaskan teacher Martha Demientieff has discovered that her students find "book language" baffling. To help them gain access to this unfamiliar use of language, she contrasts the "wordy," academic way of saying things with the metaphoric style of Athabaskan. The students discuss how book language always uses more words, but how in Heritage language, brevity is always best. Students then work in pairs, groups, or individually to write papers in the academic way, discussing with Martha and with each other whether they believe they have said enough to "sound like a book." Next they take those papers and try to reduce the meaning to a few sentences. Finally, students further reduce the message to a "saying" brief enough to go on the front of a T-shirt, and the sayings are put on little paper tee shirts that the students cut out and hang throughout the room. Sometimes the students reduce other authors' wordy texts to their essential meanings as well. Thus, through winding back and forth through orality and literacy, the students begin to

"Say 'Ask', Deneese" by A.J. Verdelle

A young girl from the South goes North, attends school and finds her grammar consistently corrected by a teacher whom she at once admires and despises.

"Where is your grandmother, Deneese?" Missus James ask me.

I sure do like the way she talk. She so crisp and proper and even like a drum. All this rumination and I done forgot the question.

"Scuse me, what you ax me?" I have to ask again.

She wince. I realize I seen her do that before. I think, dog, after I done answered smart, now I'm askin stupid. I feel like runnin out, but I just picked up one foot and start to rub it on my other sock.

Missus James looked down at my feet, me standin next to her desk and all. "Stop scratching, Deneese," she say.

I put my foot back down.

First, she sighs. "Neesey, do you know your language is atrocious?"

This halts my thinkin altogether. She returns to our conversation then as if I don't look blank or smacked down, as if she has not expected me to answer after all. Atrocious, I decide to wonder what is that. "I ask-eduh where your grandmother lives," she say.

She might as well say Cakka Lakky at the end. She leave a space between her words, like I don't know where they start and finish. She makin me nervous.

"Down home in Fuhginia," I answer. "Down Souf," I add, quietlike. I try to leave some space between my words.

"South," Missus James say back to me, and she aims her head at mine and holds her tongue between her teeth like beef in bread.

"Say it, Deneese," she say to me; "say South." Tongue sandwich again.

"Say ask, Deneese," she say to me, "ask." She still looks at me straight on, close like I'm a newspaper.

I run out the room. Then I start to hope that my socks are soakin up the pee, cause before I got through the schoolhouse door, it's just a-runnin. I hear Josephus callin t'me and I imagine he will catch up, but finally he doesn't come along. I decide he has left me alone to my shame, and so I forget all about him.

I didn't run all the way home cause it's a long way, but I ran four corners away from the school, had my coat in my hand and my geography book pressed close to my chest. Missus James sure did get my shame to racin that day. I am a country gal, and I don't know top or bottom a them city sounds she be makin. I keep hearin her say that word ask, could hear it only in my head on account a I don't have no ability to make no sound like that, not with the mouth I got, at least. Sound to me like somebody in a hurry to leave the table, rushin, got the chair cocked on the back legs, and they mind already in the next room.

The walk home was all the way one wet step on ask, the next wet step on south, big tongue a beef sandwich between my teeth. My socks just squished, gettin clammy in the cole. My freezin cole feet in my wet socks is what reminded me to put my coat on. I had it on my arm while I was lookin inside my head at Missus James movin her tongue round. I wished I could make the right pronunciations. Exchange for the nice coat she give me. I wished I hadn't a peed and run off like I did. I wants to stand forward like somebody with sense.

From *The Good Negress* by A.J. Verdelle. © 1995 by the author. Reprinted by permission of Algonquin Books of Chapel Hill, a division of Workman Publishing.

For reflection

1. Ask students: Have you every felt like Deneese did in school that day? If so, what was the situation?

2. Ask some students to enact the story as it is written. Then ask them to enact it again, but this time have the person playing Ms. James modify her approach based on some of the recommendations in the article by Lisa Delpit. Discuss the 'mini-plays.'

understand the stylistic differences between their own language and that of standard text.

Functions of Print

Print may serve different functions in some communities than it does in others, and some children may be unaccustomed to using print or seeing it used in the ways that schools demand. Shirley Brice Heath, for example, found that the Black children in the community she called Trackton engaged with print as a group activity for specific real-life purposes, such as reading food labels when shopping, reading fix-it books to repair or modify toys, reading the names of cars to identify a wished-for model, or reading to participate in church. There was seldom a time anyone in the community would read as a solitary recreational activity; indeed, anyone who did so was thought to be a little strange.[21]

The children in Trackton, in short, read to learn things, for real purposes. When these children arrived in school they faced another reality. They were required, instead, to "learn to read," that is, they were told to focus on the *process* of reading with little apparent real purposes in mind other than to get through a basal page or complete a worksheet — and much of this they were to accomplish in isolation. Needless to say, they were not successful at the decontextualized, individualized school reading tasks.

Researchers have identified other differences in the use of language in print as well. For example, Ron Scollon and Suzanne Scollon report that, in the Athabaskan Indian approach to communicative interaction, each individual is expected to make his or her own sense of a situation and that no one can unilaterally enforce one interpretation. Consequently, they were not surprised when, in a story-retelling exercise intended to test reading comprehension, Athabaskan children tended to modify the text of the story in their retellings.[22] The school, however, would be likely to interpret these individually constructed retellings as evidence that the students had not comprehended the story.

Talk Across the Curriculum

A debate over the role of language diversity in mathematics and science education was fueled recently by the publication of a book by Eleanor Wilson Orr titled *Twice as Less — Black English and the Performance of Black Students in Mathematics and Science*.[23] Orr is a teacher of math and science who, as director of the elite Hawthorne School, worked out a cooperative program with the District of Co-

lumbia to allow several Washington, D.C. public high school students to attend the prestigious school. Orr and her colleagues were dismayed to find that despite their faithfully following time-tested teaching strategies, and despite the Black D.C. students' high motivation and hard work, the newcomers were failing an alarming percentage of their math and science courses.

Noting the differences in the language the Black students used, Orr decided to investigate the possibility that speaking Black English was preventing these students from excelling in math and science. In a detailed argument she contends that the students' nonstandard language is both the cause and the expression of the real problem — their "*nonstandard perceptions*."[24] She cites student statements such as "So the car traveling *twice as faster* will take *twice as less* hours" to support her thesis, and suggests that it is the difference between Black English and Standard English forms in the use of prepositions, conjunctions, and relative pronouns that is the basis for the students' failures.

It is important to critique this position in order that the failures of those responsible for teaching mathematics and science to poor and Black students not be attributed to the students themselves, that is, so that the victims not be blamed. There are many problems with the Orr argument. One is her assumption that Black students, by virtue of speaking Black English, do not have access to certain concepts needed in mathematical problem solving. For example, she makes much of the lack of the "as as" comparison, but I have recorded Black English-speaking six- to eleven-year-olds frequently making such statements as, "She big as you" and "I can too run fast as you."

A second problem is that Orr compares the language and performance of low-income, ill-prepared students with upper-income students who have had superior scholastic preparation. I contend that it was not their language which confused the D.C. students, but mathematics itself! Any students with a similar level of preparation and experience, no matter what their color or language variety, would probably have had the same difficulties.

The most basic problem with the Orr argument, however, is Orr's apparent belief that somehow mathematics is linked to the syntactical constructions of standard English: "[T]he *grammar* of standard English provides consistently for what is *true mathematically*."[25] What about the grammar of Chinese or Arabic or German? Orr's linguistic naive determinist position can only lead to the bizarre conclusion that speakers of other languages would be equally handicapped in mathematics because they, too, lacked standard English constructions!

Even though Orr asserts that the cause of the problem is the speaking of Black English, she seems unaware that her proposed solution is not linked to this conceptualization. She does not recommend teaching Standard English, but rather, teaching *math* through the use in instruction of irregular number systems which force students to carefully work out concepts and prevent their dependence on inappropriate rote memorized patterns. One can surmise that as students and teachers work through these irregular systems, they create a shared language, developing for the students what they truly lack, a knowledge of the *content* of the language of mathematics, not the form.

Interviews with Black teachers who have enjoyed long-term success teaching math to Black-dialect-speaking students suggest that part of the solution also lies in the kind and quality of talk in the mathematics classroom. One teacher explained that her Black students were much more likely to learn a new operation successfully when they understood to what use the operation might be put in daily life. Rather than teach decontextualized operations, she would typically first pose a "real-life" problem and challenge the students to find a solution. For example, she once brought in a part of a broken wheel, saying that it came from a toy that she wished to fix for her grandson. To do so, she had to reconstruct the wheel from this tiny part. After the students tried unsuccessfully to solve the problem, she introduced a theorem related to constructing a circle given any two points on an arc, which the students quickly assimilated.

Another Black math teacher spoke of putting a problem into terms relevant to the student's life. He found that the same problem that baffled students when posed in terms of distances between two unfamiliar places or in terms of numbers of milk cans needed by a farmer, were much more readily solved when familiar locales and the amount of money needed to buy a leather jacket were substituted. I discovered a similar phenomenon when my first-grade inner-city students did much better on "word problems" on standardized tests when I merely substituted the names of people in our school for the names in the problems.

All of these modifications to the language of instruction speak to Heath's findings in Trackton: some youngsters may become more engaged in school tasks when the language of those tasks is posed in real-life contexts than when they are viewed as merely decontextualized problem completion. Since our long-term goal is producing young people who are able to think critically and creatively in real problem-solving contexts, the instructional — and linguistic — implications should be evident.

Conclusion

One of the most difficult tasks we face as human beings is communicating meaning across our individual differences, a task confounded immeasurably when we attempt to communicate across social lines, racial lines, cultural lines, or lines of unequal power. Yet, all U.S. demographic data points to a society becoming increasingly diverse, and that diversity is nowhere more evident than in our schools. Currently, "minority" students represent a majority in all but two of our twenty-five largest cities, and by some estimates, the turn of the century will find up to 40 percent nonwhite children in American classrooms. At the same time, the teaching force is becoming more homogeneously White. African-American, Asian, Hispanic, and Native American teachers now comprise only 10 percent of the teaching force, and that percentage is shrinking rapidly.

What are we educators to do? We must first decide upon a perspective from which to view the situation. We can continue to view diversity as a problem, attempting to force all differences into standardized boxes. Or we can recognize that diversity of thought, language, and worldview in our classrooms cannot only provide an exciting educational setting, but can also prepare our children for the richness of living in an increasingly diverse national community. (Would any of us really want to trade the wonderful variety of American ethnic restaurants for a standard fare of steak houses and fast-food hamburgers?)

I am suggesting that we begin with a perspective that demands finding means to celebrate, not merely tolerate, diversity in our classrooms. Not only should teachers and students who share group membership delight in their own cultural and linguistic history, but all teachers must revel in the diversity of their students and that of the world outside the classroom community. How can we accomplish these lofty goals? Certainly, given the reality of the composition of the teaching force, very few educators can join Martha Demientieff in taking advantage of her shared background with her culturally unique students and contrasting *"our Heritage language"* or *"the way we say things"* with

"Formal English." But teachers who do not share the language and culture of their students, or teachers whose students represent a variety of cultural backgrounds, can also celebrate diversity by making language diversity a part of the curriculum. Students can be asked to "teach" the teacher and other students aspects of their language variety. They can "translate" songs, poems, and stories into their own dialect or into "book language" and compare the differences across the cultural groups represented in the classroom.

Amanda Branscombe, a gifted White teacher who has often taught Black students whom other teachers have given up on, sometimes has her middle school students listen to rap songs in order to develop a rule base for their creation. The students would teach her their newly constructed "rules for writing rap," and she would in turn use this knowledge as a base to begin a discussion of the rules Shakespeare used to construct his plays, or the rules poets used to develop their sonnets.[26]

Within our celebration of diversity, we must keep in mind that education, at its best, hones and develops the knowledge and skills each student already possesses, while at the same time adding new knowledge and skills to that base. All students deserve the right both to develop the linguistic skills they bring to the classroom and to add others to their repertoires. While linguists have long proclaimed that no language variety is intrinsically "better" than another, in a stratified society such as ours, language choices are not neutral. The language associated with the power structure — "Standard English" — is the language of economic success, and all students have the right to schooling that gives them access to that language.

While it is also true, as this chapter highlights, that no one can force another to acquire an additional language variety, there are ways to point out to students both the arbitrariness of designating one variety over another as "standard," as well as the political and economic repercussions for not gaining access to that socially designated "standard." Without appearing to preach about a future which most students find hard to envision, one teacher, for example, has high school students interview various personnel officers in actual workplaces about their attitudes toward divergent styles in oral and written language and report their findings to the entire class. Another has students read or listen to a variety of oral and written language styles and discuss the impact of those styles on the message and the likely effect on different audiences. Students then recreate the texts or talks, using different language styles appropriate for different audiences (for example, a church group, academicians, rap singers, a feminist group, politicians, and so on).

Each of us belongs to many communities. Joseph Suina, a Pueblo Indian scholar, has proposed a schematic representation of at least three levels of community membership. He sets up three concentric circles. The inner circle is labeled "home/local community," the middle circle is "national community," and the outer circle represents the "global community."[27] In today's world it is vital that we all learn to become active citizens in all three communities, and one requisite skill for doing so is an ability to acquire additional linguistic codes. We can ignore or try to obliterate language diversity in the classroom, or we can encourage in our teachers and students a "mental set for diversity." If we choose the latter, the classroom can become a laboratory for developing linguistic diversity. Those who have acquired additional codes because their local language differs significantly from the language of the national culture may actually be in a better position to gain access to the global culture than "mainstream" Americans who, as Martha says, "only know one way to talk." Rather than think of these diverse students as problems, we can view them instead as resources who can help all of us learn what it feels like to move between cultures and language varieties, and thus perhaps better learn how to become citizens of the global community.

Lisa Delpit holds the Benjamin E. Mays Chair of Urban Educational Leadership at Georgia State University in Atlanta, Georgia. She is a MacArthur fellow and received the Outstanding Contribution to Education Award in 1993 from the Harvard Graduate School of Education, which hailed her as a "visionary scholar and woman of courage." Her book, Other People's Children: Cultural Conflicts in the Classroom, *won the 1995 Critic's Choice Award from the American Educational Studies Association and the* Choice Magazine's *Outstanding Academic Book Award.*

FOOTNOTES

1. Stephen D. Krashen, *Principles and Practice in Second Language Acquisition* (New York: Pergamon, 1982).

2. Ibid., p. 22

3. S. Nelson-Barber, "Phonologic Variations of Pima English," in R. St. Clair and W. Leap, eds., *Language Renewal among American Indian Tribes: Issues, Problems and Prospects* (Rosslyn, Va.: National Clearinghouse for Bilingual Education, 1982).

4. Some of these books include Lucille Clifton, *All Us Come 'Cross the Water* (New York: Holt, Rinehart and Winston, 1973); Paul Green (aided by Abbe Abbott), *I Am Eskimo— Aknik My Name* (Juneau, Alaska: Alaska Northwest Publishing, 1959); Howard Jacobs and Jim Rice, *Once upon a Bayou* (New Orleans, La.: Phideaux Publications 1983); Time Edler, *Santa Cajun's Christmas Adventure* (Baton Rouge, La.: Little Cajun Books, 1981); and a series of biographies produced by Yukon-Koyukkuk School District of Alaska and published by Hancock House Publishers in North Vancouver, British Columbia, Canada.

5. Shirley Brice Heath, *Ways with Words* (Cambridge, Eng.: Cambridge University Press, 1983).

6. S. Michaels and C.B. Cazden, "Teacher-Child Collaboration on Oral Preparation for Literacy," in B. Schieffer, ed., *Acquisition of Literacy: Ethnographic Perspectives* (Norwood, N.J.: Ablex, 1986).

7. C.B. Cazden, *Classroom Discourse* (Portsmouth, N.H.: Heinemann, 1988).

8. Ibid., p. 18

9. Ibid.

10. Heath, *Ways With Words*

11. H. Mehan, "Asking Known Information," *Theory into Practice* 28 (1979), pp. 285-94.

12. Ibid., p. 124.

13. G. Smitherman, *Talkin and Testifyin* (Boston: Houghton Mifflin, 1977).

14. R. Sims, "Dialect and Reading: Toward Redefining the Issues," in J. Langer and M.T. Smith-Burke, eds., *Reader Meets Author/Bridging the Gap* (Newark, Dela.: International Reading Association, 1982).

15. Ibid.

16. P.M. Cunningham, "Teachers' Correction Responses to Black-Dialect Miscues Which Are Nonmeaning-Changing," *Reading Research Quarterly* 12 (1976-77).

17. Robert Berdan, "Knowledge into Practice: Delivering Research to Teachers," in M.F. Whiteman, ed., *Reactions to Ann Arbort: Vernacular Black English and Education* (Arlington, Va.: Center for Applied Linguistics, 1980).

18. Ibid., p. 78.

19. R. Kaplan, "Cultural Thought Patterns in Intercultural Education, "*Language Learning* 16 (1966), pp. 1-2.

20. Cazden, *Classroom Discourse,* p. 12.

21. Heath, *Ways with Words.*

22. Ron Scollon and Suzanne B.K. Scollon, "Cooking It Up and Boiling It Down: Abstracts in Athabaskan Children's Story Retellings," in D. Tannen, ed., *Spoken and Written Language* (Norwood, N.J.: Ablex, 1979).

23. Eleanor Wilson Orr, *Twice as Less: Black English and the Performance of Black Students in Mathematics and Science* (New York: W.W. Norton, 1987)

24. Ibid., p. 30.

25. Ibid., 149 (emphasis added).

26. Personal communication, 1988.

27. Personal communication, 1989.

RACISM IN THE ENGLISH LANGUAGE

BY ROBERT B. MOORE

An integral part of any culture is its language. Language not only develops in conjunction with a society's historical, economic and political evolution; it also reflects that society's attitudes and thinking. Language not only expresses ideas and concepts but actually shapes thought. If one accepts that our dominant White culture is racist, then one would expect our language — an indispensable transmitter of culture — to be racist as well. Whites, as the dominant group, are not subjected to the same abusive characterization by our language that people of color receive. Aspects of racism in the English language that will be discussed in this article include terminology, symbolism, politics, ethnocentrism and context.

COLOR SYMBOLISM

"The English language is my enemy. It teaches the Black child 60 ways to hate himself and the White child 60 ways to aid and abet him in the crime." - Ossie Davis

The symbolism of white as positive and black as negative is pervasive in our culture. "Good guys" wear white hats and ride white horses, "bad guys" wear black hats and ride black horses. Angels are white, and devils are black. The definition of black includes "without any moral light or goodness, evil, wicked, indicating disgrace, sinful," while that of white includes "morally pure, spotless, innocent, free from evil intent."

The studies of Kenneth B. Clark, Mary Ellen Goodman, Judith Porter and others indicate that this persuasive "rightness of whiteness" in U.S. culture affects children before the age of four, providing white youngsters with a false sense of superiority and encouraging self-hatred among third world youngsters.

ETHNOCENTRISM OR FROM A WHITE PERSPECTIVE

Some words and phrases that are commonly used represent particular perspectives and frames of reference, and these often distort the understanding of the reader of listener. David R. Burgest[2] has written about the effect of using the terms "slave" or "master." He argues that the psychological impact of the statement referring to "the master raped his slave" is different from the impact of the same statement substituting the words: "the White captor raped an African woman in captivity."

Implicit in the English usage of the "master-slave" concept is the ownership of the "slave" by the "master," therefore, the "master" is merely abusing his property (slave). In reality, the captives (slave) were African individuals with human worth, right and dignity and the term "slave" denounces that human quality, thereby making the mass rape of African women by White captors more acceptable in the minds of people and setting a mental frame of reference for legitimizing the atrocities perpetuated against African people.

The term slave connotes a less than human quality and turns the captive person into a thing. For example, two McGraw-Hill Far Eastern Publishers textbooks (1970) stated, "At first it was the slaves who worked the cane and they got only food for it. Now men work cane and get money." Next time you write about slavery or read about it, try transposing all "slaves" into "African people held in captivity," "Black people forced to work for no pay" or "African people stolen from their families and societies." While it is more cumbersome, such phrasing conveys a different meaning.

PASSIVE TENSE

Another means by which language shapes our perspective has been noted by Thomas Greenfield[3] who writes that the achievements of Black people — and Black people themselves — have been hidden in:

...the linguistic ghetto of the passive voice, the subordinate clause, and the "understood" subject. The seemingly innocuous distinction (between active/passive voice) holds enormous implications for writers and speakers. When it is effectively applied, the rhetorical impact of the passive voice — the art of making the creator or instigator of action totally disappear from a reader's perception — can be devastating.

For instance, some history texts will discuss how European immigrants came to the United States seeking a better life and expanded opportunities, but will note that "slaves were brought to America."

Not only does this omit the destruction of African societies and families, but it ignores the role of northern merchants and southern slaveholders in the profitable trade in human beings. Other books will state that "the continental railroad *was built*," conveniently omitting information about the Chinese laborers who built much of it or the oppression they suffered.

While touring Monticello, Greenfield noted that the tour guide:

...made all the Black people at Monticello disappear through her use of the passive voice. While speaking of the architectural achievements of Jefferson in the active voice, she unfailingly shifted to [the] passive [voice] when speaking of the work performed by Negro slaves and skilled servants.

Noting a type of door that after 166 years continued to operate without need for repair, Greenfield remarks that the design aspect of the door was much simpler than the actual skill and work involved in building and installing it. Yet his guide stated: "Mr. Jefferson designed these doors..." while "the doors were installed in 1809." The workers who installed those doors were African people whom Jefferson held in bondage. The guide's use of the passive tense enabled her to dismiss the reality of Jefferson's slaveholding. It also meant that she did not have to make any mention of the skills of those people held in bondage.

POLITICS AND TERMINOLOGY

"Culturally deprived," "economically disadvantaged" and "underdeveloped" are other terms which mislead and distort our awareness of reality. The

LANGUAGE IS NOT NEUTRAL

BY ENID LEE

Discuss the following table and have students generate their own list of positive and negative connotations of words in different subject areas.

CONCEPT	POSITIVE CONNOTATION	CONTEXT	NEGATIVE CONNOTATION	CONTEXT
A piece of clothing worn as a garment	Clothing	The skirt of a North American woman	Costume	The sari of an Indian woman
Small dwelling of simple construction	Cottage	A shepherd's house in the Scottish hills	Hut	House of an African villager
System of institutionalized expressions of sacred beliefs, observances and social practices found within a given cultural context	Religion	Christianity	Superstition	African religions e.g. Animism
Taking the initiative, being bold and self-confident	Assertive	Male executive	Aggressive	Female executive
Battle in which one side practically eliminates the opponent	Victory	The Europeans conquering the Native people	Massacre	The Native People conquering the Europeans
State intervention in social upheaval	Maintaining law and order	British policemen quelling rioters	Introducing repressive measures	Polish government dealing with strikers
People engaged in liberation struggles	Freedom Fighters	Resistance Movement in France	Terrorists	Pre-independence period in Zimbabwe

REPRINTED FROM *LETTERS TO MARCIA: A TEACHER'S GUIDE TO ANTI-RACIST EDUCATION* BY ENID LEE (CROSS CULTURAL COMMUNICATION CENTRE, 1985.)

application of the term "culturally deprived" to third world children in this society reflects a value judgement. It assumes that the dominant Whites are cultured and all others are without culture. In fact, third world children generally are bicultural, and many are bilingual, having grown up in their own culture as well as absorbing the dominant culture. In many ways, they are equipped with skills and experiences which White youth have been deprived of, since most White youth develop in a monocultural, monolingual environment. Burgest[4] suggests that the term "culturally deprived" be replaced by "culturally dispossessed," and that the term "economically disadvantaged" be replaced by "economically exploited." Both these terms present a perspective and implication that provide an entirely different frame of reference for addressing the third world experience in U.S. society.

Similarly, many nations of the third world are described as "underdeveloped." The less wealthy nations are generally those that suffered under colonialism and neo-colonialism. The "developed" nations are those that exploited the resources and wealth of the less wealthy nations. Therefore a more appropriate and meaningful designation for less wealthy nations might be "over exploited." Again, transpose this term next time you read about "underdeveloped nations" and note the different meaning that results.

Terms such as "culturally deprived," "economically disadvantaged" and "underdeveloped" place the responsibility for their own conditions on those being so described. This is known as "blaming the victim."[5] It places responsibility for poverty on the victims of poverty. It removes the blame from those in power who benefit from, and continue to permit, poverty.

Still another example involves the use of "non-White," "minority" or "third world." While people of color are a minority in the United States, they are part of a vast majority of the world's population, in which White people are a distinct minority. Thus, by utilizing the term minority to describe people of color in the United States, we can lose sight of the global majority/minority reality — a fact of some importance in the increasing and interconnected struggles of people of color inside and outside the United States.

Use of the term third world to describe all people of color overcomes the inherent bias of "minority" and "non-white." Moreover, it connects the struggles of third world people in the United States with freedom struggles around the globe.

The term third world gained increasing usage after the 1955 Bandung Conference of "non-aligned" nations, which represented a third force outside of the two world superpowers. The "first world" represented the United States, Western Europe and their sphere of influence. The "second world" represented the Soviet Union and its sphere. The "third world" represented, for the most part, nations that were, or are, controlled by the "first world" or West. For the most part, these are the nations of Africa, Asia and Latin America.

"LOADED" WORDS AND AFRICANS

Conflicts among diverse peoples within African nations are often referred to as "tribal warfare," while conflicts among the diverse peoples within European countries are never described in such terms. If the rivalries between the Ibo and Hausa and Yoruba in Nigeria are described as "tribal," why not the rivalries between Serbs and Slavs in Yugoslavia, Scots and English in Great Britain, Protestants and Catholics in Ireland or the Basques and the Southern Spaniards in Spain? Conflicts among African peoples in a particular nation have religious, cultural, economic and/or political roots. If we can analyze the roots of conflicts among European peoples in terms other than "tribal warfare," certainly we can do the same with African peoples, including correct reference to the ethnic groups or nations involved. For example, the terms "Kaffirs," "Hottentot" or "Bushmen" are names imposed by White Europeans. The correct names are always those by which a people refer to themselves. (In these instances Xhosa, Khoi-Khoin and San are correct.[6])

The generalized application of "tribal" in reference to Africans — as well as the failure to acknowledge the religious, cultural and social diversity of African peoples — is a decidedly racist dynamic. It is part of the process whereby Euro-Americans justify, or avoid confronting their oppression of third world peoples. Africa has been particularly insulted by this dynamic, as exemplified by the pervasive "darkest Africa" image. This image, widespread in Western culture, evokes an Africa covered by jungles and inhabited by "uncivilized," "cannibalistic," "pagan," "savage" peoples. This image ignores the geographical reality. Less than 20 percent of the African continent is wooded savanna, for example. The image also ignores the history of African cultures and civilizations. Ample evidence suggests this distortion of reality was developed as a convenient rationale for the European and American slave trade and Western colonialism. The Western powers, rather than exploiting, were civilizing and Christianizing "uncivilized" and "pagan savages" (so the rationalization went). This image also served [and serves] to justify Western colonialism. From Tarzan movies to racist children's books like *Doctor Dolittle* and *Charlie and the Chocolate Factory*, the image of "savage" Africa and the myth of "the White man's burden" has been perpetuated in Western culture.

SPEAKING ENGLISH

The depiction in movies and children's books of third world people speaking English is often itself racist. Children's books about Puerto Ricans or Chicanos often connect poverty with a failure to speak English or to speak it well, thus blaming the victim and ignoring the racism which affects third world people regardless of their proficiency in English. Asian characters speak a stilted English ("Honorable so and so" or "Confucius say") or have a speech impediment ("roots or ruck," "very solly," "flied lice"). Native American characters speak another variation of stilted English ("Boy not hide. Indian take boy."), repeat certain Hollywood-Indian phrases ("Heap big." And "Many moons") or simply grunt out "Ugh" or "How." The repeated use of these language characterizations functions to make third world people seem less intelligent and less capable than the English-speaking White characters.

CONCLUSION

A *Saturday Review* editorial[7] on "The Environment of Language" stated that language

...has much to do with the philosophical and political conditioning of a society as geography or climate...people in Western cultures do not realize the extent to which their racial attitudes have been conditioned since early childhood by the power of words to ennoble or condemn, augment, or detract, glorify or demean. Negative language infects the subconscious of most Western people from the time they first learn to speak. Prejudice is not merely imparted or superimposed. It is metabolized in the bloodstream of society. What is needed is not so much a change in language as an awareness of the power of words to condition attitudes. If we can at least recognize the underpinnings of prejudice, we may be in a position to deal with the effects.

Consciousness of the influence of language on our perceptions can help to negate much of that influence. But it is not enough to simply become aware of the effects of racism in conditioning attitudes. While we may not be able to change the language, we can definitely change our usage of language. We can avoid words that degrade people. We can make a conscious effort to use terminology that reflects a progressive perspective, as opposed to a distorting perspective. It is important for educators to provide students with opportunities to explore racism in language and to increase their awareness of it, as well as learning terminology that is positive and does not perpetuate negative human values.

Dr. Robert B. Moore was an internationally recognized scholar, lecturer and activist. One of the pioneers in the field of promoting White awareness of racism, Dr. Moore had a significant impact on the anti-racist work in many schools and in the Race and Ethnic Relations Department for the Board of Education, North York, Ontario, Canada. He also served as Resource Director for the Council on Interracial Books for Children (CIBC). Dr. Moore passed away in 1991.

Reprinted from "Racism in the English Language", the Council on Interracial Books for Children (CIBC).

NOTES

1. Podair, S. "How bigotry builds through language." *Negro Digest.* March, 1967.

2. Burgest, D. "The racist use of the English language." *Black Scholar.* September, 1973.

3. Greenfield, T. "Race and passive voice at Monticello." *Crisis.* April, 1975.

4. Burgest, D. "Racism in everyday speech and social work jargon." *Social Work.* July 1973.

5. Ryan, W. 1971. *Blaming the victim.* Pantheon Books.

6. Wolf, S. "Catalogers in revolt against LC's racist, sexist headings." *Bulletin of Interracial Books for Children.* Volume 6, Nos. 3&4, 1975.

7. "The environment of language." *Saturday Review,* April 8, 1967.

YUBA CITY SCHOOL

BY CHITRA DIVAKARUNI

From the black trunk I shake out
my one American skirt, blue serge
that smells of mothballs. Again today
Neeraj came crying from school. All week
the teacher has made him sit
in the last row, next to the fat boy
who drools and mumbles,
picks at the spotted milk-blue
skin of his face, but knows
to pinch, sudden-sharp,
when she is not looking.

The books are full of black curves,
dots like the eggs the boll-weevil laid
each monsoon in the furniture-cracks
in Ludhiana. Far up in front
the teacher maces word-sounds
Neeraj does not know. They float
from her mouth-cave, he says,
in discs, each a different color.

Candy-pink for the girls
in their lace dresses, matching
shiny shoes. Silk-yellow
for the boys beside them,
crisp blond hair, hands raised
in all the right answers,
who never look back. Behind them
the Mexicans, whose older brothers,
he tells me, carry knives,

whose catcalls and whizzing rubber bands
clash, mid-air, with her
voice, its sharp purple edge.
For him, the words are
a muddy red, flying low and heavy,
and always one he has learned to understand:
idiot, idiot, idiot.

I heat the iron over the stove. Outside
evening blurs the shivering
in the eucalyptus. Neeraj's shadow
disappears into the hold
he is hollowing all afternoon.
The earth, he knows, is round, and if
one can tunnel all the way through,
he will end up in Punjab,
in his grandfather's mango orchard,
his grandmother's songs,
lighting on his head,
the old words glowing
like summer fireflies.

In the playground, Neeraj says,
invisible hands snatch at his uncut hair,
unseen feet trip him from behind,
and when he turns, ghost laughter
all around his bleeding knees.
He bites down on his lip
to keep in the crying. They are
waiting for him to open his mouth,
so they can steal his voice.

I test the iron with little drops of water
that sizzle and die. Press down
on the wrinkled doth. The room fills
with a smell like singed flesh.
Tomorrow in my blue skirt I will go
to see the teacher, my tongue
stiff and swollen
in my unwilling mouth, my few
English phrases. She will pluck them
from me, nail shut my lips. My son
will keep sitting in the last row
among the red words that drink his voice.

Chitra Divakaruni *lives in the San Francisco Bay area. She is a teacher of creative writing at Foothill College, where she is director for the annual multicultural writing conference. Her most recent poetry collection is titled* Black Candle.

Reprinted from Leaving Yuba City*, by permission of* DOUBLEDAY*, a division of Bantam Doubleday Dell Publishing Group, Inc, and the author.*

SPELLING AND SOCIAL JUSTICE

"Spelling and Social Justice" is excerpted from a keynote presentation for the DC Area Writing Project 1995 summer institute at Howard University. The photos accompanying this article are of DCAWP Teacher Consultants in the institute.

BY ENID LEE

Writing has the power to change the social order. You might say that this is a rather grand claim to make for a few scribbles on a piece of paper. It is also not what you are likely to be thinking about as you work with a group of students who cannot spell very well. Instead, you might be thinking, "We definitely need to get these sentences in order before we change the world order!" Let me suggest, however, that if our work is driven by the knowledge that we are providing our students with tools for their own empowerment and the empowerment of their communities, then the dichotomy between spelling and social justice disappears. We see that it is really spelling for social justice.

In pedagogical terms, we would have students write about things that matter, to real audiences. We would tap into our students' desire to use all of their resources to help them spell things correctly. Those resources include their own oral language(s) as a source of knowledge about how to begin spelling the words; their own devices for remembering the rules of spelling; the support and assistance of peers; and access to computer technologies such as spell-check. We find that students' spelling starts to improve when it becomes a tool for making statements about themselves and their community. It improves when it becomes a tool for naming their world. Yes, writing *does* have the power to change the social order and to bring about a new reality.

Some time ago, I read about a class which was shown a picture book called *Brides of America*. A Mexican American girl said, "This book is wrong because my mother isn't there and she is American." She could tell from the faces. She said, "You should throw the book out." This girl had learned how to read words, but she also had learned to read herself into the picture. She knew the book was incomplete. Of course, the book could be kept in the class, but it should be called *Some Brides of America* or *European American Brides*. Real literacy consists of both reading and writing ourselves, and our communities, into the texts.

As we see with even very young children, we cannot afford to become so bogged down in grammar and spelling that we forget the whole story. Every student whom we help to read and write is being provided with tools to defend herself or himself. We are helping prepare them for the onslaught of antihuman practices that this nation and other nations are facing today: racism, sexism, and the greed for money and human labor that disguises itself as "globalization." With critical literacy skills, students also learn to have a sense of reading the text of society more clearly. They ask about the missing pieces. They ask what I call 'the Columbus question': "Who else was there when Columbus arrived? And what did they have to say about their fate after they were discovered, beaten, stolen and robbed from?" Literacy is political. It is either empowering or disempowering. I hope that we are on the side of empowering.

This perspective on literacy can change the deficit model through which so many of our children are described: "They can not, they can not, they can not..." My questions are: "What can they do? What can they do? What can we in a school community create?" Notice that I said "school community." We cannot expect the individual teacher to do everything. Who can we link with? What other teachers can we work with? What kind of concerns can we put forward to the administration and staff members?

This perspective allows us to look at the agents of power and change located in our classrooms, faculty lounges and communities. This perspective also allows us to recall the histories of our people with respect to reading and writing. Personally, I seek inspiration from and share with my students the fact that Africans, while held in bondage in this country, were denied the right to learn to read. Yet through struggle and determination, at great risk and with few resources, significant numbers of African Americans managed to learn to read by the time the laws were barely off the books.

This is the politics of reading and writing. If we think of reading in a more symbolic way than simply reading from a textbook, we see that it is the native ability to use information that you have in your head, to make sense of the world around you, to make sense of the text of the world. When I say text, I want to use text broadly; not just the basal-reader, but rather the text of the environment, of the street culture of day-to-day living. Every person who comes into our class has already read the text of their lives. This is how they have made sense of what has been going on around them. The clues to them are the looks on a person's face that mean: "You are not behaving well." Or if there are smiles, the look means: "You are doing fine." The looks on people's faces constitute a code, just as the letters on a page are a code. We help students to break a new code when they learn to read print. They have broken other codes prior to coming to us. We build on their prior knowledge, for they have read other texts and have made sense of other symbols. They have used what experience they have in their heads to make sense of the world around them. We must build on these code-breaking skills.

This approach to literacy is useful especially when we hear people say, "Illiteracy is rampant." Illiteracy is a relative experience. In other words, you can be illiterate within one context, in confronting one code, but you are not inherently illiterate. You can apply this to the experience of colonization. A new code was introduced among the indigenous people of the Americas in colonial times. They read various codes and texts prior to the arrival of the Europeans, who imposed a different code. Schools are often like those colonial conquistadors. We require that the children forget what they knew before they came to us, forget the old code, forget that they were able to read and make sense of the world. Consequently they forget to think of reading as something basic and to use the information in their heads to make sense of the new code.

I remember when I had to learn how to use the computer. Prior to that, I was illiterate with respect to computers. I had to learn with the help of others to write and read in new ways. Let us not think that any person is illiterate in some permanent way. Rather, it is that we have not yet found how to help some students to interpret the new code. If you believe that, you will definitely become the kind of teacher who sees the possibility for all students. You will also be able to link the smaller activities of spelling with the larger agenda for social justice.

BILINGUAL EDUCATION: TALKING POINTS

BY J. DAVID RAMIREZ

The question of how to best educate students with limited or no English language skills is critical. Current discussion on whether these children should receive instruction in their primary language is intense and often heated. Indeed, such exchanges have become a national debate.

Knowledge and a critical appraisal of the history of language policy in the United States and of what research tells us about how quickly children develop first and second language skills leads one to conclude that these exchanges are not mere reflections of differences in pedagogical approaches. They represent a deeper historical pattern of struggle over social, economic and political power, e.g., the desire to dominate on the basis of language, language proficiency, ethnicity, race and/or gender. Language policy has been and continues to be used as a more socially acceptable surrogate for overt racism (Wiley, in press). Even the motivation and context for research has been seriously questioned for political undertones (Secada, 1993).

Exchanges regarding language of instruction are largely not about differences in pedagogy, but, perhaps, about the very nature of whether we, as a society, really commit ourselves to continue our "grand experiment" in democracy. This experiment has not yet created the conditions for full democratic participation by all members in our communities, but perpetuates traditional inequities in distribution of power, e.g., resources, decision making and well-being, among diverse groups within our society. Explication of these conditions is beyond the scope of this article, but it is provided elsewhere (Orfield, 1997; Nakagawa, 1996; Wiley, in press; Crawford, 1992; Rickford, 1997). The intent of this article is to directly address some of the more blatant misinformation proffered by members of the English-only movement, the current standard bearers for maintaining the inequitable and undemocratic status quo.

It is important that I begin by clarifying terms. First the term, "bilingual education," is itself confusing. Bilingual education, as described in federal and state legislation and budgets, refers to a range of instructional support services for students who speak a language other than English and who are for-mally identified as lacking the necessary English language skills required by traditional English only classrooms. Such students are referred to in this legislation as being "Limited English Proficient." The purpose of these special support services is to ensure school success by helping students both to learn English and to learn their academic subjects, e.g., math, science, social science and language arts. Thus, the term bilingual education is used interchangeably to refer to:

1. *English-only services* such as English as a Second Language (ESL, traditionally emphasizing English social communication language skills), content-based ESL (emphasis is placed on the development of the specific academic English language skills required by each content area, e.g., English math language, English science language, and English social science language), and sheltered English content instruction (primary emphasis is on the development of specific content skills such as mathematics, and a secondary emphasis on the development of the specific academic language skills required of the particular content area);

2. Instructional services which provide *content instruction both in English and the student's non-English primary language*. The main purpose of primary language use is to assure that the the non-English speaking students are able to learn academic subject matter in the language they know best as they acquire their English language skills. In some higher quality programs, there is an added goal of providing the students with opportunities to continue to develop their primary language skills and to become fully proficient in two languages, English and their primary language. Educational programs which provide instruction in two languages also include one or more of the English-only instructional services listed above as essential program components.

As alluded to above, these special instructional support services for students learning English tend to be funded primarily through federal and/or state monies. It is critical that the reader understand that *almost all* of currently existing specially funded so-called "bilingual education" instructional services fall into the first category above. That is, English-only instructional services comprise almost all instructional services provided through bilingual education funds. To minimize this potential confusion in the type of instructional services being discussed, I will not refer to bilingual education, but instead I will use the term multilingual education to refer to instructional programs wherein both English AND the child's primary language are used for instruction. In addition I will specify the particular English-only instructional approach under discussion.

The second important term to be clarified is "English Learner." Traditionally federal and state policy makers tend to use the more pejorative term, Limited English Proficient, which connotes a deficiency on the part of the student by emphasizing what the student does not know. In actuality, the student already knows another language and is "adding" English as a second language. From a more constructivist approach, to recognize and validate the important knowledge that these children bring to the classroom, I prefer to use the term English Learner.

ASSERTIONS VS. FACTS

The following presents a litany of the key arguments against "bilingual education" made by English-only advocates. My response follows each assertion. I present this information as a modest effort to assist local educators, parents, students, and members of the community in their quest to assure equity and access to rigorous and relevant education for ALL students in our public schools.

English-only: Bilingual Education does not work. The continued low achievement of Hispanic LEP students shows that bilingual education has failed.

Response: Data clearly shows that nationally almost all English Learners or LEP students receive an English-only program. Therefore, the low achievement of LEP students must indicate that English-only programs do not work.

As an example, almost all (over 80%) English Learners in California are in programs where no primary language is used for instruction. All of their instruction is in English. Nationally, the proportion of English Learners receiving English only instruction, under the auspices of "bilingual education," is even higher. Thus, the results of student assessments clearly demonstrate that English-only Programs do not work. There is research evidence to show that the more infrequent "multilingual education" programs (those that incorporate primary language instruction) result in significant gains in content skill development and English language proficiency.

English-only: Bilingual programs are impractical because we do not have the bilingual teachers or resources to address the needs of the over 120 primary language groups in the United States, even in heavily impacted areas such as California, New York, New Jersey, Florida and Texas.

Response: It is practical, not to mention advisable, to provide multilingual programs in schools and classroom where there are sufficient numbers of English Learners speaking the same primary language. Moreover, it does not cost any more to provide a multilingual classroom than it does to provide a traditional English-only classroom. A RAND study in 1983 and the BW Associates study for the California State Legislature in 1992 found that providing special support services to English learners does not cost any more than the cost of providing a traditional English only program.

It is important to differentiate between schools with "small and scattered primary language populations" (e.g., Urdu) from those with substantial numbers of students speaking the same primary language (e.g., Spanish, Cantonese, Vietnamese or Khmer). While I concur that it is impractical to provide a full multilingual program for small and scattered primary language groups, as a teacher I am responsible for providing meaningful instruction to each of my students. If my student is the only Urdu speaking student in my class or my school and this student does not understand any English, I need to determine how to access other primary language resources so that the content is accessible. These could include cooperative learning activities with bilingual English-Urdu speaking students, working with the parents to help their child at home, or working with a community based organization that has multilingual services to provide this student with equal access to my lessons. However, in classrooms and schools where there are substantial numbers of students who speak the same primary language, it is practical to provide these students with equal access to the core curriculum in their primary language. This can be achieved as they are in the process of learning English through the services of a bilingual teacher specially trained to provide multilingual educational services, i.e., first and second language development as well as content instruction in English and the students' primary language.

Research clearly shows that providing students with primary language instruction does not slow down their rate of English language acquisition. Research indicates that English learners do not develop English language skills any faster

© MARIE MOLL

when provided an English-only program than when provided with a program that combines quality English language development with quality primary language content instruction. National and international research indicates that it requires, on average, five or more years to develop the high level of academic English language skills required for classroom learning. This research also shows that English learners can clearly catch up to their English proficient peers in the content areas when provided access to the content in their primary language, even when they are tested in English.

Two major studies concluded that it does not cost any more to provide a multilingual classroom than it does to provide a traditional English-only classroom. A study by RAND Corporation for Congress (Samulon, 1983) and one conducted by BW Associates for the California State Legislature (BW Associates, 1992) all found that over 80% of the cost to educate a child is reflected in staff. Most districts do not pay bilingual teachers more than non-bilingual teachers and the cost of providing books and other learning materials for multilingual and traditional English-only classrooms does not differ. Therefore both studies concluded that it does not cost any more to provide a multilingual classroom than it does for a traditional English-only classroom.

English-only: Since we cannot provide bilingual services (i.e., in this context, English-only advocates are referring to multilingual instruction) to all of the over 120 primary language groups, it is not fair to provide those services to any one of them.

Response: This is absurd. We currently have a critical shortage of math and science teachers. Should we drop all math and science education from our schools? More pointedly, this position is tantamount to saying, "Because there are not enough heart donors to meet the needs of all the patients in need of a heart transplant, we therefore should prohibit all heart transplants." As stated before, I agree that it is impractical to consider providing full multilingual services in situations where there are few and scattered primary language groups. However, in schools and districts where there are substantial numbers of the same primary language groups it is practical and reasonable.

English-only: The language of this land has always been English. Bilingual education is a legacy of the 1960s, which should be eliminated.

Response: This is not true. We tend to forget that not all of the colonists came from England. The early colonists also spoke and provided schooling in German, French, Dutch and Spanish. This practice continued into the 20th century wherever large enclaves of these primary language speakers lived. In fact, German-speaking public schools thrived in the mid-West until World War II, when the anti-German sentiment forced many German Americans to disassociate themselves from their German heritage lest they be branded as being non-American and suffer the same treatment as Japanese Americans.

An examination of the history of language policy in the United States, quickly reveals that the various cycles of English-only efforts were more concerned with issues of economic and political enfranchisement of some groups over others rather than pedagogy, e.g., English-only business men over the Cherokee Nation; White landowners over Blacks in the South; and White settlers over Mexican residents in California. (Crawford, 1992)

The Articles of Confederation and the Declaration of Independence were, as a matter of course, consistently translated into these non-English languages to assure the full participation of all colonists. Attempts to have English declared as the "Official Language" (e.g., Benjamin Franklin) were soundly rejected by the Founders. They considered language a tool whose use should be determined by the individual and not the State. They clearly expressed the belief that what defined Americans was not the language they spoke, but their commitment to a democratic form of government.

Finally, the U.S. Supreme Court in 1966 clarified through the Lau decision that equal treatment alone does not guarantee equal access to educational opportunities. Instruction must be comprehensible to each student. Each school district must provide evidence documenting the efficacy for every student of whatever educational approaches are provided.

English-only: My grandparents were immigrants. They learned English without bilingual education and they were successful. Why do these groups need it?

Response: First, it is a myth that all immigrant groups were successful. While social language skills are quickly developed, e.g. on average within a year, the more demanding language skills needed for academic success requires at least 5 or more years to develop. (Ramirez, 1992; Collier, 1997) With the availability of plentiful low-skilled entry-level jobs, earlier immigrants did not need to develop high level academic skills to find a job. They could secure one with minimal social English language skills. Now, immigrants must master complicated academic skills to find employment in today's job market. To do so requires a more sophisticated mastery of academic English language skills, which requires more time to develop. There is no easy or quick fix to develop such skills.

Research documents that current immigrants are learning English at a faster rate than immigrants from prior generations. It used to take anywhere from three to four generations for the children of some immigrant groups entering prior to 1950s to enter the economic, social and political mainstream. There is substantial evidence that school failure or lack of school success was common for early immigrants. For example, Italian, Irish, Polish and Jewish immigrant children at the turn of the century left school early and did not enter high school. Data suggests that until the 1950s, immigrant and many first generation children received little formal education (e.g., Berrol, 1982; Bodnar, 1982; Fass, 1988; Perlmann, 1988).

English-only: Just because we are for English-only does not mean we are "anti-immigrant."

Response: This is not true. English-only initiatives patterned after those currently under consideration in California clearly target immigrant parents and their children. These initiatives dangerously erode the rights of all parents to determine the education that they would like for their children.

For example, under the California Unz initiative, language minority parents who want their children provided with some instruction in their primary language would be required to petition their school district for such services each year. The services would only be provided if the parents were joined in their request by at least twenty other parents. As immigrant parents typically do not speak English, are not familiar with our political process or the school system, and are typically isolated in their communities, this proposed initiative creates several substantive and significant barriers for immigrant parents seeking a meaningful education for their children. Such barriers targeted to a specific group can only be construed as being anti-immigrant.

English-only: Bilingual advocates are simply trying to protect the jobs of bilingual teachers.

Response: This is a myth and is intentionally misleading to the public. Currently there is a shortage of teachers, particularly in states attempting to reduce class size. If multilingual education were to be prohibited, all of the bilingual teachers would still have their jobs; their teaching skills are badly needed. Since bilingual teachers tend to receive the same salary as non-bilingual teachers, there is no financial incentive for bilingual teachers to advocate for multilingual education other than their concern for the achievement of their students. Lastly, state and federal monies for education all require stringent accountability. This function is fulfilled by directors of multilingual education. If multilingual education were be prohibited, such administrators would still be needed to provide program oversight.

English-only: English-only initiatives support local control.

Response: This is not true. In current practice, local school boards are able to choose from a range of educational programs the one that best suits the needs of their local community. In contrast, English-only initiatives dictate to school boards a single educational program. This shifts power away from the local communities to the state which would then have the responsibility for enforcing the provisions of the initiative.

English-only: English-only instruction supports and strengthens families.

Response: This is not true. In some instances, English-only families would be as negatively impacted by poorly constructed initiatives as language minority families. For example, the Unz initiative would prohibit the use of any language other than English in grades K-5. Instruction in a language other than English would be allowed in grades 6 and above only if the following conditions were met: parents annually petition their school board to provide their child with instruction in a language other than English, there are at least 19 other students with the same request, and each student demonstrates proficiency in English on a standardized measure by scoring 50% or higher. As written, the Unz initiative would apply to both language minority and English-only speaking families.

Language minority families would be negatively impacted. Lilly Wong-Fillmore at the University of California, Berkeley compared English Learner preschoolers who were in an English-only program to those in a Primary Language instructional program. She found that English Learner preschoolers in the primary language instructional program showed greater growth when tested in English at the end of their kindergarten year than did their peers who had participated in the English-only preschool program. Of great concern was the impact upon the family.

Dr. Wong-Fillmore found that the English Learner preschoolers in the English-only program quickly stopped speaking their primary language and switched to English. This occurred not only in school but at home. The result was that the amount and content of parent-child interactions were greatly reduced and restricted. Parents, unable to communicate in English, were speaking less to their children, limiting their conversations to caretaking activities such as "Did you clean your room?" Parents were unaware of what was happening at school and found themselves unable to support their children's learning.

In contrast, language minority parents whose children were in primary language preschool programs continued with extended parent-child interactions and complex conversations, enabling parents to support their children's learning. The Unz initiative, and similar English-only proposals would serve to weaken language minority families, and assure that these parents would not be able to support their children's learning meaningfully and actively.

English-only speaking families would also be hurt by the initiative. There is a growing number of English speaking parents who recognize the social, economic and political advantages of multilingualism and have their children placed in Two-Way Bilingual Immersion Education programs or in foreign language programs. As written the Unz initiative would prohibit these families from availing themselves of these programs at the elementary level. At the secondary level, assuming a normal distribution of test scores, one could expect that half of English speaking students currently enrolled in foreign language classes would score below 50%. Under the Unz initiative these students would be forced out of such classes. This exclusion would curtail their ability to meet foreign language requirements for college admission.

English-only: English-only instruction will strengthen communities.

Response: English-only proposals tend to weaken the social fabric of the community as well as it economic potential. Using the Unz initiative as an example, as proposed it is already exacerbating divisions between nonimmigrant and immigrant groups (even among those sharing similar language and cultural backgrounds), racial groups and English and language minority groups. If passed, the Unz initiative would also make school personnel personally liable if they use a language other than English in schools. Testimony was recently submitted in a pending court case regarding incidents in a Southern California school district, where teachers reported that "language vigilantes" comprised of "concerned citizens" went through classrooms and pulled down any signs that were not in English. (Quiroz vs. Orange Unified School District, 1997) One can only imagine how the Unz initiative, if passed, could catalyze these and other "patriotic Americans" to more extreme actions. Such a climate is not conducive towards creating a spirit of collaboration between the school, home and community.

The business community in the United States is an important part of an increasingly competitive global economy. It is clamoring for a workforce that is both multilingual and multicultural. Restricting the students' opportunities for developing multilingual language skills would limit the economic opportunities of the students and would serve to restrict the needs of our expanding labor force.

English-only: The public education bureaucracy is not responsive to the needs of local schools. Sponsors of the Unz initiative attribute their efforts to the failure of the California Department of Education in providing local school boards with the flexibility to determine the kind of education they would like to provide to their children. Only four school districts out of over a thousand districts in the State successfully obtained waivers from the California Department of Education exempting them from providing bilingual education.

Response: Such claims are examples of sensationalism and intentional misinformation. While it is true that there are over a thousand school districts in California, it is important to note that, to date, only four districts submitted such waiver requests. Thus, every district that has sought a waiver from the State has obtained one. If one is truly concerned about maximizing local control, one would think that efforts to streamline the waiver request process would be more appropriate than ones which only serve to limit choices for students, parents, school boards, and communities.

English-only: English-only initiatives unite our communities with a common language. They help to avoid the balkanization occurring in Canada and assure non-English speakers a fair chance at "The American Dream."

Response: This statement reinforces attitudes and behaviors which serve to divide communities rather than to bring them together. It also misrepresents the reality of American society.

English-only campaigns exacerbate conflicts between speakers of English and native born citizens. The English-only movement reinforces attitudes against English Learners, e.g., "They do not want to learn English," and "Their children are taking limited resources from our children." These attitudes are surprising given the research documenting that the rate of transition to English among immigrants has gone from two or three generations to one generation. Also, the demand for English classes among immigrant adults far outpaces the availability of such services. Immigrants are learning English and they are learning it at a faster rate than their predecessors.

The media has and continues to be a willing partner in creating a climate of mistrust and conflict within the community around immigrant and language issues. News articles consistently report information in a superficial, sensational, confrontational style, focusing on the extremes: "Us against them." Rather than receiving clear, direct information which would allow them to make a reasoned decision, readers are forced into taking sides. No middle ground is sought. Reacting to this critique, a reporter for the *Los Angeles Times* responded, "A balanced article does not sell papers; conflict does."

CONCLUSION

In a moment of generosity, one might assert that the unstated assumption behind English-only initiatives is the belief that English proficiency is the key to harmony within the community as well as to personal success (when combined with hard work and sacrifice). However, it has been my observation that White women are as proficient in English as White men. It is equally obvious that many members of so-called "model minorities" such as Japanese and Chinese Americans also demonstrate formidable proficiency in English, as well as high educational attainment comparable to or exceeding that of many more successful White men. Furthermore, many Latino Americans and African Americans have successfully acquired academic English language skills and advanced academic credentials. Yet, White women and men and women of color do not enjoy the same level of economic, political or social opportunity as their White male counterparts. As noted earlier, language policy in the United States has been and continues to be used as an effective tool to control access to social, economic and political resources. These examples illustrate that underlying the "language problem" are issues of racism, sexism, classicism and ethnocentrism. Consequently, the conflict within our communities will not be resolved solely by requiring that everyone speak English, but by directly addressing these underlying issues.

David Ramirez is the Director of the Center for Language Minority Education and Research, University of California at Long Beach. He is one of the leading researchers on the longitudinal impact of bilingual education.

RESEARCH/POLICY IMPLICATIONS FOR THE SERVICES PROVIDED TO ENGLISH LEARNERS AND NATIVE ENGLISH SPEAKERS

1. English language development should support the acquisition of academic language skills, e.g., English Math Language.

2. Design special content instructional services with a view to providing students with K-12 special L1 and L2 language development services.

3. Develop content and student performance standards that clearly delineate and integrate subject matter and language.

4. Provide English Learners with substantial opportunities to develop their primary language skills.

5. English language development is most successful when it is introduced systematically, e.g., content-based ESL, L1, and sheltered content instruction.

6. English Learners should be provided with access to the core curriculum in their primary language.

7. Native English Speakers should be provided access to the core curriculum in their second Language.

8. Curriculum should build upon students' prior knowledge and be relevant to their lived experience.

9. Provide students with opportunities to develop communication and group process skills to work collaboratively with others.

10. Provide students with opportunities to become information literate.

11. Provide students with opportunities to become technologically literate.

12. There should be effective outreach and collaboration with family and community.

RESEARCH ABOUT HOW TO FACILITATE
SECOND LANGUAGE LEARNING

The following is a very brief summary of the major findings from research regarding second language learning. This summary and the list on the previous page provide a framework for designing successful learning opportunities for English Learners.

1. There is a difference between social and academic language skills (Cummins, 1987; Brice-Heath, 1987).

2. Second language skills for academic learning require, on average, five or more years to develop (Ramirez, et. al., 1992; Collier, 1989; Genessee, 1989; Skutnabb-Kangas, 1981).

3. Language development requires an articulated Pre-K/Grade 12 instructional framework: Speaking, Reading, Writing and Listening Skills (Krashen and Terrell, 1983; Ferguson, 1977).

4. Increased proficiency in the primary language facilitates development of second language skills (Ramirez, et. al., 1991; Swain and Lapkin, 1992).

5. Because language acquisition is facilitated when it is used purposefully and meaningfully, content instruction in a second language should reflect a continuum of instructional approaches that considers both the students' level of second language and content skills development through an integration of second language teaching and content methodology (Mohan, 1991; Bilingual Education Office, 1990; Vygotsky, 1962; Penfield and Roberts, 1958).

6. Access to the core curriculum in the English Learners' primary language allows them to catch up to their native English speaking peers in the content areas (Ramirez, 1992; Collier, 1993, 1995).

7. The instructional program must have a strong multicultural component that is infused throughout the curriculum, because learning is most effective when it builds upon the prior knowledge of a student and is perceived as relevant by the learner (Brice-Heath, 1992; Cortes, 1992; Kagan, 1992; Grant, et. al. 1995; Walsh, 1993; Darder, 1995).

8. Providing second language instruction, including primary language instruction (for English Learners), does not cost any more than the cost of providing traditional instructional services (BW Associates, 1992; Carpenter-Huffman, P. and Samulon, M., 1981).

9. There must be effective outreach to involve ALL parents in the schooling of their children. Because school success for a student is the result of both parental involvement and the quality of instructional services (Keith, 1991; Ramirez and Douglas, 1989; Fehrman, et. al., 1987).

10. As accountability is a central component of an effective program, there must be a well delineated evaluation process to assess the delivery of services and their impact on student achievement (Ramirez, 1992).

11. The most successful program for meeting the English language and content skill needs of English Learners is also the most effective program documented in helping native English speakers acquire foreign language skills (Grey, T. & Hornberger, 1982). This program is referred to as Two-Way Bilingual Immersion Education. (Lindholm, 1996).

12. Two-Way Bilingual Immersion Education programs are the most promising educational programs which integrate issues of school reform with language, race and culture for all students (Ramirez, in press).

Linguistic Human Rights and Education

BY Alma Flor Ada

▸ A young Mexican man working as a carpenter in my house asked every day about my children's ability to speak Spanish. His insistence was surprising. Finally, with deep emotion he told me: "My mother died recently, unexpectedly. Now I realize I knew nothing about her. I always lived at home with my mother, and yet never really talked to her. Being the youngest of seven children, I don't remember having ever spoken Spanish. I always spoke English and there was always someone around who understood me. At the end, I was the one who stayed home. I know my mother loved me, she cooked for me, ironed my shirts, hugged and kissed me every day. But I never, never had a conversation with her, since she spoke only Spanish. And now I go around, begging my brothers and sisters for crumbs of my mother's memories. For me it's unbearable that I know nothing of her, of who she was, of what she thought, of what dreams or feelings she may have had. No one understands me, but my pain is unbearable. And all I can ask myself is why? Why did I not learn Spanish as a child?"

▸ At the end of one of my workshops, a school administrator in Southern California tells me about her German mother. A college professor, her mother was a well-educated woman who spoke English fluently. When the family came from Germany, she and her three sisters stopped using German and eventually forgot it. All the conversation at home happened in English. They never thought they had missed anything until the day the mother went into a coma. Having thought the mother would never recuperate, she and her sisters were resigned to the loss; then the mother awoke. She looked intently to each one of her daughters and talked to each one extensively, before dying. All three felt that the mother's words were tremendously significant, but none of them knows what the mother said. She spoke in German — the German of their childhood — which they had totally forgotten.

▸ One of my friends in New York, an only daughter who always loved and admired her learned father, now has to accept that all communication is impossible between her and her father. Her father, after a lifetime in the United States, has reverted in his old age to speaking only his native Yiddish, which she heard as a child at home but never learned to speak.

▸ A Mexican mother in Seattle tells me in anguish and despair that she is unable to speak to her teenage son. She never realized before to what extent he did not understand Spanish, the only language she speaks, because the older daughter was always there to translate. She thought that he simply preferred to speak English, like most young people. She could not even imagine that he had completely lost the ability to speak Spanish. The balanced bilingual daughter has now successfully moved on to college. The young boy is being dismissed from high school and sent to an alternative continuation school. His mother can not find out how the boy feels or what he thinks. He meanwhile is unable to understand his mother's words of encouragement and support.

▸ A group of Vietnamese parents in Portland tell me about their children (through an interpreter). If they had only guessed how far their children would drift away from them, separated by the lack of a common language in which to transmit values and family history, they would have never chosen to come to the United States. "We did not want to lose our children to the State in a communist regime, and yet we have totally lost them in a declared democracy."

▸ A bright Mexican-American high school graduate cannot enter any of the universities of her choice because she lacks sufficient second language knowledge.

▸ A young Puerto Rican engineer does not get a position he worked towards. The job goes to a person with no Hispanic heritage but who did a year of study of Spanish in Seville and can communicate with South American engineers, while the Puerto Rican can not.

A Parent's Right

Do parents have the right to be able to communicate with their children in their own language? Do children have a right to preserve the language in which their parents and relatives can transmit family history, cultural values and world view? Do minority groups have the human right to preserve the most fundamental element of their culture, their own language? Are there ethical and legal implications when a school district allows, facilitates or promotes the loss of the student's home language when that home language is also an academic subject that could offer the opportunities of advanced placement, enhance admission potential to the best universities and constitute a source of income and better jobs?

All of these questions may sound unnecessary and even absurd, but they are not. As recent as 1995 a judge in Texas ruled that speaking the mother tongue was a case of child abuse and prohibited the mother from doing so. The fact that the decision was appealed and overruled does not erase the fact that a judge would make such a ruling. The English-only movement carries on with strong economic support.

The development of human language is one of the highest achievements of human beings. Each language has taken thousands of years to develop as a comprehensive system, capable of expressing thoughts, feelings and new discoveries. Language is the tool used to describe what exists and to dream things that have never existed. It is through language that we retain the past and that each generation experiences an enriched tradition. It is through language that we engage in social action and generate projects that can shape the future

The disappearance of any one language is a terrible loss for all of humankind. To neglect the opportunity to learn a language with which one is in contact is a terrible waste. The loss of the ability to speak one's own mother tongue is a great misfortune. Linguistic human rights need to be viewed socially and individually. They are the rights of a community to its own survival and the rights of an individual to her/his full development.

LINGUICISM

Linguistic human rights are threatened by racist attitudes based on a belief in the superiority of some languages to others. Inherently all languages are equally effective tools of communication. The differences between languages are linked to the history of its speakers and their own needs. The apparent superiority (in number of speakers, in relationship to professional or scientific usage, etc.) of some languages over others is certainly not reflective of any linguistic feature, but of the relationship to power and wealth of the speakers of the language. Any language of the world can be used for any use its speakers re-

quire, be it technological, scientific or diplomatic. The fact that some languages seem to have the prerogative to be used in those contexts does not have a linguistic base, only a power base, be it political or economic or both.

Racism is the arguments and structures created to promote and maintain inequality. It aims to validate the unjust distribution of power and resources among individuals belonging to different groups. Tove Skutnabb-Kangas and Robert Phillipson have coined the term *linguicism* to refer to the institutionalized prejudice against certain languages.

Language is a gift that provides understanding of ourselves and other people. It is a gift for communication and social action. It is a gift for learning. If one language is a gift, two or more languages are a double, or a multiple gift. There is no sane argument to defend that having the ability to speak only one language is better than having the ability to speak two. Monolingual persons have to make do with the limitations that an exclusive view of the world creates. Bilinguals have the advantage afforded by a dual view of the world, and those who learn several languages have the added benefit of understanding the human experience from multiple viewpoints. The number of speakers one is able to communicate with also multiplies in proportion to the number of languages one knows.

LANGUAGE ACQUISITION

Language acquisition happens in a natural way during childhood. It is a lengthy process, but children are particularly well equipped for it. When language is presented as a desirable tool for communication, children's efforts to acquire it are seen as natural. They receive positive feedback and encouragement. When there is no stigma attached to the language, children can achieve near native or native mastery in approximately six years of constant or frequent exposure. Unfortunately, when minority students perceive their language to be considered inferior to the language of power, and/or when they are made to believe that they need to choose one above the other, they frequently lose the ability to speak their own home language. The pain involved in denying a part of themselves can cause a future inability to recapture the language.

One common attitude in the United States is that parents should shoulder all the responsibility of maintaining and developing the home language. A frequently used argument is that it is the school's responsibility to teach children English, but that if parents want children to speak the home language they should take care of that at home. The fallacy of this argument can be seen easily if we recognize that schools spend a major amount of time teaching English language arts to English speaking students, from kindergarten through college. They do not believe that the home is equipped to do this task and rather than leaving it as a parental responsibility, schools train specialized personnel and devote substantial resources to the development of curricula and the acquisition of materials for this purpose.

There is no question that the responsibilities of schools have increased noticeably in the second half of the twentieth century. The extended family has disappeared, technology has created a different kind of attention and interest in young people, and the knowledge revolution has both increased the curricular content and placed additional demands on the type of preparation needed to compete in the work force. Poverty has become more devastating, and social crime and illness have become greater threats.

Precisely for all these reasons, schools cannot afford to alienate the families or prevent them from meaningful participation in the schooling process. Rather than seeing the development and maintenance of the home language as an added burden they need to see it as a priority and a source of hope for the overall success of the students. Research has proven once and again that students who maintain their home language have, in equal conditions, a better opportunity for academic success than those who lose their home language. Adding a second, and even a third or a fourth language, as the first language's development continues, is an enriching process. Additive bilingualism contributes to developing cognitive flexibility, the ability to confront and resolve new and challenging problems, as well as enriching the child's world view. The cognitive process is not interrupted. Language abilities are transferred and the new knowledge is supported by the previous knowledge.

The typical process of supplanting the first language with another frequently leads to multiple problems: loss of self-identity, internalization of shame about parents, home and community, language uncertainties and academic difficulties. Furthermore, it is a loss for the individual, community and nation. It can make true communication within the home impossible.

The gift of two languages should not be restricted to those born to families who speak a language other than the majority language. It is a benefit that all children should enjoy.

Young children are particularly well-suited to acquire languages. Linguists and child development specialists continue to marvel at the extraordinary feats young children accomplish in the process of acquiring the phonology, morphology and syntax of the language, as well as their ability to learn many thousand words in their first few years. At an early age, children spend most of their waking hours acquiring language. Language becomes a very important tool for understanding and organizing the world, for developing a view of the world, and for relating to family and friends. The innate ability of all children should be tapped to insure that all children acquire at least a second language, preferably three or four.

We may never be able to truly understand the extent of the identification of the child with the mother tongue. It is a connection that begins in the womb. As soon as the ears of the unborn child are formed, the unborn child listens to the mother's voice. Sound is carried by amniotic fluid; the mother's voice is usually the closest and most constant sound. Her voice holds the inflections and intonations of a particular language. Babies can recognize their mother's voice among many others just a few hours after birth. That voice is intrinsically connected to the particular inflections of a given language.

One of the major stimuli of language development in children is the encouragement, praise, support and success which children experience as they say their first words and sentences. They capture the parents' and caretakers' attention. They are praised, lifted and cuddled. Many times they see their needs fulfilled by being able to ask for what they need. But the language a child learns does not belong exclusively to herself or himself, it is rather the language of the parents, the family, the home. And as such, the language is a marker of identification, of belonging. When a child's language is ignored, scorned, rejected, put down, or disregarded, the strong identification with the language causes the child, and the child's family, to feel ignored, scorned, rejected, put down or disregarded.

A Commitment to Language Diversity

The messages concerning the value of bilingualism that society and schools (except in the specific cases of two-way immersion and developmental bilingual programs) are giving young people are highly detrimental. Why is participation in bilingual programs left to the parents' discretion, when other academic decisions are not? Schools determine

Students from the Latin American Youth Center AIDS Peer Education Program host a weekly Sunday morning Spanish language talk show on Radio Mundo in Washington, D.C.

the full extent of the curriculum and the methodology to be followed without asking individual parent consent to teach their children math, spelling or social studies. Yet they are not willing to take the same academic responsibility when it comes to the teaching of a language. What message does this give parents and students?

No child coming to school with advanced knowledge in math or geography is told to forget that knowledge and not mention it in class. Yet children who speak a second language find themselves being asked to put it aside and ignore it. Students are not transferred out of math or reading, but moved forward to more advanced learning. Yet they are transferred out of bilingual education as if their literacy in another language was disposable, something to be forgotten. Their knowledge is then condemned to stagnate or die.

Alma Flor Ada is the Director of Doctoral Studies, Multicultural Program, University of San Francisco. She teaches and guides the work of educators involved with multicultural and multiethnic populations. Dr. Ada is a widely published author of children's literature and books for teachers on the uses of bilingual education in the classroom.

LESSONS FOR THE CLASSROOM

EARLY CHILDHOOD

ACTIVISM AND PRESCHOOL CHILDREN

BY LOUISE DERMAN-SPARKS

The preschool years lay the foundation for children's development of a strong, confident sense of self, empathy, positive attitudes towards people different from themselves, and social interaction skills. However, pervasive institutional and interpersonal racism and other forms of oppression in our society sabotage healthy development in these areas. Early childhood teachers and parents must help children learn how to resist.

One way to do this is to involve children in activism activities that are appropriate to their interests and abilities. The *Anti-Bias Curriculum*, developed by a multi-ethnic group of early childhood educators in Southern California suggests ways that teachers and parents can do so (Derman-Sparks and the ABC Task Force, 1989).

The four goals of the *Anti-Bias Curriculum* are to: (1) Nurture each child's construction of a knowledgeable, confident self-concept and group identity; (2) promote each child's comfortable, empathic interaction with people from diverse backgrounds; (3) foster each child's critical thinking about bias; (4) cultivate each child's ability to stand up for her/himself and for others in the face of bias.

These four goals interact with and build on each other. For children to feel proud and confident about who they are they need to develop a variety of ways for responding to prejudice and discrimination directed against themselves. For children to develop empathy and respect for diversity, they also need a variety of ways to interrupt prejudice and discrimination they see directed at others. Through activism activities children learn that injustice is not overcome by magic or by wishes, but that people make it happen and that each one of them can make it happen.

Young children have an impressive capacity for learning how to act on behalf of themselves and others — *if adults provide activities that are relevant to them, and match their developmental and cultural learning styles*. Effective activities arise out of children's lives, including the history of their ethnic group working for justice, and fit their cognitive, emotional, and behavioral abilities. Choices about activities should take into account families' various beliefs about appropriate ways to take social action, as well as about the role of children in these activities. Take time first to discuss with staff and parents the purpose of activism activities, and collaborate on which activities might best fit the children's experiences, age, and background. Keep in mind the underlying goal to provide children op-

GOALS AND DEVELOPMENTAL EXPECTATIONS OF ANTI-BIAS, MULTICULTURAL CURRICULUM FOR YOUNG CHILDREN		
2- AND 3-YEAR-OLDS ▶ Are learning acceptable ways to express their feelings when they want something or when others hurt them. **4-YEAR-OLDS** ▶ Engage in simple problem-solving and conflict-resolution techniques for dealing with incidents of teasing or rejection directed at their own and other's identity.	**5-YEAR-OLDS** ▶ Problem-solve and use ways to handle specific unfair comments and behaviors that arise in their school or home lives. ▶ Gain emotional food-for-thought from stories about adults who have worked for social justice, especially adults they know. ▶ With adult help, create and engage in simple group actions base.	**6-, 7-, AND 8-YEAR-OLDS** ▶ Develop fair classroom behavior rules for identity issues with greater understanding, more autonomy and more depth. ▶ Identify respectful ways to ask about cultural behaviors and ideas different from their own. ▶ Learn about people who work for social justice in their communities. ▶ Problem-solve conflict situations involving bias. ▶ Problem-solve specific group actions related to a concrete discriminatory situation in their school or immediate community.

© Rick Reinhard, 1990

portunities to experience their ability to take action for themselves and others, thus fostering a "habit" of empowerment.

The chart on the previous page (Derman-Sparks, 1992) identifies general developmental possibilities for children from two to eight years old. Within this framework, each teacher and parent must determine the specific individual needs of their children.

Here are some guidelines to consider when creating activism activities for the children with whom you work:

1. **Be alert for unfair practices in your school or community that directly affect your children's lives.** These can be related to any aspect of children's identity and well being. They may directly involve an incident in the classroom/center, or relate to a problem that comes from the children's wider community. Children may bring an incident to your attention. For example, a kindergarten teacher explains a method she uses:

I teach my children to call on friends when they are faced with an unfair situation. For example, last week two boys were playing on the rope swing, and two girls were waiting for a long time. The girls kept asking for a turn, and the boys ignored them. I watched and waited to see what would happen. Finally, the girls came to me and complained. I asked them, "What should we do? I could go and stop them, but that won't help you in the future.' One girl then said, 'Maybe we could get some of our friends to help us.' I responded, 'Yes, that's a good idea.' The two girls collected about four children, girls and boys, and with their friends around them told the boys to give them a turn. The boys got off the swings and complained to me that they had been chased off. I talked with the two boys about what they had done to create the need for the girls to get their friends to help them."

Staff may raise an issue, sometimes spontaneously. For example, another kindergarten teacher wrote:

One activity we did was to paint over a wall in a park that had racial slurs written on it. The day we saw it, I stopped the group and said, 'Do you know what is written on this wall? It makes me very angry.' I read the words, we talked about what they meant, how they are very hurtful to people. Then we talked about what we could do and decided to paint over the words, which we did the next day. We probably could have written to the Parks Department, telling them about the wall and what we did. It would have been interesting to see what kind of response we got.

At another time, an issue may arise from larger community concerns. For example, children and families around the nation have joined early childhood teachers in "Worthy Wage Day" activities. (One strategy of a nationwide Worthy Wages campaign www.ccw.org is to improve salaries and working conditions of preschool and child care teachers.) While this issue springs from staff concerns, it directly affects the well-being of children and families. In Pasadena, children in several childcare centers learned what "worthy wages" meant, made posters and banners, and joined together at the steps of the City Hall, where representatives of the city government and some of their teachers and parents spoke about why better wages are necessary for child care center staff.

2. **Consider the interests and developmental abilities of your group of children.** Will the problem grab their attention? Is the issue developmentally appropriate for them? Do the methods fit the way young children learn? For example, an activism activity in a mid-Western child care center began when one of the children was hospitalized because he had eaten a bottle of vitamins he thought was candy. When the teacher, the following morning, explained why the child was absent, the children talked about confusing vitamins with candy, and how that could happen. They decided that they didn't think it was fair for vitamins to look and taste like candy, and dictated a letter to the manufacturer about their concerns. They also sent a copy of the letter to their families. (Of course, they also sent get well pictures and letters to the recuperating child.)

Another activity, initiated by their teacher, focused on bandaids, a material of considerable interest to young children.

My favorite activism activity is the one I did on "flesh colored" Curads™. One day, while getting an adhesive bandage for one of my 3-year-olds, the label "flesh colored" suddenly hit me. So I said, "Look at this — it says on the box that these bandages are flesh-colored. That means they are the same color as our skin. Let's see if it is really true." We then put bandages on each child's arm and discovered that they were only like the color of some of the children, but not like the color of those with brown skin.

The next day I suggested that we do an experiment. We would invite other children from the Children's School to put on an adhesive bandage and see if it matched their skin. So, other children came to our yard and we took photos of each child's arm with a bandage on it. We made a chart and realized that the bandage didn't match a lot of children's skin.

On the third day I suggested that we write a letter to the company and tell them what we learned. The children dictated what they wanted to say, and I added an explanation of our experi-

ment. We took a trip to the post office the next day to mail our letter. We also involved the parents, sending letters home about what we were doing, and talking about it when parents came to pick up their children.

We got a letter back from Colgate-Palmolive Company which politely said, "Enclosed find some transparent strips which are more flesh-colored.' I felt it was important that we did letter writing, even if the company didn't agree with us. We told them how we felt; they told us how they felt. I think the children felt it was a success because we could get the transparent bandages. I let it go after that. Some children remember; I've heard them say, 'This doesn't match me.' Now I'm wondering if I should have taken another step such as saying to the children that if we still don't think it's fair, we can decide not to buy this brand anymore, or ask the parents to write letters too. We are just beginning. If we get the parents involved, then we are laying a longer lasting foundation.

3. **Consider your comfort.** Is the issue one you feel comfortable addressing? What type of activities do you prefer? There is a wide spectrum of possibilities. Making changes in your own classroom is one type. For example, a group of 4- to 6-year-olds created a "handicapped parking" space in their school's parking lot, and then made tickets to put on cars inappropriately parked in the space. Activities such as writing letters, speaking with people, circulating petitions, participating in an appropriate demonstration represent a second category of possibilities. Involving parents and other community people in reclaiming their culture and history is a third. In a program for migrant families in California, staff collected favorite proverbs and stories from families and created books in Spanish and in Spanish and English for the children and for the parents. Children in a 1st through 3rd grade, Los Angeles urban public school interviewed activists in their community and then developed wall posters and books which they photocopied to share with other children in the school and with their families.

4. **Consider the parents' comfort.** Discuss with parents the reasons for activism activities and your approach to them. If parents express concerns or disagreements with activism activities in general, or with specific ones, take their concerns seriously. Try to find out what underlies their concerns. Parents' disagreement may be over the topic of the activity, or it might be over the method, or how

© Rick Reinhard, 1980

the topic affects their child's feelings. For example, after addressing issues of discrimination, children may come home sad or angry. You and the parents can consider ways to address these issues together that are honest but do not undermine children's hope for the future. Ask for suggestions about what activities you might use, problem-solve together to reach a solution acceptable to you and to the parents, and invite the parents to participate in the activity.

Parents are less likely to disagree if they see that activities address issues that directly affect young children and use child-appropriate methods, rather than those that are more relevant to adults. For example, at the child care center on the campus where I teach, parents enthusiastically supported the "band-aid" activity described previously. However not all parents wanted their children to participate in the Worthy Wage Day meeting at City Hall. Those children did other Worthy Wage Day activities at their center.

5. **Engage children in a "critical thinking" discussion about the problem**. Remember that your children must believe themselves that a particular situation or incident is unfair for an activism activity to be an educational experience. For example, four-year-olds in a child development center located on the campus of a church-based college were looking through a new calendar that had arrived in the mail. One child remarked, "Those children do not look like us." All the illustrations depicted only White children. The teacher replied, "You are really thinking. Which children don't you see?" Children called out the names of several classmates. They decided that they didn't think it was fair, and that they didn't want to use the calendar.

6. **Ask children for ideas about what they might do and include your own suggestions.** Choose one or a few activities that are safe, possible, and fit the needs of your particular group of children. The children with the "calendar" problem decided to take pictures of their class and send it with a letter to the company who made the calendar, explaining their concerns and asking that next time the calendar show all kinds of children. An additional action might be: deciding to adapt the calendar, by pasting other pictures or photos over several of the months, so that more diversity is depicted. Actions should make sense to the children, even if they are not what adults would do about a particular problem. Of course, they should also be safe for them to do.

7. **Do the activity with your children**. You may also want to document it through photographs, children's comments during the activity, and their reflections afterwards about what they did. Use this documentation to inform parents, through a wall display, a class newsletter, or other such methods, and to educate other teachers in your school about this type of activity.

8. **One activity leads to further ones**. Again, using the "calendar" incident as an example, when the children did not get a reply form the calendar company, they asked their teacher to call. When they still did not get a reply, the teacher told them about how adults use a "petition" to help make changes. The children liked the idea, wrote and illustrated their own petition and collected about one hundred names of college students on their campus. The petition did get a reply — with a promise to try to make future calendars more diverse. (Unfortunately, as of press time, we don't know if the promise was kept !)

9. **Use books to support children's own activism activities.** Following are a few suggestions.

Preschoolers

Swimmy by Leo Lionni

Elizabeth Cady Stanton by Carol Hilgartner Schlank

Martin Luther King, Jr.: A Picture Story by Margaret Boone-Jones

Primary age children

Three Cheers for Mother Jones by J. Bethel

The Drinking Gourd F.N. Monjo

The Red Comb by Fernando Pico

Ribbons for Emma by New Mexico People and Energy Collective

The Streets are Free by Kurusa

Gloria Goes to Gay Pride by Leslea Newman

10. **Engage in adult activism activities yourself.** Modeling the habit of activism in our own lives, whether we be teachers or parents, is essential for helping children to learn about the role of activism in life. Preschool-age children who see family members trying to change injustices that affect their family's life, such as organizing with other people in the neighborhood for a needed traffic light or cleaning up a neighborhood park, are more likely to do the same when they experience an injustice directed against themselves or their friends. As children move into elementary school-age, it is important for them to see family members joining with others to work for change on larger social problems, such as more housing for lower-income families. This teaches empathy and responsibility for people beyond one's own family.

Similarly, teachers who incorporate activism into their lives communicate that a pro-active stance towards injustice is a desirable trait. Teachers can tell children about educational activism activities in which they are engaged, such as working with other teachers in the school to get more books about children of color; participating in a campaign to improve salaries for childcare teachers; and working in their union to get smaller classroom size. They can also share their experiences in activism work that affects the larger community. In sum, if we practice what we preach, our message will resonate the tone of authenticity!

11. **Always keep in mind that the underlying goal of activism activities is children's empowerment — not the accomplishment of adult issues.**

One of the concerns sometimes voiced by other teachers or parents it that teachers who do activism activities with young children are using them for their own adult political agenda. Of course, that would be professionally unethical. Parents may choose to involve their young children in activism activities that reflect family values and political perspectives. However, in the classroom, activism activities are only designed for children's education and growth in the needed life skills of critical thinking, taking responsibility for acting to rectify unjust situations and becoming responsible citizens of a multicultural and democratic society.

Louise Derman-Sparks is a faculty member of Pacific Oaks College in Pasadena, California. She teaches courses on anti-bias education for K-12 and adult educators, and on the sociopolitical context of human development. She is the director of the Anti-Bias Education Leadership Project. Louise Derman-Sparks offers lectures and workshops on the topic of anti-bias education at conferences both nationally and internationally. She is the author of the most widely read book on anti-bias education for the early childhood level, Anti-Bias Curriculum: Tools for Empowering Young People *(w/ the ABC Task Force, NAEYC, 1989) and the co-author of* Teaching/Learning Anti-Racism: A Developmental Approach *(w/Carol Brunson Phillips, Teachers College Press, 1997).*

REFERENCES

Derman-Sparks, L. & the ABC Task Force. 1989. *Anti-Bias Curriculum: Tools for Empowering Young Children.* Washington, DC: NAEYC.

Derman-Sparks, L. 1992 "Reaching Potentials through Anti-Bias, Multicultural Curriculum." In Bredekamp, S.& T. Rosegrant, eds. *Reaching potentials: Appropriate curriculum and assessment for young children,* Volume I. Washington, DC: NAEYC.

Redefining the Norm: Early Childhood Anti-Bias Strategies

by Ellen Wolpert

It is often assumed that young children are unaware of racial differences and that they do not discriminate on the basis of gender, relative wealth, ethnicity and other characteristics. In fact, young children do notice differences. They quickly learn from their environment to attach values to those differences and to mimic the dominant society's discriminatory behavior unless those biases and behaviors are challenged. Children need help in recognizing and challenging bias rather than internalizing it.

A multicultural/anti-bias approach can help students learn to place a positive value on those differences and to treat all people with respect. It can nurture the development of positive self identity and group identity in not only the students but also the staff and families. Education by itself cannot eliminate prejudice or injustice. But the application of an anti-bias approach in the early years can help children to develop:

▸ pride in who they are;

▸ respect for others and the ability to interact with many different perspectives and to solve problems cooperatively and creatively;

▸ critical thinking skills and the ability to recognize bias and injustice;

▸ the commitment and ability to act against bias and injustice individually and in cooperation with others.

In this article I will describe some of the strategies that can be used to create an anti-racist/anti-bias environment. Many of the ideas have been implemented at the Washington-Beech Community Preschool, where I have worked as Director since 1985. Some of the basic ways to help students address biases are listed below.

▸ Continually reevaluate ways to integrate an anti-bias approach into all aspects of the program.

▸ Watch for bias in the environment that children encounter and listen to their comments. Gather materials that contradict the stereotypes and makes the invisible visible. Make comments that contradict statements of bias.

▸ Ask questions to develop critical thinking.

▸ Create opportunities to make comparisons between stereotypical images and a variety of real images.

▸ Create opportunities for problem-solving: what would you do if....?

▸ Take action to protest bias.

We begin by focusing on the children, families, and staff represented in our programs. With them at the center, we expand outward. We start with activities that encourage children to share who they are — drawing and talking about their lives, supporting positive feelings about one's self, family, race, culture, and community. Children make comparisons among themselves, looking at the ways they are both similar and different. They learn that different is OK. This creates the foundation for respecting and valuing differences beyond their own families and communities.

One technique we use is to create interactive materials using pictures mounted on mat board, blocks and wooden tubes. Central to the picture collection are lots of photographs of the students themselves. Used in games, children interact with the pictures and discuss the anti-bias information while they simultaneously develop a wide variety of cognitive skills such as reading, printing, developing descriptive language and vocabulary skills, counting, comparing, classifying, developing visual memory, etc.

The pictures also reflect the true diversity of our society. The images are selected to challenge prevailing stereotypes to which students are exposed. There are many primary areas of bias that permeate our environment that we can directly acknowledge, discuss and challenge on a daily basis including race, age, physical abilities, physical characteristics, gender, family composition and sexual orientation, economic class, ethnicity.

Classroom Strategies

The following are some anecdotes from our work and lessons we have learned about addressing specific areas of bias.

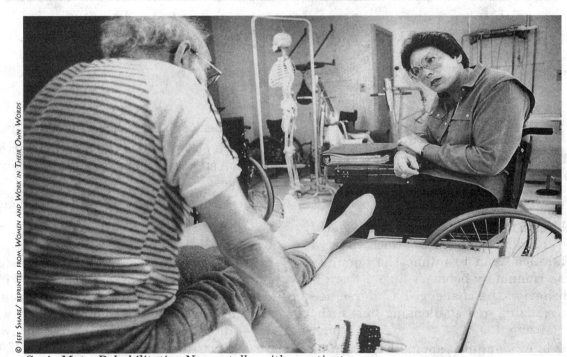

Susie Matz, Rehabilitation Nurse, talks with a patient.

RACE

▶ Many teachers believe that preschool-aged children do not notice race. One teacher was surprised when she showed a White 4-year-old boy a picture of a young Black man. The boy said, "He's a robber cuz he has a brown face like a robber..." Clearly the boy had been affected by TV news and stories repeatedly linking Black men to crime. She knew then she would have to develop anti-racist strategies. The teacher collected positive images and used them for learning games and discussions (see Photo Picture Cards following this article.) The teacher asks students, "Can you describe the people in these pictures? What skin color do they have? What are they doing?" Using a picture of an African American man teaching his son to ride a bicycle, the teacher refers specifically to skin color and the positive activities. The teachers asks: "What color skin does this man have? What is he doing in the picture? Is it like anything that happens in your family?"

▶ In Disney's *The Lion King*, the destructive hyenas have black or dark skin. Scarface, the mean lion, has a black mane. After the movie a young child says, "Black people are bad, they are bad in the movie," even though there are only animals in the movie with human voices. Racial and other forms of bias require more than an immediate response when hurtful incidents happen. We need to be proactive. Examining books and other media one can see how often the villain in children's stories is Black or dressed in black. One can assist children in recognizing this use of color and to challenge rather than internalize it. Also, purchase and create stories in which people of color are important positive characters.

▶ Heroes should be redefined as people of all races who do daily heroic things like helping a friend or helping to bring neighbors together to build a community center. It is important for children to recognize that heroes reside in their families and in the community.

▶ Children need to learn about White people who have taken a stand against racism. This teaches them the concept of solidarity. White children learn that instead of feeling guilty about racism, they can choose to work against it.

▶ Children at Washington-Beech listened to and discussed the following text from a story about two miners: *"In the morning they were clean as snow... but by night time they were black as soot, dirty as pitch."*

The students and their teacher wrote a letter to the author to protest the negative use of black in the story and the assumption that cleanliness is white.

- A White child, new in class, looked at a Black child and said, "She's still dirty. She didn't wash good." In response one can do lots of skin color activities. Bring black and white dolls to the water table and ask, "Does the color wash off? Is the doll dirty? Are all things that are dirty black or brown? When you make playdough and get the white flour and water all over your hands, are your hands dirty?" Make lists of beautiful things that are black and brown. Mix paints to match the students' and teachers' skin colors. In one class a child complained, "She won't let me play cuz I'm brown." The teacher intervened: "Saying Shade can't play because her skin is brown hurt Shade's feelings. It wouldn't be fair to say you can't play because your skin is beige. I can see you both want to play with this game. Let's think together of a different way to solve the problem."

Age

- Observing children at play quickly reveals many of their stereotypes. For example, their assumption that the elderly are all physically weak is reflected when a child bends over, uses a stick and walks slowing, saying, "I'm old." To broaden their understanding, share a variety of visual resources which demonstrate that people with canes are not all elderly, inactive or unable to contribute. Share pictures of a young man with a cane playing basketball, an elderly farm couple harvesting a crop, or an older woman playing sports. Invite older friends and relatives to share some of their experiences.

Physical Abilities

- Instead of simply contradicting the misinformation, ask questions to develop critical thinking. For example, if a child says, "People in wheelchairs can't be mommies and daddies," ask "Do you think that could be a stereotype?" Suggest simple research, "Let's look through our stories and picture collection and see if we find mommies or daddies in wheelchairs." You could find pictures such as a single mother in a wheelchair washing her infant son or a mother and father, both in wheelchairs, pushing their daughter in a baby carriage. Ask questions like: what is this woman doing to take care of the baby? Do you think she could be the baby's mommy?

- Provide crutches for the dramatic play area and borrow (or rent) a wheelchair to test getting around the room. Make group decisions on how to rearrange the room to make it more accessible to people with diverse physical abilities.

- Create persona dolls — dolls with a story that stays with that doll. One of the dolls could use a cane or wheelchair. This allows children to "interact" with people with specific issues.

- Integrate anti-bias issues into every theme. For example, during a theme on communication, have children learn sign language and develop respect for the many ways people communicate.

Physical Characteristics

- Challenge bias about physical characteristics by providing diverse body type images and supporting comments: "People come in all different shapes and sizes."

- Share the story *Fat Fat Rose Marie*. Rose Marie is teased about her size. Claire, Rose Marie's friend, stands up to the teaser. She mushes her ice cream in the teaser's face. Ask children: "What do you think of Claire's solution?" "Are there other ways Claire might have responded?" "Have you ever been teased like that?" "How did it feel?" "What can you do if someone teases you or your friend?" (*Fat Fat Rose Marie* is out of print. If you can't find the book, create your own stories using puppets.)

Gender

- Respond to play time comments such as: "You can't be the doctor. You're a girl!" by asking critical thinking questions such as "Do any of you know doctors who are women?". In the next few days, introduce visual images and books that feature women as doctors and men as nurses. In a class meeting, raise the issue: "I remember that someone said girls couldn't be doctors. What do you think about that? Do you think girls can be doctors when they grow up?". The class could visit a local clinic so children can meet a woman doctor.

- To learn about students' biases, try telling a story without showing the pictures. Use character names that can be male or female. Have children draw or describe specific characters. Compare and discuss why they thought certain characters were male and others female.

- Create a matching game of people doing similar things using lots of non-stereotypical pictures.

Include photographs of children from the class. For example, use photos of girls climbing or doing carpentry and of boys playing with dolls or helping with cleaning chores.

- Create simple dolls for the block area by wrapping non-stereotypical photographs of male and female workers around cardboard tubes that will encourage both boys and girls to play and explore diverse roles.

- Read stories which help children explore a range of roles for women. For example, *Dulci Dando Soccer Star* is about a young girl who challenges the doubts of the boys on the school soccer team and proves her skills as a soccer player.

- Play "stereotype or fact" by posing questions such as, "only boys play soccer — stereotype or fact?" In one class a child responded saying, "That's a stereotype! We got the book!"

- As adults, we must pay attention to our own comments: Do we complement girls when they wear dresses but not when they wear overalls? Do we comment on girls' appearances while focussing on boys' accomplishments? Do we encourage boys to be involved and treat the girls as if they are involved as long as they are watching?

FAMILY COMPOSITION AND SEXUAL ORIENTATION

- To support the diversity of families, create a picture collection of many kinds of families beginning with pictures of the families in your class. These can be used in a classifying and sorting game, where each child takes turns describing sets of similar families: single-parent families, group and children's homes, two-parent families, including families with two adults of the same gender. Adding the number of people in pairs of family cards, a child finds a two-parent African-American family and an extended family totaling ten people and compares that pair to a diverse age couple with their baby and a biracial family with their adopted children also totaling ten people.

- After hearing the story *Snow White*, a child announced, "Stepmothers are wicked." To encourage critical thinking the teacher asked, "Does anyone have a new mommy? What is she like? Do you know anyone who is or has a stepmommy? Have you heard other stories about stepmothers that are not wicked?"

- A child says, "You can't have two mommies." A child with gay parents is visibly upset. The

© RICK REINHARD, 1994

teacher intervenes, saying, "There are lots of different kinds of families. In some families there are two mommies. People make many different choices about who they love and who they live with." She follows up with children's books which features families with two moms like *Asha's Mums* — and another with two fathers — *Daddy's Roommate*.

▸ In one staff group at Washington-Beech there were strong disagreements about sexual orientation and implications for the classroom. In order to develop an approach that would validate children's lives and our own diversity of perspectives, we reached a compromise after several discussions. One teacher simply could not read stories she felt would advocate for a life-style which her religion strongly opposes. But, because of her deep care for the children, she was able to reassure the child of gay parents in her class when a negative remark was made. It was agreed that another teacher would read stories to the students

norm for my students. So I created new number cards with more diverse clothing images. A child collecting the number two chose pictures of two construction workers in overalls and two sisters dressed alike in red pedal pushers and plaid blouses.

▸ During a theme on housing I made 4-piece puzzles of various living situations that are inclusive of a diverse range of economic conditions including both poor and affluent scenes from urban and rural communities.

▸ During a theme on special events and celebrations, use stories like *The River That Gave Gifts* in which the best presents are made with love rather than money. Place less emphasis on individual gifts and more on things that can be shared, like new skills children can teach each other or cooperative efforts like baking bread for the whole group.

▸ Children in our classrooms learn from the media and other sources that people are poor because

---

THERE IS NO LIST OF THE THINGS WE SHOULD AND SHOULDN'T SAY. IT IS A PROCESS OF REFLECTIVE TEACHING — REFLECTING ON WHAT STUDENTS ARE LEARNING ABOUT THEMSELVES AND THE WORLD FROM OUR INTERACTION WITH THE CLASSROOM ENVIRONMENT.

---

which made reference to gay parents. This can be a difficult discussion. One of the basic principles and challenges of anti-bias curriculum is negotiating among diverse views to create environments respectful of difference that can be very controversial.

ECONOMIC CLASS

▸ Children learn through television programs that one's money is what makes a person important. Although money certainly gives a person privilege and power in this society, we want to challenge the notion that having money makes one a better person. In a theme on clothing, we can use the story *Old Hat, New Hat* to provide an alternative message. After trying on all the new and exciting hats, the best one is still the worn and familiar one.

▸ During planning for math activities, evaluate the materials. I had made number charts from a Benetton ad book with bright colors and diverse children. But I later realized how they reflect financial resources which are not the current

they are lazy, not because the system is inequitable or unfair. They also learn that certain occupations are better than others. In the classroom, we can validate the contributions that *all* workers make to society. We can incorporate visual images in our picture collection from calendars produced by a labor union and pictures of people working in the neighborhood. We can invite community workers to visit school and take field trips to see the different jobs they do. Themes can include the contributions and concerns of relevant workers. A theme on clothing can include textile factory workers. The teacher asks questions that assist children to contradict stereotypes: "Do you think the work these people are doing is important?" Children can learn about the work of all the school staff, such as the people who work in the kitchen, maintenance, administration, transportation, health room and library.

▸ Evaluate the birthday policy. Do families buy party food and favors, creating pressure to "keep up with" the more elaborate parties? Instead children can collectively prepare a celebration with handmade cards and decorations.

- When issues come up, respond in ways that create empathy rather than blame for one's poverty. Children on a field trip see a homeless mother and daughter. Back at school they talk about fairness and decide it's unfair that everyone doesn't have a home to live in. They play counting and sorting games that include pictures of people who are homeless and those organizing against poor housing. They find stories about people coming together to challenge unfairness and learn about a local organizing campaign to help people who are homeless move into abandoned buildings. Children at Washington-Beech decided to help, too, by making a support banner. At a monthly meeting, families and staff talked about the same issues and played the picture games. A parent said, "This has really changed my own attitudes. I'll never see a homeless person as just a bum anymore."

- Most children learn young that if you work hard you'll do well and will not be poor. The absence of diverse images of people who are poor from school materials means that many children will not understand the real lives and concerns of those who want jobs but are excluded because of factors such as gender, skin color, physical ability and runaway shops.

- Students seldom see images of people who work hard but receive wages too low to sustain basic needs. The common stereotype of people with low incomes is that they simply are not working hard enough. Many children will not learn to value the contributions that a majority of workers make to our society if they remain absent from school materials. We can value all workers by their inclusion in materials we create.

- In a theme on food, include pictures of farmers and farmworkers. Share stories and pictures about the work of farmworkers to protect their jobs, such as the protests against non-union fruit.

ETHNICITY

- Begin by developing awareness of and respect for the language diversity in our own community. Adding to children's knowledge of "Head, Shoulders, Knees, and Toes" in English, student intern Sook Hyun taught children to sing it in her language, which is Korean. She added picture name cards in Korean to a name photo match game. Children made Hebrew letters for an alphabet display. *Angel Child, Dragon Child* is a good story for challenging bias about language. In the story,

Ut from Viet Nam is teased by Raymond because of her accent. Raymond gets to know Ut and stops his teasing. (The story has one problem which the teacher should address. Raymond says "I can't understand her [Ut's] funny words." No one challenges his description of her language. The teacher can stop reading at this point and ask students how they would respond to this comment. Or the teacher can model a response by adding a comment from another character in the story such as, "Raymond, does Ut speak in a way you have never heard before? She speaks Vietnamese. It is not funny, just different from your language."

- A child says in a negative tone, "She's Haitian!" The teacher says positively, "Yes she is Haitian. She comes from Haiti. Did you know she can speak three languages?" Several other children proudly announce, "I'm Haitian! I can speak in Kreyol!"

- Create games that provide ongoing contact with images of people from diverse ethnic groups, beginning with ourselves. We all have ethnic origins, whether they be from Europe, Asia, Africa, the Middle East, or the Americas. The pictures go beyond our own communities to make connections to unfamiliar people doing familiar kinds of activities. Players collect pictures of people doing similar things — working with clay, riding bicycles, or playing on swings for example. Children develop sorting and classifying skills while learning to appreciate ways we are simultaneously different and alike. Children make comparisons between their stereotypes and photographs or other information.

- A child says, "Ooh, she dresses like a Puerto Rican. Those bright colors look funny." The teacher responds, "Are all the Puerto Ricans in these pictures dressed in bright colors? Is it a stereotype or fact to say that all Puerto Ricans wear bright colors?" The teacher also uses a fabric match game to point out bright color combinations and asks, "Do we all like the same colors? Why can't someone wear clothes with bright colors?"

- A child brings in a restaurant place mat of a sleepy Mexican village, a childlike man in a great big hat, a donkey and some cactus. The child, repeating a stereotype he's heard, says, "Mexicans are lazy." A teacher asks, "Is this a stereotype? Do all Mexicans live in sleepy villages and spend their time sleeping under cactus?" To contradict the stereotype, use stories like *Amelia's Road*, or *Lights on the River* about the lives of

© Rick Reinhard, 1994

Mexican farmworkers. Provide opportunities for additional research using photographs of Mexican cities or Mexicans hard at work in a car factory and ask, "Are Mexicans working in this factory lazy?" Children can see that the remark about Mexicans being lazy is a stereotype.

COOPERATIVE PROBLEM-SOLVING

To accept diverse perspectives and solve common problems related to bias, children need to develop cooperative skills rather than competitive ones. Following are some strategies that we have found helpful.

Using a picture collection with pairs of artwork or textile images, tape pictures to children's backs. They must each find another child with the same picture but they can't see their own. The game requires cooperation, as well as observation, descriptive language, and careful listening. By using artwork from diverse cultures, students can also develop an appreciation for different styles and color combinations.

We continually reevaluate activities and process. We tried musical chairs a new way, using an idea from *The Cooperative Sports and Games Book*. Instead of removing children from the game, the goal is to make space for everyone and share the seats as more chairs are removed. When I suggested

this game the teacher was very skeptical saying, "It won't work." Well, at first she was right. The children were used to competing with each other. But after several tries the new way caught on and we had no more tears. Instead children were enthusiastically saying, "You can share this seat with me, come sit with me, you can sit here." This spilled over into many other classroom activities as children felt the thrill of sharing rather than the tension and disappointment from competing.

We choose stories about cooperation, like *Swimmy* in which the little fish get together to protect themselves from the big fish. In *The Streets are Free* children organize to get a playground. The stories inspire discussions about the many ways people can challenge things they think are wrong and children apply the ideas to their own situations. One time, children were concerned about not getting enough food at lunch. They wrote letters to the food company and presented them at a meeting. The food service improved.

Some stories, such as *The Lorax*, make it appear that social change results from the goodwill of those in power or one individual. As described by Bill Bigelow in *Rethinking Schools* (4.3), *The Lorax* features an industrialist who stops polluting once he understands how harmful the poisons are to the land. The story can be used to question whether change really happens that way and to consider cooperative strategies by asking students: "Most company owners already know the impact of their factories on the land, air and people. What else could the Lorax have done? Were there other characters in *The Lorax* that could have worked together to solve the problem and if so, how?"

To encourage cooperative activities and problem-solving, I created a match game that illustrates and supports ways staff, families, and people in various communities cooperate in daily activities and challenge injustice. The pictures include photographs of children working together to make playdough, build a block structure, make a mural, bake a cake. The pictures also include a neighborhood mural about Latino concerns and scenes from a demonstration against budget cuts that would have taken away many families' daycare.

Developing the Curriculum: Reflection and Revision

On a daily basis, we reflect on the messages students are getting from the environment and ourselves. For example, without thinking a teacher made the same comment to a child she had heard when she was growing up, "Oh, don't mix all those beautiful colors together, it will come out all brown...." A child responded, "Don't you like brown. My skin is brown." As soon as she said it the teacher realized that her comment countered her efforts to encourage students to see the beauty in all colors.

There is no list of the things we should and shouldn't say. It is a process of reflective teaching — reflecting on what students are learning about themselves and the world from our interaction with the classroom environment. Following are some examples of how we have reflected on issues of bias and modified our curriculum accordingly.

As educators, we go to see the most popular children's films to be aware of the messages children are getting. For example, the opening lyrics of the film *Aladdin* are: "I come from a land, from a faraway place, where the caravan camels roam. Where they cut off your ear if they don't like your face. It's barbaric, but hey, it's home." (Protests led to changing those lines in the video.)

In the film, Aladdin the good Arab, is associated with the color white and Caucasian features and the bad one, Jafar, with the color black and Semitic features. We ask children to make comparisons between themselves and several pictures of Arabs such as an Arab man reading to his daughter. "How are people in each of picture simi-lar and different from people in our school or in your family?"

Even if children don't see the big films, they're bombarded with related toys, clothes, and advertisements wherever they go. Because it's almost impossible to avoid, we assist children in recognizing the bias so they can challenge it.

We make mistakes along the way. We learn from them and keep trying. In one class we made a puzzle chain that included pictures from Caribbean countries to make the classroom more welcoming to Caribbean immigrant students. When she saw the puzzle, a parent said, "These are great! But did you know that there are both rural villages and *cities* on the islands?" We realized that our limited image of the Caribbean as beaches and small towns was reflected in the puzzle. We added pictures of Caribbean cities.

I loved the story of *The Three Little Pigs* and suggested that it could be used during a theme on where we live because of the three different kinds of housing it introduces. After hearing the story of *The Three Little Pigs*, children saw a picture of a Yagua village in Peru in which the homes are made of trimmed tree limbs ("sticks") and built on stilts. One child remarked, "That's a stupid house."

I realized that *The Three Little Pigs* implies that stick homes are poorly built with laziness by a brother who just wants to dance and play, but brick homes are superior, strong, and built with intelligence and hard work.

To address the students' comments, we found pictures of a man in India working very hard in the hot sun to build a roof of sticks and the teacher asks, "Is the person building this house lazy? Do you think the house is strong? Could it be blown down by a wolf?" We also told a variation of *The Three Little Pigs* by replacing the wolf with an elephant. To protect their homes from the elephant's bursts of water from her trunk, the pigs in the homes of straw and sticks put them up on stilts. But the house of bricks floods. The pig in the brick house must flee to his brother's house of sticks. Students see that different materials are appropriate for different settings and conditions.

We continue by making comparisons between houses in our own environment and those in different countries, all built to address similar conditions. For example, we share pictures of houses on the Massachusetts shore with pictures of a Yagua home. Both are built on stilts, one as protection from the tides and the other to make the most of river breezes. This begins to break down stereotypes

We can include images of people standing up for their community in our wall displays and children's educational games. This picture is also a good example of how to integrate images of the use of language diversity in everyday settings.

about the inferiority of less industrialized societies.

We develop a lot of our lessons based on comments we hear from children. For example, a child sees a picture of a baby being carried in a basket and says, "Babies don't go in baskets." In response we try to encourage critical thinking and experimentation with the diverse ways familiar things can be done — such as carrying babies and bags. Pictures are provided showing the many ways people carry babies. Bags, poles, shawls, and baskets are available. A child tries using her head to support the strap of a bag and wrapping her doll on her back — learning there isn't one "regular" way but many different ways to accomplish a task.

A teacher hears a child say, "Everybody sit like Indians." To contradict the stereotype, the teacher uses a picture of a Navajo family in which people are sitting in many different ways including on a couch, a chair, cross legged on the floor, and open-legged, also on the floor. The teacher asks, "Do all Indians sit the same way?"

A match game can be created from carefully chosen, non-stereotypical images from magazines and books of Native people engaged in activities of daily life. Going to school, riding a bicycle, working as a doctor, and a grandmother and her grand-daughter out walking are just a few examples. A

variety of occupations should also be reflected, such as a tree surgeon, a welder and a doctor. Children find cards that are the same. During play we talk about the pictures. The teacher asks, "Are you surprised that these Indians are skiing or playing football?" A child says, "They're not Indians. Real Indians wear feathers." The teacher responds, "Native people have important ceremonies called pow-wows when they wear special clothes including feathers. Do you have any clothes you wear for special celebrations?"

After several weeks of activities and discussion, a child who at first argued that Indians "do toooo" always wear feathers and live in tepees was playing the match game. I asked, "Who are these pictures of?" He said: "Indians." "But where are the feathers?" I asked. He replied, proud of his new knowledge, "They're for special ceremonies."

WORKING WITH PARENTS AND FAMILIES

Parents and family members are important to the development of anti-bias curriculum. At Washington-Beech we try various strategies so that parents and families have opportunities to do the things listed below.

▶ Learn about the anti-bias curriculum approach.

▶ Experience activities children are doing in the

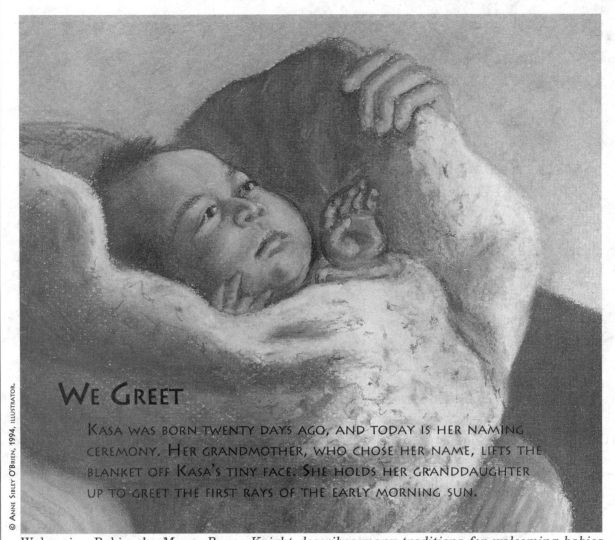

WE GREET

KASA WAS BORN TWENTY DAYS AGO, AND TODAY IS HER NAMING CEREMONY. HER GRANDMOTHER, WHO CHOSE HER NAME, LIFTS THE BLANKET OFF KASA'S TINY FACE. SHE HOLDS HER GRANDDAUGHTER UP TO GREET THE FIRST RAYS OF THE EARLY MORNING SUN.

Welcoming Babies by Margy Burns Knight describes many traditions for welcoming babies throughout the world.

classroom and teachers are using in staff development.

▸ Learn about their own biases.

▸ Share their values and expectations.

▸ Provide input and feedback.

▸ Share some of their strategies for dealing with bias.

▸ Learn ways to support their children as they begin to challenge bias.

Following are some of the ways that we have worked with parents on anti-bias education.

1. Family members explore issues of bias and anti-bias curricula at regularly scheduled family/staff meetings. Below are two examples of activities that have been tried in our meetings.

Example: Select pictures from a storybook or the newspaper, xerox and distribute to small groups. Ask the groups to describe and discuss what they see. Comparisons are then made between their perceptions and those of the actual story.

The children's book *The Streets are Free* was used for one meeting. Parents examined a picture from the book of children playing in the street. Some said that it looked like the children were trying to make trouble and get in the way of traffic. Others felt they were in the street because they had no other place to play. In this particular group the need for considering diverse perspectives was further enforced by families' direct experience. They compared the story with what happens in regard to their own neighborhoods when "outsiders" report only the bad things they "see" so their neighborhoods get the reputation of being full of crime and drugs and not full of people helping each other, getting through school, working three jobs and raising wonderful children. This activity introduced to families how and why the school helps children recognize diverse perspectives.

Example: During a family/staff meeting in November, we viewed a filmstrip used both with staff and in the classroom called "Unlearning Stereotypes about Native Americans" from The Council on Interracial Books for Children.

After the filmstrip, participants played a series of games based on familiar card games. These card games were also used with staff and in the classroom. The cards were all photographs of Native Americans in the present doing familiar activities such as reading to their children, playing football, doing the laundry, and engaged in various occupations such as surgeon, teacher, logger, farmer.

We compared these images to the stereotypes presented in the filmstrip and talked about where the stereotypes come from and the harm they do. Family members were indignant that they had never learned these things in school and that their older children were continuing to be exposed to stereotypes and "mis-education." They became enthusiastic supporters of the anti-bias approach. We talked about ways of supporting each other in the work to have all our lives and histories better represented and respected in public schools.

2. Family members critique materials, books and activities that deal with themes relevant to their own experiences.

Example: *How Long to America: A Thanksgiving Story* is written for young children about refugees fleeing their country by boat and the perilous journey they experience to get to the United States. Upon arrival they are welcomed with open arms and celebrate their good fortune with the Thanksgiving holiday.

I shared this book with a Haitian parent to get her opinion. She felt that the book was not appropriate as written because it did not portray the reality of the difficult conditions making it necessary for the family to leave their home country. Even worse, the book romanticized the families' arrival, showing them being welcomed when in fact many refugees face rejection. This is particularly true for Haitian refugees whose treatment by the United States even after a brutal coup led to international condemnation of U.S. refugee policy.

With this new knowledge, staff discussed how to edit the story by eliminating certain pictures or text, or changing some of the words so it could still be used to develop empathy for the difficulties classmates or community members have faced. They searched for other stories that would present other perspectives of the immigrant experience like *Friends from the Other Side*. In this book, a Mexican child who has come into the United States is teased and threatened by children here. He is then befriended by a young girl.

3. Family members tell their own stories. At family/staff meetings, family stories can be shared as a way of:

▸ Learning about each other's experiences and values.

▸ Exploring similarities and differences.

▸ Thinking about our own school and life experiences and using them to think about what we want children to learn.

▸ Developing our own heroes.

Example: In one group we had been struggling to deal with December holidays in a way that would be anti-bias. We decided to do a theme on all the special things we celebrate. We didn't want to focus on December holidays but we didn't want to ignore them for many reasons. For example, we wanted children to learn that not everyone celebrates those holidays and those who do, do so in many different ways.

With families, we had a big discussion about the things we all liked and didn't like about the "December holiday syndrome." This discussion helped people see, from their own experiences, the reasons we had identified for not focusing so heavily on Christmas in particular.

We asked people to share stories of other things they celebrate in their families from homecomings to naming ceremonies to learning new things. Many of these stories were then shared with the children as part of the theme on special things we celebrate. A recommended book for this theme is *Welcoming Babies*. It celebrates the diversity of ways new babies are welcomed into families.

4. Family members can provide photographs for wall displays or big books illustrating all the different kinds of families represented in the class. Photographs of the jobs family members do, such as women and men doing nontraditional activities can be added to photograph games.

5. Family members can provide music. Music children hear at home can be incorporated into class-

room activities and nap time.

6. Families can provide translations of common phrases helpful in staff/child relationships, for favorite songs, and for various theme-related words and phrases.

7. Families can often share information about how discrimination affects them, their children and/or their community.

Example: "He said he'd help our people but he doesn't do what he said he would." Several Haitian children in one group cut out a photograph from the newspaper of President Clinton talking to a group of people. The children described the picture saying, "This is Bill Clinton. He's telling our people he will help us but he doesn't do what he says he would." When family members were told about this they came in and talked to staff about the coup in Haiti that ousted their beloved President Aristide and its effect on families and their children here. The discussion helped staff better understand what people were experiencing and how to strategize for the classroom.

8. Visits to the classroom. Although it is often difficult for parents and other family members who are working to come into class there are occasions when it is possible.

Example: Developing our own heroes. One group of parents wanted to redefine heroism from the qualities of a "superhero" to the qualities of heroes in our daily lives. Family members and friends were invited to share "hero" stories with the class. One grandmother came to school to share her recent success at having gone back to school and having just received her high school diploma

Example: "But won't she die of starvation if she goes to Africa?" A Nigerian child and her family were planning a visit home. Children in the class who had seen various newscasts were afraid their classmate would die of starvation while visiting Nigeria. The child's father came to school to talk

© DEBORAH MENKART

Photos such as this one of a neighborhood store can be used for many learning activities. Classroom use of images from the students' neighborhood can help to link the school and the community.

about what his home country was like and challenged some of the stereotypes the children were learning about Africa. I made a big book of African cities as a follow-up to his visit.

9. Receive assistance with issues of bias.

Example: "Won't my son be gay if he plays with dolls?" A parent came to me because her son wanted a doll after playing with dolls at school. She received a lot of resistance from friends and family who felt that dolls for boys were inappropriate. I asked her what kind of help she wanted from her husband in caring for her own kids and what kind of a father she hoped her son would become. I suggested that playing with dolls might be a way for him to practice. Feeling much more comfortable, the parent did decide to buy her son a doll. Later this parent was able to share her story with another parent who was struggling with the same situation.

▶ ▶ ▶

Many teachers fear the resistance they will get from family members as they attempt to implement an anti-bias curriculum approach. It is true that this can be a very difficult process. Many family members have faced similar difficulties in trying to get teachers and school personnel to respect their race, culture, class, gender, physical abilities, and family composition.

Although sometimes it is difficult sharing information and experiences like those described above, really listening to peoples' concerns has proven to be extraordinarily helpful. Meeting as frequently as possible, having an open-door policy in between, and creating opportunities for small groups to talk and do activities together during the meetings generally has ensured that people speak up when opinions are expressed that they don't like. Parents and family members in the program rarely all agree with each other so when there is a disagreement there are usually adults other than staff who will argue for an anti-bias approach.

CONCLUSION

Education by itself cannot eliminate prejudice or injustice. But schools and families together can help develop proud and powerful children so that together we can all create a more just society.

Ellen Wolpert has been an early childhood educator since 1970 and is presently the Director of Education and Dissemination at The Washington-Beech Community Preschool in Boston, Massachusetts. She offers staff development and training on creating anti-bias early education environments and is available for consulting and technical assistance. For consulting or training call: 617-522-8778 or send e-mail to: ewolpert@igc.apc.org © Ellen J. Wolpert, 1997.

REFERENCES

Altman, L. & E. Sanchez. 1993. *Amelia's road.* New York: Lee & Low Books Inc.

Anzaldua, G. 1993. *Friends from the other side/Amigos del otro lado.* San Francisco: Children's Book Press.

Berenstain, S. & J. 1970. *Old hat, new hat.* New York: Random House Bright and Early Book.

Bunting, E. 1988. *How many days to America: A Thanksgiving story.* New York: Clarion.

Elwin, R. & M. Paulse. 1990. *Asha's mums.* Toronto: Women's Press.

Humphrey, M. 1986. *The river that gave gifts.* San Francisco: Children's Book Press.

Knight, M.B. 1994. *Welcoming babies.* Gardiner, ME: Tilbury House. Call or write for free catalog: Tilbury House, 132 Water Street, Gardiner, ME 04345 or call 800-582-1899.

Kurusa. 1995 *The streets are free.* New York: Annick Press.

Lionni, L. 1963. *Swimmy.* New York: Knopf.

Passen, L. 1991. *Fat, fat Rose Marie.* New York: Henry Holt.

Stops, S. 1992. *Dulci Dando soccer star.* New York: Henry Holt.

Surat, M. 1983. *Angel child, dragon child.* New York: Scholastic.

Willhoite, M. 1991 *Daddy's roommate.* Boston: Alyson Wonderland.

Thomas, J. 1994. *Lights on the river.* New York: Hyperion.

Orlick, T. 1978. *The cooperative sports and games book: Challenge without competition.* New York: Pantheon Books.

Seuss, D. 1971. *The lorax.* New York: Random House.

Unlearning Indian Stereotypes filmstrip by the Council on Interracial Books for Children (CIBC). The CIBC is no longer operating. Some school or public libraries have copies of the filmstrip which is dated but still useful.

PHOTO PICTURE CARDS: A KEY TOOL FOR THE ANTI-BIAS CLASSROOM

BY ELLEN WOLPERT

Photographs are central to the anti-bias curriculum approach for the early childhood classroom, as explained in the previous article. In this article I will describe in more detail how they are used and how to mount the photos on picture cards. Some suggestions for photographs include:

▸ People with diverse physical abilities in active roles

▸ Elderly people doing interesting things

▸ A wide variety of family composition

▸ Positive portraits of poor and working-class people doing a wide variety of jobs

▸ Men and women in nontraditional roles

▸ Positive portraits of people of all shapes and sizes

▸ People of diverse racial and cultural backgrounds

▸ Photographs of the children, families, and staff in your program. This can help to demonstrate that we are all part of, not separate from, the diversity

Photographs should provide non-stereotypical representations of people in and outside the classroom involved in familiar activities — activities that are familiar to the children in the classroom and activities from daily life rather than special events and holidays.

Include groups of people often absent from school materials based on race, ethnicity, economic class, physical abilities and characteristics, gender, age, and family composition. The absence of many groups from school materials contributes to minimizing their importance, dismissing their concerns and facilitating the acceptance of stereotypes about them. For example, many groups of workers (factory workers, waitresses, custodians) are rarely pictured in school materials. This perpetuates the thinking that they are not as important to society as those who are more visible (doctors, teachers.) Their invisibility makes children more susceptible to absorbing stereotypes such as those that suggest falsely that these workers contribute less or earn less because they are lazy and work less.

Be careful not to think of or portray others as exotic and ourselves as the norm. Pictures of people should represent daily ways of dressing. Therefore it is best, for example, not to choose photographs that represent holiday dress and celebrations, unless you are specifically doing a theme on diverse special celebrations. In this case, plan how to avoid leaving children with the association of that special way of dressing to define any group of people or to define all people other than themselves — understanding that young children retain the most salient and most visible details. For example, if you wish to challenge stereotypes about Native People and several of your pictures are of current-day Pow-wows, you run the risk of simply perpetuating stereotypes — Indians as dancers, drummers, dressed in traditional clothing and beads — rather than helping children connect to the daily lives of Native People involved in work, school, family life and friendships, and recreation.

Photographs can be used for many purposes in many ways:

1. Photographs of the staff, families, and children in our own program validate who we are and help to develop an understanding of and a respect for differences. Create wall displays such as family photo boards, cubby and art labels, and attendance boards. Make games such as concentration and lotto, and photograph/name match games. For the creation of matching games, develop photographs at labs which offer "two for the price of one."

Create labels with the names of children, their family and their friends. Play games in which children match the photos with the names. Children will develop reading skills at the same time they feel proud because of the inclusion of their own images in the materials. The photographs can be useful in discussions of ways we and our families are similar and different.

2. As children describe their reactions to various pictures, they will express their ideas about themselves and others. These comments help staff to determine what biases they will need to challenge through the curriculum. To elicit children's ideas about particular groups of people, children can be

© Deborah Menkart

asked to tell stories about the people in the pictures. To elicit their ideas about who can be friends or who can be in the same family, they can be asked to combine photographs into friendship and family groups.

3. Children can make comparisons among photographs that will acknowledge and support our similarities and our differences.

For example, children might assume that eating with a fork is the norm, while eating with chopsticks or one's hands is exotic or bad. By exposing students to diverse images of people eating, they can learn to see them as simply different. We want to develop respect for differences at the same time we create a sense of similarity of purpose. We all eat. We all use something to pick up our food with — forks, chopsticks, hands, leaves, bread.

4. Children telling stories about the photographs will integrate the anti-bias information into their thinking as well as increase their language skills. Adults creating stories can address issues of bias children have expressed or that adults know they are being exposed to.

Example: A photograph of a young girl in a wheelchair at school (from *We Can Do It*) can be used to tell a story about how some children are refusing to play with her. Children can be asked

why this is happening. They can be given information that contradicts their fears and stereotypes. And they can be asked what they could do to make her feel more welcome.

5. In response to stereotypes, children can be asked to look through picture collections to find images that either verify or challenge their stereotypes.

6. Comparisons can be made between the stereotypes and non-stereotypical collections so children learn to recognize stereotypes and to see they are unfair because they are untrue.

7. Photographs mounted on cardboard can be slipped into plastic stands (available from restaurant supply house) or pictures can be mounted on cardboard tubes. Used in the block area or other dramatic play, children will have anti-bias images to weave into their role development play. Mounted on cardboard with popsicle sticks attached, pictures become puppets for use in stories that expose children to diverse people or for problem-solving stories about issues of bias. The puppets can be used to act out scenarios. Children can be asked what the puppets could do to solve the problem.

Example: Children are teasing Angela because she speaks Spanish. The teacher creates a puppet play similar to what is happening in the classroom.

She changes the names and some of the details. She asks the children, "Why are the children teasing Pablo (the puppet)? Why does Pablo speak differently than the other children? How do you think Pablo feels? Have you ever been teased? How did it feel? Did anyone do anything to help you feel better? What can the other puppets do to make Pablo feel better? What could Pablo say to the teasers?"

8. In school we use games all the time to help children develop age-appropriate cognitive skills such as visual discrimination and memory skills, sorting and classifying, language and math skills. We can use the same games for the same skill development, but simply change the images so that the games simultaneously provide anti-bias messages. Games and other interactive materials from photographs provide multiple opportunities for children to have close contact with photographic images and the messages they convey. The game rules themselves can be changed to meet the needs and interests of any particular group of children and any age or developmental level.

Games can be created based on familiar formats such as Concentration, Lotto, Bingo, Rummy, Uno, 21, Go Fish, Dominoes, and Puzzles. The cards can also be used for the learning activities described below.

Matching: Matching games help children develop extensive language skills, including learning to recognize letters, read their own names and read those of others in the pictures. They learn letter sounds, math skills, sorting and classifying, visual discrimination and visual memory.

Have children match word cards to cards with both the photograph and word written on it. If you don't have two copies of the pictures, xerox the pictures to get multiple copies.

Begin with children's own photographs and their names. Children's names can be written in different languages. Next introduce pictures of objects. Children at later developmental levels can match words to photographs.

When playing match games, start with the cards face up and have children find the matching pairs. Then try playing with the cards face down. Children turn over two cards at a time trying to remember where the matching pairs are.

Sorting and Classifying: There are many ways the cards can be sorted or classified.

- Young children will enjoy sorting cards that include photographs of themselves with their own names written on them. They can sort the cards by those with names beginning or ending with the same letter or names with the same number of letters;

- Children can describe ways that people in pictures who appear very different also have things in common. For example: A person in a wheelchair pushing a baby carriage and a person walking pushing a baby carriage; pictures of all the different ways people use their bodies to carry things — on their heads, shoulders, back, in their hands; a 60-year-old woman and a 20-year-old man on skateboards;

- Players can collect cards with the same number of people in them. More difficult mathematical operations can be done with children who are developmentally ready. The number of people in pairs or groups of cards can be added, subtracted, multiplied or divided.

Puzzles: Picture cards can be cut into 2, 3, 4 or more pieces. Large posters can be made into more difficult puzzles. Lots of pictures can be made into a puzzle chain or other configuration. Puzzle games can be developed similar to Memory or Concentration. For example, puzzle pieces are placed face down and players turn over two pieces. Either or both of these pieces can be left face up if they go to the same puzzle or complete a puzzle.

How to Make the Picture Cards

Materials

- **Clear Contact paper.** Order from educational catalogues or purchase by the roll at local hardware stores.

- **Mat board.** Mat board is relatively expensive to purchase; scraps can often be obtained from picture framing establishments. Other stiff cardboards can be used, but the advantage of mat board is that it does not bend. Establish standard sizes and cut all your game boards to these sizes so that picture collections that can be shuffled and sorted depending on the theme or goal you are working with. Sizes I use are:

    7-1/2" x 11" (full page for most magazines)
    7-1/2" x 8-1/2" (mid size)
    7 or 7-1/2" x 5" (photograph size)

- **Paper cutter.** It is best to have a paper cutter that is at least as large as your boards. The smaller cutters — 18" or 12" — are easier to handle with smaller mat boards.

- **Double stick tape**

- **Scissors**
- **Marking pens.** Extra Fine or Fine Point Permanent Markers.

PREPARATION

1. Keep an ongoing collection of pictures. When you cut them out, write down information about the picture or cut out the information and keep it with the picture. You may not think you will need the information, but a need for it may arise later. Sort the pictures by category and keep them in files.

2. Cut the mat board into standard sizes.

3. Place pictures on the mat board using the double stick tape. Place the pictures near the bottom or top of the board leaving room for labels you may want to attach later.

4. Cut contact paper about 1.5 inches larger all the way around than the mat board you are covering.

5. Peel contact paper and place it sticky side up on your work surface.

6. Place the mat board with picture on it, face down in the center of the contact paper.

7. Cut the contact paper from the corners. Pull away the corners. Cutting this way will prevent the contact paper from overlapping on itself.

8. Use a work surface that the contact paper won't stick to and turn the board and contact paper sticky side down. Starting from the center of the picture, carefully rub towards the edge to remove any air bubbles.

9. Tightly fold up the contact paper edges.

SOURCES FOR PHOTOGRAPHS

Andrews, N. 1994. *Family: A portrait of gay and lesbian America.* San Francisco: HarperCollins.

Arnold, E. 1983. *In America.* New York: Alfred A. Knopf. Diverse collection of photographs from the United States.

Begleiter, S. *Fathers and sons.* Abbeville Press.

Cohn, A. and L. Leach., eds. 1987. *Generations: A universal family album.* New York: Pantheon

Books. Available from the Smithsonian Institution Traveling Exhibition Service in Washington, DC. Many wonderful photographs of men and women with children.

Easter, E., et al. 1992. *Songs of my people: African Americans: A self portrait.* Little, Brown and Co. Photographs of African-Americans.

Inner London Education Authority. *Copyart.* I obtained this collection through the Development Education Centre, Selly Oak Colleges, Bristol Rd, Birmingham England, B29 6LE. Phone: 021-472-3255 ask for the bookstore. Collection of line drawings of men and women in nontraditional roles. Drawings of people with diverse physical abilities.

Michelson, M. 1994. *Women & work: In their own words.* Troutdale, OR: New Sage Press.

Morris, A. *Loving.* Lothrop, Lee and Shepard Books. Photographs reflecting the diversity within the United States and internationally. There are other useful books in this series such as *Bread, Hats, Homes,* and *Transportation.*

Nestor, H. 1992. *Family portraits in changing times.* New Sage Press. Collection of photographs of diverse families.

Calendars and magazines. Good source, but be selective. Mainstream magazines tend to have an overabundance of middle class, "perfect" clothes, skin, and body size images.

Children's Books. Children's photographic essay books are a source of pictures. Story books often are illustrated with diverse art styles and depictions of diverse people in non-stereotypical roles. If you do not wish to cut up books that are in good condition, you can wait until they are well-used and beginning to fall apart.

Cards. Syracuse Cultural Workers, Northland Poster, and the National Women's History Project have diverse images on postcards. (See Resource Guide.)

Your Own Camera. The best photos can be the ones you take yourself in your school and the neighborhood. Students appreciate photos of the local grocery stores, laundry, playground, apartments, park, places of worship and other familiar sites.

Social Studies
and
Language Arts

STUDENTS' STORIES IN ACTION COMICS

Debbie Wei describes how she connects the lives of her ESL students to the curriculum in her work as teacher in the Philadelphia Public Schools. Following this article are a collection of drawings in comic book format and essays by her students in which they describe their experiences with discrimination.

BY DEBBIE WEI

Many of my ESL students leave the terror of war and persecution in their home country only to face violence and discrimination here in the United States. They are marginalized in the United States due to their race, class and English language ability. While teaching them to read and write I try to help them explore their unique position in U.S. society, both as immigrants and people of color. This is the text of their daily lives and must be the central theme of our studies.

THE SCHOOL YEAR BEGINS: GAINING STUDENT TRUST

I begin by establishing an atmosphere of trust and respect in my classroom. I let the students know that I will fight for them, but that they in turn will have to attend class, work hard, respect others' right to speak, and do homework. I tell them all this, but it is only when my words are followed by action that they really know what I mean. For example, I don't write up students for being absent. Instead I hit the streets during lunch and after school to find them. After a few years I have learned where all the major hangouts are (the pool hall on 40th Street and the Burger King on Walnut Street are the two favorites). I start this process early and since many students already know my reputation, attendance is usually dealt with. More importantly, I don't treat the truant student as if they are the problem. Instead I ask them what we can do to improve the class or what else is going on in their lives to make school attendance difficult. I am intensely aware that all too often the students who "drop out" are actually pushed out by a system which often oppresses them. Sometimes, just this shift in approach is enough to get youth to try school out again. All too often, it takes a whole lot more.

For this reason, I also advocate for the students in the building, and am involved in different levels of community organizing projects. It has been very important for my work as a teacher to maintain a constant contact with my community through the volunteer work I do. I work closely with Asian Americans United (AAU), a community organization in Philadelphia. I actively seek to tie my work in the classroom together with my work in the community. This is not difficult to do.

In the past, when AAU was working on organizing an apartment building in the neighborhood where I was teaching, I was able to incorporate the organizing by doing a lesson on reading charts. I asked students to do a home survey, based on the City's guidelines for housing inspections. The surveys were then analyzed to determine whether the apartments met minimum standards of the housing code. After determining which parts of the code were being violated, the students then worked to learn how to write a business letter by writing to the landlords asking for repairs to be made. We incorporated math skills by figuring out the amount of profit the landlords made on the various buildings the kids lived in. We studied the cost of various repairs which needed to be done. This work in the classroom was taking place while families in one building were mobilizing to organize a rent strike. Although not all of my students lived in this particular apartment complex, the content of the class was relevant to all of them.

Students come to recognize my classroom as a place where their experiences are respected. They also know that I don't just talk about equality and social justice. For students who have been exposed to a lot of hypocrisy and abuse, it is essential that they see teachers practice what they preach. This requires constant self-examination and reflection.

COMMUNITY ISSUES ARE THE CLASS TEXT

Critical issues affecting the community of my students become the theme of our classroom. In 1991 seven young Vietnamese men had been arrested and charged with first degree murder. A racial incident in southwest Philadelphia had resulted in the stabbing death of a young White male. Five of the seven young men held responsible were students from my school. My students knew the students who were arrested and knew they were not typically "trouble makers." In addition, they saw that the media left out a lot of information about the case. For example, the media never reported that the Vietnamese students were attacked first by a hostile group of Whites who told them that "chinks" did not belong in the playground they were in.

My students wrote letters to the youth in prison and some attended rallies. Intense discussions about the link between race and the justice system filled the classroom. The students were eventually tried, convicted and sentenced to various prison terms. While we cried at our loss, we also gained collective strength in knowing the truth behind it all.

In order to broaden the connections for students, we study the experiences of other ethnic and racial minorities in the United States. For example we study contemporary issues in American Indian communities such as maintenance of language and tradition as resistance. I ask them to write about the maintenance of their own native language. Not everyone agrees on this topic, but at least students get a chance to reflect on the importance of their native language and to voice their opinions.

We end the thematic unit with a discussion of U.S. holidays such as Columbus Day and Thanksgiving from an American Indian perspective. This leads into debates about holidays in their own countries. If you are Chinese, do you recognize October 1 (Establishment of the People's Republic of China) or do you recognize October 10 (Establishment of the Republic of China)? Which flag is recognized in a country? Which national song? What are the implications of choices students make? Many students from the same country disagreed with each other. Students usually learned how to discuss these emotionally charged differences in a respectful manner. I've also learned a little distance is important here as well. Some students' families fought on opposite sides of conflicts. It's critical to have a good knowledge of your students' backgrounds here so you don't surface painful, angry memories that may still be raw. In those cases it's best to pick a conflict students families aren't directly involved in.

At the same time, we raised critical questions regarding "traditional holiday" celebrations the students themselves faced in U.S. schools. Usually students whose cultures and backgrounds are not of the "mainstream" never see their experiences honored in the classroom. Even where schools make some kind of attempt to honor students' culture — students lives end up being treated as "commodities." It amazes me that Asian American culture,

for example, is only honored during "International Day," where international cuisine — prepared by the families of the students — becomes the food for the day. I have never figured out how having Asian students cook food and serve it to others actually serves to break down stereotypes.

There are no easy answers here. In a discussion of culture and tradition, there are many hard questions. Often, issues of sexism or classism in traditional cultures are just some of the many issues raised. [See "Negotiating Pitfalls and Possibilities: Presenting Folk Arts in the Schools."]

The next unit I introduce is the Civil Rights movement. We learn about various forms of discrimination such as racism and sexism and the relationship between power and oppression. We review documentaries and read speeches, poems, short stories and historical accounts. The final project for this unit is to have students talk about forms of discrimination that they have experienced directly. These discussions lead to essays.

STUDENT-FRIENDLY PUBLISHING: COMIC STRIPS

I am always looking for alternative means of establishing "voice" for my students. Many read and write on a first or second grade level. I've explored music and drama. But in 1992, our class turned their essays about discrimination into a comic book. A graduate student conducting research in my classroom, Lou Ann Merkle, proposed the idea. She had experience with comic book production and offered to help.

The students loved it. The finished art work and stories were displayed at the University of the Arts. The students and their families proudly attended the opening reception. Unfortunately, not a single school-based administrator nor any other teachers (other than my team teacher) came to the exhibit. Nor have I had any success in mounting the exhibit at the school. This was just one more example of the marginilization of English as a Second Language (ESL) students.

But the students were not discouraged. The power of their work was confirmed by the attendance of lots of people from the community and university. There were subsequent requests for the artwork to be shown in community sites around Philadelphia.

The day after the opening, twenty of my students came with me on a cold, wet, rainy morning to participate in a walk-a-thon to raise money to build a school in a village in El Salvador. This was a follow-up activity to a unit I had presented on war and peace. The previous school in El Salvador had been destroyed in the war. Many of my students had seen schools and homes in their own countries destroyed by bombs. By walking to help the children in El Salvador, they were taking a positive step for justice everywhere. The action served as a step toward taking back some of what they had lost. Also, two students had their work published in a community paper about the Vietnamese youth who were arrested. My students began to see the power of their words and organized action to create change.

The comic book format could be used in other classrooms in collaboration with the art teacher or a volunteer from the arts community. And in schools where the administration is more receptive, these stories could be shared throughout the school to build bridges of understanding and respect.

Debbie Wei is an activist and an educator. She works as a curriculum specialist in Asian American studies for the School District of Philadelphia. She is also an active member of Asian Americans United, a grassroots based social justice organization in Philadelphia. She is co-editor of the children's book, In My Heart, I Am A Dancer. *E-mail: dwei@sdp2.philsch.k12.pa.us*

REFERENCES

Lee, S. & Buscema, J. 1984. How to draw comics the Marvel way. *New York: Simon and Schuster.*

MAKING COMIC STRIPS

BY LOU ANN MERKLE AND DEBBIE WEI

Transforming student essays into a comic book format is a dynamic process. As the story in the comic strip develops from a piece of prose, the students revise the prose by adding more dialogue and action. Following are the steps we recommend based on our experience.

Have students review lots of comic books. Ask them to critique the books' portrayal of women and minorities and their inclusion of gratuitous violence. Whose lives do the books portray? Who has enough money to own a publishing company? Also ask them to reflect on the value of comic books. Who reads them? Are they widely read? What makes them so appealing?

Then ask students if they would like to make their own books, based on their own life experiences. If the answer is yes, have them select an essay from their writing folder about their own lives. For our class we picked the common theme of discrimination since the stories were to be compiled in an anthology.

Have each student transform her or his essay into a script by using a chart listing setting, time, characters, important points, action/dialogue and questions. To introduce this activity, use a sample story of past student work and develop a script collectively so they get the idea.

Then introduce some of the art concepts needed for comic book illustration. Few of our students had taken any art classes, so it seemed overwhelming to expect them to illustrate a comic book story. *Marvel How-to Draw Comics* became the text and for two weeks we spent each day learning a new basic drawing skill: line and shapes into forms and things, principles of perspective, rooms and landscapes, figures, portraits, and composition and layout.

Returning to their action/dialogue script, students sketched ideas for each frame of their story using the comic book format. We supplied pre-printed sketch paper for students to block out ideas. The papers had various sizes of blocks — vertical and horizontal rectangles and squares. We didn't use circles or other shapes for the blocks, though that certainly would have been an option. Teachers can also take the opportunity to use the blocking process as a mathematics/problem solving task for students. Over the next month, we continued working until the drawings were redrawn on good paper and "inked" in felt tip pens.

Students said that when they did portraits of each other, they looked more closely at their classmates than ever before. They also said the project helped them to demonstrate their feelings. The writing and drawing helped them to improve their thinking about their own lives and society.

LUN LY

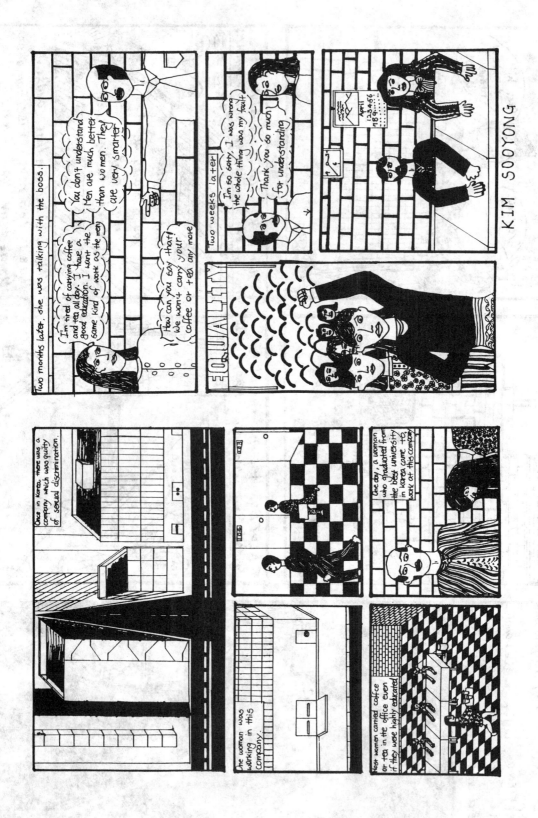

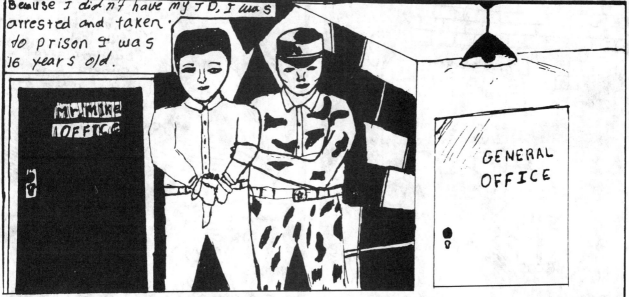

Binyam Laine

ALMAZ HABTETSION

COPS Always Pick on Asians

NO Justice

CHHAILA SOT

NO peace

JINHO LEE

RENE VILLAGRANA

Rene J. Villagrana.

STUDENTS' ESSAYS

LUN LY

On Tuesday of spring vacation this year, I was visiting some friends in Southwest Philadelphia. I was going to take the trolley to go home and I was making a telephone call from a pay phone. A bunch of White kids started to chase me. They had baseball bats and they wanted to hit me. I tried to run away from them. I ran to the 7th Police District station because I thought if the police saw these boys they would stop them. I called for help and there were some police outside, but they ignored me.

Then I ran to my friend's house. He saw that these guys were chasing me. They hit me on the neck. My friend ran out of his house with a knife. When the White kids saw him, they got scared and ran away. I was hurt in the neck. I was really angry with the police. That night when I went home, my brother saw that I was beat up and he got angry with me. He doesn't understand when I have some problems. I think a lot of families of kids don't understand when they have some problems.

SOOYONG KIM

In the world, there are many people. The human race is made up of males and females. Females have always been working in the society, but sometimes females face sexual discrimination. This is a big problem in society. Let me give you an example. If a man and woman both go to an office or company to apply for a job, most bosses would choose the man because they think men work better than women. But I don't think men are better than women. Not all men are good. Most men are good, but some are cruel. One thing I think is interesting is that most robbers are men. I never heard of women robbers, at least not big robbers. And most killers are men too.

Another thing is that in the home, women are usually harder working. Most women clean the house and wash the clothes every day. Most women are tired after work, but men don't work in the house. Most men watch T.V. or read the newspaper.

I think in most countries, women face sexual discrimination. I saw this problem in my country too. One woman in Korea was working in a company. She graduated from the best university in Korea, but she was not allowed to have advanced work. She only carried drinks or cleaned the office. She wanted to work so she told her company boss, but the boss said, "Women are not as good as men." So all the women didn't work and they demonstrated against the company. After a week, the boss gave in to the women.

In my own family, my father is good because he does wash the dishes and sometimes he cooks for my family. My mother doesn't face sexual discrimination in my home. In my opinion, women should be treated the same as men. When I graduate from school, and after I get married, I want to treat women equally and I will try to help my wife so she won't have to face sexual discrimination.

BINYAM LAINE

Discrimination is not good for anyone. In my county, Ethiopian soldiers discriminated against Eritrean people. They killed them. In my town, every corner had one or two Ethiopian soldiers.

When I walked up the street, one soldier asked me to stop walking. Then he asked me to come to him. I walked close to him. He asked me who I was. At that time, I did not have any identification with me because I was not an adult. In my country, all adults had to carry identification, but children did not. But the soldier took me to prison anyway. I was in prison for three days.

Another time, when I was 15 years old, we heard the news from the government that a new law required that every man from 16 to 30 years old had to register to go to be a soldier, but I did not register because I am Eritrean. Why should I register to kill my brothers? I decided to leave my country. I moved to a friend's house. When the army came to look for me, they couldn't find me. Then I moved to a big city. I was alone. I was 17 years old. After a lot of trouble, I left my country and came to the U.S. to try and escape that discrimination.

ALMAZ HABTETSION

One day when I was thirteen years old and I was living in my country, my mother sent me to buy some sugar from a shop. On my way, I saw one of the Ethiopian soldiers that was in our country at that time. He asked me, "Where are you from?" and I answered, "I am from Eritrea." Then he said to me, "Is there a country that is called Eritrea? Where is it located?" I said "Yes, it is located on the Red Sea coast, north of Ethiopia." He hit me and said, "Who told you that there is a country called Eritrea?" I answered, "My mother." He asked me all these questions because the Ethiopian government was saying that Eritrea was part of Ethiopia. Then he took all my money and said to me, "Tell your mother that there is no country which is called Eritrea."

At that time I felt very bad and went back to my home. Now our country is free and the people are living under a good condition. Now the Ethiopian people are living in a peaceful way with the Eritrean people.

CHHAILA SOT

I want to talk about discrimination with the police. One day I walked with my friend and my cousin. We went to 45th Street and a policeman stopped us and cursed at us for no reason. He cursed at my friend and me. The policeman came and asked my friend, "Have you ever been in jail?" My friend said, "no" and the policeman said, "F_you. You Chink. You B_S_." Then I felt sad. The police don't have the right to do that. The police always say bad things to Asian people.

The next day, my cousin and I were walking home from school and the police followed us. The police called my cousin over to him and he asked my cousin, "Where are you coming from?" My cousin said, "We're coming from school." The police thought we were coming from the game room. There had been a fight there and they were trying to say that we were involved just because we are Asian boys.

One week I walked to 45th Street to the game room and the cops called me to come over. I refused. Then one cop followed me inside the game room to take me out. He threatened to hit me and I said, "Go ahead and hit me." He didn't hit me because I said, "If you hit me, I'll sue you."

Last year, the cops called my friend and me over and took our picture. The police think we are in a gang. My friend told them we are not in a gang. They do this to Asians because we come from different countries. It makes me feel sad and angry because they don't have the right to discriminate against Asians like this.

JINHO LEE

In my opinion, there is a lot of discrimination in the world. First, some people discriminate against each other because of the color of their skin. We call this racial discrimination. America has serious racial discrimination because a lot of different kinds of people live in America. The most serious racial discrimination is White people against Black people. A long time ago, Black people were brought to America as slaves. At that time, they could not have freedom and they could not be citizens. They could not use the same restaurants, parks, or buses, and could not go to the same school as White people. This was not fair. My American history teacher said, "Slavery is the saddest part of American history." This tells us how bad discrimination is.

A second kind of discrimination is sexual discrimination. A long time ago in my country, women could not have freedom. Men could leave their home, but women could not. Women could only take care of babies and make clothes at home for men. Some women could never see the outside world. If you look at things from the standpoint of these women in my country a long time ago, then you will understand how it felt for them to be prisoners in their own homes. A long time ago, people liked sons more than daughters.

In my home, my mother likes me more than my sister. For example, at dinner time, my mother gives me more food than my sister. I always feel sorry for my sister, because my mother doesn't treat my sister fairly. I don't like this. I don't want to be sorry for my sister forever, so I am going to try and change my mother's mind.

We must respect each other and give everyone a chance. We are not animals. We are all human beings.

RENE VILLAGRANA

Two years ago when I came to the United States, I went to Chicago with my mother because I had to work. I started to work in the same factory where my mom worked.

One day, my mother told me everything about the factory and she told me the foreman discriminated against the Mexicans or Latin people because when this foreman saw a lot of Mexicans and Latin people working there, he called the immigration department.

When this happened, my mom told me not to go to work because someone told her the immigration department would come. She told me to quit the job.

After the immigration department got the illegal [undocumented] people, some time passed and more Mexicans came to work and the same foreman reported these people again. The boss knew about that, but he didn't do anything about it. This guy kept discriminating against the Latin people, and Blacks too.

PARA TERESA

BY INÉS HERNÁNDEZ-ÁVILA

A tí-Teresa Compean
Te dedico las palabras estás
que explotan de mi corazón[1]

That day during lunch hour
at Alamo which-had-to-be-its-name
Elementary
my dear raza
That day in the bathroom
Door guarded
Myself cornered
I was accused by you, Teresa
Tú y las demás de tus amigas
Pachucas todas
Eran Uds. cinco.[2]

Me gritaban que porque me creía tan grande[3]
What was I trying to do, you growled
Show you up?
Make the teachers like me, pet me,
Tell me what a credit to my people I was?
I was playing right into their hands, you challenged
And you would have none of it.
I was to stop.

I was to be like you
I was to play your game of deadly defiance
Arrogance, refusal to submit.
The game in which the winner takes nothing
Asks for nothing
Never lets his weaknesses show.

But I didn't understand.
My fear salted with confusion
Charged me to explain to you
I did nothing *for the teachers.*
I studied for my parents and for my grandparents
Who cut out honor roll lists
Whenever their nietos'[4] names appeared
For my shy mother who mastered her terror
to demand her place in mother's clubs
For my carpenter-father who helped me patiently
with my math.
For my abuelos que me regalaron lápices en la
Navidad[5]
And for myself.
Porque reconocí en aquel entonces
una verdad tremenda
que me hizo a mi un rebelde

Aunque tú no te habías dadocuenta[6]
We were not inferior
You and I, y las demás de tus amigas
Y los demás de nuestra gente[7]
I knew it the way I know I was alive
We were good, honorable, brave
Genuine, loyal, strong

And smart.
Mine was a deadly game of defiance, also.
My contest was to prove
beyond any doubt
that we were not only equal but superior to them.
That was why I studied.
If I could do it, we all could.

You let me go then,
Your friends unblocked the way
I who-did-not-know-how-to-fight
was not made to engage with you-who-grew-up-
fighting
Tu y yo, Teresa[8]
We went in different directions
Pero fuimos juntas.[9]

In sixth grade we did not understand
Uds. with the teased, dyed-black-but-reddening
hair,
Full petticoats, red lipsticks
and sweaters with the sleeves
pushed up
Y yo conformándome con lo que deseaba mi mamá[10]
Certainly never allowed to dye, to tease, to paint
myself
I did not accept your way of anger,
Your judgements
You did not accept mine.

But now in 1975, when I am twenty-eight
Teresa Compean
I remember you.
Y sabes —
Te comprendo,
Es más, te respeto.
Y, si me permites,
Te nombro — "hermana."[11]

NOTES

1. To you, Teresa Compean, I dedicate these words that explode from my heart.

2. You and the rest of your friends, all Pachucas, there were five of you.

3. You were screaming at me, asking me why I thought I was so hot.

4. Grandchildren's.

5. Grandparents who gave me gifts of pencils at Christmas.

6. Because I recognized a great truth then that made me a rebel, even though you didn't realize it.

7. And the rest of your friends/And the rest of our people.

8. You and I.

9. But we were together.

10. And I conforming to my mother's wishes.

11. And do you know what, I understand you. Even more, I respect you. And, if you permit me, I name you my sister.

Inés Hernández-Ávila is Associate Professor and Chair of the Department of Native American Studies at the University of California, Davis. She is Nez Perce on her mother's side and Chicana on her father's side. Her poetry has been published widely. She is a scholar, a poet, a cultural worker, and a Native woman of the Americas.

TEACHING SUGGESTION

1. Have students read the poem. If the group is not bilingual in English and Spanish, read each section together. Or plan in advance to have a group of students read and prepare to enact the poem for the rest of the group. Even with the translations, some students might have questions. For example, why say "Alamo which-had-to-be-its-name." (The Alamo was the nationalist battlecry of the U.S. army when they took Texas and then the rest of Mexico's northern territories, dispossessed great numbers of the now Mexican Americans from their ancestral lands and systematically stripped Mexican Americans of their civil rights.)

2. Discuss the sequence of events. First Teresa and her friends get angry at Inés. Why? What are some of the things the Latino students are probably expected to give up to become "a credit" their race? What is Inés' response? Why do Teresa and her friends back off? What did the author mean, "We went in different directions, pero fuimos juntas [we went together]."

3. Examine the issue of identity in the school. From what we can see in the poem, the Latino students had the choice of being a teacher's pet or being defiant. Ask students to discuss which was the wiser choice and why. Then ask them to consider why students should have to make that choice at all. Ask what the school would need to do to create a third option for the Latino students, an option that was respectful of their identity (language, history, literature, family, etc.) If the point has not been raised, ask students why they think the author chose to write the poem in both English and Spanish.

4. Examine the issues of conflict and power in the poem.

   ▶ The Latino students at Alamo School were getting into fights. Why? What was making them angry enough to want to fight?

   ▶ If you were a reporter writing about the violence in the school, who would you say was responsible?

   ▶ Are the students violent, or the conditions?

   ▶ Who benefits from the fact that the students are fighting among themselves? Who loses?

5. Compare the conflict in the poem to conditions in your own school. The conflict can be within a race or ethnic group, between groups, between levels of students in a tracked school or between mainstream/special education or mainstream/ESL. In one high school where this poem was discussed students identified similar conflicts between established and newly arrived immigrant students from Central America; and between African American and Latino students at the same school. Discussing the poem helped students to reflect on their on behavior, recognizing how they were fighting each other while the roots of the conflict were not addressed.

PORTRAIT POEMS: STEPPING INTO THE WORLD OF OTHERS

BY LINDA CHRISTENSEN

Portrait poems allow students to step into the world of others, to try on the persona of people from different time periods, cultures, genders, races. Through this kind of writing students struggle to see and understand another person's point of view.

Beginning poets often write "ghost poems" — vague poems full of abstractions about their love for their mother, friend, or pet. The photo poetry assignment forces them to become concrete by describing details from the pictures, clothing their "ghosts." Although I often use the work of published poets like Lucille Clifton, Quincy Troupe, Rita Dove, Martin Espada, Sharon Olds and Carolyn Forche to demonstrate how to write about photos, I find that mixing those poets with student poets helps. The student work is sometimes more accessible than that of adult writers. Students read the poems and I/we point out concrete details. I find photo prompts in a variety of places:

1. Students look at photographs of artwork from a particular period — the Harlem Renaissance, Chinese or Chicano labor history for example, to "read" history and literature in a new way. This activity celebrates diverse cultural experiences. Students may either describe what they see in the photo/painting or they may become the person in the painting and write from that person's point of view. Jacob Lawrence's series on Toussaint L'Ouverture, Frederick Douglass, John Brown, and Harriet Tubman are great sources of inspiration.

2. I also take my class to visit our local art museum where they write about the artwork on display. For example, we took a field trip to see Jacob Lawrence's migration series and Carrie Mae Weems' photo exhibit. Students wrote stunning poetry from the trip. But we have also traveled to the Columbia Gorge to view pictographs, Native American rock drawings on the canyon walls. We have ridden buses to Waterfront Park to see the statues and rock poems of Lawson Inada and other Japanese American poets who were interned during World War II. We have walked through our school's neighborhood and written poetry about local artist Isaac Shamsudin's murals.

3. Bill Bigelow and I show our students slides from pre-European contact of African culture to establish visual images of complex and rich societies. We also show slides about the beginning of the slave trade which devastated the lives of generations of Africans. Again, students choose to describe the picture or to become a character in the picture and write from that persona. Two of these poems were published in the 1992 *Rites of Passage*. Beverly McCormick's poem came from a slide showing the thousand year old ruins of Great Zimbabwe in southern Africa. In this poem, Bev becomes an African who built the walls of Zimbabwe.

Walls of Zimbabwe

Stone upon stone
walls climb to the sky.
Blood from my hands
stain boulders
as my hard muscles
ripple setting each rock
in place.

Each time the sun sets
I climb another inch.
Pain, hard work.
My grunts and groans
caught in the wind.

On my wall
I am triumphant
proud and tall as the giraffe
strong and mighty as the elephant.

Never to know
the price my blood paid
to have someone
defile my masterpiece.
My blood cries.[1]
— *Beverly McCormick*

The inspiration for Sam Jackson's poem was a slide of a branding iron used to mark enslaved Africans. He takes on the persona of one of these branding irons:

Iron

I am just an iron,
forged of molten steel,
formed
into a stamp,
the stamp of ownership.
I am put
in raging fires,
red hot,
hot as hell.
Pushed onto a Black man's
back,
leg,
or face,
to show he is property.
Property,
like me.
It hurts me just
as much as it hurts them.
But they don't forget the pain
and humiliation.
They don't forget.
I do,
because I am
just an iron.

— Sam Jackson

A man and his grandchildren waiting to be interned on May 8, 1942 in Hayward, CA. They were among the 110,000 Japanese-Americans uprooted from their homes, communities and businesses. Reprinted with permission from Documentary Photo Aids, PO Box 956, Mount Dora, FL 32757.

I have also used the artwork from the Japanese relocation camps as prompts for writing. *Beyond Words: Images from America's Concentration Camps* edited by Deborah Gesensway and Mindy Roseman contain some powerful images of life in these "camps." I project these photos as slides. While the students are viewing the pictures, I read passages from *Nisei Daughter* by Monica Sone, *Farewell to Manzanar* by Jean Wakatsuki Houston, *Tule Lake* by James D. Houston, and the poetry of Lawson Inada and Mitsui Yamada and others. The following poem by Khalilah Joseph is from this prompt:

Becoming American[2]

I looked into the eyes of my Japanese doll
and knew I could not surrender her
to the fury of the fire.
My mother threw out the poetry
she loved;
my brother gave the fire his sword.
We worked hours
to vanish any traces of the Asian world
from our home.

Who could ask us
to destroy
gifts from a world that molded
and shaped us?

If I ate hamburgers
and apple pies,
if I wore jeans,
then would I be an American?

— Khalilah Joseph

Linda Christensen is an English teacher at Jefferson High School in Portland Oregon, poet, Director of the Portland Writing Project, an editor of Rethinking Schools *and National Coalition of Education Activists (NCEA) steering committee member. E-mail: LChrist@aol.com*

This lesson is reprinted from the 1995 Teaching Guide for the Jefferson High School student literary collection, Rites of Passage *with permission of the author.*

NOTES

1. This last stanza refers to the White gold seekers who, over the years, dynamited and ransacked Great Zimbabwe sites in their search for booty.

2. This poem was inspired by "Echoes from Pearl Harbor," a chapter from Monica Sone's autobiographical *Nisei Daughter* about the WWII internment of the Japanese Americans.

MOUNTAINS OF PREJUDICE; STREAMS OF JUSTICE:
THE CHEROKEE/SEMINOLE REMOVAL ROLE PLAY

BY BILL BIGELOW

In her book, *A Century of Dishonor*, published in 1881, Helen Hunt Jackson wrote, "There will come a time in the remote future when, to the student of American history [the Cherokee removal] will seem well-nigh incredible." The events leading up to the infamous Trail of Tears, when Cherokee Indians were marched at bayonet point almost a thousand miles from Georgia to Oklahoma, offers a window into the nature of U.S. expansion — in the early nineteenth century, but also throughout this country's history. The story of the Cherokees' uprooting may seem "well-nigh incredible" today, but it shares important characteristics with much of U.S. foreign policy: economic interests paramount, race as a key factor, legality flaunted, the use of violence to enforce U.S. will, a language of justification thick with democratic and humanitarian platitudes. The U.S. war with Mexico, the Spanish-American War, Vietnam, support of the Contras in Nicaragua, and the Gulf War come readily to mind. These are my conclusions; they needn't be my students'. Our task as teachers is not to tell kids what to think but to encourage them to search for patterns throughout history, patterns that continue into our own time.

The Cherokees were not the only indigenous people affected by the Indian Removal law and the decade of dispossession that followed. The Seminoles, living in Florida, were another group targeted for resettlement. For years, they had lived side by side with people of African ancestry, most of whom were escaped slaves or descendants of escaped slaves. Indeed, the Seminoles and Africans living with each other were not two distinct peoples. Their inclusion in this role play allows students to explore further causes for Indian removal, to see ways in which slavery was an important consideration motivating the U.S. government's hoped-for final solution to the supposed Indian problem. The role play encourages students to explore some of these dynamics from the inside. As they portray individuals in some of the groups that shaped these historical episodes, the aim is for them to see not only what happened, but why it happened — and perhaps to wonder whether there were alternatives.

In previous years of teaching this role play I did not include a "Missionaries and Northern Reformers" role. The omission of a sympathetic White role left students with the misleading impression that all White people in the country were united in the quest to forcibly move Indian tribes and nations off their lands. In fact, White people as diverse as the abolitionist William Lloyd Garrison and the Tennessee frontiersman-turned-Congressman, Davy Crockett, opposed the Indian removal bill. The vote in the U.S. House of Representatives in favor of removal was 102 to 97 — an underwhelming majority. Nonetheless, it's important that students recognize the racial and cultural biases of even those who considered themselves the Indians' friends and allies. As indicated in their role, missionaries described Cherokee families as "having risen to a level with the White people of the United States." Thus, as we seek to inform students of important currents of social reform in U.S. history, we need to do so with a critical eye.

MATERIALS NEEDED

Construction or other stiff paper for placards; crayons or markers.

SUGGESTED PROCEDURE

1. [First, a suggestion to you on how to read these lesson procedures. Rather than reading all these in one, two, three order, it may be more clear if you review the student readings in the order they are mentioned in these instructions. This will help you imagine the role play more easily, and encounter it as students might.]

Read with students the "Indian Removal Role Play: Problems to Consider" handout. Show them on a map how far it is from Georgia and Florida to Oklahoma. Tell them that each of them will be in a group representing one of five roles: Cherokees, the Andrew Jackson Administration, Plantation Owners and Farmers, Missionaries and Northern Reformers, and Black Seminoles. All of them are invited to a hearing to discuss the Indian Removal Bill before

The Trail of Tears *by Robert Lindneux. Reprinted with permission of the Woolaroc Museum, Bartlesville, Oklahoma.*

Congress. They should consider the resolution, and in their presentations should be sure to respond to the three questions — whether they support the bill, what questions they have of other groups, and how they will react if the bill passes or fails. This last question encourages students to see that simply because Congress decides something does not necessarily mean people will passively accept that decision.

[**Note**: The teacher plays the Congressman (they were all men back then) who runs the hearing. An option is to select a few students to join you or to run the meeting on their own. This choice has the advantage of giving students a group of peers as an audience for their presentations. The disadvantage is that those who will run the hearing have little to do during the session of negotiation between groups, and sometimes become targets for other students' ire if they manifest the slightest inconsistency in calling on people to speak.]

2.   Have students count off into five groups. Students from each respective group should cluster together in small circles throughout the classroom. They should begin by reading their assigned role. You can urge students into their characters by asking them to write "interior monologues" (the possible inner thoughts) about their concerns in 1830;

they might invent a more detailed persona: give themselves a name, a place of birth, family, friends, etc. This is especially valuable for students in those groups (plantation owner/farmers and missionaries/northern reformers) which include people in somewhat different circumstances. Students in each group might read these to one another. You can interview a few individuals from different groups, so others in the class can hear.

3.   Distribute placards and markers to students and ask them to write their group name and display it so that everyone can see who they represent.

4.   In each group, students should discuss their ideas on the questions they will be addressing at the Congressional Hearing. Remind them that an important question to consider is what they will do if Congress decides against them. Will they resist? If so, how? If not, what might happen to them? When it seems that students have come to some tentative conclusions, ask them to choose half their group to be traveling negotiators. These people will meet with people in the other groups to share ideas, argue, build alliances. Remind students that each of their roles includes different information, so this is an opportunity to teach each other. (To insure maximum participation of students in the class, travelers may not meet with other travelers, but only with

seated members of other groups. Travelers may travel together or separately.)

5. Begin the teaching/negotiating/alliance-building session. These discussions should last until students seem to be repeating themselves — perhaps fifteen or twenty minutes, depending on the class. During this period, I circulate to different groups, and occasionally butt in to raise questions or point out contradictions. Don't skip this step; it may be the time students are most engaged in their roles.

6. Students should return to their groups to prepare the presentations they'll make at the Congressional Hearing. In my experience, if they write these out, they think more clearly and raise more provocative points. Encourage them to use the information in their role sheet, but not merely to copy it.

7. The class should form a large circle, students sitting with their respective groups. I structure the hearing by allowing one group to make its complete presentation. Then either I or the students running the hearing raise a few questions. After this, members of other groups may question or rebut points made by the presenting group. This process continues until we've heard from all the groups. The more cross-group dialogue that occurs, the more interesting and exciting the meeting.

8. As a follow-up writing assignment, you might ask students to stay in their roles and comment on the Congressional Hearing — whose remarks most angered or troubled them? At what points did they feel most satisfied with the deliberations? Or you could ask them to speculate on what happened in real life and why. Some discussion or writing questions include:

▶ What do you think actually happened to the Cherokee and the Seminole people?

▶ Might there have been tensions between the Cherokees and Seminoles? Why?

▶ Which group might have been in a better position to resist removal? Why?

▶ What reasons did some groups offer for why the Indians should be moved? What were their real motives?

▶ Why were the Seminoles such a threat to the Southern plantation owners? Do you remember some of the laws that were passed to keep Indians and Blacks divided in early America?

▶ In real life, a slim majority of U.S. representatives and senators voted to remove the Indians. What arguments might they have found most persuasive?

▶ Do you think that all those Congressmen who voted against Indian removal did so because they cared about the Indians? Can you think of other reasons Congressmen from northern states wouldn't want the southern states to expand onto Indian territory?

▶ Do you think the missionaries would have been as sympathetic toward the Seminoles as they were toward the Cherokees? Why/why not?

▶ Do you see any similarities in the situations faced by the Cherokee and Seminole peoples and situations faced by any other groups in U.S. history? in our society today? in other parts of the world?

9. After discussion, you might assign students to do some research to see what actually happened to the Cherokee and the Seminole peoples. Pages 96 to 98 in Ronald Takaki's *A Different Mirror* (Little Brown, 1993) provide a good short summary of what happened to the Cherokee along what came to be called the Trail of Tears. Chapter four, "The Finest Looking People I Have Ever Seen," in William Loren Katz's *Black Indians: A Hidden Heritage* (Atheneum, 1986) is a valuable resource for learning more about how the Seminoles were affected by the events depicted in the role play.

Bill Bigelow teaches at Franklin High School in Portland, Oregon. He is an editor of the journal, Rethinking Schools. *E-mail: bbpdx@aol.com*

Reprinted by permission of the author. A version of this article first appeared in Mary Burke-Hengen and Tim Gillespie, eds., Building Community: Social Studies in the Middle School Years *(Heinemann, 1995).*

NOTE

The title for this lesson is borrowed from a quote by a Choctaw Indian, George W. Harkins, in a "Farewell Letter to the American People, 1832," described in Ronald Takaki's *A Different Mirror* (Boston: Little Brown, 1993; pp. 92-93). Harkins wrote that "We were hedged in by two evils [racist White Mississippi legislators and the horrors of removal], and we chose that which we thought least." Were the Choctaw to stay in Mississippi, Harkins believed, a "mountain of prejudice" would block "the streams of justice."

INDIAN REMOVAL ROLE PLAY:
PROBLEMS TO CONSIDER

The year is 1830. There is a bill before the United States Congress that would provide funds [$500,000] to move all Indians now living east of the Mississippi River to "Indian Territory" (Oklahoma) west of the Mississippi River. The Indians would be given permanent title to this land. The money would pay the Indians for any improvements made on the land in the East where they're now living. It would also cover the expenses of their transportation and for a year in their new homes in Indian Territory.

The U.S. Congress has decided to hold hearings on this bill and you are invited to give testimony and to question other individuals who will give testimony. Remember, the main question for discussion is:

SHOULD ALL INDIANS LIVING EAST OF THE MISSISSIPPI RIVER BE MOVED, BY FORCE IF NECESSARY, WEST OF THE MISSISSIPPI RIVER TO INDIAN TERRITORY?

QUESTIONS FOR EACH GROUP TO CONSIDER IN PLANNING YOUR PRESENTATION:

1. Do you support the Indian Removal Bill? Why or why not?

2. What questions do you have for members of the other groups who will be in attendance?

3. What will you do if Congress passes this bill? What will you do if Congress does not pass this bill?

CHEROKEE

Your people have lived for centuries in the area the Whites call "Georgia." This is your land. At times you've had to fight to keep it.

You've had a hard time with Whites. Ever since they began settling in Georgia they have continued to push west, plowing the land, growing their cotton and other crops. Long ago, as early as 1785, the Cherokee Nation won the right to their land by a treaty with the United States government. The United States recognized the Cherokee people as part of an independent country and not subject to the laws of the United States. After the U.S. Constitution was approved, the United States government signed another treaty with the Cherokee — in 1791, when George Washington was president. Article Seven of the Hopewell treaty said, "The United States solemnly guaranty to the Cherokee nation all their lands not hereby ceded." In other words, the government agreed not to push the Cherokee out of the land where they were living.

But now the U.S. government is about to break its own treaty and steal your land. Many Whites have already bribed and tricked lots of your people out of their land. The Whites say they need it to grow their cotton and other crops, and miners have been trespassing in the foothills looking for, and finding, gold. These Whites say you have no right to the land, that you're savages. Last year, in December of 1829, the state of Georgia passed a law saying that you are under *their* control, and must

obey their laws, their wishes. This new law forbids anyone with any Cherokee blood from testifying in court, or protesting the plans to move you out of your land. But you didn't vote for this Georgia government, and besides, you have a treaty with the federal government that says you are citizens of an independent country. When the U.S. government made a treaty with you, that proved you are a nation.

The Cherokee are one of the five "civilized tribes." Much of this "civilization" was taught to you by the Whites. You have well-cultivated farms. By 1826, members of your Cherokee nation owned 22,000 cattle, 7,600 horses, 3,000 plows, 2,500 spinning wheels, ten saw mills and eighteen schools. And like southern Whites, some of you also owned Black slaves. In 1821, Sequoya, a brilliant Cherokee Indian, invented an 85 character alphabet and now most Cherokee can read and write. It's said that more Cherokee are literate than are Whites in Georgia. You even have a regular newspaper, the Cherokee *Phoenix*. You've adopted a written Constitution for your nation very similar to that of the United States. Many of your leaders have attended White schools in the East. Even by the White man's standards you're as "civilized" as they are, if not more so. But still they want to kick you off your land and move you to a place west of the Mississippi River — a place you've never even seen. You must continue to argue your case if you are to survive as a people.

ANDREW JACKSON ADMINISTRATION

You're the President of the United States. You must deal with a serious problem in the state of Georgia. This past December, 1829, the state government said that all the land belonging to the Cherokee nation would from then on belong to Georgia. The Cherokee would have no title to their land and anyone with Cherokee blood wouldn't even have the right to testify in court. The Georgians want the Cherokee moved, by force if necessary, west of the Mississippi River. They support the Indian Removal Act, now before Congress. There is a place called "Oklahoma" set aside for all the Indians in the East, including the Cherokee. Personally, you agree that Georgia has a right to make whatever laws they want, but the Cherokee do have treaties signed by the U.S. government guaranteeing them their land forever. Of course, you personally never signed any of those treaties.

You're getting a lot of pressure on this one. On the one hand there are White missionaries and lots of northerners who say that Georgia is violating Cherokee rights. Cherokee supporters point out that the Indians have done everything they can to become like civilized White people: they invented an alphabet, started a newspaper, wrote a constitution, started farms and even wear White people's clothes. Many church groups supported your election in 1828, and you want their support when you run for re-election in 1832. On the other hand, there are a whole lot of farmers and plantation owners who would like to get on that good Cherokee land. Recently, gold was discovered on Cherokee territory, and gold-seekers are already starting to sneak onto their land. Your main base of support was in the South, especially from poor and medium-sized farmers.

From your standpoint, you have to look after the welfare of the whole country. The main crop in the South is cotton — it is a crucial crop to the prosperity of the slave-owning South and to the new cloth factories of the North. Cotton, grown with slave labor, brings in tremendous profits to slaveowners and you're a slaveowner yourself, so you understand their concerns. There is excellent land being taken up by the Cherokee, as well as some of the other Indian tribes in the region: the

Andrew Jackson, 1845. Painting by Thomas Sully (1783-1872).

© NATIONAL GALLERY OF ART, WASHINGTON, D.C.

Creeks, Choctaw, Chickasaw and Seminole — though some of these have already moved west. This land could be used to grow cotton for the world. The exports of cotton to England and other countries are vital to the health of the economy. Cotton sent North is building up young industries and you can see there is great potential for manufacturing in the North.

The Seminole Indians who live in Florida represent a special problem. For years, they have taken in escaped slaves from southern plantations. Sometimes, they've even raided plantations to free slaves. They are a threat to the whole plantation system in the South. A number of years ago, you ordered the Seminoles in Florida attacked and had their farms burned. The proposed Indian Removal Act would get rid of the Seminoles forever by moving them to Indian Territory. The escaped slaves living with them would then be taken away from them and sold.

PLANTATION OWNERS AND FARMERS

All I ask in this creation
Is a pretty little wife and a big plantation
Way up yonder in the Cherokee Nation.

That's part of a song people like you sing as you wait for the Cherokee to be kicked out of Georgia. Then you and your family can move on in. Some of you are poor farmers. You live on the worst land in Georgia and other parts of the South. The big plantation owners with all their cotton and slaves take up the best land and leave you the scraps. You've heard that the Cherokee land in Georgia is some of the most fertile land in the country. Best yet, the government of Georgia is having a lottery so that even poor farmers like you will have an equal shot at getting good land. One of the reasons you voted for Andy Jackson for president is because you knew he was an Indian fighter who beat the Creeks in a war and then took their land away from them. That's your kind of president. The Cherokee are farmers too. They grow corn, wheat and cotton. If you're lucky, you'll be able to move onto land with the crops already planted and the farmhouse already built. Others of you aren't quite as poor; you have some land, and grow corn and raise hogs, but you, too, would like to move onto better land.

Some of you are plantation owners, who grow cotton on your land and own many slaves. You live in Georgia near the coast. The problem you have is that cotton exhausts the soil, so that after a number of years, your land is not as productive as it once was. You need new land with soil that hasn't been used to grow cotton for years and years. As of now, the Cherokee are living on the land that rightfully belongs to the state of Georgia. The Georgia legislature recently voted to take over that land and divide it up so that Whites like yourself could move onto it. That's a great law, but some people in Congress and around the country want to stop you from taking this territory from the Cherokee. What's the problem? There is a place set aside for the Cherokee and other Indians west of the Mississippi River. They belong with their own kind, right? Remember, the whole country — no, the whole world — depends on cotton. Your plantation and plantations like yours are what keep this country strong and productive.

But you have another big problem. In Florida, many escaped slaves live side by side with the Seminole Indians. Slaves throughout the south know about this haven for runaways. In fact, sometimes the Seminoles and escaped slaves raid plantations, burn them down, and free the slaves. You won't stand for this. The Seminole communities must be destroyed and the Indians shipped off to Indian Territory along with the Cherokee. As for the escaped slaves who live with them, they need to be recaptured and either returned to their rightful owners or put up for sale. There's also some good land in Florida that you might want to move onto once the Seminoles are gone.

MISSIONARIES AND NORTHERN REFORMERS

Some of you are White Christian missionaries who either live amongst the Cherokee people or once did. You are not plantation owners, gold prospectors, bankers, or military people. You are simply individuals who want to preach the word of God and do what's right. You are of many different Christian denominations. At great sacrifice to yourselves, you moved away from the comfort of civilization to go live in much more difficult conditions.

You believe that the Cherokee people have made great progress advancing toward civilization. According to a resolution your missionary group recently passed, some Cherokee families have "risen to a level with the White people of the United States..." Most Cherokee now wear clothes like White people and have given up their original Indian dress. Women wear decent gowns, that cover their bodies from neck to feet. Before, the women had to do the hard work of tending the corn using hoes. Now, the men do the farming with plows. They are a much more industrious people, and own more property and better houses than in the past. Slowly some of them are becoming Christians and — thankfully — are forgetting their old Indian superstitions. As your resolution points out, "Ancient traditions are fading from memory, and can scarcely be collected..." When the Whites came upon the Cherokee, the Indians were in a "purely savage state." But this is no longer the case. Many Indians and Whites are beginning to intermix. Surely this is a good thing as it brings Indians in closer contact with civilization.

You don't know of a single Cherokee who wants to leave home and go west across the Mississippi River. As your resolution states, there is "an overwhelming torrent of national feeling in opposition to removal." And you ought to know: you live with these people. You are reluctant to take sides in political arguments, but you have to bear witness to what you see and hear.

Those of you who live in the north have read the writings of the missionaries who live amongst the Cherokee. They don't want to steal the Cherokee land, so they have no reason to lie. Senator Theodore Frelinghuysen from New Jersey has spoken eloquently about the Cherokee situation. He calls the Cherokee "the first lords of the soil." The senator puts himself in the Indians' position and asks, "If I use my land for hunting, may another take it because he needs it for agriculture?"

It's true that the richest Cherokee — about ten percent or so — own some Black slaves. Some of you are abolitionists, who want all slavery to end, and don't approve of this. However, almost everyone who ever traveled in Cherokee territory agrees that the Cherokee do not treat their slaves as harshly as the Whites treat theirs. Most slaves in Cherokee country have some rights, and individuals in families are almost never sold away from each other. But slavery is slavery, and some of you don't approve of *any* slavery.

BLACK SEMINOLES

You are Black and you are Indian, a member of the Seminole people in Florida. You are descended from enslaved Africans who ran away from British plantations in Georgia over a hundred years ago, and came to settle with Indians who left their lands farther north. This was before the United States was even a country. You are a free person. Some of the Black people who live in Seminole communities ran away from slavery in the last few years. Others were bought from White slaveowners by Seminoles. These people are still called slaves, but are not treated as slaves. They can marry anyone, can't be sold away from their families, can travel where they want, have their own land, carry guns, etc. But every year they must pay part of their crops to other Seminoles as a kind of tax.

The Indian Removal Act of 1830 is now being considered by the U.S. Congress. It calls for all Indians east of the Mississippi River to be forced off their lands and moved to a place called "Indian Territory" west of the Mississippi River. Full-blooded Seminoles would be moved. But for you, a *Black* Seminole, they would make you a slave and sell you in one of the Southern slave markets. You would be forever separated from your community, your friends, your family. You will never allow this to happen.

The White plantation owners in Georgia and throughout the South are very threatened by the Indians, free Blacks and escaped slaves living peacefully side by side. They know that their slaves hear about these Seminole communities and want to run away to join them. The Seminole communities are a kind of symbol of freedom to enslaved Black people throughout the South. In the past, your people have attacked plantations and freed the slaves on those plantations, and brought them to Florida to live with you and become Seminoles. The Whites also want to steal your land so they can grow their cotton with slave labor.

Three generations of women in a Seminole family dressed in traditional clothing. Photo taken at Cypress Swamp in 1910.

President Andrew Jackson is one of the biggest slaveholders in Tennessee. Some years ago, when he was a general in the army, he ordered his troops to attack your people and destroy your farms and homes. You know that in this debate about Indian removal he is not on your side.

He also wants to move the other Indian nations in the Southeast, especially the Cherokee. You don't have much to do with the Cherokee. You know that they own large numbers of Black slaves, though they say they treat them better than do the White plantation owners. But if this law passes, they will try to move them too.

The United States government and the White plantation owners call the Seminoles "savages." But you have farms and raise horses, cattle, hogs and chickens. And unlike White plantation owners, you know what freedom means. What is "civilized"; what is "savage"?

THE INSTITUTIONALIZATION OF RACISM

BY DEBORAH MENKART

"Racism is as American as apple pie," said civil rights activist H. Rap Brown. Yet we seldom stop to examine the history of racism. When was the 'recipe' introduced? How did it become institutionalized as part of the culture of this society? This lesson invites students to examine the roots of racism in this country and the formation of White identity.

Three readings are recommended for this lesson. The first, by Lerone Bennett, Jr., is Chapter Two (not included here) from *The Shaping of Black America: The Struggle and Triumphs of African-Americans, 1619 to the 1990s* (Penguin). It is college-level reading, but written with such force and imagery that it can engage a high school student. The second is an excerpt from *A People's History of the United States* by Howard Zinn (Harper Collins). The third reading is from *Roots of Racism* produced by the London Institute for Race Relations for high school students. If the readings by Bennett and Zinn are too difficult, use the text from *Roots of Racism* for your students. This reading is very good but not as detailed as the other two. You will need to fill in some of the historical details and analysis from the Bennett and Zinn texts.

Following is a suggested sequence for exploring the history of racism in this country. If you have already completed other lessons in this book, you may want to skip the first few steps.

1. Ask for examples of how race has played a central role in the historic events of the last 50 years. Then ask for examples of how race impacts many aspects of our personal lives such as housing, employment, education and health.

2. Explain that although race is a widely-discussed topic these days, the history of racism is seldom studied in high school or even in college. In fact, Professor James Loewen (University of Vermont) found that many currently used U.S. history textbooks do not even list racism in the index. This class will be different. The readings will be challenging, but ensure your class that you think they are up to it.

3. Ask students, working in pairs, to write on a file card when they think racism developed in the United States. Was it in the 1500s, 1600s, 1700s, 1800s or 1900s? Ask them to write a brief rationale for their selection. They can pass in their cards or post them on the wall below headings for the respective centuries. In either case, students should discuss their answers. You can also ask when they think Whites in this country developed a sense of White identity. In other words, when did they change from identifying as Polish, German, Italian, Irish, English — to identifying as White Americans? Did they identify themselves as being White before they came to America? Was it immediately upon arrival? When and why did White identity become important? And most importantly, what impact has White identity had on the history of this country?

4. Distribute the readings you have selected for students (individually or in small groups) and ask them to determine:

a. During which century was racism institutionalized in the United States?

b. What evidence is there that Whites are not born racist?

c. List some of the ways in which Whites were taught and encouraged to think of themselves as being different from and better than Blacks. Some say that the "carrot and the stick" were used to teach Whites to separate themselves from Blacks. Look over the list you prepared. Which are examples of the carrot approach and which are examples of the stick?

d. Why was racism promoted? Who benefited and who lost?

e. We often talk about the impact of slavery and racism on Blacks. But what about its impact on Whites? How has the history of White people in this country been impacted by racism?

5. To respond to the questions, ask students to create a visual representation of the history. One option is to design an illustrated timeline based on either of the readings. Another option is to cut out shapes of buildings to represent various institutions. Distribute a generic building to each small group and ask them to name one of the institutions responsible for promoting

racism and then to describe some of the strategies used. For example, a building could be labeled State Legislature and some of the Jim Crow laws could be listed. Another building could be labeled School House and the students would list the ways in which schools promoted racist thought. The buildings can be placed in a circle around a stick figure, representing the influence they have on all aspects of our lives.

6. Ask students to reflect on their assumptions at the beginning of the lesson. In what ways are they they same? Have they changed? Do they think other students should examine the history of racism in this country? Why or why not? How could they share their insights and recommendations with the social studies department or the overall school administration?

7. Follow-up questions for discussion or written reflection:

a. The readings presented the methods used to divide the races in this country hundreds of years ago. Are there forces that divide us in the same way today? Compare the role of government, schools, the media and the church today with that of the 17th and 18th century.

b. W.E.B. DuBois argued that "Race feeling and the benefits conferred by whiteness made White Southern workers forget their 'practically identical interests' with the Black poor and accept stunted lives for themselves and for those more oppressed than themselves." Put this statement into your own words. Then state whether you agree or disagree and why.

c. Howard Zinn said that, "Only one fear was greater than the fear of Black rebellion in the new American colonies. That was the fear that discontented Whites would join Black slaves to overthrow the existing order." What are the fears of those in power today? Who has the potential of uniting to change the status quo? What methods are used to divide them?

A People's History

BY HOWARD ZINN

This unequal treatment, this developing combination of contempt and oppression, feeling and action, which we call "racism" — was this the result of a "natural" antipathy of White against Black? The question is important, not just as a matter of historical accuracy, but because any emphasis on "natural" racism lightens the responsibility of the social system. If racism can't be shown to be natural, then it is the result of certain conditions, and we are impelled to eliminate those conditions.

We have no way of testing the behavior of Whites and Blacks toward one another under favorable conditions — with no history of subordination, no money incentive for exploitation and enslavement, no desperation for survival requiring forced labor. All the conditions for Black and White in seventeenth-century America were the opposite of that, all powerfully directed toward antagonism and mistreatment. Under such conditions even the slightest display of humanity between the races might be considered evidence of a basic human drive toward community.

Sometimes it is noted that, even before 1600 when the slave trade had just begun, before Africans were stamped by it — literally and symbolically — the color Black was distasteful. In England before 1600, it meant, according to the Oxford English Dictionary: "Deeply stained with dirt; soiled, dirty, foul. Having dark or deadly purposes, malignant; pertaining to or involving death, deadly; baneful, disastrous, sinister. Foul, iniquitous, atrocious, horrible, horribly wicked. Indicating disgrace, censure, liability to punishment, etc." And Elizabethan poetry often used the color white in connection with beauty.

It may be that, in the absence of any other overriding factor, darkness and blackness, associated with night and unknown, would take on those meanings. But the presence of another human being is a powerful fact, and the conditions of that presence are crucial in determining whether an initial prejudice, against a mere color, divorced from humankind, is turned into brutality and hatred.

In spite of such preconceptions about blackness, in spite of special subordination of Blacks in the American in the seventeenth century, there is evidence that where Whites and Blacks found themselves with common problems, common work, common enemy in their master, they behaved toward one another as equals. As one scholar of slavery, Kenneth Stampp, has put it, Negro and White servants of the seventeenth century were "remarkably unconcerned about the visible physical differences."

Black and White worked together, fraternized together. The very facts that laws had to be passed after a while to forbid such relations indicated the strength of that tendency. In 1661 a law was passed in Virginia that "in case any English servant shall run away in company of any Negroes" he would have to give special service for extra years to the master of the runaway Negro. In 1691, Virginia provided for the banishment of any "white man or woman being free who shall intermarry with a negro, mulatto, or Indian man or woman bond or free."

There is an enormous difference between a feeling of racial strangeness, perhaps fear, and the mass enslavement of millions of Black people that took place in the Americas. The transition from one to the other cannot be explained easily by "natural" tendencies. It is not hard to understand as the outcome of historical conditions.

From time to time, Whites were involved in the slave resistance. As early as 1663, indentured White servants and Black slaves in Gloucester County, Virginia, formed a conspiracy to rebel and gain their freedom. The plot was betrayed, and ended with executions. Mullin reports that the newspaper notices of runaways in Virginia often warned "ill disposed" Whites about harboring fugitives. Sometimes slaves and free men ran off together, or cooperated in crimes together. Sometimes, Black male slaves ran off and joined White women. From time to time, White ship captains and watermen dealt with runaways, perhaps making the slave a part of the crew.

In New York in 1741, there were ten thousand Whites in the city and two thousand Black slaves. It had been a hard winter and the poor — slave and free — had suffered greatly. When mysterious fires broke out, Blacks and Whites were accused of conspiring together. Mass hysteria developed against the accused. After a trial full of lurid accusations by informers, and forced confessions, two White men and two White women were executed, eighteen slaves were hanged, and thirteen slaves burned alive.

Only one fear was greater then the fear of Black rebellion in the new American colonies. That was the fear that discontented Whites would join Black slaves to overthrow the existing order. In the early years of slavery, especially, before racism as a way of thinking was firmly ingrained, while White indentured servants were often treated as badly as Black slaves, there was a possibility of cooperation. As Edmund Morgan sees it:

There are hints that the two despised groups initially saw each other as sharing the same predicament. It was common, for example, for servants and slaves to run away together, steal hogs together, get drunk together. It was not uncommon for them to make love together. In Bacon's Rebellion, one of the last groups to surrender was a mixed band of eighty negroes and twenty English servants.

As Morgan says, masters, "initially at least, perceived slaves in much the same way they had always perceived servants... shiftless, irresponsible, unfaithful, ungrateful, dishonest..." And "if freemen with disappointed hopes should make common cause with slaves of desperate hope, the results might be worse than anything Bacon had done."

And so, measures were taken. About the same time that slave codes, involving discipline and punishment, were passed by the Virginia Assembly.

Virginia's ruling class, having proclaimed that all white men were superior to black, went on to offer their social (but white) inferiors a number of benefits previously denied them. In 1705 a law was passed requiring masters to provide white servants whose indenture time was up with ten bushels of corn, thirty shillings, and a gun, while women servants were to get 15 bushels of corn and forty shillings. Also, the newly freed servants were to get 50 acres of land.

Morgan concludes: "Once the small planter felt less exploited by taxation and began to prosper a little, he became less turbulent, less dangerous, more respectable. He could begin to see his big neighbor not as an extortionist but as a powerful protector of their common interests."

We see now a complex web of historical threads to ensnare Blacks for slavery in America: the desperation of starving settlers, the special helplessness of the displaced African, the powerful incentive of profit for slave trader and planter, the temptation of superior status for poor Whites, the elaborate controls against escape and rebellion, the legal and social punishment of Black and White collaboration.

The point is that the elements of this web are historical, not "natural." This does not mean that they are easily disentangled, dismantled. It means only that there is a possibility for something else, under historical conditions not yet realized. And one of these conditions would be the elimination of that class exploitation which has made poor Whites desperate for small gifts of status, and has prevented the unity of Black and White necessary for joint rebellion and reconstruction.

Around 1700, the Virginia House of Burgesses declared:

The Christian Servants in this country for the most part consist of the Worser Sort of the people of Europe. And since...such numbers of Irish and other Nations have been brought in of which a great many have been soldiers in the late wars that according to our present Circumstances we can hardly governe them and if they were fitted with Armes and had the Opertunity of meeting together by Musters we have just reason to fears they may rise upon us.

It was a kind of class consciousness, a class fear. There were things happening in early Virginia, and in the other colonies, to warrant it.

Howard Zinn, *an activist and historian, is Professor Emeritus at Boston University. He is the author of numerous books including an abridged version of* A People's History of the United States *written for classroom use (New Press, 1997). His memoir is titled* You Can't Be Neutral on a Moving Train.

ROOTS OF RACISM

THE DEMAND FOR SLAVES

There is one vital element of early capitalism and colonial commerce without which the whole system would have foundered — slave labor.

From the middle of the 17th century, the trade in enslaved Africans (who were used to work the tobacco and then the cotton plantations of North America, the mines, coffee, cocoa and sugar plantations of Latin America and the sugar plantations of the West Indies) grew until it reached massive proportions, both in terms of profit and of people.

This meant terrible disruption for Africa's societies, due to the enormous and continuing loss of its young, able-bodied men and women. When Europeans first made inroads into Africa, there were many different forms of society within the continent with flourishing trade networks, developments in clothworking, gold mining, iron making, different forms of agriculture, fine cities, great temples and churches and monuments and skillfully-made works of art. But much of this development was slowly bled to death, making a continent ultimately defenseless against the full Colonial conquest that was to follow — for it was not until towards the end of the 19th century that Europe was powerful enough to subdue Africa completely.

What the slave trade meant for Europe was an enormous injection of profit and wealth that enabled its industrial development to flourish together with, as we shall see, a legacy of racism that is still imbedded in European culture.

In terms of profit, slaves were valuable in two ways; as commodities to trade in and as producers of crops and raw materials. They were the essential ingredient in what came to be known as the "triangular trade." It is easy to understand how this worked if you study the map. This trade was immensely profitable. At each stage of the journey there was a transaction — and profit — to be made.

Having made a profit for their buyers and sellers, the slaves were then set to work on the plantations to produce the sugar, cotton and tobacco that the Colonists sold to the home or 'mother' country. Since the slaves were only given the bare minimum to live on and they were forced to work until they dropped, their labor was the cheapest possible; thus enabling the plantation owner to make the greatest possible profit.

THE GROWTH OF RACISM

Although African people were taken and used by Europeans as slaves in the New World for economic reasons, there was an element of racism in this choice. It can be seen if we simply ask ourselves the question: why were Europeans taken on as indentured servants, and Africans as slaves? Or, to put it another way, why was it considered acceptable to turn African people into property, but not fellow Europeans?

We must remember that slavery had existed since the earliest times. Slaves were often captives from war. There was a flourishing slave trade in the early Middle Ages around the Mediterranean, as well as a trade in African slaves carried on by Arab merchants. In the 12th century, the Italians were using slaves, people who had been captured in war and then bought and sold on the slave markets, to grow sugar on the island of Cyprus, which had been taken from the Muslims in the Crusades. Christian merchants in Genoa sold Christian slaves to Muslim Saracens.

The early Christian church owned many slaves itself, and never seriously considered that such an institution should be abolished. In that early period there was no particular objection to the use of Christians as slaves and the majority of the slaves were of European origin. By the 15th century, the Church had come round firmly to the view that Christians should not be turned into slaves, if there was an alternative.

Although slavery had existed for centuries, there is a very important distinction to be made between the slavery of earlier periods and the enslavement of non-European peoples that was practiced under slavery and colonialism. In the earlier periods, slaves were mainly seen and treated as a class within society, a necessary part of the social order, although the very lowest part of it. There were laws and customs to regulate slavery.

Under ancient slavery, slaves could obtain their freedom and even rise to the very top of society. But with colonial slavery, a slave ceased to be regarded as a person at all. A slave had no legal rights or standing and was outside of society altogether.

They were to be regarded and treated solely as things, to be bought and sold for profit, and to be used in the same way that a factory owner would use a machine; to produce whatever was required.

Nevertheless, the fact could not be got round that Black people — even enslaved Blacks — were human beings, not things. To justify such a system of treating other human beings, Europeans came to argue that the Africans they captured, bought and sold were not fully human at all. The basis for such a belief was already there in European culture itself.

CHRISTIAN TEACHING AND PRACTICE

For centuries Catholicism had held that a person could only be fully human if he or she was a believer within the one true Church. Non-believers, which included all those non-European peoples who worshipped different gods under different religious systems, were therefore considered inferior human beings.

In Europe's early history this belief had vented itself on the Jews, who were held to be responsible for the killing of Christ. They were subjected to all sorts of tyranny and abuse and made to do much of the dirty work of business and finance that was considered dangerous for the Christian soul. Attacks on them were frequent. In 1190, 150 Jews were massacred after being besieged in York Castle. At the end of the 13th century Edward I drove Jews out of England. They were expelled from France in the 14th century and from Spain in 1492.

There was, therefore, already a basis within European culture for discriminating against and abusing a whole people on the grounds of their origin. The assumption was built into European culture that Europeans were somehow superior — an assumption which the dog-eat-dog competition in greed and aggression that had gone on for centuries between European powers had done nothing to dispel.

With the coming of the slave trade, and the institution of slavery on a scale such as the world had never seen before, these elements of European culture took on a new and terrible lease of life. The very speed and intensity with which the enslavement of Africans was carried out further reinforced the notion that they were not individuals but things.

HOW THEY JUSTIFIED SLAVERY

Europeans based their theories of African inferiority on the easily seen physical differences between themselves and Africans. Thus they began to rationalize and justify their treatment of them. In other words, arguments were put forward that, although Black people were human beings, they were in all respects inferior human beings.

They were, it was claimed, uncivilized and barbaric (though, at an earlier period, Portuguese explorers themselves had been awed by the magnificence of the great African civilizations). They were stupid, but strong (so, of course, only really suited to the arduous, menial tasks of slavery). They were lazy and cunning (if you think this contradicts the earlier statement, then you are right; but logic does not enter into these types of beliefs), and so needed constant and harsh supervision. The color of their skin was black, which had been associated for centuries in the European mind with darkness, fear, evil and as the very opposite and enemy of Christian whiteness and light. Their color, which was unchangeable, was the visible proof that they themselves could never change, develop or act as anything but slaves and servants to their White masters.

There is a passage in the *Bible* about the descendants of Noah's son, Ham (who was cursed by God), who are condemned for all eternity to be slaves and servants. In the Middle Ages, this was held by the clergy to apply to the lowest ranks of society, the poorest peasants and the serfs, whose position was considered fixed and unalterable. With the establishments of slavery in the colonial period, it came to be understood to refer exclusively to Black people.

THEORIES OF RACIAL SUPERIORITY

From such crude beginnings, a whole theory of the racial superiority of white people over Black was developed, initially to justify the slave system, and eventually to justify all the ways in which non-White people were exploited by the White colonial powers. For though slavery and the slave system came to be abolished (the constant rebellions of the slaves combined with other economic developments made slavery unprofitable), other ways were found to use the lands, the raw materials and the labor of non-White peoples to produce high profits for the colonial powers. Hand in hand with these developments over the years a whole body of 'scientific' arguments was developed and used to justify the actions of the colonial powers.

If people are held to be naturally and forever inferior, then you are justified in ruling them for their own good (and your enormous profit). You are justified in not paying them what their work is worth (so getting cheap labor which adds to your profit), or not paying them the true value of what they do produce. If you study the history of any of the colonies ruled by the European powers, you will see how racist theories and racist practices have been used to create wealth and profit for the colonial masters.

So we can say that racism is not just a set of ideas or beliefs, it has a very important economic function. It not only degrades and humiliates, but it also robs and impoverishes in every way the people who are the target. Racism made the cheap labor force that the capitalist system demanded almost free. The colonies were plundered — using that labor force — of the raw materials and natural resources needed to supply the industries of Europe. Europe was enriched and its own development stimulated at terrible cost to the colonial peoples.

So we can see that the colonial and capitalist systems, which grew up together, were also inherently and inescapably racist.

Excerpted and reprinted from Roots of Racism, *published by the Institute for Race Relations in London, England,* © 1982. *This is part of a series which includes* Patterns of Racism. *Both titles are listed in the Resource Guide.*

WHAT DO YOU THINK?

What changes in the political and economic system would be needed so that racism is not inherent or inescapable as described in this reading?

THE BUSINESS OF DRUGS

BY DEBORAH MENKART

Almost every school district has a drug policy. A substantial portion of school budgets is dedicated to controlling the drug problem. School security forces increase, health classes address the dangers of drug use, assemblies feature inspirational speakers imploring students to 'just say no,' art classes design 'anti-drug' posters, and social studies classes debate specific drug policies. Yet seldom if ever are students given the opportunity to learn about the nature of the drug crisis and develop an informed analysis of this contemporary social issue.

Without studying the drug business in the United States, students are vulnerable to the racist analysis presented in the mass media — that Black and Latino youth, and an overall 'lack of values' in urban (minority) communities, are the primary causes of the drug crisis. Next in line for blame are the third world countries (again, people of color) that grow and ship drugs to the United States. Shielded from the press are the "white collar" (and most often racially White) people and industries that make big profits from the drug business: money launderers, the multinationals, the chemists, the lawyers, the weapons manufacturers, etc.

This lesson is designed to present the full picture of the drug business, introducing students to some of the 'players' who are seldom mentioned in the press. Students can then discuss who is to blame for the drug related crimes in the United States and real solutions. They can also critique the bias of media coverage and domestic and international drug policies.

The design for the lesson is a trial. It is based on a lesson developed by Bill Bigelow for teaching about the history of the conquest of the Americas. The text for a few of the roles draws heavily from the roles in that lesson, particularly the role of the "system of profit."

The primary source of information for this lesson is the book *Pipe Dream Blues: Racism and the War on Drugs* by Clarence Lusane. We have excerpted liberally from *Pipe Dream Blues* for the handouts. It is an excellent resource on this topic and is highly recommended for teachers and high school students.

MATERIALS

▶ Handouts
▶ News clippings on drug related crimes from the paper of the last couple of weeks (collect articles for a few weeks prior to this lesson)

PROCEDURE

1. Get students into small groups with a couple of news clippings in each group. Ask them to skim the clippings and discuss who, according to the report, is to blame for the drug related crimes reported in the paper. Put their answers on the board. Then ask what most of these people have in common. They are likely to be young, male, Black or Latino.

Explain that there are other people responsible for drug-related crimes who are seldom mentioned in the press. The sale of drugs is a business, a very big business. The young men portrayed in the papers are just one tier of the business. They are the laborers. The other laborers are the peasants who grow coca leaves in Latin America. But the drug business resembles other multinational industries with many levels of employees and owners. Read to students the following quote from *Pipe Dream Blues*:

There are three general tiers within the structured illegal economy: the top level that includes the 'CEOs' (Chief Executive Officers), who principally control production, manufacturing, and international export; the middle level of managers and administrators, who control national and regional distribution, marketing, high-level security, and money-laundering; and the bottom rung, which includes couriers, peasant farmers, street-level retailers, crack-house operators, and local enforcers. (Lusane, p. 89.)

Explain that in this lesson we will learn about all three levels, particularly the levels which receive little media coverage. The other group seldom mentioned in the press are White users or consumers. As Clarence Lusane explains,

While the facts show that the majority of drug users are White, the nation and the world are bombarded with images of young Black males who are handcuffed, lying on the ground dead, or herded behind prison walls — all due to trafficking or abuse

of illegal drugs. The racist myth is that most inner-city Black males are gun-toting, crack-smoking criminals-in-waiting... Although the incidence of trafficking and drug abuse is relatively the same for Blacks and Whites, their resources and political capacity to confront the problem differ. (Lusane, p. 25.)

2. Prepare to hold a trial to determine who is responsible for the distribution of dangerous drugs and the deaths which result from the drug wars in the United States. On the board, list the names of the groups who will stand trial:

▸ Money-launderers ▸ Peasant farmers

▸ Street dealers ▸ U.S. Government

▸ Consumers ▸ System of Profit

3. Write the following indictment on the board: "You are responsible for all the robberies and murders committed over the last ten years which are related to the use and sale of drugs in the United States." Tell the students that each of them is being charged with this crime. You, the teacher, will be the prosecutor. Explain that tomorrow you will assign defendant roles and hold each group responsible for the crimes. It will be up to each group to defend itself and to argue who is really to blame. Meanwhile they need to get some background information. Distribute the pre-reading "Endless U.S. Drug War a Big Business" for homework that evening. To introduce students to the reading, draw their attention to the chart on mortality rates. Assign the questions below for homework and discuss the following day (if you can devote an extra day to the lesson.)

▸ How has the war on drugs intensified crime and violence?

▸ Draw and label pictures to symbolize the pyramids of production and distribution.

▸ According to the "U.S. drug-related mortality" chart, which drugs are the most dangerous? How did you come to this conclusion?

▸ Based on the reading, what country is the largest exporter of drugs? What kind of drugs does this country export?

▸ How does the author of this article suggest his readers help bring peace to the Americas?

4. The next day, divide the students into five groups and give them their indictments and a placard with their group title. (See handouts.) Leave extra copies of the indictments available on a table in case any of the groups want to read about the other defendants as they prepare their case.

Tell them that for the purpose of this activity, they should suspend their own personal opinions and step into the role that has been assigned. From the perspective of that role, write a collective defense. This should include why they are not guilty and which group or groups they think hold the blame, and why. If some groups are ready before others, suggest they create a witness who can speak on their behalf. They could call on one of their own group members to be a witness. For example, the peasants could call on a representative of a human rights organization to testify that the peasants had resisted being pushed off the fertile land and were literally forced into growing coca as the only way to survive.

5. When the groups have had a chance to prepare, select a jury or in smaller classes take just one person each from three of the groups. Publicly swear them to neutrality; clarify with them that they no longer represent the dealers, consumers, money launderers or anyone else. If possible, invite a guest to serve as the judge. Students may feel compelled to make their defense even stronger if a "real person" (that is, an outsider) is presiding.

6. The order of the prosecution is up to you, although you may want to begin with the low people on the income ladder and move on up, saving the System of Profit until the last. The teacher presents and pursues the indictment for each group, the group defends, the jury questions, and other groups may then question. After which the process repeats itself, with a new defendant.

7. After each group has been charged and made its defense, ask the jury to step out of the classroom and deliberate. They can assign "percentage guilt," e.g., consumers are 30%, the System of Profit is 50%, etc. They also need to offer clear explanations for why they decided as they did. As they deliberate, ask the rest of the class to step out of their roles to do in writing the same thing the jury is doing.

8. Ask the jury to return and explain its verdict. Hold a discussion. Following are some questions you can raise:

▸ Was anyone not guilty at all?

▸ Why do the young people on the street keep killing each other? Are the other youth in their neighborhoods really the enemy?

▸ Have you ever studied the drug trade in school before? Or read a mainstream article which provides the kind of information that we learned in the class? If so, where and when? If not, why do you think that is the case?

▸ Compare the list of who you determined is responsible for the drug trade and who was featured most prominently in the news articles that you read at the beginning of the lesson. Are the media providing a complete picture? What group(s), if any, are omitted from the press?

POSSIBLE FOLLOW-UP ACTIVITIES

1. Take action. You can make some suggestions and solicit more ideas from the class. Here are a few ideas:

▸ Hold a grade level teach-in on the business of drugs;

▸ Write letters to the newspaper(s) critiquing the bias in coverage and making recommendations for changes;

▸ Create an informational bulletin board for the school hallway or an informational pamphlet for parents about the business of drugs;

▸ Write a song, article or a poem for the school newspaper or to be shared at the next school assembly on drugs which conveys what they have learned. (A form for the poem could be a dialogue between two of the defendant groups in the trial — for example a dialogue between a street dealer and the system of profit, or between a peasant farmer and a street dealer.)

▸ Study their state and county policies regarding drug sales and use. Analyze the effectiveness of those policies. If it is determined that changes should be made, advocate for reform.

2. It has been said that "the nation's war on drugs has become in effect a war on Black people." Do you agree or disagree? Explain your answer.

3. Explore solutions to the drug crisis which address the more systemic issues. In Chapter Ten of *Pipe Dream Blues*, Lusane describes successful programs to address addiction. Lusane also poses the challenge of decent employment as a solution:

It is highly likely that low-level employees in the illegal drug industry, who profit little and face the most danger, may be won over to the legal labor market. Contrary to popular belief, winning these workers over does not mean dangling a large salary in front of them. It does mean making available meaningful, nonviolent, productive, and career-oriented work.

Pipe Dream Blues: Racism and the War on Drugs *by Clarence Lusane. South End Press, 1991. 293 pp. Documents the history, economics and politics of the drug crisis. Describes programs and strategies which could address the roots of the drug wars and drug abuse. Available from NECA.*

Students could explore why this has not been pursued as a national goal. An excellent reference is *The End of Work: The Decline of the Global Labor Force and the Dawn of the Post-Market Era* by Jeremy Rifkin (Tarcher/Putnam, 1995).

4. View one of the following films and discuss in light of this lesson. Available in video stores.

A Hero Ain't Nothing But A Sandwich: The story of a 12-year-old African American boy addicted to heroin and his family's struggle to help him kick the habit. The film speaks to the politics of social welfare organizations and the use of drugs as a weapon against the Black community. (Based on the book by Alice Childress.)

Panther: By Mario Van Peebles. The story of the Black Panther Party for Self-Defense. Shows how the FBI tried to destroy the Panther organization and finally attacked the whole community by flooding Panther organized neighborhoods with massive amounts of extra strong heroin.

ADDITIONAL RESOURCES

Lusane, C. 1991. *Pipe dream blues: Racism and the war on drugs*. Boston: South End Press.

Claude, J. 1990. *The political economy of cocaine*. Philadelphia: American Friends Service Committee.

ACKNOWLEDGEMENT

Thanks to Clarence Lusane, Assistant Professor in the School of International Service at American University, for permission to reprint from his book and for his feedback on the lesson.

Thanks to Bill Bigelow for the design of this lesson and his comments on the readings.

ENDLESS U.S. DRUG WAR
A BIG BUSINESS

BY MICHAEL LIVINGSTON

With a flourish and fanfare, President Clinton's 1996 State of the Union speech announced that the new federal drug czar would be General Barry McCaffrey, head of the U.S. Southern Command, the nation's key garrison in Latin America.

In Colombia, meanwhile, President Ernesto Samper faces formal charges that his 1994 election campaign took more than $3 million from the Cali drug cartel.

In Mexico, authorities are continuing investigations of Raul Salinas de Gortari, the imprisoned brother of former president Carlos Salinas de Gortari. Raul amassed as much as $3 billion in foreign bank accounts while serving in the government from 1983 to 1992. On January 14, with an eye on billions of U.S. aid dollars, the Mexican government helped capture Gulf cartel chief Juan Garcia Abrego.

In yet another part of the Americas, the U.S. Drug Enforcement Agency has discovered new evidence that top Guatemalan military officials have helped transport drugs for Colombian cartels.

And, closer to home, U.S. cities are reeling after a record year of homicides, many linked to drug peddling.

What connects these events is a hemispheric war purportedly aimed at illegal drugs, a war that seems neverending.

The drug war, it turns out, exacerbates the very problems it ostensibly seeks to stem. As elected officials score political points, the combat ensures enormous drug profits and growing numbers of casualties in the streets of the United States and Latin America.

THE INDUSTRY

Behind the drug war lies an industry with annual sales of an estimated $300 billion. Cocaine shows the industry's general structure — a pyramid for production and another for distribution.

The base of the first pyramid consists of poor peasants in Latin America. They receive much more for growing coca than other crops, making it economically essential to produce for the illegal market. At the pyramid's next level are laborers who transport and refine the leaf. Many work for the organized drug cartels, who sit at the top of the pyramid. The cartels finish processing the cocaine, handle banking and money laundering, and arrange for shipment to markets.

The other pyramid is a distribution system based largely in the United States, which consumes half of the world's illegal drugs. The cartels sell the coke to intermediaries or directly to gangs.

The growers and dealers at the bottom of both pyramids earn decent livings, considering their miserable alternatives. The peasant wages are vital for the economies of supplier nations, especially Peru, Bolivia and Colombia.

Most other Latin American countries, notably Mexico and Panama, provide transhipment and money-laundering opportunities. The bulk of the profits goes to the cartels and their bankers, who usually invest the loot in the United States and Europe.

Prohibition — making it illegal to produce, sell or use drugs — reduces casual use but not the lion share of the demand. Thus, prohibition's main consequence is to hike the selling price, a boon for organized crime.

The most dangerous drugs in the United States, as measured by mortality rates, are tobacco and alcohol (see chart). Heroin and cocaine do not come close and there has never been a recorded U.S. death from marijuana.

Drug use, of course, is linked to other problems besides death. These include family violence (tied most closely to alcohol), accidents (again tied closely to alcohol but also to other legal and illegal drugs) and lost economic productivity.

Gang murders, carjackings, burglary and theft

U.S. DRUG-RELATED MORTALITY

Drug	Users	Deaths Per Year	Per 100,000 Users
Tobacco	60,000,000	390,000	650
Alcohol	100,000,000	150,000	150
Heroin	500,000	400	80
Cocaine	5,000,000	200	4

SOURCES: U.S. SURGEON GENERAL, DEPARTMENT OF HEALTH AND HUMAN SERVICES

are not tied to drug use *per se,* but to prohibition —
the high cost of drugs and the illegal industry. Economists estimate that halting U.S. prohibition would
result in 10, 000 fewer homicides per year in this
country, a drop of almost ten percent.

Why War?

The "war on drugs," as declared by Ronald
Reagan in 1982, has failed to solve the problems
tied to substance abuse, but has intensified crime
and violence. First, the war provides a ready justification in the United States for foreign intervention. Second, across the hemisphere, the war justifies political repression.

The Bush administration, for example, promoted
the 1989 U.S. invasion of Panama on grounds that
General Manuel Noriega was trafficking drugs. But
Noriega's small-time role in the industry was only a
pretext, as evidenced when the United States replaced
him with politicians closely tied to drug-trade bankers. Even accepting Bush's rationale, the invasion was
a failure — the Panama narcotics trade has become
worse than before the invasion.

Since the incursion into Panama, according to
the Washington Office on Latin America, the drug
war has been the main justification for U.S. military intervention in Latin America. U.S. officials
have used it to justify increased military aid to Bolivia, Colombia and Peru. They have cited the war
as grounds for U.S. military exercises and for de-
ploying the Green Berets to direct and train the three
countries' armed forces. The drug war has also justified an enormous expansion of "low intensity conflict" strategies that the Pentagon developed in Central America during the 1980's.

Most of the military aid and intervention has
targeted popular protests or movements, especially
in Peru and Colombia, where the drug war is used
to violate human rights of peasants, union activists, and social critics.

Indeed, the Colombian military often cooper-
ates with drug cartels' private militaries to fight a
local war against peasant organization and unions.
Both the Colombian military and the cartels perceive their common enemy to be the people who
work for a better, more just country.

Collateral Damage

In conventional warfare, "collateral damage" is
taken for granted. The drug war is no different.
One form of collateral damage is the corruption and
undermining of civilian governments.

President Samper's crisis is but one illustration.
Honest Colombian officials who stand up to the drug
industry are killed, as happens in Guatemala, Mexico,
Peru, and Colombia. Others are purchased or intimidated. The industry is corrupting even formerly stable
democracies such as Costa Rica, now a major stop en
route to the United States.

The collateral damage occurs inside U.S. borders as well. At least half of the 1.5 million people
confined in U.S. jails or prisons were charged with
drug offenses. The soaring prison population has
led to a veritable prison-industrial complex. In states
such as California, funds for prisons exceed funds
for higher education.

The drug laws, as enforced in the United States,
are also unmistakably racist. While most users are
White, most drug convicts are people of color.

The drug war also has provoked a crisis in the legal system and a rollback of civil liberties. The *National Law Journal* reports that the United States now
spends more then $100 million on police informers.
Their unsupported claims are the sole grounds for more
than 70 percent of federal search warrants.

Hypocrisy

The United States' passionate, almost obses-
sive, drug war reeks of hypocrisy in two senses.
First, the country is not merely the world's largest
drug importer, it is the largest exporter. The difference, of course, is that the drugs we export — such
as glue, tobacco, and pesticides — are legal. Their
direct harm across the Americas far outweighs the
harm caused by both illegal drug use and
criminalization.

In the second sense, the U.S. military and CIA
have actively encouraged and participated in the
drug trade on numerous occasions, from heroin
running in Southeast Asia to cocaine transport in
Central America. While direct U.S. involvement
accounts for only a miniscule amount of the drugs
used in this country, the government participation
is criminal.

The center of the drug war is here in the United
States. Any effort to end the war must also be centered here. Only by defending human rights and
opposing military intervention across the hemisphere, and only by altering U.S. drug policies, can
we hope to bring peace in this war, a battle not
really against drugs but against each and every
one of us in the Americas.

*Michael Livingston is a psychology professor at St. John's
University in Collegeville,Minnesota.*

*Reprinted from "Endless U.S. Drug War a Big Business," Con-
nection to the Americas a monthly newsletter of the Resource
Center on the Americas (March, 1996, Volume 13, No. 2).*

MONEY LAUNDERER

INDICTMENT: YOU ARE RESPONSIBLE FOR ALL THE ROBBERIES AND MURDERS COMMITTED OVER THE LAST TEN YEARS WHICH ARE RELATED TO THE USE AND SALE OF DRUGS IN THE UNITED STATES.

You are the people that make the drug business work — you grease the wheels. Without you, the drug business would grind to a halt. Therefore you are guilty for all the distribution of dangerous drugs and the drug-related crimes. Your names do not usually appear in the paper and you seldom get arrested, but you are criminals nonetheless.

One of the biggest problems facing drug dealers is what to do with the mountains of $5, $10, and $20 bills that they accumulate. In these drug-conscious days, it takes considerable and creative financial skill to turn drug dollars into what can appear to be 'honest' money. Money launderers hide money that has been gained illegally by making it seem to have been gained legally.

Launderers can be cash-and-carry types who pack suitcases and bags with cash, leave the country, and deposit the cash in a foreign bank. Or they can be the foreign bankers who make such transactions easy to complete. Laundering can become elaborate — operations with electronic money-wiring facilities, telex machines, and automatic bill-counting equipment — but the goal is always the same, to hide the vast financial gains or to make the money impossible to connect to the dealer. The most frequent vehicles for laundering drug money are banks in the United States, the Caribbean and Hong Kong. Another way to hide the profits from drug dealing is to open a business which appears to be real as a "front." That means that you open a bank account in the name of your business front and deposit the drug profits in the account so it appears that the profits are legitimate business proceeds.

Some government action has been taken against laundering, such as the Bank Secrecy Act of 1970 and the Anti-Drug Abuse Act of 1988. The Bank Secrecy Act requires financial institutions to report cash deposits of $10,000 or more, and multiple deposits from the same depositor that add up to $10,000. Such transactions are reported to the Treasury and the U.S. Secret Service. The Money Laundering Control Act of 1986 further requires banks to have in place a reporting system to monitor cash transactions under $10,000.

Nevertheless, it is estimated that prosecutors catch only two percent of laundered money circulating in the United States. A few who have been caught include: Rep. Robert Hanrahan (R-IL) and Richard Silberan, former fundraiser for Jerry Brown in California; a former attorney general for the state of Kansas; a consortium of Pennsylvania airline pilots; and three former DEA agents.

Although you are guilty, few actions have been taken against high ranking launderers due to strong lobbying by banks to curtail government regulations and oversight. Many of these bankers had close financial and personal ties with Nixon, Bush and Reagan administration officials.

You have made big profits in this role. In certain areas of the United States, there has been a growth in cash surplus at local banks. In 1970, banks in Florida, a key drug entry point, had a currency surplus of $576 million. By 1976, this figure had grown to $1.5 billion. By 1982, the cash surplus in Jacksonville and Miami alone amounted to $5.2 billion. Similar trends exist in southern California, Texas and New Orleans.

PEASANT FARMER

INDICTMENT: YOU ARE RESPONSIBLE FOR ALL THE ROBBERIES AND MURDERS COMMITTED OVER THE LAST TEN YEARS WHICH ARE RELATED TO THE USE AND SALE OF DRUGS IN THE UNITED STATES.

You, the grower, are on the bottom of the pyramid, but you play an essential role. Without the growers, there would be no drugs to sell. The drug wars would come to a halt if you stopped growing drugs.

You have no financial security, health insurance, or the legal options that middle- and upper-class employers have. You are the first and hardest hit when the market declines and you lack the skills and resources to invest and create long-term legal sources of income. You may claim that this is your only option for employment. But are you really willing to grow a deadly product to make a living?

You have been pushed off the more fertile land by multinational growers in the last two decades. In Peru and Bolivia these large growers sell cash crops such as coffee, rice, corn and cacao which require very fertile soil and the hot climate found at lower elevations. You were left to make a living from the poor soil and rough terrain of the hills. One of the few cash crops that will survive in these conditions is the coca leaf which is the key ingredi-

ent for cocaine. Coca thrives where the soil is marginal and there is little water, at high elevations and on hillsides. In addition, after the first year it is planted, coca yields four crops a year. Before expenses, you can earn up to $2,200 a year from one hectare (2.47 acres) of coca. It may not make you rich but it does raise you out of desperate poverty. Workers who make the leaves into paste earn about $9 for the three days of work it requires to produce the paste. The mixer or chemist may earn $10/day.

But there are other options. You could organize and protest the takeover of your land by the multinationals. Of course, many people who have tried to resist in the past have been killed, but isn't it better to die for what you believe in than to survive harvesting a crop that kills others? And, look at the Zapatistas, in Mexico. They have certainly called national attention to the plight of poor farmers through their protests. Instead of standing up to the government and multinationals, you simply moved and are now growing a crop which increases the crime in your country and the United States.

STREET DEALER

INDICTMENT: YOU ARE RESPONSIBLE FOR ALL THE ROBBERIES AND MURDERS COMMITTED OVER THE LAST TEN YEARS WHICH ARE RELATED TO THE USE AND SALE OF DRUGS IN THE UNITED STATES.

You, the retailers, are on the bottom of the pyramid, but you play an essential role. Without the street dealers, there would be no sales. The drug wars would come to a halt if you stopped selling drugs.

You have no financial security, health insurance, or the legal options that middle- and upper-class employers have. You are the first and hardest hit when the market declines and you lack the skills and resources to invest and create long-term legal sources of income. You may claim that this is your only option for employment. But are you really willing to sell death to make a living?

As Clarence Lusane explains,

In the United States, the frontline is occupied by street sellers, lookouts, couriers, workers in heroin "shooting galleries," and crack-house operators. These workers, many of whom are inner-city Black and Latino youth, are the first arrested and the first killed. Although profits can sometimes be high (a low-level look-out can earn about ten times the minimum wage an hour on a good day), the risks are deadly and unforgiving.

While it is easy to enter the drug trade as a drug seller, particularly selling crack, few become rich...The big profits made from street sales are restricted to a few. According to Bruce Johnson of the Narcotics and Drug Research, Inc., 'less than 20 percent of the people engaged in drug dealing have a net-worth cash return of as much as $1,000.' ...Crack-house workers, as opposed to owners, appear to make very little. In one East Harlem neighborhood, studied by San Francisco State University's Phillippe Bourgois, crack-house workers made $50 to $70 for an eight-hour shift. This worked out to only 50 cents per vial of crack.

So for a relatively small profit, you are willing to contribute to the destruction of your community. You are selling your soul to the devil, and for a cheap price. Instead you could organize and demand jobs and education. Think about your younger sisters and brothers, what options do you want for them?

U.S. Government

INDICTMENT: YOU ARE RESPONSIBLE FOR ALL THE ROBBERIES AND MURDERS COMMITTED OVER THE LAST TEN YEARS WHICH ARE RELATED TO THE USE AND SALE OF DRUGS IN THE UNITED STATES.

Democrats and Republicans claim to have committed themselves to the cause of waging a war against drug abuse. But actually your policies have exacerbated the problem on many levels. Not only do your policies not address the root of the problem, but they are racist. The government emphasizes law and order tactics directed against third world countries and communities of color.

In recent years, Congress has cut funds from many social programs including drug treatment centers. So if an addict wants to kick their habit, they may be turned away or put on a long waiting list. But if they later commit a crime to pay for their habit, they will be locked up for many years. It will cost the taxpayers more money to lock someone up than it would have to treat them.

The government is investing a lot of money in prisons. Some companies are making big profits from what is known now as the "prison industry."

Congress has also provided minimal oversight of an influential branch of the United States government — the Central Intelligence Agency.

The Central Intelligence Agency (CIA) has received a lot of attention for its alleged involvement in the drugs for guns exchange with the Contras (U.S.-backed anti-Nicaraguan Sandinista fighters),

leading to increased quantities of drugs on the streets of Los Angeles. But this is not new. The CIA has often colluded with drug merchants in the name of national security. For example, in the fight against communism in southeast Asia, the CIA gave cash and arms to Laotian, Nationalist Chinese, and Thai mercenaries and turned a blind eye to the opium trade. Later the CIA employed Cuban exiles active in the cocaine and marijuana trade as informants and mercenaries in the fight against communism in Latin America.

The CIA kept former Panamanian President Manuel Noriega on its payroll, knowing full well of his role in drug trafficking. Some analysts argue that it was only when he refused to follow a CIA directive that the U.S. government decided to invade Panama and remove him. This was done in the name of protecting the Panamanian people from a dictator and drug dealer. But the people that the U.S. government put in his place appear to have even bigger drug trafficking connections — working directly with money laundering banks in Miami.

These are just a few examples of how the policies and practices of the United States government, both domestically and internationally, have contributed directly to the drug crisis in this country.

CONSUMER

INDICTMENT: YOU ARE RESPONSIBLE FOR ALL THE ROBBERIES AND MURDERS COMMITTED OVER THE LAST TEN YEARS WHICH ARE RELATED TO THE USE AND SALE OF DRUGS IN THE UNITED STATES.

The case against you is simple. If you did not buy drugs, this whole business would come to a halt immediately. It is estimated that 10 percent of the population in the United States uses some form of illegal drugs. U.S. citizens are estimated to spend $50 billion a year or $2000 per user, a sum greater than the per capita income of cocaine producing countries such as Peru, Bolivia or Colombia.

You are hurting yourself, your children and the community. Haven't you heard? All you have to do is "say no." Kick your habit. For those of you who can afford the drugs, why not spend the money on something more productive? And for those of you who have to steal to pay for your habit, isn't that just putting you in double jeopardy?

Although the media primarily show images of urban Black and Latino drug users, most of you are White. You may live in the city, the suburbs, small towns or rural communities.

Of course, you might argue that you have tried to receive treatment so that you can kick your habit, but the waiting list is so long that they tell you not to get your hopes up; "call back next year" they tell you. In fact, due to government cutbacks of funding, the treatment center only has enough staff for court-referred cases. You claim that if you want to get help for kicking your habit, you need to commit a crime and get arrested. And even then you may just go straight to jail with no professional help.

Well, why not help yourself?

SYSTEM OF PROFIT

INDICTMENT: YOU ARE RESPONSIBLE FOR ALL THE ROBBERIES AND MURDERS COMMITTED OVER THE LAST TEN YEARS WHICH ARE RELATED TO THE USE AND SALE OF DRUGS IN THE UNITED STATES.

This gets complicated. You are not a person or even a group of people, but a system. We like to blame crimes on people. But in this case, the real criminal is not human.

True, the dealers push the drugs and the banks make big money from them. But what makes them behave the way they do? Are they born evil and greedy? No. The real blame lies with a system that values property over people.

In order to get gold chains and new cars, young people are willing to kill. Jewelry and car dealers take money knowing full well it has probably come from an illegal drug trade, "Money is money after all" the saying goes. The government is cutting back drastically on social programs which could reduce the demand for drugs. The reason — social programs are not profitable.

The system of profit pushes people to make decisions based on financial cost effectiveness rather than what could benefit the community. This is what leads people to kill for profit. You, as a representative of this system, are guilty for the deaths from the drug wars.

Where do people learn the values of this system? Just think back to elementary school. Columbus, who killed hundreds of Native Americans in his search for gold, is touted as a hero. Each October children learn to revere a man who cared only about himself and allowed nothing to obstruct his pursuit of wealth. In fact, although schools talk about the value of collaboration, few examples are provided. Instead, children's books, movies and society at large celebrate the achievements of the individual. It is always an individual who is credited with scientific discoveries, even though research requires a large collaborative effort. Children also learn that money is the only way to motivate people. Countries which try to distribute wealth and social services more fairly are criticized as being undemocratic and lacking in freedom.

How do we know that the system is to blame? Look at how you have limited people's options. How are farmers in Bolivia to survive other than growing coca? Agribusiness has forced them off the more fertile land where they grew coffee and foods to sustain themselves. How are young adults, particularly African American and Latino, to support themselves? If people with degrees are getting laid off, how are these young people with little education or formal experience to compete for a job? If financial profits for the already wealthy were not protected by law, maybe the minimum wage could be raised, maybe jobs could be created providing badly needed social services, and maybe more money could be invested in education.

Violence, the KKK, and the Struggle for Equality

by NEA, CIB and CEA

White supremacist organizations such as the Ku Klux Klan are not just a thing of the past. The Oklahoma bombing and the shooting by soldiers in Atlanta are just a few of the recent events which alerted the nation to the contemporary existence of groups based on racial hatred. Therefore a curriculum developed in 1981 titled Violence, The Ku Klux Klan and The Struggle for Equality is still very useful today. We have reprinted three lessons from the curriculum which can help students analyze why White supremacist organizations are formed, study their impact on a democratic society and learn ways that people are countering the activities of these racial hate-groups.

Violence, The Ku Klux Klan and The Struggle for Equality was prepared by The Connecticut Education Association, The Council on Interracial Books for Children and The National Educational Association. The editors explained that the "material in this handbook has been assembled with the conviction that given the proper combination of factual resource information and positive, thoughtful analysis, classroom teachers at all grade levels can be strong and effective instruments for peacefully and creatively countering the violence of the KKK and its underlying racism and for advancing the positive struggle for equality."

Guidelines

These lessons are likely to be used in a variety of settings — in all-Black schools, all-White schools, in schools where the students body consists of students from several minority groups, in newly desegregated schools, and in several other situations. This curriculum will also be used in communities in which the Klan is and has been active. It is entirely conceivable that there will be students who have been exposed to pro-Klan sentiments by significant adults in their lives. It is also conceivable that some teachers using this curriculum may find that some of their colleagues espouse pro-Klan sentiments. In addition, there may be some students who themselves have been the victim of Klan violence. These situations may exist singly or in combinations, creating an atmosphere of tension. It is therefore of critical importance that:

▸ Basic principles which guide the discussion of any controversial issue be observed;

▸ The teacher treat this curriculum as an integral part of the total classroom experience;

▸ In the classroom there is respect for the ideas of others and appreciation of differences;

▸ The total classroom environment reflects the humanistic values and anti-racist attitudes implicit in this curriculum in terms of visual displays, classroom assignments and activity groupings;

▸ The teacher is familiar with the information and procedures in the lessons.

Procedure

1. Prior to doing these lessons, determine how much students know already and find out what they want to know. In a brainstorm, ask students to list all the names of White supremacist organizations that they can think of. Then ask them to discuss in pairs and share with the group what they know about White supremacist organizations. (If the students are quiet, you can raise some questions such as when and why do they tend to form, who joins them, who benefits and who loses from the existence of the groups, etc.) Place their answers in a column on a sheet of chart paper. Then ask them to share questions they have about these groups. Place the questions in a second column. Keep the paper to refer to during the lessons.

2. Explain to students that you are going to bring in some readings and activities that will help them explore their questions and determine whether what they knew already was fact or myth. Tell students that although the lessons focus on the KKK, this is a case study. What they learn about who benefits and who loses from the KKK and how to counter the organization can be applied to other White supremacist organizations.

You may also want to explain why you are introducing these lessons at this time. Ideally this will be part of a larger unit on U.S. history or the institutionalization of racism in this country. Within that context, you could point out that White supremacist organizations have played a role throughout U.S. history and continue to be active today in their opposition to racial equality. They are a force which should be understood in order to be effectively challenged in society today.

These readings and lessons on the Ku Klux Klan are reprinted with permission of the Connecticut Education Association (CEA). They are excerpted from Violence, The Ku Klux Klan and The Struggle for Equality (1981) *which was produced by the Council on Interracial Books for Children*

(CIBC), *the National Education Association (NEA) and the CEA. It is currently out of print.*

ADDITIONAL RESOURCES

For current information on the Ku Klux Klan and how people are working to oppose it, contact Klanwatch, *a project of the Southern Poverty Law Center at PO Box 548, Montgomery, AL 36104-0548, www.splcenter.org*

CARTOON BY STEPHANIE GARLAND, GRADE 8, RANCHO SAN JOAQUIN MIDDLE SCHOOL, IRVINE, CALIFORNIA. REPRINTED FROM EDITORIAL CARTOONS BY KIDS: 1994 WITH PERMISSION OF KNOWLEDGE UNLIMITED, INC., AND ZINO PRESS CHILDREN'S BOOKS, PO BOX 52, MADISON, WISCONSIN 53710.

BIRTH OF THE KU KLUX KLAN

OBJECTIVES

▸ Students will be able to present information about the origins and early activities of the Ku Klux Klan.

▸ Students will be able to contrast what the Klan practiced with what it preached.

▸ Students will be able to state in their own words the benefits that Reconstruction offered both Blacks and poor Whites and its potential for building a more just society.

▸ Students will be able to identify those who benefitted from the Klan and those against whose interests the Klan worked.

TIME REQUIRED

One homework assignment and one to two class periods.

MATERIALS NEEDED

▸ Copies for each student of History of the Klan.

▸ Copies of testimonies selected by teacher for each student who will present testimonies and for hearing officers.

TEACHER PREPARATION

Teacher should be familiar with the History of the Klan as well as all testimonies. Teacher should decide which of the testimonies to use given time restraints of class, being sure to include that of John B. Gordon.

STUDENT PREPARATION

Have students read History of the Klan and selected testimonies prior to the discussion.

ASSIGNMENT OF HOMEWORK

1. Tell the class that the next period will be used to reenact congressional hearings held in the 1870s to investigate Ku Klux Klan violence. (All testimonies are based on information presented at actual congressional hearings or on writings of people at that time. Some of it has been "modernized" and abbreviated to save time.)

2. Ask for or select students to testify and others to serve as hearing officers. Give these students a copy of the testimony they will present or the questions they will ask.

3. If General O.O. Howard's testimony is to be used, ask the student who will present it to become familiar with the gist of the material, be prepared to outline the scope of violence mentioned, and select a few sections to read.

4. Give all students a copy of Background Information and ask students to read these pages prior to the next class period.

CLASSROOM PROCEDURE

1. Explain that the hearings were designed to investigate Klan violence in order to learn more about what the Klan did and why.

2. Have hearing officers sit in front of the class, receiving testimony from witnesses. Witnesses can appear in any order, but it is suggested that John B. Gordon, the Georgia Klan Leader, appear last, after class has learned of Klan activities from other witnesses.

3. Initiate a class discussion of the testimony. Questions to be asked might include:

a. What targets does the testimony suggest the Klan chose for attack? (Black voters, Blacks who were farming successfully, teachers and the schools to which Blacks were flocking to learn to read and write, Blacks meeting to discuss politics and other concerns, Whites and Blacks who socialized.)

b. Why would the Klan seek to terrorize and intimidate these people? Who was threatened by industrious Black farmers, Blacks who could read and write, Blacks who attended political meetings, Blacks who voted? Who was threatened by Whites working with Blacks to build democracy and a better life for all?

c. How does the Klan's statement of purpose and testimony by the Klan leader contrast with the rest of the testimony?

d. What were some of the ways people responded to the Klan's activities? How would students feel had they been some of the people whose testimony was presented? How would they have reacted?

4. Tell students that such hearings helped bring about the passage of the Ku Klux Klan Act of 1871, which imposed heavy penalties on those "who shall conspire together, or go in disguise . . . for the purpose . . . of depriving any persons of the equal protection of the laws, or of equal privileges or immunities under the law." Tell them that in areas where officials strongly enforced the law, Klan violence declined. Ask them why they think groups working against Klan violence today believe it is crucial that local, state and federal officials strongly enforce existing laws in the face of rising Klan violence.

HISTORY OF THE KLAN

POST CIVIL WAR

Slavery ended after the Civil War with the ratification of the 13th Amendment in 1865.[1] However, the governments of the ex-Confederate states — controlled by the pro-slavery Democratic party which had governed before the war — soon created what were called the Black Codes. Although somewhat different in each state, the Black Codes generally deprived newly freed Blacks of the right to vote, hold office, serve on juries, testify in court against Whites, or assemble without official permission. Central to all the Codes were regulations restricting the freedom of Blacks to work.

The South Carolina Code, for example, required Blacks to have a special license for any job except farmhand or servant, and it required an annual tax of from $10 to $100 for the license. Mississippi's Code forbade Blacks to rent or lease land. Louisiana's required all agricultural workers to make contracts with employers during the first ten days of each January. Workers could not leave their employers until the contract expired, and refusal to work was punished by forced labor. The Black Codes thus enabled wealthy Whites who owned big plantations to make Blacks work for little or no pay, thus virtually re-enslaving them.

RECONSTRUCTION ERA

Some Republicans in Congress were genuinely concerned about the treatment of Blacks and feared that the hard-won gains of the war would be lost. Other Republicans worried that with Blacks now counted as whole persons yet denied the vote, Southern Whites would have increased representation in Congress, enabling the Democratic party to win control. Others deeply resented the South for the bloodshed and destruction of the Civil War. Thus from motives of justice, party-interest and vengeance, Republicans responded decisively to Southern developments.

In 1867, Congress passed the First Reconstruction Act, which invalidated the Black Codes, placed the South under military rule, and mandated elections in which all males over 18 — Black and White — could vote (some White men who held public office before secession and then supported the rebellion against the United States were disqualified from voting). These elections were to select delegates to state conventions that would draft new constitutions for each of the former Confederate states. In order to be accepted back into the Union, the newly reorganized states would have to ratify the 14th Amendment, which provided all citizens equal protection under the law. The U.S. Army was to protect the freedpeople from those Whites who wanted to prevent them from exercising their newly gained rights.

Reconstruction lasted ten years. During that time, a coalition of Blacks, poor Whites and some Northern Republicans who had moved South enacted far-reaching political and social reforms in the constitutional conventions and newly elected legislatures of the South. The new state constitutions provided universal male suffrage (a few state constitutions disfranchised some former public officials who supported secession, but the disqualifications were minor and temporary). This gave the vote for the first time to newly freed Black men, as well as to thousands of poor Whites, who before the Civil War had been deprived of the vote because of property-ownership qualifications. For the first time, Southern states provided free public schools for tens of thousands of poor White children who previously had been denied education. The property rights of women were protected, divorce laws written and imprisonment for debt abolished. Orphanages, asylums for the insane and schools for the blind and deaf people were established.[2]

Blacks were involved in all the state conventions that drafted the new constitutions, and many were elected to the new state legislatures. Contrary to the myth of "Black Rule" promoted by those Whites who opposed the social and political changes, Blacks made up a majority of the representatives in only one state — South Carolina — and then only in one house of the legislature. During Reconstruction, Blacks were elected lieutenant governor in three states and served in various positions — such as secretary of state and state treasurer — in others. Twenty Blacks were elected to the U.S. House of Representatives and two Blacks served in the U.S. Senate.

During Reconstruction, some Blacks and Whites worked together raising food for their families, and some pooled their money and bought land. Most poor Whites, however, had little to do with Blacks. For

© Rick Reinhard

been forced to work all their lives without pay — would have had the economic independence necessary to secure their political rights. Some successful farming communities of freedpeople developed in areas where they had access to land. For example, in 1863 the Mississippi plantations of Jefferson Davis and his brother were divided, and 70 freedpeople were given 80 acres each, while a Black regiment protected them from Confederates. This "Davis Bend" program was so successful that by 1865 another 5,000 acres were given to 1,800 Blacks organized into 181 companies. The government supplied equipment and materials, which were paid for when crops were sold. The people opened stores, established a school, set up a government and provided free medical services to all who could not afford a doctor. In 1865 they cleared $160,000 after paying expenses. But such successful ventures were destroyed when the ex-Confederates were pardoned by the federal government and given back the land.

For both Blacks and poor Whites, the Reconstruction era offered hope of significant improvement in their lives. It was a period in which the South — indeed the nation as a whole — came closer to being a truly democratic society than ever before. But the social and political changes were not welcomed by those who wanted to regain their former privileges and power. Their appeal to poor Whites for race solidarity, backed by years of intensive racist indoctrination and by great social and economic pressure to stay in line, kept most poor Whites aligned with those of similar skin color, rather than with those in a similar economic position. Control of the land and most resources enabled wealthy Whites to pressure many Blacks, who were economically dependent on them, not to exercise their political rights. Yet in spite of this economic and social power, significant numbers of Blacks and many poor Whites continued to struggle to build a more just, free and democratic society. The response was a campaign of terror, violence and intimidation designed to crush these social changes and restore the former elite to power.

BIRTH OF THE KU KLUX KLAN

After the Civil War, there was a great deal of turmoil and devastation in the South. In addition, 4 million enslaved people were now free. Even before the Black Codes were adopted, a variety of White vigilante and terrorist groups, determined to keep Blacks under White control, had sprung up across the South.

These groups had their genesis in the prewar slave patrols. The ubiquitous slave patrols had been a semiofficial force required to police 4 million en-

the most part, poor Whites had hated slavery, seeing it as the cause of their poverty. However, their anger had been directed more toward the Black slaves, whose labor they saw as competition, than at the White slavocracy that dominated and exploited both groups for its own benefit. Oppressive as their lives were, White supremacy had given them the illusion of benefit by telling them that at least they were superior to Blacks. This sense of White superiority and prejudice against Blacks was deeply ingrained.

Most poor Whites were either tenant farmers on large plantations or owned their own small plots of land, usually in the least fertile hill or mountain areas. These were all that remained after the development of large plantations pushed White small farmers out of the most fertile areas. After the war, there was talk of breaking up the massive plantations and dividing them among the roughly 4 million Blacks and 5 million poor Whites. Such land reform would no doubt have encouraged large numbers of poor Whites to cooperate more fully with Reconstruction efforts. However, the federal government (which was then giving away millions of acres of land to immigrant homesteaders and to railroad owners) refused to take this decisive step.

With land to farm, the freedpeople — who had

slaved people who lost no opportunity to escape from or rebel against the dehumanization and oppression of chattel slavery. In most of the slave states, the patrols played a major role in the system of control, and almost all adult White men, whether or not they were slave owners, were liable for periodic patrol service, generally performed at night, on horseback. The "paterollers,"[3] as an integral part of their duties, bullied, whipped, beat and intimidated Blacks, searched their homes and broke up gatherings.

In late 1865 or early 1866, six veterans of the Confederate Army formed a secret organization in Pulaski, Tennessee. They called it the Ku Klux Klan (the name supposedly derives from the Greek word for circle, kuklos, to which they added klan). While claiming to be a social club, they were soon expressing resentment at the changes taking place in Southern society. The Klan began to fight these changes, attempting to restore the old ways of White supremacy.

In the spring of 1867, delegates from Klans throughout Tennessee gathered at the newest hotel in Nashville. They were businessmen, former Confederate officers and leaders of church and state. They chose Nathan Bedford Forrest to be Grand Wizard. A former slave trader, Forrest had served as a Confederate calvary officer; his activities included the command of troops attacking Fort Pillow (near Memphis), garrisoned by Black soldiers, in April 1864. The Fort Pillow Massacre epitomized the Confederate practice of executing captured Black soldiers. Wholesale slaughter, accompanied by every sort of atrocity, followed the capture of the Fort. Approximately three hundred soldiers, plus women and children dependents, were brutally murdered.

The Klan was to become a night-riding vigilante organization for White supremacy. Under Forrest's leadership, it quickly expanded throughout the South. The Klan recruited Whites — particularly poor Whites — by appealing to racial prejudice and beliefs in White superiority. The Klan used violence and terror to intimidate Blacks and those Whites who were working to build democracy. The old ruling elite of the South supported the growth of the Klan, seeing an opportunity to regain its political power and keep Black labor (and ultimately that of poor Whites) under its control.

Counterdemonstrators numbering 350 rallied at the Maryland State House in protest of a 40 member Ku Klux Klan rally on October 29, 1995.

TERRORIST ACTIVITIES

Klansmen dressed themselves in white or black robes and wore masks and hoods. By hiding their identity, the masks made it psychologically easier for members to commit atrocities and lessened their chance of getting caught. Victims were sometimes lynched by a mob that dragged them from their beds at night, hung them from trees, beat them and then lit fires under them while they were still alive. Women were raped and children were often beaten or killed. Black homes, churches and schools were burned.

Klan terror was particularly directed at Blacks who had become successful leaders, public officials, teachers and farmers — individuals whose achievement and work clearly undermined the concept of Black inferiority and threatened White supremacy. The Klan assassinated the most competent and daring Black leaders and terrorized and drove out teachers who were helping Black people fulfill their great desire for education. The Klan sought to beat down Blacks who stood up for their rights, to prevent Blacks from gathering to discuss concerns and to keep Black labor under White control. From 1866 to 1875, the Klan killed an estimated 3,500 Blacks in the South and whipped, beat, tarred and feathered many thousands more. Many Whites who were friendly or worked with Blacks, or who supported the Republican party, received the same treatment.

Klan terror was especially great before elections. The Klan used assassination, beatings and intimidation to terrify Blacks, Republicans and sympathetic poor Whites and keep them from voting, thus enabling the Democratic party to regain control in state after state. North Carolina provides an example of the type of Klan activities that destroyed democracy across the South. As a result of a campaign of terror, 12,000 fewer Republicans voted in 1870 than in previous elections, and Democrats regained control of the legislature. One writer described events in North Carolina as follows:

District attorneys, jury commissioners, sheriffs many judges, and leading citizens of the community were members or supporters of the Klan. It was a secret, highly organized well-disciplined underground army. And it was determined to take control of the state out of the hands of Blacks, poor Whites, and Republicans....

The 1870 election was the Klan's target. On the night of February 26 they rode into Alamance and hanged Wyatt Outlaw, leader of a local campaign to get a church and a school for the Black community. They hanged him from an oak tree less than one hundred feet from [the] courthouse.

In Caswell County, the other Republican stronghold, the head of the party was a poor White man named John Stephens. Five men, all wealthy and educated, trapped him, strangled him, stabbed him, and threw his body on a woodpile.

The terror spread throughout the state during 1870.... By election day the work of the Klan had been done. Thousands of Republicans stayed away from the polls. The Democrats won the election and took control of the state legislature. One of the first laws they passed granted amnesty to anyone who had committed a crime on behalf of a secret White organization.

Far too few federal troops were stationed in the South to protect the exercise of democratic rights, and Blacks, poor Whites and Republicans became the easy targets of a violent counterrevolution of terror and assassination carried out by White men determined to regain power. Appeals to Washington from state officials and desperate citizens for additional troops were repeatedly turned down. Blacks had few guns to begin with, since they had been forbidden weapons during slavery and most were too poor to purchase them after the war. Sometimes those who did have guns were stripped of them by White sheriffs who either sympathized or belonged to the Klan. Nonetheless, Blacks attempted to resist the return of White supremacy and to defend themselves in whatever ways possible. (Reports about the removal of federal troops from South Carolina, for example, mention Black women carrying axes or hatchets hanging at their sides half-concealed by their aprons and dresses.)

Finally, Washington took some action against the White terrorists. After congressional hearings exposed the severity of Klan violence, Congress passed a series of laws making it a federal crime for individuals to deprive other citizens of their constitutional rights. The Ku Klux Klan Act of 1871 imposed heavy penalties on persons "who shall conspire together, or go in disguise...for the purpose...of depriving any persons of the equal protection under the law." In areas where the federal government acted, there was a sharp decline in terror. Where no determined force was brought to bear, the terror rapidly spread.

Some Republican officials attempted to prosecute Klansmen in federal court. There were many arrests, but relatively few convictions. Witnesses, juries, judges and sheriffs were all too often members or sympathizers of the Klan. However, by 1873 the Klan began to decline. In part this was due to federal action. In part it was because the need for the Klan diminished once its violence and terror succeeded, enabling White supremacists (sometimes called Redeemers) to regain control of state governments, courts and police. In states like Mississippi, where Republican rule outlived the Klan, mobs of armed, unmasked White men replaced the Klan, openly terrorizing and killing Blacks and reform-minded Whites and preventing free elections.

TESTIMONIES

TESTIMONY BY GENERAL O.O. HOWARD HEAD OF THE FREEDMEN'S BUREAU

From the numerous cases of murder and outrage perpetrated upon Negroes and those who befriended them during the days of reconstruction, which were reported to my officers . . . it is now clear that the main object from first to last was somehow to regain and maintain over the negro that ascendancy which slavery gave, and which was being lost by emancipation, education and suffrage.

The opposition to negro education made itself felt everywhere... In 1865, 1866 and 1867 mobs of the baser classes at intervals and in all parts of the South occasionally burned school buildings and churches used as schools, flogged teachers or drove them away and in a number of instances murdered them...

Our work of establishing schools went steadily on. Early in 1868, however, was the first appearance in my Bureau school reports of an offensive secret organization. It was from Charlestown, W.Va. Our workers received a note from the "Ku-Klux Klan." Not a White family there after that could be found willing to board the excellent lady teachers. At Frostburg a male teacher was threatened with violence, the Klan having sent him notes, ordering him to depart. Loyal West Virginians, however, stood by him and he did not go. In Maryland, also, one teacher was warned and forced to leave. The Klan signed their rough document which was placed in his hand, "Ku-Klux Klan." The face of the envelope was covered with scrawls; among these were the words: "Death! Death!" By a similar method a teacher at Hawkinsville, Ga. (a colored man), was dealt with by menace and afterwards seriously wounded. The Georgia superintendent wrote that for the last three months, April, May, and June, 1868, there had been more bitterness exhibited toward all men engaged in the work of education than ever before; and there were few but had received threats, both anonymous and open. Several freedmen had abandoned their fields from fear.

The cry from Alabama was even more alarming...schoolhouses were burned, and those left standing were in danger; teachers were hated and maltreated, two being driven from their work...

But Louisiana exceeded [Alabama's violence]; Miss Jordan's school at Gretna was entered by ruffians; the walls of her room were covered with obscene pictures and language, and threats against the teacher posted; she was insulted on the ferry and in the streets, and even annoyed in such a small way as to be required to pay twice as much ferriage as the teachers in the White schools. In Markville, the Ku-Klux Klan made more open demonstrations, but always by night. They posted their documents around the town, so terrifying the colored people that they did not dare leave their homes after dark. The night schools had to be closed. At Mary and Sabine parish; at Cherryville and Rapides parish; at Washington and Opelousas; at St. Landry parish, and elsewhere in a similar way by visitations and threats the schools were shut up and the teachers driven off...

Mrs. Baldwin, the teacher at Bowling Green, Ky., was a Christian lady of agreeable manners and unusual culture, but not one of the 27 loyal families of the place dared incur the odium of giving her a home. The Regulators had made themselves felt; men, professing to be gentlemen, insulted her upon the streets. Vile books and pictures were sent to her by mail; and, as a last resort, she was threatened with assassination if she was found in the city at the expiration of five days. Many other schools had to be maintained under military guard; five school buildings in Kentucky were burned about that time...

It became evident... that in the early summer of 1868, the former irregular and local hostility to freedmen's schools had taken on a new strength... Further examples will illustrate the procedure: On May 16th, L.S. Frost, a White teacher in Tennessee, was taken at night from his room by a mob of disguised young men and carried to a field nearby, men choking and beating him all the way; they were flourishing their pistols over his head, and threatening to kill him instantly if he did not cease resisting. They made him promise to leave town the next morning. They then blackened his face and portions of his body with a composition of spirits of turpentine, lampblack and tar, and released him. About a dozen persons were engaged in the outrage, some of whom were recognized by Mr. Frost.

John Dunlap, a teacher educated in Ohio, was

in July, 1868, in charge of a colored school at Shelbyville, Tenn. On Independence Day, about ten o'clock at night, a body of Ku-Klux, some fifty strong, masked, armed with pistols and bearing an emblem resembling the bleeding heart of a man, were paraded in front of his house. When he presented himself, they gave him commands which he resisted. They fired through his window, made him surrender his pistol, caused him to mount, and escorted him to the public square. Then they seized and secured a prominent colored man, James Franklin. Proceeding with the regularity of soldiers, a captain commanding, they marched their victims across the Duck River, where, dismounting, with something like a leathern thong or strap they first flogged Franklin, each man giving him five blows. After that, taking Dunlap to another place, with the same parade, they performed the same operation, badly lacerating his body. After directing him to leave the city the next day, they released him. Dunlap not at once complying with their demand, they served upon him a formal notice, sent in the form of an unstamped letter through the post office, ordering him to leave by July 15th, or he would be burned to death. Dunlap thereupon went to Nashville and remained two months. Then he came back. He was visited again after his return, but was now prepared with a guard. While the Ku-Klux were hallooing that they "wanted Dunlap and fried meat" and were approaching his residence, the guard fired upon them. The band retreated and did not appear in Shelbyville again...

The outcropping of cruelties in portions of Louisiana showed by the persons who were chosen as victims that the effort of the secret organization was particularly political.

On July 28, 1868, William Cooper, a White Unionist, came to our agent in the parish of Franklin. He was severely wounded, having been shot in his own house near Girard Station; a freedman named Prince was killed in the same parish, and all the teachers were so terrified by such demonstrations as to stop teaching...

At many points in Louisiana were these "bands of desperados formed in secret organization, styling themselves the Ku-Klux Klan." ...In some places negroes were taken out and whipped (as a rule by night) and there was no clue to the perpetrators. Even United States agents dared not hold a public meeting in that region — a gathering night of negroes at any place would be regarded with suspicion by the Whites and result in outrage and suffering to the Blacks...

The latter part of the year 1868, before the election of General Grant for his first term, these murderous secret societies reached their greatest activity. Even the country hamlets in the neighborhood of Chattanooga, which after the war abounded in Union men and late Union soldiers, were boldly visited by this strange horde. They came upon one commodious schoolhouse in the country and burned it to the ground; but the persistent teacher, a colored youth, though threatened by the Ku-Klux Klan with violence and death if he did not yield to their commands, made himself a brush arbor and there continued his school to the end of the term. Before the November election (the freedmen's first national suffrage) the Ku-Klux, armed and masked as usual, at night paraded the streets of several cities, and filled the freedmen with terror...

After the election, for a time, the excessive wrath abated... The two months of 1868 that followed the Presidential election and the first six in the next year, 1869, were quite free from the Ku-Klux Klan raids.

During the last half of 1869, however, there was a quickening of the secret pulse...From Kentucky, a teacher who had a remarkably good school about ten miles from Bowling Green wrote: "the Ku Klux Klan came one night and told me if I did not break up my school they would kill me." The teacher obeyed. He reported that the White people said that this action by the Ku-Klux was... because "the niggers there were getting too smart."

North Carolina, that had made such good progress in every way under our systematic work, began in some of its counties to be infested during the latter half of 1869. "There was for a time a suspension of schools in a number of districts."... Teachers became frightened, and, under the threats of violence printed on placards and put upon doors and fence posts, it was deemed best to obey the dread-inspiring foes that, many or few, were magnified by excited imaginations into multitudes. The marauders went in bands, always masked, usually in small squads, each squad having from five to ten in number...

South Carolina showed some eruptions of the same nature as late as December 24, 1869. A gentleman of good standing was building a large school structure at Newberry, S.C., for the education of the children of the freed people. He was visited by armed men and driven from the hotel where he was boarding, and a young lady teacher at the same place, sent by the Methodists from Vermont, was

subjected to the meanest sort of insults and perse-
cutions.

Testimony by Charlotte Fowler
Spartanburg, S.C., July 6, 1871

Congressional Officer: I believe all the witnesses have been sworn in. I now call on Mrs. Clarlotte Fowler. Step up. When was your husband, Wallace Fowler, killed?

Charlotte Fowler: It was the first of May.

C.O.: Tell us what happened.

C.F.: I was sick, very sick in bed with a fever, all day Wednesday and Thursday. My husband came home Thursday night from the field and he cooked for me and for our granddaughter Sophia, who was staying with us. After he went to bed I heard the dogs barking, then people banging on the door.

C.O.: Who was it

C.F.: Well, my husband opened the door and they shot him, with the little girl standing right there. I just saw two of them, but I heard more riding away.

C.O: What happened then?

C.F.: I was screaming and my granddaughter was crying. The men made Sophia light a stick in the fire so they could hold it up and see better. The man who shot my husband had a black mask with horns on it. He took the lighted stick and held it over my old man. The other man came over and dropped a chip of fire on my husband, and burnt his chest right through the shirt.

C.O.: Was he dead then?

C.F.: No. He was shot through the head, and every time he breathed, his brains would come out. But he didn't die until the next day, in the afternoon.

C.O.: Did the old man, your husband, belong to any party?

C.F.: Yes, sir. The Radical Republicans, ever since they started the voting for colored people. My husband worked for that party.

Testimony by William Coleman,
Macon, Mississippi, Nov. 6, 1871

Congressional Officer: How long have you lived in Macon?

William Coleman: I came here about the last of April.

C.O.: Where did you come from?

W.C.: I came from Winston County.

C.O.: What occasioned your coming here?

W.C.: I got run by the Ku-Klux.

C.O.: Give the particulars to the committee.

W. C.: Well, I don't know anything that I had said or done that injured any one, further than being a radical in that part of the land, and as for interrupting any one, I didn't, for I had plenty on my own of anything I wanted for myself. I had done bought my land and paid for it, and I had a great deal of hogs; I had eighteen head of hogs to kill this fall. I had twelve head of sheep, and one good milk-cow, and a yearling, and the cow had a right young calf again, and I had my mule and my filly, and all of it was paid for but my mule...

C.O.: Did the Ku-Klux come to your house?

W.C.: They did.

C.O.: In the night-time?

W.C.: They came about a half hour or more before day. . . .they were shooting and going on at me through the house, and when they busted the door open, coming in shooting, I was frightened. . . . I grabbed my ax-handle and commence fighting, and then they just took me and cut me with knives. They surrounded me on the floor... some had me by the legs and some by the arms and the neck. . . . They took me out to the big road before my gate and whipped me until I couldn't move or holler or do nothing. . . . They left me there for dead and what it was done for was because I was a radical, and I didn't deny my profession anywhere and I never will. I never will vote that conservative ticket if I die.

C.O.: Did they tell you they whipped you because you were radical?

W.C.: They told me. "God damn you, when you meet a White man in the road lift your hat; I'll learn you. God damn you, that you are a nigger, and not to be going about like you thought yourself a White man; you calls yourself like a White man. God damn you."

C.O.: Were you working on your own land?

W.C.: Yes, sir; that I bought and paid $473 for.

Testimony by Hannah Tutson
Jacksonville, Florida, Nov. 10, 1871

Congressional Officer: You are the wife of Samuel Tutson. Were you at home when he was whipped last spring?

Hannah Tutson: I was. Five men pushed the

door in. George McRae and Cabell Winn were first to take hold of me. Winn said to the others, "Come in, True-Klux." I screamed and they choked me and grabbed my littlest child by the foot, they pulled him away from me and threw him against the wall. Then lots of them dragged me outside. I saw they had more men pulling my husband and stomping on him.

C.O.: What did the True-Klux do?

H.T.: They hit my head with their pistols, tied me to a tree, puled up all my clothes and said, "God damn you. We will show you. You are living on another man's land." I said, "No. I gave $150 for this land and Captain told me to stay here."

C.O.: What did they say?

H.T.: They cursed me and beat me. Then They went away except McRae, who stayed and treated me terribly; he called, "Come here, True-Klux." then five men came back and beat me some more. But I still wanted to save our land.

C.O.: Did you know those men?

H.T.: I've been working in Winn's mother's house for three years. Even though they all painted their faces and hands so they wouldn't be recog-nized, I know Winn's voice and I know lots of those menfolks. I recognized most of them.

C.O.: Did you find your children?

H.T.: Well when they finished whipping me and went away I was bleeding from my neck to my feet. The house was broken up and I couldn't see my husband or children. I took a dress but it hurt too much to put it on, so I carried it and walked 12 miles before sunrise to show Mr. Ashley how they whipped me. He told me to find my children and go out of town. Then I went back and at noon I found my children hiding. The baby they hurt was cry-ing.

C.O.: What happened to the baby and your husband?

H.T.: The baby's hip hurt and it screamed whenever it tried to stand up. I found my husband later, whipped worse than me. He could not sit or walk.

C.O.: How long had you been living on that land you bought?

H.T.: This would have been the third crop, sir, almost three years. They had been after us for a long time, telling us to get out. They they came and whipped us out.

Testimony by John B. Gordon
Georgia Klan Leader, 1871

Preface by the Congressional Officer: In 1868, the Ku Klux Klan adopted a formal statement of character and purpose. It said that the Klan "is an institution of Chivalry, Humanity, Mercy and Patriotism; embodying in its genius and its principles all that is chivalric in conduct, noble in sentiment, generous in manhood, and patriotic in purpose." Its objects were said to be "to protect the weak, the innocent, and the defenseless, from the indignities, wrongs, and outrages of the lawless, the violent, and the brutal": to relieve and assist the injured, oppressed, suffering and unfortunate, especially widows and orphans of Confederate soldiers; and to support the United States Constitution and constitutional laws. All Klansmen were sworn to secrecy.

Congressional Officer: What do you know of any combinations in Georgia, known as Ku-Klux, or by any other name, who have been violating the law?

John B. Gordon: I do not know anything about any Ku-Klux organization... I have never heard of anything of that sort except in the papers...but I do know that an organization did exist in Georgia at one time in 1868.... I was approached and asked to attach myself to a secret organization... by some of the very best citizens of the State — some of the most peaceable, law-abiding men, men of property, who had large interests in the State....

C.O.: Tell us about what that organization was.

J.B.G.: The organization was simply...a brotherhood of the property-holders, the peaceable, law-abiding citizens of the State, for self-protection. The instinct of self-protection prompted that organization; the sense of insecurity and danger, particularly in those neighborhoods where the negro population largely predominated. The reasons which led to this organization were three or four. The first and main reason was the organization of the Union League [established by the Republican party to organize Black voters] which we knew nothing more than this: that the negroes would desert the plantations, and go off at night in large numbers; and on being asked they had been, would reply, sometimes, "We have been to the muster"; sometimes, "We have been to the lodge"; sometimes, "We have been to the meeting."...We knew that the "carpetbaggers,"...these men came from a distance and had no interest at all with us... We knew of certain instances where great crime had been committed; where overseers had been driven from plantations, and the negroes had asserted their right to hold the property for their own benefit. Apprehension took possession of the entire public mind of the State. Men were in many instances afraid to go away from their homes and leave their wives and children, for fear of outrage.... There was this general organization of the Black race on the one hand and an entire organization of the Black race on the other hand. We were afraid to have a public organization; because we supposed it could be construed at once, by authorities in Washington, as an organization antagonistic to the Government of the United States.

C.O.: Did it have any antagonism toward either the State or the Federal Government?

J.B.G.: None on earth — not a particle. On the contrary, it was purely a peace police organization, and I do know of some instances where it did prevent bloodshed on a large scale...

C.O.: You had no riding about at nights?

J.B.G.: None on earth. I have no doubt that such things have occurred in Georgia....There is not a good man in Georgia who does not deplore that thing just as much as any radical deplores it. When I use the term "radical," I do not mean to reflect upon the republican party generally; but in our State a republican is a very different sort of man from a republican generally in the Northern States. In our State republicanism means nothing in the world but creating disturbance, riot, and animosity, and filching and plundering. That is what it means in our State — nothing else....I do not believe that any crime has ever been committed by [the Klan]... I believe it was purely a peace police — a law-abiding concern. That was its whole object, and it never would have existed but for the apprehension in the minds of our people of a conflict in which we would have had no sympathy and no protection. We apprehended that the sympathy of the entire Government would be against us; and nothing in the world but the instinct of self-protection promoted that organization. We felt that we must at any cost protect ourselves, our homes, our wives and children from outrage. We would have preferred death rather than to have submitted to what we supposed was coming upon us....

Gordon's testimony excerpted from Richard N. Current, ed. 1965. Reconstruction [1865-1877]. Englewod Cliffs, NJ: Prentice Hall, Inc.

"Why I Quit the Klan" by C. P. Ellis is a fascinating and moving account of C.P. Ellis's transformation from a Ku Klux Klan member to a civil rights advocate and union leader. This reading shows clearly that given the right experiences, not just arguments, people can change deeply rooted attitudes.

OBJECTIVES

▸ Students will be able to state some of the conditions that make Klan membership attractive to some people, and some of the strategies that the Klan uses to maintain its membership.

▸ Students will understand how racism divides potential allies.

▸ Students will understand that racist beliefs can be changed.

TIME REQUIRED

One or two homework assignments and one class period.

MATERIALS NEEDED

A copy for each student of "Why I Quit the Klan," an interview with C.P. Ellis by Studs Terkel.

TEACHER PREPARATION

Read C.P. Ellis interview and consider a time in your own life when you have made a change to share as an example with students as an additional prompt for their own sharing and writing.

ASSIGNMENT PROCEDURE

Give all students a copy of the Ellis interview and ask that they read it before class the next day. Tell them that Ellis was a member of the Klan, serving for a time as Exalted Cyclops (president) of the Durham, North Carolina chapter.

CLASSROOM PROCEDURE

1. Initiate a class discussion of the article, giving students an opportunity to share reactions and feelings. Some discussion questions to consider include:

a. What were some conditions in C.P. Ellis' life that made him receptive to the racist explanations of the Klan and willing to join?

b. What did the Klan offer Ellis? Are there other ways to meet these needs that would unite people rather than divide them?

c. What does Ellis tell us about the background of many Klan members?

d. Whom does Ellis believe that the Klan benefited? How did those people "behind the scenes" benefit?

e. Why do you think Ellis's father — a Klansman — and many other Klan members are working to keep White and Black people from organizing into unions?

f. What did Ellis think of Blacks, Jews and Catholics?

g. What caused him to change his views? How did his views change? Which way of thinking was of most benefit to him and why?

h. While Ellis came to understand that he was being used by people in high places, other Klan members refused to believe this. Why do you think this was the case? Was Ellis simply "smarter," or could there be other reasons Klan members would resist seeing how they were being used?

2. At this point ask students to write before they share their comments. Point out that some of Ellis's old White friends accused him of "selling out the White race." Ask students to imagine that they are Ellis writing a response to some of his old friends. Explain why you have made the changes that you did. Appeal to your old friends to change too, but in a way that addresses their concerns rather than ignoring them. Give students a few minutes to write and then ask a few to share their letters.

3. Ellis changed his attitudes in ways that, earlier, he would not have thought possible. To put students in touch with their own potential to make dramatic changes, ask class members to think of times in their lives when they changed in ways that they would never have anticipated. Ask them to list a number of instances and then have volunteers share from their lists. From these lists, students should write in story form an account of a particular change. (This can be done in class or as a homework assignment.)

CONTINUED ON PAGE 271

C.P. Ellis

C.P. Ellis was born in 1927 and was fifty-three years old at the time of this interview with Studs Terkel. At one time he was president (Exalted Cyclops) of the Durham chapter of the Ku Klux Klan, and lived in Durham, North Carolina.

All my life, I had work, never a day without work, worked all the overtime I could get and still could not survive financially. I began to see there's something wrong with this country. I worked my butt off and just never seemed to break even. I had some real great ideas about this nation. They say to abide by the law, go to church, do right and live for the Lord, and everything'll work out. But it didn't work out. It just kept getting worse and worse...

Tryin to come out of that hole, I just couldn't do it. I really began to get bitter. I didn't know who to blame. I tried to find somebody. Hatin America is hard to do because you can't see it to hate it. You gotta have somethin to look at to hate. The natural person for me to hate would be Black people, because my father before me was a member of the Klan...

So I began to admire the Klan... To be part of somethin. ... The first night I went with the fellas . . . I was led into a large meeting room, and this was the time of my life! It was thrilling. Here's a guy who's worked all his life and struggled all his life to be something, and here's the moment to be something. I will never forget it. Four robed Klansmen led me into the hall. The lights were dim and the only thing you could see was an illuminated cross... After I had taken my oath, there was loud applause goin throughout the buildin, musta been at least four hundred people. For this one little ol person. It was a thrilling moment for C.P. Ellis...

The majority of [the Klansmen] are low-income Whites, people who really don't have a part in something. They have been shut out as well as Blacks. Some are not very well educated either. Just like myself. We had a lot of support from doctors and lawyers and police officers.

Maybe they've had bitter experiences in this life and they had to hate somebody. So the natural person to hate would be the Black person. He's beginnin to come up, he's beginnin to . . . start votin and run for political office. Here are White people who are supposed to be superior to them, and we're shut out... Shut out. Deep down inside, we want to be part of this great society. Nobody listens, so we join these groups...

We would go to the city council meetings and the Blacks would be there and we'd be there. It was a confrontation every time... We began to make some inroads with the city councilmen and county commissioners. They began to call us friend. Call us at night on the telephone: "C.P., glad you came to that meeting last night." They didn't want integration either, but they did it secretively, in order to get elected. They couldn't stand up openly and say it, but they were glad somebody was sayin it. We visited some of the city leaders in their homes and talked to em privately. It wasn't long before councilmen would call me up: "The Blacks are comin up tonight and makin outrageous demands. How about some of you people showin up and have a little balance?"...

We'd load up our cars and we'd fill up half the council chambers, and the Blacks the other half. During these times, I carried weapons to the meetings, outside my belt. We'd go there armed. We would wind up just hollerin and fussin at each other. What happened? As a result of our fightin one another, the city council still had their way. They didn't want to give up control to the Blacks nor the Klan. They were usin us. I began to realize this later down the road. One day I was walkin downtown and a certain city council member saw me comin. I expected him to shake my hand because he was talkin to me at night on the telephone. I had been in his home and visited with him. He crossed the street [to avoid me]... I began to think, somethin's wrong here. Most of em are merchants or maybe an attorney, an insurance agent, people like that. As long as they kept low-income Whites and low-income Blacks fightin, they're gonna maintain control. I began to get that feelin after I was ignored in public. I thought: . . . you're not gonna use me any more. That's when I began to do some real serious thinkin.

The same thing is happening in this country today. People are being used by those in control, those who have all the wealth. I'm not espousing communism. We got the greatest system of government in the world. But those who have it simply don't want those who don't have it to have any part of it. Black and White. When it comes to money, the green, the other colors make no difference.

I spent a lot of sleepless nights. I still didn't like Blacks. I didn't want to associate with them. Blacks, Jews, or Catholics. My father said: "Don't have anything to do with em." I didn't until I met a Black person and talked with him, eyeball to eyeball, and met a Jewish person and talked to him, eyeball to eyeball. I found they're people just like me. They cried, they cussed, they prayed, they had desires. Just like myself. Thank God, I got to the point where I can look past labels. But at that time, my mind was closed.

I remember one Monday night Klan meeting. I said something was wrong. Our city fathers were using us. And I didn't like to be used. The reactions of the others was not too pleasant: "Let's just keep fightin them niggers."

I'd go home at night and I'd have to wrestle with myself. I'd look at a Black person walkin down the street, and the guy'd have ragged shoes or his clothes would be worn. That began to do something to me inside. I went through this for about six months. I felt I just had to get out of the Klan. But I wouldn't get out...

[Ellis was invited, as a Klansman, to join a committee of people from all walks of life to make recommendations on how to solve racial problems in the school system. He very reluctantly accepted. After a few stormy meetings, he was elected co-chair of the committee, along with Ann Atwater, a Black woman who for years had been leading local efforts for civil rights.]

A Klansman and a militant Black woman, co-chairmen of the school committee. It was impossible. How could I work with her? But it was in our hands. We had to make it a success. This gave me another sense of belongin, a sense of pride. This helped the inferiority feeling I had. A man who has stood up publicly and said he despised Black people, all of a sudden he was willin to work with em. Here's a chance for a low-income White man to be somethin. In spite of all my hatred for Blacks and Jews and liberals, I accepted the job. Her and I began to reluctantly work together. She had as many problems workin with me as I had workin with her.

One night, I called her: "Ann, you and I should have a lot of differences and we got em now. But there's somethin laid out here before us, and if it's gonna be a success, you and I are gonna have to make it one. Can we lay aside some of these feelins?" She said: "I'm willing if you are." I said: "Let's do it."

My old friends would call me at night: "C.P., what the hell is wrong with you? You're sellin out

the White race." This begin to make me have guilt feeling Am I doin right? Am I doin wrong? Here I am all of a sudden makin an about-face and tryin to deal with my feelins, my heart. My mind was beginnin to open up. I was beginnin to see what was right and what was wrong. I don't want the kids to fight forever...

One day, Ann and I went back to the school and we sat down. We began to talk and just reflect... I begin to see, here we are, two people from the far ends of the fence, havin identical problems, except hers bein Black and me bein White... The amazing thing about it, her and I, up to that point, has cussed each other, bawled each other, we hated each other. Up to that point, we didn't know each other. We didn't know we had things in common...

The whole world was openin up, and I was learning new truths that I had never learned before. I was beginning to look at a Black person, shake hands with him, and see him as a human bein. I hadn't got rid of all this stuff. I've still got a little bit of it. But somethin was happenin to me...

I come to work one morning and some guys says: "We need a union." At this time I wasn't pro-union. My daddy was antilabor too. We're not gettin paid much, we're havin to work seven days in a row. We're all starvin to death... I didn't know nothin about organizin unions, but I knew how to organize people, stir people up. That's how I got to be business agent for the union.

When I began to organize, I began to see far deeper. I begin to see people again bein used. Blacks against Whites... There are two things management wants to keep: all the money and all the say-so. They don't want none of these poorworkin folks to have none of that. I begin to see management fightin me with everythin they had. Hire antiunion law firms, badmouth unions. The people were makin $1.95 an hour, barely able to get through weekends...

It makes you feel good to go into a plant and ... see Black people and White people join hands and defeat the racist issues [union-busters] use against people...

I tell people there's a tremendous possibility in this country to stop wars, the battles, the struggles, the fights between people. People say: "That's an impossible dream. You sound like Martin Luther King." An ex-Klansman who sounds like Martin Luther King. I don't think it's an impossible dream. It's happened in my life. It's happened in other people's lives in America...

When the news came over the radio that Martin Luther King was assassinated, I got on the telephone and begin to call other Klansmen... We just had a real party... Really rejoicin cause the son of a bitch was dead. Our troubles are over with. They say the older you get, the harder it is for you to change. That's not necessarily true. Since I changed, I've set down and listened to tapes of Martin Luther King. I listen to it and tears come to my eyes cause I know what he's sayin now. I know what's happenin.

From Terkel, S. 1980. American Dreams: Lost and Found. *Pantheon Books, Random House, Inc.*

CONTINUED FROM PAGE 268

Optional Follow-Up Activity

Have students read "Let America Be America Again" by Langston Hughes (available in many anthologies). Point out to students that the poem was written many years ago and that the poet used the term "man" in the generic sense to mean all people, female and male. Possible questions for discussion include:

a. C.P. Ellis believes "there's a tremendous possibility in this country to stop wars, the battles, the struggles, the fights between people.... I don't think it's an impossible dream." Compare the dream that Ellis writes about to the one referred to by Langston Hughes below.

> *O, let America be America again—*
> *The land that never has been yet—*
> *And yet must be —*
> *the land where every man is free.*

b. What lessons did C.P. Ellis learn that support the poet's phrase, "I am the poor White, fooled and pushed apart?"

c. Which items in the poem represent the principles and creed that make up the dream of the United States.

d. What groups does the poem indicate have been denied realization of the dream?

e. The Ku Klux Klan cloaks itself in patriotism. In what ways might the poet's phrase "false patriotic wreath" apply to the Klan's brand of patriotism?

This lesson is from the CIBC/CEA/NEA curriculum. Text and questions have been added from a lesson based on the same reading by C.P. Ellis in Power in Our Hands: A Curriculum on the History of Work and Workers in the United States *by Bill Bigelow and Norm Diamond (Monthly Review, 1988).*

OBJECTIVES

▶ Students will be able to compare and contrast the Klan's vision of the United States with some of the country's basic principles and creed.

▶ Students will be able to give reasons why people should act against the Klan and be able to identify some appropriate and feasible activities that they might undertake.

TIME REQUIRED

One to two class periods.

TEACHER PREPARATION

Identify local groups who are working to oppose the White supremacist organizations.

CLASSROOM PROCEDURE

1. Review with students what they have learned about the Klan so far. Major points which should be included:

a. The Klan is an openly racist, White supremacist organization which claims that Whites are superior to all other peoples.

b. The Klan seeks to maintain White control of power and authority to protect the special privileges, benefits and advantages Whites gain because of racism.

c. The Klan opposes Blacks and Whites intermarrying, being friends, going to school together, having social or equal contact.

d. The Klan is against Blacks, Jews, people who want to organize Whites and Blacks into unions, people who believe in any economic alternatives to capitalism, lesbians and gay men, feminists who work for equal rights for women, refugees and immigrants from Latin America, the Caribbean, Africa and Asia and Whites who socialize with Blacks or work for equal rights for all.

e. The Klan uses violence, intimidation and terror against those people it opposes.

2. Write the following quote on the board: "Racial separation, preferably through Black repatriation to Africa, is the final and only desirable solution to America's racial problem." Tell students that this quote is from *The Klansman*, the newspaper of the Invisible Empire of the Ku Klux Klan.

3. Distribute copies of excerpts from Martin Luther King's speech, "I Have A Dream". Ask students to read the speech. (If possible, play a recording of the actual speech.)

4. Ask students to discuss the two visions of North America — the Klan's and Dr. King's. Some suggested questions include:

a. What are the elements of Dr. King's vision?

b. What is the Klan's vision?

c. Which of these visions more accurately reflects the ideals of the United States or Canada? Which of these visions would bring closer a "sweet land of liberty" and "let freedom ring"?

5. (Skip this step if you have shared the Niemoller quote in another lesson.) Tell students that Martin Niemoller was a German pastor who actively opposed the Nazis. In the late 1930s the Gestapo put him in a concentration camp. In 1945, Allied troops liberated Dachau and Neimoller was freed. Ask students to read Niemoller's quote and discuss its implications for them in terms of the Klan. What groups could be included in such a quote today?

6. Ask students to consider ways in which the Klan can be opposed and liberty, justice and equality promoted. Ask students to present their ideas, listing them on the board. Included might be:

a. Contact organizations working to oppose the Klan for information on their efforts. (Invite a representative to speak in the class.)

b. Organize a committee of students to develop activities which will inform students about the Klan and raise awareness of racism.

c. Organize an interracial committee of students to work at increasing communication and cooperation in schools experiencing interracial conflict and tension.

d. Write letters to local newspapers stating opposition to Klan activities and calling for people to speak out and act.

e. Write letters to state and national legislators asking for investigations into the activities of White supremacist groups.

f. Visit religious leaders to ask for anti-Klan sermons and educational campaigns against the bigotry and violence of White supremacist groups.

g. In areas of Klan violence, suggest that a community meeting of concerned citizens be called to discuss steps that can be taken.

h. Speak up whenever discriminatory behavior is observed or racist remarks, jokes or comments are heard.

7. Provide opportunities for students to report and discuss in class their activities related to this curriculum.

THEN THEY CAME
BY MARTIN D. NIEMOLLER

In Germany, they came first for the communists, and I didn't speak up because I was not a communist. Then, they came for the Jews and I didn't speak up because I was not a Jew. Then, they came for the trade unionists, and I didn't speak up for them because I was not a trade unionist. Then, they came for the Catholics, and I didn't speak up for them because I was a Protestant. Then, they came for me and by that time, no one was left to speak up.

I HAVE A DREAM
BY MARTIN LUTHER KING, JR.

On August 28, 1963, more than 250,000 people participated in a March on Washington for civil rights. Martin Luther King, Jr., a prominent civil rights leader, addressed the marchers from the steps of the Lincoln Memorial. The following is an excerpt from his speech.

I say to you today, my friends, even though we face the difficulties of today and tomorrow, I still have a dream. It is a dream deeply rooted in the American dream. I have a dream that one day this nation will rise up and live out the true meaning of its creed: "We hold these truths to be self-evident that all men are created equal."

I have a dream that one day on the red hills of Georgia the sons of former slaves and the sons of former slave-owners will be able to sit down together at the table of brotherhood.

I have a dream that one day even the State of Mississippi, a state sweltering with the heat of injustice, sweltering with the heat of oppression, will be transformed into an oasis of freedom and justice. I have a dream that my four little children will one day live in a nation where they will not be judged by the color of their skin but by the content of their character. I have a dream today.

I have a dream that one day down in Alabama with its vicious racists, with its Governor having

his lips dripping with the words of interposition and nullification — one day right there in Alabama, little Black boys and Black girls will be able to join hands with little White boys and White girls as sisters and brothers.

I have a dream today.... This is our hope ... to transform the jangling discords of our nation into a beautiful symphony of brotherhood . . . to work together, to pray together, to struggle together, to go to jail together, to stand up for freedom together, knowing that we will be free one day.

This will be the day when all of God's children will be able to sing with new meaning: "My country 'tis of thee, sweet land of liberty, of thee I sing. Land where my fathers died, land of the pilgrims' pride, from every mountain-side, Let Freedom ring."

And if America is to be a great nation, this must become true.... From every mountainside, let freedom ring. And when we allow freedom to ring, when we let it ring from every village, from every hamlet, from every state and every city, we will be able to speed up that day when all of God's children, Black men and White men, Jews and Gentiles, Protestants and Catholics, will be able to join hands and sing in the words of the old Negro spiritual: "Free at last! free at last! thank God almighty, we are free at last!"

THE COST OF AN ELECTION

BY BEN FORBES

During the 1992 Presidential election, my daughter's grade 5/6 class did a lesson on the presidential race. They studied the candidates' positions, asked parents to tell about their experiences as campaign volunteers, and even invited a worker from the Paul Tsongas campaign to come speak. The lesson was to end with a mock election.

As a parent, I was glad my daughter's class was studying "real life" issues but, at the same time, I was worried. With all the focus on the elections, I feared that my daughter and her classmates might be left with the impression that the U.S. system of electing presidents presented real choices to the voters and constituted a real democracy.

Rather, I wanted my daughter's class to grapple with such critical questions as: who gets to run in presidential elections? Which of the candidates are considered "major" and how is that decided? Whose interests do those major candidates represent? How do the issues presented by the candidates reflect the interests of specific constituencies, especially working-class people, women, people of color, and other oppressed groups? I also wanted my daughter to be exposed to an alternative viewpoint: that progressive social change results when groups of people from the "bottom" organize themselves into movements, and not just from appealing to those on the "top" (including elected officials.)

When I voiced my concerns to my daughter's teacher, Polly Brown, she eagerly invited me to present these issues to the class. As a literacy teacher myself, interested in critical pedagogy and whole language development, I wanted to plan a lesson based on

OCCUPATIONS/INCOMES
CEO of Finest Automobile Company
$2,000,000: 2000 M&Ms
CEO of Super Electronics Corp.
$2,000,000: 2000 M&Ms
Doctor
$150,000: 50 M&Ms
Lawyer
$150,000: 150 M&Ms
Small business owner
$50,000: 50 M&Ms
Teacher
$35,000: 35 M&Ms
Factory worker (boy, automobile)
$30,000: 30 M&Ms
Factory worker (girl, garment)
$17,000: 17 M&Ms
Farmer
$20,000: 20 M&Ms
Unemployed (unemployment comp)
$7,000: 7 M&Ms
Homeless
$500 in charity: 1/2 M&M

principles of active learning and direct experience. Rather than planning a session where I would present facts and figures, lecture about the inequities in the U.S. electoral system, and have the students passively listen (an example of what Paulo Freire calls the "banking" method of education), I designed a role-play. I thought an experiential method, followed by group reflection, might be a good way to get the students as involved as possible within the hour and a half block Ms. Brown had given me. This is what happened.

PROCEDURE

"Where does the money come from?"

To introduce the theme of the role-play, I told the students about a recent newspaper article stating that campaign costs for the presidential election were totaling more than $400 million. I then posed some questions.

▶ Where does the money come from?

▶ Why would someone give a large sum of money, like ten million dollars, to a campaign?

▶ What obligation would the candidate then have to that donor?

This initial questioning helped me get a sense of the students' prior thinking on the issue. I found that most of these fifth and sixth graders believed the presidential campaign was paid for by the contributions of ordinary people. Most thought that anybody with good ideas, who speaks about them loudly enough, will be heard by the candidates.

Next, I announced that we were going to act out a kind of mini-play to explore this issue more, and I briefly explained the role-play. I began by telling the students that, in keeping with the

"American way," the CEOs and the major presidential candidate would have to be played by boys. Two students were assigned to be his campaign managers. I then randomly handed out construction-paper labels indicating various occupations and incomes. Next I distributed plastic bags of M&Ms to represent each student's annual income, based on the equivalence of one M&M per $1000. (Any object that will dramatize the inequality may be used for this purpose, such as peanuts and paper clips.) The occupations and incomes are listed in the chart on the previous page.

The students gasped when they saw the gallon-size bags bursting with M&Ms I gave to the CEOs, in comparison with the almost empty pint-size bags the others received.

I handed out script sheets for each role-player, which listed a few of their "wants," and what actions they would take upon the arrival of the candidate. The Campaign Managers had the busiest role to play, acting as intermediaries between the candidate and the others. One by one the players acted out their scripts.

"I WANT TO TALK TO THE CANDIDATE!"

First, the students playing homeless persons approached the Campaign Managers to tell them they needed a place to sleep. After hurriedly explaining that the candidate was indeed concerned about homeless people, the managers told them they couldn't stay near the candidate and physically escorted them off to the side of the classroom. The two homeless persons then got into an argument over how to split the one M&M representing their $500 charity payment.

Next, the unemployed persons demanded that they get a chance to talk to the candidate. Again, the managers quickly said the candidate truly cares about unemployed persons, but he was not available at the moment. While being escorted to the side of the room, the unemployed began chanting "We want jobs!"

The farmers then told the Campaign Managers they wanted to talk to the candidate. The managers said to them that the candidate thought farmers are important and doing a great job, but that he was too busy to speak with them. The managers gave the farmers some campaign newspapers to read about the candidate.

When the factory workers asked to see the candidate, they were told that he was at an important meeting, but if they waited awhile they might get a chance to wave at him from a distance. The Cam-

paign Managers then suggested to the candidate that he wave to the factory workers, and perhaps make a speech at a factory next week.

The teacher and the small business owner told the Campaign Managers that they wished to talk to the presidential candidate. The managers said that, even though the candidate was extremely busy, he would talk to them for just one minute. But as soon as the teacher and small business owner told the candidate what they want, the managers told them their time was up and escorted them away.

The doctor and lawyer told the Campaign Managers they would like to talk with the candidate, and would be willing to pay $1000 to have dinner with him. The managers let the doctor and lawyer shake the candidate's hand and talk a few minutes, but then quickly showed them to seats at a table far away from the candidate's own table.

Finally, the two CEOs told the Campaign Managers they would be willing to contribute $10 million to the campaign — provided the candidate made his platform favorable to what they wanted. The managers encouraged the CEOs to make themselves comfortable at the table with the candidate. In a friendly tone of voice, the managers offered them something to eat and drink; inviting the CEOs to spend as much time as they like with the candidate. The CEOs then began to talk about what they want in return for their contribution. The candidate listened attentively.

I was pleased the students quickly got involved in the role-play, and even embellished their scripts with spontaneous gestures and dialogues. After acting out their individual parts, they easily became an attentive audience as they watched the drama unfold.

"MARCH OR DEMONSTRATE!"

When the role-play ended, I asked the students how they felt about their roles and about what happened. One student exclaimed, "The more money you had, the more the candidate listened to you!" Another said, "He only promised things to people with lots of money!" We then entered into a lively discussion on campaign financing and the relative influence different groups had upon the candidate's platform.

Then I asked, "what could you do if the candidate won't pay attention to your needs?" "What are some other ways you could get your needs met?" One student blurted out "Go on TV like Ross Perot!" but then thought for a moment and added, "If you're rich." Someone suggested that we could tell people the candidate is only listening to rich people. Someone else proposed that we could "march or demonstrate all around town." "Go on a bus to other states and spread the message," added another. One student despaired at the powerlessness of the homeless. Another lamented, "If all the candidates are slime balls, we have a really messed up country!"

After lots of animated, yet thoughtful discussion, I showed the students a copy of *Business Week's* 1989 Special Bonus Issue entitled "The Corporate Elite: Chief Executives of the Business Week 1000." I flipped through the pages showing them photos of the CEOs and read aloud some of their names. I asked them what they noticed. After a moment of silence, someone called out, "They're all wearing suits!" Another commented, "They're all White, male and rich!" Then I held up a Boston Globe photo showing all the presidential candidates — including socialist and alternative candidates. They seemed surprised at how many they hadn't heard of. We discussed why no one in the class had heard of Lenore Fulani, for example, and why there weren't more women candidates, particularly women of color candidates.

My time was up, but it was hard to leave the spirited discussion. I left the class with a copy of the *Social Stratification Poster* which graphically displays how wealth is distributed in the United States and Ms. Brown tacked it onto the wall for future discussion.

REFLECTIONS

Looking back, I realize I could have done some things differently. Next time, I would arrange the classroom with a table and row of five chairs in the front, facing the class, and describe the front of the classroom as the meeting room of a fancy downtown hotel. At the other end and the sides, toward the back of the classroom, I would post the following signs in different places: "unemployment office," "farm," "factory," "park bench," and "neighborhood." Doing this would set the stage for a discussion about grassroots organizing and alliance-building. I would ask the students to think about the effect and implications of each identified group standing in their respective places, such as the homeless per-

The Social Stratification book includes data about wealth distribution in the United States and a large pull-out poster with the image shown on the book cover. Published by New Press.

sons at the park bench and factory workers at the factory. After each person played their part, they would be asked to move to their designated places in the classroom. By raising questions related to their location, we could talk about factors such as social categories, labels, prejudices and physical structures (such as location of neighborhoods) that often prevent people from becoming friends and allies with one another.

In this lesson, I also had to oversimplify many of the complex issues surrounding the electoral process since the exercise was just a brief, one-time activity. It omitted important topics like the struggles of women, African Americans and others to win the right to vote; the ongoing battle for equity in representation and related issues, such as the histories of the labor and the civil rights movements. These should be included in an expanded unit on the electoral process.

Even in this abbreviated form, however, the

role-play succeeded as a catalyst for getting Ms. Brown's students to look more critically at elections. She told me later that the experience had a profound effect upon her students, with comments about it coming up over and over in class discussions. She mentioned one boy who was "radicalized" as a result of the role-play. Describing him as a student who "needs to act it out to 'have it,'" she felt it stirred up his strong sense of fairness and made him think about the issues with greater depth. One of the girls thought about her anger at not being allowed to play the part of the candidate. According to Ms. Brown, in their evaluations the students repeatedly referred to the role-play as a valuable part of the election unit. Several of them even ended up voting for alternative candidates in their class mock election!

As a lesson in critical literacy, the role-play experience helped my daughter and her classmates, in Freire's words, to "read the world" — know and understand the events going on around them — so as to "read the word" — know and understand the real meanings of particular words, especially those that are used sometimes to hide certain realities and effects. The role-play provided a means for these fifth and sixth graders to begin asking critical questions about race, class, gender and power in electoral politics (reading the world), about what constitutes authentic democracy (reading the word), and about the potential for progressive mass movements to attain social and economic justice.

Ben Forbes is as an Early Childhood Resource Specialist in the Cambridge, Massachusetts public schools, with an interest in multicultural education and critical literacy. He is also a doctoral student in the Reading & Writing Program of the University of Massachusetts, Amherst, School of Education.

I wish to thank Polly Brown, teacher at Touchstone Community School, Grafton, Massachusetts, for inviting me into her classroom. I also want to acknowledge Mike Charney, teacher and activist in Cleveland, and Bill Bigelow, an editor of Rethinking Schools, *for providing me with powerful models for doing role-plays in the classroom.*

REFERENCES

Freire, P. 1986. *Pedagogy of the oppressed.* New York: Continum Books.

Rose, S. 1996. *Social stratification in the United States.* New York: New Press. Full-color poster, based on U.S. census statistics, compares social groups, tracks the disappearing middle class and relates income to race, gender, education and occupation. Poster and 48-page study guide. Available from NECA for $15.

Chief Executive Officer (CEO) (MALE)

Job: Boss of Finest Automobile Company.
Income: $2,000,000 per year.

What you want: In return for your $10,000,000 contribution, you want the government to:

▸ Limit the number of foreign-made cars that can be sold in the U.S. to reduce the competition.

▸ Keep wages low for your workers to hold your costs down in order to increase your profits.

▸ Force your workers to pay more for their health insurance because health care costs for your workers are rapidly going up for you.

▸ Make weak or no environmental laws because strong ones would increase your operating costs.

What you do: Tell the presidential candidate that if his platform is favorable to the things you want, you will give him a $10,000,000 contribution to his campaign.

Chief Executive Officer (CEO) (MALE)

Job: Boss of Super Electronics Corporation
Income: *$2,000,000 per year.*

What you want: In return for your $10,000,000 contribution, you want the government to:

▸ Limit the amount of foreign electronic products that can be sold here to reduce the competition.

▸ Keep wages low for your workers to hold your costs down in order to increase your profits.

▸ Help make your workers pay more for their health insurance because health care costs for your workers are rapidly going up for you.

▸ Push for weak or no environmental laws because strong ones would increase your operating costs.

What you do: Tell the presidential candidate that if his platform is favorable to the things you want, you will give him a $10,000,000 contribution to his campaign.

Doctor at a community health center

Income: $150,000 per year.

What you want: In return for your $1,000 contribution, you want the government to:

▸ Build new hospitals.

▸ Pay for health costs for more patients.

▸ Help poor people make more money so they can stay healthy.

▸ Make strong laws to make, and keep, the environment clean so that people don't get sick.

What you do: Tell the Campaign Managers you want to talk to the presidential candidate. Tell them you will contribute to the campaign by paying $1,000 so you can have dinner with the candidate and shake his hand.

Lawyer

Income: $150,000 per year.

What you want: In return for your $1,000 contribution, you want the government to:

▸ Pay for new courthouses.

▸ Pay legal costs for poor people.

▸ Build better prisons.

▸ Protect the environment.

What you do: Tell the Campaign Managers what you want to talk to the presidential candidate. Tell him you will contribute to the campaign by paying $1,000 so you can have dinner with the candidate and shake his hand.

Teacher

Income: $35,000 a year.

What you want: You want the government to:

▸ Pay more money for education — for better schools, books and materials.

▸ Protect the environment.

▸ Help poor people to have better jobs so they can have better housing, food and neighborhoods.

▸ Pay for health care for all people.

What you do: Tell the Campaign Managers you wish to talk to the presidential candidate about what you want.

Owner of small computer store

Income: $50,000 a year.

What you want: You want the government to:

▶ Give more loans to small businesses

▶ Protect the environment.

▶ Pay for health care for all people.

What you do: Tell the Campaign Managers you wish to talk to the presidential candidate about what you want.

Factory Worker in a

garment factory

Income: $17,000 a year.

What you want: You want the government to:

▶ Increase the wages.

▶ Pay for health care.

▶ Improve the schools in your community so your children can get a good education.

▶ Encourage the companies to increase their benefits, like paid time off to be with your family when they are sick.

What you do: Tell the Campaign Managers you want to talk to the presidential candidate. If they won't let you, go to the side of the room marked "factory" and wave to the candidate.

Factory Worker in an

automobile factory

Income: $30,000 a year.

What you want: You want the government to:

▶ Increase the wages.

▶ Pay for health care.

▶ Improve the schools in your community so your children can get a good education.

▶ Encourage the companies to increase their benefits, like paid time off to be with your family when they are sick.

▶ Stop clean air laws, because they might cause your company to lose money, and cause you to be laid off.

What you do: Tell the Campaign Managers you want to talk to the presidential candidate. If they won't let you, go to the side of the room marked "factory" and wave to the candidate.

Farmer

Income: $20,000 a year.

What you want: You want the government to:

▶ Give you loans.

▶ Get cheap gas to enable you to run your farm equipment.

▶ Pay for health care.

What you do: Tell the Campaign Managers you want to talk to the presidential candidate. If they won't let you, move to place in the room labeled "farm" and read about the campaign in their newspaper.

Unemployed Person

Income: $7,000 you receive from unemployment compensation

What you want: You want the government to:

▶ Create more jobs so you can work.

▶ Give more money for Food Stamps to help you buy food.

▶ Pay for health care.

▶ Provide better services, like public transportation, schools, housing.

What you do: Tell the Campaign Managers you want to talk to the presidential candidate. If they won't let you, start chanting: "We want a job! We want a job!" Then go line up at the Employment Office to collect your Unemployment Compensation.

Presidential Candidate (boy)

What you want: $20,000,000 (20 million) to pay for your campaign costs.

What you do: Wait until your Campaign Managers tell you who has appointments to see you. When the doctor and lawyer are introduced to you, quickly shake their hands, smile, thank them for their small donation, and walk away. When the CEO of Finest Automobile Company and the CEO of Acme Electronics Company come to see you, have them sit down and be nice to them. Agree to put what they want on your platform so you can get the money they are offering to contribute to your campaign.

HOMELESS PERSON

You are a war veteran who has been unemployed for many years due to disabilities as the result of war injuries.

Income: None; you must share $500 the local charity gave to you and the other homeless persons

What you want: You want the government to:

▸ Provide a clean and safe place to live.

▸ Provide rehabilitation treatment, and job training.

▸ Create well-paying jobs that will hire people with disabilities.

▸ Pay for health care.

▸ Make laws for a cleaner environment.

What you do: Go to the Campaign Managers and tell them you need a place to sleep. When you are thrown out, get into an argument with the other homeless persons about who gets the $500 given by the charity. Then walk around the room looking for the place marked "park bench."

HOMELESS PERSON

You are homeless. You are a mother of two small children who has been unemployed for several months since the sewing factory closed down when the company decided to move it to a foreign company so they can pay the workers less money than they were paying you.

Income: None; you must share $500 the local charity gave to you and the other homeless persons

What you want: You want the government to:

▸ Provide a clean and safe place for you and your children to live.

▸ Pay for you to enroll in a job-training program

▸ Create well-paying jobs that match your training.

▸ Pay for health care and day care.

▸ Make laws for a cleaner environment.

What you do: Go up to the Campaign Managers and tell them you need a place to sleep. When you are thrown out, get into an argument with the other homeless persons about who gets the $500 given by the charity. Then walk around the room looking for the place marked "park bench."

CAMPAIGN MANAGER

Your job is to do everything possible to get your candidate elected.

▸ Tell the homeless people the candidate is concerned about their needs, but they can't stay near the candidate. Escort them to the side of the room.

▸ Tell the unemployed people the candidate cares about them, but he is not available. Escort them to the side of the room.

▸ Tell the farmers the candidate thinks farmers are important and are doing a great job, but he is too busy to see them now. Give them a newspaper to read about the candidate.

▸ Tell the factory workers the candidate is not available at the moment — he's at an important meeting.

▸ Tell the candidate to wave to the farmers.

▸ Tell the candidate he should make a speech at a factory next week.

▸ Tell the teacher and small business owner that the candidate is very busy, but they may talk to him for just one minute. Give them a few minutes to tell him what they want; interrupt them before they are finished and tell them their time is up.

▸ Tell the Doctor and Lawyer that they may sit down at the dinner, but don't let them sit too close to the candidate. Let them shake hands with him but quickly take them to their seats.

▸ Nicely invite the CEOs to sit down and make themselves comfortable. Tell them to spend as much time as they like with the candidate. Offer them something to drink and eat. Be really nice to them.

EXCLUSION — CHINESE IN 19TH CENTURY AMERICA

BY DEBBIE WEI

OBJECTIVES

Students will:

▸ Know about the lives and contributions of Chinese immigrants in the United States in the nineteenth century.

▸ Analyze the roots of anti-immigrant sentiment which led to the passage of the Chinese Exclusion Acts.

PROCEDURE

1. Ask students to visualize a pioneer in the 1800s. Ask them to describe what they see. This should include what the pioneer looks like and also his or her surroundings. If the students don't volunteer the information, ask what race or ethnicity the pioneer is. Ask about the surroundings — are there other people there? If so, who?

2. Distribute blank maps of the world. Ask students to:

a. Draw lines indicating where the pioneers who settled in the United States came from to where they landed in the United States.

b. Draw a line to indicate their routes of travel (if they moved from where they landed) to their final destination.

c. List who would already be living in the various parts of the United States where the pioneers traveled.

Have students post their maps. Summarize what you see in most of the maps. Students are likely to show people coming from Europe to the East Coast, then traveling West. They may list Native Americans as living here.

3. Ask students: Was the movement only from East to West, or could it also have been from West to East?

Explain to students that there were in fact large numbers of immigrants from Asia to the United States during the 1800s, just as there was large immigration from Europe. Post a flip chart with the following excerpt from Ronald Takaki's *Strangers*

from a Different Shore to illustrate your point: "By 1870, there were 63,000 Chinese in the United States. Most of them — 77 percent — were in California, but they were also elsewhere in the West as well as in the Southwest, New England and the South. The Chinese constituted a sizable proportion of the population in certain areas: 29 percent in Idaho, 10 percent in Montana, and 9 percent in California. Virtually all adult males, they had a greater economic significance than their numbers would indicate: in California, the Chinese represented 25 percent of the entire work force."

4. Have students become familiar with the economic and political history of Chinese immigration to the United States as described in the reading titled "Chinese in the Gold Mountain." Divide up sections of the history among small groups to have them develop a visual timeline of their section or to dramatize it for the rest of the group. Following the presentations, ask students to discuss what they have learned. Use the following questions:

▸ Why did people have to leave China?

▸ What were their experiences in the United States in general?

▸ What were their experiences working on the railroad? How did the railroad shape the history of the Pacific Coast?

▸ Describe some parallels between the Chinese experience and the work lives and social lives of recent immigrants?

▸ Why did Chinese immigration eventually stop?

Record the students' answers and let them know that they will explore the answer to the last question in the next reading and discussion.

5. Have students read the handout entitled "Anti-Asian Violence — 19th Century." Ask students to brainstorm about why the Chinese were targeted. (Add to their list if not included: Scapegoats were needed to take the blame away from the wealthy bankers and industrialists during the economic depression; the Chinese were racially identifiable.) Ask students to consider:

▸ Which was the worst episode? Why?

▸ Why was it acceptable to the majority for Asian Americans to be treated in this way?

6. Have students read "Anti-Immigrant Rhetoric — 19th Century," and the mining songs. Ask students:

- What images do the quotes and song evoke?

- What is the relationship between these documents and the violence described in the article, "Anti-Asian Violence"?

- What other institutions contributed to, or at least gave tacit approval for, the discrimination against the Chinese? (legal system, unions, media)

- What sentiments (such as the notion that immigrants take jobs away from "Americans") can still be found today?

7. Distribute the handout by Patrick Buchanan. Ask students to discuss current popular views on immigration. Can they cite any other evidence of popular culture being used to foment anti-immigrant sentiment? Can they find similarities in the two centuries of rhetoric?

OPTIONAL

1. Stage a debate on the rights of immigrants. Some students could play the part of people today and some could represent people from the 19th century.

2. Ask the students to write a poem, song or design an ad which directly challenges a particular stereotype. The song, John Chinaman's Appeal and the poem "So Mexican's Are Taking Jobs" (see "Critical Literacy" section) can be shared as examples.

CHINESE IN THE GOLD MOUNTAIN

BY DEBBIE WEI

In the 1800s, many Chinese emigrated from China to places all over the world. Chinese went to Southeast Asia, Australia, Canada, South America and the Caribbean as well as to the United States.

Several factors contributed to the immigration of Chinese to the United States:

In the 1700s European and American colonial powers had begun to invade Asia; initially, traders went to China in search of "tea and spices" and also porcelain. China was so famous for the fine quality of its ceramics that even today, well made dishware is referred to as "china." But the American and European traders did not have goods which the Chinese wanted for trade. Instead, they were forced to trade with gold and silver, creating what would be called in modern terms a "trade deficit" between China and Europe and the U.S. In response to this trade deficit, European and American traders decided to develop drug trafficking as a means to balance the trade. They began importing opium into China[1], against the wishes of the Chinese government. Many Chinese became addicted to the illicit drug. China went to war with Britain to stop the opium trade, but lost the war. Poor peasants and city dwellers suffered greatly because of the economic devastation resulting from the opium wars and the corruption in government and they began to look overseas for work.

Around the same time, the end of slavery in the United States created a great need for cheap labor. Industrialists began to look all over the world for cheap contract labor to bring to the United States to work in various industries. On the east coast, they looked to poorer European countries. One of the biggest sources for cheap labor was Ireland. On the west coast, industrialists began to look toward Asia.

In 1849, gold was found in California. Miners surged into the area and with them came the need for labor and service workers to meet their needs. The 1849 Gold Rush drew tens of thousands of Chinese across the Pacific Ocean in search of a better means to provide for their families.

Most of the Chinese who emigrated were men. The uncertainty of life waiting for the Chinese laborers in America, and the fact that traditionally, women were expected to care for their spouse's parents initially limited the numbers of women. Later, racist immigration laws designed to ensure a cheap, but temporary, labor force, severely restricted Chinese women from coming to America. In addition, Chinese men already in America were forbidden by law to marry other races. To ensure that Chinese did not create families in America, further laws were passed that stated that U.S. citizens who married Chinese would automatically lose their citizenship.

In China, America was referred to as "Gold Mountain." These 'Gold Mountain Men' planned to find gold and then voyage back to their families in China. Most of these seekers were unable to strike it rich. They found that they could not compete in the mining business with White miners. Unlike White miners, Chinese workers' earnings were taxed, and the Chinese were only allowed to work mines which had already been deserted by Whites. Many of the miners turned their labor to providing services for the mining community. Their wages were meager and the work long and hard. Yet their families in China relied on whatever earnings they could send back in order to survive. As the mining boom drew to a close, the Chinese stayed on and began to work in other fields, most notably in building the railroads and in reclaiming useless marsh and swamp land throughout California.

This back-breaking work is described in the quotes below.

That first winter (1865) was the harshest on record. (The Chinese) lived like moles. They dug tunnels through forty-foot snowdrifts and continued to lay track. Avalanches whisked men away, tunnels collapsed. Still the work went on. When the spring thaws came, men were uncovered still standing and holding their tools, their faces frozen in death masks of horror. By the summer of 1868, nine-tenths of the fourteen thousand railroad workers on the Central Pacific were Chinese — nearly one-quarter of the total population of Chinese in the country. They dynamited through 1,695 feet of solid rock to create the Donner Tunnels. While the workers on the Union Pacific rushed through the flatlands of Nebraska and the plains, the Chinese on the Central Pacific built a line that rose seven thousand feet in one hundred miles. Lowered by wicker baskets down sheer cliffs, they chis-

eled through granite and shale to carve out shelves on which to lay track...The Chinese worked 26 days...a month, from dawn to dusk. For this they earned 28 or 30 American dollars a month.

Toiling in water up to their waists, Chinese laborers built miles of levees, ditches, dikes, canals, and irrigation channels to drain the swampy land. Draft animals couldn't do the work, since their hooves sank in the mud; whites wouldn't do the work because it was too hard and unhealthy. By the time they were done, 500 million acres in the Sacramento area were reclaimed and land values rose from one dollar to one hundred dollars an acre. But the Chinese owned none of it, since the Alien Land Act of 1870 forbade the ownership of American land by Chinese...(On Gold Mountain, by Lisa See)

By the 1870s, America's economic landscape had begun a dramatic shift. Industrial companies began to grow bigger and bigger. There was a period of change in which the small manufacturing operations that used many workers began to close and large factories which used more machinery and fewer workers started to take over.

At the same time as many workers began to feel the bite of unemployment, the Transpacific Railroad was completed; thousands of former railroad workers — Chinese as well as others — entered a labor market already being sent into turmoil by the rise of large scale industrialism. As Ronald Takaki explained in *Iron Cages*, Chinese workers were a major component of the labor force in San Francisco.

By 1870, twenty-six percent of California's Chinese population lived in San Francisco, which was already, by Internal Revenue returns, the ninth leading manufacturing city in the United States. Chinese workers represented forty-six percent of the labor force in the city's four key industries — boot and shoe, woolens, cigar and tobacco, and sewing.

In 1873, the United States entered a period of a serious depression. There was extremely high unemployment, and those who had jobs worked long, hard hours for very low wages. In California, the Comstock Lode — a supply of gold that some thought would last forever — dried up and thousands of miners began to look for other work. And then in 1875, the Bank of California crashed. Its depositors lost their money. Panic began. Competition for scarce jobs increased to a fevered level, and employers responded by continuing to drop wages and lower working conditions.

Labor unions began to form to combat the abuses of employers. Unfortunately, most of the labor unions restricted membership to White men. Women and people of color were often portrayed as unwelcome competitors for American workers. With membership closed to them, even if Chinese workers wanted to unionize, they couldn't. The new labor unions exercised political influence and workers' political parties began to push for laws which would expel Chinese already in the United States and then bar Chinese from entering in the future. Campaign slogans such as "Get Rid of the Yellow Peril" and "the Chinese Must Go" became popular among candidates intent on winning elections. Newspapers quickly picked up on the trend and fanned the flames of racial hate.

The end of the 19th century brought about increased violence and anti-Chinese riots, and many Chinese were simply driven out of their adopted communities. In some of the worst cases, like Rock Springs, Wyoming or Los Angeles, Chinese were attacked and lynched. In each city, over 20 Chinese were brutally murdered in killing sprees. Accompanying the physical violence were waves of anti-Chinese legislation passed both locally and federally. San Francisco, which had a large Chinese population, passed harsh city ordinances designed to harass Chinese workers. By 1882, Congress passed the Chinese Exclusion Act which explicitly banned Chinese laborers from entering the United States. The Chinese became the first ethnic group ever to be targeted for exclusion from immigration to the U.S. based on race.

The Exclusion Laws were later expanded to include a wide range of categories and eventually all Asian groups were targeted for exclusion. The racist immigration laws had a profound historical impact on the shaping of attitudes toward race in America. They were not changed until 1965 when Civil Rights legislation made it illegal for the government to discriminate on the basis of race.

Notes

1. After the British seized control of India and destroyed the cotton weaving industry so it would not compete with their newly founded factories, they began to force subjects in their colonial holdings to grow opium to support their moves into China. Farmers who formerly spent their time and energy producing food for the populace were forced to grow opium instead, leading to widespread starvation. American traders, in the meantime, developed a vigorous trade through Turkey.

ANTI-ASIAN VIOLENCE —
19TH CENTURY

Following are just a few examples of anti-Asian violence from the 19th century.

▶ It seemed whenever the Chinese began to make a profit, the Caucasians took it from them by enacting laws — laws limiting the size of shrimping nets, laws forbidding ironing after dark...laws requiring that laundries be built of brick or stone...laws forbidding the hiring of Chinese for public works.

▶ A fifteen-dollar tax every three months was levied on laundrymen who carried their livelihoods on poles; the tax was only two dollars every quarter for those prosperous enough to own a horse and wagon — a law that clearly favored White men and hurt Chinese.

There had been laws against firecrackers and gongs...In San Francisco, if a man was arrested, his queue would be shaved...That same city passed a law requiring five hundred cubic feet of air per person in rooming houses...

▶ In Tacoma Washington, seven hundred laborers were herded into railroad cars and driven from town. Eventually all Chinese would be forced to leave that city, and for decades not a single Chinese would live within its environs. In fear, Chinese in Seattle boarded steamships for San Francisco.

▶ In Tombstone, Arizona, cowpokes cut playing cards to determine to which points of the compass the Chinese would be sent.

▶ In Tucson, a Chinese was tied to the back of a steer and sent out across the desert.

▶ In Rock Springs, Wyoming, twenty-eight Chinese were killed: eleven of them were burned alive in their homes; others were shot in the back as they tried to escape.

▶ On the Snake River in eastern Washington, thirty-one Chinese were massacred.

▶ In Alaska, Chinese miners were crowded onto small boats and set adrift.

▶ In Redlands, California — after five years of planting, pruning, harvesting, sorting and packing citrus — Chinese were barricaded in sheds as White roughnecks raided orange groves. Despite assistance from the National Guard, houses were burned and buildings looted. By 1900 the Chinese were completely driven out of California's citrus industry.

▶ In Los Angeles, on October 23, 1871, "A mob of vigilantes, composed of Mexicans and Anglos, descended on (Chinatown). Using pickaxes, they chopped into the Coronel Building, where many Chinese were hiding; others simply shot at the building. Emboldened, men stormed inside where they found...respectable Chinese men and women cowering in fear. Two dead Chinese were dragged outside, where they were kicked, pummeled, and finally hanged for good measure...a Chinese doctor was robbed, shot in the mouth, then hanged...By the end of the night, the bodies of seventeen Chinese men and boys swung from a wooden awning in front of the carriage shop, from the sides of two prairie schooners, and from the crossbeam of a gate in a nearby lumberyard. Within days, another two Chinese died from complications of gunshot wounds. At least 500 Angelenos — approximately eight percent of the city's total population — participated in the "night of horrors"

ANTI-IMMIGRATION RHETORIC —
19TH CENTURY

We have four millions of degraded negroes in the South...and if there were to be a flood-tide of Chinese population — a population befouled with all the social vices, with no knowledge or appreciation of free institutions or constitutional liberty, with heathenish souls and heathenish propensities, whose characters and habits, and modes of thought are firmly fixed by the consolidating influences of ages upon ages — we should be prepared to bid farewell to republicanism...

New York Times, September 3, 1865

No man is worthy of the name of patriot or statesman who countenances a policy which is opposed to the interests of the free White laboring industrial classes...What we desire for the permanent benefit of California is a population of White men who will make this state their home, bring up families here and meet the responsibilities and discharge the duties of freemen. We ought not to desire an effete population of Asiatics...

Governor Henry Haight, Inaugural Remarks, 1868

That he is a slave reduced to the lowest terms of beggarly economy, and is no fit competitor for an American freeman. That he herds in scores, in small dens, where a White man and wife could hardly breathe, and has none of the wants of a civilized White man. That he has neither wife, nor child, nor expects to have any. That his sister is a prostitute from instinct, religion, education and interest, and degrading to all around her. That American men, women, and children cannot be what free people should be, and compete with such degraded creatures in the labor market. That wherever they are numerous, as in San Francisco, by a secret machinery of their own, they defy the law, keep up the manners and customs of China, and utterly disregard all the laws of health, decency and morality. That they are driving the White population from the state, reducing laboring men to despair, laboring women to prostitution, and boys and girls to hoodlums and convicts. That the health, wealth, prosperity, and happiness of our State demand their expulsion from our shores.

California State Assembly, 1878

The burden of our accusation against them is that they come in conflict with our labor interests; that they can never assimilate with us; that they are a perpetual, unchanging alien element that can never be homogenous; that their civilization is demoralizing and degrading to our people; that they degrade and dishonor labor; that they can never become citizens, and that an alien, degraded labor class, without desire of citizenship, without education, and without interest in the country it inhabits, is an element both demoralizing and dangerous to the community within which it exists."

Official spokesman of San Francisco before the Joint Committee of Congress, 1876

"The Chinese must go! They are stealing our jobs!"

Denis Kearney, president, Workingman's Party, 1878

"In Congress, the arguments for exclusion were purely racist. Many of them were the same ones that had been used against the Irish decades earlier. The Chinese took jobs from "real" Americans. The Chinese were dirty, drank too much, and lived on too little money. They didn't spend their money in this country, preferring to save it and send it home. The Chinese worshipped their ancestors; wasn't that something like worshipping an idol? They worked too cheaply, and when they were out of work — unlike Americans — they became hoodlums. The Chinese carried disease; they were clannish; when they died, they sent their bones back to China, as if American soil wasn't good enough for them. In other words, the Chinese were totally unassimilable."

From On Gold Mountain by Lisa See, 1995. St. Martin's Press.

Mining Songs

John Chinaman

John Chinaman, John Chinaman,
But five short years ago,
I welcomed you from Canton, John—
But wish I hadn't though;

For then I thought you honest, John,
Not dreaming but you'd make
A citizen as useful, John,
As any in the State.

I thought you'd open wide your ports,
And let our merchants in,
To barter for their crapes and teas,
Their wares of wood and tin.

I thought you'd cut your queue off, John
And don a Yankee coat
And a collar high you'd raise, John,
Around your dusky throat.

I imagined that the truth, John,
You'd speak when under oath,
But I find you'll lie and steal too —
Yes, John, you're up to both.

I thought of rats and puppies, John,
You'd eaten your last fill,
But on such slimy pot-pies, John
I'm told you dinner still.

Oh, John, I've been deceived in you,
And in all your thieving clan,
For our gold is all you're after, John,
To get it as you can.

Text: Original California Songster

John Chinaman, My Jo

John Chinaman, my jo, John
You're coming precious fast;
Each ship that sails from Shanghai brings
An increase on the last
And when you'll stop invading us,
I'm blest, now, if I know,
You'll outnumber us poor Yankees,
John Chinaman, my jo.

John Chinaman, my jo, John,
You not only come in shoals,
But you often shake the washing stuff
And spoil the water holes;
And, of course, that riles the miners, John,
And enrages them, you know,
For they drive you frequently away;
John Chinaman, my jo.

John Chinaman, my jo, John,
You used to live on rice,
But now you purchase flour, plums,
And other things that's nice;
And I see a butcher's shop, John,
At your Chinese place below,
And you like your mutton now and then,
John Chinaman, my jo.

John Chinaman, my jo, John,
Though folks at you may rail,
Here's blessings on your head, John,
And more power to your tail;
But a bit of good advice, John.
I'll give you, ere I go —
Don't abuse the freedom you enjoy,
John Chinaman, my jo.

Air: John Anderson, My Jo
Text: Conner's Irish Song Book

JOHN CHINAMAN'S APPEAL

American now mind my song
If you would but hear me sing,
And I will tell you of the wrong,
That happened unto "Gee Sing,"

In "fifty-two" I left my home —
I bid farewell to "Hong Kong" —
I started with Cup Gee to roam
To the land where they use the "long tom."

Chorus: O ching hi ku tong mo ching ching,
O ching hi ku tong chi do,
Cup Cee hi ku tong mo ching ching
Then what could Gee or I do?

In forty days I reached the Bay,
And nearly starved I was sir,
I cooked and ate a dog one day,
I didn't know the laws sir.

But soon I found my dainty meal
Was 'gainst the city order,
The penalty I had to feel —
Confound the old Recorder.

By paying up my cost and fines
They freed me from the locker,
And then I started for the mines —
I got a pick and rocker.

I went to work in an untouched place,
I'm sure I meant no blame sir,
But a White man struck me in the face
And told me to leave his claim sir.

'Twas then I packed my tools away
And set up in a new place,
But there they would not let me stay —
They didn't like the cue race.

And then I knew not what to do,
I could not get employ,
The Know Nothings would bid me go —
'Twas tu nah mug ahoy.

I started then for Weaverville
Where Chinamen were thriving,
But found our China agents there
In ancient feuds were driving.

So I pitched into politics,
But with the weaker party;
The Canton's with their clubs and bricks,
Did drub us out "right hearty."

I started for Yreka then;
I thought that I would stay there,
But found for even Chinamen
The "diggings" wouldn't pay there.

So I set up a washing shop,
But how extremely funny,
The miners all had dirty clothes,
But not a cent of money.

I met a big stout Indian once,
He stopped me in the trail, sir,
He drew an awful scalping knife,
And I trembled for my tail, sir.

He caught me by the hair, it's true,
In a manner quite uncivil,
But when he saw my awful cue,
He thought I was the devil.

Oh, now my friends I'm going away
From this infernal place, sir;
The balance of my days I'll stay
With the Celestial race, sir.

I'll go to raising rice and tea;
I'll be a heathen ever,
For Christians all have treated me
As men should be used never.

Air: Umbrella Courtship
Text: Digger's Song Book

Patrick J. Buchanan on Immigration

Editorial

What do we want the America of the years 2000, 2020 and 2050 to be like? Do we have the right to shape the character of the country our grandchildren will live in? Or is that to be decided by whoever, outside America, decides to come here?

Now, any man or woman, of any nation or ancestry can come here — and become a good American. We know that from our history. But by my arithmetic, the chancellor is saying Hispanics, Asians and Africans will increase their present number of 65 million by at least 100 million in 60 years, a population growth larger than all of Mexico today.

If no cutoff is imposed on social benefits for those who breach our borders, and break our laws, the message will go out to a desperate world: America is wide open. All you need do is get there, and get in. Consequences will ensue. Crowding together immigrant and minority populations in our major cities must bring greater conflict.

Ethnic militancy and solidarity are on the rise in the United States; the old institutions of assimilation are not doing their work as they once did; the Melting Pot is in need of repair. On campuses we hear demands for separate dorms, eating rooms, clubs, by Black, White, Hispanic and Asian students. If this is where the campus is headed, where are our cities going?

If America is to survive as "one nation, one people" we need to call a "time-out" on immigration, to assimilate the tens of millions who have lately arrived. We need to get to know one another, to live together, to learn together America's language, history, culture and traditions of tolerance, to become a new national family, before we add a hundred million more. And we need soon to bring down the curtain on this idea of hyphenated-Americanism.

If we lack the course to make the decisions —as to what our country will look like in 2050 — others will make those decisions for us, not all of whom share our love of the America that seems to be fading away. Illegal aliens, unfunded federal mandates, control of land, guns — these are the issues driving a gathering national rebellion.

From "Immigration Time-out" by Patrick J. Buchanan (October 31, 1994)

Fundraising Letter

Dear Friends

...I believe the explosion in illegal immigration is causing massive crime, social disruption and an enormous financial drain on government services. ...That's why I favor strong action to stem the tide of illegal immigration:

(1) Denying all federal social benefits to illegal aliens.
(2) Building permanent, un-climbable fences at targeted urban border crossings, such as San Diego and El Paso, where 90 percent of illegal aliens enter our country.
(3) Full funding [for] 6,000 new Border Patrol agents, and providing them with the vehicles and technology they need to carry out their mission...
(4) Deporting illegal aliens to the interior of their country of origin, instead of just dropping them off on the other side of the border.

...Beyond the financial costs of uncontrolled immigration, America pays even more dearly in the priceless coin of national unity. For decades now our institutions of assimilation have been battered by liberals ashamed of America's heritage and by multiculturalists who despise it.

...Due in large part to uncontrolled illegal immigration, America is being "Balkanized" today. That's one of the major reasons I've stepped forward to run for President. But to keep our campaign for immigration reform on the agenda, I need your help. Please send Buchanan for President your largest possible financial contribution to help me carry our platform for immigration reform into the presidential primaries. Your check for $25, $50, $100, $250, $500 or even $1,000 will help me pay for Issues, brochures, posters, bumper stickers and TV ads.

I need your help so that the truth about the illegal immigration crisis can be aired, discussed and effectively addressed by out national leaders. Working together, you and I can take back America for the values that were instilled in us as children. We want to leave for future generations an America that resonates with the traditions upon which our nation was founded, and for which men and women have fought and died for more than 200 years...There is no time to waste.

Your Friend, Patrick Buchanan

From a fundraising letter, Fall, 1995

ANGEL ISLAND

BY DEBBIE WEI

PROCEDURE

1. Ask students if they have ever heard of Ellis Island. If they have (which is likely) ask them to tell you a little bit about it, such as which countries people came from. Then ask if they have heard of Angel Island. If not, explain that it was a "West Coast version" of Ellis Island primarily for Chinese immigrants. If more students were familiar with Ellis Island than Angel Island, ask students to consider and discuss why that was the case.

2. Using a classroom map of the United States, ask students to locate Ellis Island and Angel Island. Show the students the correct locations, near New York City and near San Francisco.

3. Ask students to quickly write down the answers to the following questions.

"What is the birthdate of <u>each</u> member of your family?" (including grandparents, uncles, aunts)

"Who lives in the third house from the corner two blocks to the north of where you live?"

After only a minute or so, ask how many have answered both questions successfully. Tell them that those that have failed the quiz will be put back one grade.

4. Explain to students that this was a simulation and that of course the exercise has no impact on their grade placement. However, these are the kinds of questions asked of detainees during intensive interrogation on Angel Island between 1910-1940. Explain that most detainees were sponsored by relatives and called "paper sons." They had to produce papers from China to prove that they were sons of Chinese already in the United States. (Note that Chinese women were barred from entering the United States unless their husbands were from the merchant class — thus the Chinese community in the U.S. was largely a bachelor society consisting of single men or married men living without their spouses.) If they could not answer the questions during interrogation, even for reasons such as nervousness or their inability to understand English, they were detained and deported. Many men spent years there and some eventually committed suicide. Ask students: How do you think the detainees felt when being asked questions like the ones I just asked you? (Repeat the questions if needed for emphasis.)

5. Pass out the poetry to the students and explain that they are translations of poems carved or painted onto the walls of buildings on Angel Island by detainees as they waited to be either deported from or admitted to the United States. Ask them to read the poetry and consider the feelings of the men who wrote them. Do you think the feelings were justified? Why or why not?

IN THE WALLS OF ANGEL ISLAND

The poems on this page were carved in the walls of Angel Island by detainees. The conditions on the Island are described by a Chinese immigrant: "I had nothing to do there. During the day, we stared at the scenery beyond the barbed wires — the sea and sky and clouds that were separated from us. Besides listening to the birds outside the fence, we could listen to records and talk to old-timers in the barracks. Some, due to faulty responses during the interrogation and lengthy appeal procedures, had been there for years. They poured out their sorrow unceasingly... A few committed suicide in the detention barracks... It was indeed a most humiliating imprisonment."

▶ ▶ ▶ ▶ ▶ ▶ ▶ ▶

When I began reflecting, I became sad and composed a poem.

It was because my family was poor that I left for the country of the flowery flag.

I only hoped that when I arrived, it would be easy to go ashore.

Who was to know the barbarians would change the regulations?

They stab the ear to test the blood and in addition, they examine the excrement.

If there is even a shadow of hookworms, one must be transferred to undergo a cure.

They took several dozen foreign dollars. Imprisoned in this hospital, I was miserable with grief and sorrow.

I do not know when I will be cured.

If one day I can escape and rise to my aspirations, I will leave this place once and for all and not be dependent on her.

To avoid humiliation and oppression by the devils,

My fellow villagers seeing this should take heed and remember,

I write my wild words to let those after me know.

▶ ▶ ▶ ▶ ▶ ▶ ▶ ▶

Instead of remaining a citizen of China, I willingly became an ox.

I intended to come to America to earn a living.

The Western-styled buildings are lofty; but I have not the luck to live in them.

How was anyone to know that my dwelling place would be a prison?

▶ ▶ ▶ ▶ ▶ ▶ ▶ ▶

America has power, but not justice.

In prison, we were victimized as if we were guilty.

Given no opportunity to explain, it was really brutal,

I bow my head in reflection, but there is nothing I can do.

▶ ▶ ▶ ▶ ▶ ▶ ▶ ▶

PARADISE AND THE POLITICS OF TOURIST HAWAI'I

BY WAYNE AU

Almost everyone on the continental United States has some preconceived notion of what Hawai'i [1] looks like. In particular, people here maintain an idea of Hawai'i that matches the propaganda that the tourist industry churns out in endless amounts: *hula*, surfing, palm trees, sun, fun, beautiful women, friendly natives, and paradise.

In *Hawai'i Recalls: Selling Romance to America* the author briefly discusses the history of America's images of Hawai'i:

During this time — from about 1910 up through the 1950's — an imaginary version of Hawaii was fabricated by the businesses that really needed to make the rest of the country and the world aware of the islands: the steamship companies and airlines, the tour guide and car rental firms, and even the pineapple growers and aloha wear manufacturers... They were selling romance... (Brown, 1982)

I use this quote to re-frame our thinking about tourist Hawai'i a little differently. Brown points out that this myth of Hawai'i is not only historically based in the economics of capitalistic tourism, but it was also a *consciously* propagated lie in an attempt to lure people to spend money. It was not inevitable that the Hawaiian Islands were to be exploited by tourism, nor is tourism the natural outcome of Native Hawaiian culture. Tourist Hawai'i, the Hawai'i that students know, is a fantasy, a fabrication, a neatly wrapped gift, made perfectly for the carefree uses that tourism advocates.

This lesson is aimed at using this nearly universal image of Hawai'i as an entry point into studying Hawai'i in general. Mainly, the focus here is to do some critical reading and deconstruction of tourist brochures — the number one form of marketing Hawai'i as paradise to would-be tourists. Students will explore questions like: Who is supposed to be coming to Hawai'i? Who is there for entertainment? How much is fake? What are the purposes of tourism and their brochures? What are the long term effects of tourism?

OBJECTIVES

▸ To introduce students to Hawai'i and the political, cultural, and economic effects of tourism.

▸ To help students develop a better understanding of their own views of the Hawaiian Islands and Hawaiian Culture, in particular how they are shaped and formed through tourism and tourist advertising.

MATERIALS NEEDED

▸ Tourist brochures. These should be available, for free and in large quantities from any travel agency. Preferably enough for each student.

▸ Handout: "What the Tour Guides Tell Us"

▸ Handout: "From A Native Daughter: Colonialism & Sovereignty In Hawai'i"

SUGGESTED PROCEDURE

1. Write the word "Hawai'i" on the board, and ask the class what images, sights, smells, sounds, etc. come to mind. As a large group, brainstorm on our ideas and conceptions of "Hawai'i." Compile a class list on the board. In the event that someone in the class is from Hawai'i, review the lesson with them in advance and have them observe what their peers have to say about their former home.

2. Ask the students to get in groups of four or five. Pass out student handout: "What The Tour Guides Tell Us" and go over it with the class. Give each group a few tourist brochures — enough for one for each person if possible. The best brochures are those with lots of pictures of people and landscapes. The students' job is to examine their brochures as a group and analyze them in terms of Hawai'i's history, the culture of native Hawai'ins and other issues related to tourism. They should provide information for each of the squares in Column One of the chart based on what is stated in the brochures. This should take them to the end of the period, and possibly into the next day.

3. For homework, provide the following assignment: "Using only the information in the brochures, write a profile of "Tourist Hawai'i." Include the climate, ge-

ography, architecture, plants, and animals. Describe the people including dress, race, gender and temperament. Are they all happy? Do they have a care in the world? What do they look like? Describe their culture. What do people like to do there? What do they eat? Write about the Hawai'i that the brochure has defined for you. Feel free to get creative with your writing, use poetry, prose, fiction, and/or fact, but make sure you base most of it on the information provided by the brochures."

4. After they have finished Column One of their charts and the writing assignment, convene for a group discussion. Ask them what they learned. Have the class share their descriptions of "Tourist Hawai'i."

5. Based on this information begin a class discussion. The following questions are provided as a guideline:

▶ How is Hawai'i depicted?

▶ What does the land look like?

▶ Who are these brochures supposed to sell Hawai'i to?

▶ Whose point of view of Hawai'i is represented in the brochures?

▶ Who and what is being sold as an attraction?

▶ How are Pacific Islanders depicted in your brochures?

▶ What kind of definition of Hawai'i do the brochures provide us with?

6. Hand out the excerpts of *From A Native Daughter* by Haunani-Kay Trask. Have them read the article, either for homework or in class. Before they begin, make sure students are familiar with the following words in the reading.

Colonization: When one country or nation forcibly takes over another. Colonization has cultural, political, economic, and mental aspects.

De-Colonization: The effort of the colonized to undo colonization and its effects.

Propaganda: Publicity intended to spread information in order to persuade or convince.

Complicitous: Contributing to or allowing wrongdoing.

Collaborationist: Someone who works together with someone else.

Cosmogonic: Theory of the creation of the universe.

Ideological: The ideas that form the basis of a political, religious or economic theory.

Commercialization: Taking something and making it into a packaged, sellable product with disregard to truth or history of the product.

Indigenous: Native to a region.

Dispossess: To deprive of possession, to take away.

7. Back in their small groups, have students fill in Column Two of their charts.

8. In the large group, have them discuss how the columns compare. In what ways are they similar (if any)? How do they differ? Which do they believe and why? Why are the two perspectives so different? Who benefits from the perspective presented in the brochures? Who loses?

9. As a closing activity, students should write a letter to their local travel agency, airline, or travel section from a local paper that compares what they found in the tourist literature/brochures with what they learned from the article by Trask. Their letters should include how they think Hawai'i should be portrayed in promotional literature, if at all.

Wayne Wah Kwai Au is a humanities teacher at Middle College High School, an alternative public school in Seattle, Washington. Aside from teaching, he writes on questions of radical pedagogy, Hawai'i and Hip Hop in urban classrooms. E-mail: WAU@CKS.SSD.K12.WA.US

NOTES

1. I use "Hawai'i" instead of "Hawaii" because it reflects a more culturally and linguistically correct spelling. The (') represents the guttural stop commonly used in the Hawaiian language.

SOURCES

Brown, D. 1982. *Hawaii recalls: Selling romance to America: Nostalgic images of the Hawaiian islands, 1910 - 1950.* Honolulu: Editions Limited.

Trask, H. 1993. *From a native daughter.* Monroe, Maine: Common Courage Press.

WHAT THE TOUR GUIDES TELL US
TOUR GUIDES VS. TRASK

Using the following chart as a guide, compare the Hawai'i described by the tourist brochures with the Hawai'i described in Trask's article.

CATEGORY	COLUMN 1: TOUR GUIDES	COLUMN 2: TRASK
HISTORY OF HAWAI'I		
NATIVE HAWAIIAN CULTURE		
HAWAI'I'S ENVIRONMENT		
TOURIST LIFESTYLE		
TOURIST ECONOMICS		
POLITICS OF TOURISM		

FROM A NATIVE DAUGHTER: COLONIALISM & SOVEREIGNTY IN HAWAI'I

BY HAUNANI-KAY TRASK

I am certain that most, if not all, Americans have heard of Hawai'i and have wished, at some time in their lives, to visit my Native land. But I doubt that the history of how Hawai'i came to be territorially incorporated, and economically, politically, and culturally subordinated to the United States is known to most Americans. Nor is it common knowledge that Hawaiians have been struggling for over twenty years to achieve a land base and some form of political sovereignty on the same level as American Indians. Finally, I would imagine that most Americans could not place Hawai'i or any other Pacific island on a map of the Pacific. But despite all of this appalling ignorance, five million Americans will vacation in my homeland this year *and* the next, and so on into the foreseeable capitalist future.

Just five hours away by plane from California, Hawai'i is a thousand light years away in fantasy. Mostly a state of mind, Hawai'i is the image of escape from the rawness and violence of daily American life. Hawai'i — the word, the vision, the sound in the mind — is the fragrance and feel of soft kindness. Above all, Hawai'i is "she," the Western image of the Native "female" in her magical allure. And if luck prevails, some of "her" will rub off on you, the visitor.

The attraction of Hawai'i is stimulated by slick Hollywood movies, saccharine Andy Williams music, and the constant psychological deprivations of maniacal American life. Tourists flock to my Native land for escape, but they are escaping into a state of mind while participating in the destruction of a host people in a Native place.

HISTORY

Before there existed an England, an English language, or an Anglo-Saxon people, our Native culture was forming. And is was as antithetical to the European developments of Christianity, capitalism and predatory individualism as any society could have been.

The economy of pre-*haole* Hawai'i depended primarily on a balanced use of the products of the land and sea[1] ...The *'ohana* (family) was the core economic unit in Hawaiian society.

As in most indigenous societies, there was no money, no idea of financial profit from exchange... In other words, there was no basis for economic exploitation in pre-*haole* Hawai'i.

Exchange between *'ohana* who lived near the sea with *'ohana* who lived inland constituted the economic life of the communities which densely populated the Hawaiian islands... As historian Marion Kelly has written, "Under the Hawaiian system of land-use rights, the people living in each *ahupua'a* [land area] had access to all the necessities of life," thus establishing an independence founded upon the availability of "forest land, taro and sweet potato areas, and fishing grounds."[2]

The genius of the mutually beneficial political system of pre-*haole* Hawai'i was simply that an interdependence was created whereby the *maka'ainana* [people of the land] were free to move with their *'ohana* to live under an *ali'i* [chiefs] of their choosing, while the *ali'i* increased their status and material prosperity by having more people living within their *moku* or domain. The result was an incentive for the society's leaders to provide for all their constituent's well-being and contentment. To fail to do so meant the loss of status for the *ali'i*.

...My people believed that all living things had spirit and, indeed, consciousness, and that gods were many and not singular. Since the land was an ancestor, no living thing could be foreign. The cosmos, like the natural world, was a universe of familial relations. And human beings were but on constituent link in the larger family...Nature was not objectified but personified, resulting in an extraordinary respect for the life of the sea, the heavens, and the earth. Our poetry and dance reveal this great depth of sensual feeling — of love — for the beautiful world we inhabited.

When Captain James Cook stumbled upon this interdependent and wise society in 1778, he brought an entirely foreign system into the lives of my ancestors... He brought capitalism, Western political ideas, and Christianity. Most destructive of all, he brought diseases that ravaged my people until we were but a remnant of what we had been on contact with his crew.

In less than a hundred years after Cook's arrival, my people had been dispossessed of our religion, our moral order, our form of chiefly government, many of our cultural practices, and our lands and waters. Diseases, from syphilis and gonorrhea to tuberculosis, small pox, measles, leprosy and typhoid fever killed Hawaiians by the hundreds of thousands, reducing our Native population (from an estimated one million at contact) to less than 40,000 by 1890. [3]

In [1893], the "missionary gang" of White planters and businessmen plotted with the American Minister to Hawai'i, John L. Stevens, to overthrow the lawful Native government of our last ruling *ali'i,* [Queen] Lili'uokalani.

As they had rehearsed so many times before, the *haole* businessmen and their foreign supporters immediately organized themselves as a "Committee of Safety" to create a new, all-White regime and to seek immediate military help from Minister Stevens. Agreeing to land the Marines and to recognize the *haole* "Provisional Government," Stevens played out his imperialist role.

Confronted by the American-recognized provisional government, and facing an occupying U.S. military force across from her palace, Lili'uokalani ceded her authority — not to the provisional government but to the United States — on January 17, 1893.

As a result of these actions, Hawaiians became a conquered people, our lands and culture subordinated to another nation. Made to feel and survive as inferiors when our sovereignty as a nation was forcibly ended, we were rendered politically and economically powerless by the turn of the century...

Since 1970, Tolelo Hawai'i, or the Hawaiian language has undergone a tremendous revival, including the rise of language immersion schools. The State of Hawai'i now has two official languages, Hawaiian and English, and the call for Hawaiian language speakers and teachers grows louder by the day. [4]

Along with the flowering of Hawaiian language has come a flowering of Hawaiian dance, especially in its ancient form, called *hula kahiko.* Dance academics known as *halau,* have proliferated throughout Hawai'i as have *kumu hula,* or dance masters, and formal competitions where all-night presentations continue for three or four days to throngs of appreciative listeners. Indeed, among Pacific Islanders, Hawaiian dance is considered one of the finest Polynesian art forms today.

[Nevertheless] Hawaiians continue to suffer the effects of *haole* colonization. Under foreign control, we have been overrun by settlers: missionaries and capitalists (often the same people), adventurers and, of course, hordes of tourists.

In Hawai'i, the destruction of our land and the prostitution of our culture is planned and executed by multinational corporations (both foreign-based and Hawai'i-based), by huge landowners (like the missionary-descended Castle and Cook — of Dole Pineapple fame — and others) and by collaborationist state and county governments. The ideological gloss that claims tourism to be our economic savior and the "natural" result of Hawaiian culture is manufactured by ad agencies (like the state supported Hawai'i Visitor's Bureau) and tour companies (many of which are owned by airlines), and spewed out to the public through complicitous cultural engines like film, television and radio, and the daily newspapers. As for the local labor unions, both rank and file and management clamor for more tourists while the construction industry lobbies incessantly for larger resorts.

Despite our similarities with other major tourist destinations, the statistical picture of the effects of corporate tourism in Hawai'i is shocking:

Fact: Over thirty years ago, at statehood, Hawai'i residents outnumbered tourists by more than 2 to 1. Today, tourists outnumber residents by 6 to 1; they outnumber Native Hawaiians by 30 to 1.

Fact: According to independent economists and criminologists, "tourism has been the single most powerful factor in O'ahu's crime rate," including crimes against people and property.

Fact: Independent demographers have been pointing out for years that "tourism is the major source of population growth in Hawai'i" and that "rapid growth of the tourist industry ensures the trend toward a rapidly expanded population that receives lower per capita income."

Fact: The Bank of Hawai'i has reported that the average real incomes of Hawai'i residents grew only one percent during the period from the early seventies through the early eighties, when tourism was booming. The Census Bureau reports that personal income growth in Hawai'i during the same time was the lowest by far of any of the 50 American states.

Fact: Ground water supplies on O'ahu will be insufficient to meet the needs of residents and tourists by the year 2000...

Fact: More plants and animals from Hawai'i are now extinct or on the endangered species list than in the rest of the United States.

Fact: More than 20,500 families are on the Hawaiian trust lands' list, waiting for housing or pastoral lots.

Fact: The median cost of a home on the most populated island of O'ahu is $450,000.

Fact: Hawai'i has by far the worst ratio of average family income to average housing costs in the country. This explains why families spend nearly 52 percent of their gross income for housing costs.

Fact: Nearly one-fifth of Hawai'i's resident population is classified as near-homeless, that is, those for whom any mishap results in immediate on-the-street homelessness.

These kinds of random statistics render a very bleak picture, not at all what the posters and jingoistic tourist promoters would have you believe about Hawai'i.

...[T]he commercialization of Hawaiian culture proceeds with calls for more sensitive marketing of our Native values and practices. After all, a prostitute is only as good as her income producing talents. These talents, in Hawaiian terms, are the *hula;* the generosity, or *aloha*, of our people; the *u'i* or youthful beauty of our women and men; and the continuing allure of our lands and waters, that is, of our place, Hawai'i.

The point, of course, is that everything in Hawai'i can be yours, that is, you the tourist, non-Native, the visitor. The place, the people, the culture, even our identity as a "Native" people is for sale. Thus, the magazine, like the airline that prints it, is called Aloha. The use of this word in a capitalist context is so far removed from any Hawaiian cultural sense that it is, literally, meaningless.

Thus, Hawai'i, like a lovely woman, is there for the taking. Hawaiians, meanwhile, have little choice in all this. We can fill up the unemployment lines, enter the military, work in the tourist industry, or leave Hawai'i. Increasingly, Hawaiians are leaving, not by choice but out of economic necessity.

...Now that you have heard a Native view, let me just leave this thought behind. If you are thinking of visiting my homeland, please don't. We don't want or need any more tourists, and we certainly don't like them. If you want to help our cause, pass this message on to your friends.

Haunani-Kay Trask is the head of the Center for Hawaiian studies at the University of Hawai'i, Manoa campus. She has been published widely for both her poetry and prose, and as a Native Hawaiian activist, she has been on the forefront of the fight for Native Hawaiian sovereignty and justice.

Excerpted and reprinted from From a Native Daughter: Colonialism and Sovereignty in Hawai'i *by Haunani-Kay Trask (Common Courage Press.) This book is currently out of print. Request a copy from your local library. Other fine books are available from Common Courage, PO Box 702, Monroe, ME 04951.*

Notes

1. The word *haole* means White foreigner in Hawaiian. "Prehaole" refers to the period before contact with the White foreign world in 1778.

2. Marion Kelly, *Majestic Ka'u* (Honolulu: Bishop Museum Press, 1980), p. vii.

3. See David Stannard, "Disease and Infertility: A New Look at the Demographic Collapse of Native Populations in the Wake of Western Contact," *Journal of American Studies,* 24 (1990) 3, 325-350.

4. See Larry Kimura, "Native Hawaiian Culture", in *Native Hawaiians Study Commission Report*, Vol. 1, p. 173-197.

MATHEMATICS

Exploring Economic Inequities

BY JAN M. GOODMAN

Skills

Interpretation of graphs, cooperative problem-solving, integration of mathematical and social studies.

Grades

4-9

Materials

▸ White paper
▸ Overhead copies of graphs
▸ A dollar bill
▸ Seventy cents in coins
▸ Two small chalkboards or two identical squares drawn on one large chalkboard
▸ Two erasers
▸ Calculators

Description

This open-ended activity encourages students to examine salary discrimination by gender in the United States. Students interpret a series of graphs constructed from government statistics and then develop possible solutions to end this economic injustice.

Procedure

1. Ask students to watch carefully as you cover both chalkboards (or identical squares) with chalk.

2. Tell your students that you need to hire two people to clean the boards. Select a male and a female volunteer. Interview each student with the following questions.

   a. Do you know how to use an eraser?

   b. Have you ever erased a chalkboard?

   c. Would you do a good job if hired to erase the board?

3. Hire both students. Then, direct them to erase the boards. When the students have completed the task, ask the class to confirm that both boards were erased equally well.

4. Announce that it is payday! Pay the male student $1.00 and count out 70 cents in coins for the female. Ask the two students to describe their feelings at payday. When students state that the wages are unfair, explain that females earn 70 cents for every dollar earned by males in our country.

5. To support your statement, show the students Graph #1: Median Income For Full-time Workers (By Gender). Use calculators to divide $21,440 by $30,358 to prove that females earn 70% of what males earn.

6. Ask students to hypothesize why men earn more than women in our country. Accept all responses.

7. Tell the students that you have information that will shed more light on the subject. Split the class into at least two groups. Each group will analyze one of the graphs and report their findings to the class: Graph #2: Median Weekly Salaries of Females and Males in the Same Job; Graph #3: Percentages of Males and Females Employed in Various Professions.

8. To prepare for their report, ask each group to:

▸ Develop and record at least four conclusions that can be reached from their graph.

▸ Explain how their graph relates to Graph #1.

9. Have a reporter from each group present Graphs #2 and #3. The graphs should be projected on the overhead or distributed to class members. Encourage classmates to ask questions about the graphs.

10. Discuss the relationships between the graphs. Here are some points that may be raised by students:

▸ Women earn less than men because they are traditionally in lower-paying jobs.

▸ Women earn less than men because they don't get paid the same wages when they do the same jobs.

▸ Ask students to hypothesize as to whether there are similar disparities of income based on race. Have them look at Graph #4. Calculate the percentage difference for White males vs. Hispanic females. Try other combinations.

11. After the graphs have been discussed, ask groups to explore what could be done to remedy this discrimination. Here are some solutions that have been raised by students:

▸ Collect all the money in the country and redistribute it.

▸ Pass a law to have equal pay for equal work.

▸ Freeze the salaries of males or raise the salaries of women until income is equal between the sexes.

▸ Pay women to have children.

12. Encourage students to take their solutions home, share them with their family and bring feedback to school. You may also wish to invite your local representative or senator to discuss the problem and potential remedies with your class.

EXTENSIONS

Explore Graph #5 with students and discuss its implication. The table shows how income is unequally distributed in our country. For example, almost 3/4 (75%) of our country's wealth is possessed by the top two-fifths (40%) of the population. The lowest two-fifths of our country's population possesses less than 15% of the income.

Jan M. Goodman is currently the principal of Jefferson Elementary School in Berkeley, California. A longtime educator and activist, she strongly believes that schools should encourage and support students to work for social change. E-mail: Goodjan@aol.com

Reprinted by permission of the author from Goodman, Jan. 1991. "Mathematics For Social Change." ComMuniCator (Special Edition) 14-15.

■ ■ ■ ■ SOCIAL ISSUES THROUGH MATH ■ ■ ■ ■

Both articles in this section describe how math can be a powerful tool for examining social issues. Students can learn math skills as they analyze the world in which they live. Following is a list of selected resources that provide social statistics and charts for these lessons.

INTERNET

▸ The Sentencing Project. Detailed information about criminal justice and sentencing issues. On their web-site one can access current data about the United States' high rate of incarceration as compared to the rest of the world, the demographics of who is incarcerated in this country which reveals the racism in the justice system and pending legislation. *www.sentencingproject.org*

▸ *Children's Defense Fund.* News and links to other sites with information about all aspects of the well-being of children including health, education, and housing. *www.childrensdefense.org*

▸ *Dollars and Sense.* As the name implies, this organization provides information to help the lay person make sense of the economy. See address in Resource Guide: Journals. *www.igc.apc.org/dollars/*

▸ *Campaign for Labor Rights.* Information about campaigns to improve working conditions in major industries. Data on workers' wages, cost of living and company profits. *www.summersault.com/~agj/clr/*

BOOKS

The publications below have a wealth of data and charts. Additional information is available about each book in the Resource Guide.

▸ *New Field Guide to the Economy* (New Press)

▸ *Social Stratification Book and Poster* (New Press)

▸ *Mythbuster: Current Issues Education Packet* (AFSC)

▸ *The War on the Poor* (New Press)

▸ *Looking Forward: Participatory Economics for the Twenty-First Century* (South End Press)

GRAPH #1: MEDIAN ANNUAL EARNINGS FOR FULL TIME WORKERS, BY GENDER (1997)

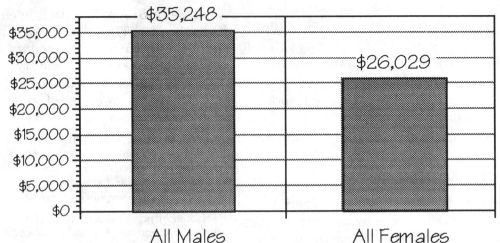

GRAPH #4: MEDIAN ANNUAL EARNINGS FOR FULL TIME WORKERS, BY GENDER, RACE AND ETHNIC ORIGIN (1997)

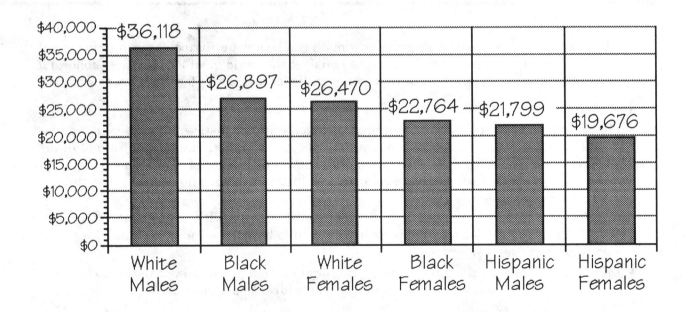

Note: The terms "Black" and "Hispanic" are classifications used by the Bureau of the Census. There are currently other terms in use to describe people of these origins, i.e., "African American," "Latino/Latina" and "Latin American." The Bureau classifies "Hispanics" as people with origins in Mexico; Puerto Rico; Cuba; Central or South American nations; and other Spanish-speaking countries, i.e., Spain.

Fact Source: U.S. Bureau of the Census, Current Population Reports, P60-200, "Money Income in the United States, 1997," Table #7, Washington, D.C., 1998. Graphs by Jan M. Goodman, copyright 1998.

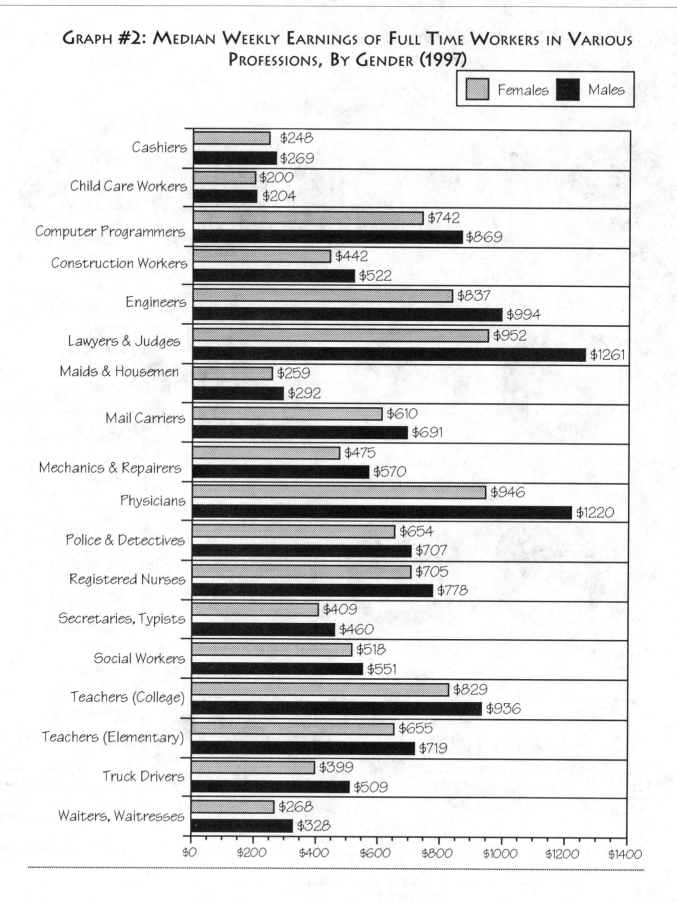

GRAPH #2: MEDIAN WEEKLY EARNINGS OF FULL TIME WORKERS IN VARIOUS PROFESSIONS, BY GENDER (1997)

Females ☐   Males ■

Profession	Females	Males
Cashiers	$248	$269
Child Care Workers	$200	$204
Computer Programmers	$742	$869
Construction Workers	$442	$522
Engineers	$837	$994
Lawyers & Judges	$952	$1261
Maids & Housemen	$259	$292
Mail Carriers	$610	$691
Mechanics & Repairers	$475	$570
Physicians	$946	$1220
Police & Detectives	$654	$707
Registered Nurses	$705	$778
Secretaries, Typists	$409	$460
Social Workers	$518	$551
Teachers (College)	$829	$936
Teachers (Elementary)	$655	$719
Truck Drivers	$399	$509
Waiters, Waitresses	$268	$328

$0 $200 $400 $600 $800 $1000 $1200 $1400

Fact Source: U.S. Department of Labor, Bureau of Labor Statistics, "Employment & Earnings," Volume 45, #1, Table #39, January, 1998. Graph by Jan M. Goodman, copyright 1998.

GRAPH #3: PERCENTAGE OF MALE AND FEMALE WORKERS EMPLOYED FULLTIME IN VARIOUS PROFESSIONS (1997)

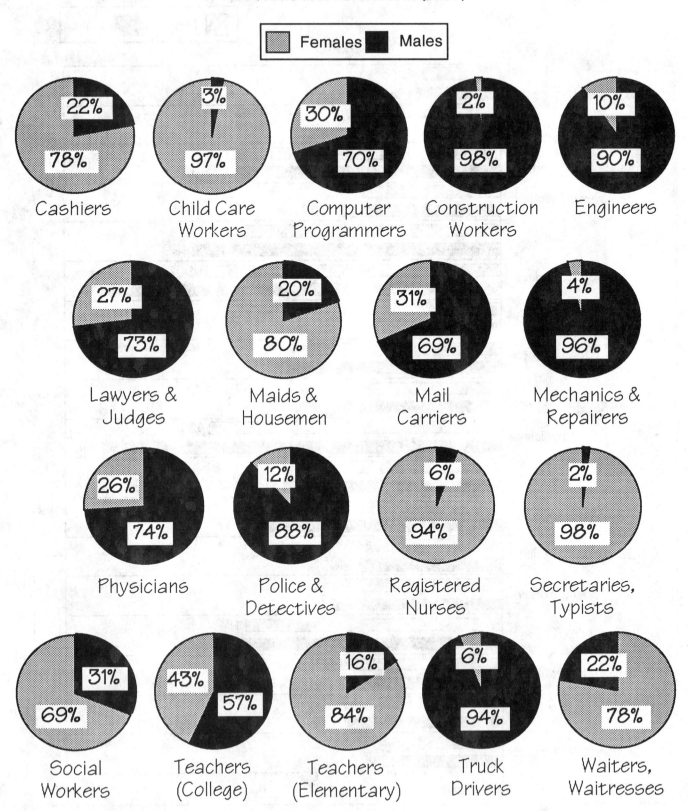

Females | Males

Cashiers
22%
78%

Child Care Workers
3%
97%

Computer Programmers
30%
70%

Construction Workers
2%
98%

Engineers
10%
90%

Lawyers & Judges
27%
73%

Maids & Housemen
20%
80%

Mail Carriers
31%
69%

Mechanics & Repairers
4%
96%

Physicians
26%
74%

Police & Detectives
12%
88%

Registered Nurses
6%
94%

Secretaries, Typists
2%
98%

Social Workers
31%
69%

Teachers (College)
43%
57%

Teachers (Elementary)
16%
84%

Truck Drivers
6%
94%

Waiters, Waitresses
22%
78%

Fact Source: U.S. Department of Labor, Bureau of Labor Statistics, "Employment & Earnings," Volume 45, #1, Table #11, January, 1998. Graph by Jan M. Goodman, copyright 1998.

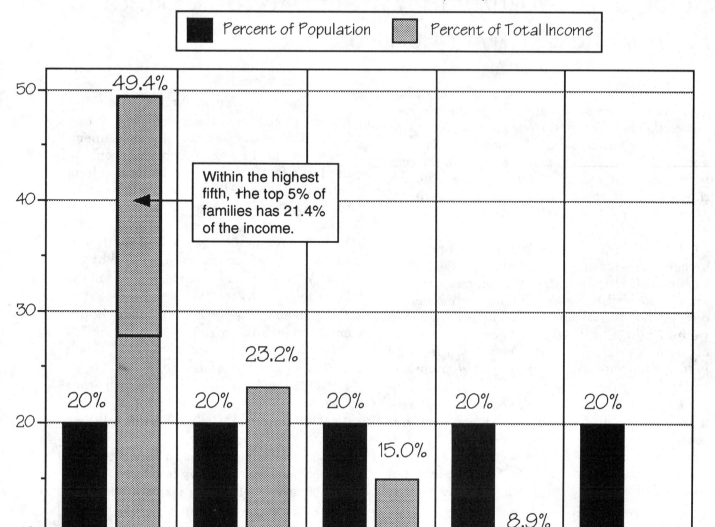

GRAPH #5: SHARE OF AGGREGATE INCOME RECEIVED BY HOUSEHOLDS IN THE UNITED STATES (1997)

Legend:
- ■ Percent of Population
- ▨ Percent of Total Income

Within the highest fifth, the top 5% of families has 21.4% of the income.

	Highest Fifth	Fourth Fifth	Third Fifth	Second Fifth	Lowest Fifth
Percent of Population	20%	20%	20%	20%	20%
Percent of Total Income	49.4%	23.2%	15.0%	8.9%	3.6%

NOTES: Aggregate income includes money received from the following sources during the calendar year: 1) earnings from all jobs; 2) unemployment and worker's compensation; 3) Social Security; 4) Supplemental Security income; 5) public assistance; 6) veteran's payment; 7) survivor benefits; 8) disability benefits; 9) pension or retirment income; 10) interest; 11) dividends; 12) rents, royalties, and estates and trusts; 13) alimony; 14) child support; 15) educational assistance; 16) financial assistance from outside of the household, and other periodic income.

Fact Source: U.S. Bureau of the Census, Current Population Reports, P60-200, "Money Income in the United States: 1997," Table # B-3, Washington, D.C., 1998. Graph by Jan M. Goodman, copyright 1998.

READING THE WORLD WITH MATH: GOALS FOR A CRITICAL MATHEMATICAL LITERACY CURRICULUM

Marilyn Frankenstein suggests ways that teachers can introduce math as a tool to interpret and challenge inequities in our society. Her teaching methods also make math more accessible and applicable because the math is learned in the context of real-life, meaningful experiences. This article is particularly useful for teachers who are creating an interdisciplinary math and social studies curriculum.

Professor Frankenstein's examples are based on her work teaching at the College of Public and Community Service, UMass/Boston. Her students are primarily working-class adults who did not receive adequate mathematics instruction when they were in high school. Many of them were tracked out of college preparation. Therefore, the ideas presented in this article can be applied to the secondary classroom.

For a more detailed description as well as a more theoretical discussion of the concepts presented in this paper, please refer to the publications listed in the reference section by Frankenstein and those coauthored by Frankenstein and Arthur Powell.

BY MARILYN FRANKENSTEIN

When my students examine data and questions such as the ones shown on this page (in the box) they are introduced to the four goals of the criticalmathematical literacy curriculum.

1. Understanding the mathematics.

2. Understanding the mathematics of political knowledge.

3. Understanding the politics of mathematical knowledge.

4. Understanding the politics of knowledge.

Clearly, calculating the various percentages for the unemployment rate requires goal number one, an understanding of mathematics. Criticalmathematical literacy goes beyond this to include the other three goals mentioned above. The mathematics of political knowledge is illustrated here by reflecting on how

---

Example: Unemployment Rate

In the United States, the unemployment rate is defined as the number of people unemployed, divided by the number of people in the labor force. Here are some figures from December 1994. (All numbers in thousands, rounded off to the nearest hundred thousand.)

• In your opinion, which of these groups should be considered unemployed? Why?

• Which should be considered part of the labor force? Why?

• Given your selections, calculate the unemployment rate in 1994.

1. 101,400: Employed full-time

2. 19,000: Employed part-time, want part-time work

3. 4,000: Employed part-time, want full-time work

4. 5,600: Not employed, looked for work in last month, not on temporary layoff

5. 1,100: Not employed, on temporary layoff

6. 400: Not employed, want a job now, looked for work in last year, stopped looking because discouraged about prospects of finding work

7. 1,400: Not employed, want a job now, looked for work in last year, stopped looking for other reasons

8. 3,800: Not employed, want a job now, have not looked for work in the last year

9. 60,700: Not employed, don't want a job now (adults)

For discussion: The U.S. official definition counts 4 and 5 as unemployed and 1 through 5 as part of the labor force, giving an unemployment rate of 5.1%. If we count 4 through 8 plus half of 3 as unemployed, the rate would be 9.3%. Further, in 1994 the Bureau of Labor Statistics stopped issuing its U-7 rate, a measure which included categories 2 and 3 and 6 through 8, so now researchers will not be able to determine "alternative" unemployment rates (Saunders, 1994).[1]

the unemployment data deepens our understanding of the situation of working people in the United States. The politics of mathematical knowledge involves the choice of who counts as unemployed. In class, I emphasize that once we decide which categories make up the numerator (number of unemployed) and the denominator (total labor force), changing that fraction to a decimal fraction and then to a percent does not involve political struggle — that involves understanding the mathematics. But, the decision of who counts where does involve political struggle — so the unemployment rate is not a neutral description of the situation of working people in the United States. And, this discussion generalizes to a consideration of the politics of all knowledge.

In this article, I will develop the meaning of each of these goals, focusing on illustrations of how to realize them in their interconnected complexity. Underlying all these ideas is my belief that the development of self-confidence is a prerequisite for all learning, and that self-confidence develops from grappling with complex material and from understanding the politics of knowledge.

GOAL #1: UNDERSTANDING THE MATHEMATICS

Almost all my students know how to do basic addition, subtraction, multiplication and division, although many would have trouble multiplying decimal fractions, adding fractions or doing long division. All can pronounce the words, but many have trouble succinctly expressing the main idea of a reading. Almost all have trouble with basic math word problems. Most have internalized negative self-images about their knowledge and ability in mathematics. In my beginning lessons I have students read excerpts where the main idea is supported by numerical details and where the politics of mathematical knowledge is brought to the fore. Then the curriculum moves on to the development of the Hindu-Arabic place-value numeral system, the meaning of numbers, and the meaning of the operations.

I start lessons with a graph, chart, or short reading which requires knowledge of the math skill scheduled for that day. When the discussion runs into a question about a math skill, I stop and teach that skill. This is a non-linear way of learning basic numeracy because questions often arise that involve future math topics. I handle this by *previewing*. The scheduled topic is *formally* taught. Other topics are also discussed so that students' immediate questions are answered and so that when the *formal* time

comes for them in the syllabus, students will already have some familiarity with them. For example, if we are studying the meaning of fractions and find that in 1985, 2/100 of the Senate were women, we usually *preview* how to change this fraction to a percent. We also discuss how no learning is linear and how all of us are continually *reviewing, recreating*, as well as *previewing* in the ongoing process of making meaning. Further, there are other aspects about learning which greatly strengthen students' understandings of mathematics:

(a) breaking down the dichotomy between learning and teaching mathematics;

(b) considering the interactions of culture and the development of mathematical knowledge; and

(c) studying even the simplest of mathematical topics through deep and complicated questions.

These are explained in more detail below.

(a) **Breaking Down the Dichotomy between Learning and Teaching Mathematics.** When students teach, rather than explain, they learn more mathematics, and they also learn about teaching. They are then empowered to proceed to learn more mathematics. As humanistic, politically concerned educators, we often talk about what we learn from our students when we teach. Peggy McIntosh (1990) goes so far as to define teaching as "the development of self through the development of others." Certainly when we teach we learn about learning. I also introduce research on math education so that students can analyze for themselves why they did not previously learn mathematics. I argue that learning develops through teaching and through reflecting on teaching and learning. So, students' mathematical understandings are deepened when they learn about mathematics teaching as they learn mathematics. Underlying this argument is Paulo Freire's concept that learning and teaching are part of the same process, and are different moments in the cycle of gaining existing knowledge, re-creating that knowledge and producing new knowledge (Freire, 1982).

Students gain greater control over mathematics problem-solving when, in addition to evaluating their own work, they can create their own problems. When students can understand what questions it makes sense to ask from given numerical information, and can identify decisions that are involved in creating different kinds of problems, they can more easily solve problems others create. Further, criticalmathematical literacy involves both interpreting and critically analyzing other people's use of numbers in arguments. To do the latter you need practice in determining what kinds of questions can be asked and answered from the available numerical data, and what kinds of situations can be clarified through numerical data. Freire's concept of problem-posing education emphasizes that problems with neat, pared down data and clear-cut solutions give a false picture of how mathematics can help us "read the world." Real life is messy, with many problems intersecting and interacting. Real life poses problems whose solutions require dialogue and collective action. Traditional problem-solving curricula isolate and simplify particular aspects of reality in order to give students practice in techniques. Freirian problem-posing is intended to reveal the inter-connections and complexities of real-life situations where "often, problems are not solved, only a better understanding of their nature may be possible" (Connolly, 1981). A classroom application of this idea is to have students create their own reviews and tests. In this way they learn to grapple with mathematics pedagogy issues such as: what are the key concepts and topics to include on a review of a particular curriculum unit? What are clear, fair and challenging questions to ask in order to evaluate understanding of those concepts and topics?

(b) **Considering the Interactions of Culture and the Development of Mathematical Knowledge.** This aspect is best described with the following example.

Example: When we are learning the algorithm for comparing the size of numbers, I ask students to think about how culture interacts with mathematical knowledge in the following situation:

> Steve Lerman (1993) was working with two 5-year-olds in a London classroom. He recounts how they "were happy to compare two objects put in front of them and tell me why they had chosen the one they had [as bigger]. However, when I allocated the multilinks to them (the girl had 8 and the boy had 5) to make a tower...and I asked them who had the taller one, the girl answered correctly but the boy insisted that he did. Up to this point the boy had been putting the objects together and comparing them. He would not do so on this occasion and when I asked him how we could find out whose tower was the taller he became very angry. I asked him why he thought that his tower was taller and he just replied 'Because IT IS!' He would go no further than this and seemed to be almost on the verge of tears."

At first students try to explain the boy's answer by hypothesizing that each of the girl's links was smaller than each of the boy's or that she built a wider, shorter tower. But after reading the information, they see that this could not be the case, since the girl's answer was correct. We speculate about how the culture of sexism — that boys always do better or have more than girls — blocked the knowledge of comparing sizes that the boy clearly understood in a different situation.

(c) **Studying Mathematical Topics through Deep and Complicated Questions**. Most educational materials and learning environments in the United States, especially those labeled as "developmental" or "remedial," consist of very superficial, easy work. They involve rote or formulaic problem-solving experiences. Students get trained to think about successful learning as getting high marks on school or standardized tests. I argue that this is a major reason that what is learned is not retained and not used. Further, making the curriculum more complicated, where each problem contains a variety of learning experiences, teaches in the non-linear, holistic way in which knowledge is developed in context. This way of teaching leads to a more clear understanding of the subject matter.

Example: In the text below, Sklar and Sleicher demonstrate how numbers presented out of context can be very misleading. I ask students to read the text and discuss the calculations Sklar and Sleicher performed to get their calculation of the U.S. expenditure on the 1990 Nicaraguan election. ($17.5 million ÷ population of Nicaragua = $5 per person). This reviews their understanding of the meaning of the operations. Then I ask the students to consider the complexities of understanding the $17.5 million expenditure. This deepens their understanding of how different numerical descriptions illuminate or obscure the context of U.S. policy in Nicaragua, and how in real-life just comparing the size of the numbers, out of context, obscures understanding.

> On the basis of relative population, Holly Sklar has calculated that the $17.5 million U.S. expenditure on the Nicaraguan election is $5 per person and is equivalent to an expenditure of $1.2 billion in the United States. That's one comparison all right, but it may be more relevant to base the comparison on the effect of the expenditure on the economy or on the election, i.e. to account for the difference in per capita income, which is at least 30/1 or an equivalent election expenditure in the United States of a staggering $30 billion! Is there any doubt that such an expenditure would decisively affect a U.S. election? (Sleicher, 1990)

GOAL #2: UNDERSTANDING THE MATHEMATICS OF POLITICAL KNOWLEDGE

I argue, along with Freire (1970) and Freire and Macedo (1987), that the underlying context for critical adult education, and criticalmathematical literacy, is "to read the world." To accomplish this goal, students learn how mathematics skills and concepts can be used to understand the institutional structures of our society. This happens through:

a. understanding the different kinds of numerical descriptions of the world (such as fractions, percents, graphs) and the meaning of the sizes of numbers, and

b. using calculations to follow and verify the logic of someone's argument, to restate information, and to understand how raw data are collected and transformed into numerical descriptions of the world. The purpose underlying all the calculations is to understand better the information and the arguments and to be able to question the decisions that were involved in choosing the numbers and the operations.

Example: I ask students to create and solve some mathematics problems using the information in the following article (*In These Times*, April 29-May 5, 1992). Doing the division problems implicit in this article deepens understanding of the economic data, and shows how powerfully numerical data reveal the structure of our institutions.

Drowning by numbers

It may be lonely at the top, but it can't be boring — at least not with all that money. Last week the federal government released figures showing that the richest 1 percent of American households was worth more than the bottom 90 percent combined. And while these numbers were widely reported, we found them so shocking that we thought they were worth repeating. So here goes: In 1989 the top 1 percent of Americans (about 934,000 households) combined for a net worth of $5.7 trillion; the bottom 90 percent (about 84 million households) could only scrape together $4.8 trillion in net worth.

Example: Students practice reading a complicated graph and solving multiplication and divi-

sion problems in order to understand how particular payment structures transfer money from the poor to the rich.[2]

The Rate Watcher's Guide (Morgan, 1980) details why under declining block rate structures, low-income citizens who use electricity only for basic necessities pay the highest rates, and large users with luxuries like trash compactors, heated swimming pools or central air-conditioning pay the lowest rates. A 1972 study conducted in Michigan, for example, found that residents of a poor urban area in Detroit paid 66% more *per unit* of electricity than did wealthy residents of nearby Bloomfield Hills. Researchers concluded that "approximately $10,000,000 every year leave the city of Detroit to support the quantity discounts of suburban residents." To understand why this happens, use the graph above which illustrates a typical "declining block rate" payment structure to (a) compute the bill of a family which uses 700 kwh of electricity per month and the bill of a family which uses 1400 kwh; (b) calculate each family's average cost per kwh; (c) discuss numerically how the declining block rate structure functions and what other kinds of payment structures could be instituted. Which would you support and why?

Example: Students are asked to discuss how numbers support Helen Keller's main point and to reflect on why she sometimes uses fractions and

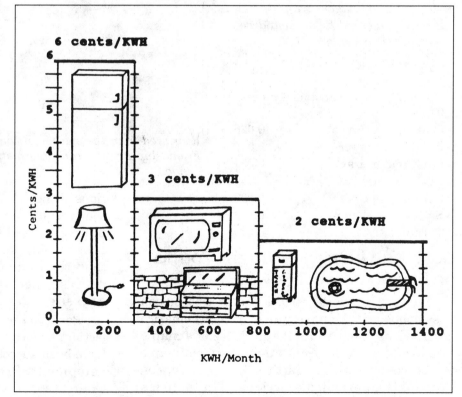

Chart reprinted with permission from the Journal of Negro Education *(Vol. 59, No. 3, 1990).*

other times uses whole numbers. Information about the politics of knowledge is included as a context in which to set her views.

Although Helen Keller was blind and deaf, she fought with her spirit and her pen. When she became an active socialist, a newspaper wrote that "her mistakes spring out of the...limits of her development." This newspaper had treated her as a hero before she was openly socialist. In 1911, Helen Keller wrote to a suffragist in England: "You ask for votes for women. What good can votes do when ten-elevenths of the land of Great Britain belongs to 200,000 people and only one-eleventh of the land belongs to the other 40,000,000 people? Have your men with their millions of votes freed themselves from this injustice?" (Zinn, 1980)

Example: Students are asked to discuss what numerical understandings they need in order to decipher the following chart. They see that a recognition of how very small these decimal fractions are, so small that watches cannot even measure the units of time, illuminates the viciousness of time-motion studies in capitalist management strategies.

Samples from time-and-motion studies, conducted by General Electric. Published in a 1960 handbook to provide office managers with standards by which clerical labor should be organized (Braverman, 1974).

Open and close
Minutes

Open side drawer of standard desk 0.014	
Open center drawer	0.026
Close side drawer	0.015
Close center drawer	0.027
Chair activity	
Get up from chair	0.039
Sit down in chair	0.033
Turn in swivel chair	0.009

GOAL #3: UNDERSTANDING THE POLITICS OF MATHEMATICAL KNOWLEDGE

Perhaps the most dramatic example of the politics involved in seemingly neutral mathematical descriptions of our world is the choice of a map to visualize that world. Any two-dimensional map of our three-dimensional Earth will, of course, contain mathematical distortions. The political struggle/choice centers around which of these distortions are acceptable to us and what other un-

derstandings of ours are distorted by these false pictures. For example, the map with which most people are familiar, the Mercator map, greatly enlarges the size of "Europe"[3] and shrinks the size of Africa. Most people do not realize that the area of what is commonly referred to as "Europe" is smaller than 20% of the area of Africa. Created in 1569, the Mercator map highly distorts land areas, but preserves compass direction, making it very helpful to navigators who sailed from Europe in the sixteenth century.

When used in textbooks and other media, combined with the general (mis)perception that size relates to various measures of so-called "significance," the Mercator map distorts popular percep-

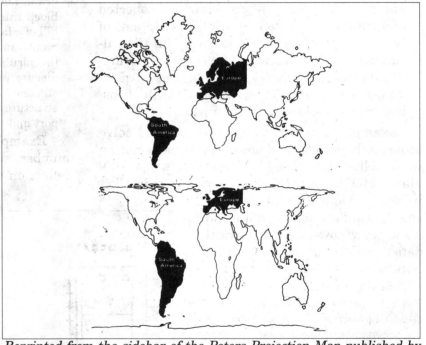

Reprinted from the sidebar of the Peters Projection Map published by Friendship Press. Order information in poster section of the Resource Guide.

tions of the relative importance of various areas of the world. For example, when a U.S. university professor asked his students to rank certain countries by size they "rated the Soviet Union larger than the continent of Africa, though in fact it is much smaller" (Kaiser, 1991), associating "power" with size.

Political struggles to change to the Peter's projection, a more accurate map in terms of land area, have been successful with the United Nations Development Program, the World Council of Churches, and some educational institutions (Kaiser, 1991). However, anecdotal evidence from many talks I've given around the world suggest that the

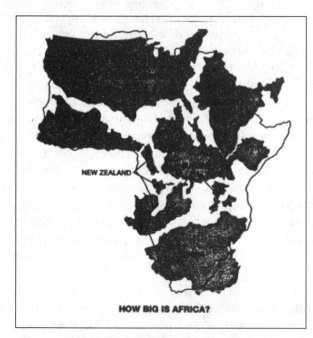

NEW ZEALAND

HOW BIG IS AFRICA?

Reprinted from the sidebar to a map of Africa published by Friendship Press. Order information in poster section of the Resource Guide.

Mercator is still widely perceived as the way the world *really* looks.

As Wood (1992) emphasizes:

The map is not an innocent witness...silently recording what would otherwise take place without it, but a committed participant, as often as not driving the very acts of identifying and naming, bounding and inventorying it pretends to no more than observe.

In a variety of situations, statistical descriptions don't simply or neutrally record what's out there. There are political struggles/choices involved in: which data are collected; which numbers represent the most accurate data; which definitions should guide how the data are counted; which methods should guide how the data are collected; which ways the data should be disaggregated; and which are the most truthful ways to describe the data to the public.

Example: Political struggle/choice over which numbers represent the most accurate data. To justify the Eurocentric argument that the Native American population could not have been so great, various "scholars" have concluded that about one million people were living in North America in 1500. Yet, other academics "argued on the basis of burial mound archeology and other evidence that the population of the Ohio River Valley alone had been [that] great," (Stiffarm & Lane, 1992) and that "a pre-contact North American Indian popu-

lation of fifteen million is perhaps the best and most accurate working number available." Admitting the latter figure would also require admitting extensive agricultural institutions, as opposed to the less reliable hunting and gathering. Cultivators of land are "primarily sedentary rather than nomadic...and residents of permanent towns rather than wandering occupants of a barren wilderness."

Example: Political struggle/choice over which definitions should guide how data are counted. In 1988, the U.S. Census Bureau introduced an "alternative poverty line," changing the figure for a family of three from $9453 to $8580, thereby preventing 3.6 million people whose family income fell between those figures from receiving food stamps, free school meals and other welfare benefits. At the same time, the Joint Economic Committee of Congress argued that "updating the assessments of household consumption needs... would almost double the poverty rate, to 24 percent" (Cockburn, 1989). Note that the U.S. poverty line is startlingly low. Various assessments of the smallest amount needed by a family of four to purchase basic necessities in 1991 was 155% of the official poverty line. "Since the [census] bureau defines the [working poor] out of poverty, the dominant image of the poor that remains is of people who are unemployed or on the welfare rolls. The real poverty line reveals the opposite: a majority of the poor among able-bodied, non-elderly heads of households normally work full-time. The total number of adults who remain poor despite normally working full-time is nearly 10 million more than double the number of adults on welfare. Two-thirds of them are high school or college-educated and half are over 33. Poverty in the U.S. is a problem of low-wage jobs far more than it is of welfare dependency, lack of education or work inexperience. Defining families who earn less than 155% of the official poverty line as poor would result in about one person in every four being considered poor in the United States." (Schwartz & Volgy, 1993)

Example: Political struggle/choice over which ways data should be disaggregated. The U.S. Government rarely collects health data broken down by social class. In 1986, when it did this for heart and cerebrovascular disease, it found enormous gaps:

"The death rate from heart disease, for example, was 2.3 times higher among unskilled blue-collar operators than among managers and professionals. By contrast, the mortality rate from heart disease in 1986 for blacks was 1.3 times higher than for whites...the way in which statistics are kept does not help to make white and black workers aware of the commonality of their predicament." (Navarro, 1991)

GOAL #4: UNDERSTANDING THE POLITICS OF KNOWLEDGE

There are many aspects of the politics of knowledge that are integrated into this curriculum. Some involve reconsidering what counts as mathematical knowledge and re-presenting an accurate picture of the contributions of all the world's peoples to the development of mathematical knowledge. Others involve how mathematical knowledge is learned in schools. Winter (1991), for example, theorizes that the problems so many encounter in understanding mathematics are not due to the discipline's "difficult abstractions," but due to the cultural *form* in which mathematics is presented. Sklar (1993), for a different aspect, cites a U.S. study that recorded the differential treatment of Black and White students in math classes.

Sixty-six student teachers were told to teach a math concept to four pupils — two White and two Black. All the pupils were of equal, average intelligence. The student-teachers were told that in each set of four, one White and one Black student was intellectually gifted, the others were labeled as average. The student teachers were monitored through a one-way mirror to see how they reinforced their students' efforts. The "superior" White pupils received two positive reinforcements for every negative one. The "average" White students received one positive reinforcement for every negative reinforcement. The "average" Black student received 1.5 negative reinforcements, while the "superior" Black students received one positive response for every 3.5 negative ones.

Discussing the above study in class brings up the math topics of ratios and forming matrix charts to visualize the data more clearly. It also involves students who are themselves learning mathematics in reflecting on topics in mathematics education. This is another example of breaking down the dichotomy between learning and teaching, a category discussed in the above section on *Understanding the Mathematics.*

And, of course, Freire (1970) theorizes about the politics of "banking education," when teachers deposit knowledge in students' empty minds.

Underlying all these issues are more general concerns I argue should form the foundation of all learning, concerns about what counts as knowledge and why. I think that one of the most significant contributions of Paulo Freire (1982) to the development of a critical literacy is the idea that:

Our task is not to teach students to think — they can already think, but to exchange our ways of thinking with each other and look together for better ways of approaching the decodification of an object.

This idea is critically important because it implies a fundamentally different set of assumptions about people, pedagogy and knowledge-creation. Because some people in the United States, for example, need to learn to write in "standard" English, *it does not follow* that they cannot express very complex analyses of social, political, economic, ethical and other issues. And many people with an excellent grasp of reading, writing and mathematics skills need to learn about the world, about philosophy, about psychology, about justice and many other areas in order to deepen their understandings.

In a non-trivial way we can learn a great deal from intellectual diversity. Most of the burning social, political, economic and ethical questions of our time remain unanswered. In the United States we live in a society of enormous wealth and we have significant hunger and homelessness; although we have engaged in medical and scientific research for scores of years, we are not any closer to changing the prognosis for most cancers. Certainly we can learn from the perspectives and philosophies of people whose knowledge has developed in a variety of intellectual and experiential conditions. Currently "the intellectual activity of those without power is always labeled non-intellectual" (Freire & Macedo, 1987). When we see this as a political situation, as part of our "regime of truth," we can realize that all people have knowledge, all people are continually creating knowledge, doing intellectual work, and all of us have a lot to learn.

Marilyn Frankenstein is one of a group of scholars and activists in the field of mathematics education from a critical perspective. She is co-founder, along with Arthur B. Powell and John Volmink, of the Criticalmathematics Educators Group (CmEG) and the author of numerous articles and books on criticalmathematics (see References below.) She is a Professor of Applied Language and Mathematics, College of Public and Community Service, University of Massachusetts-Boston, Boston, MA 02125. E-mail: frankie@ umbsky.cc.umb.edu

NOTES

1. Thanks to my friend, UMass/Lowell economist Chris Tilly, for this problem.

2. This situation has changed in Massachusetts, which now has a flat rate structure, and my reference did not contain real data for Michigan. So although the context-setting data are real, the numbers used to understand the concept of declining block rates are realistic, but not real.

3. Grossman (1994) argues that "Europe has always been a political and cultural definition. Geographically, Europe does not ex-

ist, since it is only a peninsula on the vast Eurasian continent." He goes on to discuss the history and various contradictions of geographers' attempts to "draw the eastern limits of 'western civilization' and the white race" (p. 39).

REFERENCES

Braverman, H. 1974. *Labor and monopoly capital.* New York: Monthly Review Press.

Connolly, R. 1981. "Freire, praxis, and education." In R. Mackie (Ed.) *Literacy and revolution: The pedagogy of Paulo Freire.* New York: Continuum Press.

Cockburn, A. 1989, December 11. "Calculating an end to poverty." *The Nation.*

Frankenstein, M. 1983. "Critical mathematics education: An application of Paulo Freire's Epistemology." *Journal of Education.* 165.4:315-340.

——. 1989. *Relearning mathematics: A different third r radical maths.* London: Free Association Books.

——. 1990. "Incorporating race, class, and gender issues into a critical mathematical literacy curriculum." *Journal of Negro Education.* 59.3:336-347.

——. 1994, Spring. "Understanding the politics of mathematical knowledge as an integral part of becoming critically numerate." *Radical Statistics.* 56:22-40.

——. 1995. "Equity in mathematics education: Class in the world outside the class." In W.G. Secada, E. Fennema, & L.B. Adajian, (Eds.) *New directions for equity in mathematics education.* pp. 165-190. Cambridge, UK: Cambridge University Press.

——. 1997. "Breaking down the dichotomy between teaching and learning mathematics." In Freire, P., J. Fraser, D. Macedo, et al. (Eds.) *Mentoring the mentor: a critical dialogue with Paulo Freire.* pp 59-88. New York: Peter Lang.

——. 1997. "In addition to the mathematics: Including equity issues in the curriculum." In J. Trentacosta (Ed.) *Multicultural and gender equity in the mathematics classroom: The gift of diversity.* pp 10-22. Reston , VA: National Council of Teachers of Mathematics.

Frankenstein, M., & Powell, A.B. 1989. "Empowering non-traditional college students: On social ideology and mathematics education." *Science and Nature.* 9.10:100-112.

——. 1994. "Toward liberatory mathematics: Paulo Freire's epistemology and ethnomathematics." In P. McLaren & C. Lankshear (Eds.) *Politics of liberation: Paths from Freire.* pp. 74-99. London: Routledge.

Freire, P. 1970. *Pedagogy of the oppressed.* New York: Seabury.

——. 1982 Education for critical consciousness. Unpublished Boston College course notes taken by Frankenstein, M. July 5-15.

Freire, P., & Macedo, D. 1987. *Literacy: Reading the word and the world.* South Hadley, MA: Bergen & Garvey.

Grossman, Z. 1994. "Erecting the new wall: Geopolitics and the restructuring of Europe." *Z Magazine.* 39-45.

Kaiser, W.L. 1991, May/June "New global map presents accurate views of the world." *Rethinking Schools.* 12-13.

Lerman, S. 1993. Personal communication with the author. March 26.

McIntosh, P. 1990, November 14. "Interactive phases of personal and pedagogical change." Talk at Rutgers University/Newark, NJ.

Morgan, R.E. 1980. *The rate watcher's guide.* Washington, DC: Environmental Action Foundation.

Navarro, V. 1991, April 8. "The class gap." *The Nation.* 436-437.

Orenstein, R. E. 1972. *The psychology of consciousness.* San Francisco: W. H. Freeman.

Powell, A.B., & Frankenstein, M. 1997. *Ethnomathematics: Challenging Eurocentrism in mathematics education.* Albany, NY: SUNY Press.

Saunders, B. 1994, September 26. "Number game." *The Nation.* 259.9:295-296.

Schwarz, J.E., & Volgy, T.J. 1993, February 15. "One-fourth of nation: Above the poverty line — but poor." *The Nation.* 191-192.

Sklar, H. 1993, July/August. "Young and guilty by stereotype." *Z Magazine.* 52-61.

Sleicher, C. 1990, February. "Letter to the editor." *Z Magazine.* 6.

Stiffarm, L.A., & Lane, P. Jr. 1992. "Demography of Native North America: A question of American Indian survival." In M. A. Jaimes (Ed.) *The State of Native America.* pp. 23-53. Boston: South End Press.

Winter, R. 1991. "Mathophobia, Pythagoras and roller-skating." In *Science as culture,* Vol. 10. London: Free Association Books.

Wood, D. 1992. *The power of maps.* New York: The Guilford Press.

Zinn, H. 1995. *A people's history of the United States.* New York: Harper & Row.

THE ALGEBRA PROJECT

BY LIZ HOTTEL

In 1964, Robert Moses helped to organize the Student Nonviolent Coordinating Committee (SNCC) and the voter-registration drive known as Freedom Summer. The success of these movements led to the 1965 Voting Rights Act. Eighteen years later, Moses found himself fighting another kind of institutional racism. Through involvement with his children's school in Cambridge, Massachusetts, he saw that African American students were consistently placed in below-grade level math classes. A Harvard-educated mathematician, Moses began to design a curriculum which helped the students get up to grade-level. Implicit in this curriculum was an understanding of the need for a more humane teaching approach to math and the history of inequality in math tracking. The Algebra Project was born.

> "ALGEBRA IS TO ECONOMIC ACCESS WHAT THE VOTE WAS TO POLITICAL ACCESS."

"The ongoing struggle for citizenship and equality for minority people is now linked to math and science literacy," explains Robert Moses. (*The Nation*, March 4, 1996) The Algebra Project aims to have every student complete the college preparatory math sequence in high school, including Algebra by 9th grade and precalculus or calculus by 12th. The program begins with a yearlong curriculum for the 6th grade. To participate, schools must make a three-year commitment and must train teachers in the principles of the project. In The Algebra Project, students:

1. experience a physical event.

2. draw pictures and/or make graphic representation of the event.

3. discuss and write about the event in their own natural, intuitive language.

4. engage in a process of regimenting or structuring the language they use to describe the event.

5. develop and use abstract symbolic representation of the event.

A useful illustration of these principles can be found in what are known as "Trip-Lines." The students take field trips which link social history with technological discovery. They often visit the homes of local civil rights leaders (such as Medgar Evers). The trajectory of their trip functions as an integer line, with each stop representing a positive number. Later, they are asked to write about the experience in their own words. Some programs work with the arts, including music and dance, deconstructing the tempos and beats and exploring questions of space and geometry through the movements of the students' bodies.

The interconnection between the students' learning, teachers and the community is central to the philosophy of the program. The importance of these connections was learned through the Civil Rights movement. Meetings between people with different experiences and levels of involvement are stressed, following an organizational model used by the Freedom Riders.

The Algebra Project excites students interest in math outside the classroom and boosts self-esteem about their capacity to learn. One example of this is The Math League Games, competitive after-school events, which function in much the same way as intramural sports. Faced with a program that is heavily invested in them and their future, students have responded personally and academically. Discipline problems have been greatly reduced in schools participating in the project, and teachers confess to a new feeling of hopefulness about teaching kids math.

Moses maintains that the time to increase comprehensive math literacy is limited, and is threatened by the reduction of funds to school systems, the growing social stratification and the divisiveness of the current educational system.

The Algebra Project acknowledges the presence of racial and economic inequality in education and addresses them methodically and with hope and humanity. Indeed, if as Moses suggests, "Algebra is to economic access what the vote was to political access," the classroom is where the fight for racial and economic equality must be fought today. For more information contact:

The Algebra Project, Inc.
99 Bishop Richard Allen Drive
Cambridge, MA 02139
(617) 491-0200 Fax: (617) 491-0499

SCIENCE
AND
GEOGRAPHY

A Question of Biology: Are the Races Different?

by Richard C. Lewontin

Racism claims there are major inherited differences in temperament, mental abilities, energy, and so on between human groups even though no evidence exists for such inherited differences. Racism draws credibility from what seem to be obvious differences in some physical traits like color, hair form, or facial features. "After all," it is argued, "races differ so markedly in such inherited physical traits, so isn't it reasonable that they would differ in mental ones as well?" To understand the real situation we need to look at what is really known about genetic differences between people and to examine the very concept of "race" itself.

Race is Only So Deep

In the nineteenth century and before, "race" was a fuzzy concept that included many kinds of relationships. Sometimes it meant the whole species as "the human race"; sometimes a nation or tribe as "the race of Englishmen"; and sometimes merely a family as "He is the last of his race." All that held these notions together was that members of a "race" were somehow related by ties of kinship and that their shared characteristics were somehow passed from generation to generation.

Beginning in the middle of the nineteenth century, with the popularity of Darwin's theory of evolution, biologists began to use the concept of "race" in a different way. It simply came to mean "kind," an identifiably different form of organism within a species. So there were light-bellied and dark-bellied "races" of mice or banded or unbanded shell "races" of snails. But defining "races" simply as observable kinds produced two curious situations. First, members of different "races" often existed side by side within a population. There might be 25 different "races" of beetles, all members of the same species, living side by side in the same local population. Second, brothers and sisters might be members of two different races, since the characters that differentiated races were sometimes influenced by alternative forms of a single gene. So, a female mouse of the light-bellied "race" could produce offspring of both light-bellied and dark-bellied races, depending on her mate. Obviously there was no limit to the number of "races" that could be described

BEYOND HEROES AND HOLIDAYS

within a species, depending on the whim of the observer.

Around 1940, biologists, under the influence of discoveries in population genetics, made a major change in their understanding of race. Experiments on the genetics of organisms taken from natural populations made it clear that there was a great deal of genetic variation between individuals even in the same family, not to speak of the same population. It was discovered that many of the "races" of animals previously described and named were simply alternative hereditary forms that could appear within a family. Different local geographic populations did not differ from each other absolutely, but only in the relative frequency of different characters. For example, in human blood groups, some individuals were type A, some type B, some AB, and some O. No population was exclusively of one blood type. The difference between African, Asian, and European populations was only in the proportion of the four kinds.

These findings led to the concept of "geographical race," as a population of varying individuals, freely mating among each other, but different in average proportions of various genes from other populations. Any local random breeding population that was even slightly different in proportion of different gene forms from other populations was a geographical race. This new view of race had two powerful effects. First, no individual could be regarded as a "typical" member of a race. Older textbooks of anthropology would often show photographs of "typical" Australian aborigines, tropical Africans, and Japanese, listing as many as 50 or 100 "races," each with its typical example. Once it was recognized that every population was highly variable and differed largely in average proportions of different forms from other populations, the concept of the type specimen became meaningless.

The second consequence of the new view of race was that since every population differs slightly from every other one on the average, all local interbreeding populations are "races," so race really loses its significance as a concept. The Kikuyu of East Africa differ from the Japanese in gene frequencies, but they also differ from their neighbors, the Masai, and although the extent of the differences might be less in one case than in the other, it is only a matter of degree. This means that the *social* and *historical* definitions of race that put the two East African tribes in the same "race," but put the Japanese in a different "race," were purely arbitrary. How much difference in the frequencies of A, B, AB, and O blood groups does one require before deciding it is large enough to declare two local populations are in separate "races"?

ALL PEOPLE LOOK ALIKE

In ordinary parlance we still speak of Africans as one race, Europeans as another, Asians as another. And this distinction corresponds to our everyday sensory impressions. No one would mistake a Masai for a Japanese or either for a Finn. Despite variation from individual to individual within these groups, the differences between groups in skin color, hair form, and some facial features makes them clearly different. Racism takes these evident differences and claims that they demonstrate major genetic separation between "races." Is there any truth in this assertion?

We must remember that we are conditioned to observe precisely those features and that our ability to distinguish individuals as opposed to types is an artifact of our upbringing. We have no difficulty at all in telling apart individuals in our own group, but "they" all look alike. Once, in upper Egypt, my wife was approached by an Egyptian who began a lively conversation with her under the impression that he knew her. After she repeatedly protested that he was mistaken, he apologized, saying, in effect, "I'm sorry but all you European women look alike."

SUPERIORITY IS IN THE EYES OF THE BEHOLDER

If we could look at a random sample of different genes, not biased by our socialization, how much difference would there be between major geographical groups, say between Africans and Australian aborigines, as opposed to the differences between individuals within these groups? It is, in fact, possible to answer that question.

During the last 40 years, using the techniques of immunology and of protein chemistry, it has been possible to identify a large number of human genes that code for specific enzymes and other proteins. Very large numbers of individuals from all over the world have been tested to determine their genetic constitution with respect to such proteins, since only a small sample of blood is needed to make these determinations. About 150 different genetically coded proteins have been examined and the results are very illuminating for our understanding of human genetic variation.

It turns out that 75 percent of the different kinds of proteins are identical in all individuals tested from whatever population, with the exception of an occasional rare mutation. These so-called *monomorphic* proteins are common to all human beings of all races, and the species is essentially uniform with respect to the genes that code them. The other 25 percent are *polymorphic* proteins. That is, there exist two or more alternative forms of the protein, coded by alternative forms of a gene, that are reasonably common in our species. We can use these polymorphic genes to ask how much difference there is between populations, as compared with the difference between individuals within populations.

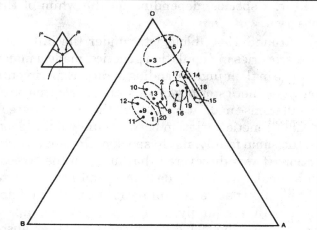

Figure 1. *Triallelic diagram of the ABO blood-group allele frequencies for human populations. Each represents a population; the perpendicular distances from the point to the sides represents the allele frequencies as indicated in the small triangle. Populations 1-3 are African, 4-7 are American Indians, 8-13 are Asians, 14-15 are Australian aborigines and 16-20 are Europeans. Dashed lines enclose arbitrary classes with similar gene frequencies, which do not correspond to "racial" classes.*

Table 1: Examples of extreme differentiation and close similarity in blood-group allele frequencies in three racial groups.

Gene	Allele	Population Caucasoid	Negroid	Mongoloid
Duffy	Fy	0.0300	0.9393	0.0985
	Fy^a	0.4208	0.0607	0.9015
	Fy^b	0.5492	0.0000	0.0000
Rhesus	R$_0$	0.0186	0.7395	0.0409
	R$_1$	0.4036	0.0256	0.7591
	R$_2$	0.1670	0.0427	0.1951
	r	0.3820	0.1184	0.0049
	r^1	0.0049	0.0707	0.0000
	Others	0.0239	0.0021	0.0000
P	P$_1$	0.5161	0.8911	0.1677
	P$_2$	0.4839	0.1089	0.8323
Auberger	Au^a	0.6213	0.6419	--------
	Au	0.3787	0.3581	--------
Xg	Xg^a	0.67	0.55	0.54
	Xg	0.33	0.45	0.46
Secretor	Se	0.5233	0.5727	--------
	Se	0.4767	0.4273	--------

Source: L.L. Cavalli-Storza and W. F. Bodmer, The Genetics of Human Populations, *W.H. Freeman and Company, 1971.*

Table I shows the three polymorphic genes that are most different between "races" and the three that are most similar among the "races." The first column gives the name of the protein or blood group and the second column gives the symbols of the alternative forms (alleles) of the gene that is varying. As the table shows there are big differences in relative frequencies of the allele of the Duffy, Rhesus, & P blood groups from "race" to "race," and there may be an allele like FY^b that is found only in one group, but no group is "pure" for any genes. In contrast, the Auberger, Xg, & Secretor proteins are very polymorphic within each "race," but the difference between groups is very small. It must be remembered that 75% of known genes in humans do not vary at all, but are totally monomorphic throughout the species.

Table 1

An example of a highly polymorphic gene is the one that determines the ABA blood type. There are three alternative forms of the gene which we will symbolize by A, B and O and every population in the world is characterized by some particular mixture of the three. For example, Belgians have about 26 percent A, 6 percent B, and the remaining 68 percent is O. Among Pygmies of the Congo, the proportions are 23 percent A, 22 percent B and 55 percent O. The frequencies can be depicted as a triangular diagram as shown in Figure 1. Each point represents a population, and the proportion of each gene form can be read as the perpendicular distance from the point to the appropriate side of the triangle. As the figure shows, all human populations are clustered fairly close together in one part of the frequency space. For example, there are no populations with very high A and very low B and O (lower right hand corner). The figure also shows that populations that belong to what we call major "races" in our everyday usage do not cluster together. The dashed lines have been put around populations that are similar in ABA frequencies, but these do not mark off racial groups. For example, the cluster made up of populations 2, 8, 10, 13, and 20 include an African, three Asian, and one European population.

A major finding from the study of such polymorphic genes is that none of these genes perfectly

Table 2: Allelic frequencies at seven polymorphic loci in Europeans and Black Africans.

Locus	Europeans Allele 1	Allele 2	Allele 3	Africans Allele 1	Allele 2	Allele 3
Red-cell acid phosphatase	0.36	0.60	0.04	0.17	0.83	0.00
Phosphoglucomutase-1	0.77	0.23	0.00	0.79	0.21	0.00
Phosphoglucomutase-3	0.74	0.26	0.00	0.37	0.63	0.00
Adenylate kinase	0.95	0.05	0.00	1.00	0.00	0.00
Peptidase A	0.76	0.00	0.24	0.90	0.10	0.00
Peptidase D	0.99	0.01	0.00	0.95	0.03	0.02
Adenosine deaminase	0.94	0.06	0.00	0.97	0.03	0.00

Source: R.C. Lewontin, The Genetic Basis of Evolutionary Change, *Columbia University Press, 1974. Adapted from H. Harris,* The Principles of Human Biochemical Genetics, *North Holland, Amsterdam and London, 1970.*

Table 2

discriminates one "racial" group from another. That is, there is no gene known that is 100 percent of one form in one race and 100 percent of a different form in some other race. Reciprocally, some genes that are very variable from individual to individual show no average difference at all between major races. (See Table 1.)

Rather than picking out the genes that are the most different or the most similar between groups, what do we see if we pick genes at random? Table 2 shows the outcome of such a random sample. Seven enzymes known to be polymorphic were tested in a group of Europeans and Africans (actually Black Londoners who had come from West Africa and White Londoners). In this random sample of genes there is a remarkable similarity between groups. With the exception of phosphoglucomutase-3, for which there is a reversal between groups, the most common form of each gene in Africans is the same form as for the Europeans, and the proportions themselves are very close. Such a result would lead us to conclude that the genetic difference between Blacks and Whites is negligible as compared with the polymorphism within each group.

The kind of question asked in Table 2 can in fact be asked in a very general way for large numbers of populations for about 20 genes that have been widely studied all over the world. Suppose we measure the variation among humans for some particular gene by the probability that a gene taken from one individual is a different alternative form (allele) than that taken from another individual at random from the human species as a whole. We can then ask how much less variation there would be if we chose the two individuals from the same "race." The difference between the variation over the whole species and the variation within a "race" would measure the proportion of all human variation that is accounted for by racial differences. In like manner we could ask how much of the variation within a "race" is accounted for by differences between tribes or nations that belong to the same "race," as opposed to the variation between individuals within the same tribe or nation. In this way we can divide the totality of human genetic variation in a portion between individuals within populations, between local populations within major "races," and between major "races." That calculation has been carried out independently by three different groups of geneticists using slightly different data and somewhat different statistical methods but with the identical result. Of all human genetic variation known for enzymes and other proteins, where it has been possible to actually count up the frequencies of different forms of the genes and so get an objective estimate of genetic variation, 85 percent turns out to be between individuals within the same local population, tribe, or nation. A further 8 percent is between tribes or nations within a major "race," and the remaining 7 percent is between major "races." That means that the genetic variation between one Spaniard and another, or between one Masai and another, is 85 percent of all human genetic variation, while only 15 percent is accounted for by breaking people up into groups. If everyone on earth became extinct except for the Kikuyu of East Africa, about 85 percent of all human variability would still be present in the reconstituted species. A few gene forms would be lost like the FY[b] allele of the Duffy blood group that is known only in American Indians, but little else would be changed.

WHO'S WHO?

The reader will have noticed that to carry out the calculation of partitioning variation between "races," some method must have been used for assigning each nation or tribe to a "race." The problem of what one means by a "race" comes out forcible when making such assignments. Are the Hungarians Europeans? They certainly *look* like Europeans, yet they (like Finns) speak a language that is totally unrelated to European language and belongs to the Turkic family of languages from Central Asia. And what about the modern-day Turks? Are they Europeans, or should they be lumped together with the Mongoloids? And then there are the Urdu and Hindi speaking people of India. They are the de-

© RICK REINHARD, 1990

scendants of a mixture of Aryan invaders form the north, the Persians from the West, and Vedic tribes of the Indian subcontinent. One solution is to make them a separate race. Even the Australian aborigines, who have often been put to one side as a separate race, mixed with Papuans and with Polynesian immigrants from the Pacific well before Europeans arrived. No group is more hybrid in its origin than the present-day Europeans, who are a mixture of Huns, Ostrogoths and Vandals from the east, Arabs from the south, and Indo-Europeans from the Caucasus. In practice, "racial" categories are established that correspond to major skin color groups, and all of the borderline cases are distributed among these or made into new races according to the whim of the scientist. But it turns out not to matter how the groups are assigned because the differences between major "racial" categories, no matter how defined, turn out to be small.

The result of the study of genetic variation is in sharp contrast with the everyday impression that major "races" are well differentiated. Clearly, those superficial differences in hair form, skin color, and facial features that are used to distinguish "races"

from each other are not typical of human genes in general. Human "racial" differentiation is, indeed, only skin deep. Any use of racial categories must take its justification from some source other than biology. The remarkable feature of human evolution and history has been the very small degree of divergence between geographical populations as compared with the genetic variation among individuals.

Richard C. Lewontin is a population geneticist at the Museum of Comparative Zoology at Harvard University. He was a long time member of Science for the People *and is the author of* Biology as Ideology *and* Human Diversity.

Reprinted with permission of the author from Science for the People, *March/April 1982.*

ADDITIONAL RESOURCES

Gould, S. 1981. *The mismeasure of man.* New York: W.W. Norton.

Lindqvist, S. 1995. *The skull measurer's mistake and other portraits of men and women who spoke out against racism.* New York: New Press.

Tobach, E. & Rosoff, B. Eds. 1994. *Challenging racism and sexism: Alternatives to genetic explanations.* New York: Feminist Press.

AN ISSUES APPROACH TO CHEMISTRY

The chart below is reprinted from the book Anti-Racist Science Teaching *(Free Association Books, London, 1987). It suggests some themes that can be used to link chemistry concepts to social issues.*

16+ (FOURTH AND FIFTH YEAR) CHEMISTRY COURSE 'ISSUES'

Entry Issues	Questions that can be asked	Chemistry content that could be included
A. Energy Matters 'Save it!' stickers Nuclear energy: No thanks! Poisoned by fire!	Why are we 'short' of energy? What is 'nuclear' energy? What is radioactivity? Which fuel is best? What happens in combustion? Is it OK to use up all the coal and oil? What else is oil used for?	Atomic structure: energy in nucleus atoms change. Combustion: energy obtained from rearrangement of atoms which are unchanged. Concept of molecule. Measurement of heat of combustion of carbon, methane, etc. Products of combustion, incomplete combustion of plastics. C-Chemistry: hydrocarbons plastics, fermentation (alcohol). Fuel cells, other cells.
B. Hunt Down the Lead Lead in petrol Lead in water Lead in dust	What is the evidence for toxicity? Why is/was it used in the first place? Can we do without it? What is the cost? How else does lead get into us? Why are some waters safe? Why does lead behave as it does? What are the alternatives?	Internal combustion engine, 'anti-knock', combustion hydrocarbons. Properties of metallic lead, ease of extraction, use by plumbers (*in situ*). Density (relative atomic mass). Hardness, pH of water, Copper, plastics.
C. Water: What's In It? Acid Rain Smog. Toxic effluent.	What does water normally contain? Where does the acid come from? What does acid do to the soil? Why is the sea salty? What are salts?	Acidity/alkalinity, pH, pH salt solutions, water cycle, natural waters, hardness of water, composition of sea water, 'salts from the sea', halogens (elements, compounds, ionic bonds, Group 7), $S + 2O_2$ + sulphuric acid, nitric acid. Preparation of salts (ionic equation) simple geology, composition of soils.
D. The Carbon Dioxide Story Destruction of ozone layer. 'Greenhouse' effect.	What's in the atmosphere? What effect does it have? Has it always been the same? How did the oxygen get there? How is it maintained? What happens to CO_2?	Photosynthesis, respiration, combustion, carbon cycle. Stability of CO_2, heat of formation CO_2 is water, action on limestone (equilibria, reversible reactions), C^{14} dating (isotopes).
E. Food and Fertilizers Beware nitrates! World food problem. Butter mountains.	What do foods contain? How do they get there? What do foods need to grow? What grows where? Is there a shortage? What is fertilizer? Which is the best? How are they made? How much do they cost? Are there side effects? What's in a diet?	Composition of foods, N cycle, sewage treatment, Haber process (rates, equilibria, catalyst), soils, pH, chemistry of ammonia, nitric acid. Food and medicine.

THE DEVELOPMENT FOR THIS PROPOSAL WAS CARRIED OUT BY THE PGCE CHEMISTRY STUDENTS (1982/3) AT CHELSEA COLLEGE, CENTRE FOR SCIENCE AND MATHEMATICS EDUCATION, IN COLLABORATION WITH CO-TUTORS IN TEACHING PRACTICE SCHOOLS AND THEIR CENTRE SUPERVISING TUTORS DRS ERICA GLYNN, JOHN HEAD, JAN HARDING.

A Theme for Biology: Crop Diversity

By Louis Werner

Profit-driven commercial breeding and hybridizing — aimed at pleasing consumers and industrial food processors — have also reduced the taste spectrum and genetic fingerprint of what we eat. If store-bought tomatoes seem to taste and look more and more the same, one can be sure also that they ripen at the same time, require the same pesticides and fertilizers, and resist the same known diseases and weather fluctuations.

But with this loss of diversity comes vulnerability to the unpredictable. Witness the Irish potato famine of the 1850s, when a new fungus swept every field in the country, and the more recent corn leaf blight of 1970, when disease reduced the U.S. crop — most of it a single hybrid — by 700 million bushels. The next year's harvest was saved only by crossing the modern hybrid with a seed-banked variety not commercially grown, yet resistant to that particular fungus.

Excerpted from Werner, L. 1996. "Saving the Seed Spectrum." Americas. 48.2:2. With permission from Americas, a bimonthly magazine published by the General Secretariat of the Organization of American States in English and Spanish.

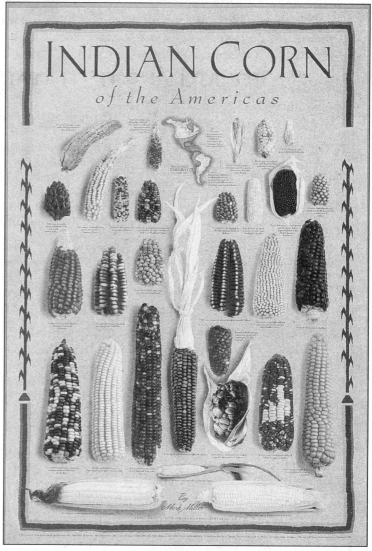

Indian Corn of the Americas

The full color poster of Indian Corn of the Americas (24" x 36") is printed by and available from Celestial Arts for $15 + $3.50 shipping. Can be ordered with a beige or black background. Similar posters reflecting the diversity of chiles, fruit, lettuce and tomatoes are also available. To purchase a poster or request a catalog, contact Celestial Arts, PO Box 7123, Berkeley, CA 94707, 510-559-1600 or 800-841-2665.

Research Questions

The theme of diversity in crops could lead to an interdisciplinary lesson investigating questions such as the ones below.

▶ What is the relationship between crop diversity and resistance to disease and insects?

▶ What is the relationship between crop diversity and the need for chemical fertilizers and insecticides?

▶ When did the movement to cultivate just one hybrid crop begin? Why? What impact has this policy had on the environment?

▶ What efforts are being made to promote crop diversity?

GETTING THE LEAD OUT

Lead poisoning has been defined as the number one environmental health threat for children in the United States with over one million children having elevated blood lead levels. Lead can cause permanent damage to a child which can affect achievement potential.

Galvanized by a crisis of lead contamination in the nearby neighborhood of Avanti, Gail Anderson's high school students are educating their community about the hazards of lead in the environment. They felt that if the residents of Avanti could live in pollution for so long without knowing it, it was possible that they were doing the same thing in their own town of Noblesville, Indiana. Because lead has its most toxic effects in children, they decided to develop an education program for elementary schools. They developed a mini-textbook with accompanying activities for elementary teachers to use with the kids.

They made several trips to fourth grade classes where they showed samples of articles with lead, lead contiminated soil, and lead-based paint chips, while pointing out that lead cannot actually be seen. The fourth graders brought paint samples from their homes which the high school students took back to their school to test. In older neighborhoods, as many as fifty percent of the homes tested positive. The students sent information letters to the parents of each student who brought in positive paint chips.

Gail Anderson has developed a lead literacy unit for high school classes which includes background information, labs, parent permission slips for soil tests, information letters for positive paint chip results, soil test result letters, pamphlets, and a sample letter for elementary school teachers to see if they are interested in participating. An elementary unit is also available. Both are on disk so that teachers can customize the materials for their classes. The cost is $7 for each unit (specify MAC or DOS; elementary or secondary). Write to:

Gail Anderson
Noblesville HS
18111 Cumberland Road
Noblesville, IN 46060

TESTING PAINT CHIPS FOR LEAD

1. Place between 0.05 and 0.20 gram of crumbled paint chips in a test tube. Avoid pieces of wallboard or wood.

2. Carefully add 15 drops of concentrated nitric acid (HNO_3).

3. Place the test tube in a boiling-water bath for 10-15 minutes. Make sure the room is well ventilated. (During this time, any lead in the paint chip will dissolve and go into the acid as lead ions.)

4. Remove from water bath and add 2 ml distilled water.

5. Allow the test tube to stand undisturbed for 10 minutes to let any undissolved material settle.

6. Decant the semi-clear liquid into a clean test tube.

7. Let the new test tube cool for 5 minutes.

8. Add 10 drops of 20% KI, letting it fall directly onto the liquid in the tube. Do not shake. (20% KI: Add 20.0 g potassium iodide per 100 ml solution)

9. If a bright yellow precipitate appears as the drops hit, the test is positive. If there is no yellow precipitate, the test is negative. If a reddish or orange-red precipitate occurs, the test is negative. If there is any doubt, retest. Do not record results until you are sure.

Note: Because this lab is time intensive, make good use of the time by doing several tests at once. If you don't have many samples, have several lab groups test the same sample to make sure that results agree.

Adapted with permission from GREEN TEACHER: Education for Planet Earth, *1996. Subscriptions are $22/year for four issues from:* GREEN TEACHER, *PO Box 1431, Lewiston, NY 14092, (416) 960-1244.*

ENVIRONMENTAL RACISM AND NATIVE AMERICAN RESERVATIONS

BY LYNETTE SELKURT

This lesson for middle school uses examples from one state to help students understand institutional racism. Similar lessons can be developed in other states, drawing on the particulars of how groups are located within the state or even within in a city. This lesson can also be used as part of a larger unit on the contemporary reality of Native Americans.

TIME

Three or four class periods.

OBJECTIVES

▸ Identify areas of relative soil quality on a map.

▸ Analyze the distribution of agricultural land to Whites and American Indians and the consequences of land distribution.

▸ Construct bar graphs from numerical data.

▸ Distinguish between institutional racism and individual prejudice.

▸ Define environmental racism.

SUGGESTED PROCEDURES

1. Introduce the lesson. We do not provide a suggestion for this step because your comments or questions for the students will vary depending on whether this is part of a larger unit on environmental racism, Native American issues, or the history of your state.

2. Pass out a soil map and a growing season map (Figure 1). Discuss with students which land they would like to own if they were farmers and why.

3. Pass out the Wisconsin Reservation map (Figure 2). Ask students to compare the locations of Indian reservations with the most and least arable farmland. (If possible, transfer the maps to overhead transparencies. Place the reservation map over the soil map to highlight the relationship between the two.)

4. Divide the class into small groups and distribute the Housing and Social Characteristics Chart. Have each group construct a bar graph using the data. For example, one group could construct a bar graph depicting, for Indians and all races, the percentage of:

▸ Families in poverty.

▸ Families headed by a female.

▸ Total persons in poverty.

5. Have students present their bar graphs and explain them to the class.

6. Ask students to analyze the relationship between the information on the bar graphs and the arability of soil on the reservations. As they point to the role of the government in discriminating against Native Americans, explain that this is called institutional racism. If you have not discussed the term in the past, you can ask students for more examples of institutional racism. How does this differ from individual racism? How are the two related?

7. Tell students that one type of institutional racism is called environmental racism. What do they think it means? Can they think of any more examples in their community, this country and the world? Are there examples in their own community of the distribution of land and resources being unequal? For example, in many towns and cities the lower-income neighborhoods have less parks and are closer to sources of environmental pollution such as used car lots, dumps, incinerators, etc.

8. Bring in resources about local and national groups working to address environmental racism and/or the contemporary rights of Native Americans.

9. Encourage students to take action.

Adapted from a lesson by Lynette Selkurt titled "American Indians and Institutional Racism," in Sleeter, C. and C. Grant.1989. Turning on Learning. NY: Merrill/Macmillan.

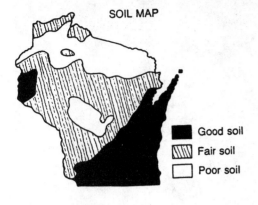

SOIL MAP

Good soil
Fair soil
Poor soil

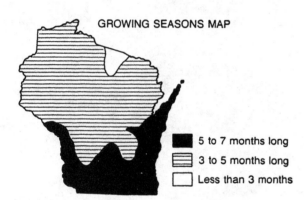

GROWING SEASONS MAP

5 to 7 months long
3 to 5 months long
Less than 3 months

Figure 1.

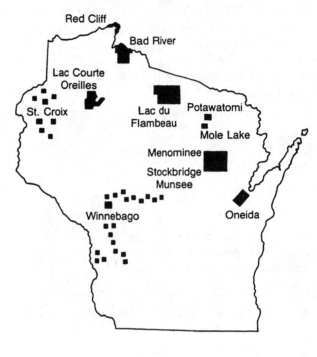

WISCONSIN INDIAN RESERVATIONS—1970

Red Cliff
Bad River
Lac Courte Oreilles
St. Croix
Lac du Flambeau
Potawatomi
Mole Lake
Menominee
Stockbridge Munsee
Winnebago
Oneida

Figure 2.

HOUSING AND SOCIAL CHARACTERISTICS CHART, 1990

Characteristics	Wisconsin Native Americans	All Races
Median Income	$9855	$13,207
Percentage of families in poverty	26%	6.9%
Percentage of poverty families headed by female	58.2%	32.4%
Percentage of unemployed	11.1%	2.8%
Median number of school years completed of population age 25+	8.9 years	12.3 years
Total persons in poverty	27.1%	4.6%

Sources: General Social and Economic Characteristics, (Wisconsin) 1990 Census Report, American Indians

THE ARTS

TAKING A STAND: STUDENT LED DRAMA AND DIALOGUE

BY KAREN DONALDSON

Most staff in schools in the United States do not view racism as a major deterrent to student learning. Yet, many students do. Students have stated that they feel anger, depression and exclusion and cannot concentrate on school work. Numerous students get so discouraged they opt not to attend school or classes. They also feel they are being deprived and cheated out of a full education when curriculum does not include the contributions and experiences of all people. One solution to this dilemma is for teachers to create avenues of leadership for students to become empowered to address issues of racism in school, since many school systems are hesitant to rally for such change. With regard to racism, students have the most at stake, and by taking an active role in their education many will value it more.

To assess the impact of an anti-racist arts curriculum on high school students in a peer education program, I conducted a project study in the Branchard Public School system (pseudonym). An overview of this study, described in detail in *Through Students' Eyes: Combatting Racism in United States Schools* (Donaldson, 1996), is provided in this article.

As with many school systems today, the Branchard Public School System encountered media exposure for its numerous racist incidents such as: students of color being disproportionately suspended from school; a high school teacher writing disparaging comments about the lack of abilities, promiscuity and violent behavior of students of color; and the lack of people of color in administrative positions. With a student population of 25,000 and the ethnic ratio reflecting 37% European-American, 33% African-American, 28% Hispanic-American and 2% Asian-American, the community and school system rose to address their racial problems. Community organizations, along with the school department, began with an educational summit, in which people from all sectors of the community attended to voice their concerns. This summit was followed by a student race relations survey which was administered to 2,000 students in grades eight and eleven. The survey results revealed that 88% of these students perceived rac-

ism in their schools. Following the summit and survey, community/school ad-hoc committees were formulated to make recommendations for school improvement. Recommendations from each committee were submitted. One of these suggested that a task force of secondary students be established to address issues of racism and culture via training in areas such as bias awareness and communication skills. The students would study racism, multicultural understanding and sensitivity and student-student, student-staff, student-community relations. It was in response to this recommendation that the student anti-racist project was developed.

This project, called "Let's Stop Racism In Our Schools," was administered at one of the local high schools. Although the administration felt it could benefit from such a project, teachers were very reluctant to support it. Nonetheless, fliers announcing the "Let's Stop Racism in Our School" project were posted throughout the school, promoting it as a peer education project. A diverse group of students from the Peer Education Program, African-American Society Club, Honors Club and individual students attended the first meeting. An introductory workshop to highlight the roots of racism was scheduled.

In addition to responding to racism in the schools, the purpose of the project was also to research the perceptions of the student participants on how racism influences learning; and the effectiveness of empowering students through anti-racist/multicultural education arts curriculum. Very often students' views are omitted from research studies and curriculum development.

Our introductory workshop focused on the history of indigenous groups and enslaved Africans in the United States. It began with drumming, dance and storytelling of Africa, the cradle of civilization. Students reenacted the forced migration of over fifty million Africans brought to the Americas and sold into slavery, and the slaughtering of Native Americans for land and gold. They discussed these beginnings of the racist ideology now embedded in our society and possible ways to reduce both institutional and individual racism.

The arts, as students admitted, are one way to make others aware of racism in U.S. schools. Many students agreed that visual teaching and doing hands-on activities enhanced their interest and comprehension in school subjects. Furthermore, the arts are the way of life and a vehicle to teach traditions, experiences and her/history for numerous cultural groups. The arts are also multi-sensory and incorporate a variety of learning and teaching styles into any curriculum. Therefore, the arts can be a significant component of anti-racist/multicultural education curriculum.

With this art appreciation in mind, auditions were held and a core group of twenty committed students were enrolled in the project. Their commitment was to attend racism education classes twice a week for sixteen weeks, formulate an anti-racist support/performing group and perform/lecture for various schools within and without the school system, as well as volunteer as human research subjects, sharing their reactions to the project.

Students shared experiences with racism, which included comments such as:

"I was put into special classes because of my accent, and stayed there half a year before they discovered I did not belong there."

"I was placed in an advanced math class, but as I entered the class the teacher insisted I didn't belong there, I know it was because I was Spanish and all the other students in the class were white."

"I was told by my teacher to prove others wrong and not get pregnant by the age of sixteen like all the other Puerto Rican girls."

With the knowledge gained from their lessons and their sharing of personal experiences with racism, students wrote a script entitled "Let's Stop Racism In Our Schools." Students rehearsed the performance and practiced mock answers to simulated questions which could be posed by student audiences.

The production — combining poetry, drama, dance and song — consists of four brief scenes:

▶ Protest March: Students begin with a march against racism, followed by personal expressions/experiences with racism in schools

▶ Definition and History of Racism in the U.S.

▶ Racial Prejudice and Racial Stereotyping: an Outgrowth of Racism: Students explode with common prejudices and anger to exhibit what we as American people do to one another

▶ Finale: Students recite some solutions to the

problem of racism in schools. They close with an original song entitled "Let's Stop Racism In Our Schools."

During the study, the students performed several productions. The first production was an in-house, work-in-progress performance for teachers, administrators, parents and interested community members. Out of a large teaching faculty, only three teachers attended. Two of these teachers were African-American. After the performance, the cast spoke with the audience. Students wanted to know why the teachers did not come to support their efforts, but no clear explanation was evident. The African-American teachers shared that students are not the only people who experience racist attitudes in schools; teachers do also. They gave examples of students not respecting teachers of color and colleagues not wanting them to be a part of the faculty. At this time, community people such as the chairperson of the education committee for the N.A.A.C.P., the Deputy School Superintendent, the Peer Education Director and community organizations gave words of encouragement to the students. They told them that in spite of the unpopularity of an anti-racism production. They said they should continue to stand up and deliver the message that students and others need to hear.

The second performance was at an almost all-white middle school for 600 students. The cast received a standing ovation and numerous questions from the student audience, i.e.: "What should I do when my friend is calling other students racist names?" One of the cast members replied, "Take a stand. Tell your friend you'll have no part in it." One week after the performance, the cast was notified that the students at the middle school were still talking about the production and the general consensus of the middle school audience was that the group was courageous. Because they were young like them, these students could relate far better to the high school students than to adults telling them what is not right. The cast members were elated from this performance and response. It was then they realized the potential of their efforts to reduce racism in schools. The students felt proud and empowered and subsequently united to form S.A.R.I.S. (Students Against Racism In Schools).

The third performance discouraged the cast again. It was in front of their peers. Administrators did not notify teachers and students about the performance until two minutes before the bell, at which time they were only told to file into the auditorium. Teachers were upset because of the disruption in their class schedules. They stood on the sides and in the rear of the auditorium, away from their students. Of one principal and four assistant principals, none came to the auditorium to announce the performance. Much of the student audience was loud and unruly throughout the performance and those who tried to hear the show could not. This situation devastated the cast. After meeting and sharing their sentiments with one another, they decided to visit the principal's office. It was there that one of the assistant principals listened to their grievances, apologized and promised to do it right the coming year. The cast was not satisfied. Yet, through it all, the participants discovered their empowerment rendered both support and resistance. This acknowledgment solidified the need for their work and heightened their determination not to give up.

When interviewed about their experiences in the project, students still felt that using the arts to teach about racism is a highly effective medium. This diverse group of students learned that camaraderie between ethnic groups is a strong force to reckon with, on stage or otherwise. They learned they had the power to lead young people in a peaceful and critically conscious direction, and how some of their friends and teachers support racist views. Students remarked that doing the project helped them in many ways. They could clearly see from their experiences with the project how racism permeates our lives. With that understanding, they were able to temper their frustrations by making positive changes within themselves and their schoolwork, which further enabled them to honorably accept the challenge of being role models and leaders of social change for other youth, schools and community.

There were many responses to my major research question, *how does racism affect student learning?*, such as "Racism affects my learning because if I have the slightest feeling a teacher is racist toward me, then I kind of work toward that racist expectation"; "If I know a teacher is racist, I won't want to do anything in that class, I'll just sit there"; "All my life, teachers and students have made racist remarks or treated me differently because of my race. I hated it and that hate grew inside. How can I like school, when it teaches me to hate myself and others?" Their comments indicate that if we are to develop well-educated, healthy youth we must address this dilemma now. We must recognize the urgency of providing anti-racist curricula at all levels, and give students the opportunity to share their feelings, assist in the development of curriculum and take social action and leadership approaches to addressing issues of racism in their schools.

Karen B. Donaldson, Ed.D. is an assistant professor of Multicultural Education for the Curriculum and Instruction Department/School of Education at Iowa State University, Ames, Iowa. Dr. Donaldson is the author of Through Students' Eyes: Combatting Racism in United States Schools *(Greenwood Publishers, 1996) and is currently completing her second book,* Shattering the Denial: Proactive Protocols for the Classroom and Beyond *(Greenwood Publishers, 1998.) E-mail: PROFK@iastate.edu*

REFERENCES

Donaldson, K. 1996. *Through students' eyes: Racism in United States schools.* Westport, CT: Greenwood Publishers.

Hart, T. E. and L. Lumsden. May 1989. *Confronting racism in the schools.* Oregon School Study Council, University of Oregon (ED 306 705).

Hidalgo, N. M., C. L. McDowell and E.V. Siddle, eds. 1992. *Facing racism in education.* Cambridge: Harvard Educational Review.

Mizell, L. 1992. *Think about racism.* New York: Walker and Company.

Murray, C. B. and R.M. Clark. June 1990. *Targets of racism.* The American School Board Journal.

Nieto, S. 1996. 2nd ed. *Affirming diversity: The sociopolitical context of multicultural education.* New York: Longman.

Pine, G. J. and A.G. Hilliard III. April 1990. *Rx for racism: Imperatives for America's schools.* Phi Delta Kappan.

Busting Ads with Art

BY LIZ HOTTEL

The Adbusters Media Foundation is dedicated to deconstructing the myths of advertising and commercial media. They describe themselves as "a global network of artists, activists, educators, guerilla tacticians." Their goal is to "build the new social activist movement of our information age. Our mission is to take on the archetypal mind polluters — Marlboro, Absolut, McDonald's, Calvin Klein, Nissan, Time-Warner, Disney — and beat them at their own game; to uncool their billion-dollar image with uncommercials on television, subvertisements in magazines and anti-ads right next to theirs in the urban landscape; to take control over the role that the tobacco, alcohol, food, fashion, automobile and culture industries play in our lives, and to set new agendas in their industries."

The Adbusters Media Foundation's magazine, *Adbusters* features an array of art and articles which help readers to re-examine the influence of advertising in our lives and challenge what we have learned to take for granted as "marketing techniques." They sponsor "Buy Nothing Day," an annual worldwide effort to spotlight out-of-control consumerism. All three major television networks rejected television spots for the campaign, one calling it "Un-American." In addition, they create ad parodies, "subvertisements," subverting ubiquitous images such as "Joe Camel" into a hospital-bound, cancer-ridden "Joe Chemo," to show that what is depicted as glamorous and manly — smoking — is really anything but.

Classroom Exercise

Kids are natural critics. They miss very little and are often adept at determining what is "fair" and what's "not fair." Draw on this ability by having them develop some of their own ad parodies using the classroom exercise below.

Procedure

Materials

▸ Commercial ads from magazines or the postcard ads available for free in many stores and coffeehouses.

▸ Adbuster ads. Use the samples provided and/or order more from the Adbuster Media Foundation.

Step One

Post both sets of ads on the chalkboard. Ask kids to pick the commercial ad from the *Adbuster* advertisement. How could they tell? What was its message? Was the ad parody effective? If so, what strategies did the artist employ?

Discuss the ways people of different races, ethnicities and gender are portrayed in the media. Why are all the cleaning, cooking and childcare products addressed to women? Why are the commercials for athletic shoes and hardware directed towards men? Do students think its because these groups just "naturally" want these things or are we socially conditioned to want them? Address the influence of advertising on linking brand-name clothing, cigarettes and other items with happiness. How does advertising influence cultural norms? Is the marketing "fair?"

Step Two

Have the students make an adbuster or a subvertisement. Suggest that they use whatever medium you are currently using in your art class. (They could also cut up the magazine advertisements, paste over them, alter the given image to become part of their own.) The 'adbusters' can be posted in your school, submitted to the school or other local papers and/or sent to the Adbusters Media Foundation.

Resources

Adbusters Media Foundation
1243 West 7th Avenue
Vancouver, BC, V6H 1B7, Canada
(607) 736-9401
http://www.adbusters.org
E-mail: adbusters@adbusters.org

The Ad and the Ego Video
This video describes the direct influence of advertising on American culture today. Would be useful viewing in conjunction with this art lesson. The video comes with a teaching guide. Ordering information is in the Resource Guide.

ADBUSTERS

Illustration: Ron Turner Concept: Scott Plous

Joe CHEMO

THE SURGEON GENERAL WARNS THAT SMOKING IS A FREQUENT CAUSE OF WASTED POTENTIAL AND FATAL REGRET.

Photo: Nancy Bleck

YOU'RE RUNNING BECAUSE YOU WANT THAT RAISE, TO BE ALL YOU CAN BE. **BUT IT'S NOT EASY** WHEN YOU **WORK** SIXTY HOURS A WEEK MAKING SNEAKERS IN AN **INDONESIAN FACTORY** AND YOUR FRIENDS **DISAPPEAR** WHEN THEY ASK FOR A RAISE. **SO THINK** GLOBALLY BEFORE YOU DECIDE **IT'S SO COOL TO WEAR** NIKE

Ad Parody: Abrupt—www.abrupt.org

Nature...

IT'LL GROW BACK

DAMAGE

POISON FOR THE ROAD

These images are just a few of the many 'adbusters' displayed in the Adbuster Media Foundation magazine and on their postcards. See information under Resources on previous page.

TECHNOLOGY

Global Learning Networks: Gaining Perspective on Our Lives with Distance

by Kristin Brown, Jim Cummins, Enid Figueroa and Dennis Sayers

We would do well to listen to the teachers who have attempted to raise and confront issues of racism through global learning networks, in which students and teachers take advantage of the Internet to engage in collaborative projects with distant classes, for they have much to tell us.

Tracy Miller, an elementary bilingual (Spanish-English) program teacher from San Francisco whose students, primarily of Mexican and Central American descent, had just completed a video exchange with another bilingual class in Brooklyn with children of Afro-Caribbean heritage, principally from Puerto Rico and Santo Domingo. Ms. Miller's goal had been to confront her students' negative feelings toward their African-American schoolmates in San Francisco by providing positive experiences with distant students who share similar linguistic and cultural attributes together with recent life experiences as immigrants, but who differ as "visible minorities." Here is what Tracy Miller had to say:

> This was a good start. We still need to do so much more, to integrate the classes themselves, to have after-school programs where all students play and work together. It's a very slow process, but there was real understanding, and one thing leads to another. Some schools don't do anything but this was a good starting point.

Global learning networks are a starting point; where would she go from here?

> I'd definitely like to continue the video exchange with the Afro-Caribbean class in New York. I'd like my students to learn more about the histories and cultures of African and Latino people in the Caribbean, in Latin America, in New York and right here in San Francisco. We've really only just begun. The students are observant but don't necessarily raise questions about the bigger issues. I can see how the teacher can do even more to help ask those questions and to help students think about what they are observing. I want to use the video exchange to help raise questions about the issues that divide and to explore with my students how the anti-immigrant sentiment in our state fueled by Proposition 187 has contributed to tensions and negative feelings among students at

our school. But also to look at how the groups have come together in the past and how to work together in the future to heal the divisions and begin to solve the problems that our communities face.

This article represents a stage in a continuing dialogue about how to create contexts of empowerment in schools. We explore how power can be generated collaboratively in the technology-mediated interactions between educators, students and communities and how these interactions can simultaneously challenge structures of injustice in schools and other institutions of society. Clearly, the task of creating anti-racist schools is ambitious and will require a careful selection of tools, strategies and educational approaches to help students, teachers and parents confront inequity from both a personal and a broader socio-political perspective. Technology-enhanced global learning networks provide one approach to teaching and learning that brings edu-

Sending a message over the telecommunications network — Orillas student at Club TechByte, an after-school computer program in Tijuana, Mexico, communicates with a partner class in another part of the world.

cational communities together across cultural, racial and national boundaries to analyze critically and seek to improve the world in which they live.

We believe that global learning networks represent a powerful tool for creating contexts of empowerment for both teachers and students. We are using the term "empowerment" in a very specific sense to mean "the collaborative creation of power." Power is created in the relationship between individuals (or groups or countries) and shared among participants. As implied by this definition, power relations are embedded in all the interactions that take place between educators and students in the school context. These relationships can range across a continuum from collaborative to coercive. We define coercive relations of power as the exercise of power by a dominant group (or individual or country) in a way that harms a subordinated group (or individual or country). Examples in education include various forms of racism (e.g. a curriculum that omits the experiences and perspectives of people of color) and the disparagement of bilingual students' language and culture (e.g. through prohibiting students from using their home language). The assumption is that there is a fixed quantity of power that operates according to a zero-sum logic; in other words, the more power one group has the less is left for other groups.

Collaborative relations of power, on the other hand, operate on the assumption that power is not a fixed predetermined quantity but rather can be *generated* in interpersonal and intergroup relations. In other words, participants in the relationship are *empowered* through their collaboration such that each is more affirmed in her or his identity and is better able to create change in his or her life or social situation. The power relationship is *additive* rather than *subtractive*. Power is *created with* others rather than being *imposed on* or *exercised over* others. From this perspective the interactions that take place between educators and students in school are never neutral. They are always either challenging patterns of coercive relations of power that exist in the wider society (e.g. through anti-racist education) or reinforcing these coercive relations of power.

How can communication across distances be designed to help create more collaborative relations of power? What opportunities are created when we introduce communication across distances in our classrooms? Paulo Freire and Celestin Freinet, two progressive educators whose ground-breaking work began earlier this century, felt strongly that it is not until people are forced to take a step back

and rethink the world in which they live — a distancing process — that they can reanalyze their own worlds, enhance their understanding of their own lives and day-to-day realities, and finally reflect on that world and take decisive action to improve it. We have termed this process a "pedagogy of distancing." Technology-enhanced global learning networks give us new and rich opportunities for engaging in a pedagogy of distancing. We feel that a pedagogy of distancing, greatly facilitated through global learning networks, is one that changes attitudes and fosters learning and critical questioning through dialogue within classes and between classes — across cultures, distances and differences. In this article we discuss the potential of global learning networks for creating the kinds of contexts for sustained dialogue, collaboration, and critical inquiry that we feel will help restructure power relations in schools and society.

> Distancing becomes...
> ...analysis
> ...perspective
> ...taking stock
> ...stepping back
> ...sharing across differences[1]

OVERVIEW

Part One of this article provides a series of vignettes illustrating the many ways in which progressive educators have begun to use networking opportunities to develop an anti-racist curriculum in their schools. Through these examples, we introduce the concept of "distancing." Part Two then traces the history of a pedagogy of distancing through the work of two critical educators: Paulo Freire and Celestin Freinet. Part Three examines the processes that help drive contexts for collaborative critical inquiry and provides specific suggestions for educators interested in implementing a pedagogy of distancing in their own classrooms.

PART ONE: VIGNETTES OF GLOBAL LEARNING NETWORKS

What kinds of projects take place in classrooms helping to forge global learning networks? The classroom examples that follow illustrate ways in which challenging content and ambitious teaching and learning strategies are being linked to real world issues by innovative educators, parents and students. These examples speak forcefully to the question: what are schools for? The resounding answer is that schools can assume a powerful role in helping to build community, expose injustices, consider alternatives to the way things are and engage students and adults in generating the knowledge and skills to improve society for everyone.

In these networking projects teachers are using a wide range of technologies, including electronic mail, the Internet, video tapes, audio tapes and speaker phones, to create learning environments that will equip their students with the intellectual and cultural resources crucial for success in the multicultural national and global societies they will help form. The global learning networks we advocate often employ technology. Yet the kinds of intercultural collaboration we are proposing derive their impact and momentum not from the technology itself but from a vision of how education can be organized to restructure power relations in both local and global arenas.

The vignettes we offer here are organized by the main themes they address:

a) Confronting social and economic strife globally and locally.

▶ With a desire to understand more clearly the damage perpetuated by social and economic strife and to promote international solidarity, teachers in Catalonia, Spain donated a computer and a modem in 1993 to a refugee camp for Bosnian children in Savudrija, Croatia. When messages were received in Bosanki, the native language of the children in Bosnia, the students in Catalonia took advantage of the Internet to find translators who could share the messages in English and other more widely spoken languages. The letters spoke powerfully about the experiences of the Bosnian students and their families. A multi-school project was launched extending to other refugee camps in the former Yugoslavia, Palestine, Chiapas in Mexico, Brazil and Algeria. For the students from the refugee camps, the network provided a welcome opportunity to increase awareness globally about the international economic and political forces leading to conflict in their countries and the direct impact of war on their lives. For the students who heard directly from their peers in refugee camps, themselves from many different cultural and linguistic backgrounds, "ethnic cleansing" is no longer an abstract concept; it has a human face and voice that bring home to them the personal and collective costs of intolerance and oppression. This communication, while at times uncomfortable, has generated a resolve among many

students to understand the roots of discrimination and to confront its manifestations in their own societies as well as the roots of conflicts in other parts of the world and how their own countries may be implicated. Many of the students involved in this project have gained a keen interest in current events as a result of the personal contact and immediacy made possible by the telecommunications. Teachers have responded by making these communications an integral part of real world lessons in social studies, history, language arts, math and science in their schools. (More information about this project can be found in English, Spanish and Catalan on the WWW: <http://www.pangea.org/org/psf/history2.html>. For information about multilingual and anti-racist projects on I*EARN contact <krbrown@igc.apc.org>. For general information on I*EARN in the United States, see http://www.iearn.org/iearn/.)

▶ Teachers in the U.S. are using networking to confront prejudice among students in their inner city schools. At a San Francisco elementary school, tensions were high among Latino bilingual students who had been bussed into a school in a primarily African American neighborhood under a desegregation order. A Spanish-speaking bilingual teacher and her African American colleague initiated a long-distance team-teaching partnership with a bilingual teacher in New York City who worked with Spanish-speaking students from the Caribbean. How might this exchange begin to address the tensions at the San Francisco school? The San Francisco teachers explained,

> Since our partner class in New York would include Spanish-speaking Latino students of African descent, we would be linking San Francisco's Latino students with faraway colleagues who in many ways were like them — immigrant students who spoke the same mother tongue and shared the experience of learning English as a second language — but whose physical attributes and pride in their African heritage more closely resembled their African American schoolmates. In this way we hoped to provide a bridge between the African Americans and the Latinos who saw one another every day at school but whose interactions were distorted by fears.

The two classes in San Francisco and their New York colleagues shared videos and other projects for a year. One example was an intergenerational study of folk games from Mexican, Caribbean and African American cultures, a topic that fits in well with both the African American teacher's thematic unit on ancestors, and the bilingual teacher's interest in oral and written language. The teachers carefully designed each activity to provide opportunities for sharing among students within each school, in small racially-mixed groups, as well as between schools.

By showing the links between Latinos and African Americans in the Caribbean culture and by serving as a catalyst for greater interaction among students at each school site, the exchange was an important step in beginning to break down the racial isolation and prejudice locally at the San Francisco school. New friendships that developed among students led to three African American families enrolling their children in the bilingual program the next year and to every girl in the bilingual class joining the Girl Scouts so they could continue to collaborate with their new-found friends on projects after school.

The students concluded, "We learned that in this world there is a friend for everyone. This is a project we'd like to continue." The teachers in San Francisco also reflected on what they'd learned from the exchange. In the words of the bilingual teacher, "The students are observant but don't necessarily raise questions about the larger issues that divide. I can see now how the teacher can do more to help raise those questions." The San Francisco teachers, aware that short-term intercultural sharing is only a first step to bringing their students together for discussions about the roots of the tensions at school, are eager to continue the project. In future exchanges they hope to explore with their students how issues of race and power get played out in different settings, such as how the anti-immigrant sentiment in California has contributed to negative feelings among students at the school. (This exchange took place as part of the Project "De Orilla a Orilla" (From Shore to Shore). For information about participation, contact Enid Figueroa <efigueroa@igc.apc.org>, Dennis Sayers <dmsayers@ucdavis.edu>, and Kristin Brown <krbrown@igc.apc.org>.)

b) Creating a greater sense of solidarity within and between groups: bridging geographic, linguistic, and cultural differences

▶ Neighborhood computer centers and on-line networks are being organized by underserved communities to ensure that low-income residents have both affordable access to the Internet and the tools and skills to design technology projects around their needs. Plugged In is a nonprofit organization which has received funds from businesses and public agencies to address the increasing gap between the information "haves" and "have-nots" by setting up a community computer center in East Palo Alto, CA. Teens involved in the after-school "Street.Net" project at Plugged In have used communications technologies to link with the Street Level Youth Media Project in Chicago, IL to engage in a critical analysis of national urban issues and other issues of relevance to them and their communities. Street.Net seeks to provide a forum for communication among youth in urban areas across the country. Participants use computer networking to share writings about issues such as violence, poverty, ghettoization, cultural values and urban stereotypes. These investigations often lead to community action or efforts to make those outside the communities more aware of community concerns. For example, a videotape was produced focusing on the bussing situation in a district, based on interviews with the students actually involved. Street.Net participants learn to access the vast information resources available on the Internet while working together to find solutions to the common problems they face.

This year at Plugged In, an after-school technology networking program is helping to bridge another kind of distance; the social distance between youth from East Palo Alto and teens from the more affluent Palo Alto just a few miles away on the other side of the freeway. For the first time in the memory of the directors and youths at Plugged In in East Palo Alto, white high school students are coming to this primarily African American, Latino and Asian-Pacific Islander community for after-school enrichment activities. What has drawn them together is the oppportunity to help facilitate a weekly on-line dialogue, established by the center in East Palo Alto, which is open to young people across the nation to air their views on selected topics of current interest to teens. The team of ten students who facilitate the dialogue is composed of three African American students, four white students, and three students who identify themselves as having mixed heritage. The facilitation team meets regularly to select topics for discussion that will maintain the interest of other teens and deal with meaningful themes. Recent topics have included Ebonics and teen suicide. The students discuss their roles and responsibilities in moderating the discussion, at first dealing with such challenges as keeping the conversation going and responding to inappropriate comments. Recently they have collaborated with a journalist on an article entitled, "What Color is the Net?" about racism on the Internet. (For information about Plugged In see: <http://www.pluggedin.org/> or contact Muki Izora,

Epa.net Project Director at <muki@pluggedin.org>. For information about the "Plugged In" Project, contact Elisheva Gross at <plgnsheva@aol.com>.)

▶ In Canada, the KIDS FROM KANATA Project uses computer networking to link students from First Nations (Native Canadian) and European backgrounds to help them explore Canada's diversity and develop a wider Canadian identity. Classes form triads involving one "Native" class and two "non-Native" classes who work together during an entire school year to engage in cultural explorations, comparing rural and urban experiences and discussing such issues as the roots of protest in First Nations' communities. What makes this project of particular interest to educators designing an anti-racist curriculum is the careful attention paid to "leveling the playing field" between dominant and subordinated groups and to making students aware of how unequal relations of power between ethnic groups affect social interactions. The project organizers recognize that simply linking students from diverse backgrounds in telecommunications projects doesn't necessarily lead to greater understanding. Project materials created by a curriculum development team headed by Native Canadian educators use quotes from prominent Native Canadians in guiding Canadian participants from different cultural backgrounds in establishing a productive dialogue. The curriculum guide and materials offer a number of suggestions for positive and balanced interactions, taking steps to ensure that the students from the First Nations are not merely the object of picturesque study. Elevating the power of the First Nations to name the triad is just one example of an effort to avoid letting the voice of the dominant groups take over from the beginning. Other examples of the way that power differentials are dealt with include: establishing ground rules that all groups will take part in the decision-making and directing of activity and in the revealing of their cultures; asking schools with greater resources of technology and experience to provide extra support to those who are just beginning; and explicitly teaching strategies for conflict resolution. Through this project, students are guided in constructive listening, reflecting, making their assumptions explicit, and problem solving, all key elements in intercultural communication. (For more information about KIDS FROM KANATA contact Jonn Ord at York University, Ontario, Canada <jonno@edu.yorku.ca> or on the WWW see: <http://www.web.apc.org/webhome/KFK/kfkhome.html>.)

(c) Addressing the exclusion of the voices of subordinated peoples from the histories taught in our schools.

▶ In the Holocaust-Genocide Project, elementary and secondary students from many parts of the world use a variety of on-line information tools to research the topic of genocide. For several years now, students in the I*EARN Project from North and South America, Eastern and Western Europe, Israel, Russia, Cambodia, Australia and China have published an annual magazine with student reflections on genocide and other forms of oppression. Students researching the Holocaust have used the Internet to locate various databases to gather information and establish contact with international experts on this topic. They have formed book groups to read the autobiographies of Holocaust survivors. In Australia, Argentina and the United States students are taking an active role in locating Holocaust survivors in their communities and recording their accounts. High school students have developed lessons to share the information they have found with children in nearby elementary schools. As the project has grown to include young people from more countries, the original focus of the Holocaust has expanded to include other examples of genocide and forms of oppression. Students in Cambodia, from the Khmer Students and Intellectuals Association, have discussed the mass killings that took place in their country during the Pol Pot era. They have also helped bring to the attention of their peers in other countries the role that weapon sales from foreigners may play in stepping up the scale of the violence that takes place. Students in the United States have researched hate groups and sought to raise funds for those directly affected by the burning of African American churches in their country. Koorie (indigenous) students from Australia have encouraged their peers in their own and other countries to classify "silent massacres" — such as high rates of infant mortality and incarceration ending in death — as "blatant racism." In so doing they point out that racist acts come not just from hate groups but also emerge from institutional racist practices by well-meaning individuals. (Further information can be found about this project on the WWW: <http://www.igc.org/iearn/hgp>.)

▶ The web-based "Walk to Canada" project is an example of a "virtual field trip." Unlike other "electronic" field trips, in which scientists report on their travels to distant locations, a historian who leads students on a journey back in time de-

Como se sienten
las niñas y los
niños porque no
hablan el ingles

"How boys and girls feel when they don't speak English."

Soluciones para los
niños afectados.

Que las maestras
aprendan español

Traten a todos los niños
y niñas igual

Que los traten en su
idioma para que ellos
no se sienten inferior.

"Solutions: That teachers learn Spanish. Treat all children equally. Speak in the child's language so that the children don't feel inferior."

Pages from a student-authored book about the experience of Mexican and Zapotec students in a California school. The book was created as part of the "We are Authors" project with teacher Nancy Jean Smith.

signed this project. Anthony Cohen, an African American historian from Maryland, retraced the steps of the original Underground Railroad, traveling by foot from Maryland through Pennsylvania and New York State to a destination in Ontario, Canada. Whenever possible he stayed in the same places that fleeing enslaved African Americans stayed in. Along the way Anthony collected oral histories, recorded his reflections and posted weekly reports describing places he stopped on his trip. He welcomed questions from students, which were sent to his messengers via e-mail. The messengers then delivered him the questions in person or by telegraph, the only forms of written communication available to African Americans fleeing from slavery on the Underground Railroad. The messengers then posted these questions, along with the answers offered, on the WWW. Anthony's hope of bringing this period of history to life for school children is being realized as teachers and students use his research on the Underground Railroad as a springboard for discussions and questions about the nature of slavery, oppression, and resistance. (This project was funded by the National Parks of Canada. For more information see <http://www.npca.org/walk.html>.)

(d) Counteracting the devaluation in our schools of knowledge from non-dominant cultures and the resulting alienation of students from their families.

▶ "We are Authors" is an example of an on-line "meet the author" project, conducted from an anti-racist perspective. For two years bilingual children's book author and critical educator Alma Flor Ada corresponded with Spanish- and English-speaking children in the United States, Mexico and Puerto Rico. In response to the children's e-mail asking how one becomes an author, Dr. Ada created a videotape in which she read from her books, talked about where the ideas for her stories came from and the underlying themes of cultural diversity and social justice, and encouraged each of the students and teachers to write a book of their own. As students shared their questions, successes and doubts as writers, the teachers in the project became concerned that the children who felt that there was nothing in their lives to write about tended to be students of color from the very poorest communities. Drawing on the work of Paulo Freire, Dr. Ada shared a theoretical framework for helping students draw on their lived experiences in finding ideas for their writing and for helping teachers and students see how schools often convey underlying messages about the relative importance of the different cultures that compose the school community.

The project continued for a second year as Dr. Ada guided the teachers setting up family literacy programs at the schools. Students began working with their parents, many of whom had little formal schooling, to write books on such topics as the

Alma Flor Ada with a student in an Orillas class at Escuela Don Tito in Puerto Rico.

diverse regions to collaborate rapidly in a wide-ranging investigation of proverbs. In this exchange students and their families were particularly interested in studying the social and historical contexts in which proverbs have been used. First, students consulted with grandparents and extended family members in the collection of proverbs. Key facts about each proverb — such as when grandmother used it and what she *really* meant — were typed into a computer database. Students then consulted with their partner classes as they discussed both the literal and figurative meanings of each proverb, noting the controversial, and sometimes contradictory, nature of proverbs. Not all proverbs are wise, they concluded; many are racist, sexist, and ageist. Students and their families identified and critiqued the proverbs they did not agree with, writing modern fables and opinion statements on "what's wrong with this proverb" and discussing the social fabric in which the proverbs have developed and exist. In this way, proverbs were used not only as a vehicle for students to share cultural and linguistic knowledge, but also to critique situations that we may have taken for granted in the "good old days" such as "a woman's place is in the home." (These two projects were organized by teachers in

families' hopes and visions for their futures, experiences in coming to the United States, and harsh conditions and inequities in their places of work. Participants published book after book, beginning to analyze the conditions of their lives. Students, no longer hesitant to speak out, organized research and writing projects at their schools to help make the teachers and school community aware of the ways in which certain voices are silenced, how language practices affect children of different groups, and what their recommendations are for changes in school policies. At many of the schools the family literacy programs continue and copies of the student- and parent-authored books have now been placed in the school and classroom libraries as resources for biliteracy development.

▶ Folklore collections and oral histories can be instrumental in building bridges between schools and families and within the wider community of speakers of a particular language — both among the diaspora of local immigrant communities and their cultures of origin around the world. In the Orillas International Proverbs Project, telecommunications made it possible for Spanish-, Portuguese- and English-speaking communities from

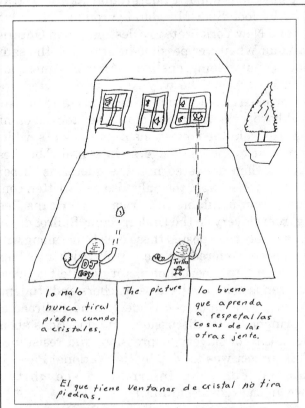

People who live in glass houses should not throw stones. Illustration by Ruben Davila, 5th grade, New Haven, CT, from the Orillas Proverbs and Beyond Tolerance Project.

the project "De Orilla a Orilla." For more information see: <http://orillas.upr.clu.edu>.)

(e) Restructuring the curriculum in schools to examine content area studies from a broader sociocultural perspective.

▶ Curricular divisions in schools usually link math with science in isolation from the social studies curriculum. When mathematics is instead taught "across the curriculum," multiple opportunities arise to use math to uncover stereotypes, understand history, and examine issues of inequality. In a telecommunications project organized by Orillas teachers in Puerto Rico, "The Power of Mathematics: Connecting Math to Our Lives," elementary and secondary students use math skills to compare and analyze data they have gathered in their schools and communities and have received from other classes on the network. Some schools are exchanging data on-line in order to investigate the wide range of income levels in society. As they analyze wage distribution based on state, country, ethnic group, gender and kind of work done, they gain real-world practice in the use of fractions, percentages, statistics and graphing. At the same time, with the help of their social studies teachers, they are learning important lessons on the value of disaggregating the data when analyzing social problems and are addressing important questions about the implications of the data they have found such as "what problems in our country would be reduced if wealth were distributed more equally?" Other schools are sharing data on the network as they examine issues of representation in schools and in the media. Participating classes have divided class members into teams to look at the ways in which different groups are represented in the instructional materials and images found at their school site. Several teams are conducting their investigations in the school library. One team analyzes the biographies on the library shelves in terms of gender, race, class and other categories of their choice. Other teams have chosen to look at how different groups are represented in the city newspapers and CD Rom encyclopedias in the reference section. Meanwhile another team tours the school campus to gather corresponding data on the images that appear on the walls of the classrooms, hallways and offices, asking not only who is represented but in what context.

Teachers report that their classes have gained a heightened awareness of these issues; students are more observant of the TV shows they watch at home and of the texts they use in the classroom, noting not only who appears in these books but what they are doing when they do appear, whose perspectives are represented, and whether the authors of the texts invite the readers to consider the biases of what they are presenting. The project also encourages students to reflect on how their research findings influence the way they think about themselves and how publishing and power operate. In their math classes students compare the percentages of the images they have found for each group with the distributions of those groups in the larger society and in their own community. Creating line and bar graphs, they present their findings in person to other students and teachers and decision-makers at their school site and on-line to students conducting parallel investigations at other sites. Through this project students are not only practicing their math skills but also learning how decisions are made in educational settings and taking action to influence future decision-making around the selection of materials and books in schools. (This project was based on an article by Bob Peterson entitled "Teaching Math Across the Curriculum: A Fifth Grade Teacher Battles 'Number Numbness.'" *Rethinking Schools*, Fall 1995, Vol. 10 No.1. For a more detailed description of the math networking activities, contact Kristin Brown at <krbrown@igc.apc.org>.)

▶ At a large high school in Oxnard, CA, immigrant students and their English as a Second Language (E.S.L.) teachers have redesigned the E.S.L. curriculum to employ more interactive teaching methods and a problem-posing approach to selecting the content through which English will be learned. Problem-posing is a process of group dialogue that helps students see the social, historical, and cultural causes of problems rather than blame themselves for having difficulty; through the dialogue they gain knowledge and self-confidence to act to make changes in their lives, in the school, and in the community. Among the problems that the immigrant students from Southeast Asia, Latin America and the Pacific Islands examined were how to involve the immigrant parents in decision-making at the school, how students in E.S.L. programs can be selected for student councils and other school activities important for inclusion on college applications, and how to name and confront racism in their classes. In the process, the students have learned not only to speak in English, but also gained the confidence to speak out. A number of these students speak so compassionately about the experiences of a newly arrived immigrant and have articulated so clearly the educational and social barriers they've confronted and effective solutions for overcoming them that they have been invited to state and regional conferences to talk to groups of teachers and parents.

The students (who have now formed a student activist group called the Students for Cultural and Linguistic Democracy (S.C.a.L.D.)) have begun using telecommunications as a tool for sharing with students at other schools some of the hard-won lessons they've learned for overcoming the isolation they sometimes feel at their own school when they raise controversial issues. The students with whom S.C.a.L.D. corresponds underscore how valuable it has been for them to meet a group of students with such clearly articulated plans for taking action in the public school system. In the New Places Project, members of S.C.a.L.D. networked with students in Argentina, Australia, China and South Africa in examining how schools deal with immigrant students. As this international team of students compared their findings about ways in which school structures may perpetuate racism and made recommendations to address these problems, the students from Oxnard described strategies for involving parents, setting up bilingual programs and

S.C.a.L.D. exchange is launched with a live audio-conference — a Mexican student in Oxnard, California discusses with Puerto Rican students in Connecticut the plans for a joint investigation on immigration.

organizing community conferences. In another exchange, S.C.a.L.D. employed computer conferencing, audio phones and video phones to communicate with a large urban high school in Hartford, CT. As a result the Puerto Rican immigrant students in Hartford have set up a similar group, in their case called Rompiendo Barreras (Breaking Barriers). S.C.a.L.D. and Rompiendo Barreras have become mutual support groups as they take the role of social change agents in their schools. (Teachers and students from S.C.a.L.D. have authored two chapters in the book, *Reclaiming Our Voices: Bilingual Education and Critical Pedagogy and Praxis* edited by J. Frederickson and a chapter in *Education Reform and Social Change* edited by C.E. Walsh.)

What makes these and other networking projects effective contexts for confronting racism? As we attempted to show in the examples, many of these educators have begun to reframe education around critical inquiry and the collaborative generation of knowledge in such a way that the experience and cultural contributions of all students are valued. Rather than passively internalizing the sanitized curriculum promoted by socially powerful groups, students are actively generating their own intercultural literacy through dialogue and collaborative research with colleagues in their own classroom and in classrooms across the globe.

Yet there is something else important happening here. By opening their classrooms and their minds to experiences from cultures other than their own, these students and teachers are not unwittingly turning their backs on their own. In fact, the students have become more aware of their own culture as a result of the contrast they have experienced with another. For example, in the proverbs project that involved scores of schools in several countries, students' cross-cultural skills were enhanced as they used telecommunications to discuss the proverbs with many other classes and compile them into a multilingual publication. At the same time, "high technology" led to intergenerational learning that in turn fostered a deeper critical understanding of each student's cultural heritage. The contexts for collaborative learning and for confronting real world issues provided by long-distance partnerships often open rich opportunities for teachers and students to learn both about the world, and through the questions that are sent from afar, about themselves. Together, the projects depicted in these vignettes illustrate in various ways what we have termed a "pedagogy of distancing."

PAINTING BY DESSIN D'HERVE PINEL FROM LE MONDE DE L'ÉDUCATION, NOVEMBER 1996

Célestin Freinet

In the next section, we'll examine in greater depth the role of distancing in the work of both Freire and Freinet. Through their work, we'll learn more about both the special role that technology can play in a pedagogy of distancing as well as the link between distancing and the kind of critical inquiry that can help form a solid foundation for addressing issues of racism.

PART TWO: HISTORICAL ROOTS OF THE "PEDAGOGY OF DISTANCING"

Too often, when analyzing the role of technology in education, our focus on recent innovation obscures the decades of hard-won achievements by progressive teachers using educational technology. The danger lies in ignoring the relationship of our work to the practice of those who have gone before, failing to do justice to the contributions of people throughout the world who have built the traditional elements which get renamed and incorporated into others' liberating practices. Questions of ownership are ignored and those with the newest technology often get credit for the ideas of others. This section draws on the work of two gound-breaking educators concerned with the link between community-based learning and action for social justice: Paulo Freire (1921-1997) and Celestin Freinet (1896 - 1966). Although both these educators began explor-

ing the use of technology to these ends before the advent of computers and the Internet, their work has important lessons for us now.

DIFFERENT HISTORIES, SIMILAR CONCERNS

After the military coup of April 1964, the Brazilian popular educator Paulo Freire was arrested, imprisoned and eventually forced into exile. Government authorities were reacting to Freire's successes in mounting massive literacy campaigns among illiterate adults. Freire's Popular Culture Movement (PCM) had been expanding to include 20,000 "Culture Circles,"each serving 25 to 30 rural and urban slum residents who were working to build both their literacy skills and an awareness of their collective ability to generate change in their communities.

Paulo Freire's writings on adult literacy have influenced educators in countless countries. Less widely known in the English-speaking world —but no less influential — has been the work of Celestin Freinet of France. As Freire himself acknowledged: "I am flattered to have my work associated with that of Celestin Freinet." Freire recognized Freinet as "one of the great contemporaries in education for freedom" (cited in Lee, 1983).

French educators Celestin and Elise Freinet founded what remains the largest school-to-school network in history — the Modern School Movement (MSM). Celestin Freinet, who remained a rural elementary school teacher all his life, and his wife Elise developed a teaching approach which has shaped the practice of educators throughout Europe and Latin America and in many African and Asian nations (Sayers 1990).

In the Freinet network, partner teachers in faraway communities worked on identical curricular projects in both their classrooms. Their students produced joint newspapers, conducted dual community surveys, collected oral histories and folklore at both sites, or mounted parallel science investigations. Using the national postal service to exchange curricular projects, Freinet established team-teaching partnerships between 10,000 schools. In fact, so many teachers in the Freinet network organized to demand government support for their inter-school exchanges that to this day every French teacher pays *nothing* to use the national postal service for educational projects.

While Freire's work centers on adult literacy education, Freinet was concerned principally with school-age students. Their experiences differ in other ways as well. Freire's literacy projects were initiated in Latin American and African countries, where he elaborated a pedagogy that has had an impact felt in many industrialized countries. Freinet, on the other hand, began his work in France and eventually established team-teaching partnerships in 33 countries on every continent but Antarctica. Freire's Culture Circles sought to confront, through *face-to-face* dialogue, the day-to-day concerns confronting urban and peasant communities, while Freinet's team-teaching exchanges *over long distances* acted as a catalyst for critical thinking and social action at the local level.

However, both Freire and Freinet recognized the pedagogical benefits of educational technology. Both employed technology in developing teaching approaches that encouraged a special brand of "distancing" by learners from their day-to-day reality, yet at the same time fostering a critical "engagement" with that reality. By examining the characteristics of "distancing" in the teaching approaches of first Paulo Freire and then Celestin and Elise Freinet, we learn more about a pedagogical approach that will be useful in developing anti-bias curriculum and restructuring our schools so that the focus is on critical thinking and inquiry.

PAULO FREIRE AND "GAINING DISTANCE"

Literacy instruction in Freire's campaigns was divided into two parts: a pre-literacy phase and a literacy-building phase. In the pre-literacy phase, slides were created that relied entirely on graphic, non-written representations. These slides, which could be projected in front of the group, depicted culture as a vital social process in which the community plays an active, determining role. During the literacy-building phase, the slides used both graphic and written representations of key community concerns — called "generative themes"— which literacy workers had identified after weeks of research with local residents.

What role does technology play in helping to create a distance between learners and their day-to-day routines? Let's take a look at the first and last slide of Freire's pre-literacy phase in examining the power of distancing. In the first slide of the series depicting a line drawing of a village scene, we

Paulo Freire

see a house, a person holding a farming tool, a pig rooting in the garden and a bird flying overhead — all commonplace elements in the lives of the villagers of Northern Brazil. Significantly, Freire chose not to show photographs but instead to use the drawings. This decision was based on the assumption that the abstract portrayal of these day-to-day elements would evoke in the cultural circle participants a greater sense of distance from the images than would a familiar photograph.

Participants in the culture circles, with the

Slide 1. (Reprinted from Literacy in 30 Hours: Paulo Freire's Process in North East Brazil *by Cynthia Brown (COLT, 1978)).*

guidance of a PCM facilitator, began to discuss not a particular pig, bird, house or person but what these elements represent in the broader socio-political context. In this simple act of creating graphic depictions that are at once one step removed from the lives of the peasants yet still grounded in their everyday realities, a process of distancing was initiated that would lead to shared critical reflection and decisive, active engagement to transform those realities. He begins the process of distancing.

The tenth and last slide of the pre-literacy phase illustrates the importance Freire placed on technology-mediated dialogue. It depicts the participants gathered around a slide projector, viewing and discussing one of the previous slides. Freire writes, "This slide represents the working of a Culture Circle. Upon seeing it, the participants easily identify with the process it depicts. They discuss culture as the systematic acquisition of knowledge, but also of the democratization of culture. ... The participants analyze the working of their Culture Circle, its dynamic sense, the creative force of dialogue and of conscientization" (1969, p. 142).

culture by making the slide's image "shareable" among all participants. Indeed, Freire wrote that "[when a] representation is projected as a slide, the learners effect an operation basic to the act of knowing: *they gain distance from the knowable object.* This experience is undergone as well by the educators, so that educators and learners together can reflect critically on the knowable object which mediates between them" (p. 15).

Particularly significant was the direct link between "distancing" and literacy development. Each slide was termed a "codification." It depicted a scene composed of elements which had been carefully selected and arranged by literacy workers to raise issues and provoke discussion. In the pre-literacy phase, as adult learners examined and discussed each of the elements composing the scene, they *decodified* the slide's meaning. Then, after arriving at a group consensus on the multiple possibilities for community action to effectively address the issue depicted in the slide, the adult learners engaged in a process of *recodification.* The fact that participants could not read was not allowed to prevent their considering highly complex issues. Having become more critically conscious of their lives and communities, they could explore together alternate realities and possibilities for improving their situation.

Slide 10. (Reprinted from Literacy in 30 Hours: Paulo Freire's Process in North East Brazil by Cynthia Brown (COLT, 1978)).

Next, in the literacy-building phase, the graphic codifications were then supplemented by a short list of written words summarizing each slide's theme. Using these slides, the *decoding* of a word by analyzing the separate syllables used to create the word — a parallel process to earlier decodifications — was introduced. Finally, through *recoding*, learners produced many new words by using the letters and syllables in the words they had learned to read as building blocks for new words — words such as people, vote, and employment. In this way they completed in the realm of phonemes and graphemes a writing process that remains squarely rooted in a reading of the adult learners' world and of the possibilities for communal social action to transform that world. In this way entire communities learned that

Every element of this slide, like the nine slides which preceded it, had been carefully arranged to encourage discussion of cultural action for change. Significantly, in this transparency the slide projector *itself* occupies a central place. Freire felt that the audiovisual technology contributed an essential element to the Culture Group's discussion, playing a central role in the democratization of they could transfer the skills they had confidently developed in "reading the world" to also "reading the word" (Freire, P. and Macedo, D. 1987).

For Freire, audiovisual technology played a large role in fostering reflective distancing. Certainly, this point was not lost on the military junta who sought to extirpate his influence in Brazil. Not surprisingly, they burned all the printed literacy materials they could lay their hands on, and thus joined ranks with book burners from reactionary regimes throughout history frightened by "subversive" ideas contained in published materials. But the military government took a further step, which shows they appreciated the dangers in Freire's use of educational technology: they also destroyed the *slide projectors* whose only crime was to display images for thousands of Culture Circles.

CELESTIN AND ELISE FREINET AND "DISTANCING OURSELVES"

In the 1920s Celestin and Elise Freinet developed three complementary teaching techniques that encouraged students to engage with their classmates, their families and the community, while at the same time gaining the necessary distance to see their familiar surroundings from new perspectives.

The first technique was the "learning walk." Weather permitting, students would join Freinet in exploratory walks through their community. During these walks, impressions were gathered which formed the basis for subsequent classroom activities in reading and writing, social studies, science and math. As a regular follow-up activity to these walks, the students authored what Freinet called "free texts," group-authored texts centering on community issues. Soon Freinet introduced his second technique — *classroom printing* — to help students place even more value on their writing. Freinet brought into classrooms the most advanced printing technologies of his time — the mimeograph machine and the movable type printing press — to produce hundreds of copies of the students' "free texts" for their families and friends. With Freinet's third technique — long-distance *class-to-class partnerships* — teachers and their students increasingly turned to educational technology as a *cultural amplifier*. Audiovisual technologies such as photos and audio tapes played the important role of "turning up the volume" and compensating for the inevitable distortions introduced as messages crossed time, space and cultures.

For Elise and Celestin Freinet, school-to-school exchanges were not an end in themselves. Rather, partnerships between faraway classes served as the indispensable precursor to a more profound and active engagement with social realities much closer to home. These long-distance learning partnerships create a context — we might even say a pretext — for students to collaborate more intensively with people in their *own* classroom and community.

When we live very close to our surroundings and to people, we eventually come not to see them.

> ... But thanks to the questions sent from our distant colleagues, our eyes are opened. We question, we investigate, we explore more deeply in order to respond with precise verifications to the inexhaustible curiosity of our distant collaborators, based on a natural motivation. This gradually leads to an awareness of our entire geographic, historic, and human environment (Gervilliers et al., 1968/1977).

Through this activity, students could come to replace an unquestioning view of their world with a more objective, conscious and critical perspective.

The student, because she needs to describe them, develops an awareness of the conditions of her life, of the life of her town or her neighborhood, even of her province.

> ... She had been living too close to these conditions and through inter-school exchanges she has distanced herself from them in order to better comprehend the conditions of her life (p. 31).

Yet "distancing" is not the only outcome. Students also discover multiple opportunities for purposeful *engagement* with their day-to-day reality. According to Freinet, reflective distancing leads to social action: "Inter-school networks ... are conducive to a true cultural formation, offering to each individual several possibilities of action over his surroundings, and causing a profound engagement with human beings and with things past, present and future" (p. 15).

IN SUMMARY

For Freire and the Freinets, critical learning involves a two-fold process of *reflective distancing* and *purposeful engagement* with the physical and social world. Educational technology played as central a role in Celestin and Elise Freinet's inter-school partnerships as it did in Paulo Freire's Culture Circles, acting as a catalyst for critical reflection in these two popular pedagogies, each of which linked distancing with social action. In the next section, we reflect further on how we might take advantage of a pedagogy of distancing in our own work.

Processes in Collaborative Critical Inquiry

A distancing context...

> Involves exchange between two or more learning partners who are unknown but knowable
>
> There are both real differences and intriguing similarities between partners
>
> There is a sharing of power, with mutual respect and greatly reduced status differentials
>
> Activity structure encourages genuine inquiry

... that encourages SELF-DISCLOSURE...

> Activity involves asynchrony, pausing, time to reflect
>
> Requires looking inward, making conscious what you already know, and externalizing this self-reflection
>
> Also requires looking outward and examining the community in which you live and learn
>
> Based on awareness that if you are not willing to reveal your own world, you cannot expect others to show you theirs, and thus cannot compare their knowledge with yours to build new meanings

... and "CROSS-CULTURAL" COMPARISONS...

> Comparing what you have learned from self-disclosure with your partner's self-portrait
>
> Noticing discrepancies, "gaps" and discontinuities between the self-portraits

... then, QUESTIONING and MORE SELF-DISCLOSURE...

> Verbalizing these discrepancies, "gaps" and discontinuities so that your partner reflect, respond, and act, that is, in written format or using another communication technology
>
> Responding to the surprising statements and inquiries of your partner in a way that encourages reflection, reacting, and action

... with NEW OPPORTUNITIES TO DISCOVER AND DISPLAY TALENTS, locally and at a distance...

> Developing a new appreciation for others in your own community as you draw on their knowledge and skills to interpret and respond to the questions raised by your partners
>
> Gaining new perspectives in analyzing problems and issues and greater awareness of how to draw on community resources to take action locally

... leading to JOINT ACTION resulting from SHARED EMPOWERMENT.

> Based on a deeper analysis of socio-political and environmental issues and how they are played out in different localities
>
> Transforming learning into action as students help one another "think globally and act locally."

Figure 3

PART THREE
CREATING CONTEXTS FOR COLLABORATIVE CRITICAL INQUIRY: GLOBAL LEARNING NETWORKS

Coercive relations of power are not inevitable. In fact, virtually all of us are familiar with an alternative way of relating among people, communities and nations. We have all experienced how power can be generated in interpersonal relationships — how the empowerment of one partner augments rather than diminishes the power of the other. This section describes how technology, when coupled with a pedagogy of distancing, can serve as a catalyst to initiate these collaborative relations of power in the classroom and school.

We attempt to sketch out how educators and students together can create, through their classroom interactions, a microcosm of the kind of society where everybody feels a strong sense of belonging regardless of race, gender, language, culture, creed or sexual orientation. The creation of these interpersonal and collective spaces, where students learn to critique the roots of inequality, represent an act of resistance to those elements within the societal power structure that are intolerant of difference and are motivated to maximize individual profit at the expense of the common good.

Briefly, the basic processes at work in creating context for critical and collaborative inquiry are summarized in Figure 3 and discussed in more detail in the section below. It is important to note that a long-distance partnership does not by itself lead to probing dialogues. The direction these dialogues take is greatly influenced by the way in which educators who are serious about anti-racist practices take advantage of "teachable moments" that arise and how these shape learning experiences.

It is also important to clarify that the processes highlighted in this overview rarely take place in a linear fashion. For example, opportunities for students to discover and display talents and experiences may arise at many points in an exchange, as can possibilities for reflection and community action. It should also be understood that the principles outlined apply regardless of whether two, three or more classes are working together or when exchanges take place between groups in non-school community-based settings.

1. THE DISTANCING CONTEXT

Distance, in the context of class-to-class exchanges, creates the possibility of collaboration with an unknown but knowable audience. It is the process of "coming to know" the other group and reflecting on what is being learned at each stage that sets into motion further inquiry and action. Careful attention to planning at the outset will help establish a context for sustained dialogue, shared decision-making, and a trusting relationship conducive to exploring issues related to racism.

COMMITMENT

Teachers attest that the most critical element in long-distance team-teaching is the quality of the working relationship between the two classes. Frequent and regular communication help forge the most satisfying relationships; silence is difficult to interpret. This may mean at times simply sending a note to let the other group know about the progress you're making, the obstacles you've encountered locally, or the lessons you're learning. Teachers also discover that long-distant partnerships may require more specific planning and timelines than they might otherwise need in their own classrooms. When both teachers keep their commitment, there are few strategies that are more exciting and rewarding; if not, the results will be measured in the frustration and disappointment of students in both classes.

CHOOSING A PARTNER

Creating a partnership where there is a social or geographical distance between the classes provides a natural opening for questions. Yet it doesn't necessarily hold true that the greater the distance the better. It is important not to overlook the possibilities that emerge for in-depth dialogues when these real differences are also accompanied by intriguing similarities. One example is the productive dialogue bilingual educators in the U.S. have found when "cross-cultural" communication takes place between students from the same culture. Even though students from the two classes may share a common heritage, for one group of recent arrivals that heritage may be a living reality while for the other students, from the same culture but born in the United States, it may be a cultural and linguistic tradition in danger of fading into another kind of distance, that of a distant memory. Similarly, when immigrant groups are linked back to their homelands, communication over geographic and cultural distance can create a context for cultural revitalization of

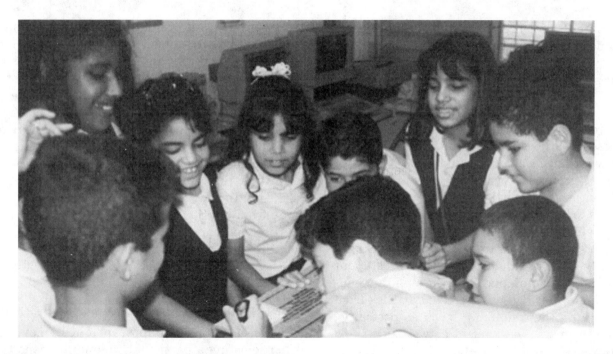

Students at Escuela Abelardo Diaz Morales in Puerto Rico open an Orillas 'culture package.' They will guess the location of their partner class based on geographical and cultural clues.

traditions that are devalued in the dominant society.

Caution should be taken that the choice of language does not place one class at an undue advantage. It shouldn't necessarily be expected that all classes work in English. If your class doesn't include native speakers of the language your partner class writes in, you may want to collaborate locally with native speakers of that language who can translate, such as parents or bilingual teachers down the hall. So that the exchange meets the needs of both classes, we encourage teachers to rephrase the question, "In which language shall we write?" to one of "What language shall we use for which activities?"

CHOOSING AN ACTIVITY STRUCTURE

Next, work with your partner to find an activity structure that will have room to encourage real questioning. Teachers new to telecommunications often wonder whether "penpals," sometimes called "keypals," offer a good place to start. Our experiences have shown that this activity is more appropriate as an advanced project or as an extracurricular exchange among a few students. There are a number of obstacles to maintaining the continuity of penpal exchanges between two classes, including frequent student absences, high student mobility rates and differing class sizes. Instead, choose an activity structure that will lead to class discussions, frequent and active dialogues involving all the students in your class.

Some examples of successful team-teaching projects include: a) shared student journalism and publishing; b) comparative investigations, including dual community surveys, joint science investigations, and contrastive geography projects; and c) oral histories and traditional and modern folklore compendia, ranging from community narratives to intergenerational collections of proverbs, game songs, children's rhymes and folktales. These projects tend to encourage collaboration and discussion through shared decision-making, interdependent cooperative activity in small groups at both sites, publications that reflect the voices of all involved, and investigations outside of school in which students interact in new ways with their families, relatives, and the elders of their community.

2. CREATING OPPORTUNITIES FOR SELF-DISCLOSURE

A partner class relationship is based on the awareness that if you are not willing to reveal your own world, you cannot expect others to show you theirs. Thus you cannot compare their knowledge with yours to build new meanings. Students' keen interest in getting to know their partner class and finding out "what it's really like over there," provides them a natural incentive to take great care not to misrepresent their own reality. This desire to be honest and correct and to double-check one's facts provides a good context in which to conduct anti-racist education.

CREATING A CLASS SELF-PORTRAIT

Before engaging in a curriculum project between two classes, teachers usually find it helpful to exchange what have come to be known as "discovery packages," "group self-portraits" or "culture packages." Whatever name is chosen, the function of the package is to break the ice and establish a common point of reference between distant classes by exchanging a group "self-portrait." Discovery packages may be envelopes or small boxes filled with student autobiographies, maps, photographs, audio and videotapes, and other carefully selected articles from the school and the community such as postcards, school newspapers, and student artwork.

Many classes find this activity so valuable that a series of packages are exchanged throughout the year, each time exploring more fully with students the provocative questions, "What is culture?" "What are the cultures represented in our class and community?" and "How might we represent our cultures to another group?" Critical educators emphasize that "one of the goals of multicultural education is to show that culture is not a collection of "quaint customs" but actually a system of "strategies for living" (Menkart). Teachers can encourage students to identify metaphors and symbols to include that represent the values, ways of knowing, and social relationships that have helped members of their culture survive and thrive. The least interesting packages are random collections of artifacts; the most interesting are carefully composed collections of symbols that reveal values and relationships within the community.

As anti-racist educators we need to help our students move beyond a discussion of the surface features of culture. When students mention food, folklore and festivals, we can push them further in their thinking to consider the historical, economic and political contexts in which these customs have evolved, asking how the customs are employed, where they come from and what they might have to do with solidarity or resistance. In a networking project involving K-12 and university level students in a study of twentieth century African American migration, one of the African American graduate students shared a recipe that had been handed down in his family from this period. A question was raised by one of the white students, "What do lemon bars have to do with the

more serious issue of migration?" A rich exchange ensued on-line in which an African American professor explained that the exchange of recipes and discussion about food was very much a part of the history of migration. The preparation for the trip north could be extensive; families were often justifiably afraid of having to stop along the way and risk not finding a restaurant willing to seat "colored" people. Why was the African American community of this era fearful? When we accept the term "migration" to describe the mass movement away from the South during this period and focus on the opportunities available to African Americans in the North, we often fail to recognize the role that the dramatic rise in the number of lynchings at that time played in the move north.

ASYNCHRONOUS VS. SYNCHRONOUS COMMUNICATION

One of the most important questions to ask when selecting a particular communications technology is whether it allows time for the students to reflect on the exchange. When given the choice between asynchronous technologies (those not occurring in "real time" such as e-mail, regular mail, or computer bulletin board conferencing) and other seemingly "higher tech" synchronous options (such as a real-time C-U-See-Me or "live" IRC relay chats), educators often choose the option which allows for reflection and local dialogue. Having extra planning time as well as opportunities to seek assistance from people locally who can serve as language and cultural resources can help share power between and within classes and build students' confidence.

3. CROSS-CULTURAL COMPARISONS

As school and community "self-portraits" are exchanged — whether they take the form of "discovery packages" at the beginning of an exchange or of shared texts as part of a jointly-planned curriculum project — partner classes begin to compare and contrast their communities and world views, which are so often taken for granted. In a partner class relationship each side becomes "the other." There are two different norms to be explored, with each reality told by those on the inside and then reexamined in response to questions from those on the outside. Through this sharing students gain new perspective-taking skills. Rarely in schools do dominant groups have a chance to see their own culture reflected back through the eyes of another. Rarely do subordinated groups have the chance to define how they would like to be seen by others and convey what they think is most significant about their culture.

Responding to Your Partner's Self-Portrait

The day that a discovery package arrives is an exciting day in any partner class. As a rule, everything else stops in the classroom as the teacher and students prepare to discover the contents of the package. Yet students' natural enthusiasm when opening the package can be channeled by teachers to further magnify the learning experience. The sending class can help the receiving class maximize the impact of the discovery package by including a detailed "packing slip." The sending class itemizes on a piece of paper what they are including in the package and why they think the partner class will find each item of interest. The receiving teacher then uses this packing slip to shape her or his class's discussions as the contents of the discovery package are revealed, item by item.

The receiving class, in turn, should take a few moments and jot down notes of their reactions to the items in the discovery package. The teacher can ask students to discuss such key topics as "what we liked best or found most interesting about the package you sent us," "questions we have after receiving your package," and "things about your class, your school, and your community that we would like to know more about" — all topics of tremendous interest to the sending class. Send these questions and comments by return post or by e-mail immediately to the distant partner class. For example, an item for a packing slip might be:

Item: An article from the most recent issue of our school newspaper

Why we thought you would find this of interest: Check out the author! Monique is one of five students in our class who is also in the journalism club. In this article she interviews the school principal about a controversial issue at our school just now: racial slurs that have appeared on the walls of the school bathrooms. Does this ever happen at your school? Why do you think students do this and what should the next steps be? Most of us agree with Monique, that although this kind of graffiti hasn't appeared before it shouldn't be considered "an isolated incident." Race relations and discrimination are issues that we'd like to see talked about more directly at our school.

4. Questioning and Further Self-Disclosure

When teachers encourage their classes to notice discrepancies, "gaps," and discontinuities between the self-portraits that are exchanged, they help their students become keen observers of social realities. Anti-racist educators can help guide students in asking questions about new or unfamiliar situations that will help the students become more aware of equity issues in different parts of the world. These questions might include: Who is affected? Who benefits? Who suffers as a result? How are the resources being shared? Who was involved in making the decision? Who is affected by it? What are the written and unwritten rules in this situation? Who determines these rules?

Another line of questioning that has proven to be particularly productive is to encourage students to reflect on the "gaps" in their own thinking and to elaborate on the difference between what they found and expected to find in the context of these exchanges. What was surprising about this? How did my expectations differ from reality? What do we know so far? What might we expect to hear? What do you predict their response will be to the questions we posed? When students receive a text or self-portrait, opportunities arise to ask not only what we are finding out about the other side but what we are learning about our own thinking. What preconceptions were we holding? How have these been deepened or changed? This, in turn, can lead to questioning how our opinions are formed. How does the media present such cultural issues? How does what we hear in the media differ from what we are finding in this first hand account? As critical educator and curriculum developer Bill Bigelow reminds us, questioning is at the heart of an anti-racist curriculum. "Multicultural education should be based on a problem-solving approach, using inequity in this society as the core problem. The curriculum should pose the big "why" questions. Why is there racism? Why is there sexism? What are the roots of social conflicts?" (Bigelow, 1993)

Engaging in a Joint Curriculum Project

In a partnership, students jointly pose a significant problem of mutual interest to be investigated locally, decide on a basis for comparison of what is being learned, discover and refine comparable tools of study, and share and compare the outcomes of parallel locally-based studies to help one another transform learning into action. Where do the topics for investigation come from? Ideally they emerge from the students' interests in both classes. The themes may emerge from a discussion that was sparked during the initial cultural package exchange, from the curriculum areas or units being studied in both classes, or from personal interests and experiences of the students.

Teachers committed to anti-racist education find ways to use students' interests as a point of departure for significant investigations. Bill Bigelow encourages critical educators to help students "find social meaning in individual experience — to push students to use their stories as windows not only on their lives, but on society" (p. 439). Partner class projects create provocative avenues for questioning as young people are stretched in their thinking to examine familiar issues from new perspectives and to consider how two seemingly unrelated local realities may be manifestations of a broader social or political issue. Projects evolve in fascinating ways as students continue to ask such questions as, "what are the real issues here?"

5. DISCOVERING AND DISPLAYING TALENTS LOCALLY

Class-to-class partnerships are characterized not only by a strong sense of inquiry between the distant classes but also by multiple opportunities for promoting new kinds of interactions at the local level. In order to respond to the probing questions that are raised by their distant colleagues, students often discover that they need to draw on a much wider range of skills and resources than are needed to complete the usual school assignments. As a result, students often gain a new appreciation for skills that they, their families and their classmates possess. For example, students who were once reluctant to speak up in class may find that they have specialized language or community-based skills that make their active participation valuable in the context of the exchange.

DESIGNING EXCHANGES TO AMPLIFY PREVIOUSLY SILENCED VOICES

When partnerships involve diverse student populations, an important dynamic is created — opportunities for renegotiating identities can take place not only at a distance but also locally. Anti-racist educator Enid Lee writes, "One of the ways that discrimination works is that it treats some people's experiences, lives and points of view as though they don't count, as though they are less valuable than other people's" (p. 20). Teachers can consciously design an exchange to help reverse patterns of discrimination at a school. In selecting a partner class and a theme to investigate, decisions can be made that privilege certain kinds of knowledge. For example, in a partnership between schools in Connecticut and Puerto Rico, a learning context was created that privileged Spanish language skills in the Connecticut school. The pres-

tige of the Spanish dominant immigrants was enhanced in the eyes of their English-speaking, Puerto Rican schoolmates who eagerly sought out their linguistic and translation skills in the context of the exchange. Other teachers consciously incorporate an oral history or community research component into project activities in order to help validate the knowledge of parents and families.

6. JOINT ACTIONS

The editors of *Rethinking Schools* have pointed out that students need opportunities to question social realities, to "talk back" to the world. Students who have edited and published newspapers and conducted opinion polls on issues of concern to communities around the world are well-equipped with research and analytical tools for effecting change and mobilizing support in their own communities. Through partner class exchanges, students also gain a deeper analysis of the need for change. They are exposed to new and more diverse perspectives in analyzing social problems through their discussions with both their partner class and other members of their community. As a result, their thinking is based on a more complete understanding of socio-political and environmental issues. Instead of seeing events in isolation, young people come to see, in a more sophisticated way, how local incidents are manifestations of broader patterns of oppression (such as how the media functions in society to validate some groups and to diminish the importance of others.) Through global learning networks, learning can be transformed into action as students learn to "think globally and act locally." At the same time this slogan is transformed into something much more personal than a political agenda, something that embodies the lived experiences, dreams and visions of the collaborating students as they build a better future.

CONCLUSION

Multicultural educators maintain a steadfast commitment to helping schools reverse patterns of failure for students of color and ensuring that all children develop the skills to succeed in our increasingly global and multicultural society. Yet at the same time, in a world where the gaps between the "haves" and the "have-nots" are widening, both in terms of information literacy and economic resources, we find ourselves needing to further our analysis. We need to ask how we can actively challenge the real causes of underachievement which are rooted in the social conditions of the schools and communities and in the way status and resources are distributed within the society.

We must be critical of technology's uses in our educational practice, especially when we are confronted daily with examples of its abuses, including technology-heavy privatization schemes, computer-"assisted" standardized testing, and the "remediation for the poor/enrichment for the rich" mindset. In this article we outlined an approach using computer technology to restructure power relations in schools and society. Yet many schools do not have access to technology or to the Internet. Although global learning networks do not depend on high technology, all teachers and students deserve a variety of tools from which to choose. Unfortunately, access to technology is still uneven, creating inequities both in access and information. Anti-racist educators can help raise the questions: In reality just how wide is the world wide web? Whose voices are there and whose are missing?

At the same time, our critical stance should not keep us from seeking out the potential of technology to promote reflective, socially engaged learning. Global learning networks, when used to promote a pedagogy of distancing, can provide an important tool in bringing educational communities together across cultural, racial and national boundaries to challenge structures of injustice in schools and other institutions of society and to seek to improve the world in which we live.

Kristin Brown specializes in the use of global learning networks to promote intercultural learning and colloborative and critical inquiry. She is a senior professional development specialist for the Pacific Southwest Regional Technology in Education Consortium (PSRTEC) at the Center for Language Minority Educational Research in Long Beach, California.

Jim Cummins teaches courses related to language learning and critical pedagogy at the Ontario Institute for Studies in Education at the University of Toronto. He has published widely on issues related to linguistic and cultural diversity and is the co-author with Dennis Sayers of Brave New Schools: Challenging Cultural Illiteracy through Global Learning Networks and the author of Negotiating Identities: Education for Empowerment in a Diverse Society.

Enid Figueroa is a specialist in curriculum and the integration of computers into the classroom. She is the co-founder, with Kristin Brown and Dennis Sayers, of the networking project "De Orilla a Orilla" and works at the University of Puerto Rico to coordinate this and other educational projects. She is currently a doctoral candidate at UPR conducting classroom-based research on the use of global learning networks to advance academic skills.

Dennis Sayers directs the Literacy, Diversity, and Technology Project at Ann Leavenworth Center for Academic Excellence in Fresno, California, a five-year teacher-researcher study of biliteracy and prosocial behavior acquisition within a two-way bilingual immersion program.

NOTE

1 For a fuller discussion see *Brave New Schools: Challenging Cultural Illiteracy through Global Learning Networks* by Jim Cummins and Dennis Sayers (1995, St. Martin's Press).

BIBLIOGRAPHY

Ada, A. F. 1995. "Fostering the home-school connection" in *Reclaiming our voices: Bilingual education, critical pedagogy & praxis*. pp. 163-178. Ontario, CA: California Association for Bilingual Education.

Allport, G. 1954 *The nature of prejudice*. Reading, MA: Addison-Wesley.

Bigelow, B., L. Christensen , S. Karp, B. Miner, and B. Peterson. 1994. "Creating classrooms for equity and social justice" in *Rethinking our classrooms: Teaching for equity and justice*. pp. 4-5. Milwaukee, WI: Rethinking Schools, Ltd.

Bigelow, B., B. Miner, and B. Peterson. 1991. "Why rethink Colombus?" in *Rethinking columbus*. p. 3. Milwaukee, WI: Rethinking Schools and NECA.

Bigelow, W. 1990. "Inside the classroom: Social vision and critical pedagogy" in *Teachers College Record*. 91.3: 437-448.

Brown, K. and J.C. Cuellar. 1995. "Global learning networks as a catalyst for change: Confronting prejudice between 'minority groups'" in *NABE News*. 18.6.

Brown, K., E. Figueroa, and D. Sayers. 1996. "What is Orillas?" in *Multicultural Education*. 3.3: 11.

Cummins, J. and D. Sayers. 1995. *Brave new schools: Challenging cultural illiteracy through global learning networks*. New York: St. Martin's Press.

Freinet, C. 1974. *Las tecnicas audiovisuales* (J. Colome, Trans). Barcelona: Editorial Laia.

Freinet, E. 1975. *Nacimiento de una pedagogia popular. Historia de una escuela moderna*. (Pere Vilanova, Trans.) Barcelona: Editorial Laia.

Freire, P. and D. Macedo. 1987. *Literacy: Reading the word and the world*. New York: Bergin and Garvey.

Freire, P. 1975. *Cultural action for freedom*. Cambridge, MA: Harvard Educational Review.

Freire, P. 1969. *La educacion como practica de la libertad*. Mexico DF: Siglo XXI Editores.

Gervilliers, D., Berteloot, C. & Lemery, J. 1977. *Las correspondencias escolares*. Barcelona: Editorial Laia.

Jasso, A. & R. 1995. "Critical pedagogy: Not a method, but a way of life" (pp. 253-259) in Frederickson, J. (Ed.) *Reclaiming our voices: Bilingual education, critical pedagogy & praxis*. Ontario, CA: California Association for Bilingual Education.

Lee, E. 1994. "Taking multicultural, anti-racist education seriously: An interview with educator Enid Lee" p. 19-22 in *Rethinking our classrooms: Teaching for equity and justice*. B. Bigelow, L. Christensen, S. Karp, B. Miner, and B. Peterson (Eds).

Lee, E. 1985. *Letters to Marcia: A teacher's guide to anti-racist education*. Toronto: Cross Cultural Communication Centre.

Lee, W. 1983. "Celestin Freinet, the unknown reformer." *Educational Forum*. 48.1: 97-113.

Levine, D., Lowe, R., Peterson, B., Tenorio, R, eds. 1995. *Rethinking schools: An agenda for change*. New York: The New Press.

Menkart, D. 1993. *Multicultural education: Strategies for linguistically diverse schools and classrooms*. Washington D.C.: National Clearinghouse for Bilingual Education.

Nieto, S. 1996. *Affirming diversity: The sociopolitical context of multicultural education*. New York: Longman.

Ord, J. 1996. KIDS FROM KANATA Materials and Personal Correspondence.

Peterson, B. 1995. "Teaching math across the curriculum: A fifth grade teacher battles number numbness." *Rethinking Schools.* 1:1: 4-5.

.Sayers, D. and Brown, K. 1993. "Freire, Freinet and Distancing: Forerunners of Technology Mediated Critical Pedagogy in Technology and Language-Minority Students" in *NABE News.* 17.3: 13, 32-33 .

Sayers, D. 1990. School-to-School exchanges in Celestin Freinet's Modern School Movement: Implications for computer-mediated global learning networks. Keynote Address, November 17, 1990. First North American Freinet Congress, St. Catharines, Ontario.

Sayers, D. 1994. "Bilingual team teaching partnerships over long distances: A technology-mediated context for intra-group language attitude change" in R. DeVillar, C. Faltis, & J. Cummins, eds. *Cultural diversity in schools: From rhetoric to practice* (pp. 299-331). Albany NY: State University of New York Press.

Students for Cultural and Linguistic Democracy 1996. "Reclaiming Our Voices" in Walsh, C., ed. *Education reform and social change: Multicultural voices, struggles, and visions* pp. 129-146. Mahwah, NJ: Lawrence Erlbaum Associates, Inc.

Skuttnab-Kangas, T. 1981. *Bilingualism or not: The education of minorities*. Clevedon, England: Multilingual Matters.

Terrazas, B. & Students for Cultural and Linguistic Democracy. 1995. "Struggling for Power and Voice: A High School Experience" in Frederickson, J., ed. *Reclaiming our voices: Bilingual education, critical pedagogy & praxis*. pp.279-309.Ontario, CA: California Association for Bilingual Education.

Zipp, S. "What Color Is the Net?" March 19,1997 *The Netizen* Internet: HotWired, Inc.

ON THE ROAD TO CULTURAL BIAS:
A CRITIQUE OF "THE OREGON TRAIL" CD-ROM

BY BILL BIGELOW

The critics all agree: *The Oregon Trail* is one of the greatest educational computer games ever produced. *Prides' Guide to Educational Software* awards it five stars for being "a wholesome, absorbing historical simulation," and "multi-ethnic," to boot (1992, p. 419). The new version, *Oregon Trail II*, is the "best history simulation we've seen to date," according to Warren Buckleitner, editor of *Children's Software Review Newsletter* (MECC, 1994). Susan Schilling, a key developer of *Oregon Trail II* and recently hired by *Star Wars* filmmaker George Lucas to head Lucas Learning Ltd., promises new interactive CD-ROMs targeted at children and concentrated in math and language arts (Armstrong, 1996, p. E-1).

Because interactive CD-ROMs like *The Oregon Trail* are encyclopedic in the amount of information they offer, and because they allow students a seemingly endless number of choices, the new software may appear educationally progressive. CD-ROMs seem tailor-made for the classrooms of tomorrow. They are hands-on and "student-centered." They are generally interdisciplinary — for example, *Oregon Trail II* blends reading, writing, history, geography, math, science, and health. And they are useful in multi-age classrooms because they allow students of various knowledge-levels to "play" and learn. But like the walls of a maze, the choices built into interactive CD-ROMs also channel participants in very definite directions. The CD-ROMs are programmed by people — people with particular cultural biases — and children who play the new computer games encounter the biases of the programmers (Bowers, 1988). Just as we would not invite a stranger into our classrooms and then leave the room, teachers need to become aware of the political perspectives of CD-ROMs, and to equip our students to "read" them critically.

At one level, this article is a critical review of the *Oregon Trail* CD-ROMs. I ask what knowledge is highlighted and what is hidden as students play the game. But I also reflect on the nature the new electronic curricula, and suggest some questions teachers can ask before choosing to use them with our students. And I offer some classroom activities that might begin to develop students' critical computer literacy.

PLAYING THE GAME

In both *Oregon Trail* and *Oregon Trail II*, students become members of families and wagon trains crossing the Plains in the 1840s or 1850s on the way to Oregon Territory. A player's objective, according to the game guidebook, is to safely reach Oregon Territory with one's family, thereby "increasing one's options for economic success" (*Oregon Trail II* "Guidebook").

The enormous number of choices offered in any one session — what to buy for the journey; the kind of wagon to take; whether to use horses, oxen, or

mules; the size of the wagon train with which to travel, whom to "talk" to along the way, when and where to hunt, when to rest, how fast to travel — is a kind of gentle seduction to students. It invites them to "try on this worldview; see how it fits." In an interactive CD-ROM, you don't merely identify with a particular character, you actually adopt his or her frame of reference and act as if you were that character (Provenzo, 1991). In *Oregon Trail*, a player quickly bonds to the "pioneer" maneuvering through the "wilderness."

In preparation for this article, I've played *Oregon Trail II* until my eyes became blurry. I can see its attraction to teachers. One can't play the game without learning a lot about the geography from Missouri to Oregon. (However, I hope I never have to ford another virtual river ever again.) Reading the trail guide as one plays teaches much about the ailments confronted on the Oregon Trail, and some of the treatments. Students can learn a tremendous amount about the details of life for the trekkers to Oregon: the kinds of wagons required, supplies needed, vegetation encountered along the route, and so forth. And the game has a certain multicultural and gender-fair veneer that, however limited, contrasts favorably with the White male dominated texts of yesteryear. But as much as the game teaches, it mis-teaches more. In fundamental respects, *Oregon Trail II* is sexist, racist, culturally insensitive, and contemptuous of the earth. It imparts bad values and wrong history.

They Look Like Women, But...

To its credit, *OT II* includes large numbers of women. Although I didn't count, women appear to make up roughly half the people students encounter as they play. But this surface equity is misleading. Women may be present, but gender is not acknowledged as an issue in *Oregon Trail*. In the opening sequences, the game requires students to select a profession, special skills they possess, the kind of wagon to take, the city they'll depart from, etc. Class is recognized as an issue — bankers begin with more money than saddlemakers, for example — but not gender or race — a player cannot choose these.

Without acknowledging it, *Oregon Trail* maneuvers students into thinking and acting as if they were all males — and, as we'll see, White males. The game highlights a male lifestyle and poses problems that historically fell within the male domain: whether and where to hunt, which route to take, whether and what to trade, whether to caulk

a wagon or ford a river. However, as I began to read more feminist scholarship on the Oregon Trail, I realized that women and men experienced the Trail very differently. It's clear from reading women's diaries of the period that women played little or no role in deciding whether to embark on the trip, where to camp, which routes to take and the like. In real life, women's decisions revolved around how to maintain a semblance of community under great stress, how "to preserve the home in transit" (Faragher and Stansell, 1992; Schlissel, 1992; Kesselman, 1976). Women decided where to look for firewood or buffalo chips, how and what to cook using hot rocks, how to care for the children, and how to resolve conflicts between travelers, especially the men.

These were real life decisions, but, with the exception of treating illness, they're missing from *The Oregon Trail*. Students are rarely required to think about the intricacies of preserving "the home in transit" for 2000 miles. An *Oregon Trail II* information box on the screen informs a player when "morale" is high or low, but other than making better male-oriented decisions, what's a player to do? *OT* offers no opportunities to encounter the choices of the Trail as women of the time would have encountered them, and to make decisions that might enhance community, and thus "morale." As Lillian Schlissel concludes in her study, *Women's Diaries of the Westward Journey*, "If ever there was a time when men and women turned their psychic energies toward opposite visions, the overland journey was that time. Sitting side by side on a wagon seat, a man and a woman felt different needs as they stared at the endless road that led into the New Country" (Schlissel, 1992, p. 15).

Similarly, *OT* fails to represent the texture of community life on the Trail. Students confront a seemingly endless stream of problems posed by *OT* programmers, but rarely encounter the details of life, especially that of women's lives. By contrast, in an article in the book, *America's Working Women*, Amy Kesselman includes a passage from the diary of one female trekker, Catherine Haun, in 1849:

We women folk visited from wagon to wagon or congenial friends spent an hour walking ever westward, and talking over our home life "back in the states" telling of the loved ones left behind; voicing our hopes for the future in the far west and even whispering, a little friendly gossip of pioneer life. High teas were not popular but tatting, knitting, crocheting, exchanging receipts for cooking *beans or dried apples or swopping food for the sake of variety kept us in practice of feminine occupations and diversions** (Kesselman, 1976, p. 71).

The male orientation of *OT* is brought into sharp relief in the game's handling of Independence Day commemoration. Students as pioneers are asked if they wish to "Celebrate the Fourth!" Click on this option, and one hears loud "Yahoos" and guns firing. Compare this to the communal preparations described in Enoch Conyers' 1852 diary (but not in *The Oregon Trail*):

A little further on is a group of young ladies seated on the grass talking over the problem of manufacturing "Old Glory" to wave over our festivities. The question arose as to where we are to obtain the material for the flag. One lady brought forth a sheet. This gave the ladies an idea. Quick as thought another brought a skirt for the red stripes... Another lady ran to her tent and brought forth a blue jacket, saying: "Here, take this; it will do for the field." Needles and thread were soon secured and the ladies went at their task with a will, one lady remarking that "Necessity is the mother of invention," and the answer came back, "Yes, and the ladies of our company are equal to the task" (Hill, 1989, p. 58).

The contrast between the "Yahoos"/gunfire of *OT* and the collective female exhilaration described in the diary excerpt is striking. This comparison alerted me to something so obvious that it took me awhile to recognize. In *OT*, people don't talk to each other, they all talk to you, the player. Everyone in the *OT*-constructed world aims her or his conversation at you — underscoring the simulation's individualistic ideology that all the world exists for you, controller of the mouse. An *OT* more alert to feminist insights and women's experiences would highlight relations between people, would focus on how the experience affects our feelings about each other, would feature how women worked with one another to survive and weave community, as women's diary entries clearly reveal.

As I indicated, large numbers of women appear throughout the *OT* simulation, and they often give good advice, perhaps better advice than the men we encounter. But *OT*'s abundance of women, and its apparent effort to be gender-fair, masks an essential problem: the choice-structure of the simulation privileges men's experience and virtually erases women's experience.

---

* Note the original spellings have been left in quotes.

AFRICAN AMERICANS AS TOKENS

From the game's beginning, when a player starts off in Independence or St. Joseph's, Missouri, African Americans dot the *Oregon Trail* landscape. However, by and large they are no more than black-colored White people. Even though Missouri was a slave state throughout the entire Oregon Trail period, I never encountered the term "slavery" while playing the game. I found race explicitly acknowledged in only one exchange, when I "talked" to an African American woman along the trail: "I'm Isabella. I'm traveling with the Raleighs and their people. My job is to keep after the cows and watch the children. My husband Fred is the ox-driver — best there is." Are they free, are they enslaved? Are we to assume the Raleighs are White? I asked to know more: "I was born in Delaware. My father used to tell me stories of Africa and promised one day we'd find ourselves going home. But I don't know if I'm getting closer or farther away with all this walking." The end. Like Missouri, Delaware was a slave state in ante bellum days, but this is not shared with students. Isabella offers provocative details, but they hide more than they reveal about her identity and culture.

Oregon Trail's treatment of African Americans reflects a very superficial multiculturalism. Black people are present, but their lives aren't. Attending to matters of race requires more than including lots of Black faces, or having little girls "talk Black:" "I think it's time we be moving on now." (This little girl reappears from time to time to repeat these same words. A man who looks Mexican likewise shows up frequently to say, with heavy accent: "Time is a-wasting. Let's head out!")

Even though one's life prospects and worldview in the 1840s and 1850s — as today — were dramatically shaped by one's race, this factor is invisible in *Oregon Trail*. *OT* players know their occupations but not their racial identities, even though this knowledge is vital to decisions participants would make before leaving on the journey as well as along the way.

For example, many of the constitutions of societies that sponsored wagon trains specifically excluded Blacks from making the trip west. Nonetheless, as Elizabeth McLagan points out in her history of Blacks in Oregon, *A Peculiar Paradise*, Blacks did travel the Oregon Trail, some as slaves, some as servants, and at least some, like George Bush, as well-to-do pioneers (McLagan, 1980). Race may not have seemed important to the *OT* programmers but race mattered a great deal to Bush: Along the Trail, he confided to another emigrant that if he experienced too much prejudice in Oregon, he would travel south to California or New Mexico and seek protection from the Mexican government (McLagan, 1980, p. 19).

And Bush had reason to be apprehensive: African Americans arriving in Oregon Territory during the 1840s and 1850s were greeted by laws barring Blacks from residency. Black exclusion laws were passed twice in Oregon Territory in the 1840s, and a clause in the Oregon state constitution barring Black residency was ratified in 1857 by a margin of eight to one — a clause, incidentally, not removed until 1926.

Upon completion of one of my simulated Oregon Trail journeys, I clicked to see how I turned out: "In 1855, Bill built a home on 463 acres of land in the Rogue River Valley of Oregon," experienced only "moderate success" and later moved to Medford, "establishing a small business that proved more stable and satisfying." Although the *OT* simulation never acknowledges it, "Bill" must have been White, because in 1850 the U.S. Congress passed the Oregon Donation Land Act granting 640 acres to free White males and their wives — only. It is unlikely that a Black man, much less a Black woman, would have been granted land in 1855 or have been allowed to start a business in Medford some years later.

Why were Whites so insistent that Blacks not live in Oregon? The preamble of one Black exclusion bill explained that "situated as the people of Oregon are, in the midst of an Indian population, it would be highly dangerous to allow free negroes and mulattoes to reside in the territory or to intermix with the Indians, instilling in their minds feelings of hostility against the White race..." (McLagan, 1980, p. 26). And Samuel Thurston, a delegate to Congress from Oregon Territory explained in 1850 why Blacks should not be entitled to homestead in Oregon:

The negroes associate with the Indians and intermarry, and, if their free ingress is encouraged or allowed, there would a relationship spring up between them and the different tribes, and a mixed race would ensue inimical to the whites; and the Indians being led on by the negro who is better acquainted with the customs, language, and manners of the whites, than the Indian, these savages would become much more formidable than they otherwise would, and long and bloody wars would be the fruits of the comingling of the races. It is

the principle of self preservation that justifies the action of the Oregon legislature (McLagan, 1980, pp. 30-31).

Thurston's argument carried the day. But *Oregon Trail* programmers have framed the issues so that race seems irrelevant. Thus, once students-as-pioneers arrive in Oregon, most of them will live happily after ever — never considering the impact that race would have on life conditions.

Just Passing Through?

Oregon Trail programmers are careful not to portray Indians as the "enemy" of westward trekkers. However, the simulation's superficial sympathy for Native groups masks a profound insensitivity to Indian cultures and to the earth that sustained these cultures. The simulation guidebook lists numerous Indian nations by name — and respectfully calls them "nations." The *OT* guidebook explains that emigrants' fear of Indians is "greatly exaggerated."

Some travelers have been known to cross the entire breadth of the continent from the Missouri River to the Sierra Nevadas without ever laying eye on an Indian, except perhaps for occasional brief sightings from a distance.

This is all well and good, for it is probably best for all parties concerned for emigrants and Indians to avoid contact with each other. Such meetings are often the source of misunderstandings, sometimes with regrettable consequences.

Emigrants often spread disease, according to the guidebook, which made the Indians "distrust and dislike" the emigrants. The guidebook further warns *OT* players not to overhunt game in any one place as "few things will incur the wrath of the Indian peoples more than an overstayed welcome accompanied by the egregious waste of the natural resources upon which they depend."

What orientation is highlighted and what is hidden in the simulation programmed for students to follow? The ideology embedded in *Oregon Trail I* and *II* is selfish and goal-driven: Care about indigenous people insofar as you need to avoid "misunderstanding" and incurring the wrath of potentially hostile natives. *OT* promotes an anthropocentric earth-as-natural-resource outlook. Nature is a thing to be consumed or overcome as people traverse the country in search of success in a faraway land. The simulation's structure coerces children into identifying with White settlers and dismissing those who weren't White. It contributes to the broader curricular racialization of identity students absorb — learning who constitutes the normalized "we" and who is excluded.

OT players need not take into account the lives of others unless it's necessary to do so in order to accomplish their personal objectives. Thus the cultures of Plains Indians are backgrounded. The game marginalizes their view of the earth. Contrast, for example, the Indians' term "mother earth" with the *Oregon Trail* term "natural resource." The metaphor of earth as mother suggests humans in a reciprocal relationship with a natural world that is alive, nourishing us, sustaining us. A resource is a thing to be used. It exists for us, outside of us, and we have no obligations in return.

The consequences of the Oregon Trail for the Plains Indians, the Indians of the Northwest and for the earth were devastating. In fairness, as they play *Oregon Trail*, students may hear some of the details of this upheaval. For example, on one trip I encountered a "Pawnee Village." Had I paid attention to the warning in the guidebook to "avoid contact" I would have ignored it and continued on my trip. But I entered and "talked" to the people I encountered there. A Pawnee woman: "Why do you bother me? I don't want to trade. The things that we get from the White travelers don't make up for all that we lose." I click to hear more. "We didn't know the whooping cough, measles, or the smallpox until your people brought them to us. Our medicine cannot cure these strange diseases, and our children are dying." I click on "Do you have any advice?" Angrily, she says, "No. I just want you to leave us alone." The implication is that if I just "leave [them] alone" and continue on the trail I can pursue my dream without hurting the Indians.

However, this interpretation hides the fact that the Oregon Trail itself, not just contact with the so-called pioneers, devastated Indian cultures and the ecology of which those cultures were an integral part. For example, pioneers — let's begin to call them their Lakota name, Wasi'chu, "greedy persons"* — cut down all the cottonwood trees found along the rich bottomlands of plains rivers — trees which "offered crucial protection during winter blizzards as well as concealing a village's

---

* The Lakota "used a metaphor to describe the newcomers. It was Wasi'chu, which means 'takes the fat,' or 'greedy person.' Within the modern Indian movement, *Wasi'chu* has come to mean those corporations and individuals, with their governmental accomplices, which continue to covet Indian lives, land, and resources for private profit. *Wasi'chu* does not describe a race; it describes a state of mind" (Johansen & Maestas, 1979, p. 6).

smoke from its enemies. In lean seasons, horses fed on its bark, which was surprisingly nourishing" (Davidson and Lytle, 1992, p. 114).

The Oregon Trail created serious wood shortages, which even the Wasi'chu acknowledged. "By the Mormon guide we here expected to find the last timber," wrote overlander A.W. Harlan, describing the Platte River, "but all had been used up by others ahead of us so we must go about 200 miles without any provisions cooked up." A few weeks later, in sight of the Black Hills, Harlan wrote: [W]e have passed many cottonwood stumps but no timber. . ." (Davidson and Lytle, 1992, p. 115)

Wasi'chu rifles also killed tremendous numbers of buffalo that Plains Indians depended upon for survival. One traveler in the 1850s wrote that "the valley of the Platte for 200 miles presents the aspect of the vicinity of a slaughter yard, dotted all over with skeletons of buffaloes" (Davidson and Lytle, 1992, p 117). Very soon after the beginning of the Oregon Trail the buffalo learned to avoid the Trail, their herds migrating both south and north. Edward Lazarus points out in *Black Hills/White Justice: The Sioux Nation Versus the United States — 1775 to the Present:* "But the Oregon Trail did more than move the buffalo; it destroyed the hunting pattern of the Sioux, forcing them to follow the herds to the fringes of their domain and to expose themselves to the raids of their enemies" (1991, p. 14).

However, wrapped in their cocoons of self-interest, *Oregon Trail* players push on, oblivious to the mayhem and misery they cause in their westward drive. This is surely an unintended, and yet intrinsic, part of the game's message: Pursue your goal as an autonomous individual, ignore the social and ecological consequences; "look out for number one."

NO VIOLENCE HERE

Oregon Trail never suggests to its simulated pioneers that they should seek permission of Indian nations to travel through their territory. And from this key omission flow other omissions. The simulation doesn't inform players that because of the disruptions wrought by the daily intrusions of the westward migration, Plains Indians regularly demanded tribute from the trekkers. As John Unruh Jr. writes in *The Plains Across:*

The natives explicitly emphasized that the throngs of overlanders were killing and scaring away buffalo and other wild game, overgrazing prairie grasses, exhausting the small quantity of available timber, and depleting water resources. The tribute payments... were demanded mainly by the Sac and Fox, Kickapoo, Pawnee, and Sioux Indians — the tribes closest to the Missouri River frontier and therefore those feeling most keenly the pressures of white men increasingly impinging upon their domains (1993, p. 169).

Wasi'chu travelers resented this Indian-imposed taxation and their resentment frequently turned to hostility and violence, especially in the later years of the Trail. The Pawnees were "hateful wretches," wrote Dr. Thomas Wolfe in 1852, for demanding a 25 cent toll at a bridge across Shell Creek near the North Platte River (Unruh, 1993, p. 171). Shell Creek and other crossings became flashpoints that escalated into violent skirmishes resulting in the deaths of settlers and Indians.

Despite the increasing violence along the Oregon Trail, one choice *OT* programmers don't offer students-as-trekkers is the choice to harm Indians. Doubtless MECC, producer of *Oregon Trail*, is not anxious to promote racism toward Native peoples. However, because simulation players can't hurt or even speak ill of Indians, the game fails to alert students that White hostility was one feature of the westward migration. The omission is significant because the sanitized non-violent *Oregon Trail* fails to equip students to reflect on the origins of conflicts between Whites and Indians. Nor does it offer students any insights into the racial antagonism that fueled this violence. In all my play of *OT* I can't recall any blatant racism directed at Indians. But as John Unruh, Jr. points out, "the callous attitude of cultural and racial superiority so many overlanders exemplified was of considerable significance in producing the volatile milieu in which more and more tragedies occurred" (Unruh, p. 186).

THE END OF THE TRAIL

Soon there will come from the rising sun a different kind of man from any you have yet seen, who will bring with them a book and will teach you everything, after that the world will fall to pieces. Spokan Prophet, 1790 (Limerick, 1987, p. 39)

Someone can spend two or three hours — or more — playing one game of *Oregon Trail* before finally reaching Oregon Territory. Once we arrive, the game awards us points and tells us how our life in Oregon turned out. And yet it fails to raise vital questions about our right to be there in the first place and what happened to the people who were there first.

In its section on the "Destination," the guidebook offers students its wisdom on how they should view life in a new land. It's a passage that underscores the messages students absorb while engaged in the simulation. These comforting words of advice and social vision are worth quoting at length:

Once you reach the end of your journey, you should go to the nearest large town to establish your land claim. If there are no large towns in the area, simply find an unclaimed tract of land and settle down. . . As they say, possession is nine-tenths of the law, and if you have settled and worked land that hasn't yet been claimed by anyone else, you should have little or no trouble legally establishing your claim at a later time.

As more and more Americans move into the region, more cities and towns will spring up, further increasing one's options for economic success. Rest assured in the facts that men and women who are willing to work hard will find their labors richly rewarded, and that you, by going west, are helping to spread American civilization from ocean to ocean across this great continent, building a glorious future for generations to come!

The Lakota scholar/activist Vine Deloria, Jr., in his book, *Indians of the Pacific Northwest* (1977), offers a less sanguine perspective than that included in the CD-ROM guidebook. People coming in on the Oregon Trail "simply arrived on the scene and started building. If there were Indians or previous settlers on the spot they were promptly run off under one pretext or another. Lawlessness and thievery dominated the area" (p. 53). From 1850 on, using provisions of the Oregon Donation Act, thousands of "pioneers" invaded "with impunity."

As Deloria points out, there were some in Congress who were aware that they were encouraging settlers to steal Indian land, and so shortly after, Congress passed the Indian Treaty Act requiring the United States to get formal agreements from Indian tribes. Anson Dart, appointed to secure land concessions, pursued this objective in a despicable fashion. For example, he refused to have the treaties translated into the Indians' languages, instead favoring "Chinook jargon," a non-language of fewer than 300 words good for trading, giving orders, and little else. Dart's mandate was to move all the Indians east of the Cascades, but he decided some tribes, like the Tillamooks and Chinooks, should keep small amounts of land as cheap labor reserves:

Almost without exception, I have found [the Indians] anxious to work at employment at common labor and willing too, to work at prices much below that demanded by the Whites. The Indians make all the rails used in fencing, and at this time do the boating upon the rivers: In consideration, therefore, of the usefulness as labourers in the settlements, it was believed to be far better for the Country that they should not be removed from the settled portion [sic] of Oregon if it were possible to do so (Deloria, 1977, p. 51).

Meanwhile, in southwestern Oregon, White vigilantes didn't wait for treaty niceties to be consummated. Between 1852 and 1856 self-proclaimed Volunteers attacked Indians for alleged misdeeds, or simply because they were Indians. In August of 1853, one Martin Angel rode into the Rogue River valley gold mining town of Jacksonville shouting, "Nits breed lice. We have been killing Indians in the valley all day," and "Exterminate the whole race." Minutes later a mob of about 800 White men hanged a seven year old Indian boy. In October 1855, a group of Whites massacred 23 Indian men, women, and children. This incident began the Rogue Indian war, which lasted until June 1856 (Beckham, 1991, p. 103). Recall that this is the same region and the same year in one *Oregon Trail* session where "Bill" built a home and experienced "moderate success" — but thanks to the *OT* programmers, learned nothing of the social conflicts swirling around him.

Nor did Bill learn that, even as a White person, he could protest the outrages committed against the Rogue River Valley Indians as did one anonymous "Volunteer" in a passionate 1853 letter to the *Oregon Statesman* newspaper:

A few years since the whole valley was theirs [the Indians'] alone. No white man's foot had ever trod it. They believed it theirs forever. But the gold digger come, with his pan and his pick and shovel, and hundreds followed. And they saw in astonishment their streams muddied, towns built, their valley fenced and taken. And where their squaws dug camus, their winter food, and their children were wont to gambol, they saw dug and plowed, and their own food sown by the hand of nature, rooted out forever, and the ground it occupied appropriated to the rearing of vegetables for the white man. Perhaps no malice yet entered the Indian breast. But when he was weary of hunting in the mountains without success, and was hungry, and approached the white man's tent for bread; where instead of bread he received curses and kicks, ye treaty kicking men — ye Indian exterminators think of these things. A Soldier (Applegate and O'Donnell, 1994, p. 34)

The *Oregon Trail* hides the nature of the Euro-American invasion in at least two ways. In the first place, the *OT* CD-ROM simply fails to inform simulation participants what happened between settlers and Indians. To the *OT* player, it doesn't feel like an invasion, it doesn't feel wrong. After one of my arrivals, in 1848, "Life in the new land turned out to be happy and successful for Bill, who always cherished bittersweet but proud memories of the months spent on the Oregon Trail." (This struck me as a rather odd account, given that I had lost all three of my children on the trip.) The only person that matters is the simulation player, in this case Bill. I was never told whether life turned out equally "happy and successful" for the Klamaths, Yakamas, Cayuses, Nez Percés, Wallawallas, and all the others, who occupied this land generations before the Wasi'chu arrived. The second way the nature of the White invasion is hidden has to do with the structure of the simulation. For a couple hours or more the player endures substantial doses of frustration, tedium, and difficulty. By the time the Willamette or Rogue Valleys come up on the screen we, the simulated trekkers, feel that we deserve the land, that our labors in transit should be "richly rewarded" with the best land we can find.

DATA DECEPTION AND THOUGHTS ON WHAT TO DO ABOUT IT

In the Beatles' song, all you need is love; in *Oregon Trail*, all you need is data. *Oregon Trail* offers students gobs of information: snake bite remedies, river locations and depths, wagon specifications, ferry costs, daily climate reports. Loaded with facts, it feels comprehensive. Loaded with people voicing contrasting opinions, it feels balanced. Loaded with choices, it feels free. But the simulation begins from no moral or ethical standpoint beyond individual material success; it contains no vision of social/ecological justice, and, hence promotes the full litany of sexism, racism, and imperialism, as well as exploitation of the earth. And simultaneously, it hides this bias. The combination is insidious, and makes interactive CD-ROMs like this one more difficult to critique than traditional textbooks or films. The forced identification of player with simulation protagonist leaves the student no option but to follow the ideological map laid out by the programmers.

Nonetheless, my critique is not a call to boycott the new "edutainment" resources. But we need to remember that these CD-ROMs are not teacher substitutes. The teacher's role in analyzing and presenting these devices in a broader ethical context is absolutely vital. Thus teachers across the country must begin a dialogue toward developing a critical computer literacy. We need to figure out ways to equip students to recognize and evaluate the deep moral/political messages imparted as they maneuver within various computer software programs.

Before choosing to use CD-ROMs that involve people and place, like *The Oregon Trail* — or, for example, its newer siblings *The Yukon Trail*, *The Amazon Trail*, and *Africa Trail* — teachers can consider a series of questions. These include:

▸ *Which social groups are students not invited to identify with in the simulation?* For example, Native Americans, African Americans, women, Latinos are superficially present in *Oregon Trail*, but the stuff of their lives is missing.

▸ *How might these social groups frame problems differently than they are framed in the simulation?* As we saw in the foregoing critique of *Oregon Trail*, women tended to focus more on maintaining community, than on hunting. Native Americans had a profoundly different relationship to the earth than did the Euro-American "tamers of the wilderness."

▸ *What decisions do simulation participants make that may have consequences for social groups not highlighted in the simulation? And what are these consequences?* Even though the very existence of the Oregon Trail contributed to the decimation of Plains and Northwest Indians, simulation participants are never asked to consider the broader effects of their decisionmaking. What may be an ethical individual choice may be unethical when multiplied several hundred thousand times. (In this respect, CD-ROM choice-making both reflects and reinforces conventional notions of "freedom" that justify disastrous social and ecological practices.)

▸ *What decisions do simulation participants make that may have consequences for the earth and non-human life?* Similarly, a simulation participant's choice to cut down trees for firewood may be "rational" for that individual, but may also have deleterious effects on the ecological balance of a particular bio-region.

▸ *If the simulation is time-specific, as in the case of The Oregon Trail, what were the social and environmental consequences after the time period covered in the simulation?* The wars between Indians and U.S. cavalry in the latter decades of the nineteenth century are inexplicable without the Oregon Trail as prologue.

▸ *Can we name the ideological orientation of a particular CD-ROM?* The question is included here simply to remind us that all computer materials — indeed, all curricula — have an ideology. Our first step is becoming aware of the nature of that ideology.

These are hardly exhaustive, but may suggest a useful direction to begin thinking, as CD-ROMs become increasingly available and as they come to cover more and more subjects.

Finally, let me use the example of *The Oregon Trail* to sketch out a number of ways that teachers can begin to foster a critical computer literacy:

▸ Once we've identified some of the social groups that are substantially missing in a CD-ROM activity like *The Oregon Trail*, we can make an effort to locate excerpts of their diaries, speeches, or other communications (to the extent that these cultures are print-oriented) and read these together.

▸ We might then engage students in a role play where, as a class, students face a number of Oregon Trail problems. For example, class members could portray women on the Oregon Trail and decide how they will attempt to maintain a community in transit. Or they might role play a possible discussion of Oglala people as they confront the increasingly disruptive presence of Wasi'chu crossing their lands.

▸ Students might be asked to list all the ways that African Americans would experience the Oregon Trail differently than Euro-Americans would — from planning to the trip itself. (It's unlikely, for example, that every White person on the streets of Independence, Missouri said a friendly "Howdy," to Blacks encountered, as each of them does to the implied but unacknowledged White male *OT* simulation player.)

▸ In playing the *OT* simulation, students could assume a particular racial, cultural, or gender identity, and note whether the choices or experiences described in the simulation make sense from the standpoint of a member of their group. For example, would a typical African American in Missouri in 1850 be allowed to choose which city to begin the trek west?

▸ As we share with students the social and ecological costs of the Oregon Trail, we could ask them to write critical letters to each of the "pioneers" they portrayed in the simulation. Some could represent Rogue Valley Indians, Shoshoni people, or even Mother Earth. For instance, how does "Mother Earth" respond to the casual felling of every cottonwood tree along the Platte River?

- A Native American elder or activist could be invited into the classroom to speak about the concerns that are important to his or her people and about the history of White-Indian relations.

- We could encourage students to think about the politics of naming in the simulation. They could suggest alternative names for the Oregon Trail itself. For example, the historian of the American West, Frederick Merk, aptly calls the Oregon Trail a "path of empire" (1978). Writer Dan Georgakas names it a "march of death" (1973). Other names might be "invasion of the West," or "the 20 year trespass." Just as with Columbus's "discovery" of America, naming shapes understanding, and we need classroom activities to uncover this process.

- Students could write and illustrate alternative children's books describing the Oregon Trail from the standpoint of women, African Americans, Native Americans, or the earth.

- Now have them "play" *The Oregon Trail* again. What do they see this time that they didn't see before? Whose worldview is highlighted and whose is hidden? If they choose, they might present their findings to other classes or to teachers who may be considering the use of CD-ROMs.

The Oregon Trail is not necessarily more morally obnoxious than other CD-ROMs or curricular materials with similar ideological biases. My aim here is broader than to merely shake a scolding finger at MECC, producer of the *OT* series. I've tried to demonstrate why teachers and students must develop a critical computer literacy. Some of the new CD-ROMs seem more socially aware than the blatantly culturally insensitive materials that still fill school libraries and bookrooms. And the flashy new computer packages also invoke terms long sacred to educators: student empowerment, individual choice, creativity, high interest. It's vital that we remember that coincident with the arrival of these new educational toys is a deepening social and ecological crisis. Global and national inequality between haves and have nots is increasing. Violence of all kinds is endemic. And the earth is being consumed at a ferocious pace. Computer programs are not politically neutral in the big moral contests of our time. Inevitably, they take sides. Thus, a critical computer literacy, one with a social/ecological conscience, is more than just a good idea — it's a basic skill.

Bill Bigelow *teaches at Franklin High School in Portland, Oregon and co-edited* Rethinking Our Classrooms: Teaching for Equity and Justice *(Rethinking Schools, 1994.)*

A version of this article first appeared in Rethinking Schools *(Fall 1995, Vol. 10, #1).*

REFERENCES

Applegate, S. & O'Donnell, T. 1994. *Talking on paper: An anthology of Oregon letters and diaries.* Corvallis, OR: Oregon State University Press.

Armstrong, D. (February 23, 1996). "Lucas getting into education via CD-ROM." *The San Francisco Examiner.*

Beckham, S. D. 1991. "Federal-Indian Relations." *The First Oregonians.* Portland, OR: Oregon Council for the Humanities.

Bowers, C.A. 1988. *The cultural dimensions of educational computing: Understanding the non-neutrality of technology.* New York: Teachers College Press.

Davidson, J. W. & Lytle, M. H. 1992. *After the fact: The art of historical detection.* New York: McGraw-Hill.

Deloria, Jr., V. 1977. *Indians of the Pacific Northwest.* Garden City, NY: Doubleday.

Faragher, J. & Stansell, C. 1992. "Women and Their Families on the Overland Trail to California and Oregon, 1842-1867." Binder, F. & Reimer, D., eds. *The way we lived: Essays and documents in American social history, Vol. I.* Lexington, MA: D.C. Heath.

Georgakas, D. 1973. *Red shadows: The history of Native Americans from 1600 to 1900, from the desert to the Pacific Coast.* Garden City, NY: Zenith.

Hill, W. E. 1989. *The Oregon Trail: Yesterday and today.* Caldwell, ID: Caxton Printers.

Johansen, B. & Maestas, R. 1979. *Wasi'chu: The continuing Indian wars.* New York: Monthly Review.

Kesselman, A. 1976. "Diaries and Reminiscences of Women on the Oregon Trail: A Study in Consciousness." Baxandall, Rosalyn; Gordon, Linda; Reverby, Susan. *America's working women: A documentary history — 1600 to the present.* New York: Vintage.

Lazarus, E. 1991. *Black Hills/White justice: The Sioux Nation versus the United States — 1775 to the present.* New York: HarperCollins.

Limerick, P. N. 1987. *The legacy of conquest: The unbroken past of the American west.* New York: W.W. Norton.

McLagan, E. 1980. *A peculiar paradise: A history of Blacks in Oregon, 1788-1940.* Portland, OR: The Georgian Press.

MECC. 1994. *The Oregon Trail II.* Minneapolis, MN.

Merk, F. 1978. *History of the westward movement.* New York: Knopf.

Pride, B. & M. 1992. *Prides' guide to educational software.* Wheaton, IL: Crossway Books.

Provenzo, Jr., E. F. 1991. *Video kids: Making sense of Nintendo.* Cambridge, MA: Harvard University Press.

Schlissel, L. 1992. *Women's diaries of the westward journey.* New York: Schocken.

Unruh, Jr., J. D. 1993. *The plains across: The overland emigrants and the trans-Mississippi west, 1840-1860.* Urbana and Chicago: University of Illinois Press.

SCHOOL WIDE ACTIVITIES

CULTURAL CLUBS IN PUBLIC SCHOOLS

BY BAKARI CHAVANU

Before becoming the Black Student Union (BSU) advisor at my school, I had little or no prior experience with high school student clubs. As a high school student myself, I had felt no inclination to join a club. No one encouraged me to be a member of any school group — except the high school track team.

Yet when I got to college I found student organizations to be central to the development of my cultural and political awareness and to affirming the importance of education. It was through student organizations that I found education to have a higher purpose than simply a degree and a job.

Outside of classrooms, athletic activities, and student government, school clubs and organizations constitute one of the most significant opportunities for students. Here students can develop leadership and organizing skills. Clubs also provide a space for cultural bonding and inclusion. In clubs students actively and constructively congregate, socialize, share experiences and concerns, plan social and cultural activities reflecting their interests, and invite others to participate in those activities.

CULTURAL CLUBS AT FLORIN HIGH

This is my fifth and most productive year as a high school club advisor. The cultural population at my school is truly diverse. The student population is White (36%), Black (17%), Latino/a (12%), Asian (10%), Filipino/a (11%), and Native American (1%). Cultural clubs include the Black Student Union, the Pacific Islanders, the European Heritage Club, the MAYA club, the Japanese Club, the Asian club, the Native American Club, and the Christian Club.

Club members responding to a survey I conducted maintained that they joined their club in order to learn more about their culture and to bring about unity and self-respect for students from their cultural background.

These clubs are supported by the school's Cultural Committee, club advisors (teachers and counselors) and our Student Activities director. A monthly program called Cultural Exchange is offered by our school's Cultural Resource Coordinator. Cultural Exchange brings at least two cultural clubs together each month, for two hours, to exchange views, concerns, and visions concerning their cultures. Clubs also participate in the school's Winter holiday and the Spring multicultural kaleidoscope assemblies. School clubs have been the most visible during the quarterly food fairs in which cultural clubs (along with other school programs) raise money selling food representing their culture. Asian American Clubs hold a yearly talent showcase featuring cultural dances and performances. This event has consistently brought a packed house of Asian American parents and relatives to the school. Other cultural club activities include going on field trips, sponsoring student speakers, designing floats and marches for the homecoming parade, and conducting community service.

These cultural bonding and celebratory activities have a positive impact on the students and their families. However it's also important for students to learn to address social and political issues which impact their race, culture, gender and which impact society as a whole.

Phron and Phebe (BSU Secretary) host the Black Family Night during Black History Month.

Activist Clubs

I wanted to share with students in the Black Student Union some of the benefits often reserved for college students of learning how to organize and challenge inequities. As historian Manning Marable points out in his essay, "The Politics of Black Student Activism" (p. 88),

As originally conceived, the Black Student Unions (BSUs) wanted to create a greater social and political awareness among African-American students, and desired to confront and to challenge White administrators on matters of educational policy. They called for the creation of the Black Studies departments, Minority Student Programs, Cultural Centers, and other institutions. The BSUs advanced the cause of affirmative action by demanding the recruitment and appointment of Black faculty and administrators. The BSUs represented a vital link between the struggles being waged in urban streets and our communities with the politics of higher education which existed at White academic institutions.

Marable writes about higher education, but high school students also need to advocate for anti-racist education and to link community issues to the school curriculum. In my work with the Black Student Union at Florin High School, we have been able to sponsor issue-oriented events such as the ones listed below.

Presentations.

▸ The Million Man March

▸ Four-part series on the contributions and significance of Malcolm X

Discussions. Group dialogues on topics of concern to students:

▸ Male/female relationships and the movie *Waiting to Exhale*

▸ Interracial dating

▸ The use of the "N" word

▸ Affirmative action

Teen Summit. We invited two representatives from each club and the school student government to give presentations on their views of cultural inclusion. This was the first panel presentation by students at the school. Hopefully it will become a model for future student forums based on student concerns.

Conferences. Members regularly attend a regional and statewide Black Student Union conference where they network and participate in workshops.

Other clubs at my school and across the country have chosen to address social and political issues. For example, when voters in California in 1995 passed the anti-immigration Proposition 187 bill, Latina/o students responded in large numbers across the state. These young people saw the racism and political scapegoating of this bill. Members of the MAYA club on my campus held their own spontaneous protest which was not officially supported by the school or district. It spawned a debate about the role of student activism, the politics of the bill, and ways teachers can support and even help students use education for social action. Furthermore, it led to a collaboration between the MAYA club advisor and me on an event about Proposition 187. We sponsored a panel presentation which was attended by over two hundred students.

Organizing Cultural Clubs and The Role of the Advisor

Student clubs are a challenge. Students often lack the experience, fortitude, and cultural awareness to build and sustain a club. The success of this year's BSU is attributed to a combination of strong student leadership, my increased level of organization as an advisor, the support of other staff members, and the willingness of many club members to take responsibility for maintaining their group.

In the last six years, the BSU has had some good leaders. However the 1995-96 leader, Phron McElroy, was able to bring the perspective and experience gained from being a member since his freshman year. His commitment and vision helped the club grow tremendously. Phron understood that maintaining the club required dedicated, consistent and positive leadership. His commitment provided me the opportunity to be a real advisor — providing him and other club officers with tools to carry out their leadership roles.

This year I decided to prepare for and treat BSU like I would my academic courses. In the past, BSU membership and activities would flounder largely because I could not provide the time it needed to be successful. I decided, along with Phron, to make the club stronger than ever before. I relinquished a few other major responsibilities to give myself more time for my role as an advisor.

With the help of a few other staff members, Phron and I actively recruited members during the first few weeks of school. Instead of just waiting to see if students would come to the first meeting on their own,

Black Student Union members.

we called everyone who had indicated interest in the BSU at the lunch time club sign-ups. This resulted in about 35 students attending the first session. We prepared club t-shirts to help recruit students to the club and establish camaraderie on the part of members.

During the first semester of school Phron and I talked on a regular basis. I showed him how to develop an agenda, plan activities, and deal with various problems in communication and club responsibilities inherent in any organization. However, getting students organized does not mean doing all the work for them. With every successful meeting and club activity, Phron and other club officers and members learned to take charge. Just as I strive to build a student-centered classroom in which students practice self-directed learning, so must club members learn to run their own group. As Phron stated, "To be a good leader, you need to form a bond with members of the organization by understanding, caring and talking with the members. You need to show members that you as a leader are their extra support."

My role is to be an advisor and watchful eye on how the club develops. I regularly advise officers on what they can or must do in order to carry out various activities. In addition to talking to officers, typing out a memo of "reminders" sometimes helps get things done.

My other suggestions for club advisors to help build a strong club include:

1. Develop a support network of teachers, counselors, administrators, parents, and staff members who can be called upon to work with and advise club officers concerning their responsibilities.

2. Organize club committees. This year, BSU committees included a cultural activities committee, a birthday/appreciation committee, a publicity committee, and a historical committee (whose role is to take photos of club activities and maintain a photo album). Political/cultural activities were loosely organized by the cultural activities committee.

3. Develop a club binder including membership attendance sheets, activities sign-up sheets, budget reports, publicity fliers produced, and written or typed plans of events.

4. Develop a monthly calendar of club events, meetings, and deadlines.

5. Develop "how-to" guides for regular events, like fund-raisers, dances, student forums, etc.

6. Develop a list of community speakers who can speak at club meetings and events.

As a club advisor, one often has to advocate for more support from the school. Clubs often operate on the periphery of the school. Meetings are usually held before or after classes. Club advisors get little or no support by way of material resources, time, and even recognition for their work. In most cases, clubs operate because of the work of a few dedicated student members and their advisor. Just like community cultural and political activities, support of club activities by students at large depends on various factors: the popular appeal of the activity, the effectiveness of the public relations work of the club, and, above all, the ability of club members to organize and carry out their plans.

Because clubs are an extracurricular activity, most club members are constantly challenged to balance their club responsibilities with academic and nonacademic expectations. Working a part-time job, in addition to meeting academic expectations, can make leading or participating in a club very difficult.

Most schools recognize the need for cultural clubs, but very few of them provide clubs with the type of support given to academic and athletic programs. Most clubs must raise their own money for club activities and club officers rarely receive professional training in leadership skills.

With a broader awareness of the history of and need for cultural clubs in an academic environment, we can see the potential of such clubs to help students make connections between their school, their community and the larger society. Cultural clubs can help increase the participation of students from different cultural backgrounds and help prepare them to meet the challenges of post-secondary education and larger social problems. Phron described this participation within a larger context, "The purpose of BSU is about respecting each other and coming together and learning from one another. It's not just to learn about historical events regarding African Americans, but it's for bonding with other African Americans to form a relationship of strength and determination."

Sustaining Social Action

Next year I want to help students identify school and community issues and problems they can address through their club. Depending on the school and the surrounding social and political environment, it's not always easy to engage students in social action. Most often, like adults, students are more reactive than they are proactive. But in viewing cultural clubs as training grounds for cultural unity, leadership skills, and social awareness, students can be invited to respond to certain political issues in different ways. They can learn how to make other students aware of issues through the use of art, writing, drama, forums, formal debates, and even political rallies. They can organize meetings, seminars, and work actively with community and national organizations. I plan to call upon community organizations, churches, and student support services to help bring more social activism to the club.

Developing cultural clubs is not easy, but it is essential to maintaining the necessary student activism that has historically challenged racism, sexism, and other forms of inequality, and above all, as Marable points out, has promoted educational awareness and self-organization.

Bakari Chavanu teaches English and African American cultural studies at Florin High School in Sacramento, CA. His work has been published in Rethinking Schools *and* Multicultural Education. *He is a Steering Committee member of the National Coalition of Education Activists. He can be reached by e-mail — BakariC@aol.com or at Florin High School, 7956 Cottonwood Lane, 95828.*

School Mascots

BY BARBARA MINER

Go White Boys!
Victory to the Black Skins!
Rah Rah Chinamen!

Can you imagine any school district in the country tolerating such racist cheerleading for sports teams?

Of course not. So why are millions of children attending schools with mascots and sports teams such as the Redmen, the Warriors, the Red Raiders and the Indians?

Nor are such demeaning stereotypes limited to elementary and high schools. There's also the Marquette Warriors at Marquette University in Milwaukee, the Atlanta Braves baseball team, and the Washington Redskins football team just to name a few.

"BY TOLERATING THE USE OF DEMEANING STEREOTYPES IN OUR PUBLIC SCHOOL SYSTEMS, WE DESENSITIZE ENTIRE GENERATIONS OF CHILDREN."

CONCRETE WAY TO FIGHT BIAS

Organizing against such mascots and sports names provides a concrete way to combat bias against Native Americans. At best, your efforts will lead to a change in names. At worst, it will raise consciousness about the negative nature of such mascots and names.

While some schools have gotten rid of Native American mascots, many refuse to do so. In Wisconsin, for example, there are an estimated 78 schools with Native American mascot names, according to the state's Department of Public Instruction.

The Great Lakes Inter-Tribal Council has asked Wisconsin officials to prohibit public schools from using Native American images and caricatures as mascots or in logos. Public opposition to the proposal has underscored the amount of work that needs to be done in changing attitudes.

© JAUNE QUICK-TO-SEE SMITH, 1992

Trade (Gifts for Trading Land with White People) by Jaune Quick-to-See Smith. Oil on canvas, mixed media, objects, 60 x 170" Collection: Chrysler Museum, Norfolk, VA. Courtesy Steinbaum Krauss Gallery, NYC.

In the Wisconsin town of Milton, a letter-to-the-editor reflected a common reaction to attempts to change the name of the high school's teams, the "Redmen."

"Why does one woman want to change a logo that has been used at Milton High School for over 50 years...," the letter asked. "People of Milton, don't let her get away with it. Stand up and fight like your Redmen teams do."

Native Americans make several points to counter such views:

Why are Indians used as names for teams and as mascots in the same way as badgers, gophers, or eagles? Are Indian people equated with animals and seen as less-than-human?

Mascots are often used to provide comic relief during half time; they are silly creatures not to be taken seriously. Why perpetuate such a view of Native Americans?

The mascots help people deny the modern-day existence of "real Indians" living and working in the 20th century.

The mascots perpetuate the stereotype that Native Americans are bloodthirsty and savage.

Teams and mascots aren't named the Jew Boys, or the Black Savages, or the Spics, or the Yellow Peril. Why isn't there the same sensitivity toward racism against Native Americans?

"Racially demeaning stereotypes are dangerous," notes Carol Hand, a Native American parent who has filed a legal complaint against the Milton school mascots. "By tolerating the use of demeaning stereotypes in our public school systems, we desensitize entire generations of children."

Barbara Miner *is the managing editor of* Rethinking Schools.

Reprinted with permission from Rethinking Columbus: Teaching About the 500th Anniversary of Columbus' Arrival in America, *Rethinking Schools, 1001 E. Keefe Ave., Milwaukee, WI 53212; 414-964-9646. Copies of* Rethinking Columbus *can be ordered for $8 + $2 postage.*

ADDITIONAL RESOURCES

Write to HONOR: Honor Our Neighbors Origins and Rights for information about recommended actions and a list of the addresses for the owners and commissioners of national professional teams, www.honoradvocacy.org

"We describe ourselves through stories about the land and the animals. I tell my stories in paint. Coyote makes me do it."
JAUNE QUICK-TO-SEE SMITH

ABOUT THE ARTIST:

JAUNE QUICK-TO-SEE SMITH

Born on the Flathead Reservation of the Confederated Salish and Kootenai tribes in Montana, Jaune Quick-to-See currently lives and paints in New Mexico. Much of her work, such as the painting on the previous page, features large-scale paintings of identifiable Indian icons — like a 12-foot long canoe or a buffalo — romanticized by movies, novels and the media. Close up, the paintings reveal clippings from Jaune's tribal newspaper, books and magazines that tell a different story about Indian life today.

At one time, galleries refused to exhibit Jaune's paintings saying "they weren't Indian enough." A result of this rejection was that Jaune founded two artist cooperatives. She also curates and organizes exhibitions for younger Native artists.

The information above and the poster of the artist are from the Women of Hope: Native American/Hawaiian *poster series and study guide produced by Bread and Roses Cultural Project © 1997. Packet includes 12 full color posters of Native American and Hawaiian women. See Resource Guide.*

Girl Power

BY LISA BERNDT, AMY EPSTEIN AND VALERIE MINOR

We developed "Girl Power" as a workshop for James Lick Middle School's 1995 Harmony Conference. The Harmony Conference is an annual event for students, school staff and parents with workshops focusing on equity and justice. We envisioned Girl Power as an opportunity for girls and women to come together, to explore and celebrate what it is like to be a girl.

First Steps

Resisting the impulse to immediately jump into planning activities, we reflected on our own experiences. We asked ourselves:

▸ What was it like to grow up as a girl?

▸ What messages were we told about being girls?

▸ What do we know and wonder about girls' experience today?

We found that we — diverse in terms of age, race and class background — had heard many of the same messages about being a girl. Moreover, our memories resonated with the stories of young women with whom we worked.

Making a Statement

Through journal-writing and dialogue, we produced a list of statements related to being a girl. Some of the statements were things we were often told as girls: *"Well, you know how girls are." "You're so pretty when you smile." "You're so cute when you're mad."*

Other statements described our experience as girls: *Boys disrespect you and act like it's all a joke. Gossip takes over friendships. People say it's gross for girls to have muscles and be strong. People say get good grades, but don't want to hear what you think. If I don't get my clothes and hair right, I know I'll have a horrible day. I can't go outside, I feel like I'm in a box sometimes.*

A few statements were antithetical to our experience: *My clothes let me move and act the way I want to. I can do anything I want.* Finally, many statements were open-ended:

Girls never _____.
You'd be so pretty if _____.
When I walk past a group of guys I don't know I always _____.
It's important to have a guy who _____ because _____.
My best friend is important to me because ___.
I fight with my best friend because _____.
If someone calls out my name, I would ____.
When I hear guys talk about another girl, it makes me think _____.
When I hear girls talk about another girl, it makes me think _____.
Things could be different if _____.

Preparing for the Workshop

We devised an activity for engaging with the statements we had generated; the activity is described in detail below. Preparation also included:

1. **Deciding what to tell girls about confidentiality and reporting**. At the beginning of the workshop, we talked about confidentiality and mandatory reporting. We made sure each participant understood that "everything stays in the room" except in cases of disclosure of harm or planned harm to self or others. Such disclosure, we explained, would necessitate reporting to the police or child protective services.

Editors' Note

It is sometimes easy to think about "girl" as one big group. The racial and cultural backgrounds of girls, even in the same classroom and school, affect their experiences and development in profoundly different ways. So, when considering using the lesson "Girl Power," think about how race and cultures shape their "girl-ness." The following questions may be used as one way to address the issues more directly in order to have the girls think about themselves as both gendered and racialized:

▸ *What was/is it like to grow up as an African American, Asian, Latina, Native American or mixed-race girl?*

▸ *What did you like about growing up as _____ girl? What was hard?*

▸ *How do girls and boys, as well as adults, from other racial and cultural groups see you? What do they assume about girls from your group?*

▸ *What do you want them to know about what it's really like to be a girl with your racial and cultural background?*

---

2. **Being prepared for disclosure of abuse**. We designated two trained counselors as resources in case of participant disclosure of abuse. They were prepared to meet individually with participants, providing support, referrals and advocacy as needed.

3. **Using name tags**. We brought name tags for everybody and made sure they were utilized. Dialogue was enhanced by our use of each other's names instead of "you" or "that girl over there."

4. **Preparing the Space**. Food, music, and decorations (a rug; fabric and posters on the walls) transformed a bare classroom into a warm, relaxing, and nurturing environment for the workshop.

ACTIVITY: THE STATEMENT GAME

We wanted the workshop to help participants 1) name and challenge constraining and oppressive messages about being a girl; and 2) notice, share and celebrate what girls most like and appreciate about girlhood. With these goals in mind we designed and facilitated the following activity:

1. We wrote each statement on a piece of chart paper and posted them all over the workshop room. We also posted a few blank pieces of chart paper.

2. Before the activity, we described to the participants how, through our reflection and dialogue, the statements had come into being. We mentioned the solidarity and enjoyment we had shared in working together as women to create this workshop. We discussed the importance for us of being able to speak freely about differences as well as commonalities, and briefly mentioned some differences among us related to race, class, culture and age. We emphasized our desire for Girl Power to be a space where everybody would feel that all parts of ourselves were welcome. We explained that we would be doing an activity today to share participants' knowledge and experience about being girls and women.

3. We distributed stickers of three different colors to participants, to be used to represent different intensities of response to the statements. For example, if a participant had often had "boys disrespect her and act like it was a joke," she would place a red sticker on that piece of butcher paper. If it happened to her sometimes or occasionally, she would place a green sticker on the paper. If it happened rarely, she would use a yellow sticker. If she didn't relate to the experience, she wouldn't put a sticker on the paper. [Note: Some confusion accompanied the use of the stickers. "Intensity of response" meant different things in connection with different types of statements. Participants were at times unsure of whether the placement of a sticker signaled agreement, disagreement, frequency of personal experience, or frequency of the experience for girls in general. While participants were still very enthusiastic about the use of the stickers, it may be useful to explore different, perhaps simpler ways of engaging with the statements.]

4. We handed out markers to participants, to be used to complete the open-ended statements and/ or to add statements by writing them on the posted blank pieces of chart paper.

5. We turned on popular music, and allowed about thirty minutes for participants to walk around the room, reading and responding to the statements.

6. Following a short refreshment break, we facilitated a one-hour discussion, focusing on participants' experiences of and reflections on the activity.

REACTIONS AND REFLECTIONS

Youth and adult participants noted that dialogue was characterized by unusually high levels of trust and respect, particularly for a group so diverse in terms of race, culture, class background, neighborhood affiliation and age.

Many commonalities emerged. Certain statements were met with almost universal consensus, such as "Boys disrespect you and act like it's a joke," "Gossip takes over friendships," and "I can't go outside, I feel like I'm in a box sometimes." Not one young person in the room (and only one adult!) responded affirmatively to "My clothes let me move and act the way I want to."

Some participants expressed curiosity about "how it got like this in the first place." Others stated they thought it had just always been this way for girls; "it's just the way guys are; it's just the way things are and it's never gonna change."

FIGHTING ALL FORMS OF OPPRESSION

Girl Power succeeded as a space for a diverse group of girls and women to "tell it like they see it." To this end, we consciously did the following:

▸ We were careful to reflect students' own language and concepts in the workshop statements.

▸ We specifically invited participants to bring all of the parts of themselves into the room and to feel free to speak from all of their "home" voices. It is interesting how participant experience of this invitation varied: teachers seemed to feel less confined in their teacher roles, while students seemed to feel more confident that we were prepared to hear about the diversity of their experiences rather than trying to make them conform to predetermined notions of girlhood.

▶ We "walked the walk" by speaking openly about our own process of creating Girl Power, including our need for a space in which we could be all of our selves.

We made space for each participant to speak in her own voice about her own range of experience. This posed some challenges. For example, near the end of the workshop, we invited the girls to create and perform skits. We supported the girls' efforts to name and dramatize girlhood as they experience it in their lives. Some of the White adult participants objected to the subject matter and language of the skits, which they viewed as glorifying violence. Other adult participants (Whites and people of color) disagreed, viewing the skits as genuine expressions of the girls' everyday reality, and as such, appropriate starting points for continued dialogue about — and deconstruction of — sexism.

A commitment to make space for all voices calls upon us to continually reflect on how our assumptions about what is appropriate and normal fit with our own and others' perspectives and experiences. This is particularly true for those of us — White people, men, heterosexual people, adults, and the economically privileged — who are granted privilege by mainstream society and taught to enforce a paradigm by which dominant norms are unquestioningly correct and alternative ways of being are flawed or wrong.

ADDRESSING RACE & CULTURE

While Girl Power succeeded as a vehicle for a diverse group of girls and women to communicate openly and meaningfully, attention to race and culture was primarily indirect, through the "back-door." Through reflection, we acknowledged some of the factors pushing us toward the back-door way. We discussed the depth of separation between different racial and cultural groups, and the difficulties of fully confronting this separation while simultaneously engaging in the celebration of girlhood. We also noted how often we had participated in workshops where adult naming of concepts and situations seemed to overwhelm young peoples' own voicing and dialogue.

We believe that future Girl Power workshops should do more to directly address race and culture. It is probable that this would necessitate a longer workshop format: four hours is insufficient for naming and confronting separation while simultaneously celebrating commonality, for introducing adult-named concepts (sexism, racism, internalized oppression) while simultaneously centering the dialogue in young peoples' own naming and analysis of experience. A strategy might be to include among the statements something like: "I am both a girl/woman and ____. One thing this means is _____."

Participants may name race and culture. This would then be a starting point for more direct dialogue. Likewise, participants may choose to name other things; talking about what was not named (race, culture) would also be a starting point for more direct dialogue.

YOUTH FEEDBACK

Youth feedback on our workshop included:

▶ I learned that too many young women are being disrespected by young men. I give this workshop an A+++, because a lot of young women now know how to speak out when a boy disrespects them. There should be more girls rights groups. I have sent a message across. All girls will know how to handle the situation better.

▶ I learned how boys disrespect girls and sometimes girls disrespect girls. Also about how you wear stuff to get attention. I'd give this workshop an "A" because it's something where girls can tell how they feel when boys disrespect them."

▶ I think what I learned about girls and guys is to have respect for all colors and cultures and that is why we have the Harmony Conference.

FINAL COMMENTS

Girl Power sparked greater pride and solidarity among girls and women at James Lick Middle School. It noticeably enhanced the relationships between and among participants, and catalyzed one teacher's initiation of a popular, ongoing Girl Power group. We hope that schools everywhere will offer more opportunities for young people and adults to share, celebrate and reflect on our lives, and to work together to name, deconstruct and eradicate sexism and all forms of injustice.

Lisa Berndt, Amy Epstein and *Valerie Minor* are staff members of Project Respect, a San Francisco-based school reform project working for equity in education. For more information, contact the authors at Project Respect, 1268 Noe Street, SF, CA 94114.

HOLIDAYS AND HERITAGE

GUERRILLA GIRLS' POP QUIZ.

Q. IF FEBRUARY IS BLACK HISTORY MONTH AND MARCH IS WOMEN'S HISTORY MONTH, WHAT HAPPENS THE REST OF THE YEAR?

A. DISCRIMINATION

REPRINTED WITH PERMISSION OF GUERRILLA GIRLS.

BOX 1056 Cooper Sta NY, NY 10276 **GUERRILLA GIRLS** CONSCIENCE OF THE ART WORLD

HERITAGE MONTHS AND CELEBRATIONS: SOME CONSIDERATIONS

BY DEBORAH MENKART

Many schools plan elaborate Black History Month and Hispanic Heritage Month programs. Some schools also recognize Women's History Month, Native American Heritage Month and others. It is important to acknowledge previously marginalized histories. However, special events in isolation can reinforce stereotypes rather than challenge them. For example, a student who had just attended a Hispanic Heritage assembly in a Washington, DC high school was asked what she had learned about Latinos. She answered, "Well, they are good at dancing." The assemblies in her school reinforced stereotypes about Latinos. Asked if she could name any Latinos who had made a difference in history or contemporary life, she could only think of Claribel Alegria — a Salvadoran poet that NECA and Curbstone Press had brought to the school the year before. In a school with an almost fifty percent Latino population, this student had learned nothing in any of her classes or special assemblies about Latino people or organizations.

In addition, heritage month events are often used as an excuse not to revise the overall school curriculum and school policies. There may be posters in the hallway featuring African American and Latino leaders, but a disproportionate number of Black and Latino children are suspended each week. There may be greetings in multiple languages during the morning announcements, but school policy does not encourage children to maintain their native language. Parents might be encouraged to bring in dishes for their respective heritage month, but their lives and knowledge are never connected to the curriculum.

This is not to suggest that one do away with heritage celebrations. Instead we can challenge ourselves to go deeper. In the same way that educational reform has recognized the benefit of instruction that is holistic and interdisciplinary, a similar approach is called for in addressing cultural heritage.

Listed below are some points and resources to consider when planning heritage events for your school. The books and videos mentioned are listed in the "Resource Guide." The other articles in this section of the book provide additional ideas about how to make holiday and heritage recognition more meaningful.

1. Consider what students will learn from heritage celebrations. Often a group of teachers, counselors and or parents is responsible for planning the heritage month or holiday events. If so, spend the first meeting preparing a list of instructional objectives — what is it that you want the school body to learn from these events? Too often we skip this step and go directly to drawing up a list of possible presenters. In developing the list of instructional objectives, spend some time asking members of that particular ethnic or racial heritage what they would like their peers to understand about their heritage. This is worthwhile, even if members of the particular ethnic or racial group are on the planning committee. The broader school community should provide input as to what stereotypes need to be addressed and how.

2. Examine the school's yearlong curriculum. When Carter J. Woodson first suggested a celebration in February of Black History, it was meant to build on the instruction that had gone on since September. So one of the first questions to ask is: is this a celebration of an integrated curriculum, or are we squeezing all of our Black History lessons into this month? If you find the content of the overall curriculum is still largely Eurocentric, then one can assume that students still learn that White people are most important and that everyone else plays a secondary role. In order to shift the curriculum, teachers will need to broaden their own understanding of U.S. history and identity. Honor the heritage you are celebrating by providing time for a book group to read and discuss a text on that culture's history. Teachers, other school staff, parents and members of the community could be invited to participate. The group could meet once a week before or after school. Ideally an administrator will help to arrange for a block of time for small groups of teachers and other school staff to be released from their other duties to participate. In some schools, the school will provide half an hour before or after school and the school staff will provide an additional half hour of their own time. When the school system's central administration asks for a report on the activities (assemblies) held to honor Black or Hispanic heritage, explain that this year you held fewer assemblies and instead laid the groundwork for staff to revise the yearlong curriculum. Books like *A Different Mirror* or *A People's History of the United States* are ideal for study/discussion groups. Or start with a book by Carter Woodson himself, *The Miseducation of the Negro*. Written in 1933, it is still relevant today.

3. Recognize that Latinos and Asian Americans have deep roots in the United States. There is a tendency to introduce these cultures as "international," when in reality Latinos have been on this land since before the Pilgrims and Asian Americans have been here for over 150 years.

4. Address the values, history, current reality and power relationships that shape a culture. Heritage months frequently feature the crafts, music and food of specific cultures. Crafts, music and food are an important expression of culture. However in isolation they mask the obstacles that people of color have faced, how they have confronted those obstacles, the great diversity within any cultural group and the current reality of people in the United States. *Hope and History* by Vincent Harding provides suggestions on how to teach about the role of the Civil Rights Movement in America's history. *Colonialism in the Americas* (VIDEA), *Open Veins of Latin America* (Galeano), *Dangerous Memories* (Golden, et al), *Hispanic Struggle for Social Justice* (Cockcroft), *Occupied America* (Acuña) or *Caribbean Connections: Puerto Rico* (Sunshine) are a few of the titles that could be used for Latino Heritage. Any study of foods could also include an examination of the roots of hunger, as presented in the high school curriculum *Finding Solutions to Hunger: A Hunger Program for Middle and Upper School Students* (Kempf). Teach about the people, organizations and experiences of each culture — in the context of U.S. and world history and current events.

5. Expand Black History Month to include the diaspora throughout the Americas. *Teaching About Haiti* (Sunshine), *Collective Memory* (Smith, et al) and *Caribbean Connections: Jamaica* (Sunshine) are useful references.

6. Present Native American culture not only in the past, but also in the present. Units on Native Americans invariably describe life before the conquest. It is also common at the elementary level to present all Native Americans living in teepees and wearing feathers. A deeper respect for Native Americans is taught with a curriculum which ad-

---

"A few years ago I quit accepting invitations from schools, state agencies and the private sector to make presentations for Cinco de Mayo, the annual Mexican American celebration.

Here's why. During the days prior to the celebration, school halls and classrooms are decorated with flags, pictures and other memorabilia. Once Cinco has passed, however, everything goes back into drawers and we're forgotten for the next 51 weeks. Meanwhile a preponderance of Chicano/ Latino students is having negative experiences with our educational system.

In the halls of our city, county and state governments, you hear Mexican music, see people eat Mexican food, and hear speeches about "celebrating diversity." Yet little has been done to increase the hiring and promotions of Chicanos/Latinos. Until we have parity, until you find us in board rooms instead of cloak rooms, then and only then will I speak for Cinco."

Gilbert de la O lives in Minnesota where he has been fighting for the rights of Chicanos and Latinos since the 1960s. In 1968 he founded the Brown Berets, a national Chicano organization that successfully fought for the establishment of a Chicano Studies Department at the University of Minnesota. In February of 1996 he was named "Volunteer of the Year" by the St. Paul United Way. The son of Texas-born migrant farmworkers, Gilbert de la O considers himself Mexican for his heritage, Chicano because of his movimiento (movement), and a patriotic American because he was wounded in Vietnam defending what he believed to be democratic values.

Reprinted from Connection, the Resource Center on the Americas.

---

dresses their current reality and acknowledges the great diversity among Native American cultures throughout history. The typical curriculum may move children to sympathize with the Native peoples and imagine that they would have defended their rights. But meanwhile they are oblivious to the fact that Native Americans continue to be removed from their lands and that there are opportunities to defend those rights today. Students can also learn about the lives and struggles of Native people throughout the America — in Alaska, Canada, the United States, Mexico, Central and South America. There are a number of good films including *Incident at Oglala* and *Broken Rainbow*. Rigoberta Menchu's autobiography presents a detailed description of Mayan culture and the injustices faced by Mayan people today. The Activists for Social Change section lists others people from the past and present such as Chief Joseph, Chief Wilma Mankiller and Chief Black Hawk.

7. Introduce leaders in the context of the organizations they worked with. Children are misinformed when they are told that great people make history all on their own. It is also important to study the work of organized movements for change, as is highlighted in the story of the sanitation work-

ers' strike in the video, *At the River I Stand*. Children have to learn from history about how change really happens if the curriculum is to serve as a tool for them to build their future. (See "Activists for Social Change" for more suggestions and a list of names.)

8. Recognize the diversity that exists within the United States and Canada. Often schools with diverse populations will hold an "International Festival." Everyone brings a dish or shares a tradition from their own heritage. Using the term "International" gives the impression that the dishes and traditions are foreign to the United States or Canada. Yet the fact that everyone bringing the dishes lives in North America means that the dishes and traditions actually reflect the domestic cultural diversity. Continue to hold the festival, but change the name to for example "Heritage Festival" or "Cultural Traditions Festival."

Happy Holidays?

BY JULIE BISSON

I have always loved holidays, both as an individual and as a teacher. When I was growing up, holidays were always a time of anticipation, decoration, warmth and family togetherness.

As a teacher, I carried my love of holidays into the classroom, wanting to recreate with my students what I felt in my family. It wasn't until I was working in the child-care program at Pacific Oaks Children's School and learning about anti-bias education that I began to feel some disequilibrium about what I was doing around holidays in the classroom. As I talked to other teachers and to teacher trainers, I discovered I wasn't the only one. Teachers across grade levels were feeling frustrated, overwhelmed and at a loss about how to handle holidays.

As a result, some teachers do not celebrate holidays because of pervasive commercialism and stereotypes. Other teachers center the entire year's curriculum around holidays. Still others use holidays as a basis for multicultural curricula, with "units" or "themes" centered on different countries and their celebrations (i.e., Mexicans are studied during May and Cinco de Mayo, and Chinese during January and Chinese New Year), which often leads to stereotyping and trivialization. My observations prompted me to research this topic for my master's thesis and develop guidelines for teachers.

The first step in integrating holidays into the classroom in a meaningful, respectful way is to decide on goals for holidays in the classroom. Make a list and keep them in mind as activities are planned. The next, and sometimes most difficult, step is to decide which holidays to include. It is important to honor and include all students in the class by including their holiday rituals and experiences in some way.

If holidays other than those experienced by the students are to be included, teachers must relate them to the classroom goals, as well as to such factors as developmental levels (older students are better able to understand and appreciate an unfamiliar holiday than are younger ones) and how much the students understand about the cultural group that observes the holiday. Holidays should never be used to introduce a cultural group, nor should they be the only time a particular group is discussed. Such approaches lead to stereotyping.

One way to integrate holiday activities into the regular curriculum — in a meaningful, respectful way that meets all students' needs — is to center them around the four anti-bias goals. (See Derman-Sparks, L., A.B.C. Task Force. *Anti-Bias Curriculum: Tools for Empowering Young Children.* Washington, D.C.: NAEYC.) Here are some suggestions.

1. Nurture each student's self-identity within the context of a group identity.

Find out what holidays your students celebrate and how. Plan activities, discussions and field trips that reflect home and/or family celebrations. Activities do not have to culminate in a party; some holidays can be recognized through a discussion at a group or meeting time.

2. Promote each student's comfortable interaction with people who are different from them.

Introduce holidays observed by students in the class but not generally recognized in society (i.e., other than national holidays). Perhaps a student would like to invite classmates on a field trip to attend a celebration that is important in his or her family. Help students understand that although not everyone celebrates the same events, all holidays are equally valuable. There are no "right" or "wrong" holidays.

3. Foster each student's ability to think critically about bias.

Commercial holiday decorations or cards often contain stereotypes. By comparing and contrasting Thanksgiving Day cards with real photos of contemporary Native Americans, for example, teachers can help students see the discrepancy between the portrayal of Native Americans in the media and who they really are today. Help children understand how it must feel to see yourself represented in a way that is not true and accurate. Teachers also can involve children in discussions about how many important holidays are not recognized in society. This omission hurts feelings and invalidates what is important to a person and his or her family.

Rigoberta Menchú Tum
Quiché Maya Indian ♦ Chimel, Guatemala

Rigoberta Menchu, Nobel Prize winner. Defender of the land and cultural rights of the indigenous people of Guatemala. (Poster from Syracuse Cultural Collective. See Resource Guide.)

4. Cultivate each student's ability to be an activist and stand up for himself or herself and for others in the face of bias.

By celebrating social justice holidays such as Passover, Martin Luther King, Jr.'s Birthday, Juneteenth, International Women's Day, International Worker's Day or Mexican Independence Day, we let students know that real people have fought to change bias and unfair practices. These activities can lead to discussions about real people who are struggling for justice today. Find out who the activists are in your community and introduce them to your students (either in person or in other ways). Students can take action by writing letters to card companies, letting them know that their stereotypical cards are harmful. They can let store owners know that by not including cards or decorations for non-dominant holidays, they are ignoring a large population of people. Students can also promote understanding and respect at their school for holidays which are ignored by mainstream culture.

Julie Bisson is an early childhood education trainer, author, community college instructor, and consultant on culturally relevant, anti-bias education. She is the author of Celebrate: An Anti Bias Guide to Enjoying Holidays in Early Childhood Programs *(Redleaf Press, 1997).*

Reprinted with permission of the author from the newsletter of the Peace Education Committee of the Women's International League for Peace and Freedom, Building Peace, *Summer, 1995.*

CELEBRATE LABOR ACTIVISTS

We can choose to celebrate, for example, the efforts of individuals and organizations to make safer and more humane conditions for workers throughout the world. Within this context, students can learn about the:

▸ Labor movement in the 1930s (see *Power in Our Hands* by Bigelow and Diamond for role plays on U.S. labor history and *Labor's Untold Story* for background);

▸ History of International Workers' Day (May 1) and how it is celebrated in many parts of the world;

▸ Formation and strategies of contemporary unions such as the United Farm Workers Union (UFW);

▸ Campaigns to protest unfair labor practices by multinationals. Many youth are involved in these campaigns, such as Boycott NIKE;

▸ Role of local labor activists and unions.

Students can plan how to honor the work of these people. An important part of honoring or celebrating is to carry on the work and to teach others. Ask students what the rest of the school should know about the historic and contemporary role of labor activists. How could this information be shared?

May Day Demonstration in Guatemala City. Sign says, "We are children and we have rights."

A NATIVE PERSPECTIVE ON THANKSGIVING

OBJECTIVE

Students will describe a Native perspective on Thanksgiving.

PROCEDURE

1. Ask students to describe what they know about the first Thanksgiving meal shared by Europeans and Native Americans. (Clarify that you are asking for this event in particular since most cultures throughout history have celebrated some sort of celebration of thanks or Thanksgiving for the fall harvest. The celebration usually features a meal with the fruits of that harvest.) List their ideas.

2. Explain that it is not certain just how Thanksgiving first became a holiday. However most of what we have learned in schools has been from a European American perspective. Would they like to read a story about how Thanksgiving may have started from a Native American perspective? Ask students to read the handout.

3. Were they surprised? How does this story differ from versions they have heard before? Why do they think that is?

4. Have students make up a skit or have a discussion about what the Wampanoag people may have considered or weighed before they shared their harvest feast with the colonists. Do you think that some Wampanoag people may have objected to celebrat-ing with the Pilgrims? Or, your class could have a debate or meeting, some taking the point of view of Wampanoag people who would argue for sharing their harvest food with the Pilgrims, and others arguing for not helping the Pilgrims. (Remind students that this is hypothetical, and that we do not really know if such a discussion occurred.)

5. List on the board what each group, the Pilgrims and the Wampanoags, had to be thankful for in 1621. Do you think the Wampanoags would have felt grateful to the Pilgrims? Do you think the Pilgrims would have felt grateful to the Wampanoags?

6. Today many people in the United States celebrate Thanksgiving. Although the meaning of Thanksgiving is probably a little different for each family who celebrates it, many serve a "traditional Thanksgiving dinner" that includes foods native to North America. What are some of these foods?

Many people in the United States remember the first Thanksgiving, and some consider it a day of mourning. Discuss with the class why some people might feel this way.

This lesson was adapted from The Wabanakis of Maine and the Maritimes: A Resource Book About Penobscot, Passamaquoddy, Maliseet, Micmac and Abenaki Indians *prepared for and published by the Maine Indian Program, American Friends Service Committee, 1501 Cherry Street, Philadelphia, PA 19102. This is an excellent curriculum guide which includes lesson plans for grades 4-8.*

A NATIVE PERSPECTIVE ON THANKSGIVING

When the Pilgrims arrived in 1620, they arrived at a site that had been a Pawtuxet village. A smallpox plague, which had begun a few years before, caused the village to be deserted; almost no one was left alive, and the Pilgrims claimed for their own the cleared fields that the Pawtuxet people had left.

After a few days the Pilgrims discovered that Pawtuxet people buried their dead with supplies of corn and beans. They dug up many graves, taking the food. Some Wampanoag people who saw this were deeply offended by what they regarded as flagrant disrespect for the dead, and they attacked the Pilgrims. They were frightened off by gunfire.

Several weeks later Pilgrims were working in the fields when some Native people approached. The Pilgrims ran away, leaving their tools, which the Native people took.

In February 1621, a Wabanaki man from Maine walked into the Pilgrim village speaking English. Samoset had been kidnapped by the English in Maine and taken to England; he had returned to North America six months before the Pilgrims arrived. He told the Pilgrims about the neighboring Native peoples, and their experience with Europeans. He promised their tools would be returned.

Samoset returned with 60 Native people. Massasoit was a Wampanoag *sakom* (ZAH-g'm, Passamaquody-Maliseet word for Wabanaki leader) who signed a treaty of cooperation between the Wampanoags and the Pilgrims. Tisquantum (Squanto), a Pawtuxet, had also been captured by the English and sold into slavery in Spain. He es-caped to England and came back to North America on the same ship as Samoset. Because his people had died of smallpox, he went to live with Wampanoag people. Tisquantum remained with the Pilgrims for the rest of his life, teaching them how to survive in their new environment. (The Pilgrims were mainly artisans.)

In the fall of 1621, at the Pilgrims' invitation, the Wampanoags brought to share food that they had gathered for their traditional harvest (Thanksgiving) feast. This Thanksgiving feast lasted three days. Massasoit and 90 Wampanoags celebrated with 55 Pilgrims, all that remained from the original 103. The Wampanoags had brought five deer, as well as turkeys, geese, ducks, clams, oysters, fish, fruits, corn, molasses, salads, and maple sugar.

By the time of Massasoit's death in 1622, Wampanoag people were concerned about the loss of their land to the English. In addition, the Pilgrims expected Wampanoag people to obey their laws. These included not trespassing on "English" land, whether English people were using it or not, and laws that provided the death penalty against "blasphemy." (This law is said to have applied to Native people who refused to accept the Puritan religion.) By 1675 the Wampanoags, along with other native people in the area, declared war on the English settlers. The Native people were defeated there a year later along with other Native people in the area. Many of the survivors were executed or sold into slavery.

Much of the information in the student handout is from Un-learning Indian Stereotypes, Council on Interracial Books for Children, 1977.

ASIAN AMERICAN

BY JOYCE MIYAMOTO

When I was young
kids used to ask me
what are you?
I'd tell them what my
    mom told me
I'm an American
chin chin Chinaman
you're a Jap!
flashing hot inside
I'd go home
my mom would say
don't worry
he who walks alone
walks faster

people kept asking
    me
what are you?
and I would always
    answer
I'm an American
they'd say
no, what nationality?
I'm an American
that's where I was born
flashing hot inside
and when I'd tell
    them what they
    wanted to know
Japanese....
Oh I've been to
    Japan

I'd get it over with
so they could
    catalogue and file
    me
pigeon-hole me
so they'd know just

how
to think of me
priding themselves
they could guess the
    difference
between Japanese
    and Chinese
they had me wishing
    I was what I'd been
    seeing in movies
    and on T.V., on
    billboards and in
    magazines

and I tried
while they were
    making laws in
    California against
    us owning land
we were trying to be
    American
and laws against us
    intermarrying with
    white people
we were trying to be
    American
When they put us in
    Concentration
    camps
We were trying to be
    American
Our people
    volunteered to fight
    against their own
    country
trying to be American
when they dropped
    the atom bomb on
    Hiroshima and
    Nagasaki

we were still trying.
finally we made it
most of our parents
fiercely dedicated to
    give us
a good education
to give us everything
    they never had
we made it
now they use us as
    an example
to the blacks and
    browns
how we made it
how we overcame.

but there was always
someone asking me
what are you?

now I answer
I'm an Asian
and they say
why do you want to
    separate
    yourselves?
now I say
I'm Japanese
and they say
don't you know this
    is the greatest
    country in the
    world?
now I say in America
I'm part of the third
    world people
and they say
if you don't like it
    here
why don't you go
    back.

Reprinted from Roots: An Asian American Reader *with permission from the UCLA Asian American Studies Department.*

QUESTION FOR REFLECTION

This poem was written in 1970, around the time of the start of the ethnic studies movement. Do you think things have changed since then?

ACTIVISTS FOR SOCIAL CHANGE

Students can learn a lot by studying the lives of people who have worked for social justice. Their lives can teach how to face challenges, where to gather strength to face adversity, how to relate to other people, and how to deal with defeat. Researching the life of a famous person is an assignment frequently given to youth during the heritage months. Whatever the occasion, following are some recommendations for helping students to get the most from this assignment. On the next pages are some suggestions of people and organizations for student research.

SUGGESTED GUIDELINES

1. **Enlarge and diversify the list of people you suggest for student research.** Too often students are asked to research the same names year after year — Frederick Douglass, Martin Luther King, Jr. and Harriet Tubman during Black History Month, Cesar Chavez and Roberto Clemente for Hispanic Heritage and the suffragists during Women's History Month. Rather than challenging stereotypes, this repetition can lead students to believe that there were only a few great Blacks, Hispanics and women in U.S. history. Accompanying this lesson is a list of many more activists for social change. Encourage students to refer to this list for any project you assign on people who have made a difference. We have tried to limit the list to people about whom we know students could find at least on book. Add names of people who may not be nationally known but who are familiar as local leaders.

2. **Personalize the assignment.** Ask students to write the report in first person, as if they were the person under study writing an autobiography. This can help the students get into the other person's shoes and can motivate them to learn more. The quality of the student's writing is also likely to improve. Their essay will be an engaging story rather than the all-too-frequent lifeless reports. The student could also use his/her imagination to write about how the activist felt about certain experiences.

3. **Encourage the use of varied and primary sources.** Reward students with extra points for all non-encyclopedia type references. Suggest to students that they look for autobiographies and biographies, writings by the person they have selected, information from any organizations they were affiliated with, newspaper articles, interviews with people who knew the person, etc. In the case of primary sources, challenge students to use ones that are less commonly known. For example, in the case of Martin Luther King Jr., everyone is already familiar with his speech "I Have A Dream." Powerful as it is, it is only one of hundreds of moving and powerful essays he authored on domestic and international topics. The student will learn a lot more from Dr. King if he or she broadens their reading. Another example is Helen Keller. Everyone knows her accomplishments with regards to sight and hearing, but more thorough investigation will reveal her extensive work as a political activist.

4. **Examine how the person changes over time.** This will help students to realize that learning and growing are lifelong processes. Most people they would choose to study developed their analysis and methods over time. Ask students to document some of those changes.

5. **How could the person's work have been strengthened?** Ask students what they would recommend to the person they are studying that would (or could have) increased the effectiveness of their work. Ask them to pay particular attention to the "matrix of oppression." Point out to students that in many cases the person they are studying may have been very strong in one aspect of their work, but ignored other forms of oppression. For example, if the person worked on labor issues — did they address racial and/or gender discrimination in the union? If they addressed the rights of a racial group, did they address class and gender discrimination within that group?

6. **Highlight community activists.** Encourage students to research and present the lives of people who might not be well-known, but who are active in their community or region. Local individuals may be receptive to a request for an interview from a student. Students can get ideas about who would be a good candidate for such a request from reading newspaper articles or newsletters from local chapters of activist groups, focusing on issues such

as housing, women's rights, education, labor, etc. The same sources can be good background reading for students to use to prepare their interview questions.

7. **Highlight the organizations and institutions involved in social change.** Ask the students to include in their report/essay information about the organizations with which the person worked and the forces which influenced them. Many mainstream books and poster series give students the false impression that people do great things all by themselves. Rather than inspiring the students, this can leave them feeling powerless. "I could never accomplish that by myself," students say to themselves. Well, neither did the famous person. There is barely an accomplishment in science, sports, social change movements or other fields which does not reflect group effort and/or the strong influences of family or religion. In *Rethinking Schools*, Herbert Kohl describes how Rosa Parks has been traditionally and erroneously portrayed as an old lady who one day was just too tired to go to the back of the bus. Although she was indeed always tired at the end of a long day's work, her decision was influenced by her associations with others active in the Civil Rights movement, including discussions at the Highlander Center with other activists about strategies for confronting Jim Crow. If we want students to learn from the lives of famous people, then one of the lessons to be learned is how one works with others — through organizations, family or other groups — for change.

Another option would be to ask students to study the life of an organization. They could then make reference to various key individuals, but the focus would be on the organization itself — why and how it got started, goals, methods, successes and failures, alliances, conflicts, etc. There is not room to list all of the individual organizations here. But within each of the categories listed below, there is a history of the movement and many organizations still working on the issues today.

Women's rights

Civil rights

Anti-war

Gay rights

Native American rights and sovereignty

Immigrant rights

Labor unions

Liberation movements

Environmental protection

Health issues (AIDS, infant mortality, health of people of color)

Prison reform/prisoner's rights

Rights of the physically disabled

Housing rights

Anti-police abuse/criminal justice reform

ACTIVISTS FOR SOCIAL CHANGE

These are just a few suggestions of people and current organizations that students could research. It is an alternative to the traditional lists of sports stars, musicians, actors and mainstream politicians, but it is by no means inclusive.

Each name is followed by a few descriptive words, noting the area in which she or he were active. We tried to limit our selection to people about whom students would be able to find some published information. If a book is listed about this person in the biography section of the Resource Guide in this book, her or his name is followed by an asterisk.

MUMIA ABU-JAMAL
Journalist; Black Panther; political prisoner; 20th

RUDY ACUNA
Chicano rights activist; professor, 20th

JANE ADDAMS
Developed community social services and training for people in poverty; 20th

PEDRO ALBIZU CAMPOS
Puerto Rican independence advocate; 20th

SAUL ALINSKY
Community organizer; 20th

MAYA ANGELOU
Author; activist; 20th

SUSAN B. ANTHONY
Abolitionist; suffragist; 19th-20th

JEAN-BERTRAND ARISTIDE
Haitian leader in movement for justice; former President; 20th

ELLA BAKER
Civil rights activist; 20th

JAMES BALDWIN
Novelist; essayist; lecturer; civil and gay rights advocate; 20th

DENNIS BANKS
Founded American Indian Movement (AIM); 20th

BENJAMIN BANNEKER
Mathematician; 18th

DANIEL AND PHILLIP BERRIGAN
Anti-war activists; 20th

MARY MCLEOD BETHUNE
Founder, National Council of Negro Women; educator; 20th

CHIEF BLACK HAWK
Sauk chief; led people against White settlers in Illinois; 19th

GRACE LEE BOGGS*
Chinese American active in Civil Rights Movement; 20th

SIMON BOLIVAR
Fought for the liberation of Latin America from Spain; 19th

ANNE BRADEN
Southern labor organizer; 20th

DAVID BROWER
Ecologist; environmentalist, writer; 20th

JOHN BROWN
Militant abolitionist; 19th

CARLOS BULOSAN
Migrant farmworker; documenter of Filipino-American experience; 20th

OMAR CABEZAS
Nicaraguan Sandinista; 20th

WILL CAMPBELL
Southern Baptist leader; 20th

STOKELY CARMICHAEL (KWAME TOURE)
Civil rights activist; SNCC founder; 20th

RACHEL CARSON
Founder, the environmental movement; 20th

FIDEL CASTRO
Leader of nationalist; anti-imperialist Cuban revolution; president of Cuba; 20th

JAMES EARL CHANEY
Civil rights activist; 20th

CESAR CHAVEZ
Labor leader; founder of the United Farm Workers; 20th

SHIRLEY CHISHOLM*
Politician; first Black woman elected to U.S. Congress; 20th

SEPTIMA CLARK*
Adult educator; civil rights activist; 20th

CHARLES CLEMENTS, M.D.*
American doctor; volunteered his services during the war in El Salvador; 20th

CHIEF COCHISE
Native American leader; 19th

ROBERT COLES
Psychologist; children's activist; 20th

BERT CORONA
Activist for rights of undocumented and Mexican-Americans; 20th

CHIEF CRAZY HORSE
Native American rights activist; Sioux; 19th

BENEDITA DA SILVA*
Brazilian senator; activist for the rights of the poor; 20th

ANGELA DAVIS*
Professor; activist for Black and women's rights; 20th

DOROTHY DAY
Pacifist; founder of the Catholic Worker movement; 20th

EUGENE V. DEBS
Socialist politician; labor activist; 19th-20th

MORRIS DEES*
Lawyer; anti-Klan activist; 20th

FREDERICK DOUGLASS
Abolitionist; author; statesman; 19th

W.E.B. DUBOIS*
Author; teacher; socialist; founder of NAACP; 19th-20th

VIRGINIA FOSTER DURR*
Civil rights activist; worked to abolish the poll tax; 20th

MARIAN WRIGHT EDELMAN*
Founder and current president, the Children's Defense Fund; 20th

DANIEL ELLSBERG
Anti-Vietnam war activist; European American; 20th

OLAUDAH EQUIANO*
Abolitionist; writer; 18th

MEDGAR EVERS
Civil rights leader; 20th

JAMES FARMER
Civil rights leader; national director, CORE; 20th

ELIZABETH GURLEY FLYNN
Labor organizer; feminist; 20th

MARCUS GARVEY
Advocate, rights of people of African descent in the Americas; founder, Universal Negro Improvement Association; 20th

CHIEF GERONIMO
Native American war leader; 20th

NIKKI D. GIOVANNI
Author; poet; 20th

EMMA GOLDMAN
Labor organizer; internationalist, anarchist; feminist; 20th

ANDREW GOODMAN
Civil rights activist; 20th

ANGELINA & SARAH GRIMKE
Women's rights and antislavery activists; 19th

CHE GUEVARA
Economist; doctor; guerilla; revolutionary; 20th

WOODY GUTHRIE*
Folk singer; advocate; working people's rights; 20th

JOSE ANGEL GUTIERREZ
Chicano rights activist; 20th

FANNIE LOU HAMER*
Civil rights activist; 20th

Paul Robeson. (This poster available from Syracuse Cultural Workers. See "Resource Guide.")

VINCENT HARDING
Historian; author; 20th

FRANCES ELLEN WATKINS HARPER
First known African American novelist; abolitionist; 20th.

ABRAHAM JOSHUA HESCHEL
Writer; historian of Jewish life; spiritual leader; 20th

JOE HILL
Labor activist; song writer; 20th.

MYLES HORTON*
Educator; labor and civil rights activist; founder, Highlander Center; 20th

DOLORES HUERTA
Labor organizer; cofounder, United Farm Workers; 20th

LANGSTON HUGHES
Poet; author; 20th

ZORA NEALE HURSTON
Writer; researcher; Harlem Renaissance; 20th

JESSE JACKSON
Organizer; politician; founder, Rainbow Coalition; 20th

LILLIE MAE CARROLL JACKSON
NAACP leader; 20th

MAE JEMISON
First African American astronaut; 20th

MOTHER JONES*
Labor organizer; UMW; 19th

BARBARA JORDAN
Lawyer; professor; political leader; 20th

CHIEF JOSEPH*
Native American activist for land rights; Nez Perce; 19th

BENITO JUAREZ
First indigenous person to become president of Mexico; 20th

CORETTA SCOTT KING
Civil and human rights activist; 20th

MARTIN LUTHER KING, JR.
Civil rights movement leader; anti-war activist; 20th

MAXINE HONG KINGSTON
Author; educator; 20th

ELIZABETH KOONTZ
Educator; 20th

FRED KOREMATSU*
Fought the order of internment of Japanese-Americans in WWII all the way to the Supreme Court; 20th

JONATHAN KOZOL
Author; education activist; 20th

JOHN L. LEWIS
Labor leader; organizer of industrial workers; 20th

BEN LINDER
Engineer; clown; volunteered in Nicaragua; 20th

VIOLA LIUZZO
Civil rights activist; 20th

AUDRE LORDE
Poet; activist for rights of women, gays, and people of color; 20th

TOUISSANT LOUVERTURE*
Leader, Haitian revolution; 19th

NELSON MANDELA
South African freedom fighter; president, South Africa; 20th

WILMA MANKILLER*
Principal chief, Cherokee Nation of Oklahoma; 20th

COMMONDANTE MARCOS
Militant peasant and indigenous rights activist; Zapatista leader; 20th

THURGOOD MARSHALL
First African-American Supreme Court Justice; civil rights advocate; 20th

JOSE MARTI*
Cuban independence fighter; organizer; theorist; writer; 19th

RIGOBERTA MENCHU*
Guatemalan activist for indigenous rights; Nobel Peace Prize recipient, 20th

CHICO MENDES*
Advocate, rights of Brazilian rubber tappers and protection of the Amazon rainforest; 20th

KWEISE MFUME
Politician; current president, NAACP; 20th

HARVEY MILK
Politician; gay rights activist; 20th

HO CHI MINH
Fought for independence of Vietnam from Japan, French and the U.S.; 20th

PATSY MINK
Political leader; women's rights activist; 20th

MIRABEL SISTERS*
Four women who fought the Trujillo dictatorship in the Dominican Republic; 20th

TONI MORRISON
Author; Nobel Literature Prize winner; 20th

BOB MOSES
Civil rights activist; founder, Algebra Project; 20th

PAULI MURRAY
Educator; legal and civil rights advocate; feminist; 20th

RALPH NADER
Consumer rights advocate; 20th

HOLLY NEAR
Feminist and anti-war songwriter and singer; 20th

ELLISON S. ONIZUKA
Women's rights leader

GORDON PARKS
Photographer; 20th

ROSA PARKS
Civil rights activist; 20th

LEONARD PELTIER
Imprisoned Native American rights activist; 20th

A. PHILLIP RANDOLPH
Organizer of African American workers (Pullman); socialist; civil rights activist; 20th

BERNICE JOHNSON REAGON
Political activist; historian; founder, Sweet Honey in the Rock; songwriter; 20th

JAMES REEB
Religious leader (Unitarian Church); Civil Rights worker; 20th

MARLON RIGGS
Film maker; gay rights advocate; 20th

PAUL ROBESON*
Musician; civil rights advocate; 20th

JACKIE ROBINSON
Baseball player; civil rights advocate; 20th

HELEN RODRIGUEZ-TRIAS
Doctor; women's health advocate; 20th

KEN SARO-WIWA
Nigerian environmentalist; author; Ogoni activist; 20th

ARTURO ALFONSO SCHOMBURG
Historian; 20th

MICHAEL SCHWERNER
Civil rights activist; 20th

CHIEF SEATTLE
Advocate for protection of Native Americans and the environment; 19th

CHIEF SITTING BULL
Native American chief and medicine man; 19th

GLORIA STEINEM
Women's rights leader; 20th

RON TAKAKI
Historian; author; 20th

CHIEF TECUMESH
Leader of the Shawnees who formed a confederacy to protect their lands from invasion; 19th

MARY CHURCH TERRELL
Civil rights activist; writer; 20th

PIRI THOMAS*
Writer, documenter of immigrant experience; 20th

HENRY DAVID THOREAU
Author; leader of the Transcendental movement; naturalist; 19th

JIM THORPE
Native American leader; champion athlete; 20th

SOJOURNER TRUTH
Abolitionist; itinerant preacher; women's rights advocate; African American; 19th

HARRIET TUBMAN
Abolitionist; underground railroad leader; women's rights advocate; 19th

NAT TURNER
Leader of slave revolt; 19th

DENMARK VESEY
Abolitionist; planned slave rebellion; 19th

ALICE WALKER
Author; feminist; Pulitzer Prize winner; 20th

IDA B. WELLS*
Journalist; antilynching and women's right advocate; 20th

ROY WILKINS
Civil rights activist; 20th

SARAH WINNEMUCA
Advocate for Native Americans

WILLIAM WORTHY
Journalist; anti-imperialist; 20th

CARTER G. WOODSON
Historian; educator; founder, Association for the Study of Negro Life and History; 20th

MALCOLM X
Muslim minister and spokesperson; philosopher; organizer; 20th

MINORU YASUI
Protested the internment of Japanese-Americans; 20th

HOWARD ZINN*
Professor; author; historian; civil rights activist; 20th

La Llorona: Exploring Myth and Reality

BY MARTA URQUILLA

As part of "Hispanic Heritage Month" Marian Urquilla and I were invited to present a workshop for female students at Cardozo High School in Washington, D.C. Our aim was to not only celebrate "Hispanic Heritage" but to encourage a diverse group of young women to celebrate themselves and each other.

Our teaching tool was the Mexican story of "La Llorona." La Llorona (The Crying Woman), a legendary figure in Mexico's oral tradition, killed her three children and then, upon seeing what she had done, killed herself. According to the storytellers, La Llorona's ghost can be heard flying through the trees at night, wailing for her dead children.

The group consisted of approximately 45 young women; the majority were Latinas (mostly ESL students), while the rest were African-American and African. The group represented various ages and grade levels. The workshop was conducted in English and Spanish. The highlights were:

▸ Cross-cultural communication/celebration
▸ Successful teamwork
▸ Reading and discussion
▸ Oral storytelling and performance
▸ Positive group dynamics
▸ Fun and productive learning atmosphere
▸ Teacher participation

Buzz Activity/Community-building Activity

After a brief introduction, the group assembled in a large circle. The students were asked to find a partner. We explained to the group that we would be asking a series of questions and for each question they were to switch partners, introduce themselves to one another and spend three minutes answering the question. The questions/topics were:

▸ Name something you like about yourself or something you like to do. Why?
▸ Talk about something that you are proud of — in your culture and/or country, your family or your community. Why?
▸ Imagine yourself ten years from now. Where do you see yourself? Where do you want to be? What do you want to be doing? Why?
▸ Name a woman or girl who you admire. Who is she and why do you look up to her?

After discussing the questions, the students returned to the large circle to debrief, building connections with each other as they shared their stories.

Storytelling Activity

We used an excerpt from an essay written by a high school student from New York City who in describing her cultural identity as "half-Mexican," proudly retells the story of La Llorona as she had learned it from her Mexican uncle.

The students were divided into small groups and asked to read and discuss the story together. We circulated the room to translate for the ESL students. We asked the students to consider what might have been the circumstances of La Llorona's situation. What might have led her to kill her children? Why was she so alone? Where were her family and her community? Why didn't she have anyone to support her? The students discussed whether La Llorona represented a strong or a weak woman, and they discussed what factors might have prevented her from killing her children and herself.

The groups were then asked to consider how a situation like La Llorona's might look today. What conditions might a single woman face today in our society? Following up on the students' conversations, we asked each group to imagine a contemporary figure of La Llorona: "What would she look like? Who would she be? Show us." Each small group then created and produced a role play, featuring a 90s version of La Llorona.

Three of the five groups were able to present their role plays to the entire room. In the most striking presentation, one group presented a young, single, undocumented, recent immigrant with three children who was unexpectedly fired from her job. Unemployed and alone, the woman was unable to buy food for her children or pay the rent for their apartment. They became homeless and found themselves confronted by the dangerous life of the streets. Unable to guarantee her children's safety, she chose to end their misery by killing them.

In closing, the students were asked to think

about their experience in the workshop. What had they learned about themselves and each other? We also asked them to reflect on the image of La Llorona and how she transcended culture and myth to become a woman we could all relate to. What were the possibilities demonstrated to us by this activity for building cross-cultural alliances?

Marta Urquilla *is the founder and director of Sister To Sister/Hermana A Hermana, a young women's arts and* *leadership development project in Washington D.C. She has worked with youth as a photography and writing instructor in North Carolina, Tennessee and Washington D.C. Marta is an Echoing Green Fellow.*

References

Rodriguez, S. "Being Half-Mexican," in Tashlik, P. Ed. 1994. *Hispanic, female and young: An anthology.* Houston: Pinata Books.

WHERE I'M FROM: INVITING STUDENT LIVES INTO THE CLASSROOM

BY LINDA CHRISTENSEN

I remember holding my father's hand as he read my story hanging on the display wall outside Mrs. Martin's classroom on the night of Open House. I remember the sound of change jingling in Dad's pocket, his laughter as he called my mom over and read out loud the part where I'd named the cow "Lena" after my mother and the chicken "Walt" after my father. It was a moment of sweet joy for me when my two worlds of home and school bumped together in a harmony of reading, writing, and laughter.

In my junior year of high school, I skipped most of my classes, but crawled back through the courtyard window of my English class where Ms. Carr selected novels and volumes of poetry for me to read, where she wrote notes in the margins of my papers asking me questions about my home, my mother, my sister who'd run away, my father who'd died three years before, instead of responding by correcting my errors like my other teachers.

These two events from my schooling capture part of what the editors of *Rethinking Our Classrooms* meant when we encouraged teachers to make students feel "significant" in our classrooms:

The ways we organize classroom life should seek to make children feel significant and cared about — by the teacher and by each other. Unless students feel emotionally and physically safe, they won't share real thoughts and feelings. Discussions will be tinny and dishonest. We need to design activities where students learn to trust and care for each other. Classroom

WHERE I'M FROM
GEORGE ELLA LYON

I am from clothespins,
from Clorox and carbon-tetrachloride.
I am from the dirt under the back porch.
(Black, glistening
it tasted like beets.)
I am from the forsythia bush,
the Dutch elm
whose long gone limbs I remember
as if they were my own.

I am from fudge and eyeglasses,
    from Imogene and Alafair.
I'm from the know-it-alls
    and the pass-it-ons,
from perk up and pipe down.
I'm from He restoreth my soul
    with a cottonball lamb
    and ten verses I can say myself.

I'm from Artemus and Billie's Branch,
fried corn and strong coffee.
From the finger my grandfather lost
    to the auger
the eye my father shut to keep his sight.
Under my bed was a dress box
spilling old pictures,
a sift of lost faces
to drift beneath my dreams.
I am from those moments —
snapped before I budded —
leaf-fall from the family tree.

life should, to the greatest extend possible, prefigure the kind of democratic and just society we envision and thus contribute to building that society. Together students and teachers can create a "community of conscience," as educators Asa Hilliard and George Pine call it. (p. 4)

Mrs. Martin and Ms. Carr made me feel significant and cared about because they invited my home into the classroom. When I wrote and included details about my family, they listened. They made space for me and my people in the curriculum.

Today in my classroom at Jefferson High School, I attempt to find ways to make students feel significant and cared about as well, to find space for their lives to become part of the curriculum. I do this by inviting them to write about their lives, about the worlds from which they come. Our sharing is one of the many ways we begin to build community together. It "prefigures" a world where students can hear the home language from Diovana's Pacific Islander heritage, Lurdes' Mexican family, Oretha's African American home, and my Norwegian roots and celebrate without mockery the similarities as well as the differences.

Sometimes grounding lessons in students' lives can take a more critical role by asking them to examine how they have been shaped or manipulated by the media, for example. But as critical teachers, we shouldn't overlook the necessity of connecting students around moments of joy as well.

This year I found a poem in *The United States of Poetry*[1] that I used to invite my students' families, homes, and neighborhoods into the classroom. It's called "Where I'm From" by George Ella Lyon. Lyon's poem follows a repeating pattern "I am from..." that recalls details, evokes memories — and can prompt some excellent poetry.

Lyon's poem allowed me to teach about the use of specifics in poetry, and writing in general. But the lesson also brought the class together through the sharing of details from our lives and lots of laughter and talk about the "old ones" whose language and ways continue to permeate the ways we do things today.

TEACHING PROCEDURE

1. After the students read the poem out loud together, we note that Lyon begins many of her lines with the phrase, "I am from." I remind the class of William Stafford's[2] advice to find a hook to "link the poem forward" through some kind of device like a repeating line, so the poem can develop a momentum. I suggest they might want to use the line "I am from" or create another phrase that will move the poem.

2. We go line by line through the poem and notice the details Lyon remembers about her past. After we read, I ask students to write lists that match the ones in Lyon's poem and to share them out loud. This verbal sharing sparks memories to bubble up from student to student and also gives us memories to share as we make our way through the lesson:

▸ Items found around their home: bobby pins, stacks of newspapers, grandma's teeth, discount coupons for a Mercedes. (They don't have to tell the truth.)

▸ Items found in their yard: broken rakes, dog bones, hoses coiled like green snakes. (I encourage them to think of comparisons as they list.)

▸ Items found in their neighborhood: the corner grocery, Mr. Tate's beat up Ford Fairlane, the "home base" plum tree.

▸ Names of relatives, especially ones that link them to the past: Uncle Einar and Aunt Eva, Claude, the Christensen branch.

▸ Sayings: "If I've told you once..." (The students had a great time with this one; they had a ready supply that either brought me back to childhood or made me want to steal their families' lines.)

▸ Names of foods and dishes that recall family gatherings: ludefisk or tamales or black eyed peas.

▸ Names of places they keep their childhood memories: Diaries, boxes, underwear drawers, inside the family *Bible*.

3. We share their lists out loud as we brainstorm. I encourage them to make their piece "sound like home," using the names and language of their home, their family, their neighborhood. The students who write vague nouns like "shoes" or "magazines," get more specific when they hear their classmates shout out, "Jet," "Latina," "pink tights crusted with rosin." Out of the chaos, the sounds, smells, and languages of my students' homes emerge in poetry.

4. Once they have their lists of specific words, phrases, and names, I ask them to write. I encourage them to find some kind of link or phrase like "I am from.." to weave the poem together and to end the poem with a line or two that ties their present to their past, their family history. For example, in Lyon's poem, she ends with "Under my bed was a dress box/spilling old pictures...I am from those moments..."

5. After students have written a draft, we "read around." This is an opportunity for students to feel "significant and cared about" as they share their poems. But as most teachers know, students don't automatically give their undivided attention to each other when they share pieces in the class. To facilitate the process and to make sure that students get the attention their pieces deserve, I have students write comments about each reader's piece. I do this to keep them focused on the reader, but it's also a way for them to learn from each other what makes good writing. I tell them, "Pull out a piece of paper. Write the name of the reader, then as each person reads, write what you liked about their piece. Be specific, write down what words or phrases made the piece work. Did they use a list? A metaphor? Humor?"

6. Seated in our circle, each student reads his/her poem. After the student reads, classmates raise

their hands to comment on what they like about the piece. The writer calls on his/her classmates and receives feedback about what is good in the poem. I rarely comment during this process because students pick up on all of the points I would have made. I do stop from time to time to point out that the use of a list is a technique they might "borrow" from their peer's poem and include in their next poem or in a revision; I might note that the use of Spanish or home language adds authenticity to a piece and ask them to see if they could add some to their piece. After a few read around sessions I can spot writing techniques that students have "borrowed" from each other and included in their revisions or in their next piece: Dialogue, church sayings, lists, exaggeration. The following excerpts are from student poems that Lyon's piece provoked:

I am from bobby pins, doo rags, and wide tooth combs.

I am from prayer plants that lift their stems and rejoice every night.

I am from chocolate cakes and deviled eggs from older cousins and hand-me-downs to "shut ups" and "sit downs"

I am from Genesis to Exodus,
Leviticus, too.
church to church, pew to pew

I am from a huge family tree that begins with dust
and ends with me.
— *Oretha Storey*

I am from old pictures
and hand sewn quilts.
I am from the Yerba Buena
to the old walnut tree that is no more.

I am from *carne con chile*
to *queso con tortillas.*
I am from farmers and ancient Indians
to the *frijoles* and *sopa*
they ate.
— *Lurdes Sandoval*

I am from awapuhi ginger,
sweet fields of sugar cane,
green bananas.

I am from warm rain cascading over
taro leaf umbrellas,

crouching beneath the shield of kalo.

I am from poke, brie cheese, mango, and raspberries,
from Maruitte
and Aunty Nani.

I am from Moore and Cackley
from sardines and haupia.
From Mirana's lip Djavan split
to the shrunken belly
my grandmother could not cure.
— *Djamila Moore*

I am from Aztlan
where many battles and wars were fought.
I am from the strength and courage of the Aztecs
who died for our freedom.
I am from traditions and customs
from *posadas* and *quinceñeras*
to *dia de la muerte* and *buena suerte*.

I am from the blood of my ancestors,
the dreams of my grandmother,
the faith of my mother,
and the pride of my culture.

I am from the survivors.
— *Alejandro Vidales*

I am from the land that struggles
for freedom.
I am from the rice field, water buffaloes
and cows.
I am from the place where
Blood floats like rivers.
Innocent souls are trapped
under the ground.
Dead bodies haven't yet been buried.

A beautiful barn becomes
a cemetery.

It wasn't supposed to be like this.

I am from the place I hold

now only as a memory.
I am from a family with hearts like stones.
— *Cang Dao*

"Where I'm From" is one tiny lesson in a year of critical teaching. But as we create schools and classrooms that are "laboratories for a more just society than the one we now live in," we need to remember to make our students feel significant and cared about. But these kinds of lessons keep me going, too. When the gray days of budget cuts, standardized tests, school restructuring plans gone awry, and bad teacher room talk pile up one after another like layers of old newspapers on your back porch, pull out George Ella Lyon's poem and invite the stories and voices of your students into the classroom.

Linda Christensen is an English teacher at Jefferson High School in Portland Oregon, poet, Director of the Portland Writing Project, an editor of Rethinking Schools *and* National Coalition of Education Activists (NCEA) *steering committee member. E-mail: LChrist@aol.com*

Reprinted with permission from Rethinking Schools, *Winter 1997/98, Volume 12, No. 2, pp. 22-23.*

REFERENCES

1. *United States of Poetry* is both a book and a video published by Harry N. Abrams. I use both with high school students. Some pieces, like "Where I'm From" could be used with elementary students as well. It's an MTV format, and introduces the idea of performance poetry. Most of the pieces are more appropriate for older students. *United States of Poetry* introduces students to political poetry and to some old and new poets from diverse racial, social backgrounds.

2. William Stafford, Oregon's poet laureate for many years, published many outstanding books of poetry as well as two wonderful books on writing: *Writing the Australian Crawl* and *You Must Revise Your Life*.

Negotiating Pitfalls and Possibilities: Presenting Folk Arts in the Schools

by Debora Kodish and William Westerman

There are many good reasons to bring folk arts into a classroom. They can help students think critically about what they know and what remains outside formal histories. They can show how powerful alternative knowledge — things that people can't or shouldn't commit to paper but which they must commit to memory — is actively transmitted within diverse communities. Folk arts can teach respect for different points of view and can introduce students to the complexities of culture. And yet, in the classroom, these arts are encountered away from the richly textured contexts in which they usually occur. This process often skews folk arts so they become something else entirely, perhaps useful, but not the same. What follows is intended as a tool for teachers who want to consider (and cope with) what happens to folklore and, what can happen to people — when folklore is wrenched out of context and presented in a classroom.

It's important to recognize that the classroom situation itself affects the folk art performance experience, whether the performers are visiting artists or students and their families.

Common sense tells us that folk arts are usually performed in front of audiences who know something about the art form, who speak the language, who have some sense of the history of the tradition, who can judge what makes the current performer different from those who have gone before, and who, if it is an interactive or humorous form, will get the jokes, shout back, even boo and hiss when appropriate. Yet, in a classroom, we can assume neither such a knowledge base nor the possibility of customary interaction.

It is easy to underestimate what happens when folklore is "extracted" from its community setting and inserted into the alien structure of the classroom. Think for a moment about the stories that are important in your family, or about the stories you tell about your boss, or students. Whenever

> **FOLK ARTS CAN TEACH RESPECT FOR DIFFERENT POINTS OF VIEW AND CAN INTRODUCE STUDENTS TO THE COMPLEXITIES OF CULTURE.**

any of us tell stories, we pass on not only a tale but also our attitudes about the stories; we favor (or disfavor) characters in our stories. Our own values shape our versions of folklore, and so do folk artists provide their own versions of folk art and community history. But in a classroom, when a single artist represents a culture, differences of opinion can easily vanish. Much of the sting and danger of folk arts become invisible, or dulled, when these arts are performed in a classroom context. Ironically, some of the most powerful potential for teaching may reside exactly in these uncomfortable and dangerous areas, the places where folk arts reveal conflict, deep feelings, differences of opinion.

Approaches to Including Folk Arts

A teacher can bring folk arts into the classroom without sacrificing all of the power of these traditions, and still be sensitive to how that power and danger may impact on students.

First, we shouldn't underestimate folk arts. Stereotypes about folklore dismiss these traditions as being nonthreatening, the stuff of "old wives" and children. Move past the stereotypes that trivialize. Instead, assume that folk arts are complex and powerful symbolic forms, many-layered expressions, including serious and even dangerous stuff, and make it your business to understand where the danger lies. (It may be useful to recall that some people in this society pay therapists to listen to folklore, i.e. to family stories. In a therapeutic setting, it is understood that such stories can be powerful social and personal dynamite, deeply embedded in a complex past and not easily plumbed.)

Second, look for where there is disagreement in a single community about folk arts. Folk arts are not universally beloved. Not everyone in a single community shares, knows about, or likes the same folk traditions. For one thing, no group of people is entirely homogeneous; people sharing a common ethnicity or history still differ in terms of age, class, gender, political beliefs, aesthetics, region and much else. Such diversity ensures that people have widely different attitudes toward particular folk arts. In many communities, folk artists are specialists of a sort, and their particular skills are neither universally known nor universally respected. For example, many people educated in the French colonial-based school system of Cambodia were often brought up to believe that some folk art forms were lower-class, disreputable and rude. Consequently, people looked down on these arts and those who practiced them. In many contexts, young people go through long periods when they find the folk traditions of their parents' generation confining, embarrassing, or of little value. In some immigrant communities, great gaps separate the generations, especially when elders are skilled in languages and traditions that are not valued in the United States. In these situations, some elders choose to hide their talents from the next generation and instead encourage young people to be "American," to "get ahead."

There are politics and perspectives to all arts and it is important to understand them, especially when dealing with young people struggling to make sense of their own relationships to their families and the wider world. Look for differences of opinion about folk arts, and educate yourselves about why people differ. Sometimes, showing the existence of these differences and exploring why they exist can be an important way to open a door for youth.

Third, don't get stuck in the past; try to understand what the art means now. Every folk art has its own, not always chronicled, art history, with its own masters, aesthetics, and periods of growth, change and decline. Don't join the assumption that folk arts are enduring, ageless, ancient and timeless (another way of defusing them). For example, Cambodian classical dance, as presented by local artist Chamroeun Yin is not the same classical dance as would have been practiced in Cambodia before war, famine and resettlement. The persistence, or revitalization of this art form reflects Khmer peoples' deep desires, in refugee camps after the Pol Pot regime, for beauty, and for ordered and egalitarian ways of expressing and symbolizing Khmer identity. Though connected to ancient traditions, these arts are not, and never have been, pure or unchanging. They always have meanings and functions -- often complicated, sometimes contradictory -- for people in the present. The messy and complex present history of folk arts is one of the most important tools we have for teaching about culture and diversity within any community.

Fourth, carefully examine the structure of assignments, and the nature of the relationships between teachers and students and between students and their own family histories and traditions. Many common assignments used to honor diversity can backfire because they do not take into consideration the subtleties of personal relationships. Do consider what the assignments feel like from the point of view of particular students. Fundamentally, intercultural projects are worth doing. But it is important to evaluate such assignments, separating out what works from what puts children at stress and under scrutiny and what further marginalizes them from their classmates. In short, what backfires?

PITFALLS, CONCERNS AND POSSIBILITIES

In the following list of common sorts of assignments, we use some of the possible pitfalls or concerns about each type of assignment to frame questions for discussion and we share some ideas from experienced teachers about ways to make such assignments work.

1. Telling life stories in which students are asked to report on personal and family history.

Pitfalls for discussion: How may such assignments unintentionally put a student under pressure? Does it "cheapen" or fundamentally alter the experience of immigrant students by turning their often traumatic experiences into either something valuable as a commodity (information exchanged for a grade or for acceptance from the teacher) or something exotic (further isolating and even objectifying the student)?

Possibilities: Such assignments have to begin in trusting relationships. Kids may not tell you what they want to hide, but they may still suffer from the pressure of feeling that they have to keep information hidden. They may also try to tell you what they think you, or their peers, want to hear. It's important to allow and facilitate their own control over their stories. Give kids room by inviting them to "make up" a story, or to tell someone else's story. Allow them to use indirect framing mechanisms, and to rewrite and retell. Allow privacy for writing, so that kids don't have to share.

2. Show and tell about your customs. Students who practice traditions at home that aren't part of White, Christian American culture are asked to display or report on those customs or holidays.

Pitfalls for discussion: Does this really provide "equal time" and equal respect? Aside from the fact that this gives such students extra responsibility (e.g. having to do a report on the meaning of Passover while Christian kids are not expected to do a report on the meaning of Easter), does it further mark some students as "different" or "other?" How can it stigmatize even despite the teacher's best intentions or stated goal of making the child feel "special?" Are kids competent to present complex information about holidays or are they being pushed past their level of knowledge? They are after all, not often the main producers of these events; in fact, some folk customs function to educate and socialize youth. What are the implications of pushing kids to be "authorities" on cultural traditions?

Possibilities: Collectivize the process: give kids choices such as silence or sharing. Encourage acts of responsibility and power: allow kids to own and control the process but make questioning a part of their responsibility. Consider attention to customs that hurt: like racism or sexism. Encourage kids to look for differences within a given culture. Explore the many cultures to which people "belong" at the same time (i.e. we share some customs and culture with others of our own gender, age, class, politics). What we mean by "us" and by "them" is porous, constantly shifting and dependent on who is doing the categorizing and why. Few "cultures" are "pure." Explore what we don't know about participation in customs: can you seem to do a custom you are expected to do, while resisting? Explore ways in which people "break rules" and express individuality within folk customs.

3. Do your own festival, where students and sometimes families are asked to "put on" some or all the elements of a traditional holiday, in the school.

Pitfalls for discussion: Does this safely compartmentalize culture as entertainment, as public display separate from religion and removed from a sacred and participatory cycle? Festival and ritual in their "natural" contexts tend literally to bring many people together as communities, allow many different meanings of festival to emerge, and thus avoid a single, simple "meaning." In contrast, artificial "displayed" festivals tend to generalize about the meaning of ritual and tradition for all involved, and depict it as spectacle not as participation. As in the previous example, what can children and youth, who seldom have roles as "ritual specialists" in ritual

The book In My Heart, I Am A Dancer *provides an example of how to present folkart in the context of the artist's life.*

and festival, be expected to convey? Is there a danger of pushing them beyond their level of competence?

Possibilities: Expressions (festivals, arts) have different meanings when there are different compositions of the classroom and school, i.e. whether one, twenty, or the majority of kids are from similar cultural backgrounds. Ask kids to describe different viewpoints on (for example) a birthday, or on various coming of age traditions. Create an imaginary collective, non-exploitative festival. Choose a photo of a "typical American" Christian wedding and ask kids what they can deduce from the photo. Why do they know these things? What assumptions are they making? What don't, or can't, they know from looking at the picture? Are people happy? Was someone forced into the ritual? Does it have the same meaning to all present? Do they "believe" it? Is it a first wedding? Are they all Christian? etc.

Effectively, these assignments are various ways of looking at difference, and first steps at trying to craft assignments that do not inevitably lead to one of two conclusions: either "and underneath we're all the same" or "we have differences but we're all part of the great American melting pot, or patchwork quilt?"

There are different categories for sameness and difference, and each carries connotations. Often, the only things kids are offered for self-identification are things that are "old-world," or "traditional." When youth feel, or are made to feel that "they don't know about their own culture," we are missing a chance to understand what their culture is: a complex and sometimes internally inconsistent mix of influences, expressions, responses, knowledge, and language.

In Summary

We focus here on approaches to folk arts in education that explore here-and-now issues that confront youth as points of departure, but there are no ready-made recipes for universally successful multicultural projects, and we hope that we have, at the least, encouraged distrust for these. Non-exploitative, critically valid, multicultural curricula with integrity, validity and guts need to be made by hand: shaped from long-term relationships, based on a commitment to classrooms, founded on mutual respect and equity, and rooted in a willingness to critically examine and change educational structures.

Debora Kodish is Director of the Philadelphia Folklore Project, in Philadelphia, Pennsylvania.

William Westerman runs a project responding to the needs of refugee and immigrant artists at the International Institute of New Jersey.

This essay is reprinted from the Philadelphia Folklore Project Works in Progress *magazine 9:1 (1996) which con-*

tains a number of articles on folk arts education. The Philadelphia Folklore Project is an independent folk arts agency that documents, supports and presents local folk arts and culture. They believe that folk arts are one of the chief means that we have to represent our own realities in the face of powerful institutions. They develop public programs, offer technical assistance and organize around issues of concern. For more information, call or write the Philadelphia Folklore Project, 1304 Wharton St., Philadelphia, PA 1914, 215-468-7871.

ON THE QUESTION OF RACE

BY QUIQUE AVILES AND MICHELLE BANKS

1. They ask me to write down my race
and I think
and think and consider
writing down the truth
and have my answer read

I have a dark man
listening to a bolero
lighting a match
inside this body

I have an old lady
showing pictures to her children
talking in a language called Spanish
inside this body

2. They ask me to write down my race
and I think
and think and consider
writing down the truth
and have my answer read

I have a cargo of stolen people
crossing the Atlantic
inside this body

I have a brown man
he is painting a picture
we share a secret
it hides in the memory of a kiss

3. I have a drunk man
 asking directions
he wants to go home
wants you to tell him
which highway leads to Cuzcatlán

I have a kid in the fifth grade
who says he's American
"but my father's from El Salvador
and my mother is black"

I have all these people
these *guiros*
all these *aguacates*
this prescribed latinhood
this Hispaniard name
that doesn't agree with
English only

4. I have an old man
he is singing
patting juba
passing on the tradition
through the rhythms in his hands

a school girl in Bahia
and a young man cutting cane
just outside of Santo Domingo

I have all these voices
that have not learned to speak
orisha
sewas
ancestors
all these rhythms
these languages
these songs

5. They ask me to write down my race
and I think
and think
very seriously
and consider writing down the truth
and have my answer read

6. I have my *tía* Menche
tía Zoila
a mi abuela
a la señora con chile
a la pupusa lady
and Lorenzo's
inside my body

7. I have my Aunt Josephine
my Uncle James
and my grandfather's poetry
miss mary mack
a royal crown
and king of the mountain
inside this body

8. I have 18th & Columbia Rd
15th & Irving
Petworth
Shaw
Julio lglesias
the Jackson 5
and Lilo Gonzalez
inside this body

9. I have Rare Essence
that E-flat boogie
Five Blind Boys
Sarah Vaughn

the Shrimp Boat
and a Yaqui deer song
inside this body

10. I have a son
named John Enrique
who's black and brown
and human and tender

I have you inside this body

11. I have a blanket of memory
woven from my grandmother's laughter
inside this body

12. But I stop

and simply write down

13. "Hispanic"

14. "Black"

Quique Aviles and *Michelle Banks* *wrote this when they worked with* **Latinegro Theatre***, a project of the Latin American Youth Center in Washington, D.C. They wrote and performed theatre that challenged the audience to think about contemporary social issues. Michelle Banks is currently a teacher and administrator at a small, independent school in Washington, D.C. Quique Aviles is currently developing performance/poetry works which concentrate on social issues such as race and identity. His most recent works include "Latinhood," a one-man show about the realities of Latinos living in the United States and "Chaos Standing," a piece about multicultural living and the perceptions of Blacks, Whites and Latinos towards each other.*

TEACHING IDEA

Two students can prepare to read this dialogue poem to the class. Read the bold sections in unison. Alternate reading the other sections as indicated in the numerical sequence.

Please note that the authors both live in the Washington, DC area. A number of the references to street corners and neighborhoods refer to locations in the District.

After the students have shared, ask if anyone was reminded of people and places inside of them. Share a few examples. Then ask everyone to close their eyes and conjure images of all the people and places inside. Ask them to open their eyes and write a list of these images. The list can take the form of a poem if they choose. Stress that they should name the people and places inside of them. Point out that the poem by Banks and Aviles is particularly powerful because they don't just say I have my aunts and uncles inside of me, instead they name "my Aunt Josephine," "my son John Enrique," and so on.

After everyone has had 5-10 minutes to write, ask for volunteers to share. Students are generally amazed at how good even the 'lists' sound when read aloud. They also learn a lot about each other.

Note: The poem may raise the issue of the benefits and limitations of racial categories on application forms. As the poem points out, the boxes can depersonalize and generalize our identity. However it is important to point out that they are often included for positive reasons — to promote equity. A recent development is the suggestion that the person filling out the form can "check all that apply." Much has been written on this topic as preparations are made for the next census. The Poverty Race and Research Action Council newsletter (see Journals section of "Resource Guide") is a good source for short, readable articles.

© RICK REINHARD

TALKING
BACK

LOOKING THROUGH AN ANTI-RACIST LENS

BY ENID LEE

When examining cases of racism and inequity in schools, we often explain them in terms of lack of individual effort, bad luck, human nature or the inevitability of inequality. These explanations are not grounded in a social understanding of events and processes. In contrast, viewing the same cases through an anti-racist lens allows us to see how the use of power by individuals, communities and institutions has brought about the current situation. We can see how power is used to make change or to keep things the way they are, particularly with regard to the issues of rights, respect, resources, and representation based on skin color. An anti-racist lens leads us to look at the historical roots for both explanations and solutions.

I work in many schools throughout the United States and Canada assisting teachers, students, parents, support staff and administrators to confront and dismantle systems and structures which promote racism. These structures contribute to inequitable educational outcomes for all children. Over the years, I have developed the practice of looking at the situations I find in schools through an anti-racist lens. Whether we are aware of it or not, each of us looks through a particular set of lenses. I prefer to use a lens instead of a checklist since a checklist can sometimes be too linear, not sufficiently sensitive to context. A lens on the other hand, with its curved sides, has the capacity to disperse light rays into the many dark areas which always surround cases of racism.

I will outline what I see when I look through an anti-racist lens and invite you to use this lens when you look at situations in your school.

When looking through an anti-racist lens, I am able to see how skin color, shade, texture of hair and shape of eyes influence the opportunities we have in life, the rights we enjoy, and the access we have to resources and the representation and respect we receive. The anti-racist lens helps me to bring a historical and political perspective to solving problems and to understanding the roots of these problems. I can see how the ways in which we have organized our lives and our institutions, around race and other identities, have brought us to our present positions. These other identities include language, nationality, immigration status, culture and faith, which are often racialized.

The anti-racist lens helps me to get at the ideas that support and justify practices which treat some people, based on their skin color, as superior and more deserving, while treating other people as inferior and less deserving.

The most important feature of the anti-racist lens is that it leads me to see how situations can be transformed and how injustices can be reversed. It draws my attention to the ways in which power can be used and is used at the individual, community and institutional levels for change. It reminds me that educational failure is not inevitable and that we can bring about justice in our classrooms.

SIGNPOSTS

There are several signposts I see when I look through this lens. They are:

1. **Representation and roles in terms of racial group membership.**

   Appearances and accents of those engaged in any activity.

   Leaders and supports in terms of racial group membership.

   Absences in terms of racial group membership.

2. **History and human agency.**

   The official and unofficial versions of the actions undertaken by individuals, communities and institutions which brought about this state of affairs.

   The accounts of resistance to injustice.

3. **Ideology and interests.**

   Images, statements, accounts and beliefs that are evoked to justify and maintain current situations.

   Identification of those who benefit and those who lose from current situations.

   Structures, systems, and sources of power.

   Arrangements, patterns, processes, policies, procedures and traditions in organizations and schools in particular. These are the concrete ways in which things happen.

People and committees responsible for making decisions. When you look at these places and these people racism ceases to become a mystery. We see how it happens.

4. Hope and human agency.

Accounts of the ways in which human beings have used and are using the power they have as individuals, as members of groups and as employees in institutions to bring about racial justice, to maintain that justice once it is achieved, and to encourage others to join them to work in this area.

In order to deal with the particular situations in schools and other organizations in light of the signposts listed above, I have developed a cluster of questions and actions which help me work with strategic competence in the contexts in which we encounter racism. These questions and activities have been used by teachers, parents and students as they look through an anti-racist lens to critically analyze and act upon situations in their schools.

It is important to note that we can also apply other lenses when looking at issues of equity in schools. For example, sometimes the lenses of class or gender must be brought in focus because of the context. I have found, in my work however, that even when I work with the lenses of gender and class, I often gain a greater understanding of the situations before me when I insert the race lens over the lens of gender or class. For instance, when I am trying to understand why such negativity is being expressed against working class parents and their assumed lack of interest in their children's education, and I discover that those parents are African American, African Canadian, Native American, Native Canadian or Latino. I can raise the delicate question of race and help the discussion move forward to a more positive place.

USING THE LENS:
QUESTIONS FOR REFLECTION AND ACTION

CRITICAL ANALYSIS

1. What is the specific issue being addressed?
Who is involved in terms of race, language, class, gender and other aspects of identity?

2. How did things get to be the way they are?

What were some of the needs and strengths identified? Who identified them as needs and strengths? What actions were undertaken or not undertaken by individuals, community, and institutions in the recent past and in the distant past which brought about this situation? What were the terms under which actions were undertaken? Who established those terms? Who knew about them and who did not?

3. What are some of the beliefs (prevailing ideologies) that have led to this situation? What are the beliefs that are held by those in power and by those without the power about the ability and worth of people of particular racial backgrounds?

What are the explanations that are presented to justify actions and the positions of privilege or disadvantage that members of different racial groups enjoy or endure?

4. What are some things that keep the situation the way it is?

Has there been a conscious examination of the experiences of people of color with respect to the issue? Has there been an examination of the impact of school policies and practices, connected with communication for example, on parents and students and faculty of various racial backgrounds?

How has the institutional silence on these matters helped to maintain the status quo? How has the lack of material, financial, and/or human resources contributed to the situation? How has an inadequate time commitment resulted in the situation remaining unchanged?

5. Which groups in society benefit or lose from the present situation?

Which individuals' and communities' resources (cultural, spiritual, intellectual and financial) increase or decrease because of this situation?

Where and how are the voices and views of members of various racial groups represented or excluded in this present situation? How are the rights to self-determination of racial communities ensured?

How are we challenging the pattern and practice of one community or member of a racial group speaking for and determining the activities and direction for another community or member of another racial group?

Who in terms of racial group membership is feeling respected and validated and treated with human dignity? Who in terms of racial group membership is experiencing a sense of inherent superiority and of deserving all the privileges they enjoy?

STRATEGIC ACTION

6. What would I have to change in order for the situation to be different?

Based on the responses to the questions above, I develop a strategic plan to address the roots of the problem. I gather information about the experiences of those who have been marginalized and those who have been validated by the processes. I disseminate that information through all technologies at my disposal. I, along with others, expose the sources of power and decision-making.

With all concerned constituencies, especially those who have been formerly excluded, we redefine needs, strengths and resources. Together we redefine and redistribute roles, responsibilities and resources for greater equity to the extent that we are able, well aware that facing resistance and reversals are part of the process of making change towards racial equality.

We publicize and celebrate whatever gains we make along the way as a means of encouraging ourselves and others.

7. Where can I find allies?

I cast about with my anti-racist lens and I see that allies are everywhere. I make a list of all the people who have a vested interest in addressing the situation. I look to my colleagues who say they want our organization to work well, who say they want all students to succeed. I turn to those who work for social justice. I appeal to those whose reputation for excellence makes them likely partners in the struggle for equality. "If you are good at what you do, let everyone experience it."

I look to parents of color and all of those who want their children to have access to the best quality education. I also look to parents who are White who see the situation as a matter of justice and who also feel that their children's lives are enriched by racial, cultural and linguistic diversity. I see allies among those parents, students and teachers who have been victimized because of some form of difference — gender, sexual orientation, class, etc.

I turn to the grassroots, race-specific and academic organizations in the community.

I see as some of my greatest allies those who have gone before and have struggled and resisted racism. As a woman of African descent working

between Canada and the United States, I turn often to my ally Harriet Tubman who did much anti-racist work between these two countries. She led Africans out of one kind bondage from the United States into what others might describe as another kind of bondage in Canada. Nevertheless as my ally, I feel her legacy of perseverance.

8. What kind of work can we do in the many spheres of influence in which we operate?

Interpersonal basis with one person: colleague to colleague, student to student, parent to parent.

Class level with all students through formal curriculum.

Department or faculty-level at a faculty or staff meeting.

Parent gatherings and student gatherings.

Meeting with administration and other authorities.

School community: unions, associations and clubs.

People in other schools through networks including chat lines and e-mail connections.

Organizations, institutions and individuals outside the schools.

Lawmakers: school trustees, city councilors.

Media: newsletters, newspapers, television, tapes, CD-ROMs, websites in various languages.

9. How can we institutionalize this change? How can we prevent this situation from reoccurring?

Monitor, monitor, monitor!

Keep good records.

Check all systems to ensure that outcomes are realized.

Ensure that the issue is inserted at the policy and procedural levels.

Remind everyone that intent is not what counts; it is outcome that matters.

Remind everyone that until every person regardless of racial background is experiencing equality in the areas of respect, rights to self-determination and full humanity, representation and resources, we still have a job to do.

Keep hopeful by looking at and learning from others who have worked on and are working on these issues all around the world.

Always celebrate what has been accomplished

COMPASSION AND IMPROVISATION: LEARNING TO STAND UP FOR OTHERS

BY LINDA CHRISTENSEN

"Fatty fatty two by four can't get through the kitchen door," kids yelled at my sister Tina. I remember looking at the kitchen door, painted a pumpkin spice color by our father. Tina was chubby, but she did go through the kitchen door. Sometimes they called her "Tina, the two ton tuna." We lived in a fishing community on the California coast and fishing vocabulary dotted our language.

How did Tina deal with this? She fought. She ate. Later, she smoked, drank, and cut school. She was alternatively the class clown and the best, most generous friend anyone, outside of her family, could have. Eventually, she dropped out of high school and spent years regaining what those sidewalk bullies stripped her of when she was a child.

The underlying lesson is that kids can be cruel, and their cruelty exacts a price on their victims. The targets are the weak, the overweight, the different. Sometimes the difference encompasses race, language, and gender.

But kids don't have to be cruel; in fact, part of our role as teachers and administrators in schools is to stop children from torturing others, but more importantly, educating them so that difference doesn't automatically mean outcast.

We can teach students about Rosa Parks, Dolores Huerta, Frederick Douglass, Lucretia Mott, and John Brown — larger than life heroes who struggled to end slavery and injustice, but how do we teach them to stand up for the overweight girl sitting next to them in Algebra? How do we get them to stand up for the Vietnamese student when others laugh at her pronunciation? How do we teach them to fight against racist stereotypes? How do we get them to accept the gay math teacher down the hall?

IMPROVISATIONS: LEARNING TO INTERCEDE

1. I want students to learn how to intervene when they observe others being ostracized or hurt by intolerant behavior. To facilitate the process, I create or co-create improvisations with my students. An improvisation is a mini play. I give students a scene with a conflict embedded in it. Students discuss the situation, select who will play each character, and then practice the scene. They do not write out the dialogue; they create it as they rehearse their scene. They may either discover their resolution while practicing or figure it out during group discussion. Students often come to new insights about the situation as they are playing it out.

Each improvisation is written to put students in a conflict where a character's morality is tested. Some sample improvs from our unit on compassion:

▸ Several students are in the hallway discussing a teacher rumored to be gay. The teacher walks past.

▸ A group of friends are playing ball at the park when a person of a different racial background asks if s/he can join the game.

▸ Several friends are at the beach during the summer when they spot an especially large person in a bathing suit.

▸ A group of students are in class early when a new student appears on the scene. The new student is "poorly" dressed.

▸ Several friends are at the food court at the mall waiting in line. The person in front of them has difficulty speaking English. The line is being held up because of the confusion.

2. Students work in small groups — three or four people per group — and choose two improvs from our list or create their own. After students look over their set of improvs, they decide who will play each character, and then run through the scene. I have to remind them that someone in the group has to step up and "do the right thing." Sometimes students have to regroup and do their improv over because no one disrupted the crowd's hunger for blood.

3. I spend time with each group while they are rehearsing the improvisations because they can resort to easy answers or their laughter at the homeless person or large woman in a swimsuit might overwhelm the sense of decency I try to develop. They have a hard time letting go of the laughter that is part of the social currency that

makes some "in" while the others are "out" because they fear taking the risk of being "out" too. The improvs force them to practice the role of compassion. Someone has to stand up and say, "That's not funny." Beyond mouthing the correct response, they attempt to explain why the situation isn't funny. They have to practice acting and speaking for someone's pain, but they haven't had much experience.

4. After each group of students performs, I ask students to stay in their roles "on stage," and we talk about what happened. Who defended the homeless man? Who stopped their friends from putting down a student who wears "wanna-be Nikes" or Goodwill clothes? It helps to question the characters while they are in role. "How did you feel when people made fun of you for wearing the same clothes every day? Why do you wear the same clothes? Where did you find the courage to defy your friends and stand up for the gay teacher?" Although students are willing to play most roles, often they are uncomfortable if there is an issue of homosexuality. They ask me to play the role of the gay teacher or student.

INTERIOR MONOLOGUES: STEPPING INTO FICTION

5. After all groups perform at least one improvisation, I ask students to write an interior monologue from one character's point of view. An interior monologue captures the internal thoughts and feelings of a character as they are engaged in the situation. It may have been a character they portrayed or observed.

6. As students read their monologues, they often excavate the emotional territory these pieces triggered. How do people feel when they are laughed at, left out? How do they feel when they gather the courage to stand up for someone else, when they fight back against ignorance and hate?

7. The class becomes an audience to help develop the story line. Joe Stivers piece, "Tolerance," started as an interior monologue from Derek's, his main character, point of view. He is angry that his teacher is gay. Where does he want to go with this? Does he want to follow the improv group's narrative? No. He works in bits and pieces over time. He struggles with the ending until he makes Derek's father homophobic. It takes him most of the quarter and about fifteen revisions to get there.

8. How long does this take? Probably a week or two for the initial readings, improvs and monologues. Students choose one piece out of the three sets of fiction writing we worked on — self acceptance, tolerance, and empathy. Long fiction pieces take time. We move on, but students keep going back and reworking their pieces while we move forward with the rest of the class content. During the one day we go to the computer lab, students type, write, conference with each other and me to complete their stories or other work.

REFERENCES

Bambara, T. C. 1972. "Raymond's Run," *Gorilla, My Love.* New York: Random House.

Coville, B. 1994. "Am I Blue?" *Am I Blue? Coming Out from the Silence.* New York: Harper Trophy.

Houston, J. W. 1973. "Shikata Ga Nai," *Farewell to Manzanar.* New York: Bantam Books. pp. 10-11.

McKnight, R. 1992. "A Different Kind of Light Shines on Texas," *A Different Kind of Light Shines on Texas.* Boston: Little, Brown & Co.

O'Callahan, J. 1995. "Orange Cheeks," *A Call to Character.* New York: Harper Collins.

Wong, J. S. 1995. "Fifth Chinese Daughter," *A Call to Character.* New York: Harper Collins.

The students' writings are available in *Rites of Passage: A Literary Journal* which is listed in NECA's Teaching for Change catalog.

Linda Christensen is an English teacher in Portland, Oregon and is faculty advisor for Rites of Passage, *a student literary journal. She has written numerous articles for* English Journal *and* Rethinking Schools *and is co-editor of the publication* Rethinking Our Classrooms: Teaching for Equity and Justice. *She offers staff development workshops nationally. Christensen is on the steering committee of the National Coalition of Education Activists and is an editor of Rethinking Schools. E-mail: LChrist@aol.com.*

Reprinted from Christensen, L. 1996. Writing with Attitude: Strategies for Teaching Reading and Writing, Teaching Guide for the 1995-96 Rites of Passage. *Washington, DC: NECA.*

TALKING BACK STORIES

The stories by students, teachers, parents and administrators on the following pages are included to share in workshops as examples of the many ways that we can work for justice in our schools — and more importantly, to remind us that change is possible. In the absence of these kind of stories it is all too easy to become discouraged, convinced that you just "can't change City Hall." Immersing ourselves in the stories of those who have worked for change can remind us of the power we have when we collectively mobilize and strategize.

One way to use these stories is to make enough copies so that each student (or workshop participant) has one story. If possible, add more that you have collected from local work, newspapers (like *Rethinking Schools*) and biography excerpts. Have students take on the role of the person (or one of the persons in the case of the Clemente Middle School) in the story they received. Tell students that they are at a national conference where they should meet and learn from at least two other people. They should learn what issues the other people faced, what strategies they used, and what lessons they learned. From the information they collect, the class can create a chart listing various tactics to challenge injustices. You will find that as your students take on issues in your school, they will refer back to what they learned in this lesson for strategies and inspiration.

BLACK HISTORY *is* U.S. HISTORY

One day at Moore High School in Louisville, Kentucky, a light bulb flashed in Detra Warfield's mind and she did something many of us never do. Instead of merely thinking about her idea, this fifteen-year-old embarked on a plan to tackle an issue affecting all of the schools in her county.

After reading Detra's story you might expect her to hold some elective position in student government or perhaps serve as a youth representative on the school board. However, she describes herself as a normal student who gets lots of B's, but some C's and D's too. Detra proves that many of us have untapped leadership qualities that just need a little encouragement to emerge. The support she received from her family, especially her mother and her aunt, made all the difference in her decision to make a difference.

BY DETRA WARFIELD

It was February and Black History Month. My English teacher asked us to do a report on a famous Black American who contributed something to America. So, I picked Booker T. Washington and I wrote about him. That was all we did for that month. In all my other classes, I didn't have another assignment about Black History Month.

It made me begin thinking about why we were limited to studying Black history during the shortest month of the year. I called my aunt and asked her what I should do. She writes for newspapers and she encourages me to do anything. My aunt said, "Just get a petition up first and see how many people agree with you." She told me after passing out the petitions to write a speech and go to the Board of Education.

The next week I got a petition up; I'd never done that before. I just asked people in my school — both Black and White — would they like to have a class to learn more about Black history? Some of the students wouldn't sign because they thought they would get in trouble. Some asked what it was for, and I told them it was for a good cause. I collected over one hundred names from my school.

Then I asked my friend, Ian Cooley, who is two years younger than me, to get some names from her middle school. We started collecting the signatures in March and by the third week we had col-

lected over three hundred names.

Then I just looked up the Board of Education in the telephone book and called. I asked if I could present a speech about a Black history class in the Jefferson County schools and was given a date to come in.

There were about ten school board members. Lots of people from other schools were there for other issues. I was nervous; my leg was shaking. I had practiced at home but I was still nervous. I wrote my speech all on my own, but my aunt helped me. She told me to put three questions in my speech and to get a group of Black and White students to answer them.

The first question was, "Who was the man who raced against a steam-driven machine and won?" The second question was, "Who was the woman who freed over two hundred slaves in the Underground Railroad?" And the third question was "Who was the man who chopped down the cherry tree?" Probably half the students could answer just question three. The other two questions are about African Americans and half the students probably didn't know the answers to those because they are about Black history. [Answers: John Henry; Harriet Tubman; George Washington.]

I just presented my idea that Black people have made a lot of contributions in America and some people just don't know about it. I said that a class would teach everybody who wants to know about Black history and let them appreciate the African Americans who have done so much.

I was giving my speech and my time ran out. One of the board Members — he was the only Black member — said "Let her go ahead," and I finished my speech. The Superintendent of Jefferson County Schools said, "We'll look into this." After the meeting, I had people come up to me saying that it was a great speech.

About two weeks after the speech, a newspaper reporter interviewed me and Ian. The headline was: "Discovering a Heritage: Black History Month Leaves Two Students Wanting, Asking for More."

The one Black board member got Montes Eaves, the Assistant Superintendent of Jefferson County Schools, to help me out. I met with Mr. Eaves about a month later. He was interested. It was the first time anybody showed an interest since they had a Black history class back in the 1970s. Then Mr. Eaves asked me and my mother to join a committee.

The committee included the Assistant Superintendent and his secretary, teachers, my mom, and this other student and his teacher. This guy, a junior from Manuel High, came to the meetings because he wanted the same thing I did. In the end he asked me and my friend, Ian, to come over to his school to talk about it.

The committee met about every two weeks throughout the summer. My mom and I went to every one of those meetings. We talked about what we wanted for a Black history class and what we needed, like books and how teachers would be chosen to teach this year-long class.

That summer the committee and I used the petitions to get students' names and addresses to start up a Saturday Academy from 11 a.m. to 2 p.m. for all ages and we taught people about African Americans.

By September we got an African-American History class started in four or five schools. The class for the 1991-92 school year at Moore is completely full. It's only for juniors and seniors. So far this year we've learned about the geography of Africa; and right now we are reading *Native Son*. We have a White teacher. As long as she can teach history, it's okay with me. The other students in the class said it was all right, too.

I have a dream just like Martin Luther King, Jr. and I am hoping to keep it alive. I hope that my idea will grow and that eventually the class that includes the contributions of Blacks and other people of color won't have to be called Black History. It will be called American History.

Reprinted from No Kidding Around! America's Young Activists Are Changing Our World and You Can Too *by Wendy Schaetzel Lesko of the Activism 2000 Project. Copies of the book can be ordered by sending $18.95 (plus $4 postage and handling) payable to the Activism 2000 Project, PO Box E, Kensington, MD 20895. Toll-free order line: 800-955-7693.*

CHALLENGING RACISM IN THE NEWS

BY BLAKE WEBSTER

"I wrote to the Toronto Star *about how I felt about racial discrimination. During the week of March 21, I cut out all the pictures of people. Ninety-two percent had white skin, so I wrote to the* Toronto Star *telling them I wanted more pictures of Blacks and Asians. They published my letter on Easter Sunday, April 15, 1990. I am sending you the copy of my letter in the newspaper."*

Blake Webster won the "Together We're Better!" award, given by TG Magazine, Toronto, Ontario and the Communications Branch, Multiculturalism and Citizenship Canada, Ottawa, Ontario. He was given the honor because of his initiative and courage to speak out and challenge the media. In addition, the judges praised his good research skills and the effectiveness of taking the message to a large audience.

LETTER AS IT APPEARED IN THE *TORONTO STAR*

"Print more pictures of Blacks, Orientals. March 21 is the *International Day for the Elimination of Racial Discrimination.* For one week, I cut out all picture appearing in your paper. There were few pictures of Blacks or Orientals [Asians]. I was wondering how often you interviewed Blacks and Orientals?

If I went to another country where people had a darker skin colour, I would like to see more pictures of people like me so I would feel good about myself. I have freckles, red hair and white skin.

If your newspaper had more pictures of people with darker skin colour there might be less racial discrimination. I'm only 13 years but this would mean a lot to me."

Blake Webster *is from Pickering, Ontario.*

TURN CHILDREN AWAY? THERE'S NO WAY

Ernie McCray, principal of Marvin Elementary School in Allied Gardens, is one of five San Diego city school principals who held a press conference to announce that they would not enforce Proposition 187 if it passed. Following is his statement which appeared as an editorial in the San Diego Union-Tribune Newspaper.

BY ERNIE MCCRAY

Despite the passage of Proposition 187, my disposition remains the same. I will not, in any way, play a role in willfully hurting another person. I have sat at the back of the bus. I've missed a meal because someone refused to acknowledge my hunger. I've had someone tell me to get my "black ass" out of a hotel when there were plenty of rooms available. I've skated at the rink on special "Negro" days.

I know the hurt and humiliation that come with being mistreated. So, needless to say, there is no way on God's green earth that I could ever treat fellow human beings with such disrespect that I would ask them to prove to me their right to be in this corner of the world.

Who are we to make such demands?

There is just absolutely nothing in my DNA that will allow me, without sensible reason, to stand in the way of other citizens of the world who, as I do every day, struggle to house and feed themselves and their families and to live in dignity.

As a school principal, what should I say to a family with whom I've bonded, who happens to be here illegally? Am I to smile and say something like, "So long, it's been good to know you?"

Am I to look a little child in the face and say: "I really appreciate how you've improved in your school work and how you've been such a good citizen, but I'm going to have to turn you in. It's noth-

Ernie McCray and students having lunch at Marvin Elementary School.

ing personal, you understand. Just remember those high fives we used to give each other and all the wonderful conversations we used to have, and if you're ever in Guadalajara, I'd like you to say hello to some friends of mine."

A parent has already asked me, "What are the children supposed to think if their principal breaks the law?" I told him I felt that the law is immoral and I would have no problem explaining to a child why I couldn't honor an immoral law.

What a shameful and hurtful proposition 187 is. When I reflect on it, I sometimes don't know whether to laugh at its absurdity or cry because of its cruelty. I've done both.

The laughter comes spontaneously, like the time I overheard an attorney saying to a peer: "We need Proposition 187 because people are coming over here taking our jobs." I stood to the side of those attorneys trying to imagine some illegal immigrant crawling under a barbed wire fence or risking his or her life running across eight lanes of dangerous traffic trying to get to an interview at their law firm.

"Er-uh, Mr. Lopez, how many cases of insurance fraud have you litigated?"

Mr. Lopez, wiping dirt from his travails off his shirt, says, "Que?"

"Good answer, Mr. Lopez. Get a suit that's a little less *campesino* in appearance and report here in the morning."

Come on. Who is coming to this country and taking meaningful jobs from any American? How many U.S. citizens are standing in lines for the backbreaking work that lettuce fields have to offer?

A little laughter. But then the sadness sets in and my eyes water with tears as I think of this world we live in. People don't know how to get along. They pretend to create good relations with our neighbors to the north and south with hollow schemes like the North American Free Trade Agreement (NAFTA). Right. And it doesn't snow in Minneapolis in the wintertime.

If NAFTA offers half the potential it has promised, we won't have an immigration problem with our neighbors to the south. Do we really think people want to leave the country of their birth, of their ancestry, and split up their families, living on the edge, facing a life of uncertainty?

The fact is, far too many Mexican citizens are starving. Some are forced off agricultural land that should be theirs, causing a breakdown of their traditional way of living. They flee, and all we can offer them as fellow human beings are frenzied and cold "light up the border" receptions.

How can we choose to hate and live in fear of other citizens of the world when we, because we are human beings, have the capacity to love and create a hopeful existence?

There really could be a world without borders if we stopped pinning names on each other like *illegal immigrants*. We can only do this by first accepting deep in our hearts and consciences that all people deserve to live in peace and dignity in a just world. Then we must try, via all the avenues at our disposal, to make such a reality come true.

To such principles I am bound. As a parent, a grandparent, an educator and a contributing citizen of a most incredibly beautiful planet, it is my responsibility to reach out from wherever I am with as much love as I can muster. I will not take part in the destruction of people's hopes and dreams and their struggles to maintain their dignity.

Ernie McCray is an elementary school principal, a poet, actor and activist. Since this press conference he has continued to take an active role in defending the rights of immigrants and advocating for a top quality education for all children.

Reprinted with permission by the author.

SCHOOL'S OUT: CALIFORNIA HIGH SCHOOL STUDENTS PROTEST ANTI-IMMIGRANT LEGISLATION

BY ELIZABETH KODETSKY

It was twelve days before the November 8 [1994] election, and the high school where James Dean filmed *Rebel Without a Cause* had gone on strike. Three hundred students walked out of John Marshall High to protest Proposition 187, the anti-immigrant ballot initiative. One of these students was Leyda Azañeda, who was born in Peru and may or may not be a legal resident of the United States.

"I don't think they should come up with propositions that are racist and unfair like this," Azañeda said in explanation of the walkout. "They call this a free country."

Azañeda is among the 90 percent of Marshall students who speak a language other than English at home. One teacher here estimates that half of Marshall's students would face deportation with the enactment of Proposition 187, which requires public employees to report "suspected illegals" to the Immigration and Naturalization Service. Though it is impossible to estimate the number of students who are undocumented, one indication is that over a third of the county's 1.5 million public school students speak "limited" English.

The apparent imminent passage of Prop 187 inspired a loosely organized network of these and other students to stage walkouts at virtually every high school in the city of Los Angeles in the two weeks before Election Day. Walkouts were so widespread that the L.A.P.D. was placed on tactical alert, and police in riot gear swarmed the streets in several neighborhoods and aimed pepper spray and stingball grenades at students on at least two campuses. At this writing more than 15,000 students had walked out at more than forty junior high and high schools throughout Southern California. In Pomona students boycotted school for three days while activists set up alternative classes in a nearby church. Here school officials suspended approximately seventy students, while throughout the region police arrested at least sixteen.

News reports and school administrators tended to brush off the activism as "a nice day to take a walk," but the mass walkouts and civil disobedi-ence heralded a student movement unseen since the Chicano student demonstrations of 1968. This year students began stealthily announcing impromptu walkouts at breaks before classes shortly after Los Angeles's October 16 march against 187, believed to be the largest march in L.A. history. The confluence of immigrant families and Chicano activists in that demonstration was itself a feat of grass-roots organizing that owed most of its fire to a single immigrant advocate, Juan Jose Gutierrez, and his East L.A. legal aid center, One Stop Immigration. The march drew 125,000 supporters — even after mainstream Latino groups, including MALDEF and L.A.'s Coalition for Humane Immigrant and Refugee Rights, heeded warnings of anti-187 leaders against mobilizing a "sea of brown faces."

Tapping into loose or inactive student networks, the march breathed life into groups spanning high school and college campuses, including MEChA, the Brown Berets redux, United Farm Workers solidarity contingents and the newly formed October Student Movement.

But as Election Day approached, the student walkouts seemed to be spinning from even the grasp of their grass-roots engineers. On October 26 Gutierrez and approximately 100 student organizers met to reassess a protest that, while intending to affirm a student's right to a free education, seemed to be jeopardizing that very right as administrators threatened to suspend strikers. "We're offering sit-ins to stay on campus," Angel Cervantes, a graduate student at Claremont College and a member of the October Student Movement, said after the meeting. "We're taking the moral position of not walking out but wanting to stay there to learn."

Two days later students resoundingly rejected that advice. Outside the Van Nuys Civic Center police carted protesters back to school in school buses. On one, 18-year-old Blanca was perched on her seat instructing fellow students: Walk out tomorrow, and the next day, and the next.

Several principals and teachers privately conceded that they were terrified that walkouts would escalate into violence. Approximately 1,000 Southern California teachers and administrators have already signed pledges refusing to comply with the initiative, and they begged students to "be reasonable," in the words of principal Charles Molina. But as teacher Steve Zimmer glumly forecasted, "November 9 is going to be a really ugly day."

Elizabeth Kodetsky is a writer based in Los Angeles.

Kodetsky, E. (November 21, 1994.) "School's Out." The Nation magazine. © 1994. The Nation Company, Inc. Reprinted with permission.

PHILADELPHIA STUDENTS PROTEST BUS FARE HIKE

BY ERIC JOSELYN

In November of 1994 the Southeastern Pennsylvania Transportation Authority (SEPTA) Board announced plans to hike their [bus] fares and reclaim the highest base fare of any major transit system in the nation.

Transit officials dined with the hearing examiner, lined up friendly experts for testimony and hoped for a quick and quiet approval. SEPTA's designs for raising $13.3 million in additional income from its riders, however, did not go unnoticed by those dependent on SEPTA for their education — Philadelphia's public school students.

Over a few short weeks students and community members became energized by a threat of a hike — a hike that could cut many off from school. Mobilized, they pressured and helped secure a settlement that averted a direct increase in student token costs. In addition, these actions focused attention on the burden transportation costs already place on our school children.

Student voices joined those of Community Legal Services, the Consumer Education and Protection Association and the Kensington Welfare Rights Union, as they presented testimony to show the human cost of the proposed fare hike.

The negative impact of a price rise on student attendance was not mere speculation; the School District has documented a decline in school attendance following the last fare hike in 1990.

Before hearings in December and early January, youth activists from [the local youth leadership group] Asian Americans United began a series of outreach initiatives to contact students in high schools across the city. Ten thousand fliers alerting students to the fare hike were printed and distributed, along with black arm bands, at several high schools.

On January 12, over 350 students attended a noon rally at Central High School to protest not just the increase but the existing costs of getting to school. The next day over 100 students were present to pressure the SEPTA Board as it voted on a compromise settlement. Students rallied in the wake of the final vote and gathered again on February 8th to plan the next steps.

TESTIMONY AT THE SEPTA HEARING HANG DO, CENTRAL HIGH SCHOOL

My family pays $27.00 each week since my family has three kids going to schools that don't provide transportation. One of my sisters attends Pepper Middle School. She rode a yellow school bus through sixth grade, but now she's in 7th grade and we have to pay for her tokens. Another sister is in Franklin Learning Center and she has to pay for her tokens too. My family cannot afford this kind of money. We are on welfare. Each month, my parents have to pay out $108.00 for the six kids in my family to go to school.

The government always talks about wanting to get people off welfare. Do you ever think of the long term effect this kind of spending has on the future of this city? The high price of student fares causes many students to drop out. At a lot of schools, the education isn't really that good to begin with. Most kids, if they have to pay for it, think why bother? But if kids drop out because they can't afford tokens, then they can't get a job since they don't have a good education. They will end up back on welfare.

Public schools should be open to all students. Even now, many kids can't afford what you call a public education. If you raise the fares, even the public schools will be closed to poor students. I don't think this is equal opportunity. We might not be able to go to school, but we will learn a lesson. The lesson will be one which will teach us who this society thinks should be thrown away. Is this really the lesson you want us to learn?

Nearly 31,000 public school students use SEPTA tokens. The School District has been subsidizing the student token fares by purchasing them at $1.05 and selling them to students at $.90. This fare subsidy and other free transit costs are absorbed by the School District at a cost of over $18 million a year.

The final agreement reached with SEPTA allowed the District to maintain the current costs of tokens for students through the end of the school year. At that time the increase will go into effect but it will be absorbed by the District. This arrangement will cost the students of Philadelphia in the long run, as vital resources are diverted from other areas to cover this new cost.

There are serious questions if existing student subsidies can continue. Communications director for the District, Charlie Thomson, was quoted in the *Daily News* as saying, "We are committed to protecting our students from paying the latest fare increase for as long as possible. However, we face other budget pressures which are competing for our scarce resources."

Rough Ride Ahead

It is significant that the students who came forward in the struggle were not simply willing to take their ten-cent break and return quietly home. Discussions about future directions began right outside the board room following the vote. Their position is simply that the current tab of close to $400 a year to travel to and from school is unacceptable. Nearly 110,000 students, one half the District's enrollment, are from families on welfare and thousands of these families must bear the full cost of transportation to and from school.

At a "Victory Celebration" Lai Har Cheung, a Central High School graduate stated, "The fight to enable all students to ride for free has not ended, it has just begun." She continued, "As students, we are willing to work with SEPTA and the School District to make free transportation a reality for the hundreds of thousands of students in Philadelphia. We want to form a Youth Advisory Committee with SEPTA and the School District to begin discussing ways to reduce the burden of transportation costs. We deserve to be heard."

The new rate structure continues the practice of underwriting costs for suburban riders at the expense of city riders. As initially designed, the proposal hit low-income families and the elderly the hardest.

But, contrary to the hopes of the rate hike's architects, Philadelphia students were not willing to quietly suffer a significant boost without taking action. They encountered paternalistic and condescending attitudes from the SEPTA board members, scant recognition in the press for shaping the positive outcome, and to date, no formal acknowledgment from School District officials.

They did, however, clearly demonstrate the power of students and their allies to actively shape the policies of the city and governmental agencies. The students' actions provide a stirring demonstration of an awareness of the events that shape their lives, the ability to articulate their concerns and a willingness to take part in the life of our city. Truly, these are skills our schools need to nurture in all students.

Reprinted with permission from the Philadelphia Public School Notebook, *Fall 1995. The* Notebook *is "a voice for parents, students and classroom teachers who are working for quality and equality in Philadelphia schools." It is published four times a year. Inquiries can be sent to: School Notebook, 3721 Midvale Ave., Philadelphia, PA, 19129, 215-951-0330. Subscriptions: $12/4 issues.*

VOICES FROM A SCHOOL: ROBERTO CLEMENTE

Parents, teachers and students describe how and why they organized in a neighborhood of Philadelphia to secure a new school building.

Ruth Morales (President of the Home and School Association at Roberto Clemente Middle School.)

I came here from Puerto Rico in 1989 with my family. I was shocked to see the school that my children would go to. I knew that the Clemente building was not appropriate for kids. It was falling down. There was no gym, no auditorium and not even sufficient books.

In 1989 there was almost no parent involvement in the school. A parents' meeting was held and 150 parents came. That's when we started the Home and School. Most of the parents spoke Spanish so we began by printing flyers both in Spanish and in English.

Many of us felt that our children had been pushed aside and neglected. You know, there is so much talk about child abuse, but this was also child abuse. The system was abusing our children.

I always tell parents, we are minorities, but I don't care if you're on social security, welfare, or whatever, we have a right to a good education for our children. We don't have money to leave an inheritance, but we can leave them a good education so they can earn an honest living to support themselves.

Our students at the old Clemente became very frustrated. At one point fires were set in the school. Parents and community people began to organize seriously. We held rallies outside of the school and attended many meetings with officials. We got buses and went to City Council, and we had parents speak and protest at school board meetings. The School District finally agreed to a new facility for Roberto Clemente School.

Parents were involved in the planning of the school. We formed several committees. We requested a Latino architect because we wanted someone who understood what kind of school we wanted built. For example, the colors of the building are Caribbean.

Now that we have a new beautiful building, we are asking that parents come into the school and volunteer.

But we also want the school to serve the community. That is why we asked that there be outside entrances for the auditorium and the gym for evening events. And there will be a health clinic staffed by St. Christopher's Hospital for the community.

We were sleeping for many years. What were we thinking about for so many years that we could let our kids go into a building like that?

The most important lesson, I believe, is that parents, community and teachers are a strong force. We have to be involved with our schools so that we know what is going on with our children, and we have to come together as one to change our schools so that our children can achieve.

Janet Kristman (Sixth grade teacher at Roberto Clemente for 8 years.)

In the old building I was privileged to have windows in my classroom, and I had an actual door that closed. A lot a teachers didn't even have that before. They were teaching in the middle of the building where the only light was electricity. And of course in the summer there was no air flow and it was very hot.

This new building is a dream come true. Our new library is being set up now. It will include many more ways for students to access materials. The gym is designed for sports and the new auditorium will allow students to perform and see theatre. The science labs and computer labs are modern and will encourage kids to enjoy learning outside of a regular classroom.

We hope this new building will help to create a more positive attitude and philosophy among the staff and students.

Part of the excitement is that every child deserves a quality education. The new school is a statement that says that we value them. This is a facility that was actually designed to be a school. The other building was designed to be a factory.

The efforts for the new school generated a lot of support from the teachers. Our union got involved and many teachers served on the committees that were set up. It was a team effort.

I now realize the value of parents and community. It was through their efforts that the new school got rolling. This new building says a lot about the power of parents and community to change things.

Tamaris Leon and Marlene Burgos (Eighth grade students at Clemente Middle School.)

In our old school the kids didn't care so much. Kids would write on the walls and no one cared. Now we hang our schoolwork on the walls and nobody rips it down. We all want this school to be the best.

Here we like that we have separate classrooms. In the old school, we couldn't hear our teacher. It was always so loud. The walls didn't reach to the ceiling. Kids would throw paper and books over the walls.

Now we work harder because we have no excuses not to. Before the lights would go on and off and there were big poles in the middle of the room, and many fires. We couldn't hear the teachers.

Most of the kids here are really good. We like to be respected. That's really important to us. If a teacher has an attitude towards us, we can't respect them back. So if they give us respect we respect them back. Look at the principal, you can tell you can really talk to her and everyone respects her.

Also this new building makes us be even more respectful. For instance, the kids don't spit on each other going down the stairs like in the other school.

We love having our own gym here. We used to have to get on the bus for half the period.

And it's stricter here. Lots of teacher, parents, and security. Kids don't bring weapons. There are no secret places here to hide when you cut class.

Also the streets around the school are safer. Before on the street in front there were shootings sometimes with all the drug dealers there.

But then our parents got the new school started. They pushed and pushed. They had to. Both of our parents work so they couldn't come to the rallies, but we went to the protests with the other kids.

Now we just want people to know the kids here are good, and we're a good school. Also we are proud to be the first 8th grade to graduate from the new Roberto Clemente Middle School.

Reprinted from the Philadelphia Public School Notebook, *Winter 1995, Vol. 2, No. 2. The* Notebook *provides articles about all aspects of school reform in Philadelphia. It is a useful model of an activist education paper for parents and teachers in any school district. To subscribe, or for a sample copy, write to PSN, 3721 Midvale Avenue, Philadelphia, PA 19129-1532, 215-951-0330.*

GLOSSARY

WORD POWER

---

*"LANGUAGE NOT ONLY EXPRESSES
IDEAS AND CONCEPTS, BUT IT
ACTUALLY SHAPES THOUGHT...."
– BENJAMIN WHORF*

The linguist Benjamin Whorf points out that language is more than a reflection of the communications structures in society. Language is intimately linked to the creation and perception of reality itself. Thus, eliminating biased terminology is one way to change and correct the way we view ourselves and others.

Language, which reflects society and its culture, is not static. Nor is it more sacred than anything else in the sociopolitical arena. In our racist, sexist, classist and heterosexist society, our decisions about word usage are political decisions. When we use the male pronoun to mean both sexes, one is — consciously or unconsciously — making a political statement. Likewise, the use today of outmoded terms, like "Negro" or "Oriental," has clear political implications. Words are deleted from or added to the vernacular and their meanings and connotations changed continually to reflect the political, social and economic changes in our society. Language is used as a mechanism to shape and maintain a particular kind of social order.[1]

We offer the following words and definitions to be used as a guide for non-racist/anti-oppression terminology.[2] Our purpose is supporting the ongoing efforts to restructure our society into one that is more just. Keep in mind that some of these definitions include broad generalizations and are, at best, imprecise labels to describe diverse human populations. It is important to be aware always of the terms people use to describe themselves, and to understand their reasons for these choices. When in doubt and when possible, *ask.*

Please remember that the categories and terms in this glossary are fluid and overlapping. For example, a person from Nigeria living in the United States might refer to him/herself as African, Black, Nigerian or a person of color. His/her child, if living in the United States for most of his/her life, might choose the term African American, as well as the other options listed above.

It is always best to learn how people refer to themselves. Use your best judgment, however, in situations where you will not be able to speak directly to the person. When conducting research or attempting to gather demographic information in a particular setting, be especially careful of how you classify people because certain designations paint certain pictures. For example, one picture is painted if we simply say that all the clients in an agency are "Latinos," and another if we say, "Puerto Rican," Chicano" and "Cuban." Likewise is true if all the Black students in a school are exchange students from Nigeria or newly arrived immigrants from Jamaica. Demographic information can often be vague, but it can be made more specific by paying particular attention to race, ethnicity and nationality. Specificity is necessary to identify trends and patterns in different contexts.

ABLE-BODYISM

Attitude, action and institutional practices that subordinate people with disabilities.

AFRICAN AMERICANS

People of African descent who were born in the United States.

AGEISM

Attitude, action and institutional practices that subordinate elderly persons due to their age

ASIAN AMERICANS

Refers to people of Asian descent living in the United States. They include: Chinese, Filipino, Japanese and Korean peoples; Southeast Asians, such as people of Vietnamese, Cambodian and Laotian heritage; and South Asians, such as Indian, Pakistani and Bangladeshi. The word "Oriental," coined by the early European explorers, refers to the lands east of the Mediterranean Sea, with Europe placed as the main point of reference. It is considered a pejorative because the term implies subordination in relation to "The West," emphasizes strangeness of the many Asian cultures, and exoticizes the people, especially women.

BILINGUAL EDUCATION

Bilingual education is often misunderstood as one standard of teaching methods and program philosophies. Actually, bilingual education is a term that can refer to several different methods that use two languages for instruction. Below are just a few.

Transitional bilingual education (early exit): Students in early exit programs develop basic language skills in the student's non-English dominant language in order to help the student rapidly transition to the English-language instruction. As proficiency in English increases, students are expected to transition to English-speaking classes.

Transitional bilingual education (late exit): Students in these programs first achieve literacy skills in their dominant language before introduction of reading and writing in English.

Two-way bilingual: In these classrooms, English-speaking and nonnative English-speaking children are instructed in English and a second language, with the goal of bilingual literacy for both groups.

As these options demonstrate, the term bilingual education is imprecise when used to generically describe programs that use two languages for instruction. A good deal of misunderstanding can be avoided by proper explanation and description of the bilingual program in your school or district.

BLACKS

An inclusive term referring to people of African descent who may be living in or from any part of the world.

CAPITALISM

An economic system characterized by the private ownership of the means of production. These owners are called capitalists and their main aim is to produce goods to sell at a profit. During the early phase of industrialization, the major capitalist is the factory owner. However, we can also distinguish the merchant capitalist who deals specifically in the buying and selling of wholesale commodities on an international basis.

CHICANO

A person of Mexican descent living in the United States; its use reflects a political statement connoting pride of identity in the Indian-African-Spanish heritage of the people and their historic Mexican roots in what is now the U.S. Southwest.

CIVIL RIGHTS

Constitutional rights to political equality, i.e., the right to vote, to hold public office, to testify in court and serve on juries, etc.

CLASSISM

Attitude, action and institutional practices that subordinate working-class and poor people due to their economic condition.

COLONIES, COLONIALISM

A process which describes the way in which people from major trading nations settled in other countries to ensure that the "mother country" was supplied with raw materials. These colonies also provided a market for the finished products produced in the "mother country."

CONQUISTADORES

Generally this means "conqueror," someone who takes possession by force. But it is used more specifically in reference to the Spanish conquerors of Mexico, Central America and South America in the 16th century.

DISCRIMINATION

Differential treatment that favors one individual, group or object over another. The source of discrimination is prejudice and the actions are not systematized or institutionalized.

HETEROSEXISM

Attitude, action and institutional practices that subordinate people due to their gay, lesbian, bisexual, or transgender orientation.

HORIZONTAL HOSTILITY
Discrimination and prejudice among and between members of oppressed populations.

INTERETHNIC CONFLICT
Racial, ethnic and cultural conflicts between individuals, groups, and communities of color.

LATINOS
People from Mexico, Central America (such as Guatemala, Nicaragua, El Salvador), South America (such as Argentina, Brazil, Uruguay), and the Spanish-speaking Caribbean (such as Puerto Rico, Dominican Republic, Cuba). The term also includes Chicanos and Mexican Americans. The term "Latino" refers to a shared cultural heritage (indigenous or Indian, African and Spanish), a history of colonization by Spain and a common language, Spanish. The term does not refer to people from Spain. (Although Brazil was colonized by the Portuguese, it is included in this category because of its geographic location.) In addition, the term "Hispanic" is more often heard on the East Coast of the United States and "Latino" in the West. Those on either coast who prefer to be known as "Latino," however, say that the word was coined to express the common historical and political factors listed above, and that "Hispanic" merely reflects popular usage of a European-based language.

NATIVE AMERICANS
The descendants of the original people who inhabited North, South and Central America prior to their conquest by Europeans. There is still a debate as to whether the term "Native American" or "Indian" is preferred. Many Native Americans do use "Indian" and "tribe" in referring to their own people. Other Native peoples suggest that "Indian," "tribe" and a host of similar words are incorrect and carry derogatory connotations in our society. Recommended usage is to refer to a particular people or nation by name, such as Cherokee, Hopi and Seminole.

NORTH/SOUTH
The terms "North" and "South" are used to emphasize economic inequalities between rich and poor countries, with the North being rich and the South being poor. Rich usually means rich in cash, rather than rich in land or resources, or the wealth of people's skills, creativity and hard work. The wealthy countries became wealthy by exploiting the resources of the Southern countries. The countries of the North are the same as also referred to as "First World." They include the United States and Canada in North American; France, Germany and Great Britain in Western Europe; and Japan in Asia. Southern countries, or "Third World" countries, are in Latin America, Africa, Eastern Europe, most of East and South Asia, and the Pacific except Australia.

OPPRESSION
The systematic exploitation of one social group by another for its own benefit. The phenomenon involves institutional control, ideological domination and the promulgation of the dominant group's culture on the oppressed.

PACIFIC ISLANDERS
People from the islands of the Pacific such as the Samoa, Guam and the Fiji Islands. Native Hawaiian Islanders are Pacific Islanders as well as U. S. citizens.

PEOPLE OF COLOR
A term of solidarity referring to African Americans, Native Americans, Latinos, Asians and Pacific Islanders. This term is preferred to other terms often heard, such as "minority" and "non-White." While people of color are a minority in the United States, they are the vast majority — nine-tenths — of the world's population. White people are the distinct minority. Use of the term "minority," therefore, obscures this global reality and reinforces racist assumptions. To describe people of color as "non-White" is to use the White race as the standard against which all other races are described, or as a referent in relation to whom all others are positioned. It is doubtful that White people would appreciate being called "non-Black" or men would like being called "non-women." The term "people of color" was borne out of an explicitly political statement that signaled a solidarity among progressive African Americans, Asian Americans, Latinos, Native Americans and Pacific Islanders. People may choose to identify this way for a variety of factors including race, ethnicity, culture, physical appearance, class and political perspective.

PREJUDICE
An attitude, opinion or feeling formed without adequate prior knowledge, thought, or reason. Moreover, a prejudice cannot be changed simply by presenting new facts or information that contradicts those one already has. Prejudice can be prejudgment for or against any individual, group or object. Any individual or group can hold prejudice(s) towards another individual, group or object.

RACE
A category of the human species sharing more or less distinctive physical traits transmitted in descent; a concept that has little scientific validity but continues to have a meaning in particular social contexts.

RACISM
Racial prejudice and discrimination that are supported by institutional power and authority. The critical element that differentiates racism from prejudice and discrimination is the use of institutional power and authority to support prejudices and enforce discrimi-

natory behaviors in systematic ways with far-reaching outcomes and effects. In the United States, racism is based on the ideology of White (European) supremacy and is used to the advantage of White people and the disadvantage of people of color.

SEXISM
Attitude, action and institutional practices that subordinate women because of their gender.

THIRD WORLD
The term "Third World" is used to demarcate those colonized or formerly-colonized countries of the world. These include the nations and peoples of Asia, Africa and Latin America and the Aboriginal people of Australia. They have the unique distinction of having been oppressed and pillaged by the "First World;" that is, by the European colonialists, such as the British, Dutch, French, Portuguese and Spanish, and by the colonialists from the United States. The term "America" should no longer be used to mean the United States because the United States is only one country in the Americas. Some people have re-framed the "Third World" to "First World."

WHITE SUPREMACY
Belief in the superiority of White people over people of color, including the right of Whites to keep others in subordinate roles.

NOTES

1. Council on Interracial Books for Children, *Guidelines for Selecting Bias-Free Textbooks and Storybooks*, New York, 1979, (p. 3).

2. There are other oppressive terms, of course. However, they were not included in this paper because it focuses specifically on racism.

3. The terms African American, Asian American, Latino, Native American, and Pacific Islander are social and political designations, not biological/scientific categories. "Race" is a social and political construction, not biological. For further explanation, see Michael Omi and Howard Winant, *Racial Formation in the United States*, Routledge and Kegan Paul, 1986.

4. Definitions were adapted originally from the above named source by Patricia DeRosa and Joyce King of the Multicultural Project for Community Education in Cambridge, Massachusetts. Further modifications were made by Margo Okazawa-Rey with permission from the authors.

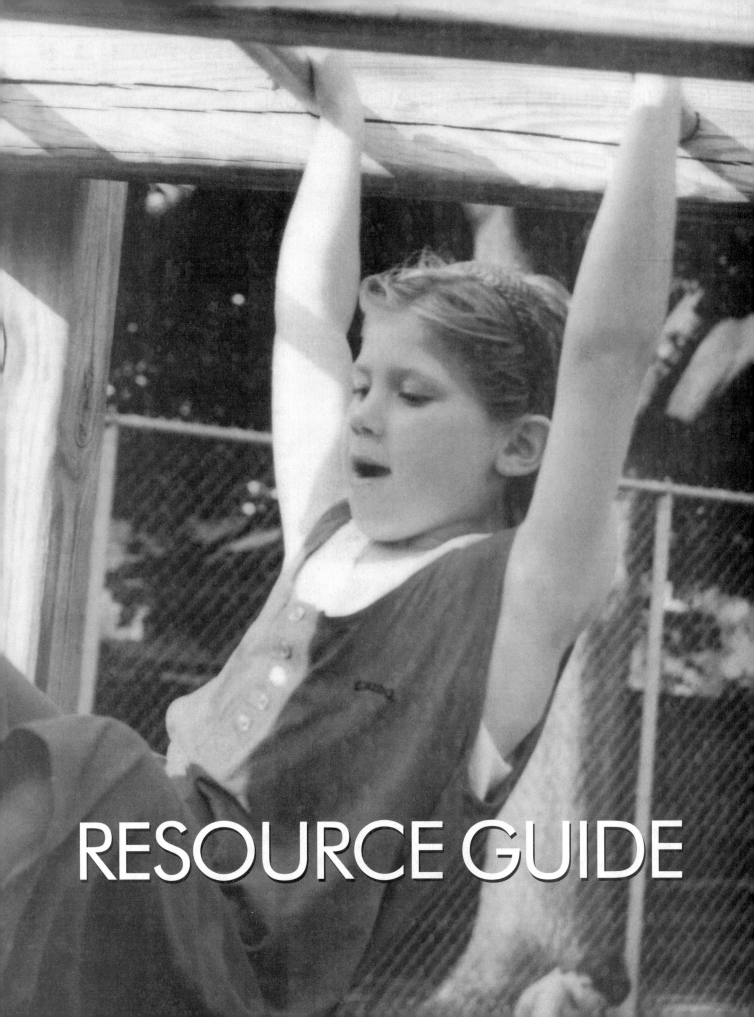

RESOURCE GUIDE

Resource Guide: Print and Audio-Visual

Contents

☒ = This item can be ordered from the Teaching for Change catalog.

Bibliographies and Annotated Resource Guides

Day, F. A. *Multicultural Voices in Contemporary Literature: A Resource for Teachers*
Information about the lives and works of thirty-nine authors and illustrators representing twenty cultures. In addition to describing the books and the reading level, Day provides classroom teaching ideas. Heinemann, 1994. 244 pp.

Harris, V. (Ed.) *Using Multiethnic Literature in the K-8 Classroom*
Chapters on Asian Pacific American, Puerto Rican, Mexican American, Native American, and African American children's literature including a critique of the literature available, key issues which should be addressed and a list of recommended children's books. Christopher-Gordon, 1997. 300 pp.☒ $30

Muse, D. (Ed.) *The New Press Guide to Multicultural Resources for Young Readers*
Over 1000 summaries and reviews of books for young people. The books are grouped under headings including: Folktales; Justice, Human Rights, Equity; Cultural Traditions, etc. Lesson plans and critical essays by prominent educators such as Sonia Nieto and Debbie Wei are included. Sections are divided into reviews of books appropriate to specific grade level. New Press, 1997.

Randolph, B. *Africa Access Review of K-12 Materials*
Detailed, critical annotations of over 200 print and audiovisual materials for teaching about Africa from K-12. *"Finally, an authoritative bibliographic resource that I can recommend to teachers and parents with confidence."* • Dr. Sulayman Nyang, Chair, African Studies Department, Howard University. Africa Access, 1992. 102 pp. ☒ $15.

Slapin, B. & Seale, D. *Through Indian Eyes: The Native American Experience in Books for Children*
Articles, stories, poetry and in-depth reviews of books about Native Americans. Oyate, 312 pp.

Stott, J. *Native Americans in Children's Literature*
Essays on the Native American presence in children's literature. Includes summaries of works by and about Native Americans. Oryx Press, 1995. 239 pp.

Biographies/Autobiographies

This section includes only a few of the powerful biographies and autobiographies which can provide insights through life stories into issues of race and racism — and an activist response. The names in bold are in "Activists for Social Change" in the "Holidays and Heritage" section of this book. Due to space restrictions we have limited ourselves to biographies which are less frequently available in school libraries. Therefore biographies by or about people such as Maya Angelou, Malcolm X, Martin Luther King, Jr., and Cesar Chavez are not included although we highly recommend their use.

Alvarez, J. *In the Time of the Butterflies*
Fictionalized account of the **Mirabel sisters**, leading opponents of the Trujillo regime in the Dominican Republic in the 1950s. Alonquin Books, 1994.

Appel, T. *Jose Marti*
Revered as a brilliant political theorist and shrewd organizer, **Jose Marti** fought for the independence of Cuba from colonialism in the late 1800s. His writings are read in schools throughout Latin America. Written for middle school readers. Chelsea House, 1992. 111 pp.

Barnard, H.F. (Ed.) *Outside the Magic Circle: The Autobiography of Virginia Foster Durr*
Tells the story of Civil Rights activist **Virginia Foster Durr**, who fought successfully to abolish the poll tax. University of Alabama Press, 1985.

Boggs, G. L. *Living for Change: An Autobiography*
Grace Lee Boggs is a first-generation Chinese American who has been a speaker, writer and activist for 55 years. University of Minnesota, 1998. 344 pp.

Brown, C. (Ed.) *Ready from Within: Septima Clark and the Civil Rights Movement*
Students can learn about the Civil Rights Movement through the life of teacher **Septima Clark**. Teachers can learn about teaching and organizing from this unsung hero of the Civil Rights Movement. Africa World Press, 1986. 134 pp. ⊠ $9

Burgos-Debray, E. *I...Rigoberta Menchú: An Indian Woman in Guatemala.*
Nobel Peace Prize winner **Rigoberta Menchú** describes the indigenous traditions of child-raising, farming, health care and spirituality. She documents her people's fight for justice and, in graphic terms, the violent government repression. Verso, 1984. 251 pp. ⊠$17

Chin, S. *When Justice Failed: The Fred Korematsu Story*
Fred Korematsu challenged his arrest and the imprisonment of over one hundred thousand Japanese Americans during WWII. Steck-Vaughn, 1993. 105 pp.

Chisholm, S. *Unbought and Unbossed*
Shirley Chisholm tells the story of her remarkable life as the first Black woman elected to the United States Congress. Houghton-Mifflin, 1970. 177 pp.

Clements, C. *Witness to War: An American Doctor in El Salvador*
Dr. Charles Clements' story of his work in the battle-ravaged countryside of El Salvador in the early 1980s. Video available with the same title. Bantam Books, 1984. 288 pp.

Da Silva, B. *Benedita Da Silva: An Afro-Brazilian Woman's Story of Politics and Love*
Brazilian Senator **Benedita Da Silva** lost two of her children to poverty. For more than 30 years she has been organizing her community and fighting for the rights of the poor. This is her story, as told to Medea Benjamin and Maisa Mendonca. Forward by Jesse Jackson. Food First, 1997.

Dallard, S. *Ella Baker: A Leader Behind the Scenes*
The life of civil rights activist **Ella Baker** written for young readers. Silver Burdett, 1990.

Davis, A. *Angela Davis: An Autobiography*
Angela Davis' account of her life as a political activist and professor since the 1950s. Random House, 1974.

Dees, M. & Fiffer, S. *A Season of Justice: A Lawyer's Own Story of Victory Over America's Hate Groups*
The life and work of anti-klan activist and lawyer **Morris Dees**. Touchstone, 1991.

Duberman, M. *Paul Robeson: A Biography.*
Paul Robeson's life as an anti-racist activist, singer, athlete and actor. Random House, 1989.

Duster, A.M. (Ed.) *Crusade for Justice: The Autobiography of Ida B. Wells*
Ida B. Wells used her talent as journalist and organizer to fight the lynching of Blacks in the United States. University of Chicago Press, 1970.

Equiano, O. *The Interesting Narrative of the Life of Olaudah Equiano, or Gustavas Vassa, the African*
Olaudah Equiano was born to a noble family in the African kingdom of Benin in 1745. While a boy he was kidnapped, enslaved and taken to the West Indies. In 1767 he gained his freedom. He wrote this life story as part of his abolitionist work in London. Dawsons, 1969. (First published, 1789.)

Equiano, O. *The Kidnapped Prince: The Life of Olaudah Equiano*
This version was adapted by Ann Cameron for upper elementary and middle school students. Knopf, 1995. 136 pp.

Garland, A. W. *Women Activists: Challenging the Abuse of Power*
Fourteen women who made a difference in their community. Feminist Press, 1988. 146 pp.

Gorfinkel, C. (Ed.) *The Evacuation Diary of Hatsuye Egami*
Hatsuye Egami's story of the treatment of Japanese-Americans in 1942 at the hands of the American government. She writes about living in Tulare Assembly Center and the day-to-day activities of life in an internment camp. International Productions, 1995. 103 pp.

Kohl, J. & Kohl, H. *The Long Haul: An Autobiography of Myles Horton*
Myles Horton founded the Highlander Folk School which played a key role in the labor movement of the 1930 and the Civil Rights Movement. This book describes not only his life and work, but also his philosophy of education which could be applied to schools today. Teachers College Press, 1998. 256 pp. ⊠ $18

Levering, D. *W.E.B. DuBois: Biography of Race, 1868-1919*
The life of **W.E.B. DuBois** who has written some of the most definitive texts on race relations in his in North America.

Mathabane, M. *Kaffir Boy: The True Story of a Black Youth's Coming of Age in Apartheid South Africa*
Mathabane's life story provides insights into the impact of apartheid. Signet Books, 1986.

Mendes, C. *Fight for the Forest*
As a trade union leader, **Chico Mendes** won international acclaim as leader of the nonviolent campaign to protect the Amazon rainforest, on which the rubber tappers depended for their living. He was assassinated because he became too successful, becoming a threat to the big landowners and business interests who profit from the forest's wholesale destruction. The book includes a history of rubber. Useful for science and social studies classes. Latin American Bureau, 1989. 96 pp.

Mills, K. *This Little Light of Mine: The Life of Fannie Lou Hamer*
Fannie Lou Hamer grew up in a family of Mississippi Delta sharecroppers. She went on to take a definitive leadership role in the Civil Rights Movement, playing a key role at the Democratic Conventions of 1964 and 1968. Penguin, 1993.

Mohr, N. *In My Own Words: Growing Up in the Sanctuary of My Imagination*
Nicholasa Mohr, an award-winning writer of fiction for all ages, describes her life growing up Puerto Rican in Spanish Harlem. It includes powerful descriptions of the racism she faced in school. Students may be familiar with her novels including *Nilda*, *Felita*, and *El Bronx Remembered*. Written for middle school on up. Simon and Schuster, 1994. 118 pp.

Moody, A. *Coming of Age in Mississippi*
Anne Moody details the experience of growing up Black in 1940s Mississippi. Bantam Doubleday, 1968. 384 pp.

Myers, W. D. & Lawrence, J. *Toussaint L'Ouverture: The Fight for Haiti's freedsom*
The story of **Toussaint L'Ouverture**, once enslaved, who became the general of the Haitian army that rose up against the French, and whose actions resulted in the independence of Haiti and the end to slavery in that country. Paintings by Jacob Lawrence. 1996. 40 pp.

Otfinosk, S. *Marian Wright Edelman, Defender of Children's Rights*
The life of Children's Defense Fund founder **Marian Wright Edelman** written for young readers. Blackbirch Press, 1991.

"An absolutely unique work: richly literary and poetic, yet urgent and politically explosive at the same time... A permanent testament to human courage and transcendence."
— Jonathan Kozol, author of *Savage Inequalities*

ALWAYS RUNNING
LA VIDA LOCA: GANG DAYS IN L.A.
LUIS J. RODRÍGUEZ

Rodriguez, L. *Always Running --La Vida Loca: Gang Days in L.A.*
Dramatic account of Chicano poet **Luis Rodríguez'** life as a gang member in the 60s and 70s, his encounters with racism in schools and on the streets, and his political activism. Written for his teenage son, excerpts are very appropriate for classroom use. Touchstone, 1993. 260 pp. ✉ $12.

Santiago, E. *When I Was Puerto Rican*
This coming-of-age memoir tells the story of Esmerelda Santiago, who went from rural Puerto Rico to New York City and on to Harvard University. Describes one woman's struggle to find acceptance in two cultures. Vintage Books, 1993. 274 pp.

Stalvey, L. *The Education of A WASP*
Autobiography of a White woman's experience learning about racism during the 1960s. She began with a naive belief that everyone experiences equal treatment. Through her increasingly active involvement with African Americans she discovered the huge difference in how America works for Whites than for Blacks. University of Wisconsin (Madison) Press, 1989.

Thomas, P. *Down These Mean Streets*
This book by **Piri Thomas** has become a classic text about the experience of growing up Puerto Rican in 1940s New York. Vintage Books, 1991 (reissue). 334 pp.

Thomas, P. *Seven Long Times*
Through his prison memoir **Piri Thomas** documents the day to day realities of life in prison, including a prisoner rebellion. Arte Publico Press, 1994. 197 pp.

Wideman, J.E. *Brothers and Keepers*
The story of two brothers who grew up in Pittsburgh. John Edgar Wideman became a college professor and award-winning novelist; his brother, Robby is serving a life sentence for murder. Both voices are used to create an account of what it means to be black men in the United States. Penguin Press, 1984. 243 pp.

Yates, D. *Chief Joseph: Thunder Rolling Down From the Mountains*
Chief Joseph called for equal rights for people of all races. During the Nez Perce-American War, he urged reconciliation and mourned the dead on both sides. In the years following the conflict, he continued to advocate self-determination for native peoples. Study guide available for this and other titles in the Unsung Americans biography series. Ward Hill Press, 1992. 141 pp.

Yates, J. *Woody Guthrie: American Balladeer*
Woody Guthrie was one of the greatest political songwriters this country has ever produced. This biography gives a detailed and loving portrait of his life and the troubled times in which he lived. Simple but com-

pelling prose for adults and students alike. Ward Hill Press, 1995. 142 pp.

Zinn, H. *You Can't Be Neutral on a Moving Train: A Personal History of Our Times*
Historian **Howard Zinn** tells his own history of thirty years of politically engaged life, dedicated to racial and social justice. Beacon Press, 1994.

FAMILY INVOLVEMENT

McCaleb, S.P. *Building Communities of Learners: A Collaboration among Teachers, Students, Families, and Community*
Through research and examples of exemplary programs the author explains how schools can develop meaningful school/family/community collaborations. St. Martin's Press, 1994. 210 pp. ⊠$20

Multicultural Coalition of Southeastern Connecticut. *Dealing with Racism in the Public School System*
Practical guide that focuses on what parents and students can do when faced with discrimination at school. The booklet contains examples of in-school racism, outlines legal rights and offers solutions for change. Includes a list of organizations fighting racism in Connecticut. Published in English and Spanish. MCSCPC, P.O. Box 1834, New London, CT 06320.

Peterson, B. *Teachers and Parents: The Milwaukee Experience*
How teachers and parents in Milwaukee won control of an inner-city elementary school. The school now has a bilingual program, uses cooperative and anti-racist teaching methods and is governed by a council of parents and teachers. City College Workshop Center, 1992. 21 pp. ⊠ $6.

Valdes, G. *Con Respeto: Bridging the Distances Between Culturally Diverse Families and Schools, An Ethnographic Portrait*
A study of ten Mexican immigrant families, with a special focus on mothers, that describes how families go about the business of surviving and learning to succeed in a new world. She places particular emphasis on the family beliefs about schools and education and contrasts those with school perceptions and policies. Teachers College Press, 1996. 237 pp.

GENDER SPECIFIC

Kirk, G. & Okazawa-Rey, M. (Eds.) *Womens 'Lives: Multicultural Perspectives*
Multidisciplinary, multicultural introduction to Women's Studies. Examines issues effecting women's lives using global, national and local contexts and social, cultural and economic analyses. Mayfield Publishing Company, 1998.

Mankiller, W., Mink, G., Navarro, M. Smith, B., & Steinam, G. (Eds.) *The Reader's Companion to U.S. Women 's History*
A ground-breaking reference on the history of the United States. This is the first book to cover the experiences and contribution of women throughout history. Includes more than 400 articles by leading feminist historians, anthropologists, politicians, social scientists and legal scholars. Houghton Mifflin, 1998.

Morgan, R. (Ed.) *Sisterhood is Global: The International Women's Movement Anthology*
Contains articles from leading feminists from over 60 countries around the world. In-depth information detailing the state of the women's movement in their countries and addressing information crucial to women's lives and health. Includes an extensive glossary and bibliography and a list of the words for "sister" in many languages. Anchor Press/Doubleday, 1984.

Ruiz, V.L. & DuBois, E.C. (Eds.) *Unequal Sisters: A Multicultural Reader in U.S. Women"s History*
Eighteen essays which address issues of race, ethnicity, region and sexuality in an attempt to provide a more accurate and more inclusive history of women in the United States. Routledge, 1994. 620 pp.

Sadker, M. & Sadker, D. *Failing at Fairness: How Our Schools Cheat Girls*
Explores how gender bias makes it impossible for girls to receive an education equal to boys. Includes examples of gender bias from American classrooms. Touchstone, 1994. 347 pp.

Stein, N. & Sjostrom, L. *Flirting or Hurting? A Teacher's Guide on Student-to-Student Sexual Harassment in Schools*
For grades 6-12. Lessons and activities on student rights, discussing sexual harassment, and creating "safe" environments. National Education Association, 1994. 106 pp.

LANGUAGE

Crawford, J. *Bilingual Education: History , Politics, Theory, and Practice*
A thorough history and analysis of both the pedagogy and politics of bilingual education. The history from this book should be woven into any course on U.S. history. Crane Publishing, 1989. 204 pp.

Cummins, J. *Negotiating Identities: Educating for Empowerment in a Diverse Society*
An accessible overview of issues of language, bilingualism and diversity with a clear understanding of power relations within our schools and society by an internationally recognized scholar on bilingual education. CABE, 1996. 290 pp. ⊠$18

Ferdman, B.M., Ramirez, A.G., & Weber, R.M. (Eds.) *Literacy Across Languages and Cultures*
Examines questions of literacy in multilingual societies. What does it mean to be "literate?" What are the issues involved when you become literate in a second language? SUNY Press, 1994. 346 pp.

Perry, T. & Delpit, L. *The Real Ebonics: Power, Language and the Education of African-American Children*
Educators, linguists, writers and students examine the lessons of the Ebonics controversy and unravel complexities of the issue that have never been acknowledged. As Dr. Asa Hilliard explains, "*This is best pragmatic and theoretical treatment of the recent Ebonics controversy. Great clarity and common sense come from an excellent selection of scholar-practitioners.*" Rethinking Schools/Beacon Press, 1998. 227 pp. ✉$10

Skuttnabb-Kangas, T., Phillipson, R., & Rannut, M. (Eds.) *Linguistic Human Rights: Overcoming Linguistic Discrimination*
Collection of articles on linguistic human rights. Mouton de Gruyter, 1995

Smitherman, G. *Talkin' and Testifyin': The Language of Black America*
Provides an understanding of Black English in the larger context of African American culture and its historical roots, and discusses attitudes toward Black English, particularly as they affect educational policy. Wayne State University Press, 1977. 285 pp. ✉ $18

Walsh, C. (Ed.) *Literacy as Praxis: Culture, Language, and Pedagogy*
Examines the relationship between literacy and empowerment for language minority students. Ablex, 1991.

TEACHING GUIDES:
ACROSS THE CURRICULUM

Creighton, A. & Kivel, P. *Helping Teens Stop Violence: A Practical Guide for Counselors, Educators and Parents*
A multicultural approach to interpersonal violence in schools and community groups using role plays and dialogue. Hunter House, 1990. 152 pp. ✉ $15

Derman-Sparks. L. & The A.B.C. Task Force. *Anti-Bias Curriculum: Tools for Empowering Young Children*
Chapters include: Learning about racial differences and similarities; Learning about gender identity; Activism;

Holiday activities; Working with parents; Ten quick ways to analyze children's books for sexism and racism and more. NAEYC, 1989. 149 pp. ✉ $10

Lee, E. *Letters to Marcia: A Teacher's Guide to Anti-Racist Education*
Practical teaching ideas from one of the leaders in the field of multicultural, anti-racist education. Cross Cultural Communication Centre, 1985. 71 pp. ✉$12

Levin, D. E. *Teaching Young Children in Violent Times: Building a Peaceable Classroom: A Pre-K-3 Violence Prevention and Conflict Resolution Guide*
How to create classrooms where children learn peaceful alternatives to the violent behaviors modeled for them in the media and beyond. Suggests use of dialogue, puppetry, games, play, class charts, curriculum webs, and graphs. ESR, 1994. 193 pp. ✉ $22

Schniedewind, N. & Davidson, E. *Open Minds to Equality: A Sourcebook of Learning Activities to Promote Race, Sex, Class and Age Equity*
Grades 3-12. Useful for teachers and parents. Packed with dozens of lessons to address building trust, communication and cooperation; stereotypes; the impact of discrimination; and creating change. Prentice Hall, 1998. 387 pp. ✉ $43

Schniedewind, N. & Davidson, E. *Cooperative Learning, Cooperative Lives: A Sourcebook of Learning Activities for Building a Peaceful World*
Over 75 interdisciplinary activities that are easily integrated into upper elementary and middle school language arts, math, social studies, art and science classes. Brown Co., 1987. 538 pp. O/P.

TEACHING GUIDES AND TEXTS: ART

Chahan, S. & Kocur, Z. *Contemporary Art and Multicultural Education*
Lessons, color reproductions, interviews with artists (in English and Spanish) and essays on art and education. The lessons use art to explore subjects such as American identity, the family, racism, the Vietnam war and the role of public art. Routledge and the New Museum of Contemporary Art, 1996. 392 pp. ✉ $39

Rohmer, H. (Ed.) *Just Like Me: Stories and Self-Portraits by Fourteen Artists*
A diverse collection of artists share their personal visions in colorful, buoyant self-portraits. Encourages self-expression by young people. Children's Book Press, 1997. 31 pp.

Teaching Guides and Texts: Language Arts

The titles in this section are ideal for interdisciplinary language arts and social studies.

Appleman, D. et al. *Braided Lives: An Anthology of Multicultural American Writing*
Brings together vivid stories and poems of Native American, Hispanic American, African American and Asian American writers and invites readers to discover the rich personal insights of cross-cultural literary study. Minnesota Humanities Commission, 1991. 287 pp. ✉ $18.

Daniels, J. (Ed.) *Letters to America: Contemporary American Poetry on Race*
This anthology features the work of poets who have had the courage to write about race with honesty and passion. Some poems celebrate racial identity while others excavate the shameful racial history of the United States. Poets include: Gwendolyn Brooks, Lucille Clifton, Joy Harjo, Langston Hughes, Garrett Hongo, Audre Lorde, Sharon Olds, Gary Soto, Gail Tremblay, Nellie Wong and more. Wayne State University Press, 1995.

Espada, M. (Ed.) *Poetry Like Bread: Poets of the Political Imagination*
This outstanding collection of political poetry is written in both Spanish and English. As Rigoberta Menchu wrote, "*the poets in the book...confront the moral crisis and desperation we witness in the gross materialism permeating our societies. With bold and simple words, they speak to us of the women and men who build hope every day.*" The poetry would be most appropriate for upper elementary through high school classrooms. Curbstone Press, 1994.

Greer, C. & Kohl, H. (Eds.) *A Call to Character: A Family Treasury of Stories, Poems, Plays, Proverbs, and Fables to Guide the Development of Values for You and Your Children*
A wonderful gift for any teacher or parent. These are the stories that encourage children to "do the right thing" for themselves and the community. Marian Wright Edelman of the Children's Defense Fund says, "*Finally, we have a book that highlights values that remind us to care about each other and not just ourselves.*" Harper-Collins, 1995. 456 pp. ✉ $15

King, L. (Ed.) *Hear My Voice: A Multicultural Anthology of Literature from the United States*
Stories, poems, essays and speeches, divided into six units: Borders; Love; Family; Society: Conflict, Struggle & Change; Personal Identity; and Celebrations. Invaluable for secondary classrooms. Includes book of readings and a teaching guide with activities designed to link social studies and language arts. Addison-Wesley,1994. 398 pp. Teaching Guide, 96 pp. ✉ $34

Miller, E. (Ed.) *In Search of Color Everywhere: A Collection of African-American Poetry*
Award-winning collection of over 200 poems which teach about freedom, the celebration of Blackness, love, family gatherings, healing, rituals, music, dance and sports, and the American journal. Stewart, Tabori, & Chang, 1996. 256 pp. ✉ $18

Muse, D. (Ed.) *Prejudice: Stories About Hate, Ignorance, Revelation and Transformation*
For children ages 12 and up. Through these thought-provoking short stories and excerpts from novels, readers will witness challenges people face in overcoming prejudice they find in others, as well as the prejudice they find in their own hearts. Hyperion Books for Children, 1995. 212 pp.

Singer, B. (Ed.) *Growing Up Gay/Growing Up Lesbian: A Literary Anthology*
Over fifty coming-of-age stories. Contributors include James Baldwin, Rita Mae Brown, Audre Lorde, plus other established and young writers. New Press, 1994. 317 pp. ✉ $10

Whaley, L. & Dodge, L. *Weaving in the Women: Transforming the High School English Curriculum*
In a lively and conversational tone, Whaley and Dodge offer a diverse selection of women writers and introduce practical ideas on how to integrate them into the curriculum. "*A pedagogical and bibliographical treasure trove of feminist scholarship and also a very friendly teachers' guidebook. I find the book both unassuming and dazzling...*" • Peggy McIntosh, Wellesley College Center for Research on Women. Boynton/Cook, 1993. 300 pp. ✉ $25

Youth Communications. *Starting With I: Personal Essays by Teenagers*
This collection of student essays is a gift to teachers who use student work as starter dough in their classes. Written from diverse racial and ethnic perspectives, these essays discuss social issues that affect youth today. As their titles suggest, these students are up front and honest: "What Would You Do If I Was Gay?" "Yo, Hollywood! Where Are The Latinos At?" "Color Me Different." These essays are a sure hit in the middle to high school classroom. Persea Books, 1997. ✉$14

Teaching Guides and Texts: Mathematics

Bazin, M. & Tamez, M. *Math Across Cultures*
Part of a Teacher Activity Series produced by the Exploratorium. Well thought-out exercises that dem-

onstrate how math is used in societies around the world, including "The Structural Patterns of Weaving" and "Incan Math." The Exploratorium, 1995. 3601 Lyon Street, San Francisco, CA, 94123 (www.exploratorium.edu)

Frankenstein, M. *Relearning Mathematics: A Different Third R --- Radical Maths*
Intended for adult learners who have been made to feel a failure at math, this book overcomes learning obstacles by developing methods that help to empower students. It sets math problems in the context of current issues around race, gender and class. Free Association Books, 1989.

Gerdes, P. *Women and Geometry in Southern Africa*
This book won an award for *"combining in an ingenious way the study of geometry with that of the visual arts..."* It de-mystifies mathematics in relation to gender and race, and erases the borders between mathematics and popular culture as experienced in the work and crafts of women in Southern Africa. Africa World Press, 1997.

Zaslvasky, C. *Africa Counts: Number and Pattern in African Culture*
Zaslavsky uses photographs, graphs, diagrams, personal anecdotes and quotations from African literature to document the contributions of African peoples to the science of mathematics. Lawrence Hill Books, 1973. 328 pp.

Zaslavsky, C. *The Multicultural Math Classroom: Bringing in the World*
Rationale for introducing multicultural, anti-racist perspectives into the math curriculum, along with practical teaching ideas. Students address community issues through math. Includes sections on numerals, recording and calculating, geometry and measurement in architecture, geometry in art, data analysis, games of many cultures and more. Heinemann, 1996. 240 pp. ⊠ $25

Teaching Guides and Texts: Science

Bazin, M. & Tamez, M. *Science Across Cultures*
Companion book to *Math Across Cultures*. Contains activities that demonstrate how cultures create methods for understanding and working in the changing world. Includes "Teacups and Temperature: Chinese Tea Drinking Traditions" and "Rain in a Bottle: Water Collection in the Kalahari Desert." The Exploratorium, 1997. (See above for address.)

Caduto, M. & Bruchac, J. *Keepers of the Earth: Native American Stories and Environmental Activities for Children*

Children ages 5-12. A collection of North American Indian stories and related hands-on activities. Emphasis is on a multidisciplinary approach to teaching about the Earth and Native American cultures. Other books in the series include *Keepers of Life* and *Keepers of the Animals*. Fulcrum, 1997. 240 pp. ⊠ $20.

Gill, D. & Levidow, L. *Anti-Racist Science Teaching*
This book shows how science and technology embody distinctive values and cultural assumptions, including racist ones. These are in turn reflected in the way science is taught in many schools. Specific case studies present anti-racist approaches to biology, nutrition, and wildlife conservation, as well as one school's experiment with reorganizing the curriculum across disciplinary boundaries. Free Association Books (London), 1987. 324 pp. (01-609-5646/0507.)

Gould, S.J. *The Mismeasure of Man*
A historical study of scientific racism. Gould illustrates the logical inconsistencies of the theories and the prejudicially motivated misuse of data. Norton, 1981. 352 pp. ⊠ $15

Kissinger, K. *All the Colors We Are: The Story of How We Get Our Skin Color*
This bilingual (English/Spanish) book uses photos and engaging language to give children the scientific truths about skin color. Redleaf, 1994. 32 pp.

Teaching Guides and Texts: Social Studies

Acuña, R. *Occupied America: A History of Chicanos*
Examines the experiences and history of Mexican peoples since the first U.S. invasion of Mexico in the early 1800s. Deals in depth with political and economic trends and issues, as well as relations with the United States. HarperCollins, 1988. 475 pp.

Albeda, R. et al. *The War on the Poor: A Defense Manual*
The facts and analysis you need to refute the right-wing assertions that poverty should be blamed on the poor. Provides data to counter the myths about welfare, followed by clear descriptions of equitable alternatives. Also examines employment, the economy, gender roles, and family. New Press, 1996. 142 pp. ⊠$12

American Social History Project. *Freedom's Unfinished Revolution: An Inquiry Into the Civil War and Reconstruction*
Lively prose, primary documents, illustrations and photographs invite students to study this period of history in-depth and critically. Includes exercises and discus-

sion questions. New Press, 1996. 302 pp. ✉ $20

Amott, T.L. & Matthaei, J. *Race, Gender & Work: A Multicultural Economic History of Women in the United States*
Traces women's work lives through the process of capitalist development, and outlines the diversity and dynamism of women's contributions to U.S. economic history. South End Press, 1991. 433 pp.

Andreas, J. *Addicted to War: Why the U.S. Can''t Kick Militarism*
A perspective you won't find in the flag-waving, everything-is-fine textbooks that fill our schools. Frankly partisan, this irreverent comic book examines who benefits from military adventures, who pays — and who dies. New Society Publishers, 1991. 65 pp. O/P.

Aptheker, H. *Anti-Racism in U.S. History: The First Two Hundred Years*
Examines the existence of anti-racism in this country — from the 1600s through the 1860s, and challenges the view that racism was universally accepted by Whites until the outbreak of the Civil War. Praeger, 1993. 246 pp.

Belli, G. et al. (Eds.) *Rediscovering America/ Redescubriendo América*
Ages 10-Adult. Folktales, short stories, essays, poetry, songs from Latin America and the Caribbean. Readings and lessons on conquest and resistance, the environment, race, the Maya, and much more. NECA, 1992. (Bulk discounts available.) 104 pp. bilingual, ✉ $5

Bennett, Jr., L. *Before the Mayflower: A History of Black America*
This comprehensive and detailed account traces black history from its origins in western Africa, through Reconstruction and the Jim Crow era, to the Civil Rights Movement of the '60s and '70s. Penguin, 1993. 713 pp. ✉$17

Bigelow, B. *Strangers in Their Own Country: A Curriculum Guide on South Africa*
Introduces students and teachers to the lives and struggles of the people of South Africa with stories, poems, role plays, news articles and historical readings. Africa World Press, 1985. 92 pp. ✉ $13

Bigelow, B. & Peterson, B. (Eds.) *Rethinking Columbus: The Next 500 Years*
K-Adult. Lessons, essays, short stories, interviews, poetry and lessons to engage students in a critique of the ethnocentric versions of the encounter and textbook bias in general. Bulk discounts available. Rethinking Schools, 1998 (second edition). 160 pp. ✉ $8.

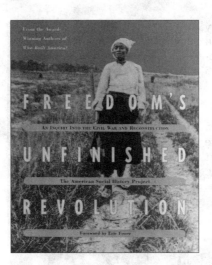

Bigelow, B. & Diamond, N. *The Power in Our Hands: A Curriculum on the History of Work and Workers in the United States*
Secondary. Role plays and writing activities project students into real-life situations where they explore the history and contemporary reality of employment (and unemployment) in the U.S. "*...one of the best social studies curricula ever produced.*" • Fred Glass, California Federation of Teachers. Monthly Review. 1988. 184 pp. ✉ $18

Bigelow, B. & Edmundson, J. *Inside the Volcano: A Case Study of U.S. Foreign Policy*
This secondary school curriculum uses Nicaragua as a case study for students on the impact of U.S. foreign policy. Calling for active participation and critical thinking, the lessons prompt students to examine their own lives so they can understand the experiences of the people in another country. NECA, 1990. 130 pp. ✉$12

Cockcroft, J. *Hispanic Struggle for Social Justice.*
Beginning with Mexican-American resistance to the Anglo takeover of their lands to the contemporary struggle of all Latinos for equity in employment, health care, education and political representation, this book presents the history of Latinos in the United States. High school reading level and above. Franklin Watts, 1994. 160 pp. ✉ $23

Cockcroft, J. *Latinos in the Making of the United States*
Uncovers the many riches of the Hispanic role in the making of the United States. Latino roles in business, education, agriculture, environmental awareness, and industry are among those addressed. Franklin Watts, 1995. 191 pp.

Cockcroft, J. *Latinos in the Struggle for Equal Education*
Presents a wealth of information on Latino contributions to education, beginning with the first mission schools in fifteenth-century Spanish settlements in California and continuing to current controversies over bilingual education and the schooling of children of immigrants. Franklin Watts. 1995. 191 pp.

Donahue, D. & Flowers, N. *The Uprooted Refugees and the United States*
A multidisciplinary teaching guide with lessons on the historical and current treatment of refugee issues. Includes real-life experiences of refugees and lessons on the complexity of immigration policy. The authors are members of the Amnesty International educators' network. Hunter House, 1995. 210 pp.

Facing History and Ourselves. *Facing History and Ourselves: Holocaust and Human Behavior*

Resource book on an interdisciplinary approach to a study of the holocaust and the consequences of discrimination, racism and antisemitism. FHFO, 1994. 576 pp. (617-232-1595.)

Fast, H. *Freedom Road*
In this riveting historical novel, Howard Fast brings the Reconstruction era alive -- and shatters many of the myths about this critical era of American history. Foreword by W.E. DuBois. M.E. Sharpe, 1944. 275 pp.

Folbre, N. *The New Field Guide to the U.S. Economy: A Compact and Irreverent Guide to Economic Life in America*
Numbers, charts, stories and cartoons on all aspects of the U.S. economy, including income, education and welfare, the environment, education and health. Documents inequities based on race and gender. *"... A rich mine of information about what has been happening to our society ... a guide for those who hope to find a way to a future that is more humane and free and just."* • Noam Chomsky. New Press, 1995. 224 pp. ⊠ $17

Gage, S. *Colonialism in the Americas: A Critical Look*
Through lively dialogue and illustrations, the book traces the history of the peoples of the Americas and examines the legacy of colonialism. VIDEA, 1991. 52 pp. ⊠ $15.

Galeano, E. *Open Veins of Latin America: Five Centuries of the Pillage of a Continent*
Eloquent and gripping history of the exploitation of the land and peoples of Latin America from the conquest to the present. Second edition with introduction by Isabel Allende. Monthly Review, 1998. 360 pp ⊠ $18

Harding, V. *Hope and History: Why We Must Share the Story of the Movement*
This series of essays emphasizes the significance of the Civil Rights movement, tracing its effects on varying spheres of life. Orbis Books, 1990. 249pp. ⊠ $17

Hartman, C. *Double Exposure: Poverty and Race in America*
Up-to-date and comprehensive review of major topics regarding the intersection of race and poverty such as: affirmative action; the "permanence of racism;" the use and utility of racial categories; multiculturalism; immigration; and democracy/equality. Useful reference for high school students and teachers. M.E. Sharpe, 1996. 280 pp. ⊠ $22

Institute of Race Relations. *Roots of Racism*
The genesis of racism traced from the Middle Ages through the Industrial Revolution. High school read-

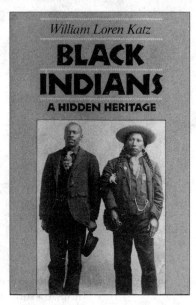

William Loren Katz
BLACK INDIANS
A HIDDEN HERITAGE

ing level. London Institute of Race Relations, 1985. 32 pp. ⊠ $10

Institute of Race Relations. *Patterns of Racism*
Covers the development of racism and colonialism in the 20th century in South Africa, Latin America, North America, Australia, the West Indies and India. High school reading level. LIRR, 1985. 48 pp. ⊠ $10

Katz, W. *Black Indians: A Hidden Heritage*
Traces the relations between Blacks and American Indians since the time of the conquest. Filled with inspiring stories of how both groups worked together to oppose White oppression. Atheneum, 1986. 198 pp. ⊠ $10

Kempf, S. *Finding Solutions to Hunger: Kids Can Make a Difference*
Engaging, interactive and challenging lessons for middle and high school students on the roots and solutions to domestic and international hunger. Examines colonialism, contemporary development projects, the media, famine vs. chronic hunger, the working poor and more. WHY, 1997. 245 pp. ⊠$22

Kiang, P. *Asian American Studies Curriculum Resource Guide*
Identifies themes such as exclusion, identity and community building and provides sample teaching activities and resources for K-12. For ordering information, write to: Peter Kiang, University of Mass. at Boston, 100 Morrissey Blvd., Boston, MA 02125.

Loewen, J. *Lies My Teacher Told Me: Everything Your American History Textbook Got Wrong*
Survey and analysis of the twelve leading high school textbooks. In addition to documenting the inaccuracies and omissions, Loewen provides the history that is missing. This is an essential resource for every history teacher. Simon and Schuster, 1995. 384 pp. ⊠ $15.

Lusane, C. *Pipe Dream Blues: Racism and the War on Drugs*
Documents the history, economics, and all politics of the drug crisis and programs to address its root causes. Data can be used in math and social studies lessons to determine who really profits from the drug trade. South End Press, 1991. 293 pp. ⊠ $14.

Maine Indian Program of the AFSC. *The Wabanakis of Maine and the Maritimes*
Information and materials for a more accurate picture of the history and culture of Indians in Maine and the Maritimes. The book is organized into four parts: historical overview, lesson plans, readings and fact

sheets for grades 4-8. AFSC, 1989. 498
pp. (See Catalog section.)

Network of Black Organizers (Ed.)
Black Prison Movements
This volume analyzes the U.S. criminal system, the prison system in general, and the reality of political prisoners, prisoners of war and prisoners
of political conscience in the U.S. Various political perspectives and voices
from behind prison walls are included.
Africa World Press, 1995. 225 pp.

Perry, T. (Ed.) *Teaching Malcolm X:
Popular Culture and Literacy*
An array of authors discuss the im-
portance of Malcolm X as a historical

figure and cultural hero and provide guidelines for
teaching about him. Contributors include Patricia Hill
Collins, Nikki Giovanni, Linda Mizell, Imani Perry and
Cornel West. Routledge, 1995. 224 pp. ✉$19

Rodney, W. *How Europe Underdeveloped Africa*
Dr. Rodney turns around the study of underdevelop-
ment in Africa. He documents the history and development of African societies and the subsequent destructive impact of European colonialism and slavery.
Howard University Press, 1982. 312 pp.

Roediger, D.R. *The Wages of Whiteness: Race and
the Making of the American Working Class*
W.E.B. DuBois once observed that low-paid White
workers in the United States 'were compensated in
part by a public and psychological wage.' This 'bonus'
was a belief in their inherent racial superiority over
non-Whites, a conviction that sustained them in their
unequal struggle with American capital. Scholarly and
accessible, with fascinating accounts of the origins of
working-class racism in colonial settler attitudes, of
the history of the ideas like 'free White labor' and of
the struggle for 'Whiteness' of the immigrant Irish
working class, Roediger's books is a key text to understanding the ideology of racial superiority. Verso, 1991.
191 pp.

Starr, J. *The Lessons of the Vietnam
War*
This book of historical documents, testimonies, personal narratives and statistical information is a landmark in honest classroom materials on the Vietnam
War. Also includes extensive coverage
of the Persian Gulf War. Center for Social Studies Education, 1996. 355 pp.

Sunshine, C. & Menkart, D. (Eds.)
Teaching About Haiti
Helps students to place in context the
current political crisis of the first
independent Black nation in the Americas. Includes: Literature; Interviews;

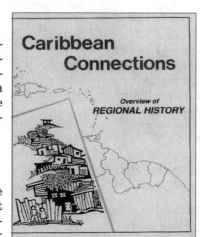

Analysis of the Roots of Poverty;
Folktales; Vodou; Songs by Boukman
Eksperyans; Teaching/Action Ideas
and Bibliography. Call for bulk discounts. 1994. 48 pp. Newsprint. ✉ $2

Sunshine, C. (Ed.) *Overview of
Regional History*
Includes essential background reading
to understand U.S.-Cuban relations
and the Cuban revolution, plus The
Arawaks and the Caribs; Bitter Sugar;
African Resistance to Slavery; India to
the Caribbean; Gunboat Diplomacy;
and more. NECA/EPICA, 1991. 178 pp.
✉ $16

Sunshine, C. (Ed.) *Caribbean
Connections: Jamaica*
Includes: brief history, Anansi and Brer Rabbit stories; Marcus Garvey Movement; Rasta to Reggae; poetry; women's theatre; socio-drama for students and
more. NECA/EPICA, 1991. 106 pp. ✉$12

Sunshine, C. & Warner, K. (Eds.) *Caribbean
Connections: Moving North*
Chronicles Caribbean life in the United States. Fea-
tures the work of noted authors such as Edwidge
Danticat, Judith Ortiz Cofer, Paule Marshall, Julia
Alvarez and others who trace their roots to Puerto
Rico, the English-speaking West Indies, the Domini-
can Republic, Cuba and Haiti. NECA, 1998. 256 pp. ✉
$18

Sunshine, C. (Ed.) *Caribbean Connections: Puerto
Rico*
Includes: Puerto Rican history, the life of Alfonso
Schomburg; interviews with Puerto Rican women in
the garment industry in New York; debate on Puerto
Rico's political status; and more. (Three selections in
Spanish.) NECA/EPICA, 1990. 106 pp. ✉ $12

Takaki, R. *A Different Mirror: A History of
Multicultural America*
Beginning with the colonization of the "New World"
and ending with the Los Angeles riots
of 1992, this book recounts U.S. history in the voices of Native Americans,
African Americans, Jews, Irish Americans, Asian Americans, Latinos and
others. Takaki turns our traditionally
Anglo-centric historical viewpoint inside out and examines the ultimate
question of what it means to be an
American. Little, Brown & Co., 1993.
508 pp. ✉ $15

Terkel, S. *Race: How Blacks and
Whites Think and Feel About The
American Obsession*
Preachers, college students, Klansmen,
interracial couples, the nephew of the

founder of apartheid, and Emmett Till's mother are among nearly 100 Americans who share their opinions and experiences in *Race*. The interviews present a diverse and complex view of race in America and are an ideal length for classroom use. New Press, 1992. 403 pp.

Wei, D., & Kamel, R. (Eds.)
Resistance in Paradise: Rethinking 100 Years of U.S. Involvement in the Caribbean and the Pacific
In 1898, the United States annexed the Pacific Islands of Guam, Hawai'i, and Somoa, as well as Cuba, Puerto Rico, and the Philippines. Annexation altered the course of history for these countries and significantly affected their cultures, political systems, and social structures. *Resistance* provides over 50 lesson plans, role plays and readings for grades 9-12 and is filled with illustrations, cartoon, maps, and photographs for classroom use. "*A major contribution in an attempt to have teachers and students rethink the causes and consequences of the Spanish-American War.*" • Franklin Odo, Smithsonian Institution, AFSC, 1998. 199 pp. ⊠ $12

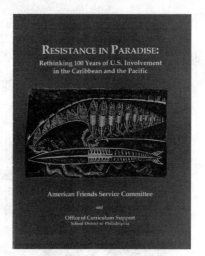

RESISTANCE IN PARADISE:
Rethinking 100 Years of U.S. Involvement in the Caribbean and the Pacific

American Friends Service Committee
and
Office of Curriculum Support
School District of Philadelphia

Zinn, H. *A People's History of the United States*
Lives and facts rarely included in textbooks — an indispensable teacher resource. "*Professor Zinn writes with an enthusiasm rarely encountered in the leaden prose of academic history, and his text is studded with telling quotations.*" • Eric Foner, *The New York Times*. Updated and expanded edition. Harper Collins, 1995. 676 pp. ⊠ $18

TESTING AND TRACKING

Wheelock, A. *Crossing the Tracks: How "Untracking" Can Save America's Schools*
One of the best resources for any school district interested in knowing why it should detrack, and how to do it. New Press, 1992. 311 pp. ⊠ $13

Implementing Performance Assessments: A Guide to Classroom, School and System Reform
Provides descriptions, examples and practical advice on projects, exhibitions, observations, interviews, performance exams and portfolios, with tips for getting started with assessment reform and an extensive resource section. FairTest, 1995. 56 pp. ⊠ $6

Fairtest. *Standardized Tests and Our Children: A Guide to Testing Reform*
Essential guide for parents and teachers on the problems with standardized testing. FairTest. 32 pp. ⊠ $4

NCEA. *Maintaining Inequality: A Background Packet on Tracking and Ability Grouping*
Articles by parents, scholars, students and teachers which critique tracking and suggest alternatives. National Coalition of Education Activists, 1992. ⊠ $6

THEORY AND ACTION

Adams, M. et al. *Teaching for Diversity and Social Justice: A Sourcebook*
Curriculum designs for courses on racism, sexism, heterosexism, antisemitism, ableism, and classism. Designed for college, non-formal education and staff development. Routledge, 1997. 374 pp. ⊠$25

Andrzejewski, J. (Ed.) *Oppression and Social Justice: Critical Frameworks*
Includes writings about how powerful groups maintain power and attempt to control dominant beliefs through the media. Ginn Press, 1993.

Ayers, W. et al. (Eds.) *Teaching for Social Justice*
Engages parents, citizens, students, and teachers in a conversation about the basis for education in a democracy. Features a unique mix of hands-on, historical, and inspirational writings. The topics covered include education through social action, writing, community building, and adult literacy. Contributors include: Bill Bigelow, Jim Carnes, Henry Giroux, Herbert Kohl, and more. New Press, 1991. 416 pp. ⊠ $19

Banks, J.A. *An Introduction to Multicultural Education*
Professor Banks is one of the world's leading scholars and researchers in multicultural education. This book is designed to introduce preservice and practicing educators to the major issues and concepts in multicultural education. Allyn and Bacon, 1994. 136 pp.

Beauboeuf-Lafontant, T. & Augustine, D. (Eds.) *Facing Racism in Education*
Collection of articles from issues of Harvard Educational Review (HER) which break the silence about the experience of people of color in education. HER Reprint Series, 1996. 360 pp.

Carew, J. *Fulcrums of Change: Origins of Racism in the Americas*
Essays on racism, exile, literature, and the Caribbean experience. Africa World Press, 1988. 170 pp.

Darder, A. *Culture and Power in the Classroom: A Critical Foundation for Bicultural Education*
Darder lays the foundation for a theory of critical bicultural education. Bergin and Garvey, 1991. 170 pp.

Delpit, L. *Other People's Children: White Teachers, Students of Color, and Cultural Conflicts in the Classroom*
MacArthur Award-winner Lisa Delpit critiques the

teaching practices of many White teachers which do not address the educational needs of students of color. She also shares ways teachers can be better "cultural translators" and addresses recruitment, teacher training, and supervision. New Press, 1995. 304 pp. ✉ $15

Derman-Sparks L., & Phillips, C.B. *Teaching/Learning Anti-Racism: A Developmental Approach*
Provides both a "how-to" and a conceptual framework to help teachers and teacher trainees adapt anti-racism education for their educators. *"The authors have offered us enlightenment, potential directions for action, and a level of hope. I do not know if the virus of racism/White supremacy can be eliminated. I believe that if it can, it will be in large measure because of the type of work presented here."* • Asa G. Hilliard, III, Georgia State University. Teachers College Press, 1997. 167 pp. ✉ $18

Donaldson, G. *The Ville: Cops and Kids in Urban America*
Documentary on the relationships between African American teenagers and police in Brownsville and East New York. Written from the perspectives of one youth and one police officer, whom the author followed for two years in their respective daily routines. Anchor, 1993. 405 pp.

Foster, M. *Black Teachers on Teaching*
A riveting and honest portrait of the politics and philosophies involved in the education of black children during the last fifty years. Black teachers go on record about mixed-race classrooms, the losses and gains accompanying desegregation, repeated cycles of attempted and abandoned reform efforts, and the differing attitudes and perceptions of black students among black and White teachers. The book offers insights into the methodologies, philosophies and experiences of a small but dedicated group of educators. New Press, 1997. 188 pp. ✉ $15

Garibaldi, A., Reed, W. & Willie, C. *The Education of African-Americans*
Contains an assessment of the educational status of African-Americans since 1940. Focuses on the connection between public policy and its impact on school reform. Includes an extensive evaluation of public spending programs (such as The Rockefeller Foundation) as well as discussions of institutional racism and class stratification. Greenwood Publishing Group, 1991.

Hollins, E. et al (Eds.) *Teaching Diverse Populations: Formulating a Knowledge Base*
This book presents current knowledge about teaching culturally diverse populations. SUNY, 1994. 289 pp.

hooks, b. *Yearning: Race, Gender, and Cultural Politics*
Recognized intellectual leader hooks examines the politics of race and gender. South End Press, 1990. (Look for other titles by hooks such as *Teaching to Transgress.*)

Katz, J. *White Awareness: A Handbook for Anti-Racism Training*
Classic text with many useful exercises for staff development. University of Oklahoma Press, 1979. O/P.

Kivel, P. *Uprooting Racism: How White People Can Work for Racial Justice.*
Features timely discussions of racism, and provides suggestions, advice, exercises and approaches for how White people can work to fight racism. New Society Publishers, 1996. 243 pp.

Kohl, H. *I Won't Learn from You and Other Thoughts on Creative Maladjustment*
Essays on the phenomenon of "not learning" or refusing to learn when a student's intelligence, dignity or integrity is compromised by a teacher, institution or a larger social mindset. The New Press, 1994. 160 pp. ✉ $12

Kuykendall, C. *From Rage to Hope: Strategies for Reclaiming Black and Hispanic Students*
Recommendations for school policies and practices. National Education Service, 1992.

Ladson-Billings, G. *The Dreamkeepers: Successful Teachers of African American Children*
Portraits of eight exemplary teachers who differ in personal style and methods but share an approach to teaching that affirms and strengthens cultural identity. Jossey-Bass, 1994. 187 pp. ✉ $17

Levine, D. et al. (Eds.) *Rethinking Schools: An Agenda for Change*
Highlights from the country's leading education reform journal. Sections on curricula, testing and tracking, national education policy, antibias education, and community. New Press, 1995. 284 pp. ✉ $16

Lindqvist, S. *Skull Measurers' Mistake and Other Portraits of Men and Women Who Spoke Out Against Racism*
Essays by twenty 19th century men and women who, while not themselves the victims of racism, went against the temper of the time to expose the many faces of prejudice. Hardback. New Press, 1995 182 pp. ✉$22

Lowe, R. & Miner, B. *Selling Out Our Schools: Vouchers, Markets and the Future of Public Education*
Articles on major issues surrounding "school choice,"

vouchers and the effort to privatize our public schools. It also contains a special section on the conservative movement and its educational reform agenda. 88 pp. ⊠ $5

Lutz, C. & Bartlett, L. *Making Soldiers in Public Schools: An Analysis of the Army JROTC Program*
Responding to recent, rapid growth of JROTC programs, particularly in the South and in schools with large minority populations, this booklet refutes claimed benefits of JROTC for students and schools. The authors argue that JROTC is at odds with the effort to provide safe, democratic schools that promote respect for others, critical thinking and basic academic skills. AFSC, 1995. 40 pp. ⊠ $4

Martin, R. (Ed.) *Practicing What We Teach: Confronting Diversity in Teacher Education*
Combines theory with concrete classroom examples of critical multicultural teaching in higher education. Includes "Creating Classroom Environments for Change," "Teaching Whites About Racism," and "Multicultural Teacher Education for a Culturally Diverse Teaching Force." SUNY Press, 1995. 282 pp. ⊠ $22

Martusewicz, R, et al. (Eds.) *Inside Out: Contemporary Critical Perspectives in Education*
Essays which help the reader look at education from the "inside" (the complex processes, relations, and methods that operate within schools) and from the "outside" (the larger social, political, economic, and historical forces that influence what goes on in schools.) St. Martin's Press, 1994. 307 pp.

Ng, R, et al. (Eds.). *Anti-Racism, Feminism, and Critical Approaches to Education*
Contributors from Canada and the United States address educational issues relevant to aboriginal peoples, people of color, and people of religious minorities in light of feminist and critical pedagogical theory. Bergin and Garvey, 1995. 171 pp.

Nieto, S. *Affirming Diversity: The Sociopolitical Context of Multicultural Education*
How personal, social, political, cultural, and educational factors interact to affect the success or failure of students. Offers a research-based rationale for multicultural education; case studies and a chapter on language diversity. Longman, 1996. 422 pp. ⊠ $50

Ogbu, J. & Gibson, M. *Minority Status and Schooling: A Comparative Study of Immigrant and Involuntary Minorities*

This volume addresses the central question of why some minority groups do better in school than others. Case studies examine the school performance of Hispanic, Sikh, Turkish, Korean, West Indian, and Mexican immigrants, as well as African American and Native American students. Garland Publishing, 1991. 407 pp.

Olsen, L., et al. *The Unfinished Journey: Restructuring Schools in a Diverse Society*
This report encapsulates the findings of a research project designed to make recommendations on how to restructure our schools to address diversity and equity issues. California Tomorrow, 1994. 362 pp.

Paley, V.G. *White Teacher*
An introspective account of a kindergarten teacher's experience coming to terms with issues of race in her classroom. Harvard University Press, 1989. 142 pp. ⊠ $12

Perry, T. & Fraser, J. (Eds.). *Freedom's Plow: Teaching in the Multicultural Classroom*
"[In] Freedom's Plow *we hear the honest voices of daily practice and we see new innovations in action. [Teachers'] stories give us a wealth of ideas."* • Rita Tenorio, co-editor, *Rethinking Schools*. Routledge, 1993. 309 pp. ⊠ $21

Rothenberg, P. (Ed.) *Racism and Sexism: An Integrated Study*
Anthology of articles on racism and sexism. St. Martin's Press, 1988. O/P

Sapon-Shevin, M. *Playing Favorites: Gifted Education and the Disruption of Community*
Examines how gifted education disrupts the classroom community, de-skills regular classroom teachers, and impairs the creation of a climate of inclusion. Sapon-Shevin suggests how schools can meet individual educational needs as well as the commitment to the education of all children. SUNY, 1994. 275 pp. ⊠$20

Shor, I. *Critical Teaching and Everyday Life*
Practical and theoretical guide to adapting the methods of Brazilian educator Paulo Freire in the classroom. University of Chicago Press. 270 pp. ⊠ $13.

Shor, I. *When Students Have Power: Negotiating Authority in a Critical Pedagogy*
Shor tells the story of trying to share power with his students. Personal, practical, and theoretical, the book honestly confronts underlying tensions that many

critical teachers will recognize. University of Chicago Press, 1996. 251 pp. ⊠$14

Shor, I. (Ed.) *Freire for the Classroom: A Sourcebook for Liberatory Teaching*
An anthology of essays by teachers using Paulo Freire methods in their classrooms. The book offers critical theory side-by-side with actual reports of teaching practice. Heinemann, 1987. 237 pp.

Sleeter, C. *Keepers of the American Dream*
Study of how 30 teachers address cultural diversity in their own teaching and how they thought about various aspects of cultural and racial diversity. Falmer Press, 1992.

Sleeter, C. & Grant, C. *Making Choices for Multicultural Education: Five Approaches to Race, Class, and Gender*
A detailed description of the five major approaches used in multicultural education: teaching the exceptional and culturally different; human relations; single-group studies, multicultural education; and education that is multicultural and social reconstructionist. Prentice Hall, 1994. 262 pp.

Sleeter, C. & McClaren, P. (Eds). *Multicultural Education, Critical Pedagogy, and the Politics of Difference*
Collection of articles by Geneva Gay, Sonia Nieto, Antonia Darder, Donaldo Macedo, the editors and more on the politics and practice of multicultural education from a critical perspective. In this book, *"the connections between multicultural education and critical pedagogy are brought into clear focus and illustrate how different ways of teaching and learning can benefit all students instead of just a few."* • Sandra M. Lawrence, Mount Holyoke College. SUNY Press, 1995. 465 pp.

Tatum, B. D. *"Why Are All the Black Kids Sitting Together in the Cafeteria?" and Other Conversations About Race*
Dr. Tatum, professor at Mount Holyoke College and psychologist, challenges the ways we talk about race and the language we use. She highlights new ways of approaching successful dialogues about racism and provides students' observations and informed psychological investigations of why segregation and racism occur in the cafeteria — and in society. HarperCollins, 1997. 270 pp. ⊠$13

Walker-Moffat, W. *The Other Side of the Asian-American Success Story*
Examines how the story of Asian American educational success deflects attention from the problems affecting Asian immigrant groups. Also contains concrete ways for schools to do a better job of educating all students

"Why Are All the Black Kids Sitting Together in the Cafeteria?"

A Psychologist Explains the Development of Racial Identity

And Other Conversations About Race
BEVERLY DANIEL TATUM, PH.D.

by involving home and community resources. Jossey-Bass, 1995. 209 pp.

Walsh, C. (Ed). *Education Reform and Social Change: Multicultural Voices, Struggles, and Visions*
A theoretical and practical framework for school reform. Examples of parent/school collaborations. Authors include Peter Kiang, Sonia Nieto, Alma Flor Ada, Peter Negroni, Tony Baez, and more. Lawrence Erlbaum, 1996. 270 pp.

Woodson, C.G. *The Mis-Education of the Negro*
A classic text on racism in education. Originally published in 1933 and still relevant today. As Dr. Woodson says, *"This crusade [to transform schools] is more important than the antilynching movement, because there would be no lynching if it did not start in the schoolroom. Why not exploit, enslave, or exterminate a class that everybody is taught to regard as inferior?"* Africa World Press, 1990 (first published in 1933). 215 pp.

Yeboah, S. *The Ideology of Racism*
Detailed analysis of the history and ideology of racism. Hansib Publishing, 1988. O/P

CATALOGS

Contact the groups below for a free copy of their catalog. More catalogs are listed in the section titled Videos.

AACP - Asian American Curriculum Project
Extensive selection of Asian American books for all ages. 234 Main Street, PO Box 1587, San Mateo, CA 94401, 800-874-2242, aacp@best.com, www.best.com/~aacp/

AFSC - American Friends Service Committee
Collection of fiction and nonfiction books and videos on a wide range of social justice issues. AFCS Literature Resources, 1501 Cherry Street, Philadelphia, PA 19102-1479, 888-588-2372, www.afsc.org

Children's Book Press
Diverse collection of award-winning, beautifully illustrated children's books. Many titles are bilingual. 246 First Street, Suite 101, San Francisco, CA 94105, 415-995-2200.

Del Sol Books
Books (for children and teachers), cassettes, and videos in English and Spanish by Alma Flor Ada. Also includes children's books recommended by Alma Flor Ada. 29257 Bassett Road, Westlake, OH 44145, 888-335-7651.

Educators for Social Responsibility
Resources for conflict resolution, violence prevention,

intergroup relations and character education. 23 Garden Street, Cambridge, MA 02138, 800-370-2515. www.esrnational.org

Labor Heritage Foundation
Videos, books and music on labor history and contemporary labor issues. 815 16th St., NW Suite 301, Washington, DC 20006.

National Women's History Project
History, literature, posters and videos on women for grades K-12. 7738 Bell Road, Windsor, CA 95492-8518, 707-838-6000, nwhp@aol.com, www.nwhp.org

Multicultural Media
Videos and CD's of music from around the world with an emphasis on the music of the people. RR3 Box 6655 Grainger Rd, Barre, VT, 05641, 802-223-1294.

Red Sea Press
Books on Africa by many publishers including Africa World Press. 11-D Princess Road, Lawrenceville, NJ 08648, 800-789-1898. www.africanworld.com

Resource Center of the Americas
Classroom resources on Central and South America, including a strong selection of works on the experience of immigrants. 317 Seventeenth Ave. SE, Minneapolis, MN 55414, 612-276-0788. www.americas.org

Resources for Social Change
Books on fundraising, community organizing, fighting the right, and public policy. Applied Research Center and Chardon Press, 3781 Broadway, Oakland, CA 94611, 888-458-8588. www.chardonpress.com

Rethinking Schools
Excellent publications on teaching and school reform. 1001 E. Keefe, Milwaukee, WI 53212, 800-669-4192, www.rethinkingschools.org

School Improvement Catalog
Resources for parents, school staff and the community from the Center for Law and Education on school reform. Lots of practical guides. 1875 Connecticut Avenue NW, #510, Washington, DC 20009, 202-986-3000 www.cleweb.org

Smithsonian Folkways: A World of Sound
Recordings from throughout North America and the world. Visit the website for video clips, sound bites and detailed information. 955 L'Enfant Plaza, Suite 7300, Wash., DC 20560, 202-357-2700, folkways@aol.com, www.si.edu/folkways

Teachers & Writers
Books on the teaching of writing by creative teachers and writers. 5 Union Square West, New York, NY 10003-3306, 888-BOOKS-TW, www.twc.org

Teaching for Change
The best collection of resources for school reform from a multicultural, anti-racist perspective. NECA, PO Box 73038, Washington, DC 20056, 800-763-9131, NECADC@aol.com, www.teachingforchange.org

WEEA — Women's Educational Equity Act
Large collection of resources for schools to promote gender equity in education. 55 Chapel Street C97, Newton, MA 02458, 800-225-3088, www.edc.org/WomensEquity

CD ROMs

American Journey: History in Your Hands
A five-disc series with the following titles: The African American Experience, The Asian American Experience, The Hispanic-American Experience, The Immigrant Experience and Women in America. Each disk has a wealth of primary source photos, illustrations and text documents. Produced by Primary Source Media. 12 Lunar Drive, Woodbridge, CT 06525. 800-444-0799.

Who Built America: From the Centennial Celebration of 1876 to the Great War of 1914.
Hundreds of adventures take students behind the printed page and back in time into the lives of the ordinary women and men who built this country. History comes to life with photos, oral history interviews, music, speeches, poetry, charts, graphs, and even many of the earliest moving pictures ever recorded. American Social History Project. Windows and MAC versions available. ✉ $50.

JOURNALS

The following are just a few of the journals which provide a perspective and facts often absent from the mainstream press. The journals are listed by theme, although many address multiple topics.

AFRICA

African Link: The Magazine of African Roots.
African Link is a quarterly magazine that analyzes issues on Africa. It covers political, economic, cultural & social issues. $14/yr. PO Box 5132, NY, NY 10185-0056.

DOMESTIC AND INTERNATIONAL NEWS

Dollars and Sense.
The economics magazine for non-economists. De-mystifies economics and provides a left analysis of a variety of trends including free trade, unemployment, school funding, the deficit, consumer debt, taxes, the environment, the decline of US manufacturing and much more. Ideal for students. Bimonthly. $18.95/yr. ind., $42/yr. inst. 1 Summer Street, Sommerville, MA 02143, 617-628-8411, www.igc.apc.org/dollars/

The Nation.
Published since 1865, *The Nation* provides consistent, up-to-date news, analysis and book/film reviews.

Weekly. $48/yr. 72 Fifth Avenue, 5th floor, New York, NY 10011, 212-242-8400, natad@aol.com.

New Internationalist.

Each month the magazine focuses on a specific issue from a global perspective, such as hunger, the arms trade, the drug wars, multinational corporations and others. Monthly. $34 per year. 1011 Bloor Street West, Suite 300, Toronto, ON Canada, M6H 1M1. Sample issue on request.

Z Magazine.

Reports and articles on domestic and US policy. Often features articles by authors such as bell hooks and Noam Chomsky. Monthly. $26/yr. 18 Millfield St., Woods Hole, MA 02543, 508-548-9063, lydia.sargent@lbbs.org

EDUCATION

Action for Better Schools.

Reports on actions by parents and teachers to reform schools with an emphasis on social justice. Quarterly publication for National Coalition of Education Activists members. For brochure, write to NCEA, PO Box 679, Rhinebeck, NY 12572, 914-876-4580, RFBS@aol.com

Fairtest Examiner.

Reports and critiques on K-12, university admissions and employment testing practices and alternatives. Quarterly. $30/yr. ind, $45/inst. 342 Broadway, Cambridge, MA 02139, 617-864-4810, fairtest@aol.com, www.fairtest.org

Journal of Negro Education

Published since 1932, the journal presents articles with current research and analysis about policies and practices impacting the education of African Americans. Quarterly. $16/yr. ind, $28/yr. inst. P.O. Box 311, Howard University, Washington, DC 20059, 202-806-8120.

Multicultural Education.

Journal on multicultural education. Quarterly. $40/yr. ind., $60/yr. inst. Caddo Gap Press, 3145 Geary Blvd., San Francisco, CA 94118, 415-392-1911, caddogap@aol.com

NOT FOR SALE!

Published by the Center for Commercial Free Education, this newsletter provides information about the work of teacher, parent and student activists across the country. Contact for subscription information and a list of publications such as Not for Sale: Student Action Guide. 1714 Franklin St. #100-306, Oakland, CA 94612, 800-UNPLUG-1, unplug@igc.org

Our Schools/Our Selves: A Magazine for Canadian Education Activists.

Many of the articles are of interest to teachers in the US too. Addresses all aspects of schooling including multicultural education, tracking, vocational education, school funding, etc. Bimonthly. $46/yr ind, $60/yr inst. (Canadian) 107 Earl Grey Road, PO Box 25215 Stn Brm B, Toronto, Ontario, M7Y 4M1.

Radical Teacher: a socialist and feminist journal on the theory and practice of teaching.

Each issue offers thought-provoking analytical essays, literature, classroom exercises, and a resource guide by school teachers and university professors. Special issues dedicated to Working-Class Studies, Lesbian/Gay/Queer Studies, and Disabilities Studies. Tri-annual. $14/yr. PO Box 383316, Harvard Square Station, Cambridge,MA 02238.

Rethinking Schools.

Every educator should subscribe to Rethinking Schools for up-to-date reports and analysis on all aspects of school reform including school funding, unions, curriculum, parental involvement, anti-racist education and more. Also features teaching ideas and resources. Quarterly. $12.50/yr. 1001 E. Keefe Ave., Milwaukee, WI 53212, 800-669-4192, RSBusiness@aol.com, www.rethinkingschools.org

ENVIRONMENT

Green Teacher.

Environmental, international development and human rights education. Each issue carries ideas for rethinking education, practical teaching suggestions and ready-to-use activities, and evaluations of dozens of new teaching resources. Quarterly. $27/yr. PO Box 1431, Lewiston, NY 14092, 416-960-1244, greentea@ web.net

Panoscope.

Articles on sustainable development from around the world. 6/year. $18/yr ind., $30/yr inst. Panos Institute, 1701 K Street NW, 11th Floor, Washington, D.C 20006. 202-223-7949, PANOS@CAIS.com.

INDIGENOUS PEOPLES/NATIVE AMERICANS

Akwesasne Notes: A Journal of Native and Natural Peoples.

The voice of indigenous peoples of the Americas. Each issue addresses the issues and concerns of Native people today. Guest essays by Native Elders and others provoke thought on such topics as the environment, land claims, sovereignty, gaming, and spirituality. Regular departments include: art; poetry; book, music art and video reviews; news from the confederacy; and Native history. Quarterly. $25/yr. Mohawk Nation, P.O. Box 196, via Rooseveltown, NY 13683-0196. 518-358-9531, fax: 613-575-2935, notes@glen-net.ca

Cultural Survival Quarterly.

Themes of past issues include: Land and Resources: The Issue of Compensation, Central America, Tourism, The Soviet Union and Eastern Europe and more. Designed to inform and to stimulate action on behalf of indigenous peoples and ethnic minorities. Quarterly. $25/yr. 96 Mount Auburn St., Cambridge, MA 02138.

Indigenous Woman

Indigenous Women's Network (IWN) is a network of indigenous women in the Americas and the Pacific. Their goal is to "work within the framework of the vision of our elders" to rebuild families, communities, and nations. The purpose of the Network is "to increase the visibility of Native women and empower them to participate in political, social and cultural processes while working toward the betterment of ourselves as Native women and improving the conditions within our communities." P. O. Box 2967, Rapid City, SD 57709-2967.

LATIN AMERICA AND THE CARIBBEAN

Centro: Journal of the Center for Puerto Rican Studies.

Themes of past issues include: Youth and Youth Culture, History and Politics, Latinos and the Media, Impact of the AIDS Epidemic and more. Semiannual. $15/yr ind, $30/yr inst. Hunter College, 695 Park Ave, Box 548, New York, NY 10021, 212-772-5688.

The Connection

Monthly digest of important news from Latin America and the Caribbean with a focus on Central America. $40/yr ind., $60/inst. Resource Center on the Americas, 317 17th Ave SE, Minneapolis, MN 55414-2077, 612-627-9445, rctamn@tc.umn.edu

NACLA Report on the Americas (North American Congress on Latin America).

Well-researched articles on Latin American and Caribbean politics and economy. Well worth getting the list of back issues as a reference for student research. Bimonthly. $27/yr ind, $47/yr inst. 475 Riverside Drive, Suite 454, NY, NY 10115, 212-870-3146, www.nacla.org

MEDIA BIAS

Adbusters: Journal of the Mental Environment

Strategies on how to "take on the archetypal mind polluters — Marlboro, Absolut, McDonalds, Calvin Klein, Nissan, Time-Warner, Disney — and beat them at their own game. Wonderful examples of ads designed to expose the reality behind commercial ads. 1243 W 7th Avenue, Vancouver, B.C. Canada, V6H 1B77, www.adbusters.org.

Extra!

Well-documented critique of media bias on current issues in the major print and television news. Provides a model for students on how to develop their own critiques of local press. Bi-monthly. $19/yr ind. Fairness and Accuracy in Reporting (FAIR), PO Box 170, Congers, NY 10920-9930, 800-847-3993, www.fair.org

MIDDLE EAST

Middle East Report (MERIP).

In-depth reporting on the Middle East and US policy. Also, cultural coverage, outstanding photographs and the best work of Middle Eastern artists and cartoonists. Bimonthly. $32/yr. Blackwell Publishers, 350 Main Street, Maiden, MA 02148, 800-835-6770.

ORGANIZING

Boycott Quarterly.

Comprehensive list of current boycotts throughout the world. In-depth reports on feature boycotts, related topics and other economic democracy topics in every issue. $22/yr ind. Center for Economic Democracy, PO Box 30727, Seattle, WA 98103-0727, BoycottGuy@aol.com.

Third Force: Issues and Actions in Communities of Color.

News and political analysis for grassroots activists in national and international communities of color. $22/yr. Center for Third World Organizing, 1218 East 21st St, Oakland, CA 94606.

RACE

Poverty and Race (Bimonthly)

Bimonthly articles and extensive resource listings from the Poverty and Race Research Action Council. $25/yr. 1711 Connecticut Avenue, NW #207, Washington, DC 20009, prrac@aol.com.

Race and Class.

Scholarly articles on global issues of race and class. $32/yr ind. Institute of Race Relations, US Mailing Agent, Mercury Airfreight International Ltd., 2323 Randolph Avenue, Avenel, NJ 07001.

RaceFile.

A critical assessment of reporting on racial issues in the established and community press. Extensive news clippings. $48/yr ind. Applied Research Center, 25 Embarcadero Cove, Oakland, CA 94606.

RESOURCE REVIEWS

MultiCultural Review.

A resource for educators who are interested in culturally diverse teaching materials and outlooks. Focus on reviews of new publications, with useful review and press indexes in the back. Quarterly. $59/yr. 88 Post Road West, PO Box 5007, Westport, CT 06881-5007, 203-226-3571.

Worldviews: A Quarterly Review of Resources For Education and Action.

Invaluable reviews of new print and audiovisual resources (including CD Roms). Each issue reviews new publications and provides a detailed resource list on a particular theme or region. Quarterly. U.S. and Canada: $25/yr ind, $50/yr inst. Outside U.S. and Canada: $45/yr. ind. , $65/yr inst. 1515 Webster St., Oakland, CA 94612, 510-451-1742, www.igc.org/worldviews/

YOUTH

Skipping Stones: A Multicultural Children's Magazine.

Award-winning, nonprofit magazine for multicultural and global awareness. Celebrates diversity by publishing folktales, original writings (sometimes, multilingual), art and photos by youth and adults. Recent themes: Challenging Disability; African, Native, and Latin American Cultures, World Religions and Celebrations; Changing Families. 36 pages. Bimonthly, $25/yr ind. $35/yr inst. Low-income discount. PO Box 3939, Eugene, OR 97403-0939, 541-342-4956, skipping@efn.org

POSTERS

The Alternative Alphabet Poster for Little and Big People

Tired of the white queen symbolizing Q and the white king representing K? This beautifully-illustrated poster introduces values of equity into one of U.S. cultures basic learning tools the alphabet poster. This clear approach incudes an image and a number of different reading-level words for each letter which can prompt inquiries and start conversations. For example, A includes: Africa, Anne Frank, apple, abolitionist and antelope. Students can develop their own alphabet poster with words from their studies and their lives, using this one as a model. Design by Karen Kerny and Melinda Matzell. Syracuse Cultural Workers. 1998 24 x 36, laminated ✉$18

Gays in History by Laurie Casagrande

Features James Baldwin, Willa Cather, Errol Flynn, Michelangelo, Edna St. Vincent Millay, Cole Porter, Eleanor Roosevelt, Bessie Smith, Walt Whitman, and Virginia Woolf. 30" X 25" ✉$10.

How Big is Africa?

This full color 17 x 22 poster shows how the continent of Europe, the United States and China combined do not cover all of Africa when their maps are superimposed. Produced by the Boston University African Studies Center Outreach Program. ✉$12

Indigenous Heroes

Images of indigenous people who have worked for social justice including: Rigoberta Menchu, Leonard Peltier, Anna Mae Aquash, Chico Mendes and more. OYATE, 1996. 18" x 24" ✉ $10.

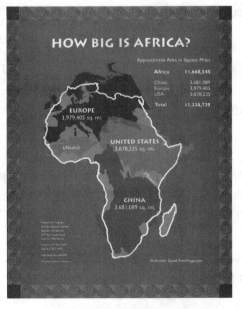

Peters' Projection World Map

New projection shows continents according to their relative size. Traditional maps make lands near the equator look smaller than they really are -- for example, South America appears smaller than Europe, when it is really more than twice Europe's size. Friendship Press. 35" x 50" folded. ✉ $11.

Women of Hope: African Americans Who Made A Difference

Full color posters of African American women who have had a profound impact on American life: Maya Angelou, Ella J. Baker, Alexa Canady, Septima P. Clark, Ruby Dee, the Delany Sisters, Marian Wright Edelman, Fannie Lou Hamer, Mae C. Jemison, Toni Morrison, Alice Walker, and Ida B. Wells. Includes 48-page study guide produced by NECA. Posters shipped flat. Bread & Roses, 1993. Twelve 17" x 22" posters.✉ $60.

Women of Hope: Asian American

Full color posters and study guide of Asian American women who were chosen by scholars and community leaders for their inspirational qualities and strength. Includes: Maya Lin, Angela Eunjin Oh, Ngoan Le, Sumi Sevilla Haru, Shamita Das Dasgupta and more. Twelve 18" x 24" posters. ✉ $60.

Women of Hope: Latinas Abriendo Camino

Color posters plus a 64-page study guide with biographies in English and Spanish, lessons and resource guide. Includes: Julia Alvarez, Sandra Cisneros, Miriam Colon, Dolores Huerta, Amalia Mesa-Bains, Nydia Velasquez and more. Bread & Roses Cultural Project, 1995. Twelve 18" x 24" posters. ✉ $60

Women of Hope: Native American/Hawaiian

Full color posters plus a 48-page study guide with biographies, lessons and resource guide. Features Joy Harjo, Winona LaDuke, Wilma Mankiller, and more. Addresses issues of sovereignty, land rights, language, the environment, dance, music, discrimination, stereotypes, and resistance. Bread & Roses Cultural Project, 1997. Twelve 18" x 24" posters and study guide. ✉$60

TAPES

Other Colors: Stories of Women Immigrants

Interviews with women immigrants to the Boston area from Central/South America, the Caribbean, Cape Verde, Eastern Europe, the former Soviet Union, China, Southeast Asia, the Middle East and Europe. Audiotapes and teacher's guide are designed for high school and adult education. PO Box 4190, Albuquerque, NM 87196, 505-265-3405.

VIDEOS

Included here are titles for staff development and/or classroom use. In all cases the videos should be screened first by the instructor/facilitator to determine the appropriateness for your particular audience. The historic videos (such as *Battle of Algiers*, *Hearts and Minds*, *Zoot Suit*) are often too long for a school class period, so sections can be selected.

The producers and/or distributors are listed below for many of the videos. Some offer a special discount to educators. Note that prices are subject to change and do not include shipping costs. Contact each of these organizations for current ordering information and for catalogs with more excellent videos.

If the video can be found in video stores, we have simply indicated at the end of the listing, "video stores."

California Newsreel, 149 Ninth St. Rm. 420, San Francisco, CA 94103, (415) 621-6196, www.newsreel.org (With these videos, the $69.95 price is for requests on K-12 school letterhead or purchase orders only, all other orders are $195.)

Maryknoll World Productions, PO Box 308, Maryknoll, NY 10545-0308, (800) 227-8523, www.maryknoll.org

NAATA, National Asian American Telecommunications Association, 346 Ninth St., 2nd Floor, San Francisco, CA 94103, (415) 552-9550, distribution@naatanet.org, www.naatanet.org/distrib (With these videos, the first price listed is the regular price. The second price, following the "/" is for K-12 schools. These orders must be on school letterhead or with a school purchase order.)

New Day Films, 22-D Hollywood Ave., Hohokus, NJ 07423, 888-367-9154.

Southwest Organizing Project, 211 10th

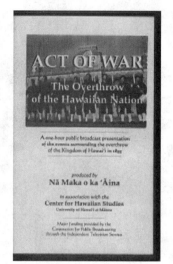

St. SW, Albuquerque, NM 87102, (505) 247-8832.

Stir Fry Productions, 470 Third St., Oakland, CA 94607, (510) 419-3930.

Third World Newsreel, 335 W. 38th St., 5th Floor, New York, NY 10018.

Act of War: The Overthrow of the Hawai'ian Nation by Puhipau & Joan Lander

This looks at the events surrounding the overthrow of the Hawai'ian monarchy in 1893 from the point of view of the Native Hawai'ians. It chronicles the conquest and colonization of the Pacific Island nation by Christian missionaries and capitalists suing archival photographs, government documents, political cartoons, and dramatic reenactments. 60 minutes. NAATA. Sale: $165/$75.

The Ad and the Ego by Harold Boihem & Chris Emmanouilides

The first comprehensive examination of advertising and the culture of consumption in the United States. The film intercuts clips from hundreds of familiar television ads with insights from media critics. As the film progresses, it shows how ads for Nike, Calvin Klein, Oil of Olay, and Suzuki are selling not only products but also values, concepts of love and sexuality, romance and success, a sense of identity, and above all, what is "normal," all of which racialized and gendered. It also analyzes the "selling" of political beliefs to demonstrate how citizenship has increasingly been replaced by spectatorship, civil society by consumer culture. 57 minutes. Free Discussion Guide. California Newsreel. ✉ $70

a.k.a. Don Bonus by Spencer Nakasako, Sokly Ny, NAATA

Emmy award winning video diary of 18-year-old Sokly Ny, Cambodian refugee living in San Francisco. This video documents the struggle of Sokly to graduate from high school as his family is being harassed in the housing project where they live and his brothers are facing difficulties of their own. Sokly shares his experiences, personal feelings, and hopes. Emmy Award winner. 55 minutes. Study guide included. NAATA, 346 Ninth St., Second Floor, San Francisco, CA 94103. Sale: $265/$85.

All Eyes on Africa by Clem Marshall

A documentary modern and ancient art and culture in Africa. 60 minutes. 1993. (416-862-2879)

Ballad of Gregorio Cortez by Robert M. Young

Compelling, at times poetic, this drama features Edward James Olmos as a young Mexican man who, in 1901, kills a sheriff in self-defense and must elude the Texas Rangers. Based on a true story which captured the imagination of the populace, with Cortez becoming a Mexican-American folk hero. 1983. 99 minutes. Video stores.

Banking on Life and Debt by Maryknoll World Productions

Over 90% of the earth's population — primarily people of color — are impacted by World Bank and IMF policies. Critics have called the policies of the World Bank and the International Monetary Fund (IMF) a "war on the poor." Viewers see the results of World Bank and International Monetary Fund (IMF) policies on the people of Ghana, Brazil and the Philippines. Narrated by Martin Sheen. 1995. 28 minutes. Maryknoll World Productions. ⊠ $20

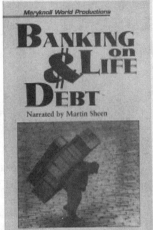

Battle of Algiers by Gillo Pontecorvo

Crisp compelling drama about the guerilla revolt against the French, waged by Algerians starting in 1954. Shot on location with a mixture of actors and real-life participants in the conflict. Provides viewers a picture of colonialism in Algeria and resistance. 1965. 122 minutes. Video stores.

Benaat Chicago: Growing Up Arab and Female in Chicago

Created by Arab American teenage women, this video addresses stereotypes, sexism and racism towards Arabs, while showing what makes many Arab Americans proud of their heritage. Interviews with young women and community leaders mixed with images from the community document the lives of Arab Americans growing up on Chicago's southwest side and show a complex picture of this rarely seen community. 30 minutes. AFSC (312-427-2533). $20.

Black Is...Black Ain't by Marlon Riggs, Nicole Atkinson, Christiane Badgley

The final film by Emmy and Peabody Award winning filmmaker Marlon Riggs tackles the explosive debates over Black identity. White Americans have always stereotyped African Americans. But the rigid definitions of "Blackness" which African Americans impose on each other, Riggs claims, have also been devastating. The video explores two central questions: Is there an essential Black identity? Is there a litmus test defining the "real" Black man and woman? Riggs mixes interviews with young and old, well-to-do and poor, urban and rural, gay and straight Black people, choreographed performance segments, and commentary by cultural critics such as Angela Davis, Cornell West, Maulana Karenga, and Barbara Smith. 87 minutes. Free discussion guide. California Newsreel. Sale: $195/$69.95.

Blue Eyed by Claus Strigel & Bertram Verhagg

Jane Elliott leads a group of 40 teachers, police, school administrators and social workers in Kansas City — Blacks, Latinos, Whites, women, and men. The blue-eyed members are subjected to pseudo-scientific explanations of their inferiority, culturally biased IQ tests and blatant discrimination. In just a few hours under Elliott's withering regime, grown professionals become despondent and distracted, stumbling over the simplest commands. This video includes a reflection by Elliott upon how the simple classroom exercise she devised for her rural Iowa elementary school children the day after Dr. Martin Luther King Jr's assassination has transformed her life. 93 minutes. Free discussion guide. California Newsreel. Sale: $195/$69.95.

Children of the Earth Series by Maryknoll World Productions

Two tapes show the customs and daily lives of children growing up in different parts of the world. In *Asia Close-Up* we are introduced to Satomi, a 13 year-old girl growing up in Kyoto, Japan, and Sok Thea, a 13 year-old boy in Cambodia who lost his in a landmine explosion. *Africa Close-Up* follows the lives of Samah, 15, growing up in Cairo, struggling between being a modern teenager in an ancient land (she takes viewers on a tour of the Nile River and the Pyramids) and Bernard, 15, who lives in rural Tanzania. Each tape is 28 minutes. Maryknoll World Productions. Sale: $16.95 each.

Earth and the American Dream by Bill Couturie

This extraordinary film examines U.S. history from the standpoint of the earth. Beginning with Columbus, it effectively blends contrasting quotes from Native American and European "settlers" with images of the environmental consequences of these ideas. *"I've never seen a film that does this so powerfully. A vital classroom resource."* Bill Bigelow, teacher and author. 1993. 77 minutes. Direct Cinema Limited. ⊠ $95

El Norte

Tells the story of a brother and sister forced to flee their home country of Guatemala where their father has dared to challenge the repressive landowners. Provides insights into the challenges faced by many Central American immigrants as they travel north and try to survive in the United States. 140 minutes. Video stores.

Ethnic Notions by Marlon Riggs

This classic documentary traces the evolution of deeply rooted stereotypes about African American women and men that have fueled anti-Black prejudice and hatred. The history of the development of the major figures — faithful Mammy, loyal Toms, carefree Sambo, male-dominating Sapphire, leering Coon, and wide-eyed Pickaninny — that have permeated U.S. popular culture from the antebellum period to the Civil Rights era is presented, with a sharp economic and political analysis and commentary about the far reaching consequences of such stereotyping. 56 minutes. California Newsreel. Sale: $49.95.

Eyes on the Prize

Six one-hour programs chronicling the emergence of the Civil Rights Movement from 1954-65. Showing even just the first episode gives a group a common historical reference point with which to begin a discussion of contemporary manifestations of racism. PBS. Video stores.

The Global Assembly Line by Lorraine Gray, Maria Patricia Fernandez Kelly, & Anne Bohlen

Inside look at the lives and working conditions of women and men employed in the "free trade zones" of North America and Asia, as U.S. companies close their factories searching the globe for a cheaper labor force. Provides a close-up of the people who make the clothes worn and electronic goods used in the U.S. 32 and 58 minute versions. New Day Films. Sale: $295/375 Rent: $65/75.

Hearts and Minds by Peter Davis

Academy Award winning, controversial documentary on the war in Vietnam, made while the War was still in progress. "...an agonizing appraisal of U.S. involvement in Vietnam, and a must for every thinking American. The urgency and power of its message hits where it hurts, and its logic and fairness are impressive." Norma McLain Stoop, After Dark. 1974. 112 minutes. Video stores.

Holding Ground: The Rebirth of Dudley Street by Mark Lipman & Leah Mahan

The video documents how a multiracial/multicultural grassroots organizing work transformed a poor, blighted Boston neighborhood into a vibrant, revitalized community. Through the voices of community residents, activists, and city officials, this moving documentary shows how the Dudley Street neighborhood was able to create and carry out its own agenda for change. 58 minutes. New Day Films. Sale: $150 Rent: $50.

Incident at Oglala by Michael Apted

Documentary of the events at the Oglala Reservation which led to the shooting of two FBI agents and the imprisonment of Native American activist Leonard Peltier. People on all sides of the issue are interviewed, allowing students to draw their own conclusion as to who was responsible. This video

serves not only as a documentary on the Peltier case, but also provides a rare picture of conditions on Native American reservations today. Narrated by Robert Redford. 1991. 89 minutes. Video stores.

Introduction to the End of an Argument (Intifada): Speaking for Oneself.../Speaking for Others by Elia Suleiman & Jayce Salloum

The filmmakers critique western-based representations of Arab culture using news sound-bytes, move clips, and documentary footages shot in the West Bank and the Gaza Strip. An evocative mix of fragmented stereotypes from mainstream movies to prime-time news. 45 minutes. Third World Newsreel. Sale: $225 Rent: $75.

It's Elementary: Talking about Gay Issues in School by Debra Chasnoff & Helen Cohen

This video examines why and how gay issues should be discussed in schools. Taking the viewpoint of elementary and middle school children, the video shows how their teachers are finding creative ways to confront anti-gay prejudice and gay invisibility. 37 minutes. New Day Films. 1997. ✉ $75 (For a longer version of the film contact New Day Films. The $75 price is limited to K-12 schools, non-profit organizations and individuals. All other institutions should contact *New Days Films.*)

The Killing Floor

Two African American men immigrate from the country to Chicago during World War I and work in a packing house. The film deals forthrightly with the racism in the workplace and the union. An excellent resource for looking at the impact of racism on U.S. labor history. 118 minutes. Video stores.

Many Voices

Nine 15 minute docudramas for grades 4-6 explore stereotyping, discrimination and racism from a child's point of view. Each open-ended program focuses on a child who is trying to come to terms with his or her background. Stories deal with language, religion, dress and ethnic and racial stereotyping. Each program leaves viewers with the child's dilemma unresolved, opening the door to classroom discussion. Accompanied by 41 page teacher's guide. 1991. TV Ontario. AGC Educational Media: 800-323-9084.

Matewan

John Sayles' feature film about a post World-War I strike in a West Virginia mining town. Mine owners bring in Black workers in an attempt to break the strike of primarily Italian immigrants and White Appalachians workers. Another excellent resource for examining how racism has had an impact on the labor movement for workers of all races. 1987. 130 minutes. Video stores.

A Matter of Respect by Ellen Frankenstein & Sharon Gmelch

This documentary discusses the meaning of tradition and change among Alaska Native peoples. Shows a range of people, from elders to youth, attempting to reconcile the traditional cultures with demands of modern life. 30 minutes. New Day Films. Sale: $150 Rent: $55.

Miles from the Border by Ellen Frankenstein

The true story of the Aparicio family who emigrated from a rural village in Mexico to a racially divided community in California. This video describes the tensions and conflicts about immigrant identity and the pressures to succeed in conventional terms. 15 minutes. New Day Films. Sale: $175 Rent: $40.

My Brown Eyes by Jay Koh

A 10-year-old Korean immigrant boy rises early and prepares for his first day of the school year. Since his immigrant parents work late into the night, he makes their breakfast and his own school lunch. Once he arrives at school, we see him become withdrawn and later get into a fight. The video provides a forum for examining the conditions in school which can serve to silence and alienate students. For grades 6-12 and staff development on issues of language and culture. 18 minutes. NAATA. ⊠ $50

Not in Our Town

The story of the people of Billings, Montana who stood up against attacks on Native Americans, African Americans and Jews by White supremacists in the early 1990s. 30 minutes. We Do the Work (510-547-8484). Sale: $89.

Off the Track: Classroom Privilege for All.

This video takes the viewer into a World Literatures classroom, where all the students in the room -- lower income, middle class, and affluent; White, Black, Asian-American and Latino; girls and boys; those automatically "advanced" and those who have been labeled in need of "special education" -- receive and produce high quality education. Ideal for staff development. 30 minutes. Teachers College Press. 1998 ⊠ $50.

Michelle Fine
Bernadette Anand
Markie Hancock
Carlton Jordan
Dana Sherman

OFF TRACK

Classroom Privilege For All

NAATA DISTRIBUTION
presents

MY BROWN EYES

Directed and Produced by
Jay Koh

"No American film is more inspiring and emotionally satisfying than this remarkable 1954 film."
—Danny Peary
Cult Movies II

THE ONLY U.S. BLACKLISTED FILM

SALT OF THE EARTH

A Question of Color by Kathe Sandler, St. Clair Bourne, & Luke Harris

This film examines the complex interplay among racial identity, culture, and self-image of African Americans in society and within themselves. It traces "colorism" — social hierarchy based on skin color — back to the sexual subjugation of Black women by slave owners and the preferential treatment their mixed-race children sometimes received. 56 minutes. California Newsreel. Sale: $195/$69.95.

Race Against Prime Time by David Shulman

The film scrutinizes how television news represents African Americans. This documentary takes viewers behind the scenes at the newsrooms of the three national network affiliates during the Liberty City uprising in Miami in the late 1980s which left 18 people dead. Provides a case study of how news gets made: what is seen and what is not. 58 minutes. California Newsreel. Sale: $195/$69.95.

Salt of the Earth by Herbert Biberman

Social drama detailing the struggle for equality of Mexican American miners and their wives. The men must fight for the rights enjoyed by their White co-workers, the women for equality with the men. Based on an actual strike in Silver City, New Mexico in 1951-52. Most of the roles played by strikers and their families. The film was financed by a miner's union. Many of the film professionals involved with the direction, writing and acting were prevented from working in Hollywood at the time due to the McCarthy hearing accusations against them. 94 minutes. 1954. Video stores.

Sankofa by Haile Gerima

The story of an African American woman who travels back in time to her capture in Africa and slavery in the United States. The title, from the Akan word, means "one must return to the past in order to move forward." One of the most powerful films ever made on the experience of slavery from through African and African American eyes. 125 minutes. Mypheduh Films. (800-524-3895)

School of Assassins by Maryknoll World Productions

This documentary exposes the United States Army School of the Americas, a facility paid for with U.S. money that has been responsible for training some of the worst human rights violators in the hemisphere, including former dictators of Argentina, Bolivia, Honduras and Panama. Details the efforts of activists to close the school. Narrated by Susan Sarandon. Study Guide. 18 minutes. Maryknoll World Productions. $15.

Skin Deep by Frances Reid

The filmmaker follows a multiracial group of students from the University of Massachusetts, Texas A&M, Chico State, and U.C. Berkeley to a challenging racial awareness workshop where they confront each other's innermost feelings about race and ethnicity. She also accompanies them back to their campuses and on visits home in an attempt to understand why they think the way they do. Issues of self-segregation on campus, feelings of hurt and discrimination, conflicts over affirmative action, and students' personal responsibility for making a difference all enter the interracial dialogue. 53 minutes. California Newsreel. Sale: $195/$69.95.

Slaying the Dragon by Deborah Gee & Asian Women United

This documentary chronicles Hollywood's one-dimensional, recycled depictions of Asian/Asian American women through film clips and interviews with media critics and Asian American actresses. The video shows the social and psychological impact of the stereotypes of the evil Dragon Lady, the seductive Suzy Wong, and the subservient Geisha Girl on Asian women. 60 minutes. NAATA. Sale: $225/$75.

The Story of Vinh by Keiko Tsuno

Story of Vinh Dinh, the son of a U.S. serviceman and Vietnamese mother who immigrates to the United States with all the hopes of fulfilling the American Dream. The film dispels the myth of the American Dream and follows Vinh on his journey from Vietnamese to American culture, from youth to manhood and from false dreams to harsh reality. 60 minutes. NAATA. Sale: $250/$75.

Tell Them Who We Are by Alexandria Levitt

An inspiring film that follows the Laquieniean Drill Team and Drum Squad of South Central LA through one competitive season, showing their hopes and dreams, failures and successes. The teenage members,

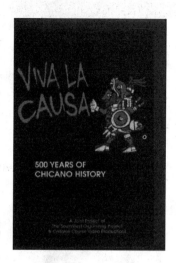

500 YEARS OF CHICANO HISTORY

their parents, and the 70-year-old founder teach about love, hope, self-esteem, and success in a tough urban environment. 29 minutes. New Day Films. Sale: $199 Rent: $60.

True Colors by ABC (20/20)

Two men, equal in all measurable aspects except that one is Black and the other is White, explore the reactions to each in a variety of situations. The hidden camera demonstrates the racism which people of color face on many fronts, as the two men try to rent an apartment, buy a car, apply for job, and shop in a store. Ideal for use in staff development settings where participants think that racism is "a thing of the past." 1989. 19 minutes.

Viva La Causa by Elizabeth Martinez & Doug Norberg

Archival footage, narrators, lively music ranging from *corridos* to rap, and photos create a compelling introduction to Mexican American history for grades 5-12 and higher education. Based on the popular book *500 Years of Chicano History in Pictures*. Fills a major gap in United States history. Available in English or Spanish. 60 minutes. Southwest Organizing Project. ✉ $35.

Young Aspirations/Young Artists (YA/YA!) by Shirley Thompson

Portrayal of youth in inner-city New Orleans who use art as a means of personal expression, vehicle for international travel, and forum for racial understanding. Shows the development of this art project that grew out of a small after-school art class. 35 and 57 minutes. Study Guide available. New Day Films. Sale $225 and 295 Rent: $75 and 85 respectively.

Zoot Suit by Luis Valdez

This musical chronicles the life of Henry Reyna, leader of a group of Mexican Americans who are set to do time in San Quentin for their part in the zoot suit riots in 1942 Los Angeles. 1981. 104 minutes. Video stores.

Visit www.teachingforchange.org for information about new videos and for links to numerous producers and distributors of progressive videos.

A Selected Annotated Listing of Internet Resources: "Information Connection" and "People Connection" Tools

by Dennis Sayers, Ed.D.,
Kristin Brown, Ed.D., Jim Cummins, Ph.D.,
Enid Figueroa, Ph.D.

Access to the Internet: Getting Connected

Any personal computer can connect to the Internet. Beyond having a computer, there are three requirements that a parent, teacher or student will need to attend to:

1. A word processor to assist in composing and revising long e-mail messages.

2. A way to connect to the Internet: In the small percentage of schools where classrooms are "wired" directly into the Internet, the school district has provided for this requirement. In most cases, however, "connecting" means:

   a. having a modem and cable that connects your computer to a phone line. Modems come in various speeds, although 28.8K bits (letters) per second (bps) is considered the standard by many, and faster connections are always preferable when you wish to access graphics-rich information on the Internet's World Wide Web. Consumers should see the cost of cable modems coming down in the next few years, access speeds many times faster than current modem devices; and

   b. having a telephone line. Any regular phone line will do, such as are found in most homes, although in some areas consumers can purchase costly ISDN or ASDN lines that permit more rapid transmission of information. Aside from installation costs, the only other fee for a normal connection is the monthly service charge for the regular phone line, since local calls to your Internet service provider are all that will be made on the line. For teachers, the ideal access method is to have a direct phone line installed in a teacher's room or the school's computer lab, if your school is not already wired for direct Internet access. Barring this, some teachers take computer disks to the principal's office where a modem is often located, and then send off their students' writings once a week, but this can be awkward. Often parents and teachers prefer to connect from home, since time is hard to find during the normal working or teaching day; and finally,

   c. paying for access to an Internet Service Provider. This could be a commercial on-line service such as America Online, Compuserve or Prodigy, all of which offer an array of services. Alternatively, a local ISP company may be available (look under "Computers: On-line Services & Internet" in your phone book), which offers bare bones but rapid Internet connections. (For a current listing of service providers devoted to K-12 education in the fifty United States, check the webpage maintained by NASA at http://quest.arc.nasa.gov/online/stindex.html; for remote areas, consider the listings at http://quest.arc.nasa.gov/online/options.html).

3. Software: A telecommunications software program to run your modem, dial the phone and help with "uploading" and "downloading." In addition, Internet "toolbox" programs that can be installed on your hard drive are extremely helpful. These include programs like Eudora (an "electronic mail reader" that helps organize and manage your e-mail) and Netscape's Navigator or Microsoft's Explorer ("information browsers" that help you locate information resources on the Internet). These programs are free to educators and are available through software companies or your Internet Service Provider.

It is possible to use any brand of personal computer, no matter how humbly equipped, to connect to the Internet. However, of course broader possibilities open up for connecting to global learning networks with a setup that includes a high-capacity hard disk, as much random access memory (RAM) as possible, a high-speed modem and a color monitor, ideally with speakers. A parent, teacher or student with such a computer setup would be in an ideal position to take advantage of the new multimedia Internet "browser" programs.

An Overview: "Information" vs. "People" Connection Tools

It is important to realize that the Internet provides access both to human resources and information resources. In other words, the Internet can connect you with new people or it can help you locate information that you need. In either case, this access takes place through the use of several main Internet communication tools. Of course, these human and information resources often are interrelated; the people you meet can help introduce you to informational resources, and often information you discover will point you to other people who share your interests. The major tool for making people connections is electronic mail, while information connections are made on websites and gophersites.

Electronic mail is based on a standard addressing system. Packets of messages are sent pony express-style over huge distances, passing through countless local computer networks on their way to be delivered at their destinations in electronic post offices around the world. We have the illusory impression of nearly instantaneous point-to-point delivery of electronic mail because each local network-to-local network transfer requires only a fraction of a second to complete. In reality, every electronic message transaction occurs locally, traversing the globe one small, yet rapid, step at a time. In similar fashion, we experience the illusion of movement every time we go to the cinema; as "motion" is conveyed through sixteen separate still images every second we are watching a film.

If electronic mail works on the principle of the pony express, then World Wide Websites and Gophersites operate much like a fire brigade. Your computer sends out buckets of commands (requests for information) from local network to local network, and other buckets of information (resources) are returned to your computer via similar routes. Again, we experience the illusion of direct, instantaneous connection with a distant network owing to the rapid local exchange of "information buckets" from network to network. We feel we are directly interacting with distant information resources housed on faraway computers.

Electronic discussion groups (e-groups) use e-mail to create a forum for people with common interests. The guiding principle behind e-groups is simple but powerful. A host computer somewhere on the Internet runs an automatic "mailing list management" program that will accept subscriptions to discussion groups on particular special interest topics, for example, "deaf education." You can subscribe to the e-group by sending a short message to the subscription address for that discussion group. From that moment on, you will be placed on the subscribers list for that e-group and will receive every message that anyone sends on deaf education to the e-group. Moreover, any message you send to the participation address of that e-group will be placed in the electronic mailbox of every other subscriber to that e-group. As a result, a discussion group is created between a broad range of people often with a wide variety of experiences yet interested in the same topic, ranging from students, parents and teachers to internationally recognized experts in a particular field.

> *Please note that the web sites listed below are subject to change. A list of these sites is available on the internet at the NECA/Teaching for Change web site:*
> **www.teachingforchange.org**
> *The sites are checked and updated periodically.*

Using an information browser like Netscape or Explorer, a parent, teacher or student can find a wealth of information by making connections either to "websites" (colorful, multimedia displays which have "hypertext" links to other webpages, sometimes called "the World Wide Web") or "gophersites" (text-only displays of written information arranged outline-style in hierarchical menus).

Gophersites and World Wide Websites can be reached by typing their correct addresses (called Uniform Resource Locators) in an information browser such as Netscape or Explorer. For example, the URL of the European Crosspoint Anti-Racism Webpage, maintained by the Netherlands International Centre for Human Rights and providing hypertext links organized by continent and country to anti-racist organizations around the world is http://www.magenta.nl/crosspoint/

Once connected to a Gopher or Web site, look for commands within your information browser program or on the screen itself which permit you to save information resources on your hard disk. Print them out or send them back to your home/school computer via electronic mail in as little as 3 seconds (but rarely more than half a minute!)

"INFORMATION CONNECTION" RESOURCES
WORLD WIDE WEBSITES (WWW) AND GOPHERSITES

Action Without Borders
www.idealist.org
A listing of links to organizations, guides and directories, and publications concerned with diversity issues in the United States.

AskERIC InfoGuides
ericir.syr.edu/Virtual/InfoGuides/
Useful InfoGuides include: American Indians and Alaska Natives, African_History, Gay and Lesbian Parents, Gender_and_Ethnic Bias in Curriculum, Holocaust Studies, Indigenous_Peoples, Mexican Americans, Migrant Education and Women's Literature.

Association For Progressive Computing (APC)
www.apc.org/index.html
APC is a global computer communications and information network serving nongovernmental organizations (NGOs) and citizen activists "working for social justice, environmental sustainability and related issues." Presently, APC is composed of 21 international member networks with the participation of 40,000 NGOs, activists, educators, policy-makers and community leaders in 133 countries.

Bilingual Education Resources on the Net
www.estrellita.com/~karenm/bil.html
Maintained by Karen Myer, author of "Estrellita Accelerated Beginning Spanish Reading," this site has a thorough listing of links to other Internet resources.

Center for the Study of White American Culture
www.euroamerican.org/
A multiracial center that examines European American Culture, with a special focus on how the prejudice of white Americans toward other ethnic and cultural groups can be confronted through anti-racist dialogue and action.

The Center For World Indigenous Studies' Fourth World Documentation Project
www.halcyon.com/FWDP/fwdp.html
This project provides access to documentation on the "social, political, strategic, economic and human rights situations being faced by Fourth World nations [indigenous peoples]." See especially "Other Indigenous

Resources," a remarkable page of links to 250 websites with information on native peoples of Africa, the Arctic/Circumpolar Regions, Asia and the Middle East, Europe, North America (Canada, Mexico, the Caribbean, and the United States), and Melanesia, Polynesia and Micronesia, including Australia.

Chicano/Latino Net

latino.sscnet.ucla.edu/

Maintained jointly by the Chicano Studies Research Center at UCLA and the Linguistic Minority Research Institute at the University of California at Santa Barbara, this webpage "brings together Chicano/Latino research as well as linguistic minority and educational research efforts being carried out at the University of California."

Community Learning Network

www.cln.org

gopher://gopher.etc.bc.ca

The British Columbia Ministry of Education present a large collection of links to networked resources, ranging from language guides to regional archives on culture, language and religion. The separate webpage titled "Curricular Resources in Aboriginal Studies" is especially notable, with links to information on Canada's First Nations (the Canadian term for the indigenous peoples of Kanata) as well as native peoples around the world.

Directory of Language Related Mailing Lists

babel.uoregon.edu/yamada/lists.html

The most extensive listing of electronic discussion groups organized by language or language family. A must for all language educators who wish to take advantage of electronic mail as a tool for promoting language learning through written communication.

The Diversity Webpage of the History/Social Studies Web Site for K-12 Teachers

www.execpc.com/~dboals/diversit.html

With several hundred annotated links to diversity resources, this webpage is an essential compendia. It focuses on the controversy surrounding immigration as well as on linguistic, ethnic, racial, gender and disability issues for educators. An unique section is "The Cultural Landscape," which gathers links relating to the functions of different kinds of communities.

The ERaM (Ethnicity, Racism and the Media) Programme

www.brad.ac.uk/bradinfo/research/eram.html

Located at the University of Bradford (UK) Department of Social and Economic Studies, ERaM provides a global forum for discussion, information dissemination, and research collaboration on issues of racism, ethnicity and the media.

ERIC

www.aspensys.com/eric/sites/barak.html

Educational Resources Information Center (ERIC) is a national information system designed to provide users with ready access to an extensive body of education-related literature. Established in 1966, it is supported by the U.S. Department of Education, the Office of Educational Research and Improvement and the National Library of Education. The most essential of all educational websites, "Links to all ERIC Resources" is an excellent candidate for every teacher or parent to enter into their computer's information browser as their "default" personal launchsite. ERIC is fully described in our "Internet Basics" section as the principal website explored by our fictional Internet explorer, the parent and teacher Olga Reyes. The various specialty ERIC Clearinghouses and adjunct services are listed separately in each subject-specific section of this Guide.

The ERIC Clearinghouse on Languages and Linguistics

www.cal.org/ericcll/

www.cal.org/NCLE

This essential clearinghouse run by the Center for Applied Linguistics (CAL) has led coordinated research into linguistics and language learning for decades. CAL also manages an adjunct clearinghouse, The National Clearinghouse for ESL Literacy, which maintains a webpage devoted to literacy education for adult immigrants limited in English proficiency.

The ERIC Clearinghouse on Rural Education and Small Schools

www.ael.org/erichp.htm

This website has many resources focused on multicultural education, migrant education and Mexican American heritage and culture.

The ERIC Clearinghouse on Urban Education

eric-web.tc.columbia.edu

Includes links to parent education Gophers and Web pages.

European Crosspoint Anti-Racism Webpage

www.magenta.nl/crosspoint/

Maintained by the Netherlands International Centre for Human Rights, this Website provides links organized by continent and country to anti-racist organizations around the world.

The First Perspective

www.mbnet.mb.ca/firstper/index.htm

Focuses on a wide range of information and resources concerning the indigenous peoples of Canada.

Facing History and Ourselves National

Foundation, Inc.
www.facing.org/
Based in Brookline, Massachusetts and with branches in six U.S. cities, Facing History and Ourselves provides a range of resources (printed, network-based, speakers' bureaus, videotapes) to confront racism, prejudice and anti-Semitism in schools and the wider society.

FLES Webpage
www.public.iastate.edu/~egarcia/fles.html
Maintained by Eduardo Garcia, the page is dedicated to providing links to Internet resources pertinent to foreign language education in elementary schools.

Gender-Related Electronic Forums
www-unix.umbc.edu/~korenman/wmst/forums.html
This webpage provides a vast listing of electronic discussion groups organized by topics including: Activism; Arts and Humanities; Education; Health; Religion and Spirituality; Science and Technology; Sexuality and Sexual Orientation; Social Science; Women of Color; and Women's Studies.

Hmong Homepage
www.stolaf.edu/people/cdr/hmong
Provides educators, parents and researchers with resources on Hmong culture and language learning.

The Holocaust/Genocide Project
www.igc.apc.org/iearn/hgp/
The website of I*EARN's award-winning project has many links to resources on combating genocide and anti-Semitism.

Human Rights Web Resources Page
www.hrweb.org
An extensive listing of links for both international and regional human rights resources on the Internet, this site is useful for activists, researchers, parents, teachers and students. The webpage of links for resources on diversity is especially interesting.

The HUMAN-LANGUAGES Page
www.hardlink.com/~chambers/HLP/
A huge and ambitious listing of pointers to language learning resources all around the world.

Index of Native American Resources on the Internet
hanksville.phast.umass.edu:80/misc/NAresources.html
A compendium of links for artistic, cultural, music, educational, historical and video resources for Native Americans, with links to other First People's nations.

InterLinks
www.nova.edu/Inter-Links/diversity.html
Nova University sponsors this thorough listing of resources for multicultural education, including African Studies Web, American Sign Language, Chicano-LatinoNet, Disability Information, Feminism Resources, Gay/Lesbian Resources and the Inter-Tribal Network for Native Americans.

Library of Congress Country Studies
lcweb.loc.gov/homepage/lchp.html
Comprehensive summaries and bibliographies on specific countries. Once connected, select "Area Handbooks."

Links to Aboriginal Resources
www.bloorstreet.com/300block/aborl.htm
A complete listing of connections to resources on indigenous peoples on every continent, with a useful rating system of Web pages devoted to Native/First Peoples. Also includes subscription information on dozens of electronic discussion groups and USENET newsgroups on topics pertinent to native peoples.

Multicultural Pavilion of the University of Virginia (MCPavilion):
curry.edschool.Virginia.edu/curry/centers/multicultural/
A well-organized "one-stop shopping" site with links to many multicultural resources around the world. MCPavilion has a well-stocked "Teacher's Corner." A related project is the MCPavilion discussion group (see below) which has also organized the MCPavilion International Project, a listing of member-contributed URLs and book reviews.

National Association for Ethnic Studies
www.ksu.edu/ameth/naes/ethnic.htm
This professional organization maintains a web page with links to key Internet resources for multicultural education.

National Clearinghouse for Bilingual Education
www.ncbe.gwu.edu
An essential website with links to hundreds of Internet resources pertinent to language and culture learning. See especially the links to "Languages & Culture," "In the Classroom," and "Success Stories" for provocative information on building bilingual competencies for both recent immigrant students and native English speakers. Also noteworthy is the webpage at http://www.ncbe.gwu.edu/classroom/bilschool.html which features links to schools with effective bilingual education programs.

NativeTech
www.nativeweb.org/NativeTech/
This beautiful series of webpages uses today's "high" technology to present the myriad expressions of na-

tive people's art and the everyday technology of lives lived close to nature. See "Internet Links" for a well-presented series of resources organized by topics.

PENN State PENpages
gopher://psupena.psu.edu
Huge, searchable listing of 13,000 full-text multicultural education resources.

The Pleiades
www.pleiades-net.com/
A site devoted exclusively to women's resources on the Internet, including an introductory tutorial designed with women's issues in mind.

Pluribus Unum
newlinks.tc.columbia.edu/~academic/newlinks/
This new website is maintained by the National Center for Restructuring Education, Schools and Teaching at Teachers College, Columbia University and is concerned with "studying diversity and pluralism in school and society."

RETAnet
ladb.unm.edu/retanet/
An outreach project of the Latin American Institute at the University of New Mexico. RETAnet works with secondary teachers, educational specialists and scholars to bring resources and curriculum materials about Latin America, the Spanish Caribbean and the U.S. Southwest into the elementary and secondary classroom. Internet access to cultural information and contacts is a key component of RETAnet.

Rethinking Schools
www.rethinkingschools.org
A publishing collective based in Milwaukee which produces the excellent Rethinking Schools newspaper and numerous in-depth analyses of educational issues from an anti-racist, social justice perspective.

Social Science Resources Page
galaxy.einet.net/GJ/social.html
A page of links that provides access to numerous Internet sites concerned with multicultural education resources.

Traces
www.trace-sc.com/index1.htm
The largest single networked information resource on Mexico, including a resource section for Mexicans living outside the nation.

Trail Guide to International Sites & Language Resources
128.172.170.24/
Maintained by Robert Godwin-Jones at Virginia Commonwealth University, the Trail Guide is an exemplar of effective webpage design. Using the metaphor of a journey on foot, Trail Guide leads foreign language learners through a vast array of resources and Internet links.

The U. S. Holocaust Memorial Museum
www.ushmm.org/index.html
Both an overview of the museum in Washington, D.C. and a site where teaching ideas may be found for integrating Holocaust studies into the curriculum.

Universal Survey of Languages
www.teleport.com:80/~napoleon/
A hugely ambitious attempt to provide connections to information on all the world's spoken and gestural languages and principal dialects.

University of Wisconsin Gopher
gopher://gopher.adp.wisc.edu
Curriculum resources for K-12 African, African American, and Islamic culture, with a search utility. Once connected, select the menu items "Course Materials and Other Educational Resources" and "African and African American Curriculum Materials K-12."

Vandergrift's Feminist Websites
www.scils.rutgers.edu/special/kay/femsites.html
Kay Vandergrift's offering of links to websites on women's issues, collected with the same sensitivity she brought to children's literature and literature for youth.

Women of Canada
www.nlc-bnc.ca/digiproj/women/ewomen.htm
The National Library of Canada sponsors a web site to showcase the achievements of 21 women who transformed Canadian and world history.

Women in Canadian History
www.niagara.com/%7Emerrwill/
Maintained by noted historian Susan Merritt, this well-designed webpage is a valuable resource in its own right through its changing focus on important women in Canadian history, but also offers useful links to related resources.

Yahoo!
www.yahoo.com/Society_and_Culture/
www.yahoo.com/Social_Science/
www.yahoo.com/Regional/Countries/
The Internet's oldest searchable index has extremely useful listings for multicultural education along with its powerful search engine on each page.

SEARCHING GOPHERSITES AND WEBSITES

Any listing of Internet resources is by definition incomplete and often rapidly outdated, since new resources are added daily and network addresses change constantly. Moreover, owing to the wide scope of multicultural education which implies access to resources for numberless cultures and languages, a key skill in effectively using the Internet is *searching*. Luckily, there are powerful "search engines" that allow a parent, teacher or student to tailor-make customized listings of all gophersites and websites around the world with resources on any given subject relating to multicultural education.

Search engines are free sites on the Internet (usually underwritten by commercial sponsors). A business that runs a commercial search engine may employ dozens of "Internet reference librarians" who spend countless hours visiting websites all over the globe, evaluating the information listings they find, and then creating indexes of categorized resources, much as librarians work to catalog and cross-reference shelves of books for their collections. Key examples include the Yahoo! and Magellan search engines; we find these search engine services to be among the most useful resources for locating information on the Internet since they deliver well-researched annotations that provide an essential "human touch."

Other search engine services (for example, Digital's Alta Vista) resort to "intelligent" robot programs or "spiders" that automatically visit websites and gophersites around the planet to gather their URLs; obviously, these services seek to compensate for their lack of depth in (humanly) informed scope with a wider-ranging selection of Internet resources, culled mechanically and automatically. Alta Vista, for example, currently provides surprisingly rapid full-text searches of 11 billion words found in over 22 million webpages; typing in the phrase "bilingual education" yields no less than 5,000 clickable links to webpages on the Internet which use this phrase, all produced in no less than 3 seconds. The word "Hmong," to offer another telling example, reveals 2,000 different webpages which mention the language or culture of this Southeast Asian immigrant group with large communities in Fresno, California, Minnesota and various other states.

We recommend that you sample the various Internet search engines (selecting from Alta Vista, Excite, Inktomi, Lycos, Magellan, Webcrawler, and Yahoo!, among others). These can be easily located by clicking on the "Net Search" button of the Internet browser you have installed on your hard drive, such as Netscape or Explorer. In addition, a series of helpful "Search Launchsites" which list all of these search engines and more specialized indi-

ces as well can be found at the following URLs:
riceinfo.rice.edu/Internet
www.search.com/
osiris.sunderland.ac.uk/rif/W3searches.html
csbh.mhv.net/~rpproctor/IRP.html

If a particular search engine appears especially successful in locating resources for your area of concern, take the extra time to learn its specialized commands for finding specific resources. This search engine should become your personalized in-depth search engine of choice. In nearly every case, the search engines available at the above addresses allow you to compose highly specific searches using "Boolean Algebra" terms such as AND, OR, and NOT (for a refresher on how these powerful connectors work, check with your school librarian).

However, you will wish to take advantage of the broader capabilities of the Metacrawler search engine (located at http://www.metacrawler.com) which supplements in its breadth of scope what your personal search engine may miss in its deeper focus. Metacrawler is a "meta" search engine that uses the single search term that you enter to explore not one but a dozen separate search engines, one by one, collating and eliminating duplicate "hits" among those it locates. While Metacrawler provides a wide range of pertinent sources, it obviously cannot offer the specialized services that a proprietary search engine is designed to deliver. Therefore, we recommend that you adopt a balanced strategy of utilizing your favorite personalized search engine in conjunction with Metacrawler.

"PEOPLE CONNECTION" RESOURCES

The day-to-day mechanics of maintaining electronic discussion groups and electronic journals over the Internet are handled automatically by a "mailing list manager," which is a computer program running at the discussion group's home network. The most common mailing list processors are LISTSERV, Listproc and Majordomo. Every discussion group, no matter what program manages its exchanges, has two addresses on the Internet: (a) the address of the mailing list management program itself, which handles requests to subscribe and "unsubscribe" from the discussion group, as well as requests to adjust other parameters for receiving messages, such as once-a-day "digests" of for especially busy exchanges [see below]; and (b) the participation address, to which any subscriber may send a message that is then bounced electronically to every other member of the discussion group's mailing list — which in many cases includes hundreds or even thousands of readers.

The basic commands for any discussion groups are "subscribe," "digest," and "unsubscribe" (referring to the commands for enrollment in a discussion group, for setting the parameters for participation so that all messages for the discussion group are delivered in a single e-mail package once a day, and for dropping the discussion group, respectively).

Here are the key commands for LISTSERV, Majordomo and Listproc discussion groups, the three major mailing list programs.

For Subscribing

LISTSERV: subscribe [listname]

Majordomo: subscribe [listname] <your full e-mail address>

Listproc: subscribe [listname] [Firstname] [Lastname]

For Unsubscribing

LISTSERV: unsubscribe [listname]

Majordomo: unsubscribe [listname] <your full e-mail address>

Listproc: unsubscribe [listname]

For Daily Digests (for high-volume groups)

LISTSERV: set [listname] mail digest

Majordomo: subscribe [listname]-digest unsubscribe [listname]

Listproc: set [listname] mail digest

(Note: With Majordomo, please note that you must subscribe to the digest and unsubscribe from the regular list in the same message; otherwise, you will receive both formats).

For e-mail newsletters, e-journals and announcement-only services, you only need the management address, as these are by definition "read-only" discussion groups. To subscribe, follow the preceding directions and include the "listname" of the e-journal where indicated.

ELECTRONIC JOURNALS AND NEWSLETTERS

LMRI Newsletter

Subscription: LISTPROC@lmri-news.ucsb.edu

The Language Minority Research Institute at the University of California-Santa Barbara publishes a monthly newsletter in both print and electronic formats.

NCBE NEWSLINE

Management: MAJORDOMO@cis.ncbe.gwu.edu

Participation: NEWSLINE@cis.ncbe.gwu.edu

In addition to discussion groups (see above), the National Clearinghouse for Bilingual Education maintains NEWSLINE as a mechanism for providing up-to-date information on news and resources relating to the education of linguistically and culturally diverse students in the United States. Unlike many e-journals, NEWSLINE is "moderated;" that is, it invites comments from its subscribers which are reviewed for accuracy and pertinence and then posted.

Wotanging.Ikche/Kanoheda Aniyvwiya

Subscriptions: GARS@netcom.com

This newsletter includes information drawn from various Internet sources relating to Native American educational issues, including TRIBALLAW, NATCHAT and NATIVE-L listservers. To subscribe include, in the body of your message, the words "sub wotanging.ikche <your email address>".

SPECIAL INTEREST ELECTRONIC DISCUSSION GROUPS (LISTSERVs)

ACTIV-L

Management: LISTSERV@umcvmb.missouri.edu

Participation: ACTIV-L@umcvmb.missouri.edu

Forum on civil and human rights, peace, and nonviolence.

AFRICA-L

Management: LISTSERV@ vtvm1.cc.vt.edu

Participation: AFRICA-L@ vtvm1.cc.vt.edu

A forum for those interested in increasing communication of all types to and from Africa.

AFRICANA-L

Management: LISTSERV@listserv.cc.wm.edu

Participation: AFRICANA-L@listserv.cc.wm.edu

Discussion focusing on the use of information technologies and networks on the continent of Africa.

AFROAM-L

Management: LISTSERV@harvarda.harvard.edu

Participation: AFROAM-L@harvarda.harvard.edu

A discussion group devoted to African-American issues. Recent projects includes "Griot" (the term for "historian" in African cultures) which has sought to link African history and the oral traditions of family ancestries maintained among the African American Diaspora.

AMNESTY

Management: MAJORDOMO@igc.org

Participation: AMNESTY@igc.org
Discussion group of Amnesty International.

BEN
Management: LISTSERV@listserv.vt.edu
Participation: BEN@listserv.vt.edu
One of the newest discussion groups with an active membership, the Bilingual ESL Network's lively debate is spiced by a mix of veteran bilingual educators and those new to the field.

BILINGUE-L
Management: LISTSERV@Reynolds.k12.or.us
Participation: BILINGUE-L@Reynolds.k12.or.us
A forum concerned with developmental bilingual elementary education, or "two-way bilingual programs," where native speakers of English learn all their regular subjects with native speakers of Spanish, with the goal of both groups becoming bilingual while performing academically on grade level. Based on the premise, according to the organizers, that "a second language is best learned not as the object of instruction, but rather as the medium of instruction, through a content-based curriculum."

CHICLE
Management: LISTSERV@unm.edu
Participation: chicle@unm.edu
General discussion of Chicano literature and culture

CULTUR-L
Management: LISTSERV@vm.temple.edu
Participation: CULTUR-L@vm.temple.edu
Discussion group for those interested in the role of cultural differences in the curriculum.

DIVERS-L
Management: LISTSERV@psuvm.psu.edu
Participation: DIVERS-L@psuvm.psu.edu
Discussion encouraging diversity in academic studies.

EDUDEAF
Management: LISTSERV@ukcc.uky.edu
Participation: EDUDEAF@ukcc.uky.edu
For teachers of the deaf and hard-of-hearing.

Ethnicity, Racism and the Media
Management: majordomo@bradford.ac.uk
Participation: eram-list@bradford.ac.uk
(ERAM-LIST: See Websites, above.)

FEMINISM-DIGEST
Management: MAJORDOMO@netcom.com
Participation: FEMINISM-DIGEST@netcom.com
Forum on women's rights.

GERMANICA-L
Management: LISTSERV@netcom.com
Participation: GERMANICA-L@netcom.com
A discussion group concerning Germanic Americans and Americans of Germanic heritage, including Austrian, Dutch, German, Germans from Russia, Franks, Lombards, Pennsylvania Dutch, Bavarian, Saxon, Silesian and Swiss.

GLGB-HS
Management: LISTSERV@ocmvm.onondaga.boces.k12.ny.us
Participation:GLGB-HS@ocmvm.onondaga.boces.k12.ny.us
Forum for teachers and secondary students of global studies.

GLOBALED-L
Management: LISTSERV@vita.org
Participation: GLOBALED-L@vita.org
Forum on curriculum issues in global education.

GNET
Subscription: GNET_REQUEST@dhvx20.csudh.edu
While global learning networks are growing rapidly, there are many parts of the world where access is as severely restricted as it is for poorer school districts in North America. This discussion group also generates an archive/journal for documents pertaining to the effort to bring the net to lesser-developed nations and the poorer parts of developed nations.

H-NET
Management: LISTSERV@uicvm.uic.ed or LISTSERV@msu.edu
Participation: Substitute the actual group name for the word "LISTSERV," e.g. H-ETHNIC@msu.edu
Not a single discussion group but a far-ranging suite of groups with 30,000 subscribers from 62 countries, "Humanities Net" is managed by the University of Illinois (Chicago) and Michigan State University. Of particular interest for multicultural studies are H-ANTIS (on anti-Semitism), H-URBAN (urban history), and HOLOCAUS (Holocaust studies) out of the University of Illinois and H-AFRICA (African history), H-ASIA (Asian history), H-DEMOG (demographic history), H-ETHNIC (ethnic, immigration and emigration studies), H-JUDAIC (Judaica, Jewish history), H-LATAM (Latin American history), H-RURAL (rural and agricultural history), H-W-CIV (teaching Western civilization), H-WOMEN (women's history), and H-WORLD (world history) out of Michigan State University.

HR-L
Management: HR-L-REQUEST@vms.cis.pitt.edu

Participation: HR-L@vms.cis.pitt.edu

Forum on international human rights issues.

INDIANnet
Management: LISTSERV@spruce.hsu.edu

Participation: INDIANNET@spruce.hsu.edu

Open forum for those interested in Native American issues.

INTCOLED
Management: MAISER@ist01.ferris.edu

Participation: INTCOLED@ist01.ferris.edu

Devoted to "international collaborative education" using the Internet.

LG-SHIFT
Management: MAILSERV@sil.org

Participation: LG-SHIFT@sil.org

A discussion group on language shift (the preservation or loss of the primary or home language among members of immigrant communities).

LMRI Discussion Groups
Management: LISTPROC@lmrinet.gse.ucsb.edu

The Language Minority Research Institute at the University of California-Santa Barbara maintains a number of discussion groups. Use the same management address to subscribe to all of these discussion groups. Once subscribed you can participate by sending a message to the discussion group's name at the lmrinet.gse.ucsb.edu computer; for example, MUJER-L@lmrinet.gse.ucsb.edu.

AERA-BILINGUAL: For bilingual education research;

BTEACHER-ED: On issues of bilingual education teacher education;

CAAPAE-L: Run by the California Association for Asian Pacific American Education, serving the educational needs of Asian Pacific American students;

LANGPOL: Discussions of language policy issues related to bilingual education;

MUJER-L: Forum for concerns pertinent to education and Latina women; and

PARA-ED: Raises issues concerned with para-educator professional development, career pathways to teacher certification, work conditions and job responsibilities.

MCPavilion
Management: majordomo@virginia.edu

Participation: mcpavilion@virginia.edu

A discussion group for K-12 educators focusing on practical classroom issues for multicultural education. (See Multicultural Pavilion under WWW, above.)

MEXICO-L
Management: LISTSERV@tecmtyvm.bitnet

Participation: MEXICO-L@tecmtyvm.bitnet

Discussion of Mexican culture, in English and Spanish.

MIGRANT-L
Management: LISTSERV@netcom.com

Participation: MIGRANT-L@netcom.com

A forum devoted to issues affecting the education of migrant students.

MULT-CUL
Management: LISTSERV@ubvm.cc.buffalo.edu

Participation: MULT-CUL@ubvm.cc.buffalo.edu

A forum on the sociopolitical context of multicultural education.

Mult-Ed
Management: LISTPROC@gmu.edu

Participation: MULT-ED@gmu.edu

Co-sponsored by the National Association for Multicultural Education and George Mason University, this is a general forum for multicultural educators.

MULTC-ED
Management: LISTSERV@umdd.umd.edu

Participation: MULTC-ED@umdd.umd.edu

Forum on Multicultural Education from K-12 through University. Contributors include educators and parents, covering the full range of diversity, including disability and gender orientation.

NAT-EDU
Management: LISTSERV@gnosys.svle.ma.us

Participation: NAT-EDU@gnosys.svle.ma.us

Principally higher education participation on issues surrounding Native American education.

NAT-LIT-L
Management: LISTSERV@cornell.edu

Participation: NAT-LIT-L@cornell.edu

Forum devoted to discussion of Native American literature.

NativeWeb
Management: LISTSERV@thecity.sfsu.edu

Participation: NativeWeb@thecity.sfsu.edu

Discussion on using the World Wide Web to promote the interests of indigenous peoples around the world, and on locating space on servers to post newly-developed Web resources.

NIFL-ESL, NIFL-FAMILY. NIFL-ALLD, and NIFL-WORKPLACE

Management: LISTPROC@novel.nifl.gov
Participation: NIFL-ESL@novel.nifl.gov
Participation: NIFL-FAMILY@novel.nifl.gov
Participation: NIFL-ALLD @novel.nifl.gov
Participation: NIFL-WORKPLACE@novel.nifl.gov

The National Institute for Literacy (NIFL) maintains four discussion groups, first on the learning of English as a Second Language for adults, second on intergenerational literacy, third on adult learners with learning disabilities and finally on adults in the workplace. All are moderated by staff from the National Clearinghouse for ESL Literacy Education.

ORTRAD-L

Management: LISTSERV@mizzou1.missouri.edu
Participation: ORTRAD-L@mizzou1.missouri.edu

A forum on living oral traditions — and texts rooted within oral traditions — with an intercultural, interdisciplinary focus.

SEASIA-L

Management: LISTSERV@msu.edu
Participation: SEASIA-L@msu.edu

Southeast Asian electronic discussion list is devoted to discussion on the languages and cultures of this key region, to which many bilingual program students trace their heritage.

SPANBORD

Management: LISTSERV@asuvm.inre.asu.edu
Participation: SPANBORD@asuvm.inre.asu.edu

Forum devoted to the history and archaeology of the Mexico-U.S. border region.

TAINO-L

Management: majordomo@corso.ccsu.ctstateu.edu
Participation: TAINO-L@corso.ccsu.ctstateu.edu

The Taino-L discussion group, in English and Spanish, is associated with the Taino Inter-Tribal Council web page (http://www.hartford-hwp.com/taino/), which focuses on the Taino nation and other Arawak-speaking peoples from the Caribbean, the United States and South America.

WOMEN

Management: LISTSERV@world.std.com
Participation: WOMEN@world.std.com

Gender issues at all levels of education.

WORLD-L

Management: LISTSERV@ubvm.cc.buffalo.edu
Participation: WORLD-L@ubvm.cc.buffalo.edu

Discussion of non-Eurocentric world history.

Y-RIGHTS

Management: LISTSERV@sjuvm.stjohns.edu
Participation: Y-RIGHTS@sjuvm.stjohns.edu

Discussion on the rights of children and adolescents.

Searching for Electronic Discussion Groups

There are several search engines available to assist educators in finding discussion groups on specific areas of interest. This is especially important as electronic discussion groups are known to migrate frequently from network to network as usage fluctuates. Also, new discussion groups arise constantly. Chief among the search engines for electronic discussion groups are:

Kovacs
http://n2h2.com/KOVACS/
scholarly and professional discussion groups

List of Lists
http://catalog.com/vivian/interest-group-search.html

Liszt
http://www.liszt.com/
Education subsection: http://www.liszt.com/select/
Education
A searchable index of 65,000 discussion groups.

Nova
http://www.nova.edu/Inter-Links/

TileNet
http://www.tile.net/tile/listserv/index.html

The University of Waterloo
http://www.lib.uwaterloo.ca/discipline/education/discussions.html.

USENET
http://WWW.Reference.com/
e-mail based or USENET discussion groups

Webcom
http://www.webcom.com/impulse/list.html

These and other search engines for discussion groups appear on the "Pitsco Launch to Electronic Discussion Groups" at http://www.pitsco.com/p/listinfo.html and at the Rice University Internet Navigation Page at http://riceiinfo.rice.edu/Internet.

Finally, there are dozens of subject-oriented guides to education-related discussion groups located at http://www.clearinghouse.net/tree/edu.html. These guides are updated by experts in numerous educational content areas and are valuable annotations of electronic discussion groups that are available on the Internet.

In recognition of the fast-moving pace of change with regard to electronic discussion groups, the preceding sections include annotations only for those electronic discussion groups that have distinguished themselves as essential resources in a particular subject area. Of all the resources listed, electronic discussion groups are the most variable and transitory with regard to location. Yet few Internet resources are more valuable than electronic discussion groups in terms of the potential for networked human interaction.

PARTNER CLASS CLEARINGHOUSES AND PROJECT-ORIENTED ACTIVITIES

In addition to engaging in discussions with colleagues on topics of common interest, multicultural educators can also establish *teaching contacts* with their counterparts throughout North American and in countries around the world — in many cases, with classrooms from the nations of origin of their students — in order to plan joint curricular projects. To do so, teachers can contact a clearinghouse which sets up partner classes and project-oriented activities. Two of the most important clearinghouses are described below.

1. Orillas

De Orilla a Orilla (Spanish for "From Shore to Shore") is a teacher-researcher project that has concentrated on documenting promising practices for intercultural and multilingual learning over global learning networks. Since 1985, Orillas has been an international networking project to promote team-teaching partnerships and group projects designed to effect social change, using modern telecommunications to extend an educational networking model first developed by the French educators Celestin and Elise Freinet in 1924.

Parents or teachers should contact Orillas if they are interested in participating in learning projects over global learning networks that:

a. Promote bilingualism and learning another language.

b. Validate traditional forms of knowledge, such as the oral traditions associated with folklore, folk games, proverbs and learning from elders through oral history.

3. Advance anti-racist multicultural education.

4. Develop new approaches to teaching and learning that encourage students, parents and communities to take action for social justice and environmental improvement.

Orillas operates over various networks; thus, cost for participation ranges from no-cost to low and moderate cost, depending on the type of service provider available to a parent or teacher. The Orillas Web page is located at http://orillas.upr.clu.edu/

For more information, contact the co-directors:
Kristin Brown, <krbrown@igc.org>

5594 Colestine Road, Hornbrook CA 96044
Enid Figueroa, <efigueroa@orillas.upr.clu.edu>

P.O. Box 7475, Caguas, Puerto Rico 00626
Dennis Sayers, <dennis_sayers@hotmail.com>

695 W. Palo Alto, Fresno CA 93704

2. I*EARN: International Education and Resource Network

The purpose of I*EARN (the International Education and Resource Network) is to enable elementary and secondary students to make a meaningful contribution to the health and welfare of the planet. Its coordinators explain, "We want to see students go beyond both simply being 'pen-pals' and working on strictly academic work to use telecommunications in joint student projects designed to make a difference in the world as part of the educational process." I*EARN is expanding to additional international sites daily and now includes about hundreds of schools in over 20 countries.

Additional information may be found at www.iearn.com, or contact International Education and Resource Network (I*EARN), 475 Riverside Drive, Room 540, New York NY 10115, phone: 212-870-2693.

NOTE

We have relied extensively upon the "Guide to the Internet for Parents and Teachers" found in *Brave New Schools: Challenging Cultural Illiteracy through Global Learning Networks* by Jim Cummins of the Ontario Institute for Studies in Education and Dennis Sayers of the University of California Educational Research Center (St. Martin's Press, ISBN 0-312-16358-4).

© Cathleen Maclearie, 1996

INDEX

Index

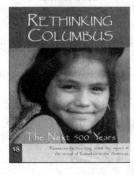

Are you ready to move beyond heroes and holidays?

If so, consider joining us in the National Coalition of Education Activists. NCEA is a multiracial network of school staff, families, union and community activists, children's advocates, and others working for equity and fundamental change in schools.

NCEA encourages and supports local activists' efforts to implement changes like those described in *Beyond Heroes and Holidays*, provide a counter to the right, and fight racism and other forms of institutional bias in schools.

Members receive:

- One year subscription to our quarterly newsletter, Action for Better Schools.
- Free access to NCEA's information bank and activist network, Resources for Better Schools.
- Priority registration for conferences and institutes.
- Opportunity to shape the organization and the movement.

NCEA believes the struggle for better schools is part of a larger movement and our efforts are guided by the following principles:

- School reform must be guided by a broad vision of social change.
- Kids should be active, critical learners and at the center of every school.
- The physical conditions in which teaching and learning take place have to improve dramatically.
  - Racism and other forms of discrimination and oppression, must be redressed.
  - Grassroots efforts, such as organizing campaigns and community mobilizations, should drive school change.

. . . .

NCEA DEPENDS ON MEMBERSHIP PARTICIPATION AND SUPPORT! PLEASE JOIN US.

_____ **YES**, I want to help build the movement for public schools that serve all children well. Enclosed is my dues chec [$100, organizations; $40, household income over $40,000; $20, $25,000-$40,000; $15, $15-25,000; $5, under $15,00

Included with your membership are free samples of the following publications. Please check the ones you'd like to rece

Name _____

Address _____

City _____ State _____ Zip _____

Phone (H) _____ (W) _____

Fax _____ E-mail _____

❑ FairTest Examiner
❑ Philadelphia Public School Notebook
❑ Rethinking Schools
❑ School Improvement Catalog, CAPS/Center for Law Education
❑ I'm not ready to join, but please send me more informa

RETURN TO: NCEA, P.O. Box 679, Rhinebeck, NY 125
914-876-4580 ■ e-mail: rfbs@aol.com

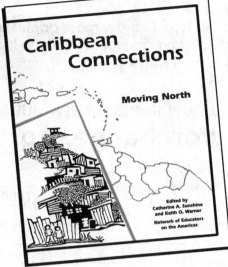
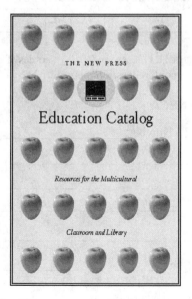

ORDER FORM

 Copy and use this order form to order more copies of *Beyond Heroes and Holidays* and for any item in the "Resource Guide" marked with the ⊠.

Additional copies of *Beyond Heroes and Holidays*:

$27 each + shipping

Call for resale and bulk rates.

Shipping Allow two weeks for **regular shipping**. We ship via UPS Ground, which can take 4-7 business days, unless another service level is requested. For faster delivery, request **rush (3-day) shipping**. Refer to chart for shipping charges.

Outside the U.S. Compute the regular charges, then add additional charge as shown below. We welcome international orders; however, we can accept payment in U.S. dollars only. International mail is sent via surface parcel post unless requested otherwise.

Shipping Charges

Total Order	Regular	Rush
Up to $15	$5	$8.50
$15.01-$40	$7	$11
$40.01-$70	$8	$15
$70.01-$200	12%	20%
over $200.01	8%	15%

For shipments outside the U.S., add

To Canada and Mexico	$10
Other outside U.S.	$20

Payment Place orders by phone (with credit card), fax, e-mail or mail. Use a check, credit card (Visa and Master Card) or purchase order.

Price Increases Due to circumstances beyond our control, prices are subject to change without notice.

Review Copies Due to a limited budget, we cannot afford to send review copies.

Taxes NECA is a 501-c-3 nonprofit organization, Federal Tax I.D. number is: 52-1616482. Only Washington, D.C. residents are required to pay sales tax on their orders.

Send orders to:

NECA, PO Box 73038,
Washington, DC 20056,
800-763-9131
202-238-0109 (fax)
necadc@aol.com

For current prices and new items, check out:
www.teachingforchange.org

Qty.	Title	Unit Price	Total
	National Coalition of Education Activists brochure Free		
	Sub-Total		
	Sales Tax: 5.75% for D.C. addresses only		
	Shipping: ❑ Regular (❑ U.P.S. or ❑ U.S. Mail) ❑ Rush		
	Tax-Deductible Donation		
	TOTAL		

I can help promote *Teaching for Change*. ❑ Please send _____ copies of the catalog to distribute at workshops/conferences/schools.

Payment: ❑ Check enclosed, payable to **NECA**

❑ Institutional Purchase Order attached. PO Number: _____

❑ VISA or MasterCard Number: _____

Expiration Date: _____ Signature: _____

Name _____

Address _____

City _____ State _____ Zip _____

Phone (h) _____ Phone (w) _____

E-mail Address _____

School/Organization _____

Position/Title _____ Subject(s) _____ Grade(s) _____